The Meaning of

The Holy Qur'an

In Today's English

Extended Study Edition

Volume 2 of 3

Presented by Yahiya Emerick

Amirah Publishing

To reorder go to: http://www.amirahpublishing.com

ISBN: 9798421973317

Table of Contents

What is the End Result?

Proving the Faith

Repentance

9 At-Tawbah
aka Al-Barā'ah
Late Medinan Period

This is the only chapter of the Qur'an that does not begin with an invocation of Allah's mercy. There have been various explanations as to why the traditional phrase of "In the Name of Allah" was left off. Many early Muslims were under the impression that it might be something of a continuation of the last chapter, (and this was the opinion of Caliph Uthman,) while the complementary view in modern times is that this chapter is unlike all other chapters both in initial tone and content, in that it seems from the outset to be stern and full of warnings to both the remaining pagans of Arabia and the hypocrites. 'Ali ibn Abi Talib explained it exactly in this way by saying that to begin in Allah's name is to have the assurance of His protection, but in this chapter, the opening lines are a revocation of Allah's protection, and thus the introductory invocation of Allah is left off. (*Ma'ariful Qur'an*)

The hidden subtext in this chapter is that Islam was now unstoppable and was clearly on track to ultimate victory. If that weren't a good enough sign for the remaining pagans of Arabia (some of whom had violated their previously signed treaties with the Prophet) and the hypocrites (who still foolishly thought they could stop the progress of Islam), then they truly were as twisted as the Qur'an made them out to be and were, by extension, unworthy of fellowship or entry into Mecca – Allah's holy sanctuary. Thus, verses 1-37 were revealed soon after the conquest of Mecca with a clear purpose: to cancel all treaties made between the treacherous pagans and the Muslim state - only guarantying the peace for the remainder of the traditional truce months. The Muslims were commanded, however, to continue to honor the treaties they had with those pagan tribes that adhered faithfully to their end of the bargain until the treaty durations expired, even as they were reminded of the looming Byzantine threat to the north.

Here is the background for the remaining verses in this chapter. Verses 38-72 were revealed in the middle part of the year 629, and they concern the Prophet's efforts to organize an army for the journey to Tabuk, a border town that was located at the northernmost reaches of Arabia. Here are the events that led up to the Prophet's call to arms. Local client rulers of the Byzantines (the Ghassanids) had murdered some of the Prophet's envoys. Thus, the Prophet felt obligated to organize a military response. Late in the year 629, he sent a force of three thousand men (under the command of his adopted son, Zayd ibn Harith) to Syria, to show that such brutality would not go unanswered. After receiving a call for help from Suhrabil ibn Amr, the king of Basra, the

Byzantine Emperor Heraclius sent an army of his own, commanded by his brother Theophanous (Theodore), which, drawing upon many local allied Arab tribes, swelled the defenders to anywhere from 10,000 to 100,000 men. (The reports differ and are sometimes greatly exaggerated.) The two armies met in Syria at the famous Battle of Mu'tah.

Regardless of the true number of enemy troops, the odds against the Muslims were bad, and by all rights the Muslims should have been vanquished handily. On the eve of battle, one companion named 'Abdullah ibn Ruwahah said to the uneasy Muslims: "Men, what you're disliking is the same thing that you've come out in search of, in other words, martyrdom. We're not fighting the enemy with numbers or the strength of multitudes, but we're confronting them with this religion that Allah has honored us with. So come on! Both prospects are fine: victory or martyrdom." Then the men said, "By Allah, Ibn Ruwahah is right."

When the battle commenced, the Byzantine's massive numbers threatened to drown out the Muslims. However, the Muslims used stunningly unorthodox cavalry tactics and were able to avoid being swallowed up by the endless sea of Byzantines. Zayd eventually fell in the battle, however, and his lieutenant, Ja'far ibn Abi Talib, took command. When he, too, fell, the third man to take control of the Muslim force, 'Abdullah ibn Ruwahah, said aloud to those around him, "O my soul! If you're not killed, you're bound to die anyway. This is the fate of death overtaking you. What you wished for, you've been granted. If you do what they (Zayd and Ja'far) have done, then you're guided aright!" He fell in the battle shortly thereafter. (Meanwhile, back in Medina, the Prophet sorrowfully informed the people about the death of those prominent companions, before news had ever reached the city. When Ja'far's family was informed of what the Prophet had foreseen, they began to weep uncontrollably, and the Prophet asked them not to weep, for Ja'far was, he explained, now in Paradise.)

After fierce and desperate fighting, Khalid ibn Walid was given command and led a fighting retreat complete with a clever ruse to make it seem as if he were receiving fresh troops. The Byzantines, being stunned by the fierce bravado of the Muslims, also withdrew, but not before claiming victory. When Khalid led the beleaguered survivors back to Medina, some people actually started berating the men as cowards who should have died on the battlefield (citing verses 8:15-16). However, the Prophet came out and stopped the people from saying this, telling them, "No, they're strugglers in Allah's cause who will fight again another day." (Verses 8:65-66 were revealed allowing Muslims to retreat if the odds were more than two to one against them.)

The bold gambit of the Muslims did impress many southern Syrian and southern Iraqi tribes, and thousands of people from these semi-independent tribes (who were previously allied to either the Byzantines or Persians) accepted Islam. According to the historian Nicephorus, Heraclius was aware of this problem and traveled to Antioch to plan his next move. His strategy would involve, not surprisingly, brute force. The Byzantines sought to crush the progress of Islam by harassing and oppressing any tribes that converted. (Eventually they began to position troops for a proposed assault on Medina, itself!) After the Byzantines began executing some tribal chieftains who had accepted Islam, and with scattered reports that the Byzantines were organizing Syrian Arabs for an invasion of the south, the Prophet had no choice but to organize an army to meet this northern threat.

Thus, in September of the year 630, the Prophet himself marched an army of 30,000 people (including many women volunteers) northward to Tabuk in response to the threat of the Byzantines. (Many hypocrites sought exemptions from service, however, and feared leaving Medina due to the fact that the Muslims were so poorly equipped. There was also a heat wave afflicting the region, dampening the enthusiasm of the weak at heart.) The Byzantines, however, still smarting from their experience at Mu'tah, wound up withdrawing all their forces from northern Arabia, and no actual fighting took place.

The Prophet used his time in the region (about twenty days) to cement further alliances and also to extract promises of tribute from those tribes that had previously helped the Byzantines, particularly the Ghassanid tribe. (Some local chieftains, impressed with the Muslims, began to convert, as well.) This successful expedition by the Prophet resulted in offers of allegiance from rulers and chiefs all over the Arabian Peninsula, southern Syria and southern Iraq. And so, the Prophet returned to Medina at the head of a triumphant mission. Then, verses 73-129 were revealed after the Prophet returned home, and they address a variety of issues related mostly to this campaign and also to the hypocrites.

Background on verses 1-2: The Prophet had peace treaties with many pagan bedouin tribes, and some honored them while others continued to raid Muslim interests. After the fall of Mecca, the Muslim situation became more secure, and the shaky treaties that provided at least a semblance of security for the Muslims in Medina could be reevaluated based on current conditions. Those bedouins who honored their treaties would continue to enjoy them, but those bedouins who used their treaties as a shield to hide behind, striking out when they pleased, were put on notice that their treaties were being cancelled after the passage of the sacred months. Thus, the Prophet was "exempted" from honoring treaties with those who did not honor them with him. This revelation gave fair warning to all of Arabia, and thus the scholars conclude that any Muslim government is required to make public its repudiation of any treaties before taking any action against its enemies.

(This is a declaration) of exemption from Allah and His Messenger to those pagan tribes with whom you've made treaties, (and who've been unfaithful to them). [1]

You (pagans) may travel (safely) anywhere you wish throughout the land during the (next) four months, but know that your (treacherous) deeds will never frustrate Allah, for Allah is certainly going to bring humiliation down upon those who reject (the truth). [2]

8

(This is) an announcement from Allah and His Messenger to all the people gathered on the day of the Great Pilgrimage (in Mecca) that Allah and His Messenger are dissolving all (treaty) obligations with the idol-worshippers.

If you (treacherous idol-worshippers) would only repent, it would be best for you, but if you turn away, then know that you can't frustrate Allah, so give the news of a painful punishment to those who suppress (their faith). [3]

(However, those treaties) that you've made with those idol-worshippers who *have been* faithful to the terms, and who *didn't* give aid to any of your enemies, are not cancelled, so fulfill your obligations with them to the end of (each treaty's) term. [1] Indeed, Allah loves those who are mindful (of their obligations). [2] [4]

Now when the sacred (truce) months have passed, [3] fight the (double-crossing) idol-worshippers wherever you find them. [4]

---

[1] This verse refers to the tribes of Banu Kinanah, Banu Damurah and Banu Mudlaj who were still honoring the terms of the treaties they agreed to with the Prophet and affirmed in the precincts of Mecca. (There were nine months left on those treaties.)

[2] Among the many slanderous and false charges made by some critics against Islam is the mistaken notion that a Muslim government can cancel any treaty it makes at a whim. They cite this chapter as proof and make all kinds of insinuations about the alleged untrustworthy nature of treaties any Muslim would sign. Their lack of understanding is pitiful, and their hypocrisy is enormous. Verses 1-4 contain principles that any modern government or international institution – even the common sense of the masses – would accept. Obey treaty obligations strictly. However, if the other side is clearly violating their end of the bargain, then such a treaty is no treaty at all and should be discarded *with fair notice*. The Prophet never broke the terms of any treaty he signed. Rather, it was the other side that would always break the deal first, and then the Prophet was free to act, such as in the case of the Meccans breaking the terms of the Treaty of Hudaybiyyah, when they supported their allies in an attack on a tribe allied with Medina.

[3] Even if individual treaties expired before the coming of the next pilgrimage season, an extension was given to each hostile tribe until the end of the truce months, so public announcements could reach all over Arabia that their day of reckoning for their treachery was due. (*Ma'ariful Qur'an*)

[4] After the customary truce months were over, the Prophet's plan was to subdue the pagan tribes who had used their treaties as a cover to create further mischief. This verse has been misinterpreted, however, by both religious extremists and critics of Islam to somehow mean that a Muslim state is meant to be in *perpetual war* against all non-Muslims all around it. Despite the fact that this is a fallacious leap of meaning, both parties fail to realize that this verse, in historical context, is directed squarely against a particular group of idol-worshippers who were guilty of a specific crime, that of betraying their treaties. If there is any wider lesson in this verse for Muslims in later times, it's that permission is

Capture them, besiege their (settlements) and ambush them at every outpost. However, if they repent, establish prayers and give in charity, then leave them to their way, for Allah is forgiving and merciful. [5]

If an individual idol-worshipper asks you for security, then grant safe passage to them so they can have the opportunity to hear the word of Allah. Then escort them to a place where they can be safe. (They deserve this gracious treatment), for they're a people who don't know (about Allah's way of life). [5] [6]

Those Who Break Treaties willfully must be Opposed

How can there be a treaty with idol-worshippers in the sight of Allah and His Messenger, other than with those with whom you've made a treaty near the Sacred Mosque? As long as they're true (in their word) to you, then stay true (in your word) to them, for Allah loves those who are mindful (of their honest obligations). [7]

Again, how can (there be treaties with idol-worshippers), [6] especially given the fact that if they overpowered you, they would

---

given to cancel the treaties and fight against those who make treaties with you but then betray the terms of those treaties first. By the way, after the Prophet's passing, the first caliph, Abu Bakr, used this verse to justify declaring war on some southern tribes who were Muslims, but who refused to pay the required charity any longer. These were called the Wars of the *Ridda*, or Apostasy.

[5] Even though a group may be an enemy, it doesn't mean that every individual among them desires to fight or work against you. An allowance must be made for such people who come to you and ask for safe passage, information or asylum. They can also have the opportunity to see Muslims firsthand and hear and experience the reality of their beliefs. Perhaps they were filled with misconceptions before. In any case, they cannot be forced to convert (see 2:256). If they desire to remain pagans, then see them to a safe land where they can dwell. The scholars say that this verse also means that non-Muslim ambassadors and emissaries are guaranteed safety during their journeys to and from the seat of the Muslim government. The Prophet always granted ambassadors and message carriers diplomatic immunity. After the conquest of Mecca, the Prophet also granted four months of immunity to those few hostile Meccans who decided to flee the Muslim advance. Later on, nearly all of them accepted Islam, even 'Ikrimah, the son of Abu Jahl!

[6] How can you contract a treaty with a people who will betray the terms of the treaty, work against you and then overpower you? How can you do it when they'll disregard all social and political norms and work to oppress you, even though you might be related to some of them by blood and even though their sworn treaties are supposed to prevent them from harming you? Think of all the international treaties that have been signed among nations in modern times from the Geneva Convention and Nuclear Non-

neither respect family ties nor treaty obligations? [7] They say what you want to hear, but their hearts are filled with loathing towards you, for most of them are disobedient wrongdoers. [8]

They've sold the signs of Allah for a miserable price and have hindered people from His way. What they've done is utterly criminal! [9] Indeed, when it comes to a believer, they neither respect family ties nor obligations, and thus they'll go beyond all bounds! [10]

Yet, despite all of that, if they repent, establish prayer and give in charity, then they'll become your brothers in religion. That's how We explain the verses for people who understand. [11] However, if they

---

Proliferation Accords to the Universal Declaration of Human Rights and the numerous conventions against torture; yet, these have been flouted by many signatory governments with impunity and hubris! When only one side keeps a promise, it is best to scrap your agreement and start over.

[7] The word *dhimmah* means contractual obligations. It's the same term used to describe the relationship between an Islamic government and the non-Muslims living under its authority and protection. In exchange for the payment of an annual tax known as the *jizyah* (which is usually slightly higher than the *zakah* rate for Muslims), Christians and Jews become *dhimmis*, or contractual citizens of the state. They are free to practice their own religion and choose their own local leaders. They are afforded all legal rights under civil law and are not obligated to be drafted into the army in times of war. For its time, this concept of legal multiculturalism was far more advanced than any other system of the day, where the usual policy of any government back then was either to kill or banish those of another religion or to convert them forcibly. (The Bible also has a system for dealing with subject peoples, though it seems very politically incorrect to discuss it. See Deuteronomy 20:10-16 for example.) It must be noted that despite the alarmist claims of some critics of Islam, the function of an Islamic state is not to subjugate non-Muslims and make them pay taxes until they convert. If non-Muslims migrate into an Islamic state to settle down, they become *dhimmis*. If a non-Muslim state makes war on the Islamic state and if the Islamic state begins to achieve victory, then when the non-Muslim state calls for a negotiated peace, the Islamic state is obligated to enter peace negotiations [2:193]. If the non-Muslim state that attacked the Islamic state does not sue for peace and is instead vanquished in the war, its citizens become *dhimmis* and are thereafter protected by the Islamic state. An Islamic state can exist side-by-side with non-Muslim states, as long as peace and good relations are maintained [2:190]. (It must be noted that Muslim countries today, with their secular leaders, kings, dictators and odd blendings of culture, Western political trappings and pseudo-religion do not generally qualify as *Islamic* states in the traditional sense.) Remember that the treaties that the Prophet made with the Jews of Medina were treaties between equal parties; they were not *dhimmi* contracts, and the Prophet never broke any treaty he made with Jewish or Christian entities. The Prophet once said, "Beware! Whoever is cruel and hard on (a non-Muslim) with whom you have a treaty, or who curtails his rights, burdens him in more than he can bear, or takes anything away from him against his will, I shall be his prosecutor on the Day of Judgment." (*Abu Dawud*) He also said, "My Lord has prohibited me from wronging anyone protected by a treaty or anyone even besides that." (*Ma'ariful Qur'an*)

11

betray their agreements after giving their word and then taunt you about your religion, [8] then fight the leaders of rejection, [9] for they have no beliefs that would constrain them. [12]

And *shouldn't* you fight against people who betray their agreements and plot to drive away the Messenger and who take aggressive action against you first? Are you scared of them? By all rights, you should fear Allah, if you truly believe. [13]

So fight against them, and Allah will punish them by your hands and humiliate them. (He'll) help you against them and heal the (bruised) feelings of the believers [14] by calming the sense of outrage within their hearts. Allah turns toward whomever He wants, and Allah is full of knowledge and wisdom. [15] Did you think you were just going to be left alone before Allah could distinguish who among you has striven hard (in His cause) and who has restrained himself from taking others as close intimates in preference to Allah, His Messenger and (the community of) believers? Allah is well-informed of all that you do. [16]

Only the Faithful should Control Places of Worship

Background on verses 17-22: It is said that this passage was revealed in response to the ongoing contention of many pagan Meccans that they were sincere custodians of Allah's holy shrine in Mecca. The words of the Prophet's uncle 'Abbas, who was captured several years before this revelation at the Battle of Badr, are indicative of this viewpoint. When he was brought to Medina, many of his relatives who had become Muslim and who had migrated with the Prophet began scolding him for believing in idols and cutting off family ties. 'Ali ibn Abi Talib was especially hard in his accusations. 'Abbas said in his defense, "What's wrong with you, for you're only mentioning our shortcomings and not our strong points?" When 'Ali asked what those were, 'Abbas replied, "We (pagans) fill the

[8] This is the verse that Muslims use to justify fighting against those who mock and belittle Islam or its Prophet. Libel against revered religious figures is a crime in Islamic law. This is not the same as criticism of the *misapplication* of that figure's teachings, it must be remembered, nor can this principle be used to stifle healthy religious diversity. It covers mocking and taunting of the sacred, and in this Islam would also extend such protections to the reputation of all other prophets such as Jesus and Moses. Western cultures used to have strong laws against the mocking of their sacred symbols, though militant secularism has made the ridicule of religion and holy figures a praiseworthy activity in modern times. (*Ibn Kathir*)

[9] In other words, don't bother with ordinary people who are being misled by their leaders, propagandists and hate-mongers. Fight against the head of the snake, for the ignorant masses don't know what they're doing or what's being done to them most of the time.

sacred shrine with pilgrims; we serve the Ka'bah, and we give water to the pilgrims while freeing those in debt." (*Asbab ul-Nuzul*) Later on, after 'Abbas had accepted Islam, he had a discussion with 'Ali ibn Abi Talib and Talhah ibn Shaybah in which he and Talhah boasted of their services to the Ka'bah. 'Ali replied that he had been praying facing the Ka'bah six months before any of them, and he also was striving with the Prophet all along, and thus his service to Allah was more valuable than their services to the Ka'bah. (*Ma'ariful Qur'an*)

It's not the place of idol-worshippers to maintain the prayer-houses [10] of Allah, for they've given proof against themselves that they reject (Him). Their efforts are useless, and they're going to dwell in the Fire. [11] [17]

Allah's prayer-houses must be maintained only by those who believe in Allah and the Last Day and who establish prayer, give in charity and fear none but Allah. [12] They're the ones who (can be considered) to be rightly guided; (so, they'll treat those places of worship with proper reverence). [18]

Are you (idol-worshippers of the opinion) that merely giving water to pilgrims and maintaining the Sacred Mosque (in Mecca) is somehow equal to (the sacrifices made for Allah's sake) by those who (truly) believe in Allah and the Last Day and who struggled in the cause of Allah? They're not equal in Allah's sight, and Allah doesn't guide an oppressive people. [19]

Those who believed (in Allah), who migrated and who struggled in the cause of Allah with their wealth and their lives, are more

---

[10] The term *masjid* is usually translated as mosque. Yet, the word means a place of prostration or worship. It is used in a general sense in this verse and can apply to any type of religious temple devoted to the One God, be it a church, synagogue or a mosque, and therefore I've translated it in the generic sense of a prayer-house, i.e., place of worship. Idol-worshippers have no business maintaining any of them.

[11] This passage points out to the pagans that those who rejected the supremacy of Allah in favor of man-made idols had no business operating a shrine dedicated to Allah – no matter how they tried to justify it. Would anyone imagine idolaters maintaining St. Peter's Basilica in Rome or any other church, mosque or synagogue? It is thoroughly illogical, and this verse points out that only those who believe in Allah sincerely, and in no other false gods or idols, have the right to be in charge of holy places dedicated solely to the One God.

[12] The Prophet once said, "If you notice that a person is at the mosque on time (for prayer,) then be assured of his true faith, for Allah the Most High said..." And then he quoted this verse [9:18]. (*Tirmidhi*)

13

valuable in the sight of Allah, and they are the ones who will be successful. [20] Their Lord has given them the good news of mercy from His Own Self, of His satisfaction and of gardens filled with everlasting delights that will (be theirs) forever! [21] They will live within them forever, and with Allah are the greatest rewards! [22]

Making the Choice

Background on verses 23-24: When new converts to Islam in Mecca were asked to migrate to Medina, they were often inundated with requests from their non-Muslim relatives to stay where they were. Even after the Conquest of Mecca, converts from the pagan tribes of the countryside continued to face this familial pressure to remain at home. This passage asks such converts to make a choice: either remain with the pagans for worldly reasons or migrate for the sake of Allah. (*Ma'ariful Qur'an*)

O you who believe! Don't take your fathers or your brothers as close friends if they love concealing (the truth of Allah) more than having faith (in Him). Anyone who does that is doing wrong. [23]

Say (to the believers, who may be inclined to remain among their pagan relatives,) *"If your fathers, brothers, spouses, relatives, financial gains, trade deals that you're afraid will suffer or the lovely homes you live in are more beloved to you than Allah, His Messenger or in struggling in His cause, then you just wait until Allah's command comes to pass.* [13] *Allah doesn't guide people who are rebellious."* [24]

Allah Helps the Righteous

As it is, Allah has already helped you on many battlefields. On the day of (the Battle of) Hunayn, however, when your great numbers made you feel overconfident - *that by itself did nothing for you.* [14] The

---

[13] The 'command' is thought to be Allah's decision of judgment against those who disobeyed the order to migrate. It could either be misfortune in this life or punishment in the next. (*Ma'ariful Qur'an*)

[14] In the year 630, just after Mecca surrendered to the Prophet, the nearby city of Ta'if organized an army to fight against the Muslims under the command of one Malik ibn 'Awf an-Nadri. The two powerful tribes of Hawazin and Thaqif, who were the nucleus of the new enemy, were so confident of victory that they ordered all their women, children, camels and sheep to accompany them to the battlefield, thinking it would make them that much more earnest to win the fight. When the Prophet received news of the march of this new foe, he organized an army that numbered over twelve thousand men

wide earth hemmed you in (as you passed through the narrow valley and were suddenly taken by surprise in ambush). Thus, you turned back in retreat. [25]

Then Allah sent His tranquility down upon the Messenger and upon the believers, and He sent forces (of angels) you couldn't even see. [15] Thus, He punished the faithless, and that's how He repays those

---

and set out from Mecca to meet this new enemy. (He asked the people of Mecca, his former foes, for the loan of weapons to equip his army. They were pleased that he asked, rather than took, and provided many weapons.) When the Muslims entered into a narrow valley named Hunayn, they were suddenly ambushed by the enemy — almost 20,000 strong - with a rain of arrows followed by an infantry charge, and the startled Muslims retreated in utter confusion. The Prophet and a few faithful companions not only stood their ground, however, but they continued to advance, and even Abu Sufyan, the recent convert, stood by the Prophet and helped defend him from the rushing assault of the enemy. (He later remarked that he would rather be ruled by a Qurayshi man than by a man of Ta'if!) The Prophet called for the Muslims to return and asked his uncle 'Abbas to shout loudly to them. 'Abbas cried out, "Companions of the Tree (from the Pledge of Ridwan), Companions of the Chapter of the Calf!" (This was a reference to chapter two of the Qur'an and it's special place in the hearts of many.) Feeling ashamed at their cowardice, the Muslims returned and drove the forces of Ta'if back. Even some embittered Meccans who had come, secretly desiring to kill the Prophet in the confusion, found faith in Allah and instead helped the Prophet! Soon the pagans were on the run. They abandoned their women, children and goods in their camp and ran all the way back to the secure walls of their city. The Muslims took some 6,000 men, women and children captive and then laid siege to the city. The companions asked the Prophet to pray for the ruin of Ta'if, but the Prophet instead prayed for their conversion. Siege engines and catapults were soon brought by the recently converted Muslim tribe of Banu Daws from the south, but after a little less than a month, the Prophet lifted the siege, realizing that a sacred truce month had just arrived. However, he vowed to the beleaguered men of Ta'if that he would return with a new force the following year unless they capitulated. Some days passed, and a delegation of men from Ta'if arrived at the Prophet's camp even before he returned to Mecca. They made offers of peace and then declared their conversion to Islam. They begged for the return of their families and goods. An-Nadri even sent word that both he and his nobles had converted. The Prophet asked the delegation to choose what they wanted returned: their captured men, women and children or their captured goods. They chose their people, and, after calling upon his men to consider freeing the captured people as a gesture of goodwill towards their new brothers-in-faith, the Prophet succeeded in getting the 6,000 captives freed. He also gave a hundred camels to an-Nadri and confirmed him as chief of the city of Ta'if. An-Nadri, who was surprised by the Prophet's generosity, then composed a poem to praise the Prophet and his graciousness. (At-Tabari)

[15] One of the Hawazin tribesmen later narrated how angels had routed them, saying, "When we met the Messenger of Allah and his companions on the Day of Hunayn, they didn't remain on the battlefield for more than the time it takes to milk a sheep! (The Muslims fled after the ambush.) When we routed them we chased them until we came upon the rider of the white mule, who was the Messenger of Allah. Suddenly, men with glowing and handsome faces intercepted us and said, 'Disgrace their faces! Go back!' So

who cover (the light of faith within their hearts). [26] Then after that, Allah accepted the repentance of whomever He wanted to from among those (who fled after the initial ambush), for Allah is the forgiving and merciful. [27]

> **Background on verse 28:** After the conquest of Mecca, pagan pilgrims continued to enter Mecca, and they continued to perform their religious rites, sometimes naked, often clapping and whistling, as they were wont to do. Thus, after a short time had passed, the Prophet forbade the future entry of idolaters into Mecca, and this verse was the source for his ruling. (*Ma'ariful Qur'an*)

O you who believe! The idol-worshippers are impure, so don't let them come near the Sacred Mosque after this year of theirs has passed. [16] If you're afraid of becoming poor (on account of the financial losses that this ban might cause), then Allah will enrich you as He wills from His Own bounty, for Allah is full of knowledge and wisdom. [28]

Be Prepared to Defend Yourselves

> **Background on verse 29:** In historical context, this verse was revealed after the Byzantine Empire had already become openly hostile to the Muslims of Medina and a war footing was in place. The purpose of this verse is as a rousing call for the Muslims to face a declared enemy that happened to be culturally Christian (the Byzantines).

---

we ran away, but (the returning Muslims) followed us, and that was the end for us." (*At-Tabari*)

[16] This verse mentions specifically that only pagans are prohibited from entering Mecca. In the years immediately following the Prophet's passing, Jews and Christians were still allowed to enter the city. The early scholar, Jabir ibn 'Abdullah, said this verse does not apply to non-Muslim servants nor to *dhimmis* (Jews and Christians under contractual relationship to the Muslim government). (*Ibn Kathir*) Later on, during the rule of 'Umar ibn 'Abdul-'Aziz (d. 720), the famed Umayyad caliph, the order was given (by his decree) to extend the ban for entering Mecca to Jews and Christians, as well. Since that time Muslim orthodoxy has enshrined this principle, leaving only the Hanafi school of Islamic Law holding that Jews and Christians are allowed to enter Mecca. (There has never been any bar on Jews and Christians (or Zoroastrians) from living elsewhere in the Arabian Peninsula.) However, all schools of law agree that no non-Muslims are allowed to preach or build houses of worship in Arabia, based upon the saying of the Prophet that Arabia cannot be home to two religions. There is no prohibition for other Muslim countries to have the presence of churches, synagogues and other non-Muslim houses of worship.

(Don't be afraid to) fight against those who don't believe in Allah and the Last Day, who don't forbid what Allah and His Messenger have forbidden, and who don't accept the true way of life. [17]

(If) those who received the scripture (before you make war upon you, then fight them) until they (agree) to pay (an annual) tax from their own hand, [18] acknowledging that they've been subdued. [19] [29]

---

[17] It could be argued that Jews and Christians, who are being referenced here, *do* believe in Allah and the Last Day, but it must be born in mind that Christians generally believe in a trinity of three beings as God, while the Jews seem to take God as something of an exclusive tribal deity. Christians have conflicting views of the Day of Judgment, thinking that a 'saved' believer will have no account for his deeds. Beyond this, the other qualifiers mentioned in this verse such as obeying the Messenger (Muhammad) and such are items Jews and Christians absolutely do not accept.

[18] There is a generally accepted rate for the *jizyah* tax, which is the tax that non-Muslim male wage-earners pay to an Islamic government to exempt them from certain duties and Islamic financial taxes and that also guarantees their people the rights of citizenship and protection. The Prophet had made a *jizyah* deal with the Christian tribe of Najran that they should forward two thousand articles of clothing to Medina annually. (Considering the large size of the Najrani Christian tribe, this amounted to about 5% of their gross domestic product. This general amount was further enshrined and confirmed by Caliph 'Umar ibn al-Khattab when he made a *jizyah* deal with the Christian tribe of Bani Taghlib and pegged the rate of annual payment to be twice the rate of the *zakat* that Muslims pay on their yearly accumulated savings and assets. Muslims pay 2.5% annually.) (*Ma'ariful Qur'an*) This prophetic practice also means that *jizyah* arrangements are to be made with the recognized leadership of non-Muslim entities, and not with individuals. The expression here referencing 'from their hand' means that only those of means can be taxed, and those who 'have nothing in their hand,' are not to be taxed. (*Baydawi*) Those non-Muslims who are categorically exempted from *jizyah* include women, children, the disabled, the handicapped, religious leaders and the very old. (*Ma'ariful Qur'an*)

[19] This verse is not suggesting that Muslims must fight against Jews and Christians for all time until they submit to taxation, as some extremists (and critics of Islam) might believe, and there are ample other verses that make it clear that in Islam war is defensive in nature. When Muslims are at peace with a Jewish or Christian entity, then there is no cause for the Muslims to fight any further or make any attempt to conquer them. This is proven by the following verses: 22:39 (where permission to fight is given only to those who have been wronged); and 2:192-193 (where the establishment of a peace treaty obligates the Muslims to stop fighting - except against evil tyrants). The Prophet concluded a peace treaty with the Christians of Najran, and the Islamic state never fought them. Likewise, the Prophet made treaties with Zoroastrians, Jews and some Christian tribes of southern Syria with no military action involved. It is only the general war with the Byzantines that this verse is referencing.

When a Holy Man is Overly Magnified

The Jews call Ezra a son of God, [20] and the Christians call the Messiah a son of God, but those are just phrases from their mouths. They do nothing more than copy what the faithless in ancient times used to say.

Allah's curse is upon them, and they're greatly deceived! [30] They've taken their theologians and saints as lords in place of Allah, and also the Messiah, the son of Mary, as well, even though they were ordered to serve none but the One God alone [21] – *there is no god besides*

----

[20] Not all seventh-century Jews called Ezra, the hero of the Babylonian Return, a 'son' of God. (Though it must be remembered that to Jews, calling someone a 'son' of God implied no biological connection, and the Old Testament labels many people as 'sons' of God to emphasize their holiness and righteousness.) At the Prophet's time, however, there was apparently a sect of Jews living in Yemen who labeled Ezra a 'son' of God, though perhaps only metaphorically. (*Encyclopedia Judaica*, vol. 6.) In addition, the ancient Jewish books of I and II Esdras do describe Ezra in fairly miraculous terms, even going so far as to assert that he was entered into heaven without having to die first.

[21] An Arab pagan named 'Adi ibn Hatim, the son of the legendary chief, Hatim Tai, of whom many stories of chivalry and generosity abound, accepted Christianity in the days before Islam came. During the war between the Meccans and the Muslims in Medina, 'Adi ibn Hatim's tribe, the Banu Tai, fought against the Muslims. Some of his family members were captured, and he felt compelled to resettle in Syria. The Prophet, however, quickly freed 'Adi's relatives, including his sister, and he even gave her generous gifts. Thereafter, she traveled to Syria to meet her brother, and she exhorted him to accept Islam and pay a visit to the Prophet in Medina. He threw caution to the wind and made the two-week journey to Medina. When he finally met the Prophet, he ('Adi) was wearing a silver cross around his neck. The Prophet saw this and recited this verse, but then 'Adi interjected, saying, "They didn't worship (their scholars and saints)!" Thereupon the Prophet replied, "Yes, they did. (Their theologians and saints) used to prohibit what was allowed (for Jews and Christians), and they allowed what was prohibited, and (their followers) obeyed them. This is how they 'worshipped' them." Then the Prophet said, "'Adi, what do you say? Did you run away (to Syria to keep from hearing,) '*Allah is the Greatest*,' proclaimed? Do you know of anything greater than Allah? What made you run away? Did you run away so (you wouldn't have to hear,) '*There is no god other than Allah*,' being proclaimed? Do you know of any god who is more worthy of worship than the One God?" Then the Prophet invited 'Adi to embrace Islam, and he eagerly accepted. Thereafter, the Prophet said, "Truly, the Jews have earned (Allah's) anger, while the Christians are (merely) mistaken." (*Ahmad, Tirmidhi*)

Him! [22] He is far more glorified than the partners they ascribe to Him! [23] [31]

This is the True Religion and it will Prevail

They want to put out the light of Allah's (truth) with their mouths, but Allah won't allow anything but the perfection of His light to be completed, no matter how much the faithless hate it. [32] He's the One Who sent His Messenger with guidance and the true way of life so that it can prevail over all other ways of life, no matter how much the idol-worshippers hate it. [24] [33]

Beware the Corruption of "Men of God"

O you who believe! Truly, there are many theologians and saints who deceptively eat up the wealth of the people, and thus they divert them from Allah's path. [25] There are those who stow away (untaxed) gold and silver without spending it in Allah's way, so give them the news of a painful punishment. [26] [34] (That will be) a day when (their

---

[22] The issue is not that they listened to their scholars, for scholars are important in learning God's religion. (See 16:43) The problem is that the Jews and Christians would ignore or bypass what their scriptures said and ask the scholars directly without bothering to read the scriptures for themselves. Thus, any scholar, priest or rabbi was free to give whatever opinion he wished without worrying that his flock would check on the truth of his ruling. Many examples of this abound, such as the priests of the Middle Ages selling 'indulgences,' which were basically tickets purchased to lessen one's stay in purgatory. Among Jewish rabbis there are also many such practices, such as the writing of spells, good luck charms and incantations for sale to the gullible public, of which many examples have been unearthed by archeologists throughout the Middle East. Muslim *imams* and scholars, by the way, are also sometimes guilty of these types of practices.

[23] As in Deuteronomy 6:4-9 or Mark 12:29-30.

[24] The Prophet said, "Allah made the eastern and western regions of the earth come close for me (to see), and the rule of my community will extend as far as I saw." (*Muslim*) The Islamic world grew and expanded continually until the fifteenth century and eventually stretched from Spain and Morocco in the west to Indonesia in the east. Thereafter, it began to shrink, and it continues to crumble around the edges as various non-Muslim powers chip away at it and absorb chunks of it into their nations, a development that the Prophet also foretold in numerous reports.

[25] Most commentators are of the opinion that this verse is a general warning for all religious leaders and that this warning also applies to Muslim religious leaders. The Prophet said, "The slaves of the dollar (*dinar*) are losers. The slaves of the silver coin (*dirham*) are losers." (*Ibn Kathir*)

[26] The famous companion of the Prophet, Salman al-Farsi, had been a Christian for a time and served various priests in Syria. He commented on seeing both honest and

19

wealth) will be made burning hot in the fires of Hell, and it will be used to brand their foreheads, their sides and their backs. [27] *"This is what you stowed away for yourselves! Now experience (the value) of what you stowed away!"* [35]

Don't Alter the Calendar to Gain an Advantage

Background on verses 36-37: Of the twelve months, the pagan Arabs set aside four as holy or truce months. During those months, people were encouraged to travel for religious purposes and for trade, and hostilities were supposed to be suspended. This was the custom since time immemorial in the Arabian Peninsula, but the various pagan groups played with this sanctity by arbitrarily postponing holy month restrictions as it suited them by changing the date or inserting an extra month at will. Thus, one side in a war between cities or tribes might stop their own offensive activities, while another might continue theirs, saying they're delaying the start of the holy month's restrictions upon them. This was, of course, a chaotic mockery of the concept of truce months.

Therefore, in their ongoing struggle with the pagans of Arabia, the Muslims were often at a disadvantage, for the pagans would postpone or advance the restrictions of the truce months at their whim. Meanwhile the Muslims would be divided about what to do when attacked in a holy month, with some wanting to defend themselves and others hesitant to respond and violate the sanctity of the truce month. This passage was revealed to inform the Muslims that if the pagans violate the truce months, then they should be united together in confronting them. *(Ibn Kathir)*

There are twelve numbered months in Allah's sight, and this was recorded by Him on the day He created the heavens and the earth. [28]

---

dishonest men of the cloth and even once witnessed a priest's hidden stash of gold being uncovered, much to the consternation of his congregation. When this verse was revealed, the Prophet exclaimed, "Perish, all gold! Perish, all silver!" He repeated this phrase three times, and then someone asked him, "Then what kind of wealth should we work towards?" Thereupon he answered him, saying, "A tongue that remembers (Allah), a submissive heart, and a spouse who supports (you) in practicing your religion." *(Zamakhshari)*

[27] The Prophet said of this verse that wealth accumulated by Muslims from which the *zakah* tax was not paid is also included as a source of condemnation on the Day of Judgment. *(Abu Dawud, Ahmad)*

[28] There are two systems in use in our world today to keep track of the passage of the years: the lunar calendar, based on the cycle of the moon; and the solar calendar, which is based on the movement of the earth around the sun. Both of them are built on the principle of twelve months consisting of around thirty days each, though the solar calendar is less accurate and requires periodic adjustment (leap years etc). The early Muslims knew of both systems, and the medieval writer, Ibn al-'Arabi, commented on the utility of both in these words: "The solar calendar is for the benefit of worldly matters, while the lunar calendar is for religious observances." So while modern Muslims (and Jews) often regulate their religious festivals by the lunar cycle, they have generally made

Four of them have sacred restrictions, and that's the established custom, so do no wrong against yourselves within them (by violating this rule). [29] Fight against the idol-worshippers in a united front, even as they fight against you in a united front (even during the restricted months,) but know that Allah is with those who are mindful (of Him). [36]

Arbitrarily postponing (restricted months) is an added degree of suppression (of Allah's truth), and those who suppress (their awareness of the truth) are led into doing wrong on account of it. They make it lawful one year (to violate a restricted month) and forbidden another year.

They adjust the number of months restricted by Allah, so (in their eyes) restricted months become lawful! The wickedness of their actions seems good to them, but Allah won't guide a people who suppress (their faith). [37]

Answer the Call to Fight

Background on verses 38-42: In the year 630, the Prophet received word from visiting Syrian olive traders that the Byzantines had amassed an army and were preparing an attack on Medina. Apparently, word of the success of Islam had reached the Byzantine emperor Heraclius, and he was not one to allow a new power to rise, especially since he had recently concluded a terrible war with the Persians in the year 627. Thus, the Byzantines mobilized and began operations against any Arab tribes that were inclined towards Islam in southern Iraq and Syria. The Prophet organized his followers to march northward to meet this new challenge. The Expedition to Tabuk, as it came to be called, saw no combat, as the Byzantines withdrew unexpectedly. Yet, the Prophet's hand was strengthened in southern Syria and Iraq when he contracted alliances with local rulers all over the area. A faction of hypocrites decided to remain in Medina and thus weakened the potential size and resources of the expedition. Their cowardice is what this passage is referencing.

---

compromises with the solar calendar currently in ascendancy in this materialistically oriented world.

[29] During the Prophet's last pilgrimage to Mecca, he actually fixed the correct start for the month of Hajj, as among the Arab tribes no one could agree on exactly what day that month started. (*Ma'ariful Qur'an*) The four sacred months are *Dhul Qa'dah*, *Dhul Hijjah*, *Muharram* and *Rajab*, and Islam retains only the emphasis that those months are times for increased worship and devotion. The first three months are contiguous in the calendar. As a note of interest, the Arabic word for month, *shahr*, is used exactly twelve times throughout the Qur'an. The word for day, *yawm*, is used 365 times. The plural term for days, *ayyam* and *yawmayn*, are used exactly 30 times. (There are usually thirty days in each month in the Islamic calendar.)

Oyou who believe! What's wrong with you? When you're called to go out and fight in the cause of Allah, suddenly you hold tightly to the earth? Do you prefer the life of this world more than the next life? But the life of this world provides such little comfort when compared to the next life! [30] [38]

If you don't go out, then He'll punish you severely, and then He'll just replace you with another people. You bring no harm upon Him at all (by refusing to answer His call), for He has power over all things. [39]

If you don't help (the Prophet against the Byzantine Romans,) then (you should know that) Allah helped him when the faithless drove him away (from Mecca and tried to hunt him down). He was just one of two (men hiding out) in a cave when he said to his companion, (Abu Bakr, who was afraid that the Meccans would capture them), *"Don't be afraid, for Allah is with us."* [31]

Then Allah sent His tranquility down upon him, and (later, at the Battle of Badr,) He strengthened him with forces (of angels) that you couldn't even see. He brought down utterly the (boasting) claims of the faithless, for Allah's word is the highest of all. [32] Allah is indeed powerful and wise. [40] March out, whether lightly or heavily

---

[30] When the Islamic governor of Egypt, 'Abdul-'Aziz ibn Marwan (the man who married 'Umar ibn al-Khattab's granddaughter and who was the father of the Umayyad Caliph, 'Umar ibn Abdul-'Aziz) was near death, he said to his assistants, "Bring the burial shroud that I will be covered in to me so I can inspect it." When it was brought before him, he looked at it and said, "Is this all that I'm going to have from this life?" He then turned his back and cried while saying, "Damn you, life! Your abundance is meager; your meagerness is short lived, and you tricked us." (*Ibn Kathir*)

[31] The Prophet and Abu Bakr hid out in a cave for three days after they fled their hometown in 622 CE, trying to escape from a Meccan assassination plot. The Meccans sent out patrols and offered a handsome reward for the one who would bring Muhammad back - *dead or alive*. One such patrol came near the cave, and its men dismounted and approached the small opening. Abu Bakr whispered to the Prophet, "If any one of them looks down by his feet, he will see us." The Prophet replied, "Abu Bakr, what do you think about two people who have Allah as their third?" The Meccan bounty hunters found a cobweb covering the cave entrance and also a pigeon's nest. They concluded that the cave had been undisturbed for some time, and they left. (*Ibn Hisham*)

[32] When the Prophet and his followers were living under persecution in Mecca, the pagans often boasted of their strength and promised that they would prevail. Now after their defeat, their boasts were brought down to nothingness, and Allah's word prevailed.

equipped, and strive with your wealth and your persons in the cause of Allah. That's best for you if you only knew. [41]

If there would be a guaranteed profit and an easy journey, then they all would follow you, but it's going to be a far distance, (and it will be hard) on them, so much so that (many of them are now falsely) swearing, *"If only we could make it, then we would certainly accompany you."* They're destroying themselves (with their false assertions), for Allah knows that they're lying. [42]

On those Who Made Excuses and Remained at Home

May Allah forgive you (Muhammad)! [33] Why did you grant anyone exemptions (from joining the Expedition to Tabuk) before you even had the opportunity to see clearly which of them were honest (in their petitions) and which of them were liars? [43]

Those who (really) believe in Allah and the Last Day would never ask to be excused from striving with their wealth and their persons, and Allah knows best who's mindful (of their duty to Him). [44] The only ones who ever ask to be excused are those who don't believe in Allah and the Last Day and whose hearts are filled with doubts - leaving them hesitant in their misgivings. [45]

If they had really intended to march out, then they would've made some kind of preparations for it. Therefore, Allah didn't like that they should march out (anyway, due to the mischief they would've caused along the way), so He hindered them further, and they lagged behind. Thus, they were told, *"Sit with those who stay and sit (at home)."* [46]

---

[33] The Prophet, being soft-hearted, began granting exemptions to people from the general mobilization he had called for earlier for the two-week march northward to Syria. (Many of these exemptions were granted to people who were otherwise fit for service.) Similar to the reason for the revelation of chapter 80, this passage contains an admonition from Allah to the Prophet for such honest errors in judgment. Allah wanted to expose for the believers what was really in their hearts, so each could understand if he was truly obedient or merely paying lip service. This is a prime example of how the Qur'an was an interactive revelation among Allah, the Prophet and those around him, both believers and unbelievers. Through this lively dialogue, if you will, between Allah and the community He was nurturing, one can more easily understand how to apply the Qur'an's guidance in his life.

If they would've marched out with you, they wouldn't have augmented (your strength).   Rather, they would've caused indiscipline (among your men) as they scurried about in your midst, sowing seeds of sedition among you.

Some of you would have listened to them, and Allah knows who the corrupt ones are. [47] As it is, they had already plotted sedition before, and had made your situation unsettled (in the past), even until the truth arrived and the order of Allah became clear, though they hated it. [34] [48]

Hypocrites are Unreliable

Background on verse 49: This was the statement of Jadd ibn Qays, who was a leader among the Banu Salamah tribe. The Prophet had asked him, "Would you like to go and fight the yellow ones (the Romans) this year?" Ibn Qays replied, "Messenger of Allah! Grant me an exemption, and don't put me in turmoil, for by Allah, my people know that there isn't a man who is more attracted to women than I, and I'm afraid that if see the women of the (Romans) that I wouldn't have any patience (to control myself)." So the Prophet granted him an exemption on such a flimsy excuse. Then the Prophet advised the rest of the Banu Salamah tribe to chose another chief. 'Abdullah ibn Ubayy of the Auws tribe also (predictably) asked for an exemption. (*Asbab ul-Nuzul*)

Among them are some who said, *"Grant me an exemption, and don't give me a hard trial to face,"* but hadn't they already been tried

---

[34] During his early days in Medina, the Prophet had to deal with a faction of hypocrites, led by 'Abdullah ibn Ubayy, who stirred up trouble at every turn. Ibn Ubayy later passed away from old age, and the Prophet buried him graciously with respect. However, the hypocrites Ibn Ubayy helped to cultivate remained and continued to work against the Prophet from behind the scenes. Even after Mecca was vanquished without a fight, making Allah's "order" clear, they still tried to create sedition at every turn. It was a faction of these hypocrites who caused two opposing Muslim forces to fight in later years during the rule of 'Ali ibn Abi Talib (the fourth caliph) at the Battle of the Camel in Iraq (656 CE). Ironically, 'Ali commanded one army, and the Prophet's widow A'ishah commanded the other. She led a coalition seeking justice against the killers of Uthman ibn Affan (d. 656), who had been the third caliph, and she and her group thought 'Ali was moving too slowly in this regard. The two groups were preparing to mediate their dispute with negotiations, but the hypocrites, who had placed men in both camps, suddenly rushed out at each other to make it seem as if a battle had been ordered. The unsuspecting men on both sides then flew at each other in a mad rush and chaos broke out. Such was the reach and devious nature of the hypocrites of Medina.

before (during previous battles)! Truly, Hellfire surrounds all those who suppress (their faith)! [49]

If something good happens to you, it bothers them, but if some disaster strikes you, they say, *"We prepared ourselves (for this setback) beforehand,"* and then they turn away self-satisfied. [50] Say (to them), *"Nothing happens to us except what Allah has already recorded for us, and He's our Protector."* So let the believers trust in Allah! [51]

Then say (to them), *"Are you expecting anything else for us other than one of two good possibilities, (either victory or martyrdom)? All the while we're expecting that you'll receive a punishment from Allah, either from His Own Self or from our hands. Just wait and see, and we'll be waiting, too."* [52]

And tell them, *"Spend whatever you want or whatever you feel compelled to (spend to support the northern expedition,) but it won't be accepted (as a good deed by Allah), for you're a rebelliously disobedient people."* [53]

Their contributions won't be accepted because they rejected Allah and His Messenger. They come to prayers lacking motivation, and they spend (in charity) only reluctantly. [54] So don't be impressed by their money or their sons. Allah wants to punish them with these things in the life of this world, so they'll leave (this life) with souls that have rejected (Allah). [35] [55]

They swear to Allah that they're on your side, but they're not on your side. They're constantly nervous (that they might be singled out)! [56] If they could find some place to escape to, either a cave or a hideout, they would turn towards it straightaway in a rush. [57]

---

[35] Remember that if a person rejects Allah, then Allah leaves him to wander in ignorance and doesn't guide him. Still the person has a chance to use his insight and turn back towards the path, and in that case, Allah will rush back to him or her and open the doors of His wisdom and forgiveness. However, if a person not only rejects Allah's good way of life, but then becomes wicked and oppressive to his fellow creatures, and worse still, if he dedicates his life to fighting against Allah, then Allah wants to punish such a person, and He makes no effort to give him hints to stoke his desire for reform. When such miserable souls die, punishment is their due reward.

Hypocrites are never Satisfied

Background on verses 58-59: When the Prophet was distributing some charity, a recent convert from among the bedouins named Hurqoos ibn Zuhayr (*aka* Dhul Huwaysira) was unsatisfied with his share, and he said, "Be fair! Be fair!" 'Umar got angry and asked the Prophet for permission to kill the disrespectful man, but the Prophet stopped him and replied to Hurqoos, "Woe to you! Who is fairer than I am?" Then the Prophet said, "If I weren't fair, then I'd be truly lost!"

After Hurqoos left, the Prophet told his companions, "Among this man's descendants will be some whose prayer, when one of you sees it, would make his own prayer seem lacking, and his fast will seem the same as compared to their fast, but they will be rebels in religion, just like an arrow goes through the body of a hunted animal. Wherever you find them, fight them, for truly they're the worst (spiritually) dead people under the cover of the sky." (*Bukhari*)

This passage was then revealed about Hurqoos. Years after the Prophet's passing, Hurqoos joined an extremist group of ultra-purists known as the *Kharajites*, and he fell in the Battle of Nahrawan against the caliph's forces. Extremist groups to this day generally follow this deviant ideology, which is based on the notion that all Muslims besides themselves are hopeless sinners in need of correction, though they've renamed themselves in recent years with a nod, ironically, towards the pious ancestors.

Among them are some who talk against you with regards to (how you're distributing) charity. If they're given some, then they're happy, but if they're not (given any), *then they're upset!* [58]

If only they would've been satisfied with what Allah and His Messenger had given them and had said, *"Allah is enough for us! Allah and His Messenger will give us something from His bounty soon enough, and we place our hopes (for material blessings) in Allah."* [59]

Those Deserving of Charity

Background on verse 60: This verse was revealed after a man had approached the Prophet, asking for some goods to be given to him out of the funds for distribution. The Prophet replied, "Allah, the Most High, never allowed any prophet to distribute the *sadaqah* by his own decision, nor did He give this power to anyone who was not a prophet. He determined from His Own Self eight categories (of people who are to receive it.) If you fall under one of those eight categories, then I can let you have some." (*Abu Dawud*)

Charity [36] is meant for the poor, for the needy, [37] for those whose profession it is to distribute it, [38] for encouraging (recent converts), [39] for the (freeing) of bonded servants, [40] for those

---

[36] There are seven types of financial collection in Islam. The first is *zakah*, which is the required 2.5% payment of one's yearly savings (also 10% of annual agricultural produce), payable to the state or other institution for distribution to the needy. The second is called *sadaqah*, which is mentioned here in this verse. *Sadaqah* (which is derived from the word for *truth*, as in being true to the cause of Allah by voluntarily spending in His cause for His reward alone) is the general charity that one gives, either formally or informally, above and beyond *zakah*, for the sake of pleasing Allah and alleviating the suffering of one's fellows in need. (Non-Muslims in need can be given *sadaqah*, as per the call of the Prophet who said, "Give *sadaqah* to the people of all religions." (*Ma'ariful Qur'an*) What if you don't have any money to give to help the needy? The Prophet said, "Even a smile is charity." The scholars also note that *imam*, missionary, teacher and scholar's salaries can also be paid out of collected *sadaqah*, as these activities are the duty of the Muslim community to support. The other four collections are: *khums*, or the fifth share. The government gets a fifth of any war booty, discovered treasure or mineral and mining proceeds. Then there are two types of capital taxes called *kharaj* and *fai'* collected from non-Muslims, based on the income of their land holdings. (Muslim owned land is taxed under *zakah* calculations.) A further tax on able-bodied, employed non-Muslim men called *jizyah* exempts them from military service. Finally, there is *daawa'i*, or abandoned property, including the wealth of a person who dies with absolutely no heirs to inherit his holdings. The government takes over this property. (*Ma'ariful Qur'an*)

[37] The difference between the poor (*fuqara*) and the needy (*miskeen*) is that the poor are people with self-respect who don't beg, whereas the needy are those who are so desperate that they feel they have no choice but to beg. Another way of looking at it is that the poor are those who have a legitimate reason for their condition, such as illness that prevents them from working, whereas the needy are able-bodied people who suffer sudden disaster. The Prophet gave the three cases when an able-bodied person can lawfully beg. These are a debtor who can no longer handle his debts, a person afflicted with disaster that impoverished him, and a man who was stricken with poverty beyond his control, so much so that three of his relatives come to know of it. (*Muslim*) What of an able-bodied person who is under no strain but who chooses to beg? The Prophet said, "Charity should not be given to a rich person or to a person who is physically fit." (*Ahmad, Abu Dawud, Tirmidhi*)

[38] People hired to supervise and distribute charity to the needy can be paid their salaries from the general charity fund.

[39] This stipulation has two purposes. The first is to help indigent or struggling converts. The second is to use cash to further solidify the loyalty of those converts whose influence or skills are useful to the Islamic movement, and for whom financial rewards would be a strong motivation to commit wholeheartedly to the cause. The Prophet employed this strategy with some notables, such as with the chief of Ta'if after he converted to Islam (though he was given gifts from the war booty), and some men received sustained payments throughout Abu Bakr's reign. During the tenure of 'Umar ibn al-Khattab, he cancelled such payments, saying, "Allah has uplifted Islam and is no longer in need of their support."

[40] Slavery, as the Western world understands it, is not a part of Islam. Captives of war can be (but do not have to be) turned into indentured or bonded servants as a consequence of being enemies of Allah's religion, but they have the same basic *human* rights in Islam as any free person and can even petition their retainer for a contract

(straining under a load) of debt, for use in the cause of Allah, [41] and also (to help stranded) travelers. These are the stipulations set by Allah, and Allah is full of knowledge and wisdom. [60]

Don't Annoy the Prophet

Background on verse 61: Some hypocrites were slandering the Prophet, and when they were told to stop, one of them said, "He'll listen to anybody." This meant that they felt they could lie to the Prophet's face and convince him that they didn't say anything wrong. This verse references that. (*Ibn Kathir*)

Among them are some who upset the Prophet when they say, *"He'll listen to anybody."* Reply to them, saying, *"He listens to what's best for you. He believes in Allah. He believes in the (integrity of) the faithful, and he's a mercy for those who believe."* Whoever upsets the Prophet will have a painful punishment. [61]

They swear to Allah in front of you to impress you, but it would be more appropriate for them to impress (both) Allah and His Messenger, if they're (sincere) believers. [42] [62] Don't they know that the fire of Hell is reserved for all who oppose Allah and His Messenger and that that's where they'll have to stay? That's the worst humiliation of all! [63]

---

whereby they can buy their freedom. Contrary to popular misconceptions about Islam in some circles, and despite abuses that may have occurred in some eras of Muslim history, the simple fact remains that from its sources, Islam does not promote the capture or holding of bonded laborers. (The Prophet said that it is forbidden to enslave a free person, so going out to kidnap people to make them slaves is forbidden in Islam, as well.) Indeed, Islam employs a mechanism to encourage, and sometimes even require, people to free their bonded servants, and the companions were well-known to free people *en masse*. A man once asked the Prophet, "Messenger of Allah, direct me to an action that will draw me closer to Paradise and keep me away from the Fire." The Prophet replied, "Emancipate a person and free the neck (of a servant)." The man asked, "Messenger of Allah, aren't they both the same thing?" The Prophet answered, "No, when you emancipate a person, you're doing it on your own, but you free a neck (from servanthood) when you help in the price (required to free someone)." (*Ahmad*) Once, when the Prophet was told that a man got angry, slapped his maidservant and then freed her out of fear of Allah, he remarked that if he hadn't have freed her, then he would have been punished by Allah.

[41] The *cause of Allah* is a general theme that early scholars unanimously understood to mean either *zakah* or *jihad*.

[42] The commentators explain that by pleasing the Prophet, one is also pleasing Allah, for the Prophet is the instrument of Allah's will on earth.

The Apprehension of the Hypocrites

Background on verse 64: During the Expedition to Tabuk, some hypocrites were ridiculing the Prophet for daring to march an army northward, saying, "This man wants to conquer all of Syria – its palaces and fortresses, and it's just not possible." Others took to belittling the sincere believers and making fun of them. This verse was revealed in response. (*Asbab ul-Nuzul*)

The hypocrites are afraid that a chapter might be revealed about them, exposing what's really in their hearts. Say (to them), *"Go ahead and make fun of (this message)! Allah will bring out whatever you're worried about (and make it known)!"* [64]

Background on verse 65: A hypocrite said in a gathering while encamped during the Expedition to Tabuk, "I've never seen any (oral) reciters like ours! They have the hungriest stomachs, the most deceitful tongues, and they're the most cowardly in battle." A sincere Muslim spoke out, saying, "You lie! You're a hypocrite, and I'm going to tell the Messenger of Allah." When the Prophet was informed, he summoned the man who said it. The man kept saying he was only joking. Then this verse was revealed. (*Ibn Kathir*)

If you ask them (what they were talking about), they say, *"We were just talking nonsense, all in good fun."* Ask them, *"Were you poking fun at Allah, His verses and His Messenger?"* [65]

Make no more excuses, you people who rejected (faith) after (supposedly) having accepted it! [43] Although We may forgive some of you, We're still going to punish others among you on account of their wickedness. [66]

Hypocrites Protect Each Other

Hypocrites, both males and females, are all alike with each other. They call (people) towards bad conduct and discourage good behavior, while closing their hands tight (to avoid giving in charity). They've forgotten Allah, so He's forgotten them. The hypocrites are certainly rebellious wrongdoers. [44] [67]

---

[43] The Prophet said, "The example of a hypocrite is that of a sheep wandering between two herds. Sometimes she goes to one of them and sometimes to the other, and she's confused over whom she should follow." (*Muslim*)

[44] Conscious hypocrisy is considered one of the gravest shortcomings in the pantheon of sins in Islam. The two-faced liar is on a much lower scale than the person who is sinful

Allah has made a promise to the hypocrites, both male and female, and to those who suppress (their faith in Him), that they will have the fires of Hell in which to dwell. [45] That will be enough for them, for Allah's curse and a relentless punishment are what they're going to get! [68]

"(All you hypocrites!) You're just like those who came before you. Yet, (the ancient peoples) had more (worldly) power, wealth and sons than you. They had their time to enjoy their share, even as you and those who came before you did, also. You even speak the same kind of nonsense that they did! Yet, their actions were useless, both in this world and the next, and they're going to be the losers (in the end, just as you will be, if you don't repent)." [46] [69]

Haven't they heard the stories of those who went before them, of the people of Noah, the (tribes) of 'Ad and Thamud, the people of Abraham, the companions of Madyan, and of the overthrown (towns of Sodom and Gomorrah)? Messengers went to all of them with clear evidence (of the truth). It wasn't Allah who did them any wrong, for they wronged their own souls. [70]

The Unbreakable Bonds of Brotherhood

The believers, both male and female, are the close protectors of one another. They command what is recognized (as good) and forbid

---

in ignorance of morality or the truth. As such, the Qur'an often speaks of hypocrites as receiving punishments far in excess of the ignorantly sinful.

[45] 'Umar ibn al-Khattab went to the main mosque in Medina and found Mu'adh ibn Jabal sitting by the Prophet's grave, weeping. 'Umar asked him why he was crying, and Mu'adh replied that it was something that he had heard from the Messenger of Allah so many years before. He said that the Prophet had said, "A little bit of hypocrisy is like making partners with Allah. Anyone who is hostile to a friend of Allah is on his way to opposing Allah. Allah loves the fair, pious and secluded people whom no one notices are absent. (They're the) people who don't receive invitations (to parties) and who are not treated with honor when they're present. Their hearts are the lamps of guidance, and they come out from every dusty and obscure place." (*Ibn Majah, Bayhaqi*)

[46] The Prophet warned Muslims, saying, "You will adopt the ways of communities that came before you, and you will copy them in everything, so much so that if you were to see one of them crawling into a lizard's hole, you would follow him." When Ibn 'Abbas heard about this saying, he mused, "How similar is our night (century) to last night (former centuries). They are the Children of Israel, and we've been likened to them." (*Qurtubi*)

what is unfamiliar (to Allah's way of life). They establish prayer, give in charity, and obey Allah and His Messenger. Allah will pour His mercy down upon them, for Allah is powerful and wise. [71]

Allah has made a promise to the believers, both male and female, of gardens beneath which rivers flow in which to dwell, and beautiful mansions in everlasting gardens of delight. [47] However, the greatest delight of all is to please Allah, and that's also the greatest success! [72]

Be Firm against Hypocrites and their Wily Ways

O Prophet! Strive hard against the faithless and the hypocrites. Be firm with them, for their dwelling place is in Hellfire – *the worst destination!* [73]

Background on the first part of verse 74: The first part of this verse references what a hypocrite named Julas said while on the expedition. Julas had just finished hearing a speech by the Prophet in which he had warned the hypocrites that their opposition to Allah was tearing them apart inside and that Allah would punish them in the next life. Julas then returned to his friends and said, "By Allah! If what Muhammad says is true, then we're worse than donkeys." A dependent of his named 'Amr ibn Qays retorted, saying, "What Muhammad says *is* true, and so you are worse than donkeys." Then he told Julas, "By Allah! Julas, you're the closest person to me; you've been the most favorable to me, and I would never want any harm to touch you more than anyone else! But you've said something that, if I told on you, then you would be exposed (as a hypocrite), but if I hid it, it would destroy me. One of them is the lesser of the two evils."

After the Muslims returned to Medina from Tabuk, 'Amr went and told the Prophet what Julas had said. The Prophet summoned him to the mosque and asked him why he said what he did. Julas invoked the curse of Allah upon himself if he was lying, and then he swore to Allah facing the pulpit of the mosque that he never said anything like that. 'Amr swore he was truthful, as well, and then said, "O Allah! Prove the truth of the honest and expose the lies of the liar." Then this verse was revealed to the Prophet, and he recited it. Thereafter, Julas repented of his words, and it is said that his repentance was sincere. He was never known to indulge in hypocrisy again (*Ibn Kathir*)

---

[47] A group of companions said to the Prophet, "Messenger of Allah, talk to us about Paradise; of what is it made?" He replied, "Bricks of gold and bricks of silver. Its cement is made of musk; its gravel is of pearls and rubies, and its sand is of saffron. Whoever enters it will enjoy its delights and will never get depressed, and they will live forever and will never die. Their clothes will never wear out, nor will their youth ever fade." (*Ahmad*)

They swear to Allah that they've never said anything (against you), but indeed they've uttered words of rejection, and they're rejecting (Allah) even after (they claimed) to have submitted (to Him).

Background on the last part of verse 74: On the journey back from the Tabuk expedition, a faction of hypocrites who had wanted 'Abdullah ibn Ubayy to be crowned king plotted to assassinate the Prophet by surrounding him slowly with their numbers and then pushing him off his mount down a cliff, if ever one appeared on the trail. However, their plot unraveled due to the vigilance of two companions who never left the Prophet's side and warned him when the men began to converge on his intended path. The Prophet shouted at them, and they fled. He asked the two men who had been watching over him, Hudhayfah and 'Ammar, if they knew who the men were. Hudhayfah replied, "No, Messenger of Allah. They were wearing masks, but we do recognize their horses."

The Prophet then said, "They're going to be hypocrites until the Day of Judgment. Do you know what they wanted to do?" The two men answered in the negative, and the Prophet said, "They wanted to surround the Messenger of Allah and throw him (down into) the valley." Hudhayfah said, "Messenger of Allah! Should you ask their tribes to send their heads to you?" The Prophet answered, "No, for I wouldn't want it to be said by the Arabs that Muhammad used some people for fighting and, after Allah gave him victory with their help, that he commanded them to be killed." Then he said, "O Allah, throw a *dubaylah* at them." The men asked the Prophet what that was, and he replied, "It's a fiery dart that falls into the heart of one of them and brings about his end." Later on someone asked Hudhayfah about those assassins, and Hudhayfah mentioned that the Prophet told him the names of all of them, and he told no one else. Thus, Hudhayfah had the nickname, "*The Holder of the Secret*." (*At-Tabari*)

They tried to (assassinate the Prophet), though they were unable to carry it out. *This was their response to the bounty with which Allah and His Messenger had enriched them!* [48] If they repent, it would be the best for them, but if they persist (in their rebellious ways,) then Allah will punish them with a painful penalty, both in this life and in the next. In that case, no one on earth would be able to protect them or help them! [74]

On Those Who Betray their Pledge

Background on verses 75-78: A man named Tha'labah went to the Prophet and asked for him to beseech Allah to make him rich. The Prophet said to him, "Woe to you, Tha'labah, a little thanks that you can give is much better than what you won't be able to handle." Then the Prophet told him that if he really wanted riches, then he could invoke Allah to give them to him. Thereupon, Tha'labah

---

[48] In other words, how thankless can they be? Islam brought civilization and order to the wild pagans of Arabia. Allah favored them in many battles with their enemies, and on top of that, the journey to Tabuk had been wildly successful for all concerned.

swore the oath that is contained in verse 75. The Prophet then gave Tha'labah a herd of sheep, and within a short amount of time the herd expanded greatly, causing Tha'labah to become very wealthy. Because of the size of his herds, though, he also had to move progressively farther from Medina, resulting in his more and more infrequent visits to worship in the mosque. Later on, when the Prophet sent people to collect the charity tax from Tha'labah, he put off the tax collectors on two separate occasions.

This passage was then revealed about him, and someone went to him and told him, "You're ruined! A passage has been revealed about you!" So Tha'labah hurried to the Prophet and begged him to accept his charitable contribution, but the Prophet told him that Allah has forbidden him from accepting his charity. Then Tha'labah began throwing dust on his own head in sorrow, and the Prophet told him, "It's because of what you did. I gave you an order, and you disobeyed it." After the Prophet's passing, Tha'labah went to Caliph Abu Bakr and begged him to accept his charity, and Abu Bakr refused, saying the Prophet never accepted it. The same thing happened during the rule of 'Umar ibn al-Khattab and Uthman ibn Affan (d. 656), and Tha'labah passed away in despair during Uthman's reign. (*Ibn Kathir*) It is said that Allah did not accept his repentance because he harbored hypocrisy in his heart. (*Ma'ariful Qur'an*)

Among them are some who made a deal with Allah that if He gave them (great riches) from His Own bounty, then they would (reciprocate) by giving (richly) in charity (in the cause of Allah), and further that they would be among the righteous. [75] Yet, when He *did* give them (riches) from His bounty, they became greedy and turned back, reluctant (to support the cause). [76]

So He let hypocrisy grow in their hearts (as a result,) and it will remain there until the day when they're going to meet Him (for judgment), and that's because they broke their deal with Allah and also because they lied. [77] Don't they realize that Allah knows all their secrets and their veiled schemes and that Allah knows what's hidden (in the deep recesses of their hearts)? [78]

Don't Belittle the Donations of the Poor

Background on verse 79: The Prophet made a public call one day for donations to support the cause. A poor man named Abu 'Aqil came and donated a small amount of dates, explaining that he worked all night drawing water, earned two measures of dates for his pay and was thus donating half of what he earned. Some hypocrites laughed and said, "Allah and His Messenger don't need this (small amount), for what benefit could it bring." The Prophet then picked up the dates with his own hands and placed it atop the pile of donated money and goods. Then a man named 'Abdurrahman ibn 'Awf came forward and asked if anyone else was going to give in charity, and the Prophet replied, "No one except you."

Thereupon 'Abdurrahman declared he was donating a huge sum of gold in charity. 'Umar ibn al-Khattab said, "Are you crazy?" 'Abdurrahman said that he wasn't and explained that he really did have that much money, and he donated it. The hypocrites defamed him and said he just wanted to show off. This verse was revealed regarding this incident and is meant to show that even a little given sincerely can mean a great deal in Allah's sight and that a lot given in Allah's cause should be praised and not ridiculed. (*Asbab ul-Nuzul*)

Those who ridicule the believers when they give in charity from their own convictions, [49] or who (ridicule those who have) nothing more to give than their own labor due to their poverty, and then who further tease them (for donating huge sums of their resources to Allah's cause, should know) that Allah will throw their ridicule back upon them and that they're going to have a painful punishment. [79]

Whether you ask for their forgiveness or not – even if you asked seventy times for their forgiveness, Allah won't forgive them because they rejected Allah and His Messenger. [50] Allah will not guide a people who are rebellious and corrupt. [80]

About Those Who Remained behind in Medina

Background on verses 81-83: There was a heat wave and famine in Medina, and the journey north to Syria was going to be a long, hard trek of two weeks. The Prophet warned his followers of this and asked for donations to cover the expenses of the mission. Many Muslims came forward, men and women, and huge sums of money were donated. However, some others warned against the discomfort of the hot journey and tried to dissuade their friends from going. This passage was revealed about them. (*Ibn Kathir*)

Those who remained behind (in Medina) rejoiced in their inaction behind the back of the Messenger of Allah. They hated (even the mere thought) of striving in the cause of Allah with their wealth and their persons, and they said, *"Don't go out (on the Expedition to Tabuk)*

---

[49] The hypocrites were never satisfied and took every opportunity to belittle those who gave to support the Islamic cause. According to Abu Mas'ud: "If a person brought a large donation, (the hypocrites) would say, 'He is only showing off for the benefit of others,' but if a person brought a small donation, they would say, 'Allah doesn't need such (a small) donation.'" (*Bukhari, Muslim*)

[50] The allusion of the number seventy is perhaps to the time when Moses chose seventy of his people to go and ask Allah for forgiveness after the incident with the golden calf. See 7:155. On a side note, in Semitic parlance the number seventy is synonymous with 'a lot' of something.

because it's far too hot (in the desert)!" Say (to them), *"The fires of Hell are even hotter!"* If they would only realize it! [81]

So let them laugh a little now, for soon they will cry much more as a payback for what they've earned (for themselves on their record of deeds.) [82]

If Allah brings you back to any of them and they ask you for (permission) to venture out (with you on some future expedition), tell them, *"You're never going to venture out with me, nor will you ever fight an enemy by my side, for you chose to sit and be inactive the first time, so now keep sitting with those who get left behind."* [83]

Don't Honor a Hypocrite

Background on verses 84-85: This passage was revealed concerning 'Abdullah ibn Ubayy, the leader of the hypocrites of Medina. He passed away, and his son, who was a committed believer, went to the Prophet and asked if he could bury his father in one of the Prophet's robes. The Prophet gave it to him, and then the son asked the Prophet to pray for his departed father. The Prophet was about to pray for him when 'Umar ibn al-Khattab objected, saying that the dead man had been a hypocrite and an enemy of Allah. The Prophet replied, "I've been given the choice of whether to pray for him or not. I know that if I pray for the forgiveness of (a hypocrite) seventy times, he won't be forgiven. Yet, if I knew that he'd be forgiven if I prayed for forgiveness more than that, then I'd do it." (*Bukhari*) The reports differ as to whether the Prophet actually offered a funeral prayer for him or merely a supplication, but this passage was revealed sometime later, forbidding funeral prayers for known hypocrites.

Why did the Prophet give his robe for the funeral? After the Battle of Badr, many years before, one of the prisoners taken was the Prophet's pagan uncle 'Abbas. He had no shirt, and because he was a tall man, the Prophet asked for the equally tall 'Abdullah ibn Ubayy to give one of his shirts to clothe 'Abbas. He did so. The Prophet then was returning the favor. (*Qurtubi*) The Prophet said of the robe that was used to bury Ibn Ubayy: "What good will my clothes or my prayers do for him against Allah? I swear to Allah that I hope he is saved more than a thousand of his people." (*Asbab ul-Nuzul*) He also later remarked that he hoped by his action that thousands of Ibn Ubayy's followers would become Muslims. (*Ma'ariful Qur'an*) Even though he caused the Prophet much grief, the Prophet knew why 'Ibn Ubayy was a hypocrite, (he would have been made king of Yathrib, but for the coming of Islam). Thus, the Prophet always treated him as a special case and with compassion, even though Ibn Ubayy clearly didn't deserve it. (A stance that was ordered of the Prophet in verse 3:186.)

Never offer a (funeral) prayer for any of them that dies, nor stand by their grave (as they're being lowered down into it), for they rejected Allah and His Messenger, and thus died in a state of defiant rebellion. [84]

So neither be impressed by their money nor their (numerous) sons, for Allah wants to punish them through these things in this world so that they'll leave this life with souls that have lost (their ability to believe in Allah). [51] [85]

When a chapter came down (asking them) to believe in Allah and to strive alongside His Messenger, the eligible ones from among them came to you and asked for exemptions, saying, *"Leave us, for we'd rather stay with those who sit (at home)."* [52] [86] They preferred to be with those who stayed behind! Their hearts are sealed shut, and they understand nothing! [87]

However, the Messenger and the believers with him strive with their wealth and their persons. Therefore, they shall have the best (reward), even as they'll be the most successful. [88] Allah has prepared gardens for them beneath which rivers flow, and there they shall remain - *and that's the ultimate success!* [89]

---

[51] They have lost the ability to believe by the time they leave this life. That is the implication of the use of the root word *kafara* that is usually rendered as 'covered over,' 'rejected' or 'suppressed.'

[52] While it is true the Qur'an and the Prophet both speak out against the relentless acquisition of wealth, at the same time it must be clarified that Islam is not against a person being financially successful. The Prophet said, "There is no harm in being wealthy for one who is mindful of Allah, the Mighty and Exalted." (*Mishkat*) Likewise, there is no special blessing in being poor, for the Prophet warned that "Poverty can cause someone to lose (his ability to have faith)." (*Mishkat*) The trick is in maintaining your faith in whatever economic station you find yourself. Don't be blinded by wealth so much that you think only of it. Don't hoard wealth and refuse to spend it in Allah's way. Don't leave money to languish, but invest it so the increase can benefit both you and the rest of humanity. Don't waste money in frivolous pursuits. Don't be lazy with your economic horizons, and always seek to improve your condition, for making money is part of the blessings that Allah will bestow upon you. Finally, don't despair from poverty so much that you curse Allah and fall into a state of helplessness. The eminent early Muslim, Sufyan al-Thawri, once said, "Whoever has money in his hand should make good use of it, for there are times when, because of some need, one may wind up 'spending' his faith in order to satisfy that need." (*Mishkat*) In other words, a person may compromise his values if his need or greed get the better of him.

The Bedouins Offered their Excuses

Some of the (bedouin) Arabs also came to you in order to offer their excuses and to claim exemptions. [53] Thus, those who were dishonest to Allah and His Messenger sat idly by. It won't be long before a painful punishment overtakes those among them who suppressed (their awareness of the truth). [90]

There's no blame, however, on those who were too weak or ill or who couldn't find the resources to spend (for the journey), [54] as long as they're sincere to Allah and His Messenger. There are no grounds of complaint against the good (people who wanted to come, but who couldn't find a way), for Allah is forgiving and merciful. [91]

No Blame for those who could not be Accommodated

Background on verse 92: A group of men volunteered for the Expedition to Tabuk, but when the Prophet explained he had insufficient resources to equip any more men, they left weeping bitterly. The Prophet later told his companions after they returned from the journey, "Some people were left behind in Medina, but it was like they were with us all the time in every valley and every mountain pass we crossed. They were left behind only for legitimate reasons." (*Bukhari, Abu Dawud*)

(There are also no grounds of complaint) against those who came to you for transportation and to whom you had to say, "*I have no transportation for you.*" They turned back with tears overflowing from their eyes at their inability to spend (money to arrange their own way). [92]

There are, however, legitimate grounds (for complaint) against those who claimed exemption even though they were independently

---

[53] Many newly converted bedouins still had the tribal mentality of self-defense of the clan above all other considerations. Some bedouins felt that if their isolated camps were short of men, hostile tribes would take that as an opportunity to strike. (*Razi*) Muhammad was trying to change that mentality, and if enough bedouins of different groups joined him, those who remained behind would be more reluctant to attack the defenseless camps of their rivals. This coming together of all bedouins represented a sea change in the lifestyle of the desert nomads.

[54] At this time there was no established public treasury in the community. Any goods that had come into the control of the Muslims up to that point had been immediately spent on charity, supporting widows, etc.

wealthy. They preferred to remain with those who stayed behind. Therefore, their hearts were sealed shut, and they understood nothing. [93]

They're going to make their excuses to you when you return to them, but say (to them), *"Don't make any excuses (for your cowardice), because we're not going to believe you. Allah already told us about your situation, and it's what you do that Allah and His Messenger will consider. In the end, you're going to be brought back to the One Who knows the hidden and the clear, and then He's going to show you the true meaning of all that you did."* [94]

When you return back to them, they're going to swear to you in Allah's (name) that you should leave them alone - so go ahead and leave them alone (by shunning them), for they're stained (by their very own sins), and Hellfire is their destination. That's the reward they deserve for what they've done. [95]

They're also going to swear to you (as to the validity of their excuses), trying to make you pleased with them. If you do become pleased with them, (then you should know) that Allah is not pleased with those who were rebelliously disobedient. [96]

The (bedouin) Arabs are the worst when it comes to rejection and hypocrisy and are thus more likely to be ignorant of the command that Allah has sent down to His Messenger. [55] Allah is full of knowledge and wisdom. [97]

Some of the (bedouin) Arabs consider what they spend (in charity) to be a financial penalty. They keep looking for disasters to come

---

[55] The two bedouin tribes of Ghatafan and Asad are the main tribes referenced here. They were so wily and without honor that the Muslims were incredulous as to their wild ways and lack of sophistication and common sense. Once the Prophet was dealing with a bedouin from one of those tribes who brought a small gift to him – but then the man demanded a large one from the Prophet in exchange. The bedouin was so uncouth and uncivilized as to defy patience, causing the Prophet to remark later, "I almost decided never to accept any gift except from people of Quraysh, Thaqif, the Ansar or the tribe of Daws." (*Nisa'i*) The groups mentioned were either urban to semi-urban village dwellers with a sense of manners. The Prophet once remarked, "The one who lives in the desert becomes hard-hearted; the one who hunts game becomes careless, and the one who associates with rulers falls into controversies." (*Ahmad*)

upon you, but let the worst disasters fall upon them, for Allah listens and knows (all about their treachery). [98]

Some of the (bedouin) Arabs, however, do believe in Allah and the Last Day. They look upon what they spend (in charity) as a way to bring themselves closer to Allah's presence and to (be worthy) of the Prophet's prayers (for their forgiveness and success.) They truly are brought closer (to Allah by their charity and sincerity), and soon Allah will admit them to His mercy, for Allah is forgiving and merciful. [99]

Forgiveness is Offered Freely to those who Desire It

The forerunners (in faith) are those who were the first to migrate (from Mecca), then those who helped them (in Medina) and finally those who followed (closely behind) them in doing what was good. [56] Allah is pleased with them and they with Him, and He's prepared for them gardens beneath which rivers flow to live within forever. That's the ultimate success! [100]

Some of the (bedouin) Arabs (that live) around you (in the countryside) are hypocrites, even as there are (hypocrites) among the people of Medina. They're persistent in hypocrisy, and although you don't know (who they are), We know who they are. We're going to punish them twice (through fear and humiliation), [57] and then they're going to be sent into an even more severe punishment after that! [58] [101]

---

[56] The three groups who are praised as being in the forefront of faith are the Immigrants (*Muhajireen*) from Mecca, the Helpers (*Ansar*) of Yathrib who welcomed the Immigrants in and supported them, and finally the general body of believers who consistently do the right thing and support Allah's cause. The Prophet was particularly fond of the *Ansar*, and he later lamented that their numbers were thinning every year while the numbers of general converts were swelling. He exhorted the rest of the Muslim community to be kind to them, for they helped him when no one else did. He also said that none of his faithful companions will enter Hell. (*Tirmidhi*)

[57] They'll be punished twice in the world through their endless fear and stress at leading a double life, which will then culminate in their ultimate destruction. Then they'll face Hellfire after Judgment Day.

[58] The commentator Qatadah wrote of this verse, "What's the matter with some people who claim to know about the fate of others, saying, 'So-and-so is in Paradise, while so-and-so is in the Fire'? If you ask any of them about their own fate, they always say, 'I don't know about me.' So do you know more about yourself than other people? You've assumed a job from which even the prophets before you refrained." (*Ibn Kathir*)

Conflicted Actions

Background on verses 102-103: Ten men who failed to respond to the mustering of the militia to march toward Tabuk felt ashamed. Some time after the army left, seven of them swore to their wives that they would tie themselves to their fence posts or to pillars in the mosque until the Prophet forgave them. When the Prophet returned about a month later, he asked about the men he saw tied to posts and poles. When he was told about their situation, he swore he would not call for them to be released until Allah forgave them. This passage of forgiveness was revealed, and the Prophet ordered them to give money in charity to atone for their cowardice. (*Asbab ul-Nuzul*) One of these men, a man named Abu Lubabah, remained at his pillar - wanting the Prophet himself to untie him. He did.

(There are) some other (people) who've admitted to their sins. They had mixed moral deeds with evil ones, but Allah will turn to them (in forgiveness), for Allah is forgiving and merciful. [59] [102] Take charity from their wealth so you can cleanse and purify them, and pray for them, for your prayers are truly a source of tranquility for them. [60] Allah hears and knows (about all things). [103]

Don't they know that Allah accepts the repentance of His servants and that He accepts their charitable contributions? Allah is the One Who Accepts Repentance, and (He truly is) the Merciful. [104]

Say (to the people who want to repent of their sins), "*Do (good deeds), for Allah will soon see the results of your efforts, even as the*

---

[59] The Prophet said, "Last night two (angels) came to me (in my dreams) and took me to a town built with gold and silver bricks. We met two men there, and one half of their bodies resembled the most handsome human beings you ever could see, but their other halves were of the most hideous human beings you ever could see. The two (angels) told those men, 'Go and submerge yourselves in that river.' So they submerged themselves in it. When they returned to us their hideousness disappeared, and they were in the most pleasing condition. The (angels) said (to me), 'The first garden (over there) is the Garden of Eden, and that's your dwelling place.' Then they said, 'As for those men who were half ugly and half handsome, they were those who mixed good deeds with bad deeds, but Allah forgave them.'" (*Bukhari*)

[60] After the Prophet passed away, some bedouins used this verse to justify withholding their charity tax payments from the Muslim government headed by Abu Bakr, the newly chosen caliph. They asserted that this verse said that people only had to pay charity *to the Prophet*, and since he passed, they were *released* from this obligation. This is how unsophisticated and simple these bedouins were in their understanding. Abu Bakr refuted this illogical position, though some of those tribes held firm and mobilized for war. Thus, the famous Wars of the Ridda occurred in which Abu Bakr put down the rebellions of such tribes and fought them until they agreed to pay their charity tax.

Messenger and the believers (will see them, as well). Soon you're going to be brought back to the One Who knows the hidden and the plainly seen, and He's going to show you the meaning of all that you did." [105]

(Indeed, among this group of people) are some who are waiting nervously for Allah's command, so they can know whether He's going to punish them or turn towards them (in forgiveness). Allah is full of knowledge and wisdom. [106]

The Mosque of Mischief

Background on verses 107-110: After the Prophet and Abu Bakr fled Mecca for the safety of Medina in 622 CE, they stopped in the small town of Quba, which was just outside the city limits of Yathrib (Medina), and stayed for a number of days. There they dedicated the first mosque of Islam, and the Prophet would often visit it thereafter. When the full might of the hypocrites of Medina came to bear upon the Prophet and his followers in subsequent years, a faction of the hypocritical tribe of Banu Ghanam built a mosque of their own in a nearby neighborhood of Quba named Dhu Awan. They used it as a base of opposition to the Prophet, while pretending to be pious Muslims. They were also allied with a notorious Christian man from Yathrib named Abu Amir, who was one of those who left Medina to join the Meccans and then fought against the Muslims at Uhud. (Abu Amir had a heated argument with the Prophet and vowed that whichever of the two men was wrong, he should die alone far from home. His son Hanzalah, by way of contrast, was a faithful supporter of the Prophet.) In addition, the mosque was partly financed by the Christian Ghassanid king of southern Syria, who wanted to use it as an intelligence gathering installation.

Before he even returned from the Expedition to Tabuk, the Prophet came to know of the linkage and also for what the mosque was being used. Several letters from Abu Amir to the hypocrites were also intercepted – letters that encouraged sedition and rebellion! When some of the hypocrites invited the Prophet to enter Quba first before Medina and to pray in their mosque, this passage was revealed. The Prophet then ordered some of his companions to go to the *Mosque of Mischief,* as it was called, and have it torn down.

One man named Thabit ibn Arqam later built a house on the site, but he had no children survive him – ever - and thus the seemingly cursed plot fell into disuse. Thereafter, the site became a garbage dump. Abu Amir did die far from home in southern Syria among strangers. *(Ma'ariful Qur'an)* Only a mosque built for sincere devotion to Allah can be called a mosque of Allah. No house of worship should be used to plot against the religion to which it is supposed to be dedicated.

There are those who built a mosque (for no other purpose) than to promote mischief and rejection (of Allah), seeking to divide the believers and to set up a rallying place for those who previously made war on Allah and His Messenger. They're going to swear that they meant nothing but good by it, but Allah declares that they're all liars. [107]

Never set foot within (their mosque), for there's (another) mosque (nearby in the town of Quba) whose foundations were laid from the first day upon mindfulness (of Allah). It's far more appropriate for you to stand within that one, for there are people inside of it who love to be purified, and Allah loves those who make themselves pure! [61] [108]

Whose (place of worship) is better: the one who lays his foundation upon mindfulness of Allah and the seeking of His pleasure, or the one who lays his foundation upon a weak sand dune that's ready to crumble at any moment? [62] It will crumble – *along with him* – and topple into the fires of Hell. Allah doesn't guide people who are wrong! [109]

Such a (weak) building site could never be anything more than a cause for nervousness in their hearts - even until their hearts are shattered (by stress)! Allah is full of knowledge and wisdom. [110]

This is Allah's Deal

Background on verses 111-112: These two verses were revealed in the Meccan Period after the last Pledge of 'Aqabah, in which some seventy visitors from Medina pledged themselves to the Prophet and invited him to resettle in their city. (There were two prior such pledges by smaller groups of six and then twelve persons respectively.) At this last pledge, taken some months before the Prophet left Mecca for the safety of Medina, one of the new converts asked the Prophet, "Messenger of Allah, we're making a deal right now. If there are any requirements from either your Lord or you, let them be enumerated at this time clearly."

---

[61] 'Umar ibn al-Khattab said, "I looked at every type of friend, and I couldn't find a better friend than controlling the tongue. I thought about every type of clothing and didn't find any better robe than mindfulness of Allah. I thought about every type of wealth, but I didn't find any better wealth than learning to be content with a small share. I thought about every type of good deeds, but I didn't find a better good deed than offering sincere advice. I looked at every type of livelihood, but I didn't find a better livelihood than learning to persevere." The Prophet also said something similar when he was asked what type of wealth a person should look for. He said, "A tongue that remembers (Allah), a heart that is thankful, and a spouse that helps you to practice your religion." (*Ibn Kathir*)
[62] Jesus is reported to have given a similar parable in Luke: 6:48-49 when he spoke of some men who built their houses on rock and sand foundations respectively. The shifting sand caused disaster for one of them.

The Prophet said, "As for Allah, I lay down the condition that you all shall worship Him and only Him. As for myself, the condition is that you should protect me as you protect your selves, wealth, property and children." Someone asked him, "If we fulfill these two conditions, what will we get in return?" The Prophet replied, "Paradise." The people exclaimed then that they accepted that deal and that they would never cancel this agreement. Then these two verses were revealed, and the Prophet recited them. The people then lined up to place their hands in his to make their solemn oaths. (*Ma'ariful Qur'an*)

Allah has bought from the believers their lives and their wealth, and in return (He'll give them) Paradise.

They will fight in His cause; they will kill and be killed – and this is a promise that He's bound by in the Torah, the Gospel and the Qur'an.

Who is more faithful to his agreement than Allah? [63] So be pleased with the bargain you've made, for that's the ultimate success! [64] [111]

---

[63] It has been a principle enshrined in all divinely revealed scriptures that the righteous have to fight against the wicked. If they don't, then wickedness spreads, and innocent men, women and children suffer under the yoke of evil and oppression. The Torah is full of instances where the righteous were exhorted to fight against evil, while the New Testament echoes this theme in Hebrews 11:32-34 and also when Jesus famously stated, "Do not think that I came to bring peace on the earth; I did not come to bring peace, but a sword. For I came to set a man against his father, and a daughter against her mother, and a daughter-in-law against her mother-in-law; and a man's enemies will be the members of his household." (Matthew 10:34-36) The caveat, however, that sets apart war for Allah's sake and distinguishes it from mere war for conquest or loot is that a just war in the name of Allah is to stop oppression, so that all people may live in peace and security with regard to their lives and property. All other causes for war are fueled by greed, and men fighting for such causes know no limits and conduct themselves like barbarians. The war for Allah's sake envisions peace at the end for both the conquered and the conquerer, while war for greed envisions nothing but the destruction and subjugation of one's enemies. Sometimes people falsely label their war for greed as a war for Allah, such as in the Christian Crusades or the campaigns of the nominally Muslim warlord Timur the Lame. In that case, even such "holy warriors" must be opposed because they fight for the things of this life. The Prophet was once asked who fought for Allah: the one who fights for fame, fortune or adventure, and the Prophet replied that the only one who is counted as fighting for Allah is the one who fights only to uphold His religion and for His sake alone. (*Bukhari, Muslim*)

[64] 'Umar ibn al-Khattab said of this verse: "How wonderful is this deal, where the item and its cost are both given to you." Hassan al-Basri said of it: "What a profitable venture Allah has made available to every believer. Allah is the One Who blessed you with wealth and property, so spend a little of it so you can get Paradise in return." (*Ma'ariful Qur'an*)

43

(The true believers are those who) turn (to Allah) in repentance, serve Him, praise Him, wander abroad (in His cause), [65] bow down in prostration before Him, command what is recognized (as good), and forbid what is unfamiliar (to Allah's way of life). They are the ones who observe Allah's limits, so now give good news to the believers! [112]

Faith and Falsehood have a Clear Divide

Background on verse 113: After the Prophet's beloved uncle, Abu Talib, passed away, affirming his allegiance to idolatry even as he breathed his last, the distraught Prophet vowed to continue to pray for his forgiveness. Later on, in the early Medinan Period, 'Ali heard a man loudly praying for his deceased pagan parents to be forgiven. When 'Ali asked the man why he was praying for his pagan parents, he explained that Abraham also prayed for his pagan father. (Based on verse 19:47.) 'Ali informed the Prophet about this, and some time later, this verse was revealed prohibiting Muslims from praying for relatives who had died while still believing in idols. (*Tirmidhi, Bukhari, Muslim*)

It's not right for the Prophet and the believers to pray for the forgiveness of idol-worshippers, even if they're close relatives, after it's been made clear to them that they're going to be companions of the raging blaze. [66] [113]

Abraham only prayed for his father's forgiveness because of a promise he had made to him. [67] However, when it became clear to him

---

[65] Early scholars such as 'Ikrimah say that this wandering consists of traveling to seek education about the religion.

[66] Even into the Medinan Period, many Muslims had pagan relatives, and when their relatives would pass away, they were torn about what to do for a eulogy. One companion bemoaned his pagan father's passing to the Prophet, and the Prophet tearfully replied that even his own mother might be destined for Hellfire, as she might have died an idolater. (*Muslim*) Even though Islam was not extant in her time, she might have had thoughts that idolatry was wrong and rejected it, as many *hanifs* or Arab monotheists of the time already had. Only Allah knows if she did, and Muslim scholars generally feel that she died as a believer in the one God. (*Ibn Kathir*) This verse sets forth the principle for Muslims not to pray for the forgiveness of those who died willingly as pagans, for they died in a state of defiance to Allah's religion. There is no prohibition, however, for praying for the forgiveness and guidance of non-Muslims while they are alive. (*Qurtubi, Ibn Kathir*)

[67] Verses 6:74-83 tell the basic story of how Abraham came to disobey his father in matters of religion. 19:41-50 adds more details of the family conflict and contains the crucial passage where Abraham promises his father he'll pray for him. The following *hadith* supplements the overall story. The Prophet said, "On the Day of Resurrection, Abraham will meet his father Azar (Terah) whose face will be overcast and dusty, and he'll say to his (father), 'Didn't I tell you not to disobey me?' His father will reply, 'This

that (his father) was an enemy of Allah, he distanced himself from him. It was just that Abraham was accustomed to invoking (Allah frequently), [68] and he was forbearing. [114]

Allah will never let a people go astray after He's (begun to invite them to) guidance, until after He's made clear to them that of which they should be aware, for Allah knows all about everything. [69] [115]

The control of the heavens and the earth belongs to Allah. He gives life, and He brings death. You have neither any protector nor helper apart from Him. [116]

Allah Tested the Believers

And so Allah turned towards the Prophet, the Immigrants, and the Helpers who followed Him during a difficult time (on the Expedition to Tabuk, for the journey was long and hard). [70]

---

day I will not disobey you any further.' Abraham will then beseech Allah, saying, 'Lord! You promised me that you wouldn't disgrace me on the Day of Judgment, but what can be more disgraceful for me than to curse or dishonor my own father?' (See 26:87 for the promise.) Then Allah will say, 'I've forbidden Paradise for those who rejected (faith). Look at what's beneath you.' Then he will look and see a blood-stained hyena being caught by the legs and thrown into the Fire." (His father was transformed into a representation of his true nature, and so Abraham wouldn't see the form of his father being cast into Hell and would thus not be overtly shamed.) (*Bukhari*) This was to emphasize to Abraham that Allah's justice is absolute and applies across the board to all. Thus, He would not show unfair favoritism to Azar when He wouldn't show it to others.
[68] The Arabic term *awwah* suggests a tender-hearted man who was so used to calling upon Allah that it was second-nature for him to also call upon Allah for the sake of His father. (*Ma'ariful Qur'an*)
[69] In other words, after Allah's guidance is first being made known to people, He won't let them completely go astray and be lost until after they understand what it is that they would be rejecting. Then if they reject it, they have no excuses on Judgment Day that they didn't know what they were doing. This is a golden time in the story of any nation who receives a prophet, for Allah will not relent in His invitation until they are in a position to make an informed decision either to accept Allah's good will or to accept Satan's wickedness and oppression.
[70] The journey northward towards Syria was so difficult in the full heat of the desert sun that even the water ran out for the army of 30,000. The men became so desperate that Abu Bakr asked the Prophet to pray for rain for them, citing the fact that Allah always listened to his call. The Prophet prayed for rain and didn't lower his hands until rain fell some hours later. Repeated rain showers fell in intervals for days after that, and the men had sufficient water to drink and wash themselves.

However, a segment of them let their hearts become crooked, (influencing them away from their duty,) but He turned towards them, as well, for He was kind and merciful towards them. [117]

The Case of the Three Who were Forgiven

Background on verse 118: There were three men named Ka'b ibn Malik, Hilal ibn Umayyah and Murarah ibn ar-Rabi' who were otherwise perfectly able-bodied and fit to answer the call for the Tabuk Expedition. They had been among the earliest converts, but they failed to muster with the rest of the militia when it was time to march northward. (Murarah was dissuaded from participation by, among other things, the fact that it was harvest time, and he became somewhat inclined to comfort and prosperity. Hilal was having a family reunion. K'ab was wealthy and couldn't bear to leave his fortune behind!)

When the Prophet returned, these men were shunned for about fifty days, and they felt miserable, so much so that it seemed (as one of them later described it) that the earth and their own souls were closing in upon them. The Christian king of the Ghassanid tribe in Syria, Suhrabil ibn Amr, received reports of the shunning of these men, and he sent a letter to Ka'b offering to take him in to his kingdom if Ka'b would renounce Islam, but Ka'b threw the letter in his cooking fire. In time, the Prophet accepted the remorse of these men, and they were welcomed back into the community upon the revelation of this verse. Ka'b left a rather lengthy account of his experience and recounted how joyful both he and the community were when it was all over. (*Bukhari, Muslim*)

(He also turned in mercy) to the three (men) who remained behind (without a valid excuse). (They were so remorseful) that the vast earth, itself, seemed to close in upon them, and their souls seemed to strangle them (with guilt), as well.

They understood that there was no running away from Allah, unless (it was on a path) that led back to Him.

So He turned towards them so they could repent, for Allah is the Acceptor of Repentance and the Merciful. [71] [118]

Reflections on the Lessons of Tabuk

O you who believe!

---

[71] Ibn Taymiyyah (d. 1328) once wrote, "Sins are like chains and locks, preventing their perpetrator from roaming the vast garden of unity (with Allah's will) and reaping the fruits of righteous actions."

Be mindful of Allah, and be among those who are truthful (to their vows). [119] It wasn't right for (some of) the people of Medina and the local desert Arabs to refuse to follow the Messenger of Allah, nor was it right that they preferred their own lives over his.

That's because there was (no sacrifice) they could've made, whether it was thirst, fatigue or hunger in the cause of Allah, nor any step (they could've taken) to raise the ire of the faithless, nor any injury they could've received from the enemy, (without being generously repaid for it by Allah). Indeed, Allah never lets the reward of those who do good become lost. [120]

They also could not have spent anything, whether a little or a lot, or trekked across a valley without having that deed recorded to their credit, and that was so Allah could reward their actions with good (in return). [72] [121]

The believers, however, should not march out all together (leaving no one behind to guard the home front).

If a certain number remains behind during every expedition, then they could exert themselves in learning the religion. [73]

Thus, they could remind the people when they return (home) that they should be on their guard (against immorality). [122]

O you who believe! Fight the faithless who are all around you, (ready to strike at you). Be resolute against them, and know that Allah is with those who are mindful (of Him). [123]

---

[72] When the Prophet was raising funds for the Tabuk Expedition, 'Umar ibn al-Khattab came forward and donated one hundred fully equipped camels. Uthman ibn Affan (d. 656) then came and donated the same measure, and when Uthman laid a thousand gold coins in the Prophet's lap, the Prophet fingered them and said, "It doesn't matter what (potential bad deeds) Uthman may do after this." (*Ahmad*) In other words, he is guaranteed Paradise for his generosity to Allah's cause.

[73] This chapter speaks very harshly of the people who remained behind and failed to participate in the Expedition to Tabuk. In order to mitigate the fears of Muslims who feel compelled to go out to fight an enemy, leaving no one behind to protect their families or keep society functioning, this verse was revealed to affirm that there are some who have to remain behind for legitimate reasons. (*Ibn Kathir*)

Be Firmly Committed to the Cause

Whenever a chapter comes down, some (of the hypocrites) say, *"So who among you feels their faith has been strengthened by it?"* Oh, but those who (truly) believe *do* have their faith strengthened by it, and they rejoice besides! [124] Those who are sick at heart find that (newly revealed verses) add nothing but doubts to their doubts; thus, they're going to die in a state of rejection. [125]

Don't they see that they're being tested at least once or twice every year. [74]

Yet, not only *do they not repent*; they don't even pay attention to the reminders! [126]

Background on verse 127: The hypocrites were constantly afraid that new Qur'anic revelations might mention them or expose their activities, so when they heard of new verses, they would ask each other if anyone was looking at them suspiciously. (*Ibn Kathir*)

Whenever a chapter comes down, they look at each other (and say), *"Is anyone looking at you?"*

Then they turn away, even as Allah has turned their hearts away, for they're a people who don't understand at all. [127]

Now a messenger has come to you from among yourselves, and he's worried sick that you might be harmed (in the cause of Allah).

In fact, he's worried sick over your (welfare), for he's truly kind and merciful to the believers. [75] [128]

---

[74] Ever since the Prophet migrated to Medina, the Muslim community had to face at least one major challenge per year, whether it was fighting off pagans, having missionaries ambushed or suffering from famines or civil disunity. Thus, the opportunity to stand up for truth in a meaningful way was a frequent occurrence. Didn't the hypocrites ever stop and think that all their slinking and cowardice were getting tired and pathetic?

[75] The Prophet said, "My example is that of a man who built a fire. When it blazed brightly, moths and insects were attracted and fell into it. Though the man tries hard to keep them away, they thwart him and dive in. This I do; I struggle to hold you back from the fire, but you leap into it." (*Bukhari*)

If they turn away, just say to them:

"Allah is enough for me.

There is no god but He.

On Him do I trust;

He's Lord of the throne supreme." [76] [129]

---

[76] Some reports claim that these last two verses [128-129] were the last ones revealed to the Prophet, just before he passed away. (*Qurtubi*)

Jonah

10 Yūnus

Late Meccan Period

This chapter is the first in a series of six late Meccan chapters that continue to address the core theological concepts of Islam. Nature and its complexity are proof of Allah's handiwork for those who care to look into it deeply. Allah communicates with humanity through messengers who receive His messages and teach them to their fellows. The reality of life is that it's a short time filled with temptations, tests and trials that we must weather. In the end, if we are successful in negotiating the storms of this world, with full faith in Allah, then we can achieve permanent success in the Hereafter, or if we succumb to immorality, vice and corruption, we may suffer punishment in Hellfire. Like a high stakes test, our conduct in this world ultimately decides our fate. Allah will punish injustice, though He is more merciful to us than we could ever deserve.

In the Name of Allah,
the Compassionate, the Merciful

Background on verses 1-2: Ibn 'Abbas (d. 687) explained the pagan position alluded to in this verse by saying, "When Allah sent Muhammad as a messenger, most of the Arabs denied him and his message, saying, 'Allah is too exalted to send a mere human being like Muhammad.'" Thus, this passage was revealed, commenting upon their objection. (*Ibn Kathir*)

*A*lif. Lām. Rā.

These are the verses of the Book of Wisdom. [1] Is it so strange to people that We've sent Our inspiration to a man from among themselves, so he could warn people (of Allah's judgment) and give the good news to the believers that they can achieve confirmed status in the sight of their Lord? Yet, the faithless say (of it), *"This is obviously just magic!"* [2]

Your Lord is Allah, the One Who created the heavens and the earth in six time periods. Then He established Himself upon the throne (of power) and began issuing commands. [77] There are no intercessors other than those whom He allows. That's your Lord Allah, so serve Him. Won't you take a reminder? [3]

All of you will return back to Him, and Allah's promise is true. He's the One Who began the process of creation and then repeats it, so that He can justly reward those who believe and do what's morally right. Those who reject Him will be forced to drink boiling muck, and they'll have a painful punishment on account of their rejection. [4]

He's the One Who caused the sun to glow brightly with multiple (colors in splendor) and the moon to be illuminated. [78] He measured out (the moon's) stations, so you could keep track of the years and the passage (of time). [79] Allah didn't create (all of these things) except for a true purpose, and He explains His verses to people who understand. [5]

Truly, in the alternation of night and day and in everything that Allah created in the heavens and the earth are proofs for those who are mindful (of Him). [6] Those who don't look forward to their meeting with Us, who are satisfied with the life of this world and who

---

[77] This is an esoteric idea that is usually understood to mean that after the physical creation of the universe, stars and planets Allah began creating systems and life of various kinds. The throne is not understood to be necessarily a chair, for the commentators are in general agreement that it is a metaphor for power that earthlings can understand.

[78] The Arabic word used here for the bright glowing or shining of the sun is in the plural. This is indicative of the many separate colors contained in sunlight — colors that can be seen individually in a rainbow after it rains. The word used to describe the moon's light is the generic term *noor*, which means any kind of light shining upon something. Thus, the two terms ascribed to each heavenly body are accurate in that the sun gives off multiple color streams, while the moon is merely lit up by something else.

[79] The Islamic calendar is based on the traditional, pre-Islamic calendar system of the Middle East, which calculates months and years by keeping track of the more dependable lunar cycle. The months are calculated by the 29 or 30 days it takes the moon to complete each of its cycles. Thus, the Islamic year has twelve months of 29 or 30 days with an average of 354 days per year. The Arabic term used in this verse, which I have translated as lunar stations, is *manazil*. Scholars say this verse is referring to the orbit of the moon through the 27 different configurations of stars in its course around the earth. Each of these stations or positions relative to the unique star configurations is called a lunar station. (The Qur'an also uses the related word *manzil* to describe its seven major sections.)

disregard Our (revealed) verses [7] - they're going to have their home in the Fire on account of what they've earned for themselves. 80 [8]

However, those who believe and do what's morally right will be guided by their Lord on account of their faith – rivers will flow beneath them in gardens of delight! [9] Their supplication within (the garden) will be, *"Glory be to You, O Allah!"* 81 Their greeting within will be, *"Peace,"* 82 and they'll end their supplications by saying, *"Praise be to Allah, the Lord of All the Worlds!"* 83 [10]

The Fickle Nature of Humanity

If Allah were to rush forward for people the evil consequences (of their deeds) in the same way that they (want) Him to rush forward the good (things that they think they deserve), then their (time) would come to an end immediately, but We leave those who don't look forward to their meeting with Us wandering in their willful blindness. [11]

When misfortune comes upon a human being, they cry out to Us while lying down on their side, sitting or standing. However, when We've removed their misfortune, they pass on their way as if they had never cried out to Us when hardship assailed them before! That's

---

80 Hasan al-Basri (d. 737) said of this verse: "They adorned (this life) and praised it until they became completely satisfied with it. They were unconcerned with Allah's signs in the universe, nor did they ponder over them. They were also unconcerned with Allah's commandments, nor did they adhere to them. Their resting place on the Day of Resurrection will be in the Fire; that's their reward for what they earned in their worldly lives through all their sins and crimes, and that's in addition to their rejection of Allah, His Messenger and the Last Day." (*Ibn Kathir*)

81 The Prophet said, "The people of Paradise will be inspired to glorify Allah and praise Him as naturally as their very breathing." (*Muslim*)

82 'Abdullah ibn Salam was a rabbi in Medina before the coming of Islam. He later said, "When the Messenger of Allah first arrived in Medina, people were scared away, and I was one of them. Then when I saw him, I realized that his face was not the face of a liar. The first thing I heard from him was his saying, 'People! Spread the greetings of peace, feed others, be dutiful to your relatives and pray at night while others are sleeping so you can enter Paradise in peace.'" (*Ahmad*)

83 The Prophet said that Allah Himself said, "A servant of Mine who is always busy glorifying Me, so much so that he hasn't the time to ask for what he should ask for, then I will grant to him the best of what anyone asks for, and that is to have his needs taken care of without his even asking for it." (*Hadith Qudsi*)

why the extravagant think their (pointless) deeds are beneficial for them. [12]

And so it was that We destroyed generations that came before you when (their people) turned into oppressors. Their messengers went to them with clear evidence; yet, they still wouldn't believe! That's how We repay the wicked. [13] Now We've caused you (Arabs) to inherit the land after them to see how you would act. [14]

Background on verse 15: Five leaders among the Quraysh went to the Prophet and asked him to alter the teachings of the Qur'an so that they could keep worshipping their idols. This verse references their request. (*Asbab ul-Nuzul*)

Yet, when Our clear verses are recited to them, those who don't look forward to their meeting with Us say, *"Bring us some other Qur'an, or change this one (to suit us)."*

Say (to them), *"It's not my place to change it, for I follow only what's being revealed to me. If I ever disobeyed my Lord (by making up verses on my own), then I would be in utter fear of the punishment of a momentous day."* [84] [15]

Then say (to them), *"If Allah had wanted, then I wouldn't be reciting (this message) to you, nor would He have made it known to you. I've lived with you for a whole lifetime before this (message came to me, and I've never spoken of religious issues before), so won't you realize (that it came suddenly and that it must be from Allah)?"* [16]

Who's more wrong than the one who invents a forgery and then attributes it to Allah or who denies (the truth of) His (authentic) verses? The wicked will never succeed! [17]

They serve in place of Allah things that can neither harm them nor benefit them, but then they (try to justify their idol-worship by) saying, *"These (idols) intercede for us with Allah."* So ask them, *"Are you really informing Allah about something in the heavens and the earth*

---

[84] The New Testament ends with a similar warning in Revelations 22:19. "And if any man shall take away from the words of the book of this prophecy, Allah shall take away his part out of the book of life…" While individuals may tamper with written texts, the original words of Allah will remain with Him for safekeeping.

about which He doesn't know?" Glory be to Him! He's so high above the partners they're assigning to Him! [18]

And what were people other than one community (in the beginning); yet, they fell into disputes (with each other and scattered away all over the world). [85] If it wasn't for a word (of command) that your Lord previously issued (to let people have free will and then be judged by what they chose), then their differences would've been settled between them (immediately). [19]

Then they ask, *"So why isn't a miracle being sent down to him from his Lord?"* [86] Answer them, saying, *"The unseen (realm of the supernatural) belongs to Allah, so wait (and see), for I'll be waiting with you."* [20]

Many don't Understand the Reality of their Lives

When We give people a taste of mercy after they had been suffering from some hardship – then look - they start plotting against Our signs straightaway! Say (to them), *"Allah's plan is even faster than that! Our (angelic) envoys are keeping track of whatever you're planning."* [21]

He's the One Who makes it easy for you to travel over the land and sea. You board ships and sail along on them with favorable winds, and (the sailors) are pleased with their (progress). [87] However, when

---

[85] The earliest human beings, if you trace back deep enough into the recesses of the past, all lived together and sprung from the same root pair of male and female. This original tribe eventually split off into different bands and scattered all over the world over many tens of thousands of years. This verse asserts that the cause for people to leave each other involved disputes. Science has accepted that all living human beings that exist today are from the same lineage going back into the earliest days of our common ancestors.

[86] The pagans kept asking for a miracle or a proof from Allah to convince them that Allah really did support Muhammad in his claims. The proof came in the ultimate triumph of the Prophet when he not only returned to Mecca in total victory after exile, but also transformed the people of Arabia and abolished all the old ways and customs. See verse 9:40.

[87] People have always romanticized sailing and the beauty of majestic ships as they ply the waves. The twelfth-century, Spanish-Muslim poet, Ibn Lubbal, once wrote of ships in these terms: "Oh, look at the boats plunging into the race like chargers one after another. Before, the neck of the river was empty; now in the darkness it's full of jewels. The lanterns are the stars; their reflections on the water are the lances stabbing the beast of the river. Like timid rabbits escaping the falcon, the little boats flee on their little oar-feet from the larger ships that swoop down upon them on the wings of their sails."

a storm arises and the waves begin to assault them from all sides, they feel as if they're going to perish. Then (they realize) that all religion belongs to Allah, so they cry out to Him, (pledging to serve Him) sincerely, saying, *"If You save us from this, then we'll be forever grateful!"* [88] [22]

Then, when He saves them, they act outrageously throughout the earth (once more) against all right! O people! Your rebellion is against your own souls! (There's only a) short time to enjoy the life of this world – and then you're going to come back to Us, and that's when We're going to tell you the meaning of everything you ever did. [89] [23]

The example of the life of this world is like the water that We send down from the sky. It mingles with the various plants of the earth and causes them to sprout (to life). (These plants) then provide food for both people and animals. (The plants keep on growing) until the earth is clothed with their (blossoms and flowers), and then it's made (beautiful).

The people who own (the land around them) think that they're in control of it, but then Our command comes upon it by night or by day. Then We reduce it to dry stubble, as if there had never been any

---

[88] Hardship and stress can destroy people and cause them to lose hope. This is not in dispute. In such times when it seems no one can help, unbelievers suffer in despair and perhaps turn to drugs and alcohol to dim their pain. A believer takes the long view and intimately understands they are only travelors in this world for a short time. Shuraih Al-Qadhi (d. 697), an Islamic judge appointed by Caliph 'Umar, said, "If I'm afflicted with a tragedy, I praise Allah for it four times: I praise Him because it wasn't worse than it was, I praise Him when He gives me the patience to bear it, I praise Him for enabling me to say *al-istirja'* ('To Allah we belong and to him we return' in the hope of a great reward, and I praise Him for not making it a tragedy in the practice of my way of life." Quoted in *Al-Dhahabi*, written by Siyar A'lam Al-Nubala'. (Also see 2:154-156)

[89] The Prophet said, "A person who had lived a prosperous life in the world will be brought forward (on Judgment Day) and dipped once in the Fire. Then he will be asked, 'Have you ever experienced any goodness or felt any comfort?' The person will cry, 'No!' Then a person who had experienced terrible deprivation in the world will be brought forward and dipped once in the ecstasy (of Paradise). Then he will be asked, 'Have you ever faced any deprivation or misery before?' The person will cry out, 'No!'" (*Muslim*) Such will be the difference between what we experience in our earthly lives, in comparison to the magnitude of what is to come, that we will forget about everything that ever happened to us before.

luxurious growth there just the day before! That's how We fully explain (Allah's) signs for those who think. [90] [24]

The Final End is Where the Outcome will Be Decided

Allah is calling (you) to the Realm of Peace, [91] and He guides whomever He wants towards a straight path. [25] Those who do good will have good (in return) – *and even more than that!* [92] There will be neither darkness nor shame upon their faces, for they're the companions of the Garden, and there they shall remain! [26]

Those who've earned evil against themselves will be rewarded similarly with evil, and they'll further be covered in disgrace. They'll have no one to defend them against Allah, and their faces will be shrouded in the darkest shades of night. They're the companions of the Fire, *and that's where they're going to stay!* [27]

One day, We're going to gather them all together, and We'll say to those who made partners (with Us), *"Go to your places! You and the idols you've made!"* Then We're going to separate them, and their partners will say, *"It wasn't us you were worshipping!* [28] *Allah is enough of a witness between you and us that we knew nothing of your worship of us."* [93] [29]

---

[90] The Prophet said, "The one who makes this world his focus, Allah will deprive him of contentment and heartfelt satisfaction. He will remain ever in greedy pursuit of wealth and unattainable desires, and he will never receive more than the share that Allah has ordained for him. Whoever makes their focus the next life, Allah will bestow contentment and heartfelt satisfaction on them. He will also protect them from being greedy for wealth, and they will get their allotted share in this world." (*At-Targheeb wa at-Tarheeb*)

[91] This is a use of the term *Dar us-Salam*, or Realm of Peace. The commentators say it refers to Paradise, as well as to the earthly territory that is under authentic Islamic rule. Any land outside of this is known as the *Dar ul-Harb*, or Realm of Conflict, as Muslims will be under constant threat there, either with regards to their faith or their physical well-being.

[92] The Prophet said, "When the people of Paradise enter into it, a caller will say, 'People of Paradise! Allah has made a promise to you that He wishes to fulfill.' They will reply, 'What can it be? Didn't He already make our scales heavy? Didn't He already brighten our faces and save us from the Fire?' Then Allah will remove the veil (that shrouds Him), and they will see Him. By Allah, they will never have been given anything more beloved by them or more delightful to them than looking at Him (directly)." (*Muslim*)

[93] Inanimate objects such as idols will be made to speak. People who were worshipped as gods, such as the pharaohs of Egypt or the early Roman emperors, will protest their innocence. However, they will all go to the same dreadful doom. One of the purposes

Then and there every soul will be tried for what it had earned (in its life) before, and they'll be turned over to Allah, their rightful guardian. Whatever they invented will leave them to languish! [30]

The Sentence is Proven True against Them

Ask them, *"Who provides resources for you from the sky and the earth? Who has power over hearing and sight? Who brings life out of death and death out of life, and who governs the course of all matters?"* [94] (After they've thought about it), they'll be sure to say, *"Allah."* Then ask them, *"So won't you then be mindful (of Him)?"* [31]

That's Allah for you, your true Lord. What is there after truth except mistakes? So how is it that you're turning away? [32] And so it is that the sentence will be proven true against those who rebel, for they won't believe. [95] [33]

Ask them, *"Is there any (idol) from among your (false gods) that can begin creation and then renew it?"* Say (to them), *"Allah began the creation, and He renews it. So how are you deceived away (from the truth)?"* [34]

Ask them, *"Are there any among your (idols) that can guide someone to the truth?"* Then say (to them), *"Allah guides to the truth. [96] So isn't the*

---

of Judgment Day is for the guilty to finally recognize and admit their own faults and sins. Only then will Allah punish them after they understand why they deserve it.

[94] The structure of this passage in verses 31-36 is fascinating in that verse 31 forces the pagans to admit that their idols do not have equal powers with the Supreme God. Then as the argument continues into verses 32 and 33, we find that the pagans are left with no choice but to recognize that there's nothing beyond the truth except errors and mistakes. Then the verses proceed onwards, proving logically that man-made idols are powerless in the face of the truth of Allah's omnipotence, a fact that the pagans had to admit at the outset!

[95] The sentence or word against them is the general prediction that Allah made that most people will be thankless and will disbelieve in Him and thus be punished by Him. See 38:84-85 and 32:13.

[96] It is a good point that for most, if not all, of the systems of idolatry in human history, none of them encompass the promotion of a moral way of life as the basis of their existence. Idolatry and paganism, in general, are more about superstition, bringing luck or good fortune, appeasing angry spirits in nature such as volcano gods and such, using divination or fortune-telling to help a person to make decisions, or witch-doctoring and

One Who guides to the truth more worthy of being followed than (an idol or false god) that will remain lost unless it's guided (itself)?" Just how do you figure things? [35] Most of them follow nothing but conjecture; yet, conjecture can never win out over the truth, and Allah knows what they're doing. [36]

About those who Say the Prophet Invented It

This Qur'an isn't something that could've been produced by any other besides Allah. On the contrary, it confirms (the truth of those revelations) that came before it, and it's a detailed explanation of the Book (of Allah). [97] There's nothing doubtful within it, (for it's a scripture revealed) from the Lord of All the Worlds! [98] [37]

Are they saying, *"He made it all up?"* Then (challenge them by) saying, *"So bring a chapter just like it, and then call upon anyone you can besides Allah (to compare the two), if you're being so honest."* [99] [38]

But no! They're denying what they can't even comprehend even before it's been fully clarified for them. [100] In the same way, those who

---

such. Compare this with the four major religions that seek a moral way of life based on personal transformation: Islam, Christianity, Judaism and Buddhism.

[97] Even Paul recognized that all religiously-based scripture was useful for learning, and thus Christians and Jews might find much in the Qur'an that will help them better understand God and the purpose of their lives. (See II Timothy 3:16.)

[98] This is an echo of verse 2:2 in which the Qur'an states quite early and adamantly that it is a book without error.

[99] In addition to what has been discussed in the footnote concerning the similar challenge issued in verse 2:23, there is another dimension to the Qur'an that is truly fascinating. When the Arabic terms used for various concepts and their opposites are enumerated, we find that many of the key concepts and their opposites appear in exact reciprocal numbers. For example, the word used for 'this world' is *dunya*, and the word for 'the hereafter' is *akhirah*. Each appears exactly 115 times throughout the Qur'an. Other pairs include the following: angels and devils - 88 times each; life and death - 145 times each; Iblis, and seeking safety from Iblis (Shaytan) - 11 times each; hardship and patience - 114 times each; man and woman - 24 times each. Truly, this is an inexplicable sign of a deeper level of uniqueness to the Qur'an.

[100] The Qur'an is such a multi-faceted book that it is foolish to deny it without ever having understood it and all of its unique features. This was, of course, what the pagans did — dismiss it out of hand without ever considering the import of its message.

came before them also denied (the truth of their revelations,) but just see how the wrongdoers came to an end! [101] [39]

Among them are some who believed in (their scriptures), while others did not, and your Lord knows best who the immoral are. [40] If they accuse you of lying, then tell them, *"My deeds belong to me, even as your deeds belong to you. You're not responsible for what I'm doing, nor am I responsible for what you're doing."* [102] [41]

Now among them are some who merely pretend to listen to you, but can you force the deaf to hear, even while (those uncaring people) have no intellect? [42] There are others among them who stare at you, but can you guide the blind, even as they refuse to see? [43] Allah is never unjust to people in the least. Rather, it's people who are unjust to their own souls. [44]

One day, He's going to gather them all together, and it'll seem (to them) as if they had passed only a single hour of a day (in their earthly lives). They're going to recognize each other's (faces), and so it will be that those who denied their meeting with Allah and who refused guidance will be lost. [45]

Whether We show you now some of what We've promised them or We take your soul (before that), they're all going to come back to Us (in the end). Then Allah will be the witness over what they've done. [46]

A messenger was sent to every community (in the world). [103] When their messenger comes before them (as a witness on the Day of

---

[101] All the previous prophets faced rejection from their people, no matter how much proof they brought. In the end, only a few ever truly believed in Allah's words.

[102] Ironically, the people who bowed down to idols they made with their own hands were accusing the Prophet of making up something. The answer then is to wait for Allah to judge between them. The hidden subtext is that the idol-worshippers have the most to lose.

[103] Islam teaches that all civilizations received some type of prophet, messenger or guide who made them aware of Allah's will. Some were major prophets with scriptures and codified laws, while most were more local and had more limited missions of preaching, teaching or living righteously among their fellows. The people could have accepted the message or rejected it, but more often than not only a few people believed. Over time their descendants mixed the true religious teachings with the superstitions of their culture,

Judgment), the issue will be decided between them with justice, and they won't be treated unfairly. [47]

(Now your people are) asking you, *"So when will this promise come to pass, if you're being so honest?"* [48]   Say (to them), *"I have no power to bring harm or benefit to myself, except as Allah wills. Every community has its own (predetermined) time limit. And when its deadline is reached, it can neither prolong it by an hour nor accelerate it."* [49]

Ask them, *"Do you see? If His punishment were to come upon you (suddenly) during the night or during the day, which part of it would the wicked want to hurry on?* [50] *Would you then finally believe in it at last?"*

"What! Will you now (believe it's real when it happens), even though you wanted to hurry it on! [51] *Then the wrongdoers will be told, 'Suffer the unending punishment! You're only getting what you deserve!'"* [52]

Now they're asking you to confirm it by saying, *"Is that the truth?"* Tell them, *"Absolutely! By my Lord, it's the truth, and you can't escape from it!"* [53]

Answer Allah's Call and be Saved

For every soul that sinned, if it had everything on earth to offer as a ransom (to save itself), it would offer it. (Nonetheless, such bribes won't be accepted,) so they're going to be filled with regret when they see the punishment. They'll be judged with justice, however, and they won't be treated unfairly. [54]

Isn't it (a fact) that whatever is in the heavens and on the earth belongs to Allah? Isn't it (a fact) that Allah's promise is a true one?

---

resulting in a wide variety of locally flavored religions. This is how a Muslim views the many religions of earth: they each began with a true prophet, but were transformed over time by each culture. That's also why Allah sent more prophets, as a way to correct the corruption that happened to His previous prophets' efforts. Thus, a Muslim is automatically supposed to be tolerant of another religion, for it might have begun from a pure divine source. On the Day of Judgment, those many and ancient prophets, most of whose names are lost to history, will confront their peoples, and the truth will be made known as to where their peoples erred.

Yet, most of them don't understand. [55] He's the One Who gives life and death, and you're going to return back to Him. [104] [56]

O people! An earnest appeal has now come to you from your Lord, as well as a healing for your hearts and guidance and mercy for the believers. [57] Say (to them), *"Let them celebrate in Allah's bounty and in His mercy."* [105] That's better than (all the money) that they stow away. [106] [58]

Ask them, *"Have you seen (and considered) all the resources that Allah sends down for you, (so you can survive in this world)?* [107] *Yet, you make some of those things forbidden (to eat) and other things lawful (to eat, for no logical reason)."* Then ask them, *"Has Allah given you permission (to do that), or are you making things up and assigning them to Allah?"* [59]

So what do those who invent lies against Allah think about the Day of Assembly? Allah is the master of endless favor towards the people (of earth); yet, most of them are thankless. [60]

---

[104] The famous Muslim mystic, Rabi'ah al-Adawiyya (d. 801), once said, "My peace, O my fellow believers, is my solitude, and my Beloved is with me always. For His love I can find no substitute, and His love is the test for me among mortal beings. Whenever I contemplate His beauty, I realize that He is my niche, and I focus all my being towards His direction. If I die of love, before having my satisfaction completed, alas, for my anxiety in the world, alas for my distress. O Healer (of souls), the heart feeds upon its desire. The striving after union with You has healed my soul, O my Joy and my eternal Life, You were the source of my life and from You also came my ecstasy. I have separated myself from all created beings, my hope is for union with You, for that is the goal of all my desires."

[105] The Prophet explained this verse by saying that the bounty is the Qur'an, and the mercy is our ability to recite it and to act according to its teachings (and thus win Allah's favor). (*Ma'ariful Qur'an*) Thus, this verse is telling the pagans that they should be happy with Allah more than they are with material possessions and worldly concerns.

[106] Caliph Az-Zuhayr ibn Amrillah was renowned for spending state resources on public works and to support the poor. Once he entered his royal treasury with an older attendant to take an account of what was in it. Upon seeing the room bare and obviously empty of funds, the attendant remarked, "This room used to be full in the time of your father." The Caliph replied, "A treasury is not meant to be full, but to be continuously emptied and distributed for good causes. Collecting things is the job of a trader." (*History of the Caliphs*, Jalaluddin as-Suyuti) See Qur'an 2:215. Also see I Timothy 6:17-19 for a similar sentiment.

[107] The 'resources' in this verse refer to the Arab superstitions regarding what cows, camels or goats they could eat depending on how they were birthed, what time of year, whether they were twin births or not and other such arbitrary things. Chapter six also contains lengthy discussions on this issue. See 6: 138-144.

Allah is always Watching Over You

There isn't a single thing that you're involved with, nor any portion of the Qur'an that you recite, nor any deed that you do without Us being there to see it, even while you're still in the middle of it!

There's nothing on the earth nor in the heavens that's hidden from your Lord – *nothing even as small as a speck* - and nothing smaller or greater than that exists without its being recorded in a clear record. [108] [61]

Truly, the closest allies of Allah will have neither fear nor sorrow! [109] [62] They're the ones who believed and who were mindful (of their duty to Him). [63] So there's good news for them in the life of this world, as well as (good news for them) in the next - *Allah's words (of prophecy) never change* - and that (promise which is from Him is indeed the signifier of) the greatest success! [64]

Don't let what (the faithless) are saying bother you, for all combined powers belong to Allah. He's the Hearing and the

---

[108] Thus, Allah encompasses all things, whether we can directly deduce His presence or not. The classical writer, Muhiyuddin Ibn 'Arabi (d. 1240), once commented on this, saying, "Whoever builds his faith only upon what can be proven before his eyes or deduced from logic builds an unreliable kind of faith, for he will be affected by the uncertainty of constant objections. True inner certainty doesn't derive from the evidence of the mind but pours out from the depths of the heart." Thus, mere logic alone is not always sufficient, and we must open our hearts to feeling the presence of Allah, as well. This is not always easy to do and has led to enormous discussions in the Muslim world about the relationship between faith, reason and logic. This issue was also touched upon by the medieval thinker, Ibn Rushd (aka Averroes, d. 1198), whose books, as summarized in the modern work, *Faith and Reason in Islam* (trans. by Ibrahim Najjar), had such an impact on European rationalist thought. Imam Abu Hamid Muhammad al-Ghazali (d. 1111), Imam Abu al-Hasan al-Ash'ari (d. 936) and many others also were involved in these types of topics, staking out various positions, some accepted by the mainstream, others rejected.

[109] The Prophet said, "Among Allah's servants will be some whom the prophets and martyrs will consider fortunate." When the people asked him who they were, the Prophet replied, "They are the people who loved each other for the sake of Allah without any other considerations, such as money or kinship. Their faces will be lit up by layers of light. They won't experience any fear when others will be afraid, nor will they feel sorrow when others are grieving (on the Day of Judgment)." Then he recited this verse. (*Abu Dawud*)

Knowing. [65] And surely, (all creatures) within the heavens and the earth belong to Allah.

So what are they following, those who call upon 'partners' in place of Allah? They're following no more than conjecture and inventing lies. [66] He's the One Who made the night for you to rest in and the day to make things clearly seen. There's evidence in these things for any who care to listen. [67]

Addressing an Outrageous Claim

Now they're claiming, "*Allah has begotten a son!*" Glory be to Him! He's the Self-Sufficient! Everything in the heavens and on the earth belongs to Him! You have no basis to make such a claim! Are you saying things about Allah about which you know nothing? [68]

Say (to them), "*Those who invent a lie against Allah will never succeed.*" [69] Just a bit of fun in the world (for them) - *and then they'll come back to Us!* Then We'll make them suffer a terrible punishment on account of their covering (over the truth). [70]

All Prophets had to Struggle

Recite for them the story of Noah, when he said to his people, "*My people! If my continued presence among you is a burden for you, even as I've been reminding you of the signs of Allah, (it doesn't matter) for I'm depending on Allah. So join together, both you and your idols, and gather your plans (against me). Don't second guess your plans. Then sentence me (to death), and give me no chances. [71] If you (do decide) to turn away (from my preaching, then consider this): I haven't been asking you for any reward (for my efforts). My reward is due from none other than Allah, and I've been commanded to be with those who submit (to His will).*" [72]

(His people ultimately) rejected him, but We saved him and whoever was with him in the boat. We let them inherit (the land), even as We overwhelmed in the flood those who rejected Our signs.

110 Now go and see how those who were warned were brought to an end! [73]

Then after him We sent messengers (all over the world) to their individual nations. They brought clear signs to them, but their (people) wouldn't believe in what they had already (decided to reject) beforehand. That's how We seal the hearts of the defiant. **111** [74]

Moses and the Sorcerers

Then after them We sent Moses and Aaron with Our signs to Pharaoh and his nobles, but (the Egyptians) were an arrogant and wicked people. [75] When the truth came to them from Us, they said of it, *"This is obviously magic!"* [76]

Moses said to them, *"Are you saying this about the truth when it's come to you? Is this what magic is like? Mere sorcerers are never successful!"* [77]

(The Egyptians responded,) saying, *"Have you come to turn us away from the traditions of our ancestors, so you and your brother can become powerful in the land? (Well, it won't work) because we're never going to*

---

110 There is no mention in the Qur'an concerning the duration of time that the flood lasted. The Bible claims it lasted for almost a year and covered the entire world under water before gradually receding. The oldest Mesopotamian records record the flood that occurred there to have been only six or seven days.

111 Human civilization is a rich tapestry of many varied and different religions and cultures. However, they all contain some basic moral ideas, even if they are not expressed or promoted strongly. This is proof that morality all comes from the same source: Allah. Why else would human beings, out of all the creatures of the earth, believe in moral codes? Squirrels, swordfish and otters don't worry about stealing from each other, coveting their neighbor's spouse or sharing food with their lame ones, but we do more so than any other creatures, even our closest genetic relatives. *Survival of the Fittest* would actually mean the cancellation of a moral and humane frame of reference. Left to our own devices, history has shown that people can be worse than animals in their capacity for greed, cruelty and selfishness. Yet, religion calls us back to morality and to righteous living among our fellows. A man may do evil, but then he is assaulted with messages of shame and repentance. Even corrupted men of Allah are indicted by the religious principles they claim to espouse, leaving us with the question: where do these eternal truths come from that have been a part of all societies? Why does it seem that religion is an external force constantly being imposed and reimposed on an unwilling and negligent humanity? It's because the Independent Allah keeps religion coming upon us in doses, like a concerned doctor giving medicine to an uncooperative patient.

believe in you!" [78] Then Pharaoh commanded, *"Bring me every skilled sorcerer (that we have)!"* [79]

When the sorcerers arrived, Moses said to them, *"Cast down whatever (spell) you wish to cast!"* [80]

After they had their turn to cast, Moses said, *"What you've brought is wizardry, but Allah will render it useless, for Allah never lets the work of the immoral triumph.* [81] *By His words, Allah will prove the truth, no matter how much the wicked hate it!"* [82]

None of (the Egyptians) believed in Moses except for some of the offspring of (Pharaoh's) people, [112] for they feared persecution from Pharaoh and his nobles. Pharaoh certainly was a tyrant in the land whose cruelty knew no bounds. [113] [83]

The Children of Israel Believe in Moses

Moses announced (to the Hebrews), *"My people! If you believe in Allah, then trust in Him, if you're truly submissive (to His will)."* [84]

---

[112] The commentators are divided as to whether this means that only a few Egyptians believed in Moses or if it refers to only some of the children of the Hebrews believing in him. Obviously, it seems clear that the Hebrews, for the most part, did believe in Moses, and they followed him as a group out of Egypt (see verses 84-86). Therefore, this reference must be about the handful of Egyptians who accepted Moses as a prophet, such as the magicians, Pharaoh's wife 'Asiyah and perhaps a few others. (Ibn Kathir was also of this view.) The entire context of verses 75-83 is about Moses interacting only with Egyptians. The next verses [10:84-86] have Moses speaking to his own Hebrew fellows and represents a transition in the story. Keep in mind that many of these 'prophet stories' contain parallels with Prophet Muhammad's own experiences as a way to tell him his experience is not unique and thus not impossible to bear. Prophet Muhammad had made a few converts from the children of the chiefs of the Quraysh, even as the top tier of the city's leadership rejected him. (Also see 7:120-122.)

[113] The Prophet said, "There are three types of people who will not have their supplications rejected: a just leader; a fasting person until he breaks his fast; and the supplication of an oppressed person, for Allah will raise (his supplications) above the clouds on the Day of Judgment. The doors of the sky will be opened for it, and Allah will say, 'By My grace! I will certainly grant it for you, even if only after some time has passed.'" (*Ahmad, Ibn Majah*)

"We trust in Allah," they answered. (Then they prayed,) *"Our Lord! Don't make us a test for the oppressors.* [114] [85] *Save us, through Your mercy, from those who reject (You)."* [86]

Then We inspired Moses and his brother, saying, *"Make homes for your people in Egypt, and turn your homes into centers (of worship). Establish prayers, and give good news to the believers."* [115] [87]

Moses prayed, *"Our Lord! You've given Pharaoh and his nobles fancy trinkets and wealth in the life of this world. Our Lord, they've mislead (many) away from Your path, so obliterate their wealth and harden their hearts so much so that they won't believe until they see the painful punishment."* [88]

"Your prayer is accepted," came the answer. *"So stand by the straight (path), and don't follow the path of those who have no knowledge."* [89]

The Children of Israel Escape from Egypt

We led the Children of Israel across the sea. Then Pharaoh and his hordes brazenly followed after them in (their blind) rage, even until he was overwhelmed and about to be drowned, at which time he said, *"Now I believe - there's no god save for the One in Whom the Children of Israel believe! Now I submit!"* [90]

"What! Now (you want to submit)?" (it was said to him.) [116] *"Just a little while ago you were the cause of great turmoil!* [91] *We're going to save*

---

[114] A significant request, as the Egyptians had many times before taken their wrath out on the Hebrews.

[115] Moses was the functional spokesman for his people in those final years in Egypt. Allah is ordering him here to maintain their social and cultural cohesion by encouraging them to live in homes and build stable families. The Egyptians were gradually losing control over their slaves, and thus the Hebrews had to learn to be independent. The Hebrews were, however, not allowed to worship publicly; thus, they were told to offer prayers and supplications in their homes. (*Ibn Kathir*) This was also the condition of the early Meccan converts who had to worship in secret behind closed doors.

[116] The Prophet said that Allah continues to accept the repentance of people all the way until the actual process of dying has started (the so-called 'death-rattle.') (*Tirmidhi*) Pharaoh was in such a state when he tried to repent, but it was too late. Thus, this pharaoh's body was recovered and preserved. Perhaps it's on display even now in some museum somewhere in the world or lying in a tomb, waiting to be discovered by modern

your body today, so you can become an example to those who will come after you. Yet, still most people are unconcerned with Our signs!" [92]

And so it was that We settled the Children of Israel in an appropriate place and provided them with wholesome resources. It was only *after* they were given knowledge that they fell into rival groups, but Allah will judge between them as to their differences on the Day of Assembly. [93]

Ask those who came Before You

If you're ever in doubt about what We're revealing to you, (Muhammad,) then just ask those who've been reading the scripture before you. [117] The truth has indeed come to you from your Lord, so don't be among the doubtful, [94] nor be among those who deny Allah's (revealed) verses, for then you'll be among the losers. [95]

Those who've had the sentence of your Lord proven against them won't believe, [96] even if every proof were presented to them – *that is until they see the painful punishment (right before their eyes)!* [97]

Of All the Cities, Who Believed?

Why hasn't there been a single settlement that believed, so that by its faith it could have prospered, other than the people of Jonah?

---

archeologists! By way of contrast, Jewish writers claim that Allah let Pharaoh live after this defeat. (See *Midrash Yalkut*, part 238.)

[117] The Prophet suffered from so many insults and accusations at the hands of his idol-worshiping critics that he, too, being only human, sometimes felt moments of weakness and uncertainty while in Mecca. Keep in mind that the message he was bringing was also new to him and completely different from what he had experienced in his cultural background living in central Arabia. This is something that many Muslims and non-Muslims fail to appreciate. We take it for granted today that people talk of prophets, monotheism, good manners, theology, an afterlife and all the rest, but Muhammad did not grow up in such an environment. Islam was as new to him as it was to his pagan critics. Here he is told that if his own heart wavers under the assault of the pagans, he can ask the people who already had a scripture if what he is bringing is, indeed, similar to what the prophets of old brought. Mecca, being a trading town, did see Christian and Jewish merchants passing through from time to time. Some of them actually converted to Islam after the Prophet shared his message with them, proclaiming it to be the completion of their own religions.

¹¹⁸ When they believed We removed the punishment of disgrace from them in the life of this world, and We allowed them to enjoy themselves for a (little) while longer. [98]

If Allah had wanted, He could've made everyone on earth into believers, (but He didn't). So how can you make people believe when they don't want to? [99] No soul can believe except by Allah's leave, and He brings dire consequences down upon those who don't use their reason. [119] [100]

Say (to them), *"Look around at all (the wonderful signs) throughout the heavens and on the earth,"* though neither proofs nor warners are of any use to a people who have decided not to believe. [101]

Do they really expect any (other fate) than what befell those who passed away before them in former days? Then say (to them), *"You just wait then, for I'll be waiting with you, as well."* [102] In the end, We saved Our messengers and those who believed, and it was entirely appropriate for Us to save those who believed. [120] [103]

---

¹¹⁸ Jonah was sent to dwell among the people of Nineveh sometime between the years 793-753 BCE, during the reign of King Jeroboam II of Israel, (according to II Kings 14:23-25). Jonah was sent to preach in that foreign city, perhaps because the land of Israel was rife with idolatry, even into the royal house where the worship of a golden calf was (once again!) in full favor. Apparently, Nineveh, the city to which Jonah was sent, which was an early capital of the ruthless Assyrian Empire, is the only major city on earth that heard a prophet's preaching and then repented from the lowest of its people up to the ruling classes. Whereas the usual pattern in all other instances has been that the poor respond to a prophet, while most of the rich people and rulers fight against him, fearing a loss in their wasteful and extravagant lifestyles. Then Allah's just punishment comes in either the form of a natural calamity or invasion from outside invaders. The name of the Assyrian king that Jonah convinced was most likely Ashur-Dan III (772-755 BCE). This king ruled over an empire in flux, with restless nobles, rebellions, and strange portents that appeared, such as a total eclipse of the sun and two separate plagues that struck the land. This had the probable effect of making the people ready to listen to the preaching of a prophet, and it fits precisely with the pattern of divine intervention so often mentioned in the Qur'an (see 6:42-45). Unfortunately, the subsequent generations of the people of Nineveh soon forgot the teachings of Jonah. The city eventually fell in 612 BCE to an invading coalition of Medes, Babylonians and Susians. Thus, they enjoyed themselves *"for a (little) while longer."*

¹¹⁹ Thus, it comes down to the individual. Whole cultures or societies will rarely believe as a group. It is every person who will make the individual choice to believe or not, despite what's happening around him in his wider social or cultural milieu.

¹²⁰ 'Abdullah ibn 'Umar relates that one night after the Prophet had led the night prayers, he turned to the congregation and said, "Do you see this night you have? One hundred years after this night, none of those who are here in this land will be alive." (*Muslim*)

A Call to those in Doubt

Say (to them), *"People! If you have any doubts about my way of life, (then know that) I don't serve what you're serving in place of Allah. Moreover, I serve Allah, the One Who will take your souls (at death), and I've been commanded to be among the faithful.* [104]

"(I've also been told), 'Set your face upon the pure natural way. [121] *Never be an idol-worshipper,* [105] *nor call upon any other besides Allah, for they're just (material) things that can neither benefit nor harm you. If you did, then you would truly be wrongdoers.'"* [106]

If Allah touches you with some harm, no one can remove it besides Him, and if He intends for any good to come your way, then no one can withhold His favor. [122] He causes it to reach whichever of His servants that He wills, for He's the Forgiving and the Merciful. [107]

Say (to them), *"People! Now the truth has come to you from your Lord! Whoever is guided is guided for the good of his own soul, and whoever goes astray does so to his own loss. It's not my place to manage your affairs."* [108]

Now follow the revelation that's being sent to you, (Muhammad,) and be patient until Allah decides the matter, for He's the best one to judge. [123] [109]

---

[121] The term *hanif* means the pure and natural religion of monotheism.

[122] The Prophet said, "No Muslim supplicates to Allah with a supplication that does not involve sinfulness or the severing of relations of the womb, but Allah will grant him one of three things: He will either respond to his supplication quickly, save it for him until the next life, or He will turn away from him an equal amount of harm." Some people asked, "What if we supplicate more?" He replied, "There is more with Allah." (*Ahmad*)

[123] Some years later, after the Muslims had fled to Medina, the Meccans and the Muslims met in the year 624 and did battle at the Wells of Badr. The outnumbered Muslims won a stunning victory, despite having odds of three-to-one against them. This battle has often been called the first distinctive 'decision' of Allah, which was meant to show the people of the region that His favor was upon the Prophet and his followers.

Hūd

11 Hūd
Late Meccan Period

This chapter is similar to the last in theme, and it continues the veiled subtext of separation. In other words, it prepares the Prophet and his followers for the possibility of abandoning their hometown. This is hard for anyone to do, let alone large groups of people. Late Meccan chapters like this continually mentioned episodes from the lives of prophets such as Noah and Moses who had to make a clean break from their people and past lives for the sake of a brighter future. When the order finally came to the Prophet to lead his followers to Medina, they would've already been well-versed in the principle of migrating for the sake of Allah's faith. Such was the tense atmosphere in the late Meccan period that it even began to show upon the appearance of the Prophet. Abu Bakr, noting that the Prophet seemed to be getting worn down, asked him, "It seems that you've been aging. Why is that?" The Prophet answered, "The chapter of Hūd and others like it have aged me." (*Tirmidhi*)

In the Name of Allah,
the Compassionate, the Merciful

*A*lif. Lām. Rā.

(This) Book contains clear injunctions that have been categorically explained by One Who is wise and well-informed. [1] Therefore, you should serve none other than Allah.

(Muhammad, say to all people,) *"I've (been sent) to you from Him both to warn and to give good news.* [2] *Therefore, seek the forgiveness of your Lord, and repent to Him, so He can provide you with good things to satisfy you (here on earth) for a while* [124] *and ultimately grant His favor upon*

---

[124] The good things that cause satisfaction do not refer to obtaining riches and material goods. As the commentators explain, they refer to Allah making a person content with what they have in this life so they no longer covet or feel ashamed on account of possessions or the lack thereof.

those who are worthy of merit. [125] *If you turn away, then I'm afraid that you'll be punished on a momentous day.* [3] *All of you will go back to Allah, and He has power over all things."* [4]

> **Background on verse 5:** Ibn 'Abbas (d. 687) was asked about this verse. He explained that it was about a superstition the pagans had in which they were afraid to expose themselves to the sky if they had to remove any of their clothes, either for answering the call of nature or from sleeping with their wives. (*Ibn Kathir*) This verse is telling them that Allah sees them no matter how much they try to hide.

As it is, they close up their hearts and try to hide from Him! However, even though they wrap themselves up in their cloaks, He still knows what they hide and what they show, for He knows (all the secrets) of the heart. [5]

The Faithless can't Hide in their Denials

There isn't a creature that moves on the earth without its being dependent upon Allah for its provisions. [126] He knows where its usual resting place is, even as He knows where it lurks for a while, [127] for everything is recorded in a distinctive ledger. [128] [6]

He's the One Who created the heavens and the earth in six time periods, and His throne was over the water. [129] (He created you) so

---

[125] A man named 'Uqbah ibn 'Amr once asked the Prophet, "What is (the best way to attain) safety (on the Day of Judgment)?" The Prophet replied, "Control your tongue, let (the walls of) your house surround you, and weep for your shortcomings." (*Tirmidhi*) This is a snapshot of the qualities of a true believer.

[126] The Prophet said, "Allah's hand is full, and it is not diminished by spending throughout the night and the day." (*Bukhari*)

[127] A creature's usual resting place can be its territory, nest or natural environment, whereas the commentators usually construe the temporary place to mean either the grave or the womb where a creature exists for time before either being born or disintegrating back into the earth.

[128] That is Allah's Own record of what occurs in the universe. Nothing is left out.

[129] There are two ways to interpret the meaning of Allah's throne being 'over the water.' It may be possible that the 'water' being referred to here is, in reality, interstellar space, given that the mention of the heavens and the earth's creation would suggest, in keeping with the Qur'anic view that celestial bodies 'swim' in orbit [36:40], that 'water' here is another metaphor for space (for a people who had no real precise word for it). Another possible interpretation is that Allah's throne, or *power*, over the water is a clear reference to His having created all life from the sea, after He created the physical structure of the planet and the sky. (See 21:30) Contrary to romantic notions, this verse does not serve the same function as Genesis 1:2 which says that Allah's face was over the water.

that He could test (you in order to bring out) which of you is most noble in conduct. However, (Muhammad), even if you told them, *"You really are going to be resurrected after death,"* those who suppress (the light of faith in their hearts) would be sure to say, *"This is obviously just magic."* [7]

Then if We delayed the punishment for some time, they would be sure to say, *"So what's holding it back?"* Oh, but on the day when it actually comes upon them - *nothing will hold it back from them then* - and they'll be completely surrounded by what they used to laugh at! [8]

Beware the Fickle Heart

If We let a human being have a taste of Our mercy, but then withdraw it from them, they become despondent and thankless. [130] [9] If We then let them experience good fortune after a bout of hardship has befallen them, they merely say, *"My streak of bad luck is over,"* and then they become proud and overconfident. [131] [10]

Although that's not the case with those who persevere and do what's morally right, for they're going to be forgiven, and they'll have a great reward. [11]

Stay the Course

Perhaps you've been tempted to abandon some of what's been revealed to you, or perhaps your heart has become filled with anxiety (at the prospect that) they might say, *"Why aren't any treasures being sent down to him, or why aren't there any angels coming along with him?"* You're only a warner, and Allah is the One Who manages all affairs! [12]

(Perhaps you're afraid) they might say, *"He made it all up!"*

---

[130] Rabi'ah al-Adawiyya (d. 801) said, "He doesn't refuse to give resources to the one who speaks ill of Him, so how could He refuse to give resources to the one who is overflowing with love for Him?"

[131] The over-reliance of people on the concept of good or bad luck leaves them open to alternating periods of despair and over-exultation. Relying upon Allah in good times and bad, however, releases people from this feeling of being at the mercy of the whims of luck.

(If they do say that, then) tell them, *"So bring ten chapters like it, and call whomever you can other than Allah (to judge them as to their similarity), if you're really so honest!* [132] [13] *And if your (idols) don't answer you, then know that this revelation is being sent down with Allah's knowledge and that there's no god besides Him. So now will you submit (to Him)?"* [14]

Those who desire the life of this world *and all its glitter* will be repaid by Us for the deeds they did within it, and (they) won't be shortchanged. [133] [15]

---

[132] This is a reverse play on the common objection of people who don't believe that the Qur'an is from God. Whereas they might say it was an invention of Muhammad, this verse challenges people to make up ten chapters that duplicate these in all respects, if they really believe it was all the invention of a human mind. Keep in mind that previous to this, the Arabs' style of poetry was completely different, as embodied in the famous *Seven Odes*, a collection of pre-Islamic epic poems about tribal exploits that were hung in the Ka'bah to honor the authors. They were similar in style to *Beowulf* or even some aspects of classic Greek storytelling, though in many respects they are hard to decipher and are filled with esoteric or flighty fits of fancy. Given that the Qur'an was in a style that was so different, the Arabs failed to meet this challenge. What further makes duplicating the Qur'an so difficult is a number of factors, among them are the following: 1) the consistent theological themes; 2) the rhythmic style, which uses various schemes and sub-styles in a harmonious interplay designed to excite and bedazzle the listener; 3) the grammar and vocabulary choices in the Arabic text are such that people get doctoral degrees in Qur'anic Arabic, alone; 4) the subtext of the Qur'an in tone is a dialogue in which Allah is calling humanity to submit to His will, and various logical and philosophical arguments are presented and interwoven within larger complex themes; and 5) then when you get into numerical miracles, dramatic prose and other aspects, you find that it is a much harder task than one would expect! Muslims are not even satisfied with translations of the Qur'an into other languages and inevitably complain of constrained meanings and unnatural boundaries imposed upon it by the strictures of languages that are not as highly developed in allegory and metaphor as Arabic.

[133] This is the foundation of the well-known principle in Islam, which was also further explained by the Prophet, that all the good deeds that a person does in this world, which are only for the sake of this world and not for Allah's sake, will be repaid to each person by Allah in this worldly life of theirs. The Prophet said the same thing when he was asked about those who lived before Islam, who did good deeds, but who were still pagans. Such people get their rewards in this life, but they get nothing in the next, for their actions were for their own sake and not done with the intention of pleasing Allah. The Prophet said, "Actions will be judged by intentions, and everyone will have what he intended. So if someone migrated for some worldly benefit or for the purpose of marrying someone, then that is for which his migration will be counted." (*Bukhari*)

73

They're the ones who will have nothing in the next life - *other than the Fire!* All the plans they made will be useless there, even as all that they did will come to nothing! [134] [16]

Are (such evil people the same as) those who accepted the (revealed scriptural) proof [135] of their Lord, which was taught by a witness sent from Him, even as the Book of Moses (was also sent) before it, as a source of guidance and mercy?

(The believers) put their faith in it, but those factions (from days gone by) who abandoned (their revelations) will have nothing but the Fire as their promised meeting place. Have no doubt about that, for it's the truth from your Lord, though most people don't believe. [17]

Who can be more wrong than the one who invents a lie against Allah? They're going to be brought back before their Lord, and then the witnessing (angels) will say, *"These are the ones who lied against their Lord!"* [136] Truly, Allah's curse will befall the corrupt! [18] They're the

---

[134] The Prophet told the following story: "Surely, the first person who will be judged on the Day of Resurrection will be a martyr. He will be brought before (Allah) Who will then list all the favors that were bestowed upon him (in the world), and he will recognize them. Then (Allah) will ask, 'What did you do with them?' He will say, 'I fought in Your cause and died a martyr.' Whereupon (Allah) will say, 'You're lying. You fought so people would call you brave, and so they said it.' Then the command will be issued, and he will be dragged on his face and thrown into Hellfire. Then, a person who acquired and taught knowledge and recited the Qur'an will be brought before (Allah) Who will remind him of the blessings (he received), and he would recognize them. (Allah) will then ask, 'What did you do with them?' He will reply, 'I acquired and taught knowledge and recited the Qur'an for Your sake.' Whereupon (Allah) will say, 'You're lying. You acquired knowledge so people would call you a scholar; you recited the Qur'an so they would call you a reader, and so you were.' Then the command will be issued, and he will be dragged on his face and thrown into Hellfire. Then a person whom Allah made affluent and who was given riches will be brought forth and informed about the favors he received, and he will recognize them. Then (Allah) will ask, 'What did you do with them?' He will reply, 'I donated to every cause that You would have wanted me to support.' (Allah) will say, 'You're lying. You donated so that people would call you generous, and so it was said.' Then the command will be issued, and he will be dragged on his face and thrown in Hell." (*Muslim*)

[135] The 'proof' is the Qur'an.

[136] The Prophet said, "Allah, the Most Exalted and Sublime, will come near to a believer and conceal him in His shade, and He will screen him from other people and make him confess his sins. 'Do you remember this sin?' He will ask. 'Do remember that sin? Do you remember the other sin?' This will go on until He makes him admit to all of his sins, so much so that the believer will think he's about to be doomed. Then Allah will say, 'I have concealed these sins for you in the life of the world, and I've forgiven them for you

ones who hinder others from following the path of Allah, trying to make it seem crooked - *all the while they're the ones who are rejecting (the concept) of the next life!* [19]

There's no way they can obstruct Allah (and His purpose) in this world, nor will they find anyone to protect them besides Allah. Their punishment will be doubled, for they (couldn't bring themselves) to hear (the message) or notice (the signs of Allah). [20] They're the ones who've lost their own souls, and whatever they invented will leave them to languish. [21] Truly, they're going to be the biggest losers in the next life! [137] [22]

Those who believed, who did what was morally right and who humbled themselves before their Lord, they'll be the companions of the Garden, *and there they shall remain!* [23]

The two classes (of people, both the faithless and the believer), can be compared to the blind and deaf and the seeing and hearing. Are they the same in comparison? [138] So won't you take a reminder? [24]

---

today.' Then the believer will be given his record of good deeds. As for the faithless and the hypocrites, the witnesses will say, '*These are the ones who lied against their Lord! Truly, Allah's curse will befall the corrupt!*'" (From verse 11:18) (*Bukhari, Muslim*)

[137] Abu Hamid Muhammad al-Ghazali (d. 1111) once wrote, "Remember your friends who have passed away and who were near in age to you. Remember the honors and awards they earned, the high positions they held, and their handsome physical appearances. Today all of them are turned to dust. They've left widows and orphans behind them; their wealth is being wasted, and their homes are turned to ruin. There is no trace left of them today, and they lie in dark holes underneath the earth. Picture their faces before your mind's eye, and then ponder."

[138] Sultan Mahmoud of Ghazni (d. 1030) was sitting at a dinner with some of his closet advisors. The men saw his magnificent crystal goblet and admired it with many compliments, and it was one of his favorite possessions. The sultan handed the goblet to his prime minister and said, "Break it!" The official replied nervously, saying, "I could not, my sultan. It's too precious, and I would not dare to destroy one of your favorite possessions." The sultan then handed the goblet to each of his advisors with the same order, and each man refused to break the magnificent goblet. Finally, he handed the goblet to his freed slave Ayaz. When he repeated to him to break the goblet, Ayaz said, "Nothing is more precious to me than obeying your command." Then he immediately threw it to the ground, shattering it into a thousand pieces. Afterwards he said to the sultan, "I would not dream of refusing your order, and so I immediately did what you told me to do." The sultan turned to the advisors and said, "Now you can see why I love and trust him so much." Obedience to Allah's commands should be that immediate for anyone who claims to believe in Him.

Noah's People Rejected Him

And so it was that We sent Noah to his people, (and he announced), *"I'm a clear warner (who's been sent) to you* [25] *(to teach you) that you should serve no one else besides Allah. I'm afraid that you might be punished on a terrible day."* [26]

The leaders of the faithless among his people said, *"We don't see anything in you more than a mortal man like ourselves, nor do we see anyone following you except the weakest and least sophisticated among us, nor do we see you as any better than the rest of us. No way (are you a messenger of Allah)! We think you (and your followers) are liars!"* [27]

(Noah) replied, *"My people! Have you considered that I (just might have) been given clear evidence from my Lord and that He might have indeed sent His mercy down upon me from His Own presence? However, if (those things) are unclear to you, then should we force you to accept (Allah's truth) when you're dead set against it?"* [139] [28]

"My people! I'm not asking you for any money in return (for my preaching). My reward is due from none other than Allah, and I'm not going to push away (the poor people) who believe, (just because you look down upon them). They're going to meet their Lord, (even as you will). It's just that I've (come to the conclusion) that you're an ignorant people." [29]

"My people! Who would help me against Allah if I pushed the (poor) away? So won't you take a reminder? [30] *I'm not telling you that I have the treasures of Allah, nor do I know what's hidden, nor do I claim to be an angel. And I won't say about the ones whom you look down upon that Allah won't grant them something good, for Allah knows what's in their souls, and if I ever were to (push the poor away), then I would be acting like a tyrant."* [31]

---

[139] Forced conversion has never been the divine way, despite the fancies of religious bigots and mistaken demogogues. From the moment that Iblis decided to challenge Allah even unto our own time, Allah allows people free reign to do their worst. He warns them, though, through revealed scripture (and even common sense coupled with our inner sense of right and wrong) that one day there will be a price to pay for injustice, arrogance and upsetting the natural and proper order of things. See 2:56.

They answered, *"Noah! You've argued with us and carried on the argument for a long time, so now bring down upon us that with which you've threatened us - that is if you're really telling the truth!"* [32]

"Allah will certainly bring it down upon you," (Noah) replied, *"but only when He wants to do it, and then you won't be able to stop it!* [33] *If Allah wants to leave you astray, then my advice won't do you any good, even though I want to advise you, for He is your Lord, and you're going to return back to Him."* [34]

(So now are the idol-worshippers of Mecca) saying, *"(Muhammad) has just made (this story) all up"?* [140] Answer them, saying, *"If I made up (the story of Noah), then it would be my fault alone, but I'm free of all your (kinds of) corruption.* [141] [35]

The Great Flood

Background on verses 36-37: Noah preached to his people for many years. After he was finally and completely rejected by his people, as evidenced by his speech contained in chapter 71, Allah decreed that he should build a boat and save the few who believed. This is perhaps the world's oldest story, and we remember it to this day for the many lessons it yields.

Noah [142] received an inspiration (from Allah) that said, *"No more of your people will believe, except for those who've already believed.*

---

[140] The Arabs of Mecca were completely ignorant of most of the stories and themes from the Judeo-Christian tradition, so when their fellow citizen Muhammad began reciting to them such stories, the pagans laughed them off as an invention. Only later on, after the pagans began asking visiting Jews and Christians about the stories Muhammad was telling, did they become familiar with them. In this way, the Prophet was providing a kind of educational course for the people of his city, whether they realized it or not.

[141] In addition to the rampant sin and debauchery of Arabia, the Meccans also practiced idolatry and mindless superstition, *and they had the nerve to accuse Muhammad of inventing the story of Noah?* Muhammad had the well-earned reputation, from an early age, of being completely honest. So how could they accuse him of blatant lying or forgery? He was free of their kind of corruption by their own witness. As the Meccans would find out later, such stories were known to other communities - even those living thousands of miles away.

[142] Is there any archeological or documentary evidence for the story of Noah and the flood, apart from the Qur'an or Bible? Ancient records that have survived from Mesopotamian civilizations such as the Sumerians, Akkadians and Babylonians, all speak of an ancient flood that devastated the region. Although the various versions of the story give differing details, the earliest accounts of the flood mention a chief named Ziasudra/Xisouthros of Shuruppak who was warned by An, the supreme god of heaven,

Therefore, don't feel any more sadness over what they're doing. [36] *Build a boat under Our watchful eye and by Our inspiration,* [143] *and don't petition Me any further about those who do wrong, for they're going to be drowned."* [144] [37]

So (Noah) began to build the boat, but every time the leaders of his people passed by him they would ridicule him. [145] He would say (to

---

to save his family from harm by constructing a large boat. Interestingly enough, the name Ziasudra means, 'he of long life.' Later versions of the story in other languages change Ziasudra's name to Utnapishtim, which means, 'he found life.' (Kramer, Samuel Noah, *Sumerian Mythology*, Harper & Brothers, New York, 1961.) Another even much later Babylonian version calls him Atramhasi. Five-thousand-year-old clay tablets unearthed in Mesopotamia record the story of Noah (Ziasudra) this way: "…and as Ziasudra stood there beside (a wall), he heard (God say): 'Step up to the wall to My left and listen! Let Me speak a word to you at the wall, that you may grasp what I say; may you heed My advice! By Our hand a flood will sweep over the cities of the half-bushel baskets and the land (of Mesopotamia); the decision that mankind is to be destroyed has been made. A verdict, a command of the assembly cannot be revoked. An order of An and Enlil (the gods of sky and earth) is not known ever to have been countermanded. The kingship (of man), their term, has been uprooted, they must bethink themselves of that. Now… this is what I have to say to you… O man of Shuruppak…build a boat…abandon possessions and seek the living…make living creatures go up into the boat…" Ziasudra is then told how to build the boat, and he and his followers enter it just in time to escape the deluge. After six or seven days, the flood subsides, and he sacrifices to Heaven in thanks. (Jacobsen, Thorkild, *The Harps That Once…: Sumerian Poetry in Translation*, Yale University Press, 1987) Of course, the story contains mention of many gods, but that's not unexpected given the many centuries that must have passed between the original event, it's first recording, and then later embellished versions that spanned over three thousand years.

[143] Noah did not know how to build a boat. Allah inspired him and showed him how to do that. According to Ibn 'Abbas, Allah told Noah to build it in the shape of a bird's breast. Supposedly it had three rooms, two for animals and one for people. (*Zamakhshari*) Although the Bible describes a large rectangular ship, a rounded boat would have been much more logical. In ancient times, boats in Mesopotamia were often more circular in shape with steep sides and a rounded bottom. This type of boat is much more stable and bobs in the water, even if it is turbulent. According to a version of the story recorded on 3,700 year old Babylonian cuneiform tablets, the boat was indeed circular in construction. The relevant text tells the erstwhile man to build the boat from plaited palm fiber, sealed with bitumen. In this version, it is the god Enki who commands thusly: "Wall, wall! Reed wall, reed wall!" says Enki. "Atram-Hasis (Noah), pay heed to my advice, that you may live forever! Destroy your house, build a boat; despise possessions and save life! Draw out the boat that you will build with a circular design; Let its length and breadth be the same."

[144] There is a similar statement in Jeremiah 7:16 in which God is said to declare the final doom of the sinners of Israel.

[145] Noah lived in Mesopotamia in a city that was far from any large body of water (other than the nearby Euphrates river), so for him to build a large boat, in an open field away from the river, must have seemed doubly ludicrous.

them in answer), *"If you're ridiculing us now, (know that) we're (soon) going to be ridiculing you.* [38] *Soon you're going to know who it is that has a humiliating penalty in store, and who it is that will have a lasting punishment."* [39]

Then Our command arrived, and the heated banks (of the rivers) [146] began to overflow! *"Board (the ship),"* We said, *"and take a pair of male and female from every kind (of useful livestock).* [147] *Load up your family, all except for those against whom the sentence has already been given,* [148] *and (load) the believers."* However, only a few had ever believed along with him. [40]

(Noah) said to (his followers), *"Set out upon (the boat), for its course and its coming to anchor will be in the name of Allah, and my Lord is truly forgiving and merciful."* [41]

(Thereafter, the ship) floated with them upon waves (that towered over them) like mountains. Noah called out to his son, who had become separated from the rest (of the faithless), *"My son! Come on board with us, and don't (share the same fate) as the faithless!"* [42]

"I'll climb upon some mountain," he called back, *"and that will save me from the (rushing) water!"* (Noah looked away in sadness and) said, *"Today, no one is safe from the command of Allah, unless He decides to be merciful to him."* Then the waves came between them, and (his son) was just another one of those who had been drowned. [43]

---

[146] See 23:27 for an explanation of this term.

[147] The commentators are divided as to which category of animals Noah was asked to take. Those who follow the Biblical line of thought view the flood as a world-wide event, and they say he took a pair of every animal, and even plants. Those commentators who believe that it was a local flood that devastated only Noah's own people say that Noah brought pairs of livestock animals that his people would need after they disembarked from the boat (to build their society anew). Today, many commentators assume it was a local flood, as nowhere in the Qur'an does it say the entire world was underwater.

[148] Noah's wife and one of his sons refused to believe him; thus, they did not enter the safety of the boat. See 66:10 and footnote.

Then the saying went out: *"Earth! Swallow your water! Sky! Clear (yourself of clouds)!"* Then the water diminished, and the matter was fulfilled. [149]

The boat came to rest upon Mount Judi, and the saying went out: *"The wrongdoing people have passed away!"* [150] [44]

Then Noah called upon his Lord and said, *"My Lord! My son was of my own family. Even still, Your promise is true, and You're the fairest judge of all."* [151] [45]

"Noah!" (Allah) replied. *"He was no longer part of your family, for his actions were other than moral, so don't ask Me about things you may know nothing about.* [152] *This is a word of caution that I'm giving to you so you won't be one of the ignorant."* [46]

"My Lord!" (Noah) answered. *"I seek Your protection so that I won't ask You about things I may know nothing about. Unless You forgive me and show me mercy, then I would surely be among the losers."* [47]

---

[149] Radio carbon dating of samples taken from a two-foot-thick layer of flood-clay from the ruined city of Shuruppak confirms a massive inundation occurred in the area about 2900 BCE. Is Noah (Nuh in Arabic) the same man as Ziasudra/Utnapishtim? It is quite probable, and the Qur'an is more flexible in assigning ancient identities than the Bible. From the basic description and similarities found in the various ancient sources, it certainly fits that the two men (Noah and Ziasudra/Utnapishtim) may be one and the same, although we must assume the original story was corrupted by the time it was finally written down, and it does, in fact, transform even further through successive versions and adds many idols and fantastic events in the mix, as well. Be that as it may, this is a fascinating and entirely plausible connection.

[150] In Arabic, the name of the mountain where Noah landed is known as Mount *Judi*, and it's thought by some modern commentators (who merely adopt the Biblical account) to be the same place as Mount Ararat, which is located in modern-day Turkey not far from Armenia, though there is no definitive proof for this at all. The name *Judi* is the ancient name of a people who dominated southeastern Turkey. They were mentioned by name in ancient Sumerian records, and their descendants are probably the Kurdish people of today. It's a rugged region that they inhabit, with high brackish lakes and varied mountainous terrain. Commentators in the classical period named the entire region of modern-day Kurdistan as *Al-Jazirah*, and they assumed that Mount Judi was located somewhere there. (*Ibn Kathir*) Today, it is thought by some maverick scholars that the mountain Noah landed on is located somewhere near Lake Van.

[151] It seems as if Noah was hoping for some leniency for his son from Allah's judgment, even after his son had perished.

[152] Allah can see into the hearts of others, while we cannot. Our assumptions do not trump Allah's hidden knowledge.

The call went forth: *"O Noah! Come down (out of the boat) with peace from Us and also with blessings upon you and upon the people who are with you, (and also upon the communities that will descend) from them – peoples to whom We'll give enjoyment, even though in the end a terrible punishment from Us will befall them."* [153] [48]

These are some of the hidden stories (that were unknown) to you (Muhammad) and that We're revealing (to you). Neither you nor your people knew them before. So bear patiently (the persecution of the Meccans), for the final (victory) is only for those who were mindful (of their duty to Allah). [49]

Hūd Calls to His People

We sent to the (people of) 'Ad their brother Hūd. He said (to them), *"My people! Serve Allah! You have no other god than Him. You've been doing nothing but inventing (false gods).* [50] *My people! I'm not asking you for any reward for this, for my reward is due from none other than the One Who created me. So won't you understand?"* [51]

"My people! Ask your Lord to forgive you, and turn to Him (in repentance). [154] *Then He'll send abundant rain down upon you and add strength to your strength. Don't turn away in wickedness!"* [52]

"Hūd!" they answered. *"You haven't brought us any convincing proof. We're not about to abandon our gods on your word alone, nor will we ever believe in you.* [53] *We'll admit to no more than to say that maybe some of our gods have afflicted you with insanity."*

---

[153] According to ancient Sumerian and Akkadian accounts of the flood, after he left the boat, Noah (Ziasudra/Utnapishtim) made an offering to heaven of reeds, pine and myrtle. Then he is quoted as saying, "I looked at the weather. Silence reigned, for all the people had returned to clay. I wept, with the tears running down my cheeks."

[154] The Prophet said, "If a person accepts Islam sincerely, then Allah will forgive all his past sins, and from that moment the record of deeds begins again. His good deeds will be rewarded from ten to seven hundred times. A sin will be recorded as it is, unless Allah forgives it. (*Bukhari*)

(Hūd) replied, *"I call upon Allah as my witness, even as you are witnesses, as well, that I'm free of your making partners* [54] *in place of Him, so plot against me all you want, and give me no chance.* [55] *I'm going to trust in Allah, the One Who is my Lord and your Lord. There isn't a creature that moves without Him having a hold on its forelock,* [155] *and my Lord is on a straight path."* [56]

"If you turn away, then (at least) I've conveyed the message to you with which I was sent. (Now it just might happen that) my Lord will cause another people to rise up in your place. (No matter how much you resist Allah,) you can't harm Him in the least. My Lord is the guardian of all things." [57]

And so when Our command came We saved Hūd and those who believed along with him by an act of Our Own mercy, and We saved them from a tremendous punishment. [58]

And so that was the (people of) 'Ad. They renounced the signs of their Lord, disobeyed His messengers, and obeyed the commands of every arrogant enemy (of faith). [59] They were pursued by a curse in this life, and on the Day of Assembly, (oh, how they'll be punished), for the 'Ad rejected their Lord, and so - *away with the 'Ad, the people of Hūd!* [60]

The Thamud Suffer a Similar Fate

We sent to (the people of) Thamud their brother Salih. He said (to them), *"My people! Serve Allah! You have no other god than Him. He's the One Who produced you from the earth and settled you upon it. Ask for His forgiveness, and turn to Him (in repentance), for my Lord is always near and ready to respond."* [61]

(His people) said, *"Salih! You were one of us, and we had always placed our best hopes in you (that you might one day be our leader). Are you now*

---

[155] Allah is aware of the life and death of every creature, regardless of whether they're large or small, for His power is a force that pervades the entire universe and all life itself. In Arabic idiom, to take a hold of a creature's forelock is to have total control of it. See 55:41 for example.

forbidding us from worshipping what our ancestors worshipped? We have serious doubts about what you're calling us towards." [62]

"My people!" (Salih) answered. *"What do you think? If I have evidence from my Lord and if He's given me mercy from His Own Self, then who could help me against Allah if I ever disobeyed Him (by giving up this mission)? So (the bribes) you're offering me (to quit) are no more than the instruments of my own ruin.* [156] [63] *My people! This camel (you see here is specially blessed) by Allah and is a sign for you. Therefore, leave her to graze on Allah's land, and do her no harm, or a swift punishment will befall you."* [64]

(Then the arrogant people among them) cut (her legs) and crippled her, so (Salih) told them, *"Enjoy yourselves in your homes for the next three days, (after which you're going to be destroyed), and that's a promise that won't be proven false."* [65]

When Our command came, We saved Salih and those who believed along with him from the humiliation of that day through an act of Our Own mercy. Your Lord is Capable and Powerful! [66]

The mighty blast overtook the wrongdoers, and they lay cowering in their homes by the morning. [67] (It looked) as if they had never lived or flourished there before! And that was (their fate), for the Thamud rejected their Lord, and so - *away with the Thamud!* [68]

The Ruin of Lot's People

Our emissaries went to Abraham with good news. They said, *"Peace,"* and *"Peace,"* he answered back. Then he hurried to serve them a roasted calf. [69]

However, when he noticed that their hands never moved to partake of (the meal), he became suspicious of them and grew afraid.

---

[156] His people dangled the prospect before him that he might be chosen as their king – if only he would give up his campaign against their idolatry.

"Don't be afraid," they said, *"for we're being sent against the people of Lot."* ¹⁵⁷ [70]

His wife just stood there and laughed when We gave her the good news of (a son named) Isaac and (a grandson named) Jacob. ¹⁵⁸ [71] *"Misfortune is mine!"* she sighed. *"How could I bear a child now, seeing that I'm an old woman and my husband here is an old man? That would be something amazing, indeed!"* [72]

"Are you amazed at Allah's command?" they asked. *"Allah's mercy and blessings are (invested in) you, the people of (this) house,* ¹⁵⁹ *and He is indeed praiseworthy and full of glory."* [73]

When Abraham's sense of unease had left him, and after he had heard the good news (of a son), he began to plead with Us on behalf of Lot's people, [74] for Abraham was (by nature) forbearing and prone to beseeching (his Lord as a matter of habit). ¹⁶⁰ [75]

"Abraham!" (the angels said.) *"Put an end (to your pleading). The command of your Lord has already gone out. They're going to receive a punishment that cannot be turned away."* [76]

---

157 The angels mentioned here were disguised as humans, so as not to arouse alarm or undue adulation. 'Abdullah ibn 'Abbas said that they were three in number and that they were the angels Gabriel, Michael and Israfil. (*Qurtubi*) According to reports mentioned in Ma'ariful Qur'an, the guests were acting strangely. They had arrow heads and were poking the food with them. Other reports derived from Jewish sources say that the angels were being evasive in their answers to Ibrahim's queries about their identity. At-Tabari reports that the angels refused the meal unless they could pay Abraham for it. Abraham asked only that they begin the meal by mentioning Allah's name and that that would be payment enough. The angels turned to one another and said that it truly is appropriate that Allah calls this man a friend.

158 Sarah's future son Isaac and her future grandson Jacob are mentioned here to give her the good news of Allah's favor upon her. Abraham already had a legitimate son Ishmael by his second wife Hagar. (Genesis 16:3 explicitly calls Hagar a *wife* of Abraham.) However, Abraham's first wife Sarah had remained barren. When Abraham first received the secret inspiration that he would have a son with Sarah, he laughed about it in incredulity (see Genesis 17:15-19). Later on, Sarah laughed when the visiting angels told her the same thing, thinking it was impossible for her to have children (see Genesis 18:12-15). Therefore, both Abraham and Sarah laughed at what they thought to be impossible. The name *Isaac* is derived from the Hebrew term 'to laugh.' Thus, due to both parents' incredulous laughing, their new son got a name that means — he laughed!

159 By referencing the household in general, the angels were making it known that Abraham's future generations were also going to benefit from Allah's blessings.

160 The story is told of Abraham's pleading for Lot and his people in Genesis chapter 18.

When Our emissaries arrived (in the district of Sodom and Gomorrah and met with) Lot, he became worried about their (safety), for he felt powerless (to protect) them (from his wicked people). [161]

"Oh, what a stressful day!" he cried out, [77] (as he noticed) his people rushing towards his (house), eager (to seize his guests), for they had long been engaged in perverted ways.

"My people!" he beseeched them. *"My daughters are here, and they're more appropriate for you!* [162] *Be mindful of Allah, and don't disgrace me with regards to my guests. Isn't there a single man among you with good sense?"* [78]

"You know we want nothing from your daughters," they answered, *"and you know quite well what we want (to do with your guests)!"* [79]

"If only I had the strength to keep you at bay," (Lot) cried out, *"or some strong force to call upon!"* [163] [80]

"Lot!" (the angels) said. *"We are emissaries from your Lord! They won't reach you, (for we're going to hold them back). Flee (this city) with*

---

[161] It was Lot's wife who informed her wicked friends of her husband's secret guests, no doubt telling them how handsome they were. Lot's wife became completely engaged in the ways of the locals and forgot about Allah. In addition, she used to tell the people about what Lot was doing, as well as inform them whenever he had guests from out of town. The riotous crowds would then come and dishonor Lot's guests in the most shameful and deplorable manner. (*Ibn Kathir*)

[162] Some commentators are of the opinion that Lot's call to offer his *daughters* should not be taken literally and that through this line of reasoning he was telling the men gathered before his door that they should give up their homosexuality, (or he was possibly using this appeal as a stalling tactic), knowing full well that the crowd would have never considered his daughters seriously at all. (See Genesis 19:8 where Lot is also quoted as offering his daughters to appease the wild mob.)

[163] The Prophet said, "May Allah have mercy on Lot! He called upon a strong pillar of support (Allah). After him, Allah sent no prophet unless he came from a respectable family among his people." (*Tirmidhi*)   Lot had no standing among the people of his adopted city, given that he was an outsider who had merely settled there, and also because he had no illustrious genealogy, foreign or domestic, upon which to stake his reputation, unlike Jonah, for example, who preached in a foreign land, but who at least had come from a noble lineage in a nearby territory. Thus, in Lot's case, he couldn't even appeal to longstanding family ties to keep his adopted people from bothering him. Even though their nations also rejected them, all later prophets had at least some respectable standing in their local communities from which they could draw legitimacy. See 11:91.

your family while some of the night still remains, and don't let anyone look back. [164] *However, your wife (is not going to leave with you). So she's going to suffer the same fate that they're going to suffer.* [165] *Their time will be up by the morning, and isn't the morning near at hand?"* [166] [81]

When Our command came, We turned (their towns) inside out and rained shower upon shower of hard-packed brimstone down upon them [82] – (each blow being) imposed by your Lord, and such (punishments) are never far from those who do wrong. [83]

Madyan was also Tested

We sent to (the people of) Madyan their brother Shu'ayb. He said, *"My people! Serve Allah! You have no other god than Him! Don't cheat when you measure or weigh (in your business dealings). I see that you're in prosperity now, but I'm afraid that you'll be punished on an overpowering day."* [84]

"My people! Weigh and measure fairly, and don't withhold from people what rightfully belongs to them. Don't spread corruption in the land with a desire to cause chaos. [167] [85] *(The fairly earned profits) that Allah has left for you are the best for you, if you only had faith! However, I haven't been given the task of watching over you."* [168] [86]

"Shu'ayb!" they answered. *"Are the prayers that you're making (to your God) telling you that we should give up worshipping what our ancestors did or give up using our property as we see fit? Oh, aren't you the one who is so forbearing and filled with common sense, (especially when you're telling others what to do)!"* [87]

---

164 It is assumed (if one follows Biblical sources) that the angels caused the crowd to become confused or blinded, thus allowing Lot and his family to escape. (See Genesis 19:11.)

165 There is no tradition in Islam that Lot's wife turned into a pillar of salt.

166 In other words, "Lot, get going now!"

167 This refers to the highway robbery and raiding that some from his tribe commonly practiced. (*Ibn Kathir*) They also shaved the edges of gold and silver coins to steal wealth, even as the coins appeared mostly normal. Thus, cutting or shaving coins has been made a crime in Islamic law. (*Ma'ariful Qur'an*)

168 In other words, he wasn't sent to be a police officer, enforcing laws and regulations. His job was to make them aware that what they were doing was wrong and that they needed to begin policing themselves.

"My people!" (Shu'ayb) replied. *"Now you just see if I have clear evidence from my Lord (to back up my claim. Here, take a look at my own business dealings), for (Allah) has given me good returns (through honest trade as a bounty) from His Own Self.* [169] *I don't want to engage in what I've been forbidden to do, unlike your own practices. My only desire is to improve (your lives) to the best of my ability. My success will come only from Allah! I trust in Him and turn to Him (in repentance)."* [88]

"My people! Don't let my opposition (to your longstanding practices) cause you to do (more) wrong (in response), for you might suffer a fate similar to that of the peoples of Noah, Hūd or Salih, and the people of Lot are not so far away from you (that you should claim ignorance). [170] [89] *Ask your Lord to forgive you, and turn towards Him (in repentance and obedience), for my Lord is full of forgiveness and loving tenderness."* [90]

"Shu'ayb!" they answered. *"We don't even understand most of what you're telling us! In fact, we think you're the weakest among us. If it wasn't for your family (connections), we would've stoned you already, because you don't have any power to prevent us."* [171] [91]

"My people!" he replied. *"Is my family's (influence) the most important factor for you to consider (in deciding whether to harm me or not), even more than (your fear of) Allah? Are you casting Him aside behind your backs (so easily)? My Lord completely surrounds whatever you're doing!* [92] *My*

---

[169] In other words, it's not necessary to cheat in order to become financially successful.

[170] The lands of Salih's people were only a short journey's south/southeast of the area where the people of Lot used to dwell. Even as Sodom and Gomorrah were destroyed by an earthquake and resultant shower of stones, Salih's people were likewise obliterated in a cataclysm. It is said that the main city in question was located in southern Jordan in a place now named Ma'an.

[171] The Prophet once asked a group of his companions, "Do you know who is really poor?" The companions replied that in their estimation a poor person was someone who had no money or possessions. Thereupon the Prophet said, "The real poor person from my community is the one who will come on Judgment Day with tremendous good deeds and a good record of prayer, fasting, charity and the like; yet, (while he was alive in the world) he had insulted people, falsely accused people, devoured people's property unjustly and had someone killed, beaten or harassed. All those oppressed people will take their complaints to Allah, and the good deeds of the oppressor will be distributed to the oppressed. Finally, when there are no good deeds left, and there are still more complaints to be settled, then the sins of the oppressed people will be transferred to the oppressor, and thus he'll be thrown into Hellfire." (*Muslim*)

people! Do whatever you can, and I'll do whatever I can, likewise. You're soon going to know who will have a humiliating punishment befall them and who is lying, so keep on watching, for I'll be watching with you." [93]

When Our command came, We saved Shu'ayb and those who believed along with him through an act of Our Own mercy, but the mighty blast took hold of the corrupt, and they lay cowering in their homes by morning. [94] (It looked) as if they had never lived and flourished there before! And so the (people of) Madyan were removed - *just like the people of Thamud!* [95]

Take Heed of the Pattern of History

And so it was that We also sent Moses with Our signs - and also with a clear mandate [96] - to Pharaoh and his nobles. However, (his nobles) obeyed Pharaoh's orders, and (obeying) Pharaoh's orders was not the most rational (thing for them to do). [97]

He's going to stand before his people on the Day of Assembly and then lead them into the Fire - *and oh, how terrible is the place into which they'll be led!* [98] They're followed by a curse in this (life), and on the Day of Assembly they're going to get an awful gift (in exchange for their awful deeds). [99]

These are some of the stories of the nations (of the past) that We're narrating to you. Some of them still exist, while others have been mowed down. [172] [100]

It wasn't We Who did them any wrong. Rather, they did wrong against their own souls. All those idols that they used to call upon besides Allah were of no use to them when Allah's command went out, nor did they add anything (to their plight) except for more destruction. [101]

---

[172] Some ancient nations that were punished by Allah still persisted, though in a diminished way, such as Egypt, which lost its power, but whose people survived. Others, like the people of 'Ad were completely obliterated. There is no trace, other than in ruins, of that civilization, which was centered in southwestern Oman.

That's what being seized by your Lord is like when He seizes towns steeped in the midst of their own corruption, and His grasp is exceedingly firm! [173] [102]

There is a sign in this for those who fear the penalty of the next life. That will be a day when all people will be gathered together, and that will be a day of giving testimony. [103] We won't delay it any more than the time that's set for it. [104]

On the day when it arrives, no soul will be allowed to speak unless it's been granted His permission. Some of those (assembled) there will be wretched, and others will be esteemed. [174] [105]

The wretched will be in the midst of the Fire, and they'll have nothing but moaning and wailing, [106] and they'll remain there for as long as the heavens and the earth endure, except as your Lord wills, and your Lord does whatever He wants. [107]

Meanwhile, those who are held in high esteem will be in the midst of the Garden, and they'll remain there for as long as the heavens and the earth endure, except as Allah wills, and it will be an unending gift. [108]

Have no doubts (about the true nature) of what these (Meccans) are worshipping, for they're worshipping nothing more than what their ancestors worshipped before them (out of blind habit). We're going to pay them back what is due to them without withholding anything. [109]

And so it was that We gave the scripture to Moses, but (later generations) differed about it. If it wasn't for the statement (of

---

[173] The Prophet said, "Allah gives some time to a wrongdoer until He seizes him, and then he cannot escape." Then the Prophet recited this verse. (*Bukhari, Muslim*)

[174] When this verse was revealed, 'Umar ibn al-Khattab asked the Prophet, "Messenger of Allah, is there some sign for us to know (of which group we will be a part)? Will it be because of something a person did or didn't do?" The Prophet replied, "'Umar, it will be due to something that he did and that was recorded by the pens (of the guardian angels), but every easy deed was created for its purpose." (*Tirmidhi*) The last part of the tradition means, as explained by another tradition, that people who are inclined towards good find the doing of good deeds easy, while those who are inclined towards evil find evil deeds easy.

principle) that went out before from your Lord (that people will have time to make their choice as to whether or not to believe), then the matter would've been decided between them. However, they persist in doubts and misgivings about it. [110]

What is a Sincere Believer?

All shall be repaid by your Lord for the result of their deeds, for He's well-informed about everything they're doing. [175] [111] Therefore, stand up firmly (for the truth) as you've been ordered to do, both you and those who are with you who turn (to Allah for guidance). Don't overstep (Allah's laws). Indeed, He's watching everything you do. [176] [112]

Don't lean towards (being on the side of) wrongdoers, or else the Fire will take hold of you. You have no other protector than Allah, and you won't be helped (by anyone else if you cross Him). [113]

Background on verse 114: A man had kissed a woman to whom he was neither married nor related, and he went to the Prophet in repentance and asked how the sin could be erased. This verse was then revealed. After the Prophet recited it, the grateful man asked, "Messenger of Allah, is this verse just for me?" The Prophet replied, "This is for all of my community." (*Bukhari*)

Establish prayer at the two ends of the day and during some hours of the night, [177] for good deeds remove evil deeds. [178] This is a reminder for those who would be reminded. [114] Bear with patience

---

[175] Scholars of the past have said that the entire religion of Islam has been summarized in verses 11:111-115.

[176] The Prophet once commented on this passage, saying that its revelation made him feel old, (in the sense of weary from heavy responsibility). (*Ma'ariful Qur'an*)

[177] Three prayers are listed here: the dawn prayer (*fajr*), the dusk prayer (*maghrib*), and the late night prayer (*isha*). It must be noted that this verse was revealed before the mandate of the standard five daily prayers, an order that the Prophet later received during his Night Journey and Ascension.

[178] The Prophet also once said, "There isn't any Muslim who commits a sin but then does ablution and prays two units of prayer, except that he will be forgiven." (*Ahmad, Ibn Majah, Abu Dawud*) The principle is enumerated that doing a pious act, such as prayer, helps to erase sins recorded on one's record. The Prophet also once asked his companions, "Do you think that if there were a flowing stream in front of the door of any of you, and he bathed in it five times a day, that any dirt would remain on him?" The people answered in the negative, so the Prophet continued saying, "This is what the five prayers are like, for Allah uses them to wash away sins and transgressions." (*Bukhari, Muslim*)

(any hardships that befall you), for Allah will never allow the reward of the righteous to be lost. [115]

Parting Thoughts on the Path of Truth

So now why weren't there - in all the generations that went before you - people with sense enough to prevent others from spreading chaos and disorder in the earth, [179] save for the very few whom We saved (from harm)? The wrongdoers followed after nothing more than what pleased them, and they were truly wicked. [180] [116] However, your Lord never destroys a settlement unjustly, (that is) as long as its people are behaving well. [117]

If your Lord had wanted, He could've made all people into a single community. However, they never cease to argue, [118] except for the ones who've been graced with your Lord's mercy, and this is the purpose for which We created them. [181] The sentence of your Lord will be fulfilled: *"I will fill Hellfire with jinn and people all together!"* [119]

---

[179] A French mathematician and author named Blaise Pascal (d. 1662) said it rightly when he wrote, "All of humanity's problems stem from man's inability to sit quietly in a room alone." People are tempted to cause disorder the minute they leave their bedrooms, even if they do not mean to do so. Normal interaction can lead to misunderstandings which can lead to chaos and hurt feelings or worse. When we see someone going off into a negative trajectory, whether it be from abusing others, using drugs or alcohol or planning some mischief, it is our job to help them not to make bad choices. The Prophet once said, "Help your brother, whether he is an oppressor or is oppressed.' A man asked: 'O Messenger of Allah! I (know how to) help him when he is oppressed, but how can I help him when he is an oppressor?' He said: 'You can restrain him from committing oppression. That will be your help to him.'" (*Bukhari and Muslim*)

[180] The eminent companion, Abu Dharr al-Ghiffari, once said of worldly-oriented people: "They give birth to what they will ultimately bury; they build what they will eventually tear down; they hold tightly to what is temporary, and they forsake what is eternal. Blessed are the two cries that people hate the most: death and poverty."

[181] The Qur'an offers the reason why Allah created living creatures. It was so that He could extend mercy towards them. Allah is love [85:14], and He extends that love to all. In the contest of free will, however, the Qur'an makes it abundantly clear that Allah does not love those who do evil on earth and harm their fellow creatures. Even in that condition, however, Allah continues to hold out the gift of repentance and forgiveness. Even an evil person can regain fellowship with Allah. The way is open for each person's entire life up until just before their death throes begin. The material world is in some ways our nemesis, however, for our flesh desires it greatly at the expense of our spiritual and intellectual well-being. It is so much easier to give in to bodily urges than to be self-controlled and thoughtful. In this the Prophet left us with this warning, "Hell is surrounded by delights, while Paradise is surrounded by hardships." (*Bukhari, Muslim*)

(The purpose) of all of these stories of (the ancient) messengers that We're relating to you is to strengthen your heart. These (stories) that are coming to you contain the truth, as well as warnings and reminders for those who believe. [120]

So say to those who don't believe, *"Do whatever you can, and we'll do whatever we can.* [121] *Wait for some time, and we'll be waiting, also."* [122]

The (knowledge) of unseen things within the heavens and the earth belongs only to Allah, and all matters will go back to Him (for their resolution), so serve Him, and trust in Him. Your Lord is not unaware of what you're doing. [123]

Joseph

12 Yūsuf

Late Meccan Period

The story of Joseph has long been considered one of the most engaging and heart-warming accounts in the Qur'an. It is also the single longest chapter with only one continuous theme and story line. It was revealed near the last days of the Prophet's stay in Mecca, at a time when the pagans and enemies of Islam were closing the noose of public enmity around the Muslims from all sides. A group of visiting Jews from the northern city of Yathrib (later to be called Medina) had doubts about the validity of Muhammad's prophethood.

Hoping to expose him as a possible fraud, they suggested to the pagans that they should ask him to narrate a Jewish story that the Arabs knew nothing about. In the main square of Mecca, a pagan man asked him, "What happened to Joseph and his brothers? How did they come to live in a far-away land among strange people?"

If Muhammad failed to answer, then it could've been said that he was a fake and not a true prophet. Muhammad exclaimed that he would wait for revelation from his Lord. A short while later, Muhammad stood out in the public forum and proceeded to recite the entire story of Joseph and his brothers - without a pause or break - until the entire length of this chapter was finished. (Verses 1-3 were revealed and added later.)

As Muhammad recited the story, the crowd fell silent. When he had finished, the Jewish visitors who witnessed the event left without saying a word. A few weeks later, several more visitors came from Yathrib, this time Arabs, and they accepted Islam at a site called 'Aqabah. The Muslim community now had two great lights to give them hope: the addition of new believers from another city; and *the most beautiful of all stories*, as the Qur'an described the story of Joseph.

In the Name of Allah,
the Compassionate, the Merciful

Alif. Lām. Rā.

These are the verses of the clear Book. [1] We've sent it (in the form of) an Arabic Qur'an so you can think (on it) deeply. [182] [2]

Now We're going to narrate to you the most beautiful story in Our revealing this portion of the Qur'an to you. [183] You didn't know (this story) before. [3]

The Dream

Joseph said to his father, "O Father! I saw (in a dream) that eleven stars, the sun and the moon were all bowing themselves to me!" [184] [4]

"My little son," his father answered. "Don't mention this vision to your brothers for they might plot against you (out of jealousy). Satan is the clear enemy of all of humanity!" [185] [5]

"(It's my feeling) that your Lord is going to choose you (to be a prophet) and teach you how to interpret (the meaning of passing events). [186] (By this

---

[182] In other words, this chapter is the retelling of a Hebrew story in the Arabic language, so the Arabs who asked the Prophet about the story of Joseph could understand it. The deep reflection and pondering comes in when people consider that the Prophet could not have known this story, for he couldn't read or speak Hebrew, nor could he read or write in any language. How then could he narrate the entire story in one sitting in a public square and fill it full of rhyme, passion and drama? (We must also remember that there were no translations of the Old Testament in Arabic at that time. This was not done until the tenth century by a Jewish scholar in Egypt named Said bin Youssuf al Fayyumi.)
[183] The classical writer, Nouruddin Jami' (d. 1492), crafted a dramatic retelling of this entire story in his book entitled, *Yusuf and Zulaikhah*. It has since been regarded as a highly spiritual exploration into the complicated lives of the two main characters, the unspoken details of which make this tale so fascinating. The tragic Arabian story of *Layla and Majnoun*, collected and assembled by Nizamuddin (d. 1209), also echoes a similar theme of romantic/spiritual tension and ultimate redemption.
[184] Verse 100 of this chapter reveals the meaning of this dream of Joseph. Dreams that come true are from Allah and are real, according to Islam. The Prophet once said, "Nothing is left of prophethood (after I pass away) except glad tidings." The people asked, "What are the glad tidings?" He replied, "True good dreams (that convey glad tidings)." (*Bukhari*) He also said, "The dream of a believer is a dialogue in which he has the honor of talking to his Lord." (*Tabarani*) In other words, the only supernatural communication between Allah and humanity after Allah's last prophet to the world passed away will be in the form of dreams that may come true, which any individual can have.
[185] In the Biblical version of this story, Joseph first told his dream to his brothers, and later to his father, who scolded him for doing so. See Genesis 37:9-11.
[186] *Taweeli al-ahadith* can mean understanding passing events or interpreting the true meaning of things that occur in sequence. In other words, Joseph would one day gain

94

gift), He will complete His favor upon you and upon the descendants of Jacob, even as He had already completed it upon your forefathers, Abraham and Isaac. Indeed, your Lord has all knowledge and wisdom." [187] [6]

And it just so happens that in (the story of) Joseph and his brothers, there are definitely lessons for (those) people who asked! [188] [7]

The Brothers Plot against Joseph

(Joseph's older brothers complained among themselves,) saying, *"Our father loves Joseph and his (younger) brother (Benjamin) more than he loves us, even though we're just as good! Our father is obviously mistaken!"* [189] [8]

(Then one of the brothers suggested), *"So then let's kill Joseph or send him away to some far off place. Then our father will give us all his attention. There'll be plenty of time for all of you to reform yourselves later on."* [9]

However, one of the other (brothers) said, *"Don't kill Joseph! Why don't you throw him down in the bottom of a well? Then some passing caravan can find him (and take him away)."* [190] [10]

(Later, the brothers approached their father and said,) *"Father! Why don't you entrust Joseph with us, since (you know) we have his best*

---

the wisdom to interpret events and explain their meaning. This ability would also extend to visions and dreams.

[187] See 2:124 where Abraham specifically prayed that his descendants would be specially blessed.

[188] In other words, the Jews of Medina put this issue to the Prophet, and the Qur'an has a ready and lengthy answer, even as the Arabs of Mecca did not know about this Biblical story at all. Thus, all parties should take note that it is Allah at work here. (*Ma'ariful Qur'an*)

[189] In the Qur'anic version of this story there is no specific mention of a 'coat of many colors,' as in the Christian tradition, causing the brothers' jealousy to explode (see Genesis 37:3 where the Hebrew term for 'long tunic' is mistranslated as a 'coat of many colors'). From the Qur'anic perspective, the root of the problem lay in Jacob's love for his two youngest sons and in the immaturity of his elder sons, who couldn't understand that human nature always inclines a parent to show more affection to the smaller and more needy of his or her offspring. (See Genesis 37:4 where the brothers' hatred is described.)

[190] The Old Testament names this more high-minded brother as Reuben. See Genesis 37:20-22.

interests at heart? [11] *Send him with us tomorrow to enjoy himself and play. We'll protect him (from any danger)."* [12]

"I'm uneasy," their father replied, *"about your desire to take him (along with you). I'm afraid that a wolf might eat him while you're not paying attention."* [13]

"If a wolf were to eat him," they answered, *"while there's so many of us (there to protect him), then we would have perished (first)!"* [14]

So, they took Joseph out with them, (after assuring their father he would be fine), but secretly they had all agreed to throw him down a well. [191]

(Then, as they seized Joseph and were about to throw him into the deep hole), We revealed (this message to) his (heart), *"One day you're going to tell them about their affair when they won't even know (who you are)!"* [15]

Then (the brothers) returned home at nightfall in tears. [16] "Oh, Father!" they cried. *"We went racing with each other and left Joseph all alone (to watch) our things. Then a huge wolf (came and) ate him up! Yet, you'll probably never believe us, even though we're telling the honest truth!"* [17]

(Then they pulled out his shirt,) which they had secretly stained with false blood. "It can't be!" Jacob cried. *"You must have made (some kind of plan) amongst yourselves! As for me, I can only wait with gracious patience. Only Allah can (help me) bear (the pain) of what you've described."* [18]

---

[191] When the brothers had Joseph out of sight of their father, they began slapping him and abusing him all the way to the well where they intended to imprison him until he either starved to death or was found by passing nomads. Joseph was begging them to let him go, but they tied him with ropes and beat him into silence. They taunted him, telling him to call on those 'eleven stars' for help. When they threw him down the deep well, he would have drowned, except he found a stone to stand upon and was able to keep his head above water. (*At-Tabari*) The commentators say that Joseph was a young teenager at the time and that he spent three horrible days in the well. (*Ma'ariful Qur'an*)

Then a caravan of travelers passed by, and when they sent their (water boy) to the well, he let down his bucket and shouted, *"Hey! (Look at this!) What a lucky break! Here's a fine young boy!"* [192]

Then they stowed him away like a treasure, though Allah knew what they were doing. [19] (Joseph's brothers) sold him (to the caravan) for the measly price of (a handful) of silver. That's how low of an opinion they had of him! [193] [20]

Joseph in Egypt

The Egyptian who bought (Joseph) said to his wife, *"Treat him honorably, for he might bring us some benefit, or we could even adopt him as a son."* [194]

This is how We settled Joseph in the land so We could teach him how to interpret passing events. Allah has complete proficiency over His affairs; yet, most people never realize it. [21]

---

[192] Some commentators hold that the name of the young man who discovered Joseph in the well was Malik ibn Du'bar. (*Ma'ariful Qur'an*) The caravan in question was an Arab caravan. The Arabs were traders linking Africa, Arabia, Syria and Asia from time immemorial. To find a lone young boy they can sell into slavery was considered by such people as a lucky break indeed.

[193] Some commentators say that the brothers went back to the well when Joseph was taken out and demanded money from the caravan owners to buy the boy (as also mentioned in the Old Testament in Genesis 37:25-28). Other commentators suggest that the brothers had no more contact with Joseph and that the caravan merely found him and took the boy away. Based on the context of these two verses [12:19-20], it seems the first view is more likely, as it was the brothers who held Joseph in contempt. According to reports in al-Qurtubi and Ibn Kathir, this type of language used here indicates, in common merchant parlance of the day, that the selling price for Joseph was under 40 silver coins and thus a 'measly' sum to well-established mobile merchants. (The Bible claims that Joseph's selling price was a mere twenty pieces of silver. See Genesis 37:28.) Although official government-stamped coinage was not yet invented, the use of gold and silver as a trade medium had long been established throughout the Middle East from as far back as 2500 BCE.

[194] Traditionally, the man who bought Joseph is known as Potiphar (Qitfir or Itfir in Arabic), while his title of *al-'Aziz*, which means powerful official, is how the Qur'an refers to him. It is thought that he served in the government of the Amalikite (Hyksos) ruler Rayyan ibn al-Walid as priest of the god named On. This king led a dynasty of foreign origin that had subjugated northern Egypt some years before. (*Zamakhshari*) Others date him earlier to the reign of the two pharaohs Sesostris the I and III. The name of Potiphar's wife has traditionally been known as Zulaikhah. Some commentators say she was also known as Ra'eel. Joseph lived in her house for about ten years, and he was approximately 17 at the time he was brought into the service of her family. (*Zamakhshari*)

In time, as Joseph became fully mature, We endowed him with sound judgment and intelligence, and that's how We reward those who are good. [22]

However, she in whose house he lived (began to feel attracted to him), and she sought to seduce him against his (moral) nature. She bolted the doors and said to him, *"I'm ready for you now, (so come to me)!"* [195]

"Allah forbid!" Joseph exclaimed. *"Your husband is my master! He's the one who made my life here tolerable! No good comes to people who do wrong!"* [23]

The fact was, however, that she desired him greatly, and he would've desired her, except that he remembered the proof of his Lord. And so, We turned him away from decadence and (the desire to do) shameful deeds, for He was one of Our sincere servants. [196] [24]

Then they raced each other to the door, and she tore his shirt from behind (as he attempted to get away). When they reached the door they found her noble (husband) standing right there! (Thinking quickly,) she said, *"What other punishment can there be for someone who wickedly (tried to seduce your wife) except prison or a painful beating!"* [25]

"But she's the one who tried to seduce me away from my own nature!" (Joseph) protested. Just then, a member of her household who witnessed (the scene as it unfolded), suggested, *"If his shirt is torn from*

---

[195] The Prophet said, "Whoever can guarantee (that they won't misuse) what is between their cheeks and between their legs, I can guarantee that they will go to Paradise." (*Bukhari*) The meaning is that if one controls his tongue from gossip, slander, lying and praising false gods and also his sexual impulses from straying outside of legal limits, then he is worthy of heaven.

[196] In classical Muslim literature, it was surmised in popular writings that Zulaikhah had portraits of herself painted all over her room, so that even if Joseph turned away from her, he would see images of her wherever he turned. The Prophet said that when Joseph was faced with the temptation to be with Zulaikhah, the angels reported to Allah that Joseph was thinking a bad thought. Allah told them to only record it as sin if he acted on it, but if he resisted the sin, then they should record it as a good deed, for he restrained himself for Allah's sake. (*Muslim*)

the front, then she's telling the truth, and he's the liar! [26] *But if his shirt is torn from the back, then she's the liar, and he's telling the truth!"* [197] [27]

When he saw that Joseph's shirt was, indeed, torn from the back, (he turned to his wife and scolded her), saying, *"Truly, this is your ploy, and your ploy is formidable!* [198] [28] *Joseph, forget any of this ever happened!"* (Turning back to his wife), he said, *"Apologize for your offense, for you're clearly at fault!"* [199] [29]

The Women of the City Find Out

(When news of the event became known), the (upper class) women of the city (began to gossip), saying, *"The wife of the great minister wants to seduce her own houseboy. He must have stricken her with passionate desire. We can see that she's clearly losing her mind!"* [200] [30]

When she heard of their malicious gossiping, she invited them and prepared a banquet for them. (After they all arrived and were seated,) she gave each of them a (fruit-cutting) knife. (While they were cutting their food), she called out to Joseph, saying, *"Come out (Joseph, and stand here) before them."*

When they saw him, (his handsome features) astounded them, and they cut right through (their fruit) to their hands! [201] *"Allah save us!"*

---

[197] The Biblical version differs here with Zulaikhah taking Joseph's shirt from him as he ran away from her advances, and then successfully framing Joseph with the shirt, causing Potiphar to send Joseph to prison himself. (See Genesis 39:7-20.)

[198] Potiphar is quoted here using the plural form of the pronoun 'you.' Thus, he is blaming women in general for their considerable talent in ensnaring men's hearts. As the commentators have pointed out, this is just Potiphar's opinion, based on perhaps his own moment of anger, and it in no way applies to all women. (*Ma'ariful Qur'an*)

[199] This wealthy and powerful man was easy going by nature, and he did not think to revenge himself upon either Joseph or his wife, which was fortunate for them both.

[200] The Prophet said, "There are three qualities with which Allah is pleased when you gain them, and there are three that displease Him when you gain them. He's pleased when you worship only Him without making any 'partners' with Him, when you unite together on the rope of Allah and don't divide yourselves, and when you give advice to whomever Allah appoints as your leader. The three things that displease Him are when you say, 'I heard,' or 'someone said,' when you ask too many needless questions, and the wasting of money." (*Muslim*)

[201] Apparently, Joseph was extremely good looking. During his journey into heaven on his Ascension, the Prophet Muhammad passed by Joseph in the third layer of heaven,

they cried. *"He's no mere mortal! This is no less than an angelic being!"* 202 [31]

"There before you now," she said, *"is the one you blamed me for! (Yes,) I did try to seduce his very soul, but he eluded me and resisted me in order to preserve his innocence! Now if he doesn't do what I command, he'll surely be thrown into prison and be with the most contemptible!"* [32]

"My Lord!" (Joseph) cried. *"I desire prison far more than what they're calling me towards, and unless You steer their ploy away from me, I might become attracted to them and act like an ignorant fool."* [33]

Then his Lord heard (his plea) and turned their ploy away from him, for truly He is the Hearing and the Knowing. 203 [34] Then, after they saw the evidence (of what was going on), it occurred to (the

---

and he commented about him, saying, "He was given half of all beauty, and the rest was spread throughout the rest of creation." (*Muslim*)

202 The word *malak* which is used here is often translated as angel, but the primary meaning of *malak* is to own, to be a king or have sovereignty over something; hence, I could have translated the term here as prince. The Egyptians did not believe in angels in any way that we do. Instead they believed in *Akiru* (plural of *Akh*) which were the spirits of departed people who could bring you good luck in your life. Especially, the spirits of pharaohs were sought out to bring fortune. Priests attended to them and gave offerings. The women were saying that Joseph looked as noble as an otherworldly spirit, angel and royal prince all in one, and that he was handsome to boot! In general, the prophets and messengers of Allah were handsome, charismatic and good looking. They had to be in order to get people to pay attention to their preaching. A'ishah, Prophet Muhammad's widow, made a two-line poem about this verse [12:31], saying, "If the friends of Zulaikhah could see the Messenger of Allah's blessed face, then they would've cut their hearts and not their hands in their place."

203 Zulaikhah wanted to turn her handsome young slave into nothing more than a plaything for her and her girlfriends' pleasure. Joseph, however, being a Godly-oriented man, cried to Allah for deliverance, for he knew the weakness of mortal man in the face of determined female charms. How did he escape the women at the banquet? What were the proofs of Allah that reminded him to be righteous? These questions were the subject of a small but persistent body of speculation in the classical period, and the great commentator at-Tabari offers several different hypotheses culled from many writers. Some early commentators have suggested he ran out of a door; others have said that the women felt powerless to take him due to the look of resoluteness on his face; yet, others have suggested that the banquet was interrupted by some of the women's husbands who arrived unexpectedly, leading into the events of verse 35. Here in the Qur'anic text, there is no clear explanation for either question offered, though this hasn't stopped Muslim writers from delving into the deeper issues raised by this tale.

husbands of the women) that it would be best to put him in prison for a while. [204] [35]

The Two Prisoners

Now along with Joseph there were two other men who were put in (the prison). [205] The first one said, *"I saw myself (in a dream) pressing wine."* [206] The second one said, *"I saw myself (in a dream) carrying bread on my head with a swarm of birds eating off it."* (Then they said to Joseph), *"Tell us the meaning of these (strange dreams), for we can tell that you're a good one (to ask)."* [36]

(Joseph) answered, *"Even before your next meal comes, I'll explain to you the meaning of (your dreams that will predict) events before they even happen to you. This is part of what my Lord has taught me. I've abandoned the customs of (these) people who disbelieve in Allah and reject the (punishment) of the next life.* [207] [37] *I follow the customs of my fathers,*

---

[204] One can imagine that after the women returned home their husbands would soon feel alarmed at how much they praised Zulaikhah's slave boy. Perhaps the men began to fear that their own wives might be tempted to act similarly with the slave boys in their own houses. In that case, they reasoned, quietly removing Joseph to prison would be the best solution until things died down.

[205] Ibn Kathir records that when Joseph was placed in prison, the officer in charge of him came to admire him and told him so. Joseph protested that no one should love him, because anytime someone came to love him, he suffered for it. Then he gave the example of how he was loved by a paternal aunt of his, and then he was falsely accused of stealing from her as a boy. When his father loved him, he found himself thrown in a well and then sold as a slave in a foreign country. When Zulaikhah loved him, he was thrown in prison. As much as Jacob grieved for his lost Joseph, one can imagine the grief of Joseph in this, his most desperate hour.

[206] The practice of dream interpretation in Islam began with the Prophet Muhammad, himself. He said that dreams that come true were one of the 46 aspects of prophethood. He also said that it was the only element of true divine communication that would remain in the world after he was gone, since he was the last messenger of Allah to the world. He used to interpret people's dreams for them sometimes, and this has given rise to a rich literature and tradition of dream interpretation all throughout Muslim civilization. Dreams are truly an indicator of that about which our conscious and unconscious minds are anxious.

[207] Egyptian beliefs evolved over time. They were centered around a whole host of gods and mysterious forces held in place by the goddess of order, who was named Mott. Originally, the afterlife for Egyptians was not a place of accountability for one's deeds. This new doctrine didn't come about until much later in Egyptian history. (A body's soul (known as the *ka* or *double*) merely 'stepped over' to continue its life over there as it was here – albeit in the presence of many gods and demigods.) Eventually, Egyptian religion adopted a kind of 'judgment day' for good and evil in the court of Osiris, one of their

Abraham, Isaac and Jacob, and none of us ever made any partners with Allah. This comes from the grace of Allah that's been bestowed upon us and upon people (in general), though most people are thankless." [38]

Then he said, "My fellow inmates! Which is better: many lords arguing among themselves, or the One, Irresistible Allah? [39] If you don't serve Him, then you're serving nothing more than names that you and your ancestors made up, and Allah gave no one permission to do that. The right to command is for none save Allah, and He has commanded that you serve nothing besides Him. That's the straight way of life, but most people don't understand." [208] [40]

"My fellow inmates," he continued. "As for the first of you, he will again pour out the wine for his master to drink. As for the other, he will be hung from a stake, and the birds will eat off his head. The matter you two asked me about has been decided." [41]

(Then Joseph) whispered to the one whom he thought would be released, "Mention me to your master." However, Satan made (the man) forget all about it, so Joseph lingered in prison for a few more years. [42]

---

gods. The heart of a person was weighed on a scale against the feather of truth. The good souls would then go to join Osiris and live in eternal delight, while the evil souls would be chewed up by a monster named Ammit, thereafter to live in a dark pit with a horrible demon named Apophis. Some centuries after that, a form of monotheism even held sway for a time under Amenhotep IV (Akhenaton). Be that as it may, the rulers of Egypt at Joseph's time certainly did not believe in the exact particulars of the next life as it had been taught by Abraham and his descendants. Rather, their afterlife was a place that merely mirrored our own lives here on earth, with themselves, the pharaohs, as rulers of the next life, as well.

[208] The Prophet said, "Allah lays out the example of the straight path and the two borders that mark the boundaries of this path. The (borders) are two walls containing doors. On each of the doors are lowered curtains. At the entrance leading towards the (straight path) is a caller saying, 'People! Come and enter the straight path all together, and don't divide yourselves.' There is another caller positioned above the path, and when he sees anyone wanting to remove a curtain from one of the doors, he says, 'You'll be ruined! Don't open that door, for if you open it, you're going to enter it!' The (straight) path is submission (to Allah). The two walls are Allah's defined limits. The open doors lead to what Allah has prohibited. The caller at the gate is Allah's Book, while the caller from above the path is Allah's admonitions in the heart of every Muslim." (Ahmad)

The Mysterious Dream

The king [209] (of Egypt called out to his nobles) and said, *"I saw (in a dream) seven fat cows being eaten by seven skinny ones and seven green shafts of grain and seven others withered. My nobles! Tell me what my vision means if you can explain the meaning of visions."* [210] [43]

"Just a confused bunch of symbols," they replied. *"We're not experts at figuring out the meaning (of such cryptic dreams)."* [44]

However, the one who had been released (from prison), and who now remembered (Joseph) after so long, said, *"I'll tell you what it really means. Send me (to the one who can solve this riddle)."* [45]

(When the wine-server arrived at the prison, he went to Joseph's cell) and said, *"Joseph, the one (who predicted the) truth (for me so long before)! Explain for us the meaning of (this new vision): seven fat cows being eaten by seven skinny ones; seven green shafts of grain followed by seven withered ones. Tell me, so I can return to the people (at the royal court) so they can know."* [46]

(Joseph) replied, *"For seven years you'll diligently grow crops like you always do, but when you harvest them leave all the grains in the stalk except for the little that you must eat. [47] Then after this will come seven dreadful years (of bad harvests), in which you will have to live off of what you had*

---

[209] Many commentators in modern times have noticed that the ruler of Egypt in this tale is called a king, while in the stories of Moses, the ruler of Egypt is called a pharaoh. It was during the beginning of the 18th Dynasty in the 16th century BCE that the title of pharaoh began to be applied to the foreign kings of Egypt. As such, the Qur'an provides some dating for both Joseph (prior to the 18th Dynasty) and Moses (after the beginning of the 18th Dynasty). This dating is consistent with Biblical dating, which places Joseph being born circa 1914 BCE and Moses leading the Exodus circa 1446 BCE. (Biblical dating is based on Solomon beginning the Temple in 966 BCE, the Temple being started 480 years after the Exodus (see I Kings 6:1), the Israelites spending 430 years in Egypt (see Exodus 12:40), and the story of Joseph in Genesis. Of note, Genesis anachronistically refers to the king of Egypt during the time of Joseph as "Pharaoh.") To Muslim scholars of the medieval period, the Egyptian king in the story of Joseph has traditionally been known as Rayyan ibn al Walid (and sometimes as Ruiyyan ibn al Usayd). (*Ma'ariful Qur'an*)

[210] The Prophet said, "If anyone of you sees a dream that he likes, then it is from Allah. He should thank Allah for it and narrate it to others. However, if he sees something else, i.e., a dream that he dislikes, then it is from Satan. He should seek refuge with Allah from its evil, and he should not mention it to anybody, for it will not harm him." (*Bukhari*)

stored up in advance, saving only small, guarded supplies. [48] *Then after that, a year will come in which the people will be delivered (from the drought), and they'll press (wine and oil once more).*" ²¹¹ [49]

Joseph in the Court of the King

(When the man returned with the meaning of the dream), the king (was impressed), and said, *"Bring him to me."* However, when the herald (of the king) went (to the prison to release Joseph, he refused to leave his cell), ²¹² saying, *"Go back to your master and ask him, 'How is it with the women who cut their hands?' My Lord is aware of their trap."* ²¹³ [50]

(The king then ordered the women who were involved in the affair to be gathered before him.) Then he asked them, *"What were your intentions when you tried to seduce Joseph's very being?"*

The women answered, *"God save us! We don't know anything bad about him!"* Then the wife of the great minister said, *"The truth has now become clear, for it was I who tried to seduce him, but he indeed remained honorable."* [51]

(When Joseph was informed of the proceedings, he exclaimed,) *"So there it is – (I desired the truth to come to light so that my master) would know that I was never unfaithful to him in his absence, and Allah never guides the plans of betrayers!* [52] *I don't deny my guilt, for the soul can descend into depravity unless my Lord is merciful. Certainly, my Lord is forgiving and merciful."* ²¹⁴ [53]

---

²¹¹ The breadbasket that is Egypt relies upon the yearly inundation of the Nile River. If there is a drought in the region and the level of the Nile diminishes, then there is less water for irrigation, and the soil is not replenished. Such conditions were soon going to strike Egypt, and this forewarning would be Joseph's ticket out of prison.

²¹² The Prophet said, "If I had stayed in prison as long as Joseph had and then the herald came, I would have responded to his call (to go out of the prison immediately)." (*Bukhari*)

²¹³ The commentators explain that Joseph did not mention Zulaikhah by name, for he wanted to save Potiphar's household from embarrassment. (*Ma'ariful Qur'an*)

²¹⁴ Some commentators believe that verses 12:52-53 are a continuation of Zulaikhah's confessional speech, while others feel that these words are the compassionate reply of Joseph who was told about Zulaikhah's heartfelt remorse. Either interpretation is equally defensible, though I have chosen to render it as the relieved words of Joseph, following

Then the king commanded, *"Bring him to me; I'm going to take him into my personal service."* When (Joseph arrived at court, the king reassured him), saying, *"Feel confident today in my presence, for your position is secure and established."* ²¹⁵ [54]

(Joseph) said, *"Put me in charge of all the granaries in the land. I'll guard them knowing (their full importance)."* [55] And so it was in this manner that We established Joseph in the position that he could take anything in the land in whatever quantity he willed.

We parcel out Our Mercy to whomever We want, and We never lose the reward of those who do good. [56] The reward of the next life is much better for those who believe and who are mindful (of Allah). [57]

The Brothers Go to Egypt

(When the foretold famine struck the region), Joseph's brothers arrived in his presence (to buy food), ²¹⁶ but they didn't recognize him, although he knew immediately who they were. ²¹⁷ [58]

---

the majority of commentators. Note how Joseph acknowledges that he could have fallen into sin and temptation, if Allah had not strengthened his spirit.

215 According to reports cited in Zamakhshari, when Joseph was brought before the king, he (Joseph) greeted him in Hebrew. The king, who knew many languages, was astonished to hear a language he did not know. After enquiring about it, he began to speak to Joseph in many different languages, and Joseph was able to respond in them all. This impressed the king, and he asked to hear Joseph's interpretation of his dream from his own mouth. After Joseph had finished, the king was so impressed with his character that he asked Joseph what he wanted to have. Thus, Joseph asked for a position in the government overseeing the grain harvests.

216 According to commentators like Ibn Kathir and al-Qurtubi, Joseph was strict in rationing supplies during the famine. He limited foreigners to purchasing no more than one camel load of grain per person, and this was why all of Joseph's older brothers traveled to Egypt (so they could bring back enough grain for each of their families). Joseph also often presided over the distributions, like the dedicated steward he was. (*Ma'ariful Qur'an*)

217 Joseph became well-versed in the gifts of his adopted nation. He obviously learned to read hieroglyphics and to do math, as this would have been essential to his role as minister of agriculture. When the brothers arrived in the grain market they had no clue that the high official presiding over the market was none other than their own brother! Joseph must have appeared as a highly educated local official. It has always been a principle in Islam that a believer must learn and absorb what is useful from any civilization. The Prophet once said, "Wisdom is the property of a Muslim. He does not mind where he

After he had provisioned them with what they needed, he told them, *"Bring me (the youngest) brother you have from the same father as yourselves. Don't you see that I give full measure and that I provide the best hospitality?* [59] *Now, if you don't bring him to me, you won't get any more (grain) from me, nor shall you ever come near me again."* [218] [60]

They answered, *"We'll certainly get our way from his father. Surely we'll do it."* [61] Then (Joseph quietly) told his servants, "Put their trade goods back into their saddlebags, (and do it in such a way) that they won't find out until after they've returned to their families, for that may spur them into returning (for more supplies)." [62]

(When the brothers) returned to their father, they said, *"Father! We won't get any more grain (unless we take our youngest brother with us next time), so send our brother (Benjamin) with us so we can get more (supplies). We'll certainly protect him."* [63]

"Should I trust you with him," (Jacob) replied, *"when I had already trusted you with his brother (Joseph) so long before? Even still, Allah is the best guardian. He's the most merciful of the merciful."* [219] [64]

---

finds it." (*Ibn Hibban*) In other words, whether wisdom and learning comes from Muslim sources or non-Muslim sources, a believer must learn it if it is beneficial to him. The eminent classical scholar, Abu Yusuf Ya'qub al-Kindi (d. 873), once wrote: "We should never be too embarrassed to appreciate the truth or to seek it from wherever it can be found, even if it comes from far away peoples or different nations. Nothing should be dearer to the seeker of truth than the truth itself, for the truth never decays, nor should he look down upon the one who speaks the truth or who conveys it."

[218] According to the eminent commentator Baydawi, Joseph accused the brothers of being spies and asked them detailed questions about their families in the process of his interrogation. The brothers told Joseph they were a family of twelve brothers, but that one of them had died before in the desert. (This had the effect of making Joseph fear for the safety of Benjamin.) When Joseph pointed out that they were ten and the last one was not present, that was when the brothers revealed that their youngest sibling remained at home to console their elderly father. Joseph then demanded that one of the ten remain as a hostage, while the others would return to their people to fetch their youngest brother to prove that they were not spies. Other commentators suggest that the brothers had asked for an extra load of grain for an absent brother of theirs, and Joseph agreed as long as they would return with that absent brother to prove they were truthful.

[219] A popular Prophetic advice when faced with overwhelming adversity is to remind oneself that Allah is in control by saying, "We trust in Allah."

Then, when they were unpacking their supplies, they found their trade goods (hidden in the grain). They said, *"Father! For what more can we ask? Our trade goods have been returned to us so we can go and get more food for our families. We'll protect our brother and get a full load of grain (extra from our host in Egypt). That's like nothing (for him to give)."* [220] [65]

Jacob said, *"I'll never send him with you unless you swear a special promise to me in Allah's name that you'll be sure to bring him back, unless you, yourselves, are trapped."* After they swore their oath, he said, *"Allah, You be the One Who guarantees what we've said!"* [66]

(Then he gave his sons the following instructions), saying, *"My sons, don't enter the city all from the same entrance, but rather each of you should pick a different entrance, not that I can help you against Allah with my advice. No one can decide (the outcome of events) except Allah. I'll trust in Him, and let everyone who would trust (in something) trust in Him."* [67]

When they entered the city in the way their father had instructed, it didn't help them in the least against (the plan of) Allah. It was just something Jacob felt he had to say, for he was - *by Our instruction* - very intelligent (and experienced), but most people don't know that. [221] [68]

Who Took the King's Cup?

(When the brothers arrived and) were admitted back into Joseph's presence, he took his (younger) brother (Benjamin) aside and insisted that he stay with him. He told him, *"(Benjamin,) surely I'm*

---

[220] The brothers were so confident of their success in their next trading expedition that they felt for sure that the government official with whom they were dealing in Egypt would reward them with another camel load of grain (for Benjamin's camel) as a gift for following his request. To a great man in Egypt, this would be only a trifling amount.

[221] Apparently, Jacob was hoping to preserve the safety of at least some of his sons by suggesting they arrive through different paths and checkpoints into the city. His experience must have been drawn from many years of skillfully dealing with the many kingdoms and wandering tribes that inhabited the Middle East.

your own brother, so don't be worried over what the (other brothers) may do." [222] [69]

Then after Joseph had given them the supplies they needed, he (secretly) put a drinking cup into his (youngest) brother's saddlebag. (When the brothers began to leave for the return journey,) an announcer shouted out after them, *"Hey, you there! In the caravan! You're surely thieves!"* [70] (The brothers turned towards the guards) and said, *"Just what is it that you're missing?"* [71]

"We're missing the great cup of the king," they replied, *"and whoever brings it back will get a camel's load (worth of valuables)."* (Then the captain of the guard said,) *"I can assure you of that!"* [72]

(The brothers protested), saying, *"By Allah! You know we didn't come here to make trouble in this land, and we're certainly not thieves!"* [73]

"So then what should the penalty be (for this crime)," the (Egyptians) asked, *"if you're found to be liars?"* [74]

"The penalty" they answered, *"should be that the owner of the saddlebag in whose possession you find the item should be held (as a slave) to pay for the crime. This is how we penalize criminals (in our country)."* [223] [75]

Then (Joseph came and) began to search their baggage first, before coming to his brother's (bag). When (he opened) the bag of his brother (Benjamin, he held up the cup), and there it was! That's how We planned it for Joseph.

---

[222] Joseph and Benjamin were from a different mother than the other brothers. This is why it was so easy for the elder brothers to discriminate against them – petty jealousy. After they did away with Joseph (or so they thought), it was only natural for them to begin persecuting Joseph's younger brother, who naturally was elevated to Jacob's favorite. Joseph sensed that Benjamin was being treated badly by his older brothers and reassured him, even as he removed him into 'protective custody' straightaway.

[223] This principle of the early Hebrews was later enshrined in Mosaic Law in Exodus 22:3, where it orders a thief to be sold into slavery if he cannot repay what he has stolen.

He couldn't hold his brother, according to the law of the king, except that Allah willed it. We increase the status of whomever We want, but over all learned masters is a more knowledgeable One. [76]

(The brothers) cried out, *"If he stole something, then you should know that he had another brother who used to steal before!"* Joseph kept his feelings to himself, so as not to give the secret away to them. Instead, he said, *"You're in the worst position, and Allah knows best the truth of what you claim!"* [224] [77]

They begged, *"Great one! He has an old and respected father! Take one of us in his place, instead. We see that you're fair (in your decisions)."* [78]

(Joseph) replied, *"Allah forbid that we should take anyone besides the one who had our property. If we did that, then we would be acting unjustly."* [79]

What will the Brothers Tell their Father?

When (the brothers) saw no chance of him changing his mind, they discussed the matter among themselves privately. The most senior one among them said, *"Don't you know that you made a promise to your father in Allah's name and that even before this you failed in your duty to Joseph? As for me, I won't leave this land until my father allows me or Allah makes a decision about me, and He's the best to decide."* [225] [80]

"Go back to your father and tell (him), 'Father! Your son stole something. We report only what we know, and we couldn't guard against what we didn't expect! [81] *Ask at the town we passed through and in the caravan in which we returned, and you'll see that we're telling the honest truth.'"* [82]

---

[224] The brothers were betraying their faith once again, and they didn't realize that one of their victims was standing over them in judgment. The Prophet once remarked, "Keep your intentions pure, and keep Allah's pleasure in mind in all things you do, for if you do, then only a few (good) deeds will be enough (for your salvation)." (*Hakim*)

[225] It is thought that this more influential brother was Reuben (or Judah?), who also spoke out against killing Joseph so many years before. He was the one who suggested leaving Joseph in the well to be found by others or sold to travelors and taken away. Thus, it shows that the brothers were not all equal in their sinfulness. (See 12:10)

(When Jacob was informed), he cried out, *"Not so! You've made up a story to cover yourselves! I can do no more than endure this (tragedy) with dignity.* [226] *Allah will bring them all back to me (somehow), for He's full of knowledge and wisdom."* [83]

Then he turned away from them and cried, *"How sad I feel for Joseph!"* Then his eyes glazed over and became white. Blinded by his sorrow, he became increasingly despondent. [227] [84]

(The brothers) shouted, *"By Allah! You'll never stop remembering Joseph until you exhaust yourself or die!"* [85]

(Jacob answered them), saying, *"I'm only complaining about my sorrow and sadness to Allah, and I know things from Allah that you don't.* [86] *My sons! Go back to Egypt, and ask about Joseph and his brother! Never give up hope of Allah's compassion. Truly, no one despairs of Allah's compassion except for those who suppress (their awareness of His power over them)."* [228] [87]

---

[226] Jacob suspected that the brothers had done something with Benjamin, even as he feared they had moved against his beloved Joseph so many years before. His only recourse was to bear the loss with patience.

[227] Political upheaval engulfed the early Muslim world during the rule of the fourth caliph, 'Ali ibn Abi Talib (d. 661). A rival in Syria named Mu'awiyah ibn Abu Sufyan (d. 680) claimed the caliphate for himself, and the two sides made strategic moves against each other until a group of extremist purists called *Kharajites* (separatists) decided to assassinate both men for impiety. Only 'Ali was successfully murdered, and thus Mu'awiyah became the caliph. When Mu'awiyah passed away, his impious son, Yazid (d. 683), desired to seize the office of caliphate, rather than wait for nomination and election, which had been the usual way of the previous caliphs. Many Muslims arose in opposition to this blatant drift towards monarchy, and among these opponents were Husayn (d. 680), the grandson of the Prophet. He was treacherously killed in an ambush along with his family and the few supporters he had with him. His son, Zayn al-Abideen (d. 713), survived only because he was too bedridden to leave his house. He suffered confinement in Damascus for a time and then was released to lead a quiet life of prayer and study in Medina. He never forgot the loss of his family, however, and whenever food was presented to him he used to weep. One day a man said to him, "O (great-grand) son of the Messenger of Allah! Isn't it time for your sorrow to come to an end?" Zayn replied, "Woe to you! The Prophet Jacob had twelve sons, and Allah made one of them disappear. His eyes turned white from constant weeping; his head turned grey out of sorrow, and his back became bent in gloom, though his son was alive in this world. However, I watched while my father, my brother, my uncle, and seventeen members of my family were slaughtered all around me. How can my sorrow come to an end?"

[228] 'Ali ibn Abi Talib once said, "The best legal judge in Islam is the one who does not let people lose hope of the mercy of Allah, does not make a person feel despondent of Allah's

(When the brothers returned to Egypt) and entered (Joseph's presence once again), they said, *"Great one! Grief has come upon our family and us. We only have a few goods left (to trade), so grant us full rations as an act of charity for us.* [229] *Allah rewards the charitable."* [230] [88]

(Then Joseph spoke), saying *"Do you remember how you dealt with Joseph and his youngest brother in your ignorance?"* [89] (When they realized who the man before them was,) they asked, *"Are you really Joseph?"*

"(Yes), I am Joseph," he replied, *"and this is my brother (Benjamin)! Allah has brought the gift (of this reunion) to all of us.* [231] *Truly, whoever is mindful (of Allah) and who patiently perseveres (through any hardships), Allah will never let the reward of those who were good become lost."* [232] [90]

(The brothers) cried out, *"By Allah! Allah has indeed preferred you over us, and we're guilty of a crime!"* [233] [91]

"Let there be no blame upon you this day," Joseph replied. *"Allah will forgive you, and He's the most merciful of the merciful.* [234] [92] *Now, go and*

---

kindness, but who also does not make him feel safe from Allah's punishment." (*Nahjul al-Balaghah*)

[229] Ahmad ibn 'Ajiba (d. 1809) once wrote, "A feeling of discouragement when you stumble is a sure sign that you put your faith in deeds." (*Al Fahrasa.*)

[230] Why did Joseph carry on the charade that he did in front of his brothers? Perhaps he wanted them to realize their mistake for themselves. This would have been far more valuable a teaching tool than merely revealing himself at the outset. In a similar way, when the Prophet's two young grandsons, Hassan and Husayn, saw an elderly man performing his ablution improperly, rather than pointing out his mistake and embarrassing him, they asked the man to watch them make ablution, under the guise that they wanted an elder to check them to make sure they were doing it right. When the man saw them do it properly, he realized his own mistake and ever after performed his own ablutions in a correct manner.

[231] The gift was the family reconciliation and return of Joseph to his family.

[232] The New Testament echoes a similar sentiment when it says, "For the Lord disciplines those whom He loves." (Hebrews 12:6)

[233] Ibn Taymiyyah (d. 1328) once wrote, "The perfection of union (with Allah's will) is found when there remains nothing in the heart except Allah, the servant is left loving those He loves and what He loves, hating those He hates and what He hates, showing allegiance to those He has allegiance to, showing enmity to those He shows enmity towards, ordering what He orders and prohibiting what He prohibits."

[234] The Prophet said, "Be merciful with those on earth, and the One in Heaven will be merciful to you." (*Ahmad, Abu Dawud, Tirmidhi*)

111

take my shirt with you; cast it over my father's face, and he will see again. Then return here all together with your families." [93]

Jacob's Premonition

Even as the caravan departed (from Egypt, Joseph's) father exclaimed (to the people around him in his encampment), "I smell the scent of Joseph, even though you may think I'm senile." [94]

"By Allah!" they replied. "But you have an old, wandering mind." [95]

However, when the herald of good news arrived and put the shirt over (Jacob's) face, he immediately regained his ability to see. Then he exclaimed (to those around him), "Didn't I say to you that I know things from Allah that you don't?" [96]

(Then the brothers) cried out, "Father! Ask forgiveness for our sins; we were truly in the wrong." [235] [97]

"Very soon will I ask my Lord to forgive you," he replied, "for He is indeed the Forgiving and the Merciful." [236] [98]

The Fulfillment of the Dream

(When Jacob and all the rest of his family) entered into Joseph's presence, he provided a home for his parents with himself, saying, "Enter safely into Egypt, if it pleases Allah." [99]

He exalted his parents onto a high place (of honor), but they all fell down prostrate before him. (Joseph) exclaimed (in wonder), "My

---

[235] The Prophet said that the following conversation took place between Allah and Satan. Satan said, "By Your power, Lord, I will keep luring Your servants (into sin) as long as their souls are in their bodies." Allah said, "By My power and majesty, I will keep on forgiving them as long as they keep asking Me for forgiveness." (*Ahmad*)

[236] The commentators suggest that Jacob delayed his supplication for forgiveness either to look for the right moment when it might be more likely to be accepted by Allah, or to see Joseph first and get his opinion on the matter, for forgiveness sometimes also depends on the wronged person feeling vindicated. (*Baydawi*)

Father! This is the completion of the vision I had so long before. [237] *Allah has made it all come true! He was good to me when He got me out of prison and then brought all of you here from out of the desert* [238] *- even after Satan had caused conflict between me and my brothers. My Lord is subtle in what He wills, for He is the Knowing and the Wise."* [100]

(Joseph prayed), *"My Lord! You've indeed given me some power and taught me how to interpret passing events. Originator of the heavens and the earth! You're my protector in this world and in the next. Take me as one surrendering (to Your will), and join me with the righteous!"* [239] [101]

This is one of the hidden stories that We're revealing to you by inspiration. [240] You weren't there among (Joseph's brothers) when they agreed on their affair and made a plot. [102] Yet, most people won't believe, no matter how hard you wish them to. [103]

The Natural Signs of Allah

Y ou're not asking (the faithless) for any reward for this - *this is no less than a reminder for all the worlds.* [104] Then how many signs in the heavens and on the earth do they pass by? Yet, they turn (their faces) away from them! [241] [105] Most of them don't believe in Allah without making (others as partners) with Him! [106]

---

[237] Verse 12:4 contains the vision of the sun, the moon and eleven stars bowing before Joseph. These would be his father and mother (or step-mother) and eleven brothers. It is interesting to note that in Genesis 37:9-11, the same interpretation of the dream is given, yet, in verses 35:16-21 (of Genesis), Joseph's biological mother Rachel is said to have died while giving birth to Benjamin. This means that "the moon" could not have been Rachel bowing to her son Joseph in the climactic scene of the story. The Qur'an makes a veiled assumption in verse 100 that it was Joseph's own mother whom he exalted, though the ambiguity in the term 'parents' can go either way.

[238] Here is a use of the word *bedu,* from which the term bedouin, or desert-dweller comes.

[239] The cousin of the Prophet, 'Ali ibn Abi Talib, once said, "Whoever desires Paradise moves towards goodness. Whoever is afraid of Hellfire avoids the call of his passions. Whoever firmly believes that death will occur to him comes to hold the worldly life in contempt. Whoever recognizes the true worthlessness of the worldly life will find that its trials become easier."

[240] What happened to Joseph after the events of this story? According to some Jewish traditions, after Potiphar passed away, the king of Egypt arranged the marriage of Joseph to Potiphar's widow Zulaikhah, and they had three children. (*Ma'ariful Qur'an*) Genesis 41:50 offers an alternative view for consideration.

[241] Al-Jahiz (d. 869) once wrote, "I would have you know that a pebble proves the existence of Allah just as much as a mountain, and the human body is evidence as strong

Do they feel safe against the overwhelming nature of Allah's wrath coming down upon them or of the sudden arrival of the (final) Hour without their even noticing it? [107]

Say (to them), *"This is my way. I'm inviting (you) to (believe in) Allah with evidence as clear as sight. (This is) my (way, and the way of) whoever follows me. Glory be to Allah! I'll never be an idolater!"* [108]

We didn't send before you any beings other than men whom We inspired, [242] and they lived in human communities. Don't they travel through the earth and see what became of those (disbelieving nations) before them? [243] (Regardless of what people acquire), the home of the next life is the best for those who are mindful (of Allah). So won't you understand? [109]

(The forces of darkness will be granted a period of ascendancy), even up to the point when the messengers begin to lose hope (of the

---

as the universe that contains our world: for this purpose the small and slight carries as much weight as the great and vast." (*Kitab al-Hayawan*)

[242] Thus, there were no female prophets or messengers for, as this verse states, they were all *rijalan*, or men. Even though Allah did send his inspiration to both men and women, only men were commissioned with the duty of prophethood. (Mary and the mother of Moses both received inspired instructions from Allah.) Prophets often endured times of persecution and torture, even as others sometimes had to lead armies into battle. Thus, males were preferred for this office on account of its many hardships and trials.

[243] There is a built-in traveling component inherent in the Islamic worldview. Whether it's for business, trade, education, missionary work or even when one goes out to struggle in Allah's cause, the Muslim is exhorted to see the world and do something good in it. When the Prophet heard about a man who had died in his hometown of Medina, the Prophet said, "If only he would have died somewhere else besides his place of birth." When a companion asked him why, the Prophet said, "When a man dies somewhere other than his place of birth, the distance between the place he was born in and the place where his footsteps end will be measured for him, (and this will be the size of his territory) in Paradise." (*Ahmad*) The Prophet is also reported to have said, "Seek knowledge, even if in China." In another saying he indicated that a student who goes far away to learn some knowledge will be counted as a martyr if he or she happens to die while conducting his or her studies. The Muslim world until very recently (when Europeans imposed artificial borders upon it) was a very cosmopolitan place with a very rich tradition of migration and movement among its various regions. If you interview the average Old World Muslim and ask about his or her family tree, regardless of their stated country of origin, you will oftentimes find ancestors from drastically different countries making up their lineage. The Pakistani poet, Muhammad Iqbal, once wrote, "The one who is devoted to Allah cares not, for he is neither of the East nor the West. He has no home, neither in Delphi, Isfahan nor Samarkand."

success of their mission) and feel they've been denied (utterly by their people). Then, (without any advance warning), Our help will come and reach them, and We'll save whomever We want, but Our punishment will never be averted from the wicked. [110]

And so it is that there are lessons in the stories (of past civilizations) for people of understanding. (This tale of Joseph) is not a fictional account, but a confirmation of (the message that came) before it. [244] It's a detailed account of all things and a guide and mercy to a believing nation. [111]

---

[244] The Hebrew story of Joseph, though embellished with many extraneous details, is still a true story in its basic form, as the Qur'an affirms. By clearing the story of additions made through the centuries, as the Qur'an implies, the basic lesson to be learned from this tale of a family's redemption can once again be appreciated.

Thunder

13 Ar-Ra'd

Late Meccan to Early Medinan Period

This chapter was mostly revealed in the later portion of the Meccan period, although a few verses date from Medina. It summarizes many of the ongoing themes touched upon in other chapters and introduces some dramatic imagery and unique doctrines related to the next life. The name of the chapter is derived from verse 13 where the very thunder itself is said to resonate with the praise of Allah.

In the Name of Allah,
the Compassionate, the Merciful

*A*lif. *Lām. Meem. Rā.*

These are the verses of the Book, the very one that's being revealed to you from your Lord, and it's the truth. Yet, most people don't believe. [1]

Allah is the One Who raised the skies without any supports that you can see. [245] Then He established Himself upon the throne (of power). He tamed the sun and the moon, (causing) each to complete its orbit in a precise amount of time. And in this way, He regulates all matters. (The reason why) He explains the proof (of His power) in such detail is so that you can believe confidently in the meeting with your Lord. [2]

---

[245] The sky, or rather the atmosphere that encircles the earth, is held aloft by a confluence of the opposing forces of gravity and centrifugal force. Thus, the sky is supported by forces (or pillars) that we cannot see. The earth's surface is literally at the bottom of a ocean of atmosphere. The sun's light heats both water and air, causing it to rise with the spinning action of the earth. Yet, gravity generated from deep within the earth prevents it from dissipating into space. Thus, the two forces create a gaseous envelope that marks the boundaries between earth and the vacuum of space.

He's the One Who spread the earth out wide and placed firm mountains within it and (flowing) rivers, as well. (He also placed upon the earth) all types of fruit in pairs, two by two, [246] and He draws the night like a veil over the day. In these things are signs for people who think. [3]

There are (distinct) regions adjoining each other on the earth, [247] as well as vineyards, fields of grain and date palms growing from either (multiple root systems) or from only one (root). They're all watered with the same water; yet, some of them (produce fruits that) are better for eating than others. [248] In these there are signs for those who reflect. [4]

If you're amazed (at how they can deny Allah, after seeing how complex the world He made is), even more amazing still is their saying, *"When we're reduced to dust, are we really going to be created as good as new?"*

They're the ones who are blatantly denying their Lord, so they're the ones around whose necks will be shackles! They'll be the companions of the Fire, *and that's where they're going to stay!* [5]

They're asking you to hurry on something awful in preference to something good. Yet, there have been many humiliating punishments (that struck previous peoples) before them. However, your Lord is full of forgiveness towards people, even in their corruption, just as He's also harsh in punishment. [6]

---

[246] Fruits have both male and female parts in the flowers that precede their formation.

[247] The terrain of this planet is classified by regions and their unique characteristics. These diverse regions border each other in a patchwork of varied terrain. There are deserts, forests, jungles, swamps, plains and mountainous regions. All of these regions support life, even as they are vastly different from each other. Is this not a sign of Allah, Who not only created the conditions for life on earth, but Who made it so adaptable to all physical conditions? Some commentators say this verse refers to the tectonic plates of the earth. The Arabic word used here, *qata'a*, means something that is cut up in pieces. If this interpretation is accepted, then it could be reworded as, "In the earth there are adjacent (landmasses) that are separated (from one another)." Either interpretation is valid.

[248] The diversity of plant life, the way in which one root system can produce many trees or only one tree and the variance in flavors among different fruits are all signs of Allah's creative genius.

And then the faithless ask, *"So why isn't a miracle being sent down to him from his Lord?"* Yet, you're only a warner and a guide for all nations. [7]

Allah Encompasses All Things

Allah knows what every female bears and how much the wombs are early or late, for everything is measured in His sight. [8] He knows what's beyond perception, as well as what's clearly seen, for He's the Great One, the Highest of All! [9]

So it's all the same whether one of you hides his words or says them openly or whether you lay hidden by night or walk about in broad daylight. [10] (Every person has angels) following him, both before him and behind him. [249] They guard him by the command of Allah.

Truly, Allah will never change the condition of a people unless they change what's in themselves. [250] Whenever Allah wants to bring misfortune down upon a people, there can be no averting it, nor will they find any protector besides Him. [11]

Thunder is a Reminder

Background on verses 12-13: There is a story that two pagan men from Mecca approached the Prophet just after he arrived in Medina and asked about Islam. One of them named 'Amr ibn at-Tufayl asked what he would get if he accepted Islam, and the Prophet replied that he would have all the rights and duties of an ordinary Muslim. 'Amr then asked if he could be made the ruler of the Muslims after the Prophet passed away, and the Prophet answered him,

---

[249] The Prophet said, "Every one of you has a companion from the jinn and a companion from the angels." The people said, "Even you, too, Messenger of Allah?" He replied, "Even I, as well, except that Allah has helped me against (the jinn), so he only influences me to do good." (*Muslim*)

[250] Thawban, the freed servant of the Prophet, related that the Prophet said, "The nations (of the world) are about to call each other and set upon you, just as diners set upon a banquet." It was asked, "Will it be because of our small numbers that day?" He replied, "Rather, on that day you will be as numerous as the foam on a river. But Allah will remove from the hearts of your enemies any fear of you, and He will throw *wahn* into your hearts." Someone asked, "O Messenger of Allah! What is *wahn*?" He answered, "Love of the world and the hatred for death." (*Abu Dawud*)

saying, "That's not your right or your people's right; however, I could appoint you as a cavalry leader." 'Amr said, "I'm already a cavalry leader in the land of Najd. What if you rule the cities and I rule the countryside?" The Prophet refused this offer, and 'Amr and his friend, a man named Arbad, left in anger, vowing to bring an army back with them to destroy the Muslims.

Before leaving town, however, they hatched a plot to kill the Prophet. While 'Amr was to engage the Prophet in conversation, Arbad would sneak up from behind the Prophet and strike him down. 'Amr returned to the Prophet and accordingly began to distract him. Arbad came from behind, but for some reason he couldn't pull his sword from its sheath. The Prophet saw Arbad behind him, trying to unsheathe his sword, and he realized what was going on, so he left them in haste. The two men fled the city, but two companions named Sa'd and Usayd came upon them and ordered them to surrender. The pair fled again, and Arbad was struck by a stray lightning bolt in the desert and died. 'Amr took refuge in a woman's house (she belonged to the tribe of the hypocrite, 'Abdullah ibn Ubayy,) and she noticed he had an ulcer growing on his leg. On his return journey to Najd, he died from that ulcer. This passage was revealed in comment on this situation. (*Ibn Kathir*)

He's the One Who shows you the lightning as a source of both fear and hope, and He's the One Who raises up the heavily laden clouds (bursting with rain). [12] The very thunder, itself, glorifies His praises, as do the angels - wonderstruck (by His power). [251]

He sends booming thunderbolts and strikes whomever He wants. Yet, these (people) are still arguing about Allah, though He's extremely cunning. [13]

Supplications are honestly due to Him alone. Those (idols) whom they call upon besides Him don't hear them any more than if they brought their empty hands to their mouths to take a sip of water and nothing reached them.

The supplications of those who cover (the light of faith within their hearts) are nothing more than blunders. [14]

---

[251] Whenever the Prophet would hear thunder he would pray, "O Allah! Don't slay us with Your anger or destroy us with Your punishment, and save us before (ever doing) that." (*Ahmad*)

All who reside within the heavens and the earth bow down before Allah, either willingly or unwillingly, as do their shadows [252] in the mornings and the evenings. [253] [15]

Ask them, *"Who is the lord of the heavens and the earth?"* (Answer for them by) saying, *"Allah."* Then say (to them), *"So are you taking protectors other than Him, things that have no power to bring either benefit or harm to themselves?"* Then ask them, *"Are the blind and the seeing the same, or is the darkness the same as the light?"*

Are they making partners with Allah – partners who (somehow managed to) create (things by themselves) that are just like what He created, so much so that (the two) creations seem the same? Say (to them), *"Allah created everything, and He's the One and the Irresistible."* [16]

He sends down water from the sky. The resulting channels flow in a measured way, and the rushing (rapids) carry away the foam that forms on its surface. [254] Likewise, a similar kind of foam also arises when they heat (ore) in the fire to make jewelry or tools. That's how Allah distinguishes the truth from falsehood, for the foam is discarded while what is useful for people remains on the earth. That's how Allah lays out His examples. [17]

Two Ways of Life, Two Results

Good things will come to those who respond to their Lord. However, those who ignore Him – even if they had everything in the

---

[252] Even if a free-willed being denies Allah, it still is a biologically based being, and its organs, cells, blood and other systems obey the natural laws Allah set for them. In addition, that living entity must exist within its environment, and it is restrained by rules for proper living within it. A man can deny Allah all day long, but he still has to breathe every moment. He still must eat, and he has to submit to the rhythms of nature on some fundamental level, even as his body regulates his life without his active input and ceases to function when his term limit of life is reached. So even though his mind or heart denies Allah, his body glorifies and submits to Allah's rule. Even his own shadow lies flat to the ground as if in prostration!

[253] After reading this verse it is customary for the one who has faith in Allah to prostrate himself on the floor and praise Allah.

[254] Some commentators say this is a kind of parable about knowledge and how much of it Allah bestows upon the worthy and how knowledge washes away ignorance. (*Ibn Kathir*)

heavens and on the earth and much more besides to offer as a bribe, (it would be of no use), for a strict accounting will be made of them. Their ultimate home will be in Hellfire, and what a terrible place to rest! [18]

Is the one who knows that what's been revealed to you from your Lord is the truth the same as someone who's blind (to that fact)? Only the thoughtful ever take reminders. [19] They're the ones who fulfill their agreement with Allah, and they don't break their word. [20]

They (have respect for the family ties) that Allah has commanded to be joined, and they fear both their Lord and the strict accounting (to come). 255 [21] They're patient and seek Allah's (approving) gaze, even as they establish prayers and spend (in charity) out of what We've supplied to them, both in secret and in public. They also ward off evil with good. 256

They're the ones who will gain the final home [22] – everlasting gardens that they'll be allowed to enter, along with the righteous among their parents, spouses and descendants. Angels will enter (upon their presence) from every gate, [23] (saying), *"Peace be upon you on account of your patient perseverance! How delightful is the final home!"* [24]

However, those who break their agreement with Allah after having given their word, who separate what Allah has ordered to be joined, and who cause chaos and disorder in the land – they'll be far removed (from Allah's mercy), and they'll have the most miserable home! [25]

---

255 The Prophet once told the following story: Death came for a man, and when there was no longer any hope for him (to recover), he said to his family, "After I've died, collect a pile of firewood (and place it all around my body). Set it ablaze, and let it burn until my flesh is consumed in it and my bones have become brittle. Then take them and grind them into powder, and scatter the ashes over the sea." They did as they were asked, but after Allah gathers him back together (at the resurrection) He will ask him, "Why did you do that?" (The man) will answer, "Because I was afraid of You." Therefore, Allah will forgive him. (*Ahmad*) The man is said to have been a gravedigger by profession.
256 The Prophet said that if a person commits a sin (and then feels remorseful and repents), he can do a good deed to help wash the sin away from his record. (*Ahmad*)

Allah increases or restricts the resources of whomever He wants. (Those who only love this life) revel in the life of this world, but the life of this world is nothing but a passing pleasure compared to the next life. [26]

Believers Know the Truth

Those who suppress (their awareness of the truth) ask, *"So why isn't a miracle coming down to him from his Lord?"*

Say (to them), *"Allah leaves astray whomever He wants, and He guides those who repent (of their sins towards the path leading back) to Him."* [257] [27]

"(They're the ones) who believe and whose hearts find relief in the remembrance of Allah, for truly, in the remembrance of Allah hearts can find relief. [258] [28] *Those who believe and do what's morally right will find the deepest satisfaction* [259] *and the finest homecoming."* [29]

Background on verse 30: The Prophet had asked some Meccans to bow down in the name of the Compassionate Allah, and they said, "Who is *the Compassionate*, and why should we bow down just because you ask us to?" That is what this verse is referencing. (*Asbab ul-Nuzul*)

---

[257] In the early days of the Prophet's mission, he brought no miracles, only the words of Allah. As such, the first believers were those who had the capacity to recognize the truth when they heard it. Later on, near the end of the Prophet's stay in Mecca, he did perform a handful of miracles, including the famous splitting of the moon incident, at which the pagans were amazed, but then later chalked up to some sort of illusion or sorcery. (See 54:1) In Medina the Prophet performed small miracles more regularly, such as putting his hand in a water jug and causing a small amount of water to suffice the needs of hundreds of people or knowing what people were thinking or planning before they even told anybody. However, the paramount miracle was the Qur'an, itself, and the spectacular visual miracles the pagans demanded would not have convinced them anyway. The Qur'an states plainly that even if the Prophet had a ladder to heaven, still they would have made up some explanation for it and continued to deny Allah's last Prophet.

[258] Rabi'ah al-Adawiyya (d. 801) was quoted as saying, "Your hope in my heart is my greatest treasure. Your name on my tongue is the sweetest word. My most splendid hours are the hours I spend with You. O Allah, I can't live in this world without remembering You."

[259] The Arabic term *tubu*, which I have rendered as the deepest satisfaction, means happiness, joy and anything that brings delight to the eye. It is also the name of a tree in Paradise whose shade is as wide as it would take a rider to travel in one hundred years. (*Ahmad*)

And so We've sent you to a community that has had many other (civilizations) pass away before it, in order for you to recite to them what We're revealing to you. Yet, they're rejecting the Compassionate! Tell them, *"He is my Lord; there is no god but He. I trust in Him, and to Him I turn."* [30]

This Qur'an is a Weighty Message

Background on verses 31-32: A Meccan named 'Abdullah ibn Umayyah approached the Prophet and said, "You're pretending that you're a prophet and that you get prophecies. Yet, Solomon was given power over the wind, Moses over the sea, and Jesus raised the dead to life. So call on your God to make the mountains move, make rivers flow in this land for irrigating fields, bring the dead body of (our legendary ancestor) Qusayy to life and make him talk and confirm whether Islam is valid or not, or turn the stones underneath you into gold so we can have enough money to last us through summer and winter - that is if you're not just pretending to be among (the ranks of the prophets)." This passage was revealed to the Prophet immediately, and he recited it.

Then the Prophet said, "I swear by the One Who holds my soul that I would be given that if I wished for it. However, (the angel) asked me to choose between two things: either to enter (Paradise) through the gate of mercy, or to leave you alone so you can choose (your fate) by yourselves and thus be misguided. So I chose the gate of mercy, knowing that he told me that if you reject faith that you'll be punished more than anyone else ever was." (*Asbab ul-Nuzul*)

If there ever was a recital (of scripture) that could move mountains or crack the earth or cause the dead to speak, (then this would be it)! But no! The command over all things rests with Allah. [260] Don't the believers realize that if Allah had wanted, He could've guided all people together? [261]

As for those who suppress (their faith), misfortune will continue to befall them because of their (misguided) actions, or it will settle in near their homes even until Allah's promise comes to pass. [262] Indeed,

---

[260] In other words, Allah is not going to respond to the taunting and challenging of people who dare Allah to give them proof. The Qur'an is weighty in and of itself, and Allah moves in His Own time.

[261] In those early days in Mecca, faith for the Muslims was often hard, and more than a few wondered why other people were so opposed to it.

[262] People who live ungodly lives invite continual disaster. The rules of all religions about personal conduct and morality try to keep people from engaging in risky behaviors that bring harm to themselves and others. All the proof that one needs for this can be found by observing the people in crisis all around him. Unfortunately, the innocent are often

Allah never fails in His word! [31] And so it was that messengers who came before you were ridiculed, [263] but I gave the faithless some time before I finally seized them, *and oh how (terrible) was My conclusion!* [32]

The Final Destination

Is the One Who stands over every soul and what it records for itself (the same as any other)? Yet, they've made partners with Allah! Ask them, *"So name them! Are you going to tell Him about something that He doesn't know on the earth, or are you just saying something (with no truth to it)?"*

No way! Those who suppress (their understanding of the truth) are pleased with their posturing, but they're really being kept away from the path (by it).

For those whom Allah leaves astray, there can be no one to guide them. [33] They're going to be punished in this worldly life, but the punishment of the next life is so much more severe, and they'll have no defender against Allah. [34]

(What's the) likeness of the Garden that's been promised to those who were mindful (of Allah)? Rivers will flow beneath (its trees)! There'll be no end to eating, nor will its shade ever cease! This is the final (destination) for those who were mindful (of Allah), while the final (destination) of those who covered up (their faith) is in the Fire. [35]

Those to whom We've given the scripture (in the past) rejoice in what We've revealed to you, but among the factions (of other

---

dragged into the drama and self-destruction of others who do not pattern their lives on longstanding spiritual advice.

263 Even when he had to endure the worst ridicule and insults, the Prophet always tried to be optimistic. Some pagans started making fun of the Prophet by calling him Mudhammam, which meant despised on, instead of his actual name Muhammad, which meant praised one. Upon hearing this one day, the Prophet exclaimed, "Does it not amaze you how Allah protects me from the Quraysh's abusing and cursing?! They abuse a man called *Mudhammam* and curse *Mudhammam,* while I am Muḥammad!" (*Bukhari*)

religions) are some who reject a part of it. [264] Say (to them), *"I'm commanded to serve Allah and not to join partners with Him. I call to Him, and back to Him is my final goal."* [36]

> **Background on verse 37:** The Prophet was told of some people who had vowed to fast every day, others who vowed to pray all night, and yet others who vowed to remain celibate for their whole lives. The Prophet ordered them not to follow through with their plans and said, "As for me, I fast, and then I break my fast. I stand in prayer at night, but then I sleep. I eat meat, and I marry women, so whoever turns away from my example is not of me." (*Bukhari, Muslim*) This verse was revealed in comment.

And so, We've revealed (the Qur'an) as an authoritative (book) in the Arabic (language).

If you were to follow their whims after already receiving knowledge, then you would find neither any best friend nor defender (to help you) against Allah. [37]

The Prophet will be Victorious over His Foes

> **Background on verses 38-39:** The background of this verse is as follows. Some Jews in Medina spoke to the Prophet and said that he had wives and was thus too busy with them to be a prophet, for if he was a real prophet, they reasoned, then he would be busier with religious duties than with women. What they didn't realize was that nearly all the prophets had a family life in addition to their spiritual ministry. Even Moses and Abraham had wives and children, and thus the Jews were being hypocritical about it.

We sent messengers before you and arranged for them to have wives and children. It was never the place of a messenger to bring a miracle unless Allah allowed it, and for every age (of history) there

---

[264] This verse is saying that those who received revelation before Islam, i.e., the Jews and Christians, can appreciate and find common ground with the Qur'an. Thus, they rejoice in seeing Allah mentioned yet again. However, some from among them agree only with small portions of the Qur'an as they see fit (if it goes along with their worldview).

has been a scripture. [265] [38] Allah rescinds or confirms whatever He wants, for He has the Mother of the Book (with Him). [266] [39]

Whether We show you now part of the (punishment) that We've promised them or take your soul back to Us (before it befalls them), your duty is only to proclaim (the message) to them. It's Our task to call them to account. [40]

Don't (the Meccans) see how We're gradually reducing the lands (over which they hold influence) from their outlying borders? Allah commands, and no one can hinder His command, and He is quick to settle accounts. [267] [41]

The (faithless) who came before (these people) also made plans, though Allah is the ultimate planner over everything at once! He knows what every soul earns for itself, and the faithless will soon know who will have the final home (of Paradise). [42]

---

[265] In every significant age of humanity there has been a defining religious text of the time. The Scrolls of Abraham, the Sutras of Buddha (whom some Muslim scholars believe may have been a prophet), the Torah of Moses, the Psalms of David, the Gospel of Jesus and the Qur'an of Muhammad all came at different turning points in human history. (Think of how many lost scriptures there have been that have passed out of human memory!) Each revelation has influenced the growth and direction of civilization in a significant way.

[266] The commentators say that this 'Mother of the Book' refers to Allah's record book in which everything that happens is recorded. The early companions and their followers also understood this verse this way. During the month of *Ramadan*, when they used to supplicate on the Night of Power, they used to ask Allah to erase their names from the list of the unfortunate sinners if their names were there, and then add their names to the list of the blessed. They used to add that if their names were already on the blessed list that they could remain there. (*Ibn Kathir*) The Prophet also taught that Allah can change the destiny He set out for people if they supplicate earnestly and often. He said, "A man may not receive a provision (that he was meant to get) on account of some sin that he committed. Only supplication can change destiny, and only righteousness can increase life span." (*Nisa'i, Ibn Majah*)

[267] The Quraysh tribe of Mecca had enjoyed unparalleled influence in the entire Arabian Peninsula. Yet, by the Prophet's last year or two in Mecca, a number of nascent signs began to gnaw away at their preeminence. Some people from Yathrib to the north had embraced Islam, dulling Meccan influence there. A few Arab bedouin tribes of the desert accepted the Prophet's call, and even within Mecca, itself, around a hundred people had quietly embraced the faith. Later on, after the Migration to Medina, the power base of the Meccans would shrink even further, year by year, until they would have no choice but to surrender. Isn't that proof enough of Allah's power that a mere man reciting some verses could overturn and remake an entire society and political order from the ground up, against all odds?

The faithless may say, *"You're not a messenger (from Allah),"* but say (to them), *"Allah is enough of a witness between you and me, even as is anyone who knows (of Allah's previously revealed) scriptures."* [268] [43]

---

[268] Christians and Jews have a similar type of religion to Islam, and thus if the Meccans object to the basic tenets of Islam, then they should take a look at other religions before being so incredulous. Thus, the reference is made to God and 'those who had knowledge of previous revelation,' both of which affirmed the truth of Muhammad's message.

Abraham

14 Ibrâhîm
Late Meccan Period

This chapter, which is something of a continuation of the arguments introduced at the conclusion of the last, was revealed during the late Meccan period when it seemed inevitable that some sort of break or separation had to occur between the pagans and the Muslims. Indeed, verses 13-15 foreshadow the ultimate action that the Meccans would take, that of threatening to drive the Prophet and his followers away. Unbeknownst to them, however, the Muslims were soon to leave on their own to a sanctuary far to the north known as Yathrib, and later as *Medinat-un-Nabi*, or the *City of the Prophet* (*Medina* for short).

In the Name of Allah,
the Compassionate, the Merciful

*A*lif. Lām. Rā.

(This is) a book that We've revealed to you so you can lead people out of every type of darkness and into light, by Allah's leave, towards the path of the Powerful and Praiseworthy. [1]

Allah is the One to Whom belongs whatever is in the heavens and whatever is on the earth. Those who suppress (their awareness of the truth) are doomed to a harsh punishment! [2]

Those who love the life of this world more than the next life, and who try to hinder others from the way of Allah - *wishing to make it seem crooked* - they're the ones who are far off in error. [269] [3]

---

[269] When a person absolutely does not accept an idea, whether it is political, religious or even an interpretation of history, they can continue in one of three ways. They can take a live-and-let-live attitude and leave others they differ with in peace. They can become actively engaged in intellectual debate and allow themselves to possibly be swayed by arguments that make more sense. However, the worst person is the one who tries to

The Messengers and Their Missions

W e never sent any messenger unless he spoke the language of
his own people, so that he could explain things to them clearly. [270]
Allah allows whomever He wills to go astray, [271] and He allows

---

openly sabotage the position of another side through slander, false interpretations or
outright lies. Making arguments is one thing, and no honest person should shy away
from having their ideas challenged for they can either strengthen their own resolve or
modify their ideas to some degree or another. But the bitter person who cannot convince
others and may be filled with rage or prejudice may sometimes resort to outright
misinformation or the actual impediment of ideas freely flowing, just because they do not
like them and will allow no one to consider them. Censorship and false reporting of
another's beliefs are not accepted in Islam. While Islamic law does draw the line at
insulting the *character* of people, such as insulting the Prophet's reputation, or the
reputations of innocent people, women and the like, intellectual debate of ideas is
encouraged. Debates were common in the Prophet's time, and he engaged in them
freely, sometimes scoring points, other times finding his message falling on deaf ears. It
was when, for example, prominent pagans twisted the Prophet's words to make them
seem like something else or told outright lies or forcibly prevented the Muslim side from
having its voice heard that a problem arose. Even today, the message of Islam is often
misrepresented, both by non-Muslim critics and even some people with Muslim-sounding
names who believe in extremist ideogies never before found in Islam. This verse
addresses the general phenomenon of misrepresenting the faith and trying to keep people
from it in a cunning and dishonest fashion.

[270] The Qur'an was revealed to Muhammad in Arabic and specifically in the dialect of
the Quraysh tribe of Mecca. Other Arab tribes in the far corners of Arabia spoke Arabic,
but with regional accents, and the Prophet beseeched Allah to allow the Qur'an to be
recited in the various dialects of the Arabs. Gabriel informed the Prophet that the Qur'an
could be recited in the seven major dialects of the Arabian peninsula, though the official
dialect decided by the companions after the Prophet's passing is the Qurayshi dialect,
based on the fact that Muhammad was from the Quraysh. (*Bukhari*) Also see 41:44 where
the explanation is given as to why the Qur'an was revealed in the Arabic language. No
prophet was sent to a nation unless he either grew up with their language or at least
learned it well enough to preach in it, such as in the cases of Lot and Jonah who both
preached in languages they had to acquire.

[271] Some critics have accused the Qur'an of suggesting that God willfully misleads
people in a vapricious or malicious way for no other reason than He is 'mean.' This is a
gross mis understanding of the situations when God would 'allow' a person to go astray
or fall further into error. When a person declares themselves a rebel against God first,
and then takes actions to oppose God, goodness and justice, then God lets them fall
further into their delusions. His Message is still there for them to see, but if they
continue to ignore, is it right to stop someone who refuses all offers of help and seeks to
fight against you? The Bible contains the exact same sentiment in 2 Thesselonians 2:11
where we read: "For this reason, God sends them a powerful delusion so that they will
believe the lie…" Also see Romans 1:24, II Chronicles 18:7 and 18:22. The New
Testament commentator Heinrich Meyer writes of this verse: "For according to the
Pauline view it is a holy ordinance of God that the wicked by their wickedness should
lose themselves always the more in wickedness, and thus sin is punished by sin. But

whomever He wills to be guided, for He's the Powerful and Wise. [272]
[4]

And so it was that We sent Moses with Our signs (and told him), *"Lead your people out of darkness and into light, and teach them to remember the days of Allah."* [273] Truly, there are signs (in this story) for every extraordinarily patient and thankful person. [274] [5]

Remember when Moses said to his people, *"Recall Allah's favors upon you when He saved you from Pharaoh's people. They mistreated you greatly - butchering your sons while leaving your daughters alive. That was an enormous test from your Lord."* [275] [6]

And remember when your Lord proclaimed (His promise to you, saying), *"If you're thankful, then I'll grant you even more (than just your freedom), and if you're ungrateful, then (know that) My punishment is harsh."* [7] Even Moses had told them, *"If you ever became ungrateful, and if everyone else on the earth likewise became ungrateful, even then Allah would have no need (for any of you), for He would still be praised (by other beings)."* [8]

Ignoring the Messengers

Haven't you heard the stories of those who lived before you – the people of Noah and 'Ad and Thamud and all those who came after them? No one knows about them more than Allah. Messengers went to each of them with clear evidence. However, their (people) invariably put their hands up over their mouths and said, *"We reject*

---

what is an ordinance of God is also accomplished by God Himself." (Meyer's New Testament Commentary, 1980 Alpha Publications edition)

[272] In other words, the message is given clearly in the language of the people. After they hear it, it's up to them whether they accept it or not. Allah won't guide those who willfully turn away from Him, though He will gladly guide any who even make even a small effort to seek His forgiveness and pleasure.

[273] The *days of Allah* that are mentioned here can mean one of two things. The first is that the Children of Israel were being asked to recall their righteous ancestors who lived by Allah's commands. The second interpretation could mean that they were being asked to remember that all time belongs to Allah, and in the end there will be a final day when people will be brought for judgment.

[274] The Prophet said, "Faith is composed of two parts: half of it is patience, and the other half is gratitude." (*Bayhaqi*)

[275] See 2:49 and footnote.

whatever you've been sent with, and we're doubtful of the value of what you're calling us towards." [9]

Their messengers would ask them, *"Do you have any doubts about (the existence of) Allah, the Creator of the heavens and the earth? He's calling you so He can forgive you your sins and give you an extension on your time limit."* (The people would always answer,) saying, *"You're no more than a mortal man like us! You just want to turn us away from what our ancestors worshipped. So bring us a clear and decisive (miracle to prove your mission is true!)"* [10]

Their messengers would answer them, saying, *"While it's true that we're no more than mortals like yourselves, Allah favors whichever of His servants that He wants. It's not our place to bring a clear and decisive (miracle) without Allah's permission. (True) believers should trust in Allah, (rather than in miracles)!* [11] *We have no reason not to trust in Allah, for He's guided us on our pathways. Therefore, we're going to patiently endure all of your abuse. Those who would trust (in something) should trust in Allah."* [12]

Then the rejecters (of truth) would tell their messengers, *"We're going to drive you out of our land, unless you return to our traditions!"*

Thereupon, their Lord would inspire (the messengers), telling them, *"We're going to destroy the wrongdoers,* [13] *though We'll lodge your (bodies) in the earth, (and you shall remain there) long after (they're gone).* 276 *That's how it is for anyone who fears his meeting (with Me) and who takes My threat (of punishment) seriously."* 277 [14]

(Even though the wrongdoers) wanted to have victory (over the righteous), each and every stubborn tyrant failed in frustration. 278 [15]

---

276 This is a veiled reminder to the believers that they shall also pass away into the earth for the 'long sleep,' as well.

277 In other words, people who appreciate the magnitude of Allah take Allah's presence and warnings seriously! If someone doesn't believe Allah is in control and pays Allah's will no mind, then he can't rightly claim to be a believer, no matter what his religion is. Only the righteous shall inherit the earth, for the wicked, even if they gain ascendancy for a time, wind up destroying themselves anyway.

278 The Prophet said, "If you see my community being afraid of telling a tyrant that he is, in fact, a tyrant, then it may be the end of my community." (*Ahmad, Bayhaqi, Tabarani*)

Hellfire is coming up ahead of each one of them. Therein he'll (be forced to) drink boiling, disgusting muck [16] in huge gulps, but he'll never be able to get it past his throat! [279] Death will confront him from every side; *yet, he'll never die*, for a relentless punishment is what he'll have to face. [17]

The Price of Evil

The example of those who reject their Lord is that their deeds are like ashes that are blown around by a strong gust of wind on a stormy day. They have no power at all over what they've earned for themselves, and that's by far the worst mistake! [280] [18]

Don't you see that Allah created the heavens and the earth for a true purpose? If it were ever His desire, He could remove you and bring about some new kind of creation, [19] and that's not too hard for Allah. [20]

(The faithless) will be marched all together before Allah. Then the weak-minded will say to (the influential) and self-assured, *"We were only following whatever you suggested, so can you do anything for us now against Allah's wrath?"*

"If Allah had guided us," they'll reply, *"then we would've guided you. It doesn't matter now whether we're outraged or resigned to our fate, for there's no way for us to escape."* [281] [21]

Once the issue has been decided, Satan will say, *"Allah made a true promise to you, but I broke my promise to you, and I had no power over you*

---

[279] The Prophet said, "On the Day of Judgment, Hellfire will be brought, and it will call to (all) creatures (assembled for judgment), saying, 'The custody of every rebellious tyrant was given to me!'" (*Tirmidhi*)

[280] The 'earnings' mentioned here are the value of the deeds that they accrue in their record of deeds. If they cared little for Allah and morality, then everything they did in their life was a waste comparable to blown ashes.

[281] There are two types of people who reject Allah: those who actively try to convince others to lead an ungodly lifestyle (the influential and haughty), and those who follow every whim of their flesh and let themselves become duped into leading a decadent and immoral lifestyle. Both groups will be rudely awakened on Judgment Day!

other than through suggestion. [282] *You listened to me, so don't blame me. You only have yourselves to blame. I can no more hear your cries than you can hear mine. I don't accept the blame for what you previously did when you joined me (in Allah's power)."* Truly, wrongdoers have a terrible punishment prepared for them! [22]

However, those who believed and did what was morally right will be admitted into gardens beneath which rivers flow, and there they shall remain, by their Lord's leave. They'll be greeted with the word, *"Peace!"* [23]

The Parable of the Two Trees

Don't you see how Allah sets forth the example of a good word? [283] It's like a good tree whose roots are strong and stable, with branches jutting up into the sky. [284] [24] It bears fruit at all times, by its

---

[282] Jinns are creatures made of a type of energy that is drawn from fire. (They are not fire, itself, but merely made of a part of that type of energy. See 15:27.) Thus, they operate on a specific plane of energy and are outside the power of our vision. Given that all of our thoughts in our brains are merely bursts of electrical energy, it is not unreasonable to understand how demonic influence assails us. Satan and his minions "whisper" or implant "suggestions" in our thoughts, and so we see our brainpower getting influenced by outside energy. One way to measure the effect of the jinn on the mind is to consider those times in which it seemed a powerful negative thought was popping into your head, seemingly out of nowhere and without your active permission. That may have been a jinn "whispering" his dark motivations in your mind. To be sure, people are perfectly capable of thinking up sinful things themselves. Yet, there are other times when our bodily urges and negative thoughts seem to coalesce without any rational explanation. As Satan said, *"I'm going to mislead them and create in them false desires."* [4:119] After the thought is placed, it is our choice either to act upon it or to call upon Allah to banish the evil thought. Depending upon our choice we either sinned or passed a test of faith.

[283] Jesus set the standard for proving wisdom in Matthew 11:19 when he said, "Wisdom is proved righteous by its works." Thus, the rightness of a person's faith is proven by what he or she does.

[284] The 'good word' mentioned here is understood to refer to the basic statement of faith, or *kalimah*, which is the phrase, "There is no god except Allah." The Prophet once said of it, "Whoever declares that there is no god but Allah will go to Paradise." Someone asked him how the sincerity of that statement could be measured, and the Prophet replied, "By accepting this phrase, you should refrain from what Allah has forbidden." (*At-Targheeb wa at-Tarheeb*) The Prophet said that the good tree mentioned in the Qur'an is the date tree and that the rotten tree is the colocynth, a kind of vine-like bush known as the vine of Sodom (which is also mentioned in the Bible in II Kings 4:39-40 as a 'wild gourd'). (*Tirmidhi, Nisa'i*)

Lord's permission. [285] Allah offers such examples for people so they can be reminded. [25] Now the example of a rotten word is like a rotten tree that's been torn out of the earth by its roots. [286] It has no way to hold itself up! [26]

Allah will support and uphold those who believe in the good word, both in this life and in the next, [287] while Allah will let the wrongdoers go astray, and Allah does whatever He wants. [288] [27]

The Unstinting Bounty of Allah

Background on verses 28-30: This passage refers to the pagan Arabs of old who transformed Abraham's shrine in Mecca over many generations into a house of idolatry and superstition. The Prophet once identified the man who instituted idolatry in Mecca. He said it was a man named Abu Khuza'ah. Tribal oral history records that he was the son of Luhay ibn Qam'ah of the tribe of Jurhum, which was the ruling tribe of Mecca before the Quraysh invaded the city and drove the Jurhumites away several centuries before the birth of Muhammad. (*Ahmad, Ibn Kathir*)

---

285 'Abdullah ibn 'Umar narrated the following story: "We were sitting with the Messenger of Allah when he asked us, 'Tell me about a tree that resembles what a Muslim is like – its leaves don't fall in the summer or winter, and it bears fruit all year round by the will of its Lord.' I thought it was the date palm tree, but I was too shy to answer, especially since I saw that Abu Bakr and (my father) 'Umar didn't say anything. Then the Messenger of Allah said, 'It's the date palm tree.' After we left I said to 'Umar, my father, 'By Allah I thought it was the date tree.' When he asked me why I didn't speak up before, I said, 'If you would have answered, it would have been dearer to me than anything.'" (*Bukhari*) Also see Matthew 7:17-19 where Jesus makes a similar parable.

286 The term *khabeethatin* has many shades of meaning, among these are offensive, repulsive, rotten, malignant (as in a disease), wicked and evil. The idea in this verse is that a good word, such as the call of belief in one god, is like a fine fruit tree that provides abundantly for all, while a rotten word, such as the call of a false way of life that teaches people to be immoral, would be like a disgusting and deformed tree that's been ripped apart and seems hopeless.

287 The Prophet explained that the reference to the next life here is specifically the time in the grave when souls will be waiting for the Day of Judgment, a time known as *barzakh*. When the angels come to the deceased person's soul the first time, they will ask it what it worshipped in the world. If it answers with the statement of faith (the 'good word' or *kalimah*), then it will sleep peacefully until resurrection. (*Ma'ariful Qur'an*)

288 Allah acts in His Own capacity, and He does whatever He wants to do. That is His prerogative, and we are not endowed with the ability to question Him on this. The New Testament echoes a similar sentiment when we read in Romans 11:33-34 the following observation of Paul: "…Oh, the depths of the riches of the wisdom and knowledge of Allah! How unsearchable His judgments…"

Haven't you seen those who paid Allah back for His favor by suppressing (accurate knowledge of Him), and who have thus brought their people into the realm of doom [28] – *Hellfire?* [289] They're going to burn in it, - *and how terrible a place to settle!* [29] They were the ones who set up rivals with Allah, in order to steer others away from the path. So say (to them), *"Enjoy yourselves now, but you're headed straight for the Fire!"* [30]

Tell My servants who believe to establish prayer and to spend (in charity) out of the resources that We've given to them, both in secret and in public, before a day arrives in which there will be neither bargaining nor friendship. [290] [31]

Allah is the One Who created the heavens and the earth. He sends down water from the sky and uses it to produce the fruits that sustain you. He put at your service the ships that sail through the sea by His command, and He also put rivers at your service, as well. [291] [32] Likewise, He put the sun and the moon at your service; they both follow their orbits without fail, even as He made the very night and day useful for you. [292] [33]

---

[289] The previous generations are already doomed to Hell for their worship of idols in place of Allah. After the Battle of Badr, the leaders of the Quraysh who died were going to be in Hellfire, themselves.

[290] The Prophet told the following story: "A man once vowed to give charity to a prostitute, so he went out one night, found one and gave her charity. The next day when people found out, they grumbled and ridiculed him for giving his charity to a prostitute. When he heard about their disapproval, he said, 'Thank you, Allah, for leading me to give charity to a prostitute.' Then he vowed to give charity to a rich man, and that night he found one and gave him charity. Again, the next day the people mocked him, this time for giving charity to a rich man. When the man heard of their disapproval, he said, 'Thank you, Allah, for leading me to give charity to a rich man.' Then he vowed to give charity to a thief, so that night he went out in search of a thief, found one and gave him charity. This also outraged the community, but the man kept on thanking Allah for guiding him to give charity to a prostitute, a rich man and a thief. Shortly afterwards the man passed away, and he was told, 'Your charity was accepted, for it may be that the prostitute will discontinue her shameful business and turn to Allah for forgiveness; it may be that the rich man will start thinking about giving in charity himself, and it may be that the thief will repent of his stealing and give it up.'" (*Muslim*)

[291] Human ingenuity allows us to dam rivers to control flooding and also to irrigate fields in barren landscapes. The point is made here that it was Allah Who gave us the capability to do these things.

[292] The sun and the moon are used by human beings to calculate time, and their orbits are so regular that we can rely upon their witness for our own planning.

He gives you everything for which you could ask! If you ever tried to count Allah's favors, you would never be able to enumerate them all! [293] Yet, still humanity is lost in corruption and ingratitude! [34]

The Prayer of Abraham

Recall when Abraham said, *"My Lord! Make this settlement (of Mecca) tranquil and secure, and keep me and my descendants away from idol-worship.* [294] [35] *My Lord! So many people have been led astray by them.*

---

[293] The Prophet was overheard supplicating, "O Allah! All praise belongs to You. (I will never) be able to thank You enough, nor do I ever wish to be cut off from You, nor do I ever (wish to arrogantly) feel too rich (to know I must) rely upon You, O Lord." (*Bukhari*)
[294] Ibn 'Abbas (d. 687) narrated the following story from the Prophet that fills in missing details from this Qur'anic episode in the story of Abraham. The story goes as follows: The first lady to use a waist strap (a kind of pocket/belt) was (Hagar), the mother of Ishmael. She used it to brush the dirt to hide her tracks from Sarah, (who was Abraham's first wife and who bullied Hagar out of jealousy. So Abraham took Hagar and Ishmael to an empty valley in Arabia (which is the place where the Ka'bah would later be built). He sat them under a large tree that was near to where the well of *Zamzam* would later sprout. At that time Mecca did not exist, and there was no water there. Abraham left them there with a bag of dates and a jug of water. When Abraham began to depart, Hagar ran after him crying, "Abraham! Where are you going? Why are you leaving us in this valley where there's no people or water?" She said this several times, but he ignored her as he rode away. Finally she called out to him, "Did Allah command you to do this?" Abraham answered, "Yes." Hagar replied, "Then He certainly won't abandon us." She then went back to the tree and sat down as Abraham made his way out of the valley. When he was out of sight, Abraham prayed for them (and then returned to Palestine). Hagar took care of her son Ishmael, who was barely more than an infant, but then the water ran out, and they became wracked with thirst. Hagar saw her son dehydrating on the ground, and she frantically ran back and forth between two hills that were later named Safa and Marwa, searching in vain for any sign of other people. She had to raise her sleeve (over her eyes to shield them from the hot sun). She ran back and forth to the top of each hill seven times but saw no one… On the fourth circuit, however, she heard a sudden voice out of nowhere that said, "Shush." She craned her head to listen for the source of the sound but then gave up, saying, "I heard you! Do you have anything to help us?" Then she looked and saw an angel poking the ground with his wing, and water began to flow, so much so that she cried, "Enough! Enough! (*Zam! Zam!*)" That's the Well of *Zamzam* today. She ran to the water spout and began cupping it in her hands. Then she began digging around it to make it a small pool. She filled up her water jug, and the water didn't stop flowing…The angel then said to her, "Don't fear abandonment, for the House of Allah will be built in this place by this boy and his father, and Allah never abandons His people." (*Bukhari*) Some time later, a group of bedouins from the tribe of Jurhum saw birds circling over a distant valley. Thinking there might be water there, they came upon the well and noticed the mother and her son. They decided to settle there, and Ishmael later married one of their women, thus mingling the seed of Abraham with the bedouins to form a new ethnic group: the northern Arabs. When Abraham returned to visit some years later, he saw the beginnings of a settlement

Whoever follows me is of the same mind as me, and whoever disobeys me –
well, You're forgiving and merciful." [295] [36]

"Our Lord!" (he continued,) "I've settled some of my descendants in
this barren valley [296] next to Your Sacred House, so they can, our Lord,
establish prayer. So make some people sympathetic towards them, and supply
them with fruits so they can learn to be thankful." [37]

"Our Lord! You know what we conceal and what we reveal, for nothing
at all can ever be hidden from Allah, neither on the earth nor in the sky. [38]
Praise be to Allah Who has given me my sons, Ishmael and Isaac, even in my
old age, for My Lord hears all requests! [39] My Lord! Make me a prayerful
person, and make my descendants prayerful, as well. Our Lord! Hear my
request. [40] Our Lord! Forgive me and my parents and all those who believe
on the Day of Account." [41]

Allah Delays Punishment for a Reason

Don't think for a moment that Allah ignores the actions of the
wrongdoers. He's only giving them a break until the day comes when
eyes will stare unblinking, [42] when they'll run around in a frenzy with
heads raised, not looking at themselves, and feeling a void in their
guts! [43]

So warn people of the day when the punishment will come upon
them, when the wrongdoers will cry, "Our Lord! Give us more time,
even just a little! We'll surely answer Your call and follow the messengers
then!"

(However, they'll be told,) "Weren't you the ones who swore before
that you would never be brought down (from your powerful positions)? [44]
You lived (near the ruins of past civilizations) who had done wrong against

---

that would one day grow into Mecca. (The prayer contained in verses 35-41 is what
Abraham then said in thanks.)

[295] Ibrahim ibn Adham (d. 777) once wrote, "We live such a life (of pleasure in Allah's
service) that if kings knew about it, they would take up arms against us (to steal it from
us)." He himself gave up a throne to devote himself to religious studies and preaching.

[296] *Lit.* a valley where no crops of any kind are grown.

their own souls! You clearly saw how We dealt with them, and We offered so many examples to you!" [45]

They wove their mighty schemes, but their schemes were in Allah's full view (and thus could never succeed) - *even though (their plans) seemed strong enough to shake the mountains!* [297] [46] So don't ever think that Allah will fail in what He's promised to His messengers, for Allah is Powerful and a master of retribution. [47]

The Promise of a Day of Justice

A day will come when the earth will be transformed into a different earth, even as the skies will be transformed, as well, and then everyone will be marched before Allah, the One, the Irresistible. [48]

That day you'll see the sinners all tied together in chains; [49] their only clothing will be burning, oozing tar, even as their faces will be enveloped in fire. [50] (That'll be their fate), so that Allah can repay every soul with what it deserves, for Allah is swift in settling accounts. [51]

This announcement (is a message) for all humanity, so let them be warned by it, and let them know that He is only One God. Let thoughtful people then be reminded. [52]

---

[297] Jalaluddin Rumi (d. 1273) once wrote: "Even though he was as strong as a mountain and relied upon his own firmness, a small flood swept him away. When the command of destiny pokes its head out of heaven, then even the most learned become blind and deaf; fish are thrown out of the sea; traps cruelly catch the bird as he flies; genies and devils are put back in the bottle; even the ruler of Babylon falls. Everyone is then lost, save for the one who found safety within the command of destiny; no ill-reading of the planets ever touches him. Unless you find your safety within the command of destiny, then nothing you ever do can release you from it." (*Mathnawi* III, 468-473)

138

The Stony Ground

15 Al Hijr
Late Meccan Period

By the late Meccan period the Prophet was feeling continuously fatigued. The constant persecution that he and his followers were facing, the daily insults, the stories of woe that his followers brought to him of their own travails and suffering, and the fact that, despite all the logical arguments he brought to prove that idolatry was false, the majority of his people still clung to ignorant traditions – all of these things began to take a toll on the Prophet. This chapter was revealed to the Prophet partly to console him and partly to convince him to remain steadfast, hoping upon the favor of Allah to change his circumstances and those of his followers who believed in his message and suffered on account of it.

In the Name of Allah,
the Compassionate, the Merciful

Alif. Lām. Rā.

These are the verses of the Book and a clear recitation. [1] It just may happen that (one day) those who covered (the light of faith within their hearts) will wish that they had surrendered (to Allah), [2] but leave them alone to eat and make merry – preoccupied in their false hopes, for soon they'll know (the truth)! [3]

We've never destroyed any settlement without setting their time limit in advance, [4] nor can any community know when its term is up, nor can they delay it. [298] [5]

---

298 Abu Darda, a prominent companion of the Prophet, once gave a sermon in Damascus in his waning years in which he said, "O people of Damascus! Would you pay heed to the words of this sympathetic brother of yours? Then listen to me. Prominent people before you amassed huge fortunes, collected gold and possessions, built huge mansions and made long-term plans for the future. Today they're all dust. Their graves are their homes, and all their precious hopes and plans have been proven to be no more than an

The Mocking of the Faithless

(The Meccans) say, *"Hey you, the one who's getting this 'revealed message.' (We think) you're crazy!* [6] *So why aren't you bringing angels down to show us if you're really so honest?"* [7]

However, We never send angels down except for a compelling reason, and (if they did happen to come), then the (faithless) would get no relief! [299] [8]

We're sending the message down to you, (Muhammad,) and We're going to protect it. [9] We sent messengers before your time among the religious sects of the past, [10] but no messenger ever came to them without them mocking him. [11]

That's how We (allow the notion) to seep into the hearts of the wicked [12] that they can disbelieve in (the message because it's so easy to insult Allah's prophets). However, the customs of the ancients have passed away! [13]

Even if We opened up a door to the sky for them and they climbed ever farther up into it, [14] they would still say, *"Our eyes are just blurry – no, wait! We've been (the victims) of some kind of sorcery!"* [15]

---

illusion. Near you lived the people of 'Ad who had filled their land with warriors, wealth, possessions, weapons and horses. Is there anyone here who will give me two silver coins to buy what remains of their legacy?" (*Ma'ariful Qur'an*)

[299] The Prophet said, "How will you react when five (types of disaster) befall you? I seek Allah's refuge that you'll never have to experience them and that you'll never have (the sins) within you (that would bring those disasters upon you). Whenever public wickedness prevails in a community, they're struck with plagues and diseases that were unknown to their ancestors. Whenever a segment of society stops paying charity, then they're deprived of rain from the sky. It's only on account of the animals (that live in that region that any rain would fall on them at all). Whenever a segment of society cheats people in measuring amounts accurately, then they'll surely be stricken with drought, famine and oppression from a tyrant leader. Any time the leaders of a nation rule by other than what Allah revealed, then they're afflicted with enemies who will deprive them of some of their power. When they stop ruling themselves altogether by (revealed scripture) and the example of their prophet, then they seek to overpower each other (through civil war and strife)." (*Ahmad, Ibn Majah*)

And so it was that We placed the constellations in the sky and made them as decorations for all who see them. [300] [16] We're also guarding them from every outcast devil. [17] If any of them secretly tries to hear something, he's chased away by a brilliant shooting star. [301] [18]

---

[300] Some critics of Islam have suggested that Muhammad subscribed to an Aristotelian order to the heavens, that he believed the earth was stationary and flat and that the heavenly bodies were suspended from a kind of glass ceiling. These critics offer verses from the Qur'an such as those that say that Allah spread the earth out wide [78:6] or that there are seven heavens [78:12] as proof. Beyond the fact that Muhammad never went to a school to learn prevailing astronomical theories, and besides the fact that ancient Greek learning, especially the teachings of Aristotle, never reached the wilds of Arabia, the Qur'an does not advance Aristotelian views. If anything, the Qur'an is mostly general in its descriptions of the sky, the heavens and the heavenly bodies. If it were somehow 'influenced' by Greek science (how that is supposed to have occurred when Greek learning never penetrated Arabia is a mystery), then there are many more precise ideas that could have been expressed. If one is supposed to be acquainted with something, then you would not expect him to give mostly general descriptions that could be interpreted in multiple ways. For Aristotle, the earth was the center of the universe, and it did not move. Stars and planets orbited in a spherical motion and were fixed on something akin to a glass ceiling. Air, fire and water were each contained in shells around the earth, which was made of the heaviest element, but because of imperfections, land protruded above the water. The Aristotelian world view goes on into further error, but the point is made: the Qur'an doesn't mention these types of things when it describes the universe. It has its own way of presenting the phenomena of the heavens. It is the Bible that subscribes to a quasi-Aristotelian view of the universe. The Biblical tradition teaches a vision of the earth as a flat plane under a domed sphere with a deep chamber for dead souls underneath the soil called Sheol. Storage tanks for snow, hail, wind and rain lie up in the sky, and the celestial bodies revolve around the earth. For a full discussion of the historical Biblical view of the universe, see appropriate entries in either *The HarperCollins Bible Dictionary* (HarperCollins, New York, 1996) or the *Eerdman's Bible Dictionary* (Eerdmans, Grand Rapids, 1987). One famous Christian leader, Martin Luther, even called Johannes Kepler crazy for suggesting that the earth spins and revolves around the sun, for the Bible in Joshua 10:12-14 *proved* the earth is stationary and the sun moves around it.

[301] The idea, as understood by traditional scholars, is that the next realm of Heaven lies beyond the veil of physical existence, i.e., space. Between the earth and the unseen realm lies the rest of the physical universe, including the stars and other planets. The angels approach the earth and sometimes remain in the sky and discuss what will happen on earth. The evil jinn try to approach them to hear the secrets spoken by the angels. This is in keeping with the chief devil's goal (i.e., Satan) to corrupt humanity (to prove to Allah that jinns are superior to humans). These evil jinns, or devils, then seek to rush back to the surface of the earth to whisper what they heard into the hearts of fortune-tellers, astrologers and other people engaged in predicting the future. [72:8-10] The people make their predictions, and some of them come true. Thus, people become dazzled, are misled away from Allah and come to rely upon fortune-tellers and the like for guidance in worldly affairs. (The Prophet did say that for every truth the fortune-tellers say, there

We spread the earth out (wide like a carpet) and placed within it steady mountains. [302] We developed everything on earth in a balanced way [19] and provided resources for the survival of both you and the (many creatures) that are not your responsibility. [20]

There's nothing (that exists) without its proper resources being (arranged for it) in Our sight, and We release nothing (of those resources) unless it's measured out accordingly. [21]

We send the fertilizing winds [303] and cause water to fall from the sky to provide you with water, even though you're not in charge of its supply. [22] We're responsible for bringing life and death, and We're going to inherit (all things after they die). [23]

> **Background on verses 24-25:** Ibn 'Abbas (d. 687) explained the reason for the revelation of these two verses. He said, "A beautiful woman, among the most beautiful of women, used to come (to the mosque) and pray behind the Prophet. Some of the men used to intentionally seek out the rows closest to the front so they wouldn't be able to see her (by making furtive glances back at the women's prayer lines). Other men would pray in the last row (of the men's lines) so they could peek back under their raised arms (when they were prostrating) and look at her. Because of this, Allah revealed this passage." (*Ibn Majah, Abu Dawud, Ahmad, Tirmidhi, Nisa'i*)

As it is, We know who among you moves ahead and who falls behind. [304] [24] Your Lord is the One Who will gather them all together, for He's full of wisdom and knowledge. [25]

---

are 99 lies.) To guard against the devils doing this with impunity, flaming fireballs, i.e., shooting stars, chase the devils away from the upper atmosphere. This doesn't mean that every shooting star we see throughout the year is chasing a devil, but traditionally Muslim scholars have held that this is the technique Allah uses to guard the secrets of the angels from the evil jinns that seek to destroy us humans. The Prophet did tell his companions that shooting stars have nothing to do with predicting events on earth, a belief that pre-Islamic Arabs held. (*Muslim*) Also see 37:6-10.

[302] The Earth's crust is literally like a 'carpet' or layer lying over the surface of the rocky core of the planet, and the mountains are the barriers formed between tectonic plates that slow their movement and the resulting commotion that could ensue.

[303] This is a reference to the role of wind in spreading pollen far and wide to assist in the fertilization of plants. No one alive in the seventh century had such knowledge.

[304] As the background commentary explained, this verse was revealed with regards to gender locations during congregational prayers. There are many points of etiquette for the spiritual maintenance of a mosque vis-à-vis the presence of mixed genders. To begin with, there was no partition of any kind separating the men and the women in the Prophet's mosque. There was a women's section in the rear and a men's section in the

The Fall of Satan

And We indeed created human beings from pliable clay - from mere molded mud, [305] [26] and We created the jinns, even before (human beings), from the intense heat (of pure energy). [306] [27]

Your Lord said to the angels, *"I'm going to create mortal man from mineral-rich clay, from molded mud.* [28] *After I've constructed him and breathed into him (something of) My spirit,* [307] *you must all bow down to him (out of respect)."* [29]

---

front. Thus, if both genders are going to be present in the same room, then they had better focus on prayer and not on each other. Indeed, this verse is telling the Muslims that Allah knows if they're thinking of Him or of something else. The Prophet once said that the prayer lines that are best for men are in the very front and best for women in the very back, and this utterance is probably connected to this episode. This is a practical arrangement and is in no way sexist or suggestive of a lower status for women. This arrangement is just to insure that the attention of men is solely upon Allah, so that is why they are asked to sit in the front and keep their eyes forward. (Also see 24:30-31.)

[305] If all of the components that make up the human body were separated, the majority of our mass would consist of water. The rest would be made up of essentially earth elements, minerals, trace metals, and various other substances. If these resulting separate parts were mixed together in a bowl with water, it would be clay or pliable *mud*!

[306] Jinns are elemental creatures made from a component of fire. However, they are not 'fire' as we know it, for the Arabic term, *samoum*, used here, means that part of the fire that is above the tip of the visible flame where no color is seen, but the burning heat is still felt. Think of invisible white-hot fire. (Some translators render this word as scorching wind from a smokeless fire.) Thus, jinns exist on something of an infrared or even more intense plane of being – almost electrical in nature. They communicate with human beings by 'whispering' in our minds. Since our thoughts are nothing more than impulses of energy, the jinns merely attempt to alter the course of our thoughts slightly or try to bend them to their will. It is up to us, when we feel such negative influences in our thoughts, either to follow through with them or to seek Allah's protection. If we do the latter, Allah promised that it will cancel the Satanic influence.

[307] What is meant by 'His spirit?' There are mixed views on this issue, with some scholars postulating that the soul that we humans are endowed with is a small sample taken from the same spirit-matter that makes up Allah. This in no way means that we are gods ourselves, and no scholar has ever assumed such. Instead, it is akin to taking a cup of water from the sea. Is the water in the cup still the sea? No, it is separated and disconnected. It may be consumed, cycled through the environment, bottled and even used to create electricity, but eventually it may find itself back in the sea from whence it came, but until then, it's just water. Likewise, when the child in the womb has reached 120 days of development (according to the explanation of the Prophet), an angel comes and breathes a *spirit from Allah* into the baby. Assuming the child is born and lives its life (for good or evil), one day he or she will die, releasing that spirit back into the universe where it rejoins its master essence. (See 2:28) This *ruh* (spirit or divine gift) is what sets us apart from all other life forms that we know about. From this we can conceive of

The angels fell down in prostration all together, [30] but Iblis didn't (join with the angels), for he refused to be one of those who bowed. [308] [31] Then Allah asked, *"Iblis! What's wrong with you that you didn't join those who bowed down?"* [32]

"I'm not going to bow down to a mortal man," Iblis answered, *"for You created him from mineral-rich clay, from mere molded mud!"* [33]

"Then get out of here!" Allah ordered. *"You're an outcast, [34] and you'll be cursed all the way to the Day of Judgment!"* [309] [35]

"My Lord!" Iblis cried out. *"Give me some time (to prove my case) up until they're resurrected."* [36]

"You'll have your time," (Allah said), [37] *"until a day whose arrival is appointed."* [38]

"My Lord!" (Iblis) said. *"Since You made me slip up, I'm going to make (immorality and wickedness) seem proper and good to those on earth, and*

---

morality, justice and truth, even as we can use our hyper-expanded imagination to peer into the recesses of the very meaning of the universe itself. Our use (or misuse) of this *spirit* will determine whether our unique personality (called a *nafs* or individual self) enters Paradise or is doomed to Hell. (See 33:72-73) The Sufis often take this concept (of having a spirit on loan from Allah) as the basis for their poetry and philosophy. To achieve union with Allah, in their view, is not *becoming* Allah, but rather returning your soul back to its rightful master (a state they equate with being drunk with ecstacy, no less!) The Day of Judgment is when our *nafs*, or individual essence, is judged on how well we took care of the spirit that was loaned to us. (See 16:111, 29:57-59 and 21:35, for example.) Other scholars contend that the 'spirit' was especially created matter from Allah's creative will and implanted in human beings to give us our essential quality and unique nature.

308 Remember that Iblis was a jinn who was often in the company of the angels, and he did not bow down when the angels did 'all together.' Verse 7:12 specifically mentions that Allah included more than just the angels in His command to bow down. Also see 2:34 and footnote.

309 The Arabic term *deen* is derived from the root word *dana*, which means to profess a set of beliefs. It also means something that is owed. Thus, in the religious sense, the Day of Judgment or *Youm ud-Deen* is the day when our religious obligations to our Creator will be examined and judged. Muslims often state that Islam is not a religion, in the conventional sense, for it colors every aspect of life; thus, it is more of a code that believers follow, for they owe a debt of gratitude to Allah for their very existence and chance at achieving eternal reward.

I'm going to deviate all of them (morally) [39] - *except, (of course), for Your sincere servants among them."* [40]

"The path (that they follow) will be the straight one that leads back to Me," (Allah) answered, [41] "and you'll have no power over My servants, except for the ones who put themselves in the wrong and follow you." [310] [42] Hellfire is the promised destination of them all! [311] [43] There will be seven gates (leading within it) – one gate for each class (of sinners). [312] [44]

Now as for those who were mindful (of their duty to Allah), they will be among gardens and springs. [45] (They'll be told,) "Enter within in peace and safety!" [46] Then We're going to cleanse their hearts of any lurking sense of bitterness (so they'll truly) be brothers as they face each other, (relaxing) on couches. [313] [47]

---

[310] The Prophet said (in a lengthy tradition) that Satan puts doubts in the mind of a son of Adam when he considers accepting Islam and that if he is thwarted and the person becomes a believer in Allah, then Satan merely moves to another perch from which to strike. When the believer feels he must migrate to a safer place to preserve his religion and family, Satan puts more doubts in his head about it. If the believer ignores Satan, then Satan merely moves to an even newer perch down the line. If a believer is asked to fight evil, then Satan assails him with thoughts of death, his widow marrying someone else or of losing all his wealth. If a believer resists and ignores Satan, then Allah will send such a staunch believer to Paradise if any of the following four things ever happen to him: if he dies naturally, if he's killed in a just cause, if he drowns, or if an animal breaks his neck. (*Ahmad*)

[311] Adam asked Allah for forgiveness, while all Satan asked for was time to prove himself right (that jinns were superior to humans). Thus, the descendants of Adam can hope for Paradise while those who follow Satan will have only Hellfire. Allah gave to both Adam and Satan that for which they asked.

[312] The commentators differ as to whether the seven gates represent the main general entrance to Hell or if they are the names of the seven distinct levels of Hellfire. The names of each of the seven levels of Hell are as follows: (1) *Jaheem*, (2) *Jahannam*, (3) *Sa'ir*, (4) *Saqar*, (5) *Nata*, (6) *Hawiya* and (7) *Hutama*. (From *The Spectacle of Death and Glimpses of the Life Hereafter* by K.M. Islam)

[313] When people are raised up for Judgment Day, they will be themselves as they were on earth with full memories intact. Even though two people may pass judgment successfully and be entered into Paradise, it may be that one of those people did something to the other in their worldly life that would still bother them in Paradise. To alleviate all of this, just before people enter in Paradise, they will spend a moment getting all their feelings out to address every slight, no matter how small, that may assail the peace of their mind. That way, in Paradise, there will be no lingering memory of hurt or bitterness, and all can be truly brothers and sisters in Allah's playground of eternal delight.

They'll feel no exhaustion, nor will they ever be asked to leave. [48] So announce to My servants that I am *indeed* the Forgiving and the Merciful [49] and that My punishment will be a terrible punishment. [50]

Who were the Guests of Abraham?

Tell them about the guests of Abraham. [51] When they came before him and said, "*Peace,*" he answered them back, saying, "*We're uneasy about you.*" [52] They said, "*Don't feel uneasy, for we're here to give you the good news of a son who will be exceedingly perceptive.*" [53]

(Abraham) asked, "*Are you coming here to give me this good news now that I'm an old man? So what kind of good news is that!*" [54]

"*We're bringing you this good news in all truth, so don't be discouraged!*" [55]

(Then Abraham realized his folly and) said, "*Who can be discouraged at Allah's mercy except for those who are astray?*" [56] Then he asked, "*So what's the errand that's brought you here, emissaries (of Allah)?*" [57]

"*We're being sent (to destroy) a wicked people,*" they answered, [58] "*except for the family of Lot, whom we're supposed to save all together,* [59] *though not his wife, whom we've determined will remain behind.*" [314] [60]

In the Cities of the Plain

When the messenger (angels) came to Lot's family, [61] (Lot) said, "*You seem to be strangers (to this city).*" [62]

"*Yes,*" they answered, "*and we've come to you to bring about (the order of destruction from Allah that the faithless) have been doubting.* [63] *And so, we've come here to bring the reality home to you, and we're honest in what we say.* [64] *So travel by night with your family when there's only a little of*

---

314 Abraham was the uncle of Lot and they had parted ways some years before. While Lot was still clinging to faith, his wife was a sinner, having become influenced by the ways of the evil people in her city. She would betray her husband by informing the masses whenever her husband had guests in the house. The wicked people would then come and violate his guests. On account of that, Allah had no interest in saving her.

the night left, and you, yourself, must be the one (who guards) the rear. Let no one look back, and keep going onward to where you're told to go." [65]

And so, We let him know about the command that the roots of (the wicked) were going to be cut off by the morning. [66]

The local people of the city came running excitedly (when they learned there were strange men in Lot's house). [67] (Lot) said to them, *"These are my guests, so don't disgrace me.* [68] *Rather, be mindful of Allah, and don't dishonor me!"* [69]

"Didn't we forbid you from (hiding) anyone at all (from us!)" they shouted. [70]

"My daughters are here," (Lot) pleaded, *"if you have to do something."* [315] [71]

By your very life, (Muhammad), they were milling about wildly in their drunkenness! [316] [72] Then the powerful blast overtook them before morning. [73] We turned (their city) upside down and rained down upon them a shower of hardened stones! [74]

Truly, there are signs in this (incident) for those who consider. [75] Even though the (city) was located on a highly (traveled) road, (now it can no longer be found)! [76] So truly, there are signs in this for those who believe. [77]

---

315 The mob wanted to seize the strangers who were with Lot for the mob's lowly passions, but Lot couldn't conceive that angels from the Lord should be so treated, that's why he offered his daughters to them for their lusts. It may seem like a callous act on the part of the father, but remember his options: let the crowd rape an angel or his daughter. He was scared, confused and certainly didn't want to have a messenger from Allah, under his care, treated so. What Lot didn't realize was that the angels could take care of themselves. In addition, perhaps Lot wasn't so callous after all, because he knew the men wouldn't be interested in his daughters anyway. They said as much in verse 11:79!

316 Muhammad is the only prophet who received the honor of having Allah swear by his life as to the truth of a matter. This is a reflection of the special status Allah has bestowed upon His last messenger to the world. (*Ma'ariful Qur'an*) As a prophetic rule, we human beings are not allowed to swear by anyone's name other than Allah's. (*Abu Dawud, Nisa'i*)

Destroyed Nations

The Companions of the Thicket were also wrongdoers, [78] and likewise We took vengeance upon them. They were located on a clearly marked route, (but their prominence did nothing to save them). [317] [79]

The Companions of the Stony Ground also denied their messengers. [318] [80] We sent Our signs to them, but they kept turning away from them. [81] They used to carve their dwellings out of mountain cliffs, (thinking they were) secure. [82] Then the powerful blast seized them one morning, [83] and nothing they prepared was of any use to them. [84]

Don't Lose Heart

We didn't create the heavens and the earth and everything in between them except for a true purpose. The Hour (of Judgment) is certainly drawing near, so excuse (the shortcomings) of others with gracious detachment. [319] [85]

Your Lord is the Most Knowledgeable Creator! [86] And so it is that We've given you the seven frequently repeated verses, (so you can gain inspiration and strength), and a majestic Qur'an. [320] [87]

---

317 The Companions of the Thicket were the ancient people of Madyan, who worshipped a thicket of trees.

318 The Companions of the Stony Ground refers to the people of a region of northern Arabia, where the land is rocky and somewhat craggy. There are ruins of an ancient people there in the hills. Those ruins are carved dwellings in rock faces.

319 The Prophet said, "Bring good news, and don't drive people away. Make things easy, and don't make them hard. Obey each other, and don't differ among yourselves." (*Bukhari*)

320 This passage refers to the first chapter of the Qur'an, which has seven verses and is recited (at the minimum) seventeen times a day in an individual's ritual prayers. The reminder of this essential chapter, coming as it is after the exhortation to be gracious with people, is quite appropriate given that the opening chapter reminds us that Allah is the ultimate source of our well being. Who can be overly cross or angry with people when we desire that Allah overlooks our own mistakes! For Muslims, the first chapter of the Qur'an is akin to the Lord's prayer for Christians. The Prophet said of chapter one of the Qur'an: "By the One Who holds my soul in His hands, Allah did not reveal in the Torah, in the Gospel, in the Psalms or in the (rest of the) Qur'an anything like [this chapter]; it is the seven frequently repeated verses." (*Bukhari*)

Don't strain your eyes longingly at what We've given certain classes (of people in power and wealth,) nor should you feel sorry for them (because they're blinded by those things). Rather, you should (focus yourself) on lowering your wing (in kindness) to the believers. [88] (All you need to) say (to the arrogant ones is), *"I'm the one who's warning you plainly."* [321] [89]

> **Background on verses 90-91:** The pagans would go out and meet incoming caravans to warn the new visitors not to believe in the call of a man among them named Muhammad, and they also warned that he was a sorcerer. They would recite scattered phrases of the Qur'an to the visitors and ridicule its message, (without reciting anything in context); thus, they 'sectioned' it up. *(Ibn Kathir)* Strangely enough, this seems to be the same practice of modern critics of Islam.

(And so, you must continue your preaching,) even as We're directing (Our revelations) to those who are dividing themselves (up into different camps concerning the truth of this message), [90] and who also try to slice this Qur'an up into disjointed sections (by quoting it out of context in order to ridicule it). [322] [91]

And so, by your Lord, We're going to question all of them together [92] about what they've done. [323] [93] So call to them openly with whatever you're commanded, and turn away from those who make partners (with Allah). [94]

We're enough (of a protector) for you against those who ridicule you [95] and against those who set up a rival god with Allah. Soon they're going to know (the truth)! [96] We know how your heart aches

---

[321] The Prophet said, "The example of both me and that with which Allah sent me is that of a man who went to his people and said, 'People! I've seen an (invading) army with my own eyes! I'm clearly warning you! Flee! Flee!' Some of his people believed him, and they left by nightfall at a slow pace and escaped. Others didn't believe him and remained where they were until the morning when the army overtook them and utterly destroyed them. This is the example of the one who obeys me and follows what I've brought and the example of the one who disobeys me and rejects the truth that I've brought." *(Bukhari, Muslim)*

[322] A few commentators have suggested that this passage is referring to Jews and Christians who believed in some of the Qur'an but not the rest, but this is a highly unlikely interpretation given the time and the context of the entire passage.

[323] When the companions asked the Prophet about this passage and asked what they will be questioned about, the Prophet replied that people will be questioned about whether they believed in the one God or not and their commitment to Him. *(Qurtubi)*

at what they're saying, [97] but glorify and praise your Lord, be among those who bow down prostrate, [98] and serve your Lord until what is certain comes to you. [99]

The Bee

16 An-Nahl
(aka An-Ni'am)
Late Meccan Period

This chapter was revealed after the migrations of some of the Prophet's followers to Abyssinia. Although the migrants eventually returned after hearing false reports that Meccan persecution had eased, the situation of the fledgling religious sect was uncertain and seemingly grim. The mention of plots against the believers of ancient days is also a clear reference to the ongoing schemes and plots that the idolaters were continually hatching against the followers of the Prophet.

No greater example is there of the ability of otherwise normal people to become oppressors and mean-spirited purveyors of cruelty than in the way that the Meccans, who thought so highly of themselves, became so wicked and gratuitously violent against those who disagreed with the backward superstitions that held sway in that culture. The Muslims were not calling for a violent overthrow of the society. Rather, they called for reforming personal conduct, establishing a social safety net to support the weak and poverty-stricken, and considering abandoning idolatry and the many invented superstitions that had no basis in logic or reason.

In the Name of Allah,
the Compassionate, the Merciful

Background on verses 1-4: Some of the pagans used to ridicule the Prophet because the foretold punishment from Allah wasn't materializing upon them. A pagan poet named an-Nadr ibn al-Harith even taunted the Prophet, saying, "O Allah! If it's within Your power, then throw stones down upon us to hasten our suffering!" This passage was revealed in response to their ridicule, promising that the punishment would come one day, but not when they wanted. *(Asbab ul-Nuzul)*

Allah's command will come to pass, so don't seek to rush it. [324]
All glory be to Him! He's so high above the partners they assign to

---

[324] About two or three years after this verse was revealed, the entire leadership of the Meccan pagans fell in the Battle of Badr, save for Abu Lahab, who remained in Mecca but died soon thereafter from an infection. (See chapter 111. Within approximately six years after that, the Prophet returned to Mecca at the head of an army, ten thousand

Him! [1] He sends the angels with the spirit of His command and bestows it upon whichever of His servants that He wants, (saying): *"Warn (people) that there is no god but I, so be mindful of Me."* [325] [2]

He created the heavens and the earth for a true purpose. He's so high above the partners they assign to Him! [3] He created human beings from a drop of mingled fluids, and look how that same (human) becomes openly quarrelsome! [326] [4]

What has Allah Provided for Us?

He created livestock (animals) for you. You use (their hides) for warmth and make other useful products, even as you eat them, as well. [327] [5] You feel delighted at their sight as you corral them (in the evening) and when you lead them out to pasture (in the morning). [328] [6]

They carry your heavy loads to places that you couldn't get to (by yourselves), unless you were to exhaust yourself on the journey! (Allah provided you with these beasts of burden), for your Lord is kind and merciful. [7]

---

strong, and forced the peaceful surrender of the city. When all the Meccan pagans were in his power on that day of victory, he pardoned them and left them alone, causing them to convert *en masse* in wonder over his noble generosity.

[325] The Prophet said that Allah, Himself, said, "I created My servants to be natural (monotheists), but the devils came to them and deviated them from their (original) religion." (*Muslim*)

[326] A Jewish man in Medina once approached Muhammad and asked, "Muhammad! From what are human beings created?" The Prophet replied, "O Jew! (Human beings) are created from both the man's drop and the woman's drop." (*Ahmad*) Humans are created from a male sperm and a female ovum. On another occasion, the Prophet spit in his hand, and then he told those around him that Allah, Himself, said, "Son of Adam! How could you ever be as powerful as I, when I created you from something like this, and when I fashioned you perfectly and made you complete? You walk around wearing your two garments (pants and a shirt), and the earth echoes (under your footsteps). You gather money, but you don't share any of it with anybody. Then when the soul of a dying person reaches the throat, you say, 'Now I want to give in charity', but it will be too late for charity then." (*Ahmad, Ibn Majah*) Traces of human DNA are contained even in spittle.

[327] People are allowed to eat all types of domesticated livestock, except for donkeys, mules and pigs.

[328] This verse gives a reference to the cultural value of cattle to the Arabs. A man's wealth was literally counted in the livestock he owned, so when he would see his flocks and herds taken out for the day or brought in for the night, he would feel pleased with himself. (*Ma'ariful Qur'an*)

(He also created) fancy horses, [329] mules and donkeys for you to ride, and for you to parade about in exhibitions. [330] He will create other (modes of transportation) that you (currently) know nothing about. [331] [8]

It's Allah's (prerogative) to point out the right path, because there are other paths that swerve aside. If Allah had wanted, He could've guided you all (by giving you no choice but to be believers). [9]

He's the One Who sends water down from the sky. You drink from it, and from it grows the bushes [332] upon which you graze your cattle. [10] He also uses (the same water) to produce for you the grains, olives, dates, grapes and all the other types of fruit. There is a sign in this for those who reflect. [11]

He made the night and the day, the sun and the moon and the very stars themselves useful for you by His command. There are signs in these (things), as well, for those who use their reason. [12]

There is also, in all the things that He's multiplied for you in the earth and that encompass every shade of color, a sign for people who remember (the favors of Allah). [333] [13]

---

[329] The type of horse known as *khayl* in Arabic is considered by many bedouin horse-breeding tribes to be the quintessential Arabian show horse.

[330] These three animals are mentioned separately, for unlike cattle and sheep, these provide little benefit in the way of milk or meat. All schools of Islamic Law agree that eating the meat of donkeys or mules is forbidden. As for consuming horse meat, only the Hanafi school allows it, though that school of thought labels it as an undesirable practice. (*Ma'ariful Qur'an*)

[331] At the beginning of verse five, the past tense of the verb "to create" is used, while here the present/future tense of the verb is used (creates or will create). Several modern scholars have postulated that with this subtle shift in tense, the Qur'an was pre-envisioning the introduction of non-animal powered modes of transportation such as cars, planes and trains. (*Ma'ariful Qur'an*)

[332] The Arabic term *shajara* means a tree or a tall bush. In times of drought or in places with little grass, herders move their cattle close to any bushes or low hanging trees they can find so the animals can eat the leaves.

[333] What is the position of the Qur'an on evolution? In general, the Qur'an is fairly ambiguous and can be interpreted to reflect both creationist or evolutionary ideas. Modern-day Islamic scholars take divergent views on this issue, and sometimes argue one position or the other, oftentimes with great passion. (Compare the views on evolution of Palestinian scholar Adnan Ibrahim and the Pakistani American scholar Yasir Qadhi, for

He's the One Who tamed the sea for you, so you could eat fresh meat from it and also so that you could harvest (the pearls and shells) that you wear as ornaments. [334] You see the ships sailing through the waves that allow you to seek out Allah's bounty. (And so, the many resources that you gain should) give you (further reason) to be grateful. [14]

He set up firm highlands in the earth to minimize the effects of earthquakes upon you, [335] and (He laid out) rivers and passes (in the world), so that you could be guided on your travels. [15]

---

example.) Earlier generations of Muslim scientists were not troubled by this science vs faith argument that modern Muslims unwittingly inherited from fundamentalist Christians. Indeed, ten centuries before Darwin's theories, Muslims were already speculating on the effects of natural selection and evolution. For example, the ninth-century social commentator and zoologist, al-Jahiz, observed the following phenomena concerning natural selection: "Animals engage in a struggle for existence; for resources, to avoid being eaten and to breed. Environmental factors influence organisms to develop new characteristics to ensure survival, thus transforming them into new species. Animals that survive to breed can pass on their successful characteristics to offspring." (Kitab al-Hayawan) This is proven science, though science cannot explain the rise of life itself from lifeless matter and it is especially helpless in explaining human consciousness in a world where no other example exists. Rather than hold to arguments defined by modern passions and outside forces, it may be that the Qur'an presents something of a compromise between science and religion, and this middle ground is found precisely in its ambiguity. A Muslim can choose to believe in both science and God (or intelligent design) and not feel any unease about it. See 7:185 for the Qur'an's practical and poetic take on this subject. Also see 35:27-28 where variation within species is clearly laid out.

[334] In other words, people can sail in boats and navigate. This verse is cited as proof that there are no particular slaughtering rituals that must be performed when it comes to seafood. While the other schools of Islamic Law allow the eating of shellfish, clams and all other forms of seafood, the Hanafi scholars generally forbid eating anything from the sea other than fish, though there is some disagreement among them on this issue. I would suggest that the practice of boiling lobsters and clams alive, or allowing fish to suffocate to death are against basic Islamic principles of humane treatment – principles afforded to land animals by Shari'ah Law – and the conscientious Muslim would do well to make sure even sea creatures die a quick and painless death before preparing them for a meal. The Prophet specifically noted that animals we torture to death would be present on Judgment Day to testify to our cruelty. (For example, there is the famous story in which the Prophet noted that a certain woman who abused and starved a cat to death would be attacked by that cat in revenge on Judgment Day.)

[335] Lit. 'so (the earth) wouldn't shake with you,' i.e., to minimize the effects of earthquakes when the earth's plates collide. The mountains keep the plates from colliding even more violently than they already do. This is a part of the process of gradation and uplift ,which is a science well known to geologists.

(He also provided the many natural) landmarks and even the stars above by which (travelers) may orient themselves. [16]

So is the One Who can create (such) things equal to the one who can create nothing at all? Won't you take a reminder? [17]

If you ever tried to add up all of Allah's favors, you would never be able to count them all! Indeed, Allah is forgiving and merciful! [336] [18]

Allah knows what you conceal and what you reveal. [19] The (statues) that they call upon besides Allah can create nothing, for they themselves are merely created (things) [20] - *dead and lifeless*! They don't even know (if or) when they'll be resurrected! [337] [21]

The Two Potential Results

Your god is One God. Those who have no faith in the next life have stubborn hearts, and they're arrogant besides! [22]

Truly Allah knows what they're (doing both) in secret, as well as out in the open, and He has no love for the arrogant. [338] [23]

---

[336] Abu Hamid Muhammad al-Ghazali (d. 1111) once recorded how an awakened mind begins to appreciate the wonders of life and its bounties in these words: "Listen then and know that the first thing that awakens a person from the deep sleep of forgetfulness and turns him towards the straight path is Allah's bounteous favor, which stirs the mind to think the following thoughts: '*I've been given so many gifts- life, power, reason, speech, and I find myself mysteriously protected from so many trials and tribulations. Who is my benefactor? Who is my savior? I must be grateful to Him in a fitting manner, otherwise the gifts might be taken away, and I'll be finished off forever! These gifts have revealed their purpose to me, like tools in the hands of an artist, and the world appears to me like a beautiful picture leading my thoughts towards the Artist.*'" (From *The Allegory of the Seven Valleys.*)

[337] Even though idols of wood and stone are not alive, on Judgment Day, they're going to be animated so they can testify during Allah's court proceedings against those who falsely worshipped them and ascribed divinity and magical powers to them. Only creatures such as humans and jinn have been given certain forewarning of a future resurrection.

[338] Arrogance is a mental and spiritual sickness that people manifest in physical ways. It is a rejection of humbleness and needs validation from others. For this reason, arrogant people make a big show of themselves to others, and this often involves physical displays of wealth, power and 'identity' to intimidate people. One common method of doing this is in the wearing of clothes that project power and authority. Think of those who buy the most expensive clothes, jewelry and accessories to show others an 'image.' Mu'adh bin Anas RA reported about: Messenger of Allah (peace be upon him) said, "Whoever Gives up wearing elegant and expensive garments out of humbleness, When

When they're asked, *"What has your Lord revealed?"* They answer, *"Tales from long ago!"* [24]

On the Day of Assembly they can bear their own burdens in full, as well as the burden (of the crime they committed against) the unsuspecting (people) whom they misled! *Oh, how terrible the burdens they will bear!* [25]

And so it was that those who came before (these Meccans) also schemed (against Allah), but Allah knocked out the foundation of their structure, and the roof caved in upon them! [339] The wrath (of Allah) took hold of them from directions they never even expected! [26]

On the Day of Assembly, He's going to cover them in shame and say, *"So where are all My partners about which you used to argue?"*

The people of knowledge will remark, *"Today, those who covered (the light of faith within their hearts) are truly covered in shame and misery.* [27] *They're the ones who had their souls taken by the angels while they were in a state of corruption against their own selves."* [340]

He can do so, Allah will call him on the Day of Resurrection and before all the creations, He will give him the choice to wear whichever garment of Iman he Would like to wear. " (*Tirmidhi*) For a true believer in the Lord, simple clothes are the best reflection of a genuine, humble heart. This can also combat latent feelings of arrogance that Shaytan tries to inject in all of us.

[339] The Meccan idolaters tried many ways to stop the Prophet and his message, even going so far as to try and assassinate him. Nothing worked and then the thing they tried to stamp out came back to eventually accept their allegiance.

[340] The Prophet once told a group of people waiting for a funeral, "When a believer is about to leave this world and go forward to the next world, angels with faces white as the sun come down to him from heaven with one of the shrouds of Paradise - and some of the perfume of Paradise. They sit away from him as far as the eye can see. Then the angel of death comes and sits at his head and says, 'Good soul, come out to forgiveness and acceptance from Allah.' (The soul) then comes out as a drop flows from a water-skin, and he seizes it. When he does so, (the other angels) don't leave it in his hand for an instant but take it and place it in that perfumed shroud, and from it there comes forth a fragrance like that of the sweetest musk found on the face of the earth. They then take it up and do not bring it past a company of angels without their asking, 'Who is this good soul?' To which they reply, 'So and so, the child of so and so', using the best names by which people called him on the earth. They then bring him to the lowest heaven and ask that the gate should be opened for him. This is done, and from every heaven its archangels escort him to the next heaven until he is brought to the seventh heaven, and

(Then the doomed sinners) will offer their abject submission, saying, *"We didn't do anything wrong (intentionally)."* (However, it will be said to them), *"That's not true, for Allah knows what you were doing.*

Allah Who is great and glorious says, 'Record the book of My servant in the vault and take him back to earth, for I created humanity from it, I shall return them into it, and from it I shall bring them forth another time.' His soul is then restored to his body, and two angels come to him, making him sit up, and say to him, 'Who is your Lord?' He replies, 'My Lord is Allah.' They ask, 'What is your religion?' He replies, 'My religion is Islam.' They ask, 'Who is this man who was sent among you?' He replies, 'He is Allah's Messenger.' They ask, 'What is your (source of) knowledge?' He replies, 'I have read Allah's Book, believed in it and declared it to be true.' Then a voice cries from heaven, 'My servant has spoken the truth, so spread out carpets for him from Paradise, and open a gate for him into Paradise.' Then some of its joy and its fragrance comes to him; his grave is made spacious for him as far as the eye can see, and a man with a beautiful face, beautiful garments and a sweet odor comes to him and says, 'Rejoice in what pleases you for this is your day, which you have been promised.' He asks, 'Who are you, for your face is perfectly beautiful and brings good?' He replies, 'I am your good deeds.' He then says, 'My Lord, bring the last hour; my Lord, bring the last hour, so I can return to my people and my property.' On the other hand, when a faithless person is about to leave the world and proceed to the next world, angels with dark faces come down to him from heaven with woolen cloth and sit away from him as far as the eye can see. Then the angel of death comes and sits at his head and says, 'Wicked soul, come out to displeasure from Allah.' Then it becomes dissipated in his body, and he draws it out as a prickly stick is drawn out from moistened wool. He then seizes (the soul), and when he does so (the other angels) do not leave it in his hand for an instant but put it in that woolen cloth and from it comes forth a stench like the most offensive corpse found on the face of the earth. They then take it up and do not bring it past a company of angels without their saying, 'Who is this wicked soul?' To which they reply, 'So and so, the child of so and so', using the worst names that he was called in the world. When he is brought to the lowest heaven, a request is made that the gate be opened for him, but it is not opened for him." (The Prophet then recited the verse, "The gates of heaven will not be opened for them, and they will not enter Paradise until a twisted rope can pass through the eye of a needle." Then the Prophet continued his story, saying, "Allah, Who is the most Great and Glorious, then says, 'Record his book in the pit in the lowest part of the earth,' and his soul is thrown down." (Then the Prophet recited the verse, "He who assigns partners to Allah – it's as if he had fallen down from the sky and been snatched up by the birds or made to fall by the wind in a far off place." Then the Prophet continued his story, saying,) "His soul is then restored to his body, and two angels come to him, make him sit up, and say to him, 'Who is your Lord?' He replies, 'Alas, alas, I do not know.' They ask, 'What is your religion?' He replies, 'Alas, alas, I do not know.' They ask 'Who is this man who was sent among you?' He replies, 'Alas, alas, I do not know.' Then one cries out from the sky, 'He has lied, so spread out carpets from Hell for him, and open a gate for him into Hell.' Then some of its heat and hot air comes to him. His grave is made narrow for him up until his ribs are pressed together in it, and a man with an ugly face, ugly garments and a bad smell comes to him and says, 'Be grieved with what displeases you, for this is your day which you have been promised.' He asks 'Who are you, for your face is ugly and it brings evil?' He replies, 'I'm your wicked deeds.' The (unfortunate soul) then says, 'O My Lord, don't bring the last hour.'"

[28] *So enter into the gates of Hellfire, and stay in there!"* The home of the arrogant is an awful one indeed! [29]

When those who are mindful (of Allah) are asked, *"What has your Lord revealed?"* they say, *"Only the best!"* For those who do good, there will be good in this world, and the home of the next life is even better! How excellent is the home of those who were mindful! [30]

They'll be admitted into eternal gardens beneath which rivers flow! They'll have everything there they ever wished for, and that's how Allah rewards those who were mindful (of Him). [31] They're the ones who will be taken by the angels (at death) in a state of purity, and who will be told, *"Peace be upon you. Enter the Garden on account of what you did (in the world)."* [32]

Are (the faithless) just waiting (for the time when) the angels come for them, or (are they waiting) for the arrival of the command of your Lord? [341]

That's what those who went before them did, but Allah never did any injustice to them (when He punished them), for they had been doing injustice against their own souls. [33] The evil of their deeds overtook them, and the very thing at which they used to laugh closed in upon them from all sides! [34]

Allah Keeps His Promises

Those who make partners (with Allah) say, *"If Allah had wanted to (prevent us), then we would've never worshipped anything besides Him - neither ourselves nor our ancestors - and we would never have prohibited anything in preference to His (laws)."* [342] That's how others before them

---

[341] The implication is that they're as foolish as a man sitting on train tracks, who assumes that since he doesn't see any train coming, he will be safe and therefore lies down on them to rest.

[342] This is the standard argument of those who want to absolve themselves of any responsibility for their actions. If Allah really wanted people to be believers, they reason, then He wouldn't have let them become idol-worshippers, nor would He have let them make superstitious restrictions on which animals could be eaten and which could not, based on such things as if it was a twin birth of calves and such. Strangely enough, these are the same types of people who would be the first to object if they thought their power

behaved. What else is there for the messengers to do other than to convey the message clearly? [35]

And so it was that We sent to every community a messenger (who said), *"Serve Allah, and shun falsehood."* Among them were some who were guided by Allah, while others among them had (the consequences of) their mistaken ways proven true against them.

So travel all over the world, and see what happened to those who denied (Allah). [36] If you're anxious for them to be guided, (know that) Allah doesn't guide those whom He leaves astray, and there will be no one to help them. [37]

They swear by Allah – *using their strongest oaths* – that Allah will never raise the dead to life. But no! It's a promise He's going to keep, though most people don't know it, [38] so that He can present to them the meaning of those things in which they differed, and so that those who covered (the light of faith within their hearts) can finally know that they were indeed liars. [39] When We want something to happen, We only need to say, *"Be,"* - and there it is! [40]

Migration for Faith will be Rewarded

We're going to give a fine (reward) in this world to those who migrated (from their homes in the cause of Allah) after suffering under persecution. 343 However, the reward of the next life will be even greater, if they only knew! [41] (They were the ones) who persevered patiently and who placed their trust in their Lord. [42]

---

of decision making was going to be taken away from them. How hypocritical people can be! Allah gave people the ability to make free individual choices regarding their emotional and spiritual condition in their lives. He sent ample religious messages in the world for people everywhere from which to gain wisdom, and He even put a moral and ethical compass within each and every one of us. Now it's up to us either to pay attention and move towards the light or to get lazy and go with the flow, even if the river carries us over the falls. Allah did His part, now it's all on us.

343 This verse refers to the nearly eighty men, women and children who fled Meccan persecution to Abyssinia in the year 615. Later on, the Muslims were settled in lush Medina, a "fine" homeland indeed!

Muhammad, You are One of the Chosen

Background on verses 43-44: The pagan Meccans disbelieved in the Prophet, saying that if Allah was truly powerful, then He would've sent an angel to warn them. This verse, which references the ancient human prophets that were revered by the Jews and Christians, was revealed in response to reassure Muhammad that Allah had really chosen him, even though he was only a man, because it's what Allah has always done. It is thought that after this passage was revealed and made known to the Meccan public, that the pagans of Mecca were motivated to send emissaries to the Jews of Medina to ask them about the validity of Muhammad's teachings. Thereafter, passages in both chapters 17 and 18 were revealed to address some of the issues about which the Jews told the pagans to ask Muhammad.

The messengers that We sent before you, (Muhammad), were no more than (mortal) men (like yourself) to whom We granted revelation. Just ask the people who received the message before you, if you don't know about it. [43] (We sent them) clear evidence and scripture, just as We're also sending the message down to you, so you can convey clearly to people what's been sent for them, and so they can also think about it. [44]

So do those who make evil schemes feel so safe that Allah won't cause the earth to swallow them up or that the punishment won't come upon them suddenly from where they least expect it? [45]

(Do they feel so safe that they don't think) He'll take a hold of them while they're in the middle of their affairs, having no chance to prevent it, [46] or that He won't take a hold of them by gradually eroding (their power)? Your Lord is kind and merciful, (and He may take that slower route in order to give them time to repent). [47]

Don't they look at what Allah has created, even (at the small) things, like the way in which their shadows bend to the right and the left, prostrating themselves before Allah in the most humble way? [344] [48]

---

[344] This is a practical example of the Qur'anic principle that asserts that all things submit to Allah's will. Even though human beings have some type of free will to accept or deny their Lord, even their very shadows follow the law that Allah set for them, as shadows move throughout the day depending upon the position of the sun in the sky. Won't we allow our arrogance to come down enough to see that?

Whatever is in the heavens and whatever is on the earth bows down to Allah, from crawling creatures all the way up to the angels. None of them are too proud (to submit to His will). [49] (The angels) stand in awe of their Lord Who towers over them, and they do everything they're commanded to do. [345] [50]

On Dual Gods

Allah has said, *"Don't take gods in pairs, (saying there is one god of good and another god of evil), for He is only One God, so be in awe of Me."* [346] [51] Whatever is in the heavens and the earth belongs to Him, and sincere obedience is due only to Him. *So should you be mindful of any other besides Allah?* [52]

How do People Disobey Their Lord?

Nothing good ever comes to you except that it comes from Allah. Whenever you're stricken with hardship, you cry out to Him in desperation. [53] Yet, when He removes your hardship, some of you make partners with their Lord, [54] as if to show their ingratitude for the favors We've granted them. *So enjoy yourselves now, but soon you'll know (the truth)!* [55]

The Foolish Tenets of Paganism

The (Meccans) set aside a portion of the resources that We've provided to them for their survival. [347] (Then they offer that portion) to (their idols), *not even knowing (if they're real or not)!* By Allah! You're going to be questioned about all of your superstitions! [56]

---

[345] After reading this verse it is customary for the one who has faith in Allah to prostrate himself on the floor and praise Allah.

[346] The Zoroastrians of Persia held that there were two, coequal gods: one of light and the other of darkness or evil. Some Gnostic Christian groups also held similar ideas. The pagan Arabs were inclined towards these dualistic ideas and sometimes made pairs of gods themselves to represent different extremes. This is what this verse is referencing.

[347] The pagans of Arabia used to reserve a portion of their produce for their idols, in the same way that Hinduism and even some forms of Buddhism reserve a share of food to "feed" their idols. (Also see 6:136.)

Then they assign daughters (as offspring) to Allah - *all glory belongs to Him!* – even as they keep for themselves (the sons) that they desire! [348] [57] When the news is brought to one of them of (the birth) of a female (child), his face darkens, and he's filled with anguish. [349] [58] He hides himself from his fellows in shame, on account of the unwelcome news he's received.

Should"keep (the baby girl) in contempt or bury her in the sand? *Oh, what a terrible predicament on which they must decide!* [59] This is the vile example of those who don't believe in the next life, while the highest example belongs to Allah, for He's the Powerful and the Wise. [350] [60]

If Allah were to seize people (and punish them) for their corruption (according to what they deserve), then He wouldn't leave a single creature alive (on the earth)! However, He gives them a break

---

[348] The pagans said that Allah had daughters - but then they would kill their unwanted baby girls in favor of sons! Thus, their evil custom went against their own logic of what is worthy of divinity.

[349] Pagan Arab men believed that women were inferior to them in all respects. Daughters were seen as burdens because they couldn't fight, hunt or labor as hard as men, and when they married they went to live with their husbands' families and thus took resources away from their own family. For this daughters were looked down upon, and fathers would sometimes take their newborn baby girls and bury them alive in the sand. As verse 59 points out, the pagans have set up for themselves an evil choice on account of their disregard for the value of females, and so their example is one of evil upon evil, whereas Allah's way takes the high road. If they only believed in the true God, then they wouldn't have put themselves in such a bad position when daughters were born. The Prophet said, "When a daughter is born in a house, Allah sends angels to that house who say, 'All you who live in the house! Peace be upon you!' After they have said that, they take the daughter under the protection of their wings, and moving their hands softly upon her head, they say, 'Here is a frail being, born to another frail being.' Allah will extend His support to whomever will look after her and bring her up." (*Tabarani*) The Qur'an brought unheard of reforms to the status and well-being of women that one writer remarked, "Among the Quran's most detailed legislation is that designed to improve the status of women. The Quran is the only major religious text to acknowledge misogyny and enjoin correctives." (Tamara Sonn, *The Blackwell Companion to the Qur'an*, 2006)

[350] The scholars explain that the import of the mention of Allah's wisdom here is to emphasize to the pagans that in Allah's wisdom both male and female children must be valued equally. The pagan custom of killing unwanted infant girls goes against the order that Allah created, as evidenced in verse 4:1. The Prophet promised Paradise to any man who had at least two daughters and then raised them properly, educated them and treated them right. He, himself, had four daughters.

for a set amount of time. When that time limit expires, then they have no way to delay (their due punishment) - no, not even for an hour, just as they have no way to advance it. [351] [61]

They attribute to Allah what they hate (for themselves), even as their tongues express the lie that they deserve everything that's good for themselves. [352] Yet, surely the Fire (is all that) they're going to get, and they're going to be among the first to be ushered into it! [62]

By Allah! We sent (prophets) to those nations that went before you, but Satan made their (evil) actions seem appropriate and good to them. He's also the patron (of these Meccans) here today, but they're going to receive a painful punishment. [63]

We didn't send the Book to you for any other purpose than for you to explain to them clearly those things about which they've been arguing, [353] and also so it could be a guide and a mercy for those who believe. [64]

Ponder these Signs of Allah

Allah sends water down from the sky, and He uses it to give life to the earth after it was dead. There is a sign in this for people who listen. [65] There is another sign in livestock (animals), for We produce (milk) for you to drink from a place within their bodies between the

---

[351] 'Ali ibn Abi Talib was once speaking to some people about the magnitude of the Day of Judgment. Then he remarked, "By Allah! If I'm forced to spend from dawn to dusk lying on a bed of thorns, with my hands and feet in chains, and if I were dragged through the streets and markets like that, it would be better for me than to present myself in the court of Allah if I have committed an oppression against any one of His creatures or if I have usurped the rights of another." (*Nahjul-Balaghah*)

[352] Again, the pagans thought male children were better, but then they said that Allah had daughters. Thus, they're saying they deserve better than Allah!

[353] An anonymous writer once wrote, "The two most important days in your life are the day you are born, and the day when you find out why." (Quoted in a sermon by Earnest T. Campbell in 1970) When you consider the topics of 'argument' mentioned in this verse, the pagans were arguing about life after death, the purpose of life and whether a person should do good or evil, but one day the argument will be settled one way or another.

contents of their intestines and blood, a drink pure and tasty for any who drink it! [354] [66]

And from the fruit of the date palm and from grapevines you get alcoholic beverages and wholesome (non-alcoholic) products, as well. [355] In this is a sign for people who are wise. [67]

Your Lord inspired the bee to build its nests in hillsides, on trees, and in (the structures that people) erect. [356] [68] Then (He inspired it) to eat of the many (flowering) fruits and to follow humbly the wide paths of its Lord. [357] They produce from within their bodies a drink of varying shades of color that is a source of healing for humanity. [358] In this is a sign for those who reflect. [69]

Allah creates you, and then He causes you to die. Among you are some who are reduced to a state of senility (in your old age), so much

---

[354] Milk is created when nutrients from the intestinal tract are carried by the blood to the mammary glands, a fact that was unknown in seventh-century Arabia.

[355] This verse, mentioning that alcoholic drinks are a by-product of some fruits, was revealed before intoxicants were made forbidden. In any case, it's not telling anyone to drink them, for the Arabs of Mecca were already regular drinkers. It merely points out the many uses humans have in the things that Allah created. Grape juice, dried date cakes and vinegar, which are useful and wholesome, also come from those sources. (*Ma'ariful Qur'an*)

[356] 'Ali ibn Abi Talib once said, "Be like a bee. Anything it eats is clean; anything it drops is sweet, and any branch it sits on remains unbroken." (*Nahjul Balagha*)

[357] The ability of bees to know direction and then to communicate the location of distant flowering fields to their fellows through a kind of ritual dance is well known. The bees then follow these paths straight to their goal. The prominence of the bee mentioned here is reflected in the classic treatise, *The Island of Animals*, penned by a group of tenth-century, medieval Muslim philosophers known as the Brethren of Purity. In this tale, the animals of the world put mankind on trial for mistreating them. The bee is one of the main litigants who complains that humans steal its honey, which is its only food for its children. As the bee so poignantly observed, "It is well known about man that he never sees anybody else's point of view." (See *The Island of Animals*, trans. by Denys-Johnson Davies or *The Animals' Lawsuit Against Humanity*, trans. by rabbis Anson Laytner and Dan Bridge.)

[358] Bees produce honey from their bodies after ingesting flower pollen and other nectars. It comes in many shades of brown and amber, and its healing and healthful qualities both as a food and as a topical disinfectant are well known. The sign, or miracle, is clearly evident: how can humans have such a wonderful and healthy beverage made from flying insects who eat from flowers? 'Ali ibn Abi Talib once said, "The finest dress of the children of Adam is made from bug secretions (silk), and his finest drink is made from bee spit." (*Ma'ariful Qur'an*) Interestingly enough, the Qur'an uses the feminine form of the verb *their bodies* here, indicating that it is the female bees that make the honey. No one alive in the seventh century could have known that the worker bees are all females. By the way, the Prophet prohibited the killing of bees. (*Abu Dawud*)

so that you know nothing, even though you had known much before. [359] (Allah can do this) for Allah is full of knowledge and power. [70]

The Folly of Idolatry

Allah has favored some (of you) with more (material) blessings than others. [360] Those who've been favored with more resources aren't going to cast them at those whom they control to make them equal with them. Would they so eagerly scorn Allah's bounty like that? [361] [71]

Allah has given you mates of your own kind, and from your mates He's produced for you sons, daughters and grandchildren, even as He's given you so many wholesome resources besides. [362] Would it then be right for (your descendants) to believe in falsehood and be thankless towards Allah's bounty [72] and to worship others in place of Allah - beings who have no power to provide them with resources from the heavens or the earth, and who could never gain the ability to do so? [73] So then don't invent (false) representations of Allah, for Allah knows (what He's really like), and you don't know. [363] [74]

---

[359] A man went to the Prophet and said, "Messenger of Allah, the commandments of Islam have become too hard for me, and I'm now old, so tell me of something that I can keep doing." The Prophet answered, "Keep your tongue moist with the remembrance of Allah." The early scholar of the Qur'an, 'Ikrimah ibn Abi Jahl, once said of this verse that senility will not affect the one who has the habit of reciting the Qur'an often. (*Ma'ariful Qur'an*) Modern research has concluded that those whose minds are more active are, in fact, less affected by the degeneration of mental capacity.

[360] This verse is cited as proof that Islam allows people to have differing levels of wealth, and thus Islam is opposed to communism. (*Ma'ariful Qur'an*)

[361] The argument in this passage [16:71-74] is basically pointing out how foolish people are when it comes to their conception of Allah. Would Allah throw away some of His power and distribute it to idols or demigods to make them equals with Him? Well, no rich man would spread his money around among his servants to make them his equals. How then are people so ignorant when it comes to Allah?

[362] The Prophet said, "Allah will speak to His servant on the Day of Judgment and remind him of His blessings, saying, 'Didn't I give you a spouse? Didn't I honor you? Didn't I subject horses and camels to your use and make you ascend to a position of leadership and honor?'" (*Muslim*)

[363] People always try to put a face on God. The religious art of the last 10,000 years is evidence of humanity's preoccupation with making the unseen more like themselves and what they understand. Is it any wonder that all cultures on earth, except for Islam and Judaism, represent their main god(s) as human beings or other fantastic creatures? The Christian tradition makes God out to be something of an old man on a chair, with a handsome son and perhaps a semi-divine mother for His son. Many Buddhists have elevated the image of their founder, Siddhartha Guatama, into an object of worship.

Allah lays out the example of a slave under the control of another. He has no power at all, while another (person) to whom We've given Our favors (freely) spends (of his wealth without restriction) in private and in public. Are the two equal? [364] Then praise be to Allah, but most of them don't understand. [75]

Allah lays out the further example of two men. One of them is dumb and has no ability to do anything. He's a constant headache to his guardian. No matter where he sends him, he does nothing right. Is this kind of man equal with someone who commands justice (with full confidence) and is on a straight path? [365] [76]

What are Some of the Things that Allah has Done for You?

To Allah belongs whatever is beyond human perception in the heavens and the earth. What is the command of the Hour (of Judgment) but the twinkling of an eye or even quicker? Truly, Allah has power over all things! [77]

He's the One Who brought you out of the wombs of your mothers when you didn't know a single thing. Then He placed within you the abilities of hearing and sight, as well as intelligence and affection, so you could learn to be grateful. [366] [78] Haven't they seen the birds held

---

Taoism has adopted the traditional pagan gods of China. Hinduism and the related mythologies of the Aztecs, Mayans, Greeks and the Romans all have creature or human-like gods. Only the Qur'an has advanced the notion that nothing we can conceive of is equal to God. In that, Islam, along with Judaism, have been called the purist forms of monotheism in the world.

[364] The servant has no power and is thus a representation of what an idol is like, even as the person in charge is free to do whatever he likes. The boss never has a limit on his activities, and this is what Allah is like in comparison to the false idols people invent.

[365] This next example is of a person who is an aimless unbeliever who lives without guidance and makes sins and mistakes everywhere he goes, while the second person is the believer in Allah who lives by a definite code of conduct. Thus, the latter person avoids most sins and calls people to justice.

[366] These four qualities of newborns are given in exactly the proper order that a baby develops them. A baby develops hearing in the womb. Thus, when it is first born it can hear before it can see. As its awareness (intelligence) grows slowly, it soon comes to love its mother in an ever increasing way, whereas it had no conception of love before – just its constant sense of need.

aloft in the midst of the sky? Nothing holds them in place save Allah, and that is a sign for those who believe. [367] [79]

Allah provided you homes as places of rest and tranquility. He provided for you (the knowledge of how to make) tents out of animal skins, which you find so light (and easy to handle) when you travel, as well as when you stop (to make camp). [368]

Out of their wool, their fur and their hair, (you make) things (like clothing and blankets) that you can use for a while for your comfort. [369] [80]

Allah has also provided for you, out of what He's created, things (like trees) that can give you shade. He provided the mountains wherein you can find shelter. He produced clothing for you to protect yourselves from the heat and armored vests to protect you from violence against each other (in warfare).

That's how He completes His favors upon you, so you can submit (to His will in thanks). [81]

---

[367] Allah gave creatures the power to fly under their own power. No creature could have evolved this power on its own through natural selection, for as has often been pointed out, intermediate forms of flightless creatures would have had no advantage in survival. The creature can either fly from the start, or it will never develop flight at all, no matter how many 'mutations' occur. Thus, it was Allah Whose master plan called for the genetic appearance of flight in some creatures, and His power is seen clearly in this amazing ability of the birds. The complexity of bird flight, especially in long distance migrations and in the choreographed, synchronized movements of flocks of birds, shows that only Allah has designed them and given them the ability to do what they do. Some critics of Islam have suggested that there is a problem in this verse because it says that Allah is holding the birds aloft. They think that it is contrary to the fact that birds can fly under their own power. Such critics are discounting the poetic meaning of what this verse is saying. No Muslim commentator, either classical or modern, has ever interpreted this verse to mean that Allah is somehow putting an invisible hand under the birds and 'holding' them so literally. It is a verse that has, by universal recognition, no other implication than that it was Allah who gave the birds *the ability* to fly from His Own devices and that no one else could have ever created for those creatures the ability to do what has been a marvel of life ever since the first insect or dinosaur spread its wings and took to the air.

[368] We are 'nesting' creatures, in that we build permanent homes such as in buildings and such. When we travel, in order to bring our sense of safety with us, we bring tents along to make artificial 'nests' within which we can rest and rejuvenate, making us ready for the next day's challenge.

[369] Clothing, blankets, carpets, shoes, etc…

However, if they turn away, (know that) your only duty is to convey the message clearly. [82] They recognize Allah's favors; yet, then they deny them (by denying the One Who provided them). So, most of them are thankless. [83]

The Witnesses Testify

One day We're going to raise a witness from every community. Then there won't be any more excuses accepted from those who covered (the light of faith within their hearts), nor will they be allowed to make up (for their sins). [84] When the wrongdoers see the punishment (right there before them), it won't be lessened, nor will they receive any break (from it). [85]

When those who associated partners with Allah actually see their partners, they're going to say, "*Our Lord! These are our (idols) whom we used to call upon besides You.*" However, (the idols) will throw their statement back at them, saying, "*You're all liars!*" [86]

On that day they're going to validate their utter dependence on Allah, and all their inventions will leave them to languish. [87] Those who rejected (Allah) and who hindered (people) from the path of Allah will have punishment upon punishment, for they used to cause trouble. [88]

One day We're going to raise a witness out of every community drawn from among their own, and We'll bring you out as a witness against these (people of Mecca). [370] We've sent down to you the Book that explains everything. It's a guide, a mercy and a source of good news for those who've submitted (to Allah). [89]

Fulfill Your Agreement with Allah

Background on verse 90: The Prophet invited a passing acquaintance named Uthman ibn Madh'un into his courtyard one day. As the two men were sitting and conversing, the Prophet suddenly gazed up into the sky and fell silent for some time. Then he looked at the ground and shook his head as if to remember something, and then he looked up into the sky once more. After some time passed, Uthman asked him what he was doing and noted that he had never seen him act that way before. The Prophet replied that the angel Gabriel had come

---

[370] These would be the prophets, messengers, oracles and religious leaders whom Allah appointed to call their communities towards faith. They're going to witness against their people that they were, in fact, warned of Allah's punishment, but they chose to ignore the warnings,

to him while they were sitting. Uthman asked the Prophet what Gabriel had told him, and the Prophet recited this verse. Uthman later remarked that on account of this experience, his faith was made rock solid and his love for the Prophet was settled in his heart for good. (*Ma'ariful Qur'an*)

Allah commands that justice be done, that good be implemented and that relatives be treated with generosity. He forbids all shameful acts, as well as criminal behavior and rebellion. [371] This is how He's instructing you so you can be warned. [372] [90]

Fulfill the agreement of Allah after you've agreed to it, and don't break your oaths after you've sworn upon them. [373] You've made Allah your guarantee, and Allah knows everything that you do. [91]

Don't be like a woman who pulls apart the yarn she's just spun, even after it became strong, nor use your oaths to deceive each other, just so that one group can have an advantage over the others (through making temporary alliances). Allah will test you in this, and on the Day of Assembly He's going to clear up for you the matters about which you argued. [92]

---

[371] After the Umayyad dynasty came to power upon the death of 'Ali ibn Abi Talib in 661, early Umayyad caliphs used to order that 'Ali's name be cursed after Friday prayers. (Mu'awiyah, the first Umayyad caliph, had struggled for power with 'Ali and essentially won the contest making the caliphate hereditary in the process.) This was a gross and unnecessary policy, as 'Ali was the Prophet's cousin and son-in-law and was well known as a sincere believer. (There are also prophetic traditions that forbid the cursing of companions.) When the pious Umayyad caliph, 'Umar ibn 'Abdul-'Aziz (d. 720), was chosen to head the government, he immediately ordered the cursing of 'Ali to be abolished. In its place, he ordered that the first part of this verse of the Qur'an be read instead after Friday sermons. "*Allah commands that justice be done, that good be implemented and that relatives be treated with generosity.*" From that time until today, it is a commonly recited part of the concluding supplication in sermons all over the Muslim world.

[372] 'Abdullah ibn Mas'ud once said that this one verse is the most comprehensive one in the entire Qur'an. (*Ibn Kathir*)

[373] It was common for the Arabs to ally with one another, through swearing an oath of loyalty, for the gain of a temporary advantage. If they thought they would be more powerful by canceling their current alliance and allying with another group, they would. Thus, they made their oaths a joke. This verse forbids this misuse of oaths in making alliances. In fact, the Prophet eventually forbade the making of oaths for any other purpose than personal goals. He said, "There is no oath-making (for political alliances) in Islam, and any oaths made in the days of ignorance are only reinforced in Islam." (*Ahmad*) In other words, making personal pacts between non-governmental groups is forbidden, unless they were made before Islam's coming, in which case they must be honestly observed. Personal vows and formal political treaties between governments are, of course, exempted from this ban.

If Allah had wanted, He could've made you all into one unified community, but He leaves astray whomever He wants, and He guides whomever He wants, though you will all be questioned about what you've done. [93]

So don't use your oaths to deceive each other, for the foot that was firmly planted might begin to slip, causing you to suffer the evil (consequences) of having hindered others from the path of Allah. You would then have a severe punishment befall you. [94]

Don't sell the agreement of Allah for a miserable price, for there's (a reward) with Allah that's far better for you if you only knew. [374] [95] Whatever (material goods) you have will vanish, but whatever lies with Allah will last forever. We're going to compensate those who patiently persevered by rewarding them according to the best of their deeds. [375] [96]

Whoever does what's morally right, whether male or female, and has faith, We're going to give him a new life that's a life of purity. We're going to reward them according to the best of their deeds. [376] [97]

---

[374] This is against those who would betray their principles for some bribe. The classical scholar, Ibn 'Atiyyah, defined an illegal bribe as: doing something for a fee that a person was supposed to do for his religion's sake for free, or not doing something for a fee that he was supposed to do for his religion's sake. (*Ma'ariful Qur'an*)

[375] The Prophet said, "He will have achieved success, the one who submits (to Allah), and who is then given enough resources, and who is content with Allah for what He has given him." (*Muslim, Ahmad*)

[376] In Allah's sight, men and women are absolutely equal in status. There is no difference in the way Allah responds to the supplications or services offered by either, as affirmed by all traditional and modern scholars. (See Qur'an 9:75 and 40:40.) The religious duties of each are nearly identical, as well. The differences are generally in minor details that are appropriate to the individual requirements of each gender. For example, a woman is asked to cover her hair in public, while a man is required to spend his money on the family, etc... Going beyond such things as prayer, pilgrimage and fasting, which have nearly identical stipulations for both males and females, as well, women have equal rights to participate in collective communal action, such as in attending prayer services in the mosque, doing missionary work, voting for political leaders and, when necessary, in participating in the defense of the homeland. As for voting, the Prophet took the pledge of allegiance (*baya'*) from many women, including Nusaybah bint Ka'b, Umm Muni' Asma' bint 'Amr, etc... (*Ibn Hisham al-Mu'afiri*) After the conquest of Mecca, the Prophet took a public pledge of loyalty from the crowds of men near Mount Safa, and then later on the same day, he asked the women of the city to be gathered, and he took their public pledge of allegiance, as well. Even Hind, the wife of Abu Sufyan participated, though she felt remorseful and embarrassed at how much of an enemy to Islam she had been.

Whenever you read the Qur'an, ask for Allah's protection against Satan, the outcast. [377] [98] He has no authority over those who believe and who place their trust in their Lord. [99] He only has authority over those who take him as their patron and who make partners (with Allah). [100]

When We substitute one verse for another, and Allah knows what He's gradually revealing, they (object) by saying, "*You're just a lying fraud.*" Certainly not! Yet, most of them don't understand. [378] [101]

(*Ma'ariful Qur'an*) As for participating in the military, the Prophet accepted the efforts of Umm Amarah Nusaybah bint Ka'b, who was instrumental in helping to save his life when the Battle of Uhud took an unexpected turn for the worse. He even praised her greatly and extolled her bravery for sustaining twelve wounds while still bearing arms. (It is not preferred, however, for women to engage in combat duty, and the Prophet once remarked that the best type of struggle for women is in making the pilgrimage.) During the rule of Abu Bakr, when Nusaybah petitioned to join the army again, Abu Bakr agreed, commenting that he knew of her fighting prowess. (*Futuhati-Islamia*) The Prophet also predicted to one woman, Umm Haram bint Mulham, that she would one day fight in a naval battle, and in later years, she followed her husband, Ubadah ibn as-Samit, on board an early Muslim naval expedition and fought the Byzantines at sea. (*Ibn Hajar al-Asqalani*) Thus, although by custom men are supposed to make up the bulk of the military, there is no prohibition in Islam against women being a part of the force, with the caveat that combat is not preferable for them. In the Prophet's own practice, women were a vital part of the war effort as medical personnel, logistics specialists, as well as fighters in emergency situations. (They even get an equal share in any booty collected per a report in Abu Dawud about participating women who received a share after the subjugation of Khaybar.) In Islam, then, we see that men and women are considered equals in all respects, save for some minor details related to gender requirements. Many Muslim cultures have not realized this ideal, however, and have, over the centuries, regressed into typical pre-Islamic patriarchal patterns of chauvinistic social order. Today, Islamic feminists and scholars of both genders are challenging unIslamic cultural values that have taken away women's legitimate rights, even as some extremists have, unfortunately, confused such reforms with undermining Islam. Too many traditionally-minded people equate the cultures they have grown up in with Islam, when in many cases, such cultural practices are the antithesis of Islam. (For example, many Muslims in India reverse the recipient of dowry at marriage and force the parents of the bride to pay the family of the groom!)

377 This verse requires that before a person begins reading the Qur'an, he or she should say, "I seek the protection of Allah from Satan, the Outcast." This is to help clear the mind and emphasize the purity of the exercise that the person is about to undertake. Reading Allah's scripture is serious business, and even the possibility of foolish thoughts entering the mind must be done away with.

378 The Qur'an was a growing body of verses all throughout the Prophet's mission. Occasionally, the Prophet would be given new verses that would supersede the rulings of

Tell them, *"The Holy Spirit* [379] *is bringing the revelation from your Lord in all truth, in order to strengthen (the faith) of the believers, and as a source of guidance and good news to those who've submitted themselves (to Allah)."*
[102]

---

previously revealed ones, (as the times and circumstances of his movement changed). This only happened a handful of times during the twenty-three year history of revelation. In most cases, the superseded verses remained part of the preserved text and the first generation of Muslims knew which verses were the most up-to-date rulings from Allah. Only in a few reported instances were some older verses ordered by the Prophet to be removed from the official canon. He would explain that Allah had ordered such verses to be *forgotten, lifted* or *dropped*. (*at-Tabari, as-Suyuti, Abu Ubayd*, etc…) The technical terms are *unsiya, rufi'a* and *usqita*, respectively. As an example, Anas bin Malik claimed to have known about a verse that was revealed after some Muslims had perished in a skirmish, but then that verse was later dropped. That report is found with *at-Tabari*. In another instance, 'Umar recalled that there was an early dropped verse that talked about proper manners while respecting parents, which had addressed a peculiar Arab shortcoming. When the minor issue was corrected in the culture, it was no longer an issue of importance. While early Muslims were aware of this revelatory process and took it as a natural part of the evolution of Allah's scripture in the first Islamic community (*Bayhaqi*), nevertheless the Prophet's pagan critics would seize upon this issue with the charge that Muhammad himself was the author of the message, and not Allah, given that in a few instances a new revelation would abrogate (or eliminate) an old one. This is the issue that this passage is referencing. However, such a charge is without standing when, for example, you consider all of the gradual changes that Islam was making in Arabian culture. Should every minor revelation correcting every bad pagan habit remain in the final canon, when Allah has the power to keep the Qur'an in its most current and relevant form until the end of the Prophet's mission? Given that only a handful of verses met this fate, is the issue even that relevant? Furthermore, such was the nature of the Prophet's ministry: fluid change and evolution in the complexity of Islam and its scripture as circumstances evolved. Asking the Arabs to change their culture in an instant and then constantly reminding them of each and every small change in an ever-growing compendium would have been counter-productive (not to mention the fact that the length of the Qur'an might have been much longer and its relevance and majesty diluted. Are there no Biblical verses that abrogate each other? Is there no evidence of Biblical verses being dropped, especially when different ancient manuscripts are compared? Don't we know so little about the actual process of the recording and editing of the laws and teachings of Moses? Don't Christians claim that Jesus' teachings trump the laws of Moses? Aren't there writings of Paul that abrogate other verses in the Bible? Didn't Paul make up some laws on his own?) Evolutionary change in the revelation - stretched out over many years - made the process of Quranic growth and regrowth seem relatively unobtrusive and organic. By the time Islam was a firmly-rooted tradition at the end of the Prophet's mission, its holy book was complete, finalized by prophetic edict and ready to take on the ideologies of the wider world and beyond. Muslims believe that Allah designed it to be so, and Muslims have never had a problem with this knowledge.

[379] i.e., Angel Gabriel.

No One is Teaching Muhammad Anything

Background on verses 103-105: There were several young foreign slaves in Mecca who were originally from Persian or Byzantine-controlled lands. Two of these young slaves, named Jabr and Yasar, worked as blacksmiths, and it is said that they knew some passages from the Bible and used to say them. The Prophet sometimes stopped at the young men's workshop to talk to them, perhaps hoping to have an affinity with others who believed in one God, but this made the tongues of the Meccans begin to wag. Since they couldn't find any other plausible explanation for the Prophet's constant revelations, they began to insinuate that these teenage slaves were teaching Muhammad about religion and that somehow those boys were the source of Islam! When one of those boys was asked if he were teaching Muhammad, the boy replied, "No, Muhammad is teaching me!" This passage was revealed in response. (*Zamakhshari*)

We know that they're saying, *"It's a man who's teaching him,"* but the tongue of the (foreign slave) to whom they're pointing is not fluent (in Arabic), [380] while this (Qur'an) is in the purest and most precise Arabic. [381] [103] Those who don't believe in Allah's (revealed) verses will not be guided by Allah, and they're going to have a painful punishment. [104] It's those who don't believe in Allah's verses who are frauds, and they're all liars! [105]

---

[380] Lit., that person has crooked or unclear knowledge of Arabic. (*Zamakhshari*)

[381] Could any random person, such as the two slave boys (or any other foreign slave) being referenced here, be the source for the thousands of verses of the Qur'an? The Qur'an itself points out that the young man/men in question only spoke broken, rudimentary Arabic, whereas the Qur'an was in flawless Arabic prose and diction. On account of the baseless allegations of the pagans, however, the Prophet stopped visiting those young men in order to silence his critics. (Meanwhile, the revelations kept on coming to the tune of thousands of more verses.) There is also another interesting point to ponder. The foreign slaves such as Jabr, Yasar, Ya'ish, Qays and Addas, who are so often suggested as 'the source' of Muhammad's teachings, were all cultural Christians (and most probably not of the fiery evangelist kind, which did not exist yet). Even further, the Qur'an does not reflect any form of Christian doctrines or theology, such as it was in Byzantine Orthodox lands. (Even the person of Jesus is given less coverage than Moses, and there is no mention of Paul, the trinity, cryptic signs of the apocalypse, the four Gospels, atonement, Joseph, carpentry, Roman and Greek cities, Pontius Pilate, etc...) If Muhammad were somehow making the rounds among busy, illiterate young slaves to get source material for "his" scripture, then it would have certainly reflected the beliefs of the purported religion of those slaves. (In addition, when the Prophet was later in Medina, surrounded by eager - and often nosy - followers for ten years, who was supposedly teaching him then?) Such an idea is preposterous! Sadly, even to this day critics of Islam keep searching for 'the human source' of Muhammad's revelation. Many of these critics react in horror when asked if Jesus or Moses had any human 'sources' or 'influences!' (And we know so precious little historically about both men!) Why not let Allah be the source of them all?

Faith Renounced Under Duress is Still Valid

Background on verses 106-109: When Meccan persecution against the Muslims mutated into murder, some Muslims felt compelled to recant their faith to save their lives, even though they secretly held onto faith. The worst incident was when the pagans seized a man named Ammar, along with his father Yasir and his mother Sumayah and some others, and took them to a field to be tortured. They tied Sumayah and Yasir to the ground and speared them to death.

They then roughed up Ammar and threatened to kill him, like his parents, if he didn't renounce his faith. Ammar did so weeping and out of fear and then later went to the Prophet in mortal fear of displeasing Allah. The Prophet accepted that Ammar never really gave up Islam, and he counseled the young man to tell the pagans the exact same thing that he said before if they ever threatened him again. This passage was revealed in response, giving hope to those whose fear of pain would make them say anything to avoid it. (*Asbab ul-Nuzul*)

Whoever rejects Allah after having accepted faith in Him - unless he's been forced to (renounce it) while his heart remains committed - and who has opened his heart to rejection, Allah's wrath is upon (all such people). They're going to have a severe punishment, [106] and that's because they love the life of this world more than the next life. Allah will never guide people who reject (Him by choice). [107]

They're the ones who've had their hearts, ears and eyes sealed up by Allah, and they're unconcerned (about it). [382] [108] Truly, they're going to be losers in the next life. [109]

However, your Lord – for those who migrated (from their homes) after having been persecuted and who then struggled and persevered – after all of this, your Lord is forgiving and merciful. [383] [110]

One day every soul will come forward to plead for itself. Every soul will then be repaid for what it has done, and none of them will be treated unfairly. [111]

---

[382] See 2:6-7.

[383] This verse, which again references the flight of the Muslim refugees to Abyssinia, also seems to foreshadow the coming exodus of Muslims from Mecca to Medina.

The Example of a Prophet to His People

Allah lays out the example of a society enjoying peace and security, even as it was amply supplied with resources from every quarter. Yet, it was thankless towards Allah's favors.

Therefore, Allah caused it to experience both hunger and panic. (It encircled them) like a cloak (wrapped around them), all on account of (the evil in which its people) used to indulge. [384] [112] Then a messenger came to them, who arose from among themselves, but they denied him. And so, the punishment seized them even as they were still busy in their corruption. [113]

Some Dietary Restrictions

Eat from the resources that Allah has provided for you that are lawful and pure, and be thankful for Allah's favor, if it's Him you really serve. [385] [114] He's only forbidden you (to eat) dead carcasses, blood, pork, and anything that's had a name other than Allah's name invoked over it.

---

[384] This is an interesting verse on account of all the various interpretations the commentators have offered, and it is an excellent example of the diversity of opinion about the meaning of unclear or obscure references that arose in the classical age of commentary. Some say it refers to Mecca, and thus to the famine of which 44:10-12 speaks, while others say it is a general reference to any society or town that rejects its Prophet, while a third opinion is that it is about the return of the Prophet *after* the conquest of Mecca. One of the keys to understanding verses of this type is to try and pin down the historical context and chronology of the passage in question, coupled with the internal textual references. Since this passage speaks of famine *before* a messenger was sent to the people, it cannot be a reference to the famine that the Qur'an foretold in chapter 44. It also cannot refer to the return of the Prophet during the conquest of Mecca given that these verses were revealed before that event. Thus, if Mecca is really being referenced here, then the famine would have to have been something the Meccans experienced *before* Prophet Muhammad began his message. Thus, this reference is a reminder to them of how Allah controls their ultimate fate, no matter how well off they are at any given time.
[385] The Prophet said, "Allah will be pleased with His servant if, when he eats or drinks something, he praises Allah for it." (*Muslim, Ahmad, Tirmidhi, Nisa'i*) The standard after meal supplication is, "Praise be to Allah, the One Who has fed us, given us drink, and made us Muslims." The Prophet also told his followers to begin their meals by saying, "In the Name of Allah." A longer pre-meal supplication is, "O Allah, bless us in what You've provided for us, and protect us from the punishment of the Fire."

However, if someone is forced by necessity (to eat of these forbidden things in order to avoid starvation) and does so only reluctantly, without indulging in it more than necessary, then Allah is forgiving and merciful. [115]

(All you people!) Make no statements in support of the lies that your tongues may promote, arbitrarily declaring, *"This is lawful, while that's forbidden,"* in order to somehow attribute fraudulent lies to Allah. Those who invent fraudulent claims and assign them to Allah will never succeed. [116] There's only a slight profit (to be made in promoting such lies), but then they'll have a painful punishment. [117]

We prohibited for the followers of Judaism what We already told you about before, and We were never unfair to them. [386] Rather, they were unjust against their own selves. [118] However, your Lord - to those who do wrong in ignorance and who then thereafter repent and reform (themselves) - after all of that, your Lord is indeed forgiving and merciful. [119]

Follow the Path of Abraham

Abraham was a model of devotion to Allah, for he was a natural monotheist, [387] and he never made partners (with Allah). [120] He was thankful for Allah's favors, for He chose him and guided him to a straight way. [121] We gave him good in this world, and in the next life he's going to be among the righteous. [122] Then We inspired you, (Muhammad,) with the message that you should follow the creed of Abraham, the natural monotheist, and he never made partners (with Allah). [123]

---

[386] See 6:146. Also compare with Deuteronomy 32:4.

[387] The Arabic term *hanif* means someone who follows the natural and pure religion of monotheism. It was a term used by Syrian Christians for the Arabs who were neither Jews nor Christians, but who followed a primitive form of Abrahamic religion easily distinguishable from idolatry. (*Hanephe* in their language.) Before Islam there were a few people in Arabia who shunned idol-worship in favor of a simple belief in one God that was purported to have survived in one form or another from the time of Abraham. Abraham is described in the Qur'an as being a *hanif*.

Wisdom in Dialogue

Background on verses 124-125: Although this is a Meccan chapter, these last verses [124-128] were revealed in Medina and were tacked on at the end of this chapter by the Prophet's order. These few verses in particular make mention of one of the many issues that were coming out in the growing interfaith dialogue between the Muslims and the Jews.

From the context of verses 118-125 we can deduce that the Arab converts in Medina had probably asked if there was a Sabbath for them as there was for the Jews (or perhaps the Jews had suggested to them that they should have one). This passage points out that in Abraham's original religion there was no Sabbath and that the Jews were given harsh dietary requirements and difficult Sabbath regulations on account of their disobedience to Moses. Verse 16:125 advises the Muslims to talk rationally and politely when these kinds of issues are raised.

The (restrictions) of the Sabbath were only imposed upon (the Jews) who argued (about Allah's commands), but Allah will judge between them in what they've been arguing about. [124]

Invite (others) to the way of your Lord with wisdom and beautiful preaching, and reason with them in ways that are best. [388] *Your Lord knows best who is straying from His path and who is being guided (towards it).* [125]

Take the High Road

Background on verses 126-128: This passage is sometimes understood to be a continuation of verses 118-125, in that an interfaith issue involving the status of the Sabbath came up in Medina, and an argument might have ensued, save for the patience of the Muslim side. Under that line of reasoning, this passage is telling the Prophet to keep on preaching and to be high-minded about it, even if the listeners, who in this case would be Jews, have some objections to his views on the subject. Then verse 126 would say that if the preacher could score a point, as it were, in the interfaith debate, that he shouldn't go overboard in pressing his advantage, for it would only put the listener on the defensive.

---

[388] The Prophet was a preacher in the main; yet, his speeches were known to be short with few digressions. He did not give lectures everyday, so as not to tire people out, and in dialogue he was known to be respectful and high-minded. He even tried to avoid purposefully embarrassing individuals by not pointing out to them directly when he saw them doing wrong. Instead, he would say the general phrase, "What's going on that people should be acting like this?" (*Ma'ariful Qur'an*) He once said, "Make things easy (for people) and not difficult. Give glad tidings, and don't alienate (other people)." (*Bukhari*) Thus, the Prophet embodied the best principles for a missionary of the faith. 'Abdullah ibn Mubarak (d. 797) once said, "The beginning of knowledge is the intention, then listening, then understanding, then action, then preservation, and then spreading it." After these steps have been achieved, then an Islamic missionary will be said to be a master at his craft.

When you score a point of logic, be patient and resist the urge to pounce too eagerly on the weakness in your opponent, that is if you want to make him feel respected and welcomed enough so you can perhaps one day open his heart to faith and not just tear him down.

Other commentators say this passage is not connected with the preceding verses [118-125] at all and that it was revealed after the Battle of Uhud, when the Muslims, who had narrowly escaped destruction, returned to the battlefield the next day to find that the pagans had mutilated the dead Muslim fighters. When the Prophet saw the body of his beloved uncle Hamza badly cut up, he became very distraught and called for revenge upon the pagans many times beyond what they did to Hamza.

This verse, then, would be telling the Prophet not to go beyond the limits of what was done to him. After he recited it, the Prophet said, "We will be patient. We will not take revenge out on anyone." Then the Prophet made up for his thoughtless oath as outlined in 5:89. (*Ma'ariful Qur'an*) Given the change of tone in verses 126-128, the second view seems more likely, i.e., that this passage is referring to self-restraint in the face of atrocity, and Allah knows best.

If you can bring consequences against them, don't bring any consequences against them that are worse than what you've suffered. However, if you persevere patiently instead (and suppress the urge to retaliate), then that's the best for those who are patient. [126]

Therefore, be patient, for your patience is due to none other than Allah. Don't feel sorry for them, and don't be worried on account of their scheming. [127] Allah is with those who are mindful (of Him), and He's with those who (promote) what's good. [128]

The Night Journey

17 Al Isrā'

aka Bani Isrā'il

Late Meccan Period

This chapter was revealed mainly in the year 621, with a few portions being revealed earlier. This was about one year before the migration to Medina, and the unmistakable tone of closure presented in this chapter clearly shows that the Muslims were expecting that they would soon abandon Mecca for a safer place. Already Islam was growing in the northern city of Yathrib, due to the efforts of some very dedicated new converts there, and the Muslims in Mecca were restive as they chafed under Meccan persecution. Some Muslim converts had already been murdered by the pagans, and the tension was apparent and palpable.

With regards to the Night Journey and Ascension, the Prophet's cousin, Hind bint Abi Talib (aka Umm Hani), said, "The Messenger of Allah spent the night in my house. He said his night prayers and went to sleep. Just before dawn, he woke us up, and we all prayed the dawn prayer together. When the prayer was finished, he said, 'Umm Hani. I prayed with you the night prayer in this place, then I went to (Jerusalem) and prayed there, and as you can see, I've just finished praying the dawn prayer here with you.' I said, 'Messenger of Allah, don't tell people about this for they'll ridicule you and hurt you.' He replied, 'By Allah, I'm going to tell them.'" *(At-Tabari)*

Then the Prophet went out of her family home and told people the following account: "While I was in Mecca, the roof of the house was opened, and Gabriel descended. He opened my chest and washed it with Zamzam water. Then he brought a golden tray full of wisdom and faith, and having poured its contents into my chest, he closed it. Then a creature that was all white was brought, which was smaller than a mule but bigger than a donkey. The creature's stride was so wide that it reached the farthest point of its eyesight in just one step. I was carried on it."

The Prophet then explained that he was taken to Jerusalem on that mount, which flew at a dazzling rate of speed, and that he was deposited on the Temple Mount. There the spirits of the prophets of old materialized behind him, and he led them in prayer. Then the Prophet continued his account, saying: "Gabriel then took my hand and ascended with me to the nearest heaven." The Prophet was then taken into the otherworldly dimension of the *Akhirah*, or Hereafter.

As he passed further through its levels, he saw various prophets from ancient days, including Adam, Abraham, Moses and Jesus. Each of them welcomed him with warm greetings as he went by them. When he was taken into the seventh and highest layer of Paradise, he saw innumerable wondrous sights, including the delights of Paradise and the coming and going of multitudes of angels. The Prophet continued his story, saying, "Then (Gabriel) took me until we reached the *Sidrat-il-Muntaha* (the Lote Tree of the Furthest Boundary), which was shrouded in colors I can hardly describe." (See Qur'an 53:1-18] "Then I was (brought close) to the *House of Ma'moor* (in which 70,000 angels visit everyday), and three containers were offered to me. One had wine, the other milk and the third honey. I took the milk. Gabriel said, 'This is the Islamic way of life, which you and your followers are following.'"

Next, Gabriel brought Muhammad closer to the highest boundary of Paradise, beyond which the full manifestation of Allah's power exists. The Prophet described that he couldn't even comprehend the wonders of creation that he was witnessing. In later years when someone asked the Prophet what he saw at that point and if he, in fact, saw Allah, he said, "Only blinding light, how could I then see Him?" (*Ahmad*) It was during this part of the journey that Muhammad received the direct command from Allah that his followers were to offer prayers *fifty* times in a day.

When the Prophet was being taken back down through the seventh layer of Paradise, Moses stopped him and convinced him to go back to Allah and ask for a reduction. Moses pointed out that he had had a hard enough time with the Children of Israel and that fifty prayers upon his followers would be too much. The Prophet did accordingly, and Moses convinced him to ask for further reductions. Eventually the prayers were reduced to five times a day, and the Prophet told Moses he was too shy to ask for any further reductions after that. Muhammad was then brought back down to the Temple Mount in Jerusalem, and from there the mysterious steed carried him back to Mecca, where he was finally deposited back in his bed.

Predictably, when the Prophet told his story, the Meccans ridiculed him fiercely. A few converts to Islam actually renounced their faith, thinking that the Prophet was saying something totally preposterous. *How could a man go to Jerusalem and back in one night?* Some people went to Abu Bakr and told him what had happened, and they asked him if he believed it was true.

He replied, "By Allah! If Muhammad, himself, has said it, then it's true. He tells us that the word of Allah comes to him directly from Heaven to Earth at any hour of the night or day, and we believe him. Isn't this a greater miracle than what we're questioning here today." Then Abu Bakr led a crowd to the Prophet, and they all listened to his story directly. When the Prophet finished describing Jerusalem, a city to which he had never been, and recounted what he had seen of its streets and buildings, those who were present, and who had been to Jerusalem before, agreed that it was an accurate description of the city.

Abu Bakr, who had himself visited Jerusalem many times, declared, "You spoke the truth, Messenger of Allah." Then the Prophet announced that on his way back to Mecca from Jerusalem, he saw a caravan on the road leading towards Mecca. He said that he had called to the leaders of that caravan to point out to them where one of their animals had wandered off in the desert and that he drank from a water jar on the back of one of those camels. He also predicted when that caravan would return (at sunrise on such-and-such day) and that a gray camel would be in the front of the line.

On the appointed day, a caravan did enter Mecca at sunrise, led by a gray camel, and when the leaders of that caravan were questioned, they described how they were led by a stranger's voice to their lost animal in the desert. It was also found that one of their camels was carrying a water jar on its back that had a broken seal. Due to his affirming the truth of the Prophet's story, Abu Bakr earned the nickname, *As-Sadeeq*, which means the one who affirms the truth. Verses 1-3, like most in this surah, are from the Meccan Period, while a few of the verses are Medinan.

In the Name of Allah,
the Compassionate, the Merciful

Background on verse 1: The Prophet was taken from his bed one evening on a fantastic journey so that Allah could show him what the next realm actually was like. The first part of his journey (the *Isra'*, or Night Journey) was when the angel Gabriel came to him at night and took him on a winged steed called the *Buraq* all the way to Jerusalem at a very fast rate of speed. The second part of his journey consisted of rising from the Temple Mount up to Heaven to see what the next life was like and to have his faith strengthened. (This is called the *Mir'aj*, or Ascension to Heaven.)

Glory be to the One Who took His servant on a journey by night from the sacred place of prostration (in Mecca) to the faraway place of prostration (in Jerusalem) [389] - *to an area that We've specially blessed -*

---

[389] Translators of this verse usually render the two place names as *the closest mosque* and *the farthest mosque*, and this sometimes gives rise to unnecessary charges of historical inaccuracy. It is true that there was no *mosque* in Jerusalem at that time, but for that matter there was no *mosque* in Mecca, either, if you understand the word mosque to mean a typical Islamic house of worship. When you look at the meaning of the Arabic word used here, however, you find that the word *masjid*, often rendered as *mosque*, literally means *a place to prostrate in worship*. While there was no mosque in Jerusalem, there was a *masjid*, namely the ruins of the so-called Second Temple, which was *a place of prostration for worship*, and Jerusalem has always been associated with the worship of God. The Ka'bah was also not a mosque in the modern sense of the word, but it was *a place of prostration*, as well. So Muhammad's journey was from the "sacred place of prostration" in Mecca to the "faraway place of prostration" in Jerusalem. The first actual "mosque" in Islam wasn't built until the year 622 in the town of Quba, just south of the city of Medina (Yathrib), while the Dome of the Rock, which is often known as "*Masjid al-Aqsa*" or the faraway place of prostration, wasn't built until the year 687 by the Caliph 'Abdul Malik, who intended it to be a symbol of unity among the three Abrahamic faiths. It sits near the ruins of the Second Temple of antiquity.

so We could show him some of Our signs. [390] Indeed, He's the One Who Hears and Observes (all things). [1]

The Children of Israel Were Punished for their Sins

We gave the scripture to Moses and made it a source of guidance for the Children of Israel. [391] So don't take anyone other than Me as your keeper, [2] all you (Jews) who are descended from those whom We carried with Noah! He was a truly thankful servant! [3]

We warned the Children of Israel in (their) scripture that they would twice cause corruption in the earth and be filled with conceited arrogance, (and thus they would be punished twice). [4]

When the first warning came to pass, We sent Our servants, (the Babylonians), against you, *and they were greatly skilled in warfare.* [392]

---

[390] The Prophet said, "On the night when I was taken on the Night Journey, I awoke back in Mecca the next morning filled with anxiety, for I knew that my people wouldn't believe me." He sat outside pensively, and then his biggest critic, his indirect paternal relative Abu Jahl, came by and asked him with a sneer, "Is there anything new?" The Prophet then told of his Night Journey and Ascension to Heaven, and Abu Jahl excitedly called for a crowd to come and hear Muhammad speak, hoping it would prove once and for all that his nephew was crazy. The crowd became astonished at his tale, and they began to laugh. Then some of the people asked him to describe Jerusalem, for Muhammad had never been there before. He described it accurately, causing some to say, "By Allah, he got the description right." (*Ahmad*) In accepted Catholic tradition, a woman named Mary of Jesus of Agreda (d. 1665) also claimed to be mystically transported to a far distant place, the deserts of New Mexico to be exact, where she preached to Jumano Indians. This doctrine in the Catholic Church is called "bilocation." Among Mormons, Prophet Jesus also was said to have been transported to the New World to preach the message of God after he was taken up to heaven from the Middle East. Other famous Christian Saints who are also said to have experienced bilocation are: Anthony of Padua, Ambrose of Milan, Severus of Ravenna, Padre Pio of Italy and Alphonsus Maria d'Ligouri. Tantric Buddhism also accepts this doctrine of bilocation and instantaneous mystical travel. The Qur'an does not assert that Muhammad was in two locations at once however, but that he was taken from one place to another and then returned through mystical means. Many scholars hold that it was his spirit that was taken, and not his physical body.

[391] The Prophet said, "Convey these teachings to people, even if it's only one verse. Discuss with others the stories of the Children of Israel, for it's not wrong to do so. Whoever tells a lie concerning me intentionally, then let him take his seat in the Fire." (*Bukhari*)

[392] The Jewish prophets are recorded in the Old Testament issuing scathing words of warning to their people for their constant backsliding into idolatry and corruption. (See II Kings 22:16-17) Isaiah, particularly, warned of the coming judgments of Allah against his people. See Isaiah 3:16-26, 5:20-30 and 8:3-4, for example. The first 'overwhelming

They rampaged through every part of your homes, and thus it was a warning fulfilled! [5]

Then We allowed you to return (to the land of Israel, after your captivity in Babylon), as a kind of (victory for you) over them. We also added to your wealth and sons and allowed your population to increase. [6]

If you were any good at all, you were good for the benefit of your own souls, and if you were evil, it was to the detriment of your own souls.

Then later, when the second warning came to pass, (after you had become disobedient once more), your faces were framed in disgrace as (the Romans) entered into your temple of prayer, even as (the Babylonians) had done so (long before), and they destroyed whatever they laid their hands on. [393] [7]

Your Lord will show you mercy (yet again, by allowing you to recover and rebuild), but if you return (to sinful ways), then We'll return (with a third penalty). [394] We established Hellfire as a prison for those who cover (the light of faith within their hearts). [8]

---

punishment' was the invasion of the Babylonians (586 BCE), who wiped what remained of Israel off the map and forced many of the Jews into exile in Babylon. The Biblical book of Lamentations is a sorrowful reflection on their plight. (The Assyrians had already attacked and subsumed northern Israel in 721 BCE but had not completely destroyed the independence of the rest of the Jews of the south in Judea.) After the Babylonians were defeated by a new rising empire, the new Persian king, Cyrus the Great, allowed the Jews to return home in about 520 BCE. The Jews then tried to resurrect Judaism and owe the most to the efforts of their great scholar Ezra, who tried to recreate all the knowledge that was lost. Also see Leviticus 26:14-39, which contains dire threats from Allah against the Jews if they disobey Him further.

[393] The second major catastrophe that befell the Jews came after they rejected Jesus as God's messenger. (See the book entitled *Jesus in the Talmud* by Peter Schafer for a more thorough discussion of this issue.) Even though Jewish nationalists rose in revolt against their Roman overlords in the first century CE, the important point was not the mere gaining of independence – they had rejected God's chosen messenger! So the second cataclysmic event was the resultant destruction of Jerusalem by the Romans in the year 70 CE and the forced dispersal of the Jews throughout the Roman world, i.e., the *Diaspora*.

[394] The warning is clear. After two great calamities caused by their sinfulness and forgetfulness of their Creator, the Jews may expect a third terrible punishment like the predations of the Babylonians and the Romans to befall them. This is also, of course, a wider message to all civilizations, not just those who experience foreign invasions, exile,

The Reality of History

Background on verses 9-11: Some commentators believe this passage is referring to the taunting of an-Nadr ibn al-Harith, when he dared Allah to send down destruction upon him and his fellow pagans. (*Ma'ariful Qur'an*)

This Qur'an certainly guides (people) towards stability (in their lives and societies) and gives good news to the believers who do what's morally right that they shall have a great reward. [395] [9]

Those who don't believe in the next life (should know) that We've prepared a painful punishment for them. [10] A person (inadvertently) cries out for evil when his cry should be for good, but people are impatient by nature. [396] [11]

We made the night and the day as two (of Our) signs. We darkened the sign of the night, even as We illuminated the sign of the day, so you can go out and look for the bounty of your Lord, and also so you can keep track of and count the passage of years. And this is how We explain everything in detail. [12]

We All Have to Make Choices

Background on verses 13-14: The pagan Arabs used to try and predict the future by looking at which way the birds flew (similar to what the ancient Romans did). This passage is making a play on that by saying that a person's fortune is with them and their own deeds, rather than being determined by something external to them like bird patterns. (*Asbab ul-Nuzul*)

---

genocide or worse, that if they become sinful and wicked – harming their fellows, indulging in moral depravity and forgetting God's good way of life – then God may allow someone else to gain power over them and destroy their civilization, lest their own wickedness grow out of control and engulf the earth in chaos.

[395] Imam ash-Shafi'i' (d. 820) said, "All people are dead, except for those who have knowledge. All people with knowledge are asleep, except for those who do good. Those who do good are deceived, except for the sincere. Those who are sincere are always in a state of anxiety."

[396] Indeed, people are quick to arrogance when they're angry or overconfident. Yet, they should be more patient and good. People who don't believe in Allah dare His prophets to bring on Allah's punishment, when they should rather submit to His good will and live righteously, but we are, as a species, often given to impatience. (Also see 70:19-22.)

We've tied the bird (of his fortune) around the neck of every human being, and on the Day of Assembly We're going to bring out a record that he'll see laid out in the open. [13] *"Read your record! Today your own soul is enough to account against you!"* [14]

Whoever finds guidance is guided for the benefit of his own soul, while whoever goes astray does so to the detriment of his own soul. No bearer of burdens can bear the burden of another. We never brought Our punishment down upon any nation unless We raised for them a messenger (to warn them first). [15]

When We decide that a nation is to be destroyed, We send Our command to those who are lost in the pursuit of pleasure, (telling them that they must reform or else face the consequences), so the sentence can be proven true against them (that they deserve their punishment). *Then We destroy them completely!* [397] [16] How many generations have We destroyed after Noah? It's a fact that your Lord is well-informed and observant of the sins of His servants. [17]

Whoever desires the temporary things (of this world) will have them in whatever quantity We wish to give, but afterwards We're going to give them Hellfire so they can burn within it in humiliation and disgrace. [18] Whoever desires the next life, *who makes an effort to achieve it as is required,* and who has faith, their efforts will be appreciated (by Allah). [398] [19]

Both (the believers and the faithless) have Our bounty showered down upon them, for the bounties of your Lord are not withheld. [20] Have you noticed how We've given more to some than to others?

---

[397] The Prophet narrated that on the Day of Judgment four types of people will come forward and rightfully claim that they truly had no way to hear Allah's message. They are the deaf, the insane, the senile old person and a person who lived at a time when there was no active revelation coming in among his people. Allah will accept their pledge of obedience, but they will still have to go into Hell, though the Fire will be forbidden to harm them. They will live in coolness (until Allah sends them into Paradise). (*Ahmad*) Children who die below the age of puberty also automatically go to Heaven, regardless of the religion in which their parents raised them.

[398] Jesus is quoted as expressing a similar sentiment in John 12:25: "He that loveth his life shall lose it; and he that hateth his life in this world shall keep it unto eternal life." (KJV)

However, the next life is where the higher status and greater bounty awaits. [21]

Your Lord Commands Kindness to Parents

Don't set up other gods alongside of Allah, or you'll end up humiliated and forsaken. [399] [22] Your Lord has decided that you must serve no one else but Him and that you should be kind to your parents. Whether one or both of them becomes old in your lifetime, never speak to them disrespectfully nor scold them, but rather speak to them in generous terms. [400] [23]

Kindly lower the wing of humility towards them and say, *"My Lord! Be merciful to them even as they cherished me when I was small."* [401] [24] Your Lord knows what's in your heart, so if you behave in a moral fashion, then He's forgiving to those who repent (of their sins). [402] [25]

Sharing the Wealth

Give what's rightly due to your relatives, the needy and (stranded) travelers. Don't waste your money like a squanderer. [26]

---

[399] 'Abdullah ibn 'Abbas held that verses 17:22-39 are a basic summation of the entire heart of the Torah. (*Ma'ariful Qur'an*)

[400] The classical writer, Sa'di Shirazi (d. 1291), once wrote: "In the folly of youth, I one day shouted at my mother, who then sat down with a grieved heart in a corner and said, while weeping, 'Have you so forgotten your infancy that you've now become so harsh towards me?' How sweetly said the old woman to her son, whom she saw could overpower a tiger and had become as strong as an elephant: 'If you had remembered the time of your infancy - how helpless you were in my arms - you wouldn't this day have been so harsh, for you're now a man who is as strong as a lion, but only because I'm an old woman now.'" (*Ghulistan*)

[401] The Prophet said, "Treat the elderly with respect, for being respectful to the elderly is honoring Allah. Whoever does not treat them with respect is not one of us." (*Mishkat*)

[402] The Qur'an places great emphasis on respecting one's parents. The Prophet said that Paradise lies under the feet of mothers. This is a way of saying that the mother is the first person to instill good values in the child. He also said, "A father is the main gate to Paradise. Now it's up to you to use it or waste it." (*Ahmad, Tirmidhi, Ibn Majah*) This implies that a father teaches a child other important aspects of faith and sets the tone in the family. Even if one's parents are not Muslims, one still has to accord them respect.

Squanderers are like the brothers of devils, and Satan was ungrateful to his Lord. [403] [27]

> **Background on verse 28:** Some people asked the Prophet for a share in some cloth that had been donated, but he had none left to give. This verse was revealed to tell the Prophet what to do in their case. (*Ma'ariful Qur'an*)

If you (don't have any money to give to the poor) and are forced to turn away from them, though in the expectant hope that some mercy might come to you from your Lord (that you can later share with them), at the very least say something to put them at ease. [404] [28]

> **Background on verses 29-30:** There is a story told that a poor boy went to the Prophet and asked for a shirt and that the Prophet gave his only good shirt to him, leaving him with nothing to wear. As such, he remained in his home without a shirt until someone gave one to him. This passage was then revealed. (*Ma'ariful Qur'an, Asbab ul-Nuzul*)

Don't tie your hand to your neck (like a miser), nor extend it out so far (in donating) that you become guilty (of causing your own) poverty. [405] [29] Your Lord provides abundant resources to whomever He wants, and He measures (out slimmer resources to whomever He

---

[403] People who waste their money foolishly are compared to Satan's example, for he was given so many blessings; yet, he wasted them on his foolish belief that he knew more than Allah.

[404] The Prophet once said, "To smile in your brother's company is charity. To command good deeds and to prevent others from doing wrong is charity. To guide a person who is in a place where he might go astray is charity. To remove dangers from the road like thorns or sharp objects is charity. To pour water from your jug into your brother's jug is charity. To guide a person on his way who has defective eyesight is charity." (*Bukhari*)

[405] In this verse, the basic principle is that no one should bring about his own poverty by giving away everything in charity. There are quite a few traditions in which people went to the Prophet and asked if they should give all their wealth away in charity, and he always told them to keep some of it back for their family. Only Abu Bakr ever gave all he had in the Islamic cause, but he was a special case, a man blessed of Allah (and alluded to be such in the Qur'an,) and he quickly made his fortune back through trade and business, only to continue spending it in the cause of Allah! The Prophet once said, "The example of the miser and the one who freely gives is that of two people who are both wearing armored shirts from their chests to their necks. When the giver gives in charity, the armor grows in size until it covers his whole body (like a protective shield), and it hides his fingertips and erases his tracks (i.e., forgives sins). Yet, when the miser wants to spend in charity, it sticks closer to him, and every ring (of the chain mail) gets stuck in place. When he tries to loosen it, it doesn't get any wider." (*Bukhari, Muslim*)

wants, as well). Indeed, He is well-informed and watchful (over the needs) of His servants. [406] [30]

Seven Pillars of Righteousness

Don't kill your children because you're afraid of becoming poor. We'll provide resources for them, as well as for you. Indeed, killing them is an enormous crime. [407] [31]

Don't go anywhere near any unlawful sexual activity [408] for it's a shameful practice [409] and opens the way (to even greater sins and dangers.) [410] [32]

---

[406] There is an interesting saying of the Prophet in which he says that Allah keeps some people in poverty out of His mercy, because if those people became rich, they would become arrogant and sinful.

[407] Beyond the infanticide that is referenced here, some Muslim legal traditions (*Maliki, Ja'fari*) also cite this verse in justifying a total ban on abortion, save only for preserving the life of the mother. In a narration, the Prophet explained that a fetus is given a soul at 120 days, and based on this report, other schools of law in the Islamic tradition allow abortion (for a valid reason) until that time limit is reached. (These would be the *Hanafi, Shafi'i* and *Hanbali* schools.) Regardless, after 120 days of gestation all schools of thought forbid abortion save for preserving the life of the mother.

[408] Unlawful sexual activity (*zina*) consists of adultery and fornication. When a person breaches the barrier of what is proper, he becomes open to depravity, and an avalanche of sins beset him or her, leading to his or her own ruin.

[409] This verse labels adultery and fornication (*zina*) generically as *faahisha*, or shameful behavior. Elsewhere, however, the Qur'an separates the particulars of each sin and gives differing penalties to each. See 24:2 for the penalty for adultery and fornication (*zina*) and 4:15 for the penalty for shameful behavior (*faahisha*), which is thought by some to be the Qur'an's way of referring to homosexuality and lesbianism (as suggested by verse 7:80).

[410] Such wisdom, if only people would think! Rampant promiscuity, lies, unfaithfulness, substance abuse, perversions and the like lead to broken homes and broken, cynical people. The 'termination' of 'mistakes,' sexually transmitted diseases, crimes of passion, the cycle of financial dependency due to poor personal choices, the use of drugs and alcohol to forget the sorrows brought upon by all the lies, cheating, heartache and abuse, the lewdness and the constant fear of betrayal – all of these are from the Pandora's Box of crossing beyond Allah's boundaries. (The Prophet said, "When your sense of shyness departs, you'll do any (bad) thing.") Islam says 'away' with all of that: stay away from all intoxicants, don't act recklessly, live faithfully to your spouse, abstain from intimacy before marriage, and live by an ethical code of manners and high character. This is the wholesome way of life; as such, Islam considers the family as the barometer of the health of the entire society. Most people don't realize that their own seemingly individual actions have repercussions in the lives of those around them. That's why Islam is *so* strict about sexual ethics in order to prevent the cascade effect that inevitably follows a loosening of personal and social morality. Modern secular society is a good enough example of how a 'sexual revolution' can lead to utter chaos in the personal and family

Don't take the life of anyone (whose life) Allah has forbidden (to be taken), except for a just cause (under the law). If anyone is killed wrongfully, then We've given their heir the power (to either demand punishment, take monetary restitution or forgive). However, don't let them go beyond the limits (in their legal right) to take a life, (as they might bring harm to the innocent), for they're already being supported (by the law and should be satisfied with their options). [411] [33]

Don't (tamper with) an orphan's property before they reach the age of full strength (at maturity), unless you plan to improve it. Fulfill every agreement, for every agreement (that you make) will be asked about (on the Day of Judgment). [412] [34]

Give full measure (to your customers) when you measure (for them), and weigh with an accurate scale, for that's best for achieving a good result. [35]

Don't get involved with things about which you know nothing, for every act of hearing, seeing or (feeling in) the heart will be asked about (on the Day of Judgment). [413] [36]

Don't strut through the earth acting like you're so great, for (you're not strong enough) to rip the earth apart, nor can you grow as tall as the mountains. [37]

---

lives of hundreds of millions. A functioning Islamic society (that is modeled after the Prophet's society in Medina), while not always perfect (for as we know people *are* fallible), would at least not be under constant assault from all the voluminous ills that threaten the stability of many modern societies today.

[411] In other words, if the family of a murder victim demands that the killer be executed, they have to confine their retribution to the killer only and not demand others to be killed, also. (In pre-Islamic Arabia, those seeking revenge against an individual would often ply their wrath against the person's relatives, as well.) According to this verse, only the one who did the evil deed can be brought to justice – not the rest of his family or friends – and if anyone goes beyond the legal limit in seeking retribution, he must be stopped, for the law has already given the family of the murder victim its just rights.

[412] If you took on the responsibility of looking after an orphan and any property he or she may have inherited, then be true to your trust and agreement, and return the property to the orphan when he or she comes of age.

[413] This is a catch-all injunction advising us to mind our own business and avoid getting involved in the affairs of other people when we have no knowledge of what's going on.

All sinful practices like those are despicable in the sight of your Lord. [38] These are among the (pillars of) wisdom that your Lord has revealed to you, so don't take any other god alongside of Allah, or you just might find yourself being cast into Hellfire in disgrace - with (only yourself) to blame! [39]

Pagans don't Understand the Use of Reason

Background on verse 40: The pagans believed that the angels were the female daughters of Allah, while they (the pagans) valued sons for themselves above daughters. Thus, by attributing to Allah what they didn't want for themselves, they were making Allah seem shortchanged.

Has your Lord chosen to give you sons, while taking daughters for Himself among the angels? You're making an outrageous assertion! [40] And so it is that We've explained (the issues in) various (ways) in this Qur'an, so they can be reminded, but it only seems to make them distance themselves from it even more! [41]

Say (to them), *"If there were (other, lesser) gods (existing) alongside of Him,"* - as they claim – *"then they would surely (be working hard to do those things) that would bring them closer to the Lord of the throne, (in their efforts to win His favor.)"* [414] [42] Glory be to Him! He's high above all the things that they're saying (about Him) – infinitely higher! [43]

The seven heavens, the very earth and all who (live) within them glorify Him! There isn't anything that exists that doesn't glorify His

---

[414] This verse has been interpreted in two different ways. The basic premise is that for the pagans of Arabia, their idols were subordinate gods that people could pray to for favors and such, while the supreme God *Allah* was remote and disinterested in human affairs. So these demigods were, like in Greek mythology, the link between human beings and the Great Originator, (which for the Greeks was Chaos). The first opinion about the meaning of this verse is that it is posing the simple question: "If there were mini-gods, then wouldn't they try to unseat the top god and steal his throne, such as Zeus and the gods of Olympus did in unseating the Titans?" The second opinion, which has much more merit, is that this verse is saying that if there were mini-gods, wouldn't they themselves be trying to outdo each other to please the top god, just like human beings should be doing? The subtext is simply this: if your gods are subordinate and seeking to please God, then shouldn't you do so likewise?

praise, even if you don't understand how they glorify Him. [415] He is indeed forbearing and forgiving. [416] [44]

What do the Faithless Seek in the Qur'an?

When you recite the Qur'an, (Muhammad), We put an invisible screen between you and those who don't believe in the next life. [417] [45] We put wrappings over their hearts to prevent them from understanding the Qur'an and also a deafness in their ears. When you're remembering your one Lord in the Qur'an, they just turn their backs in disgust. [46]

Background on verses 47-48: The Prophet would often recite the Qur'an aloud in his house at night. Even though the Meccan leadership officially

---

[415] How do the animals, the mountains or the stars praise Allah? Is it in the way they submit to their instinct or their natural or biological underpinnings? Is there something deeper, perhaps at the molecular level, that displays Allah's glory? We don't know, but as Allah says, it doesn't matter if we don't know, because He knows. Once the Prophet came upon some people who were sitting on their mounts while conversing with each other. He said to them, "Ride them safely and then leave them safely, but don't use them as chairs for you to hold conversations in the streets and marketplaces, for the one who is being ridden upon may be better than the one doing the riding, and it may remember Allah more than he does." (Ahmad) The Prophet also forbade the killing of frogs (Nisa'i), and some early Muslims thought it was due to their croaking being equated with a kind of praise of Allah, but this assumption has not been corroborated by any surviving traditions.

[416] There are countless verses of the Qur'an that mention some type of sin or shortcoming into which a person can fall. The amazing thing is that nearly all of them end with some type of refrain or reminder that even after all their bad behavior, Allah is still forbearing (patient with us), forgiving, merciful, kind, compassionate, etc... The way Allah portrays Himself in the Qur'an, which some people foolishly believe is as a harsh and angry God, is actually the most loving Being of all. We do every foolish and sinful thing, but He constantly reminds us that His forgiveness and mercy are always waiting. The Prophet said that Allah, Himself, said, "O son of Adam, even if you came to me with an earth full of sins, and you met me not holding any other as My equal, then I would meet you with forgiveness equal to that." (Hadith Qudsi)

[417] Because the wicked chose to be wicked and then magnified their hatred of Allah, Allah makes no effort to guide them and will only move towards them if they, themselves, have an inner glimmer of faith or budding curiosity in one of Allah's signs. In that case, as the tradition of the Prophet says, "Allah will come to them running." Until that time occurs, Allah will put up barriers to their understanding of the Qur'an as a punishment so they don't bring their corruption in the circles of the believers. By itself, the Qur'an is an interesting book, and if a person who doesn't believe in it, yet who is still attracted to its charm, frequents the company of the believers only to instill doubts and create mischief, then that would make the attractive power of the Qur'an counterproductive. In addition, some very wicked people only listen to the Qur'an to find things to criticize. See the introduction to chapter 111 where this verse is practically applied.

disavowed and scorned him, still the verses themselves were often mesmerizing, giving rise to their charges that he was a sorcerer who bewitched men with his verses. One night three prominent idolaters snuck near the windows of the Prophet's house, but each came alone and wasn't aware of the others. These three men, Abu Jahl, Abu Sufyan and Al-Akhnas ibn Shurayq, stayed listening until the dawn. They noticed each other when they were leaving, and when they each admitted to stealthily listening to the Qur'an, they swore they wouldn't do it again, lest the young men of the tribe start to do the same. The next night, however, each of the three returned, thinking that he alone would not keep his word.

When they noticed each other again, they took to swearing and vowing to keep their word this time, but the same incident occurred the next night, as well. In the morning Al-Akhnas went to Abu Sufyan and asked his opinion about what Muhammad was saying. Abu Sufyan replied, "By Allah, I heard some things I recognized and knew what they were about, but I heard other things whose meaning and import I didn't know." Al-Akhnas nodded his agreement and left.

Later on, he went to Abu Jahl and asked his opinion, and Abu Jahl answered, "We've always been in competition with the Bani 'Abd Manaf, (the Prophet's sub-clan). We fed (the poor) when they did, and we gave away (in charity) as they did. So when we were running neck and neck with them like in a horserace, they said, 'There's a Prophet among us to whom revelation comes from Heaven.' So how can we compete with that? By Allah we will never believe in him nor accept what he says." Then Al-Akhnas left. (*Ibn Hisham*) This passage is a reference to this kind of behavior on the part of the Meccans. They would also look for snippets of the Qur'an that could be willfully misinterpreted or ridiculed publicly to make Islam seem like something it was not.

We know what they're really listening for when they listen to you, (for they merely wish to find something to criticize) so they can talk about it in their private conversations, saying, *"You (Muslims) are following nothing more than a man who's been bewitched!"* [47] Do you see what kind of an example they're making of you! However, they're the ones who've gone astray, and they'll never find a way (out of their mistaken beliefs). [48]

The Faithless Object to the Resurrection

"What!" they exclaim. *"When we've rotted away to dust and bones, are we really going to be made like new?"* [49] Say (to them), *"(Yes, indeed), even if you were made of stone or iron, [50] or some other created material that's even harder than (the hearts) in your chests!"* Then they ask, *"So who's going to bring us back (to life)?"*

Tell them, *"The One Who created (you) the first time!"* However, they just bob [418] their heads towards you (condescendingly) and say, *"So when will all this come to pass?"*

Then say (to them), *"The time might be close at hand, [51] and it will be a day when He calls you, and you'll (be forced to) answer with His praise, even as you'll think you only stayed (in the world) for a little while."* [419] [52]

Beware of Your Constant Enemy

Background on verse 53: It is said that this verse was revealed after some of the Prophet's companions asked him how they should respond to the insults of the pagans. (*Asbab ul-Nuzul*)

Tell My servants that they should only speak of good things, for Satan tries to make divisions among them. [420] Satan is the obvious enemy of humanity! [53] Your Lord knows you best. If He wants to be merciful to you, then He'll do so, and if He wants to punish you, then He'll do so. We haven't sent you to be their warden. [421] [54]

Your Lord knows (all about every creature) that (exists) within the heavens and the earth. We gave some prophets more gifts than others, even as We gave the Psalms to David. [422] [55]

---

[418] The Arabic word used here to describe how they shake their heads condescendingly is the same word used to describe the bobbing of a young ostrich's head when it walks. (*Ibn Kathir*)

[419] On the Day of Judgment no one will have any choice but to acknowledge their Lord, even if they spent their whole life rejecting Him or being unconcerned with spiritual truths.

[420] Words. Mere words. How dangerous a weapon they are! How prone to misuse. If we fear the control panel that will launch weapons of mass destruction, how much more should we fear the tongue that would put such evil in motion. The Prophet touched his tongue one day and told his followers that it is the tongue (and what it says) that will send a person to Paradise or Hellfire. How many strong groups have there been that have been broken and disunited from within, based on the mere wagging of idle tongues? Satan rejoices when we gossip, backbite and boast, for this is how he disunites us and destroys us. (Also see 7:17) The Prophet was so concerned with good decorum among each other that he forbade people from pointing weapons at each other, even for fun! (*Bukhari, Muslim*)

[421] In other words, it's not the Prophet's job to be some type of sheriff or law enforcer in his society. He just has to explain Allah's rules, and then it's up to the people to implement them or not.

[422] Every prophet had different circumstances with which to deal, and some got greater miracles (*lit.* Allah's favors) and such than others. Some prophets, like David, received

There is no Escaping the True Conclusion

Say (to them), "(Go ahead and) call upon all those whom you pretend (to be gods) besides Him! They have no power to solve your troubles, nor can they ward them off." [56]

Those upon whom they're calling (for favors) are themselves trying to find their own way to their Lord, even if they're already close (to Him)! [423] They ardently desire to receive His mercy, even as they're in mortal fear of His punishment, *for your Lord's punishment is truly something to think about!* [57]

There's not a single settlement that will escape Our annihilation, or at the very least (have a taste of) a strong punishment, [424] before the Day of Assembly (arrives), and that (statement has been) recorded in the Book (of Decrees). [425] [58]

We never withhold sending miracles for any other reason than the fact that ancient peoples (so frequently) called them lies. We sent a (special) camel [426] to the (people of) Thamud for them to see, but they treated her badly. And so it is that We only send miracles (in order to make people) afraid (of the coming punishment). [427] [59]

---

beautiful words of praise and thanks as their revelations (see I Chronicles 16:7-36 for an example of one of David's psalms). Others didn't get any scriptural material at all but rather received only commandments, prophecies or the mission to preach only general things without any legal specifics.

[423] Many commentators say this verse is referencing not only the pagan idols, but the personages of Jesus, Mary, Ezra and other famous, saintly people whom later followers took to be gods or god-like in their own right. This verse is pointing out that even all of the people who have been elevated to the status of gods or who are deemed god-like are, themselves, merely striving to get close to God.

[424] Even the city of Nineveh eventually fell to ruin after a series of disasters, though it was spared for a time due to the efforts of the Prophet Jonah. No city lasts forever, and they usually fall due to some sort of calamity, whether manmade or natural.

[425] This is Allah's rule book, which He wrote Himself and in which is every rule and principle by which the universe will be governed. He began this ledger, even before the creation, by inscribing it with the rule: My mercy will prevail over My wrath. (*Bukhari*) See 6:12.

[426] See 7:73 and the footnote for the miracle of the camel.

[427] Foolish people believe that miracles are for their entertainment, much like a magician would do magic tricks to amaze and astound us. However, this verse, which is the most precise comment on the purpose of miracles in the Qur'an, tells us that they are

(Remember) when We told you, *"Your Lord surrounds people (in His power)!"* We didn't send the vision (of the next life) down upon you for any other purpose than to be a test for people. (The mention of) the cursed tree (of Zaqqum) in the Qur'an (was for the same purpose), as well. [428] We (only use such symbols) to instill fear in them (so that they'll perhaps be inclined to listen), but it only adds to their immense suppression (of faith). [60]

Satan's Challenge to Allah

When We told the angels, *"Bow down (in respect) to Adam,"* they all bowed down. Iblis, however, (who was a jinn in their company, did not bow along with them).

"How can I bow down to a creature that You made from mud?" he asked. [61] *"Look at that!"* he continued. *"This (human) is the one whom You're honoring over me! If You give me a chance until the Day of Assembly, I'll make his descendants blindly obedient (to me), all but (maybe) a few!"* [62]

"Go away," (Allah) replied, *"and if any of them follow you, then Hellfire will be enough of a reward for you all! [63] Mesmerize any of them that you can with your (alluring) voice (of temptation). Assail them with your*

---

something of a last warning from Allah to people. In effect, a miracle is saying that if Allah can cause this amazing thing to happen, watch out! You're about to feel the full force of His might!

[428] Supernatural things like the Prophet's journey to Jerusalem and Paradise, and then back again in one night, and the mention of things like a cursed tree in Hell make doubtful people even more doubtful. This is what happens even though by all rights they should be afraid, especially given all the other proofs and logic of Islam. Indeed, they must realize that they just might really have to face some very dire consequences one day if they continue to reject the One Who created them. Verses 37:62 and 44:43 also mention the cursed tree of which the residents of Hellfire will partake, and those verses predate the revelation of this chapter. When Abu Jahl first heard of the tree of *Zaqqum*, he ordered dates and butter to be brought to him, and he ate them, saying, "Let us have some more *zaqqum*, for we don't know of any other *zaqqum* than this." (*Ibn Kathir*) He thus increased in his suppression of faith, as this verse notes. Also see 37:62.

cavalry and with your infantry. [429] *Share in their wealth and children,* [430] *and make promises to them - even though the promises of Satan are nothing more than deception.* [64] *As for My servants, however, you will have no power over them. Your Lord is quite enough to take care (of them)."* [65]

Your only Safety Lies with Allah

Your Lord is the One Who makes ships sail smoothly through the sea so you can seek of His bounty (through fishing or trade), for He is merciful to you. [66] When a calamity seizes you at sea, however, all those (false gods) that you call upon besides Him leave you to languish! Though when (Allah) returns you safely to land once more, you turn away (from Him), for human beings are thankless! [67]

Do you feel so safe then that He won't make a part of the earth swallow you up when you're back on (dry) land? (Do you feel so safe) that He won't send a windstorm against you that'll leave you helpless to take care of yourself? [68]

Do you feel so safe that He won't send you back out to sea (on a subsequent voyage) and then send a heavy gale against you to drown you on account of your ingratitude? Even still, you won't have anyone to avenge yourself against Us! [69]

(So be grateful), for We've been generous to the sons of Adam by providing them with transportation on both land and sea, by giving them resources that are wholesome and by granting them favors more advantageous than most of the rest of creation ever received. [70]

---

[429] Satan's followers among the jinn are known as the *shayateen*, or the devils (lit. the *separators*). Human beings also become the obedient slaves of Satan, and they ever try to drag their fellows down into corruption; thus, they're 'devils' themselves.

[430] Satan will tempt people to mix corruption with wealth through gambling, theft, living extravagantly, sinful trade and miserliness. He will tempt people to take too much pride in their children, spoiling them, or he may use their children to bring about anxiety and fear within them, or he may make them adulterous and thus have broken families, or he may tempt them to harm their children through infanticide of female offspring (in their desire for sons). (*At-Tabari*).

The Record will be Complete

One day, We're going to call out the leaders of every people. Those who receive their records in their right hand will read their records, and they won't be wronged in the least. [71] However, those who were blind (to the truth) in this world will be blind (to it) in the next life, [431] for they had veered off the path. [72]

> **Background on verses 73-77:** This passage was revealed in response to some pagans who asked the Prophet to give them special treatment in exchange for their conversion. One report says that it refers to the leaders of Mecca who told the Prophet they would be more inclined to follow him if he drove away his poor underclass followers. (*Ma'ariful Qur'an*) Another report says that members from the tribe of Thaqif visited the Prophet and offered conversion if he would exempt them from charity and prayer, exempt them from having to cancel the interest owed to them, even as they could continue to charge interest, and that their sacred trees would be protected and inviolate. According to this report, the Prophet was in the midst of having his secretary write this contract for the tribe, when this verse was revealed telling him not to cave in to their demands. (*Zamakhshari*) Yet, a third incident attributed to this revelation is that the Quraysh asked Muhammad to alter a verse of the Qur'an to their liking. In desperation he almost agreed with them, but this passage told him to stand firm and warned him to be on his guard against the subtle suggestions of those who would have him compromise. (*Zamakhshari*)

Their plan was to tempt you away from what We were revealing to you and to get you to substitute in Our name (principles) that were quite different. (If you had done so), then (those evil people) would've become your closest friends! [73]

If We hadn't given you strength, then you probably would've inclined a little towards (their requests). [74] In that case, We would've made you suffer equal amounts (of punishment), both in this life and after death, and you wouldn't have had anyone to help you against Us! [75]

Their (ultimate) plan was to try and frighten you into fleeing from (your) hometown, so they could keep you away in exile. If they (had succeeded in driving you away), then they would've remained (safe in their homes) only a little while longer after you (left, before We

---

[431] The 'blindness' on the Day of Judgment, as explained by the commentators, means they will be unable to acquire or obtain any faith or forgiveness at that time, for they will *see* no way to do it. It doesn't mean they will lose the ability to see with their eyes. This interpretation is confirmed by relevant prophetic traditions. (*Ma'ariful Qur'an*)

destroyed them). [432] [76] This has been our mode of operation with the messengers We sent before you, and you will never find any change in how We operate. [77]

Strengthen Yourselves for What Lies Ahead

Establish prayers after the sun begins to decline (at noon) until the onset of nightfall, and recite (the Qur'an) at dawn, for reciting (the Qur'an) at dawn is witnessed (by the angels). [433] [78]

Pray in the late hours of the night, as well, as an extra bonus for you (above and beyond what's required), [434] for your Lord will shortly raise you to a highly regarded position. [435] [79]

Now utter (this supplication, and then prepare yourself to migrate to Medina), *"My Lord! Let my entrance be an honest entrance, let my exit be an honest exit, and bestow upon me power from You to help me."* [80] And also declare (this phrase in order to strengthen your resolve for the coming migration), *"The truth has arrived, and falsehood will vanish, for falsehood always vanishes!"* [436] [81]

---

[432] One of the alternative plans of the Meccans was to capture the Prophet in the street, tie him up, deposit him in a faraway land, and then prevent him from returning for fear of his life.

[433] According to a saying of the Prophet, the angels work in two shifts, and they change their shifts at *fajr* time, or the prayer just before dawn, and at *'asr* time or the late afternoon prayer. Thus, if we are praying, they will tell Allah we were praying when they came upon us and praying when they left us. (*Bukhari, Muslim*) What a wonderful report to be given to our Lord!

[434] This bonus prayer is known as *tahajjud* prayer. It is not obligatory, but it is highly praised in Allah's sight. After people go to bed and sleep for most of the night, they get up to pray a two-unit prayer an hour or two before the first light of dawn appears. They can pray additional times as they wish. The Prophet made it his habit to pray the *tahajjud* prayer, and in time many other people began to join him. Later on in Medina, he skipped doing it in the mosque one night, and this confused some people who had always looked forward to joining him. When they asked him about it the next morning, the Prophet explained that he skipped doing it in the mosque one night, because he was afraid it would be made an obligatory prayer on the community, (given how its practice was rising in popularity). He also counseled people to make *tahajjud* a regular habit or not to do it at all, rather than doing it only haphazardly with no regularity. A person who goes to bed with the intention of praying *tahajjud* later, but then sleeps through it inadvertently, still gets the reward of having done it. (*Nisa'i, Ibn Majah*)

[435] This is thought to be the Prophet's exalted status on the Day of Judgment when he will be given the right to intercede on behalf of people to save them from Hellfire.

[436] This verse is something of a "throwing down the gauntlet" phrase to let the pagans know that the next phase of the Prophet's mission, that of fighting back, is coming near

We're sending down in this Qur'an that which is a source of healing and mercy for the believers, even as it causes nothing but loss to the wrongdoers. [437] [82]

Each will Act according to His Nature

Whenever We bestow Our favors upon a human being, they turn away and become aloof, but when calamity strikes them, they descend into deep despair. [438] [83]   Say (to them), *"Everyone acts according to their own disposition, but your Lord knows best who is being guided on the way."* [84]

What is the Nature of the Human Spirit?

Background on verse 85: 'Abdullah ibn Mas'ud (d. 653) reported the following incident that caused the revelation of this verse: "While I was strolling with the Prophet through a desolate patch, he stopped to rest on a palm leaf stalk. Some Jews passed by, and one of them said to the others, 'Ask him about the spirit.' Another one said, 'Why do you want to ask him about that?' A third man among them said, 'Don't ask him, or you might get an answer you won't like.' Finally they agreed on: 'Let's all ask him.' Then they asked the Prophet, but he didn't answer, and then I knew he was receiving revelation, so I stayed where I was. Then the new revelation was received, and the Prophet recited (this verse)." (*Bukhari*)

Now they're asking you about the spirit. Tell them, *"The spirit is under the command of my Lord, and no knowledge of it has ever come to you except for a little."* [439] [85]

---

to hand. Ironically, eight years after this verse was revealed, in the year 630 when the Prophet returned triumphantly to Mecca at the head of ten thousand followers, he recited this very ending phrase from this verse as he began toppling the 360 idols that were in and around the Ka'bah.

[437] Most commentators say that this passage [80-82] was the actual command for the Prophet that informed him that he would have to exit from Mecca and enter into Yathrib (later to be called Medina). It counseled him to remember that he was migrating for pure motives to assuage any latent fears or misgivings. The predictions here proved true. The Prophet returned any money with which he was entrusted to their rightful owners before he left Mecca, and when he entered Medina, people lined up in throngs, welcoming him, singing songs and begging for the honor of housing him.

[438] Isn't this verse a true commentary on worldly-oriented people!

[439] The "spirit" is thought to be Angel Gabriel. Others have said it is the spirit or soul that resides within each person. The scholars differ as to whether this verse was revealed in the late Meccan or early Medinan periods.

If We ever wanted, We could take away (this message) with which We've been inspiring you, and then you wouldn't have anyone to represent you in your claim against Us. [86] However, (the extent of) your Lord's mercy and His favor towards you is indeed tremendous! [440] [87]

Say (to them), *"If the whole of humanity and all the jinns were to gather together to produce something similar to this Qur'an, they could never produce the like of it, even if they all worked together and pooled their resources."* [88] And so it is that We've explained for people in this Qur'an every type of example (so they can ponder over them). Yet, most people are unwilling to accept it and are thankless. [89]

Answering a Flurry of Objections

Background on verses 90-93: This passage recounts a relentless assault from the pagans, who said all of these things to the Prophet in a huge outdoor gathering that they arranged. (The entire incident is recounted in *at-Tabari.*) After they asked for many miracles to benefit their city and themselves, the Prophet told them, "I won't do any of that, and I won't ask my Lord for these things. I wasn't sent for this reason; rather, Allah sent me to you to bring you good news and warnings. If you accept what I've brought you, then it will be good fortune for you in this world and in the next, but if you reject it, then I will wait patiently for the command of Allah until Allah judges between me and you." So that's when they asked the Prophet to make the sky fall upon them. The Prophet then said, "That's for Allah to decide, and if He wants to, He will do that to you." These verses were revealed about that incident. (*Asbab ul-Nuzul*)

They say, *"We're never going to believe in you until you make a spring gush forth for us from the earth,* [90] *or until you have a garden filled with date palms and grapevines and rushing streams flowing abundantly in their midst,* [91] *or until you make the sky shatter and fall down upon us, as you pretend will happen, or until you bring Allah and the angels here in front of us,* [92] *or until you have a house decorated with gold, or until you have a ladder that can reach right up into the sky! Even then, we won't believe you ever climbed up there, unless you send a book down to us that we can read (for ourselves)."*

---

[440] The Author of the Qur'an is reminding Muhammad that He can take the Qur'an away from him, if He so chose, as a way to emphasize that He has power over *all* things – especially the foolish people who are opposing His Own Prophet.

Say (to them), *"Glory be to my Lord! Am I not a messenger who's just a mortal man?"* [441] [93]

Nothing prevented the people (of former nations) from believing when guidance came to them, except for their saying, *"Has Allah really sent a mortal man as a messenger?"* [94]

Say (to them), *"If the earth were populated by angels, going about their business quietly, then We would've certainly sent an angel down from the sky to be a messenger for them."* [95] Then say, *"Allah is enough of a witness between you and me, for He's well-informed and watchful over His servants."* [96]

For the one who is guided by Allah, such a one is truly guided, but for the one whom He leaves astray – *you won't find any protector for him in place of (Allah)!* On the Day of Assembly, We're going to gather them together, flat on their faces – *blind, mute and deaf* - and then their destination will be in Hellfire. Every time (the heat of the fire) seems to wane, *We'll stoke the fire back to its full intensity!* [97]

That's the compensation that they're going to receive because they rejected Our (revealed) verses and said, *"What! When we've rotted away to dust and bones, are we really going to be made like new once more?"* [442] [98]

Don't they see that Allah, the One Who created the heavens and the earth, has the power to create them as they were (before)? It's only because He's set a specific time-limit for them - *and there's no doubt about that* - but still the wrongdoers do nothing more than thanklessly refuse (the invitation of salvation). [99]

Say (to them), *"If you had control over all the treasures that (emanate from) the mercy of my Lord, you would be unwilling to share them (with*

---

[441] The irony is that they wanted Muhammad to do so many supernatural things before they would believe in him, even though he was bringing them the Qur'an, filled as it was with so many noble teachings; yet, all the while they were believing in their idols without one shred of proof that their gods of sticks and stones were real. In the end the pagans ridiculed the Prophet, and he returned home shaken by their harsh words.

[442] This verse reconnects us with an earlier verse in this chapter [17:49] to bring the purpose of this chapter into clearer focus.

others) [443] out of the fear of spending too much, for human beings are tightfisted!" [100]

Take the Example of Moses

And so it was that We gave nine evident miracles to Moses when he came (before Pharaoh and his nobles) [444] – just ask the Children of Israel! Pharaoh said to him, *"Moses! I think you've been bewitched!"* [101]

"You know full well," (Moses) replied, *"that these (miracles) have been sent down by none other than the Lord of the heavens and the earth, as clear evidence for all to see. I think that you, Pharaoh, are doomed to perish!"* [102]

And so, (Pharaoh) resolved to wipe (the Hebrews) off the face of the earth, but We drowned him and all those who were with him, [103] and We said to the Children of Israel, *"Dwell upon the earth, but when the final promise comes to pass, We're going to gather you in a mixed crowd (on the Day of Judgment)."* [104]

The Qur'an is the Truth

We sent (the Qur'an) down for a true purpose, and it has, indeed, been sent down for that true purpose. We didn't send it to you for any other reason than to give good news and also to warn. [105]

We divided this Qur'an (into sections) so you could recite it to people in intervals, and (that's why) We've been revealing it in successive stages. [445] [106]

---

[443] The subtext is that Allah is so generous; yet, people who deny Allah, thinking they are better than He, would behave disgracefully if they ever had absolute power in the universe. The old adage is that those who wish to be king for a day will find that they would be wholly unfit for the office!

[444] See 7:133 and footnote for the nine miracles of Moses.

[445] The Qur'an is designed for easy reading. The entire book is divided up into thirty divisions (each is called a *juz*) so that it can be read in a month's time. It also has seven larger divisions (each called a *manzil*) so the more ambitious can read it in a week. On a more merciful level, it has divisions (called *hizb*, quarters or groupings) that comprise groups of 20 or more lines for even easier reading. All of this is in addition to the standard division of 114 chapters. Take your pick - set reading portions are already tailor-made for you so you can read it at your own pace!

Tell (the idol-worshippers of Mecca), *"Whether you believe in it or not, the (Jews and Christians) who were given knowledge (of Allah's revelations) before you fall down on their faces humbly when they hear it being recited to them,* [107] *and they say, 'Glory be to our Lord! Our Lord's promise has been fulfilled!'* [108] *They fall down on their faces weeping,* [446] *and it increases their humble (submission)."* [447] [109]

Background on the first part of verse 110: The Prophet was prostrating and calling upon Allah, saying, "O Compassionate, O Merciful," when a pagan man happened by. The ignorant pagan said out loud, "He claims to pray to one (Allah), but he's praying to two!" Then this verse was revealed mentioning that Allah has many holy names by which He can be invoked. (*Ibn Kathir*)

Also tell them, *"Call upon Allah, or call upon the Compassionate,* [448] *for regardless of whatever name you use to invoke Him, the most beautiful names belong to Him."*

How should we Recite the Qur'an?

Background on verse 110: This verse was revealed in Mecca at a time when the pagans would ridicule the Qur'an whenever they heard it being recited. The Prophet used to recite it in a strong and clear voice, but it would often attract needless heckling from the pagans. However, if he recited it too softly, his companions and also interested pagans wouldn't be able to hear it from him and learn it, so this verse tells him to take a middle ground. After the migration to Medina, these restrictions were no longer as essential and didn't apply, though the commentators say it remains as a general principle for the believers not to shout or whisper in their prayers, but to take a middle course. (*Ibn Kathir, Bukhari*)

(Muhammad!) Don't recite (the Qur'an) in your prayers too loudly or too softly, but recite in an even tone in between the two

---

[446] The Prophet had made some Jewish and Christian converts by this point in his ministry, in the last stages of the Meccan period. See 61:6 and footnotes for a discussion of Jesus' promise of a future prophet after him, as contained in John 14:16 and 16:5-14.

[447] After reading this verse it is customary for the one who has faith in Allah to prostrate himself on the floor and praise Allah.

[448] In Yemen, which lies at the extreme southwest of Arabia, ancient Himyaritic inscriptions that predate Islam by centuries have been discovered that show that ancient Jews and at least some Christian and pagan Yemenis there called upon Allah by the name of *Rachman*. This term also can be found in Talmudic literature as a reference to Allah. Thus, this verse is emphasizing that Allah can be called upon by many titles, as long as those titles are befitting the majesty of Allah. It's not, then, the exact name that is so important, but the faith of the one who is calling upon his Lord. (See: *The Himyarite-Ethiopian War and the Ethiopian Occupation of South Arabia in the Acts of Gregentuius*, Vassilios Christides, 1972)

extremes. [110] **Then say, "*Praise be to Allah, Who doesn't give birth to children, nor does He have any partner in His kingdom, nor does He need anyone to protect Him from weakness, so magnify Him greatly!*"** [449] [111]

---

[449] The word *takbeer* that is used here is taken as a rallying cry by Muslims. Whenever someone shouts this word, which means, "Magnify the greatness (of Allah)!" People respond by saying "*Allahu Akbar,*" which is literally an incomplete sentence in Arabic. It means, "Allah is greater than…," and the ending is left purposefully unsaid, for the ending includes anything and everything you could imagine or suggest. Allah is greater than it all!

The Cave

18 Al Kahf
Late Meccan Period

This chapter holds a special place in the imagination of Muslims. The Prophet once said of this chapter: "Whoever recites the Chapter of the Cave on Friday, it will illuminate him with light from one Friday to the next." *(Al-Hakim)* On another occasion he said, "Whoever memorizes ten verses from the beginning of the Chapter of the Cave will be protected from the Anti-Christ." *(Ahmad)* Finally, he also once said of this chapter, "Whoever recites the first and last verses of this chapter, there will be a (spiritual) light from his feet to his head, and if he were to recite the entire chapter, for him there is light from the earth to the sky." *(Ahmad)*

This portion of revelation came during a particularly difficult time. Due to relentless Meccan persecution, a large number of Muslims had migrated to Abyssinia for safety. Meanwhile, back in Mecca, the leaders of the Quraysh sent two messengers (an-Nadr ibn al-Harith and 'Uqbah ibn Abi Mu'ayt) to Yathrib (Medina) to ask the Jews about Muhammad and to get their opinion as to whether he was a true prophet or not.

The Jews sent back a suggested list of three topics about which they could ask him. "Ask him," the rabbis said, "about the reason for why the young men left their city and sought refuge in a cave and then what happened next, for this is a unique event. Ask him about the man who traveled both to the east and the west of the earth and what happened to him. Finally, ask him about the spirit and what it was." *(at-Tabari)* Those three questions are the reason for revelation of some of the portions of this chapter. When the Meccan messengers returned, they asked the Prophet about these issues. At first Muhammad said that he would have the answer right away, but he forgot to say, "As Allah wills." To teach him a lesson - that he could not order Allah to reveal things - no new revelation came for fifteen days. The Prophet realized his mistake and repented. Then verses 18:23-24 were revealed to explain the reason for the delay, and then finally the answers came.

Be that as it may, the Meccans were unfazed by the fine answers given in this chapter. They decided to punish Muhammad and the two clans to which he was most closely related, and from which many of his followers came, by forcibly ejecting them from the city and isolating them in a barren desert valley. They wrote their decree on vellum and hung it in the Ka'bah for effect. This was known as the Boycott, and for three years the Meccans refused to trade with the exiles, sell them food or allow them to leave the valley. The Muslims suffered deprivation on an appalling scale. If it wasn't for secret food deliveries smuggled in by sympathetic Meccans in the night, the Muslims would surely have perished.

Visiting Arab chieftains from the countryside eventually shamed the Meccans into lifting their cruel policy. When the document hung within the Ka'bah, wherein was written the decree, was examined, it was found that ants had eaten away all the ink, leaving the sheet blank. It was little consolation for the Prophet, however, for in the same year the Boycott was lifted, his beloved wife and soul-mate Khadijah passed away, a death no doubt hastened by the many years of suffering in the open desert during the Boycott. The Prophet's uncle and only political protection, Abu Talib, also passed away, leaving the Prophet more vulnerable to violence than ever before. Perhaps the story of the Sleepers of the Cave contained within this chapter is a veiled note of hope for the Prophet that persecution doesn't last forever and that eventually the truth will prevail over ignorance.

In the Name of Allah,
the Compassionate, the Merciful

Praise be to Allah, the One Who sent down to His servant a Book in which He allowed no crookedness. [1] (It's a Book that's) straightforward (and clear), so He can warn (all people) of a terrible penalty from Him, and so that He can give good news to the believers who do what's morally right that they're going to have an excellent reward [2] - (a reward) that will stay with them forever. [3]

(It's also a message that's been revealed) so He can warn those who say, "*Allah has begotten a son.*" [4] They have no knowledge (that could justify their claim), nor did their forefathers (have any certain proof), either. It's such an outrageous statement that's coming from their mouths, for what they're saying is no more than a lie! 450 [5]

Perhaps you'll worry yourself to death as you follow after them, distressed that they're not believing in this narration. [6] Whatever (riches and distractions) that We've placed in the earth are but a dazzling display by which We test them, in order to bring out those whose conduct is the best. [7] (In the end), We're going to reduce whatever is upon (the earth) to dry dust. [8]

---

450 Even though this chapter was revealed in pagan Mecca and the many dialogues with Christians were still in the distant future, the Qur'an takes many pre-emptive positions. The denial of Allah giving birth to sons is one of them.

The Companions of the Cave

Background on verses 9-22: Jewish visitors from Yathrib (Medina) were trying to help the Meccan idol-worshippers expose Muhammad as a fraud by providing them with questions that they could ask him, hoping he would stumble. They told the Meccans to ask Muhammad about the Companions of the Cave, and this story contained in verses 9-22 was revealed in response.

Have you ever considered that the Companions of the Cave and the inscribed writings might be among Our wondrous signs? [451] [9]

---

[451] Who were the Companions of the Cave? Most of the classical commentators usually say this story refers to the Christian legend of the Seven Sleepers of Ephesus, and they take all the details from early Christian sources and repeat them. Basically, a group of Christian young men fled persecution from the Roman emperor Decius in approximately the year 250 CE and slept in a cave in some kind of a coma until sometime in the early fifth century, when they awoke to find their religion was now the law of the land under the converted emperor Theodosious. An inscription written in lead was placed by the cave to let people know who was in there. All of this is according to Jacob of Serugh (d. 521) who wrote about them in a poem. Other Muslim commentators offer a whole host of supernatural "sleeper" events from Spain to Iraq, and they include convoluted and very suspect narratives culled from unreliable sources. A handful of more discerning commentators suggest that this story is really about an earlier group of Jews who fled persecution under Roman rule, and this is what Ibn Kathir postulates in his commentary on verse 13. Is there a possible identification for this earlier episode? During the years 66-70 CE, a faction of puritanical Jews in Palestine rose up in revolt against the Roman occupation. It was a foolish gamble, and the Jews were all but routed. As the Romans were near achieving total victory, a group of these purists (sometimes known as Essenes and other times known as the renegade sons of the priest Zadok, who were banished by the Greek rulers of Jerusalem) fled to the desert and stowed their holy writings away in some caves at Qumran, even as they lived in them for a time. This group, which labeled itself as the 'Sons of Light' or 'Men of Holiness,' was faithful to the Torah and refused to compromise with the assimilated rabbis of the cities who allowed elements of pagan superstition to seep into their religion. This group of Jews remained apart from society for a number of years - *completely isolated* - and later left their caves and rejoined their countrymen when open persecution had ended. The writings they left behind were discovered only in 1947 and are known as the Dead Sea Scrolls. Those who favor the opinion that a group of these Jewish purists were the Companions of the Cave offer as evidence the fact that the challenge to the Prophet on this topic came from the Jews, who would seemingly have had no interest in maintaining or circulating Christian legends whose locus was hundreds of miles away in the Greek and Syriac speaking Anatolian Peninsula and Levant. In addition, the Arabic term *ar-raqeem* that is used here means 'inscribed or imprinted writings,' which could be a reference to the Dead Sea Scrolls, which were written between 200 BCE and 68 CE. At least one of them was imprinted on copper and is known as a treasure map today! (The scrolls have been called the most spectacular discovery of ancient manuscripts in history - *perhaps a wondrous sign of Allah*.) For these reasons it just may be that the story in this chapter is referring to a righteous group of Jewish young men of a puritanical sect. This view is further strengthened by this description of the Essenes (or the sons of Rabbi Zadok, who was a spiritual leader

When the young men fled (from persecution) to the cave, they said, *"Our Lord! Be merciful to us, and resolve our situation in the most appropriate way."* [10]

Then We boxed up their ears for a number of years in the cave, (so they would have no news of the outside world). [452] [11] Then, (after some time had passed), We awakened them to test which of the two sides (among them) would be better able to calculate the length of their stay. [12]

We're telling you their story truthfully, for they were young men who believed in their Lord. Therefore, We increased them in guidance. [13]

Indeed, We fortified their hearts when they had confronted (their people), saying to them, *"Our Lord is the Lord of the heavens and the earth, and we're never going to call upon any god besides Him. If we did that, then we would be saying something blasphemous. [14] These people of ours have taken other gods in place of Him, so why don't they bring some clear authority to justify what they've done? Who can be more wrong than the one who invents a lie against Allah?"* [453] [15]

---

from David's time) left by an early Church father named Hippolytus (d. 235). He wrote, "These (purists) practice a more devotional life (than the Pharisees and Sadducees), being filled with mutual love…they turn away from every act of inordinate desire…they renounce matrimony, but they take the boys of others, (to raise as their own). They lead these adoptive children into an observance of their own peculiar customs…they despise wealth, and do not turn away from sharing their goods with those that are destitute. When an individual joins the sect he must sell his possessions and present the proceeds to the community…the head of the order distributes it to all (members) according to their needs." (As quoted in Vol. V of *The Anti-Nicene Fathers*, ed. by Rev. Alexander Roberts and James Donaldson. Wm. B. Eerdmans Publishing Co., Grand Rapids, 1951.) In this Qur'anic telling of the story, it is teenage boys, seemingly unconnected to any parents, who flee as a group. They are deeply religious, an obvious sign of sustained indoctrination. They take only coins with them, a sign of the habit of their sect to distribute coins to all members. Finally, their leader freely distributes the coins to the one charged with finding food for them all.

[452] Literally it says that Allah "boxed their ears up" as in a boxer landing a blow on an opponent so he is knocked out cold. What does this colorful idiom mean? Were they lulled into a deep stasis-like condition and slept for many years, or did they live in such isolation for years that it was as good as being *dead* and *deafened* to the outside world? Were they constantly in prayer and so people who peered in their caves saw them prone on the ground all the time? The choice of meaning is yours, for either interpretation is possible, depending on how you wish to look at this episode.

[453] Further clues that these youths were not necessarily Christians struggling against Roman idolatry are contained in this speech of theirs. The context makes it seem as if

(Then they made a plan to escape the wrath of their people, saying to each other), *"After you've turned away from them and all that they serve besides Allah, then seek refuge in the cave. Your Lord will shower His mercy upon you and make your situation easy to bear."* [454] [16]

The World Transforms

(If you were looking out from) the cave's entrance, you would've seen the sun as it rose away leaning to the right. When it set, it would move away from them and then down to the left, all the while they remained there, lying in the middle of the cave. [455] These are among the signs of Allah. Whomever Allah guides is guided (to the straight path), while whomever Allah leaves astray – *you won't find any right-minded best friend for him!* [17]

You would have thought they were awake (if you saw them), but they were asleep! We turned them on their right sides and their left,

---

they were protesting against something their people were doing *recently*, and that their people were replacing their former 'good teachings' with 'new false teachings.' Roman and Greek idolatry was centuries old and was still the religion of most people in the Roman heartland in the early third century, so any youths chastising their people for abandoning their former good ways would make little sense, and also by this time the authentic teachings of Jesus were already a distant memory having been corrupted in the first and second centuries by Paul and others, not that any of those teachings were officially adopted by any communities in public. Among the Jews of Palestine, encroaching idol-worship and pagan values were a recurring danger to Jewish religious life, and one or the other periodically appeared among Jews. Thus, if the Essenes were protesting the appearance of idolatry or pagan customs in their people's religion, then the reference would tend to be more relevant. Even Jesus in the Gospels is reported to have complained about the very same issues of hypocrisy, false teachings and so on in the official practices of the religious establishment. (See John 15:1-14 for example.)

[454] The principle of migration or flight for the sake of one's religion is well established in the Qur'an. Like-minded people of faith who are powerless to confront the corruption of their people must sometimes flee to preserve themselves. On this the Prophet once remarked, "There will come a time when the best wealth any of you can have will be the sheep that he can follow to the tops of the mountains and to places where rain falls, (in his flight) from tribulation for the sake of his religion." (*Bukhari*) The Prophet also said, "Souls are like soldiers. Those that recognize one another will come together, while those that don't recognize one another will turn away from each other." (*Muslim*)

[455] The described motion of the sun means that the cave was facing in a direction in which the occupants would have rarely been disturbed by the sun's direct light. It would be interesting to look into the caves that are thought to have been the principle cave in question and see which of them is facing in the correct direction vis-à-vis the description given here.

while their dog stretched out his two forelegs at the entrance. If you would have come upon them, you would have run away in abject terror of them! [18] That's (how they were) when We awakened them, so they could ask each other (about their situation.) One of them asked, *"How long have you all been here?"*

"We've been here a day or maybe part of a day at most," (they answered, but after a long discussion), they (all agreed that they weren't sure), and so they said, *"Allah knows best how long you've been here. Let's send one of you with his money to the city to see which is the best kind of food he can bring, so you can at least satisfy (your hunger) with it. Let him be discreet, and let him not talk to anyone about (the rest of us),* [19] *because if they come upon (you), then they'll stone you or force you to return to their traditions. Then you'll never succeed."* [20]

It was (on account of his antique coins and dress) that We made people aware of their situation. (This was so) they could know that Allah's promise is true and that there can be no doubt about the Hour. [456] Later on, (after the youths grew old and died, the people) disagreed among themselves about how (best to commemorate) their case.

"Let's construct a (monumental) structure over (their graves)," (some people suggested), but their Lord knew about them (and their less than honest intentions). [457] However, those who won the decision said, *"We're going to build a house of prayer over (their graves)."* [458] [21]

---

[456] Coinage in the Roman dominated world was constantly shifting in appearance as new emperors had their names and dates stamped upon money. Even coins used by Jews in those days were often Roman ones. According to most commentators, the money that the Companions of the Cave had was apparently out-of-date, given that they had withdrawn from society for so many years. When their fellow companion, who was sent to scout out the area, went to buy food in a village market as instructed, the sellers noticed his old money, vintage clothing and probably an old-fashioned accent in his speech. They ordered the youth to take them to the cave, and he did. Thus, people became aware of their case.

[457] Perhaps those people who wanted to build a massive monument were more interested in the worldly benefits that would come from erecting what would surely become a kind of tourist trap.

[458] If the Companions of the Cave were the Seven Sleepers of Ephesus, there is a cave there today that is purported to be the cave used by those youth. Both the cave and a nearby shrine dedicated to them have been a tourist trap for centuries. If the cave in question was a hideout of the Essenes and is somewhere in Palestine, then that location would have been remembered for a time as a holy place, before being lost to the recesses

(The people who know about this story differ over the details, with some) saying that there were three (young people in the cave) and that their dog was the fourth among them. (Others) said they were five, with their dog being the sixth, but they're just guessing about what they haven't seen. (Others even assert that) they were seven, with their dog being the eighth. [459]

Say (to them), *"My Lord knows best what their exact number was, and only a few (people) know for sure (how many they were)."* [460]

So don't get drawn into arguments with them (on such speculative issues), but rather (talk to them) only on topics that have clear resolutions, and don't consult any of them at all about (such obscure topics). [22]

Don't Forget to Account for the Will of Allah

Background on verses 23-24: When the Prophet was first asked about the Companions of the Cave, he said he would have the answer the next day by the latest, but he failed to add the required addendum for future plans, "If Allah wills." Thus, as a penalty, the answer to the question was delayed for over a week. Then, along with the revelation of the Sleeper's story, verses 23-26 also came to admonish the Prophet about this. (*Asbab ul-Nuzul, Ibn Kathir*)

---

of time. In addition to the Qumran site, in nearby Jordan there is a another cave at Abu 'Alanda which locals claim is the one mentioned in this chapter. There was a shrine built over it, though it has fallen into disrepair in modern times. (In 2011, 70 metal-plate books with imprinted Judeo-Christian writings were discovered in a cave not far from there.) Only Allah knows which location is correct.

[459] While the issue of the Companions of the Cave was still being discussed publicly, visiting Christians from Najran (who would have presumably preferred the Ephesus connection) were divided amongst themselves as to how many young men went into the cave to escape persecution. Their various answers are quoted here. The verse advises the Prophet not to dwell on speculation, and that Allah alone knows the true number. This information was (wisely) not revealed, as it was unnecessary, and the argumentative people would have disputed the figure anyway.

[460] When the clumsy Meccans, egged on by the Jews, asked the Prophet to tell them about the Companions of the Cave, you can imagine how they would throw out questions in a disorganized manner. "Who were they?" "The people say they were four. Is that true?" "No, they say they were they five!" "No, were they seven?" "What about their dog, what color was it?" The Meccans didn't care about the story or its lessons. They only desired to trip the Prophet's tongue and find something, anything, to catch him up on.

Never say of anything, *"I'll do it tomorrow,"* [23] without adding, *"If Allah wills."* If you forget (to add this phrase), then remember your Lord (when you recall your lapse) and say, *"I hope that my Lord guides me closer to the rightly guided way."* [461] [24]

(Some people say that the Companions of the Cave) stayed in their cave for three hundred years, and (others) add nine (more years to that figure). [25]

Tell them, *"Allah knows better how long they stayed, for the unseen (secrets) of the heavens and the earth belong to Him. He sees them and listens (to all things). (Nothing that exists) has any protector besides Him, and He never shares His rule with anyone."* [26]

Choose Your Side

Recite what's been revealed to you of the Book of your Lord. No one can change His words (of command), [462] and you'll never find anyone who can save you besides Him. [27]

---

[461] This seemingly divergent passage is not a random insertion of unrelated text within the larger surrounding narrative. (See textual background note above.) In Arabic this passage [18:23-24] is completely part of the surrounding rhythm and rhyme scheme, and in the context of the larger story it can also emphasize that Allah's will is paramount, for even as the Companions of the Cave fled in fear of their lives, Allah's will changed their fear into a new day of security. Thus, we must always make an allowance for the will of Allah both in small things and in large ones. He knows the future, and we do not. It also skillfully foreshadows the coming story in verses 18:32-44, causing the reader to make connections between different areas of the same chapter. (*Ibn Kathir*)

[462] All commentators have understood "words" here to mean the decreed commands of Allah. Some ill-informed critics of Islam have suggested that the Muslim position - that the previous revelations of the Torah and the Gospel have been tampered with - is incompatible with verses like this, which seem to say that no one can change Allah's 'revelations.' But this verse is not referring to whether or not people can tamper with written texts, but to the uttered *commands* that Allah gives. Anyone can erase a word on a page, but Allah's spoken commands will endure. In addition, His revelations will always remain in pristine form with Him, no matter what people do to books on earth. An identical understanding is contained in I Peter 1:25 of the New Testament! (Compare a KJV, NIV or RSV of the Bible, and one will find many alterations, but it's not the written text that is Allah's 'word' but the commands!) The term used here for words is *kalimat*. This term is not usually equated with prophetic revelation in Islamic parlance. Rather, words such as *dhikr, nuzul, kitab, qur'an, zabur* and the like are used for organized and collected scriptures or bodies of teachings. This verse is in effect saying, "Recite the Qur'an, for no one can stop you from succeeding in your mission because no one can change Allah's *word of command* that His side will be the winner in the end." As for

Background on verse 28: Some of the Prophet's companions in Mecca were poor and wore tattered clothing. One day a group of pagans went to the Prophet, and one of them, Uyaynah ibn Hisn, asked Muhammad to exclude such coarse and rough people from his gatherings if he wanted them to join in the meetings. Another prominent pagan named Umayyah ibn Khalaf had also advised the Prophet in this regard. This verse was revealed in response, directing the Prophet to prefer the company of the sincere, no matter their socio-economic status. (*Muslim*)

Keep your soul content with those who call upon their Lord in the morning and in the evening, seeking His face. Don't let your eyes pass beyond them, desiring the flashy glitter of this world's life. [463] Don't obey anyone whose heart We've allowed to become careless of Our remembrance, who follows his own whims and whose purpose (in life) is lost. [464] [28]

Say (to them), *"The truth (has now come to you) from your Lord."* Whoever wants to believe (in it), will do so. Whoever wants to reject it, will do so. We've prepared for the wrongdoers a fire whose (flames) will surround them like walls. Every time they ask for relief (from the heat), they'll have scalding water poured over them as hot as molten brass! It'll sear their faces! *Oh, how awful a drink and how horrible a place to rest!* [29]

As for those who believed and did what was morally right, *We're never going to lose track of the reward of anyone who did good!* [30] For them

---

protecting books recorded by human scribes, Islam makes no claim that they cannot be changed. The Prophet used to forbid his followers from taking written pages of the Qur'an into enemy territories for fear that 'unbelievers' would deface, destroy or disrespect the revelation of Allah. So if he knew that people could manipulate a written page for good or ill, then the Muslim position still stands that the Torah and the Gospel of today are not the originals given to the ancient prophets, even though the originals still survive with Allah. (For example, see the book entitled, *Who Wrote the Bible?* by Richard Elliot Friedman for an objective, scholarly study into how the scriptures have been manipulated and edited for a variety of reasons in ancient times.)

[463] The Prophet said, "Whoever adopts a simple mode of dress, in spite of his (vast) wealth and affluence, only for the sake of humbleness and modesty, Allah, the Exalted, will dress him in the clothes of nobility and wisdom." (*Abu Dawud*) 'Umar ibn al-Khattab said in later years: "Get used to rough living, for luxury doesn't last forever."

[464] Ibn al-Qayyum (d. 1350) once wrote, "If you're forced to talk to someone who is unbearable, lend him your body and deny him your spirit, and travel away with your soul. Lend him a deaf ear and a blind eye until Allah makes a way to separate you from him."

are everlasting gardens beneath which rivers flow. They'll be adorned with gold bracelets while wearing embroidered robes of green silk. They'll relax on couches within (the garden) - *oh, how wonderful a payment and how excellent a place to rest!* [31]

The Story of the Boastful Gardener

Lay out for them the example of two men. We gave one of them two gardens of grapevines, surrounded them with date palms, and then placed grain fields in between. [32] Both of the gardens produced abundantly, and there was never a bad harvest, and in their midst We let a gentle stream flow. [33]

His harvests were truly grand, so (one day) he had a tense conversation with his companion during which he boasted, *"I have more wealth than you, and I have more (influence in society than you on account of my) many followers!"* [34]

Then he went into his garden in a state of injustice against his own soul. (Looking around, he then said to himself,) *"I don't think any of this will ever perish, [35] nor do I think the Hour (of Judgment) will ever come. Even if I was brought back to my Lord, I'm sure I'll find something there even better in exchange."* [36]

His companion had told him, when they had talked before, *"Are you going to reject the One Who made you from dust, then from mingled fluids, and then crafted you into a man? [37] As for me, (I believe) that He's my Lord Allah, and I'll never make any partners with Him."* [38]

"Whenever you go into your garden, why don't you say, 'It is as Allah wills,' [465] *and 'There is no strength except with Allah?' If you've noticed that I have less money and fewer children than you, [39] it's because my Lord will give me something better (in the afterlife) than your (earthly) garden. Perhaps He might send thunderbolts from the sky (down upon you) and turn*

---

[465] The phrase *masha'llah*, or *it is as Allah wills*, is the phrase Muslims should say whenever they see something that pleases them in the material world, such as a nice view, beautiful art, something that someone accomplished, an achievement made or anything that is amazing.

(your garden) into shifting sand, [40] or maybe your water supply will sink in the earth so deep that you'll never be able to recover it." [41]

And so it came to pass that the fruits (of his labor) were encompassed (in utter destruction). He just stood there, wringing his hands in worry over what he had invested on his property, which was now destroyed down to its very foundations!

All he could say was, *"I'm ruined! [466] If only I had never made partners with my Lord!"* [467] [42] He had no group of supporters (to help him) against Allah, nor was he even able to save himself! [43]

(On the Day of Judgment), the only protection that will be available will be from Allah, the Ultimate Reality. He's the best One to reward and the best One to bring matters to a close. [44]

What is this World Really About?

Lay out for them the example of what this world is really like. It's like the water that We send down from the sky. The plants of the earth absorb it, but soon afterwards they become as dry stubble to be blown about by the winds. Allah is the only One Who prevails over all things! [45]

---

[466] 'Abdul Qadir al-Jilani (d. 1166) once wrote, "All you who complain to other people about your misfortunes! What good does it do you to complain to creatures like yourselves? They can't bring you any harm or benefit. If you rely only upon them, then you'll be associating partners with the Lord of Truth, and they'll make you distant from Him and plunge you into His displeasure."

[467] His making 'partners' with Allah doesn't necessarily mean that he was an idol-worshipper. The Prophet defined two levels of doing *shirk*, or making partners in Allah's divinity and power. The first level is in the obvious worship of idols or elevating any creature into a divine role besides Allah. The second level is in what the Prophet coined as *al-riya'*, or showing off. In other words, when we think we're so great and mighty, we're placing ourselves in competition with Allah's power. The Prophet said, "I'm most afraid for you about little *shirk*." When he was asked what that was, he replied, "Showing off. Allah will say on the Day of Judgment, as people are being rewarded or punished for their deeds, 'Go to the one for whom you were showing off in the world, and see if you will get any rewards from him.'" (*Ahmad*) Also see 17:37 for the perfect statement against ever feeling arrogant.

Wealth and children are merely the glitter of the life of this world, but the moral deeds that endure are the best in the sight of your Lord, and the best on which to hope (for the future). [468] [46]

One day We're going to send the mountains away, and you're going to see the land as a level plain. Then We're going to gather all of them together, leaving no one behind. [47] They'll all be standing at attention before your Lord in rows, (and they'll be told), *"So now you've come back to Us (as naked) as (the day) We created you the first time. But no! You never thought We would bring about your appointed meeting!"* [469] [48]

(Each person's) record (of deeds) will be placed (before him), and you'll see the wrongdoers in a state of panic on account of what (their records) contain. *"We're doomed!"* they'll cry out. *"What kind of book is this! It leaves out nothing small or great, and it makes mention of everything!"*

And so, they'll find out about everything they ever did, for it will all be right there, laid out before them, and your Lord won't treat anyone unfairly. [470] [49]

When We are Questioned

We told the angels, *"Bow down to Adam,"* and they all bowed down, except for Iblis, who was one of the jinns. He broke away from

---

[468] The Prophet said, "Well done! Well done for doing five things that will weigh (heavily) in the balance: (saying), 'There is no god besides Allah,' 'Allah is greater,' 'Glory be to Allah,' and 'Praise be to Allah'; and finally a righteous child who dies and his parents seek Allah's reward (by not becoming bitter or despairing overly much)." (*Ahmad*)

[469] The Prophet said, "Allah will gather people on the Day of Judgment naked, uncircumcised and *buhman*." When the Prophet was asked what *buhman* meant, he replied, "They will have nothing at all with them. Then a voice will call out to them that could be easily heard by all those near or far, saying, 'I am the King. I am the Judge. None of the people of Hell will enter Hell if he is owed something by one of the people of Paradise, until I have settled the matter, and none of the people of Paradise will enter Paradise if he is owed something by one of the people of Hellfire, until I have settled the matter, even if it's only as small as a slap.'" When people asked the Prophet how people could be recompensed from each other when they came with nothing, the Prophet replied, "By good deeds and evil deeds." (*Ahmad*)

[470] The Prophet said, "On the Day of Judgment, everyone who betrayed something will have a banner (behind him) by which he will be known." (*Ahmad*)

his Lord's command. So are you now going to take him and his descendants as protectors besides Me? They're your enemies, so it's a truly bad deal that the wrongdoers are making! [50] I didn't let them witness the creation of the heavens and the earth - *no, not even their own creation* - nor would I take such misleaders as assistants. [51]

One day (Allah) will say, "*Call upon those whom you assumed were My partners.*" They'll call out to them, but they won't answer back. Then We'll erect a dreadful prison wall [471] between them. [52] The wicked will see the Fire and feel themselves falling into it, and they'll find no way out. [53]

Many will Turn Away

We've given detailed explanations in this Qur'an, using every kind of example for people (to ponder). Yet, human beings argue over most things. [472] [54] There's nothing to prevent people from believing – especially now since guidance has come to them - nor from asking for their Lord's forgiveness, except that they've followed the pattern of ancient peoples (who denied that Allah would ever send His revelations to a mortal man) or that they would suffer from the onslaught of (Allah's) punishment. [55]

We only send messengers to give good news and to warn, but the faithless argue over foolish points in an effort to weaken the truth (in the eyes of their fellows). They take My (revealed) verses and what they've been warned with as a joke. [56]

Who's more wrong than the one who's reminded of the signs of his Lord but then turns away from them in forgetfulness because of what his hands have done? (As a penalty), We've wrapped veils over their hearts to prevent them from understanding and placed a

---

[471] The Arabic term *mawbiqa* means a jail cell, prison wall, or a place of destruction.
[472] The Prophet went to visit his daughter Fatimah and her husband 'Ali one night in Medina. They were about to go to bed and hadn't prayed any further that night. The Prophet asked them, "Aren't you going to pray?" 'Ali replied, "Messenger of Allah, our souls are in the hand of Allah. If He wants to wake us, He will." The Prophet chuckled and then walked away slapping his thigh as he recited the ending of this verse, "...*human beings argue over most things.*" (*Ahmad*)

deafness in their ears. Even if you called them to guidance, they'd never agree to be guided. [57]

Even still, your Lord is the Forgiving and a master at showing mercy. If He were to take a hold of them (immediately and punish them) for what they've earned for themselves (on their record of deeds), then He would've certainly hurried their punishment forward.

However, they have their time limit, and after that they'll have no place to be safe. [58] (This is the pattern of previous) generations that We destroyed. When they were immersed in corruption, We fixed a final date for their destruction. [59]

Moses Seeks a Teacher

Background on verse 60: Moses was often disobeyed by his people, and they were prone to arguing with him. After one such episode, Moses lost his temper and said, "Who's the smartest man among the people? It's me - I'm the smartest!" Because Moses didn't say Allah was the most knowledgeable of all, Allah made him go on a quest to learn patience. Allah told him to go to the coast (of the Red Sea) where the Gulf (of 'Aqabah) and the Gulf (of the Suez) meet at the bottom tip of the Sinai Peninsula and look for a person there who was more learned than even he. Moses asked Allah, "How can I find him?" Allah inspired him with the following instructions: "Take a fish in a container, and you will find him where you lose that fish." So Moses set out with his servant, bringing a fish in a container, on the journey to find the wisest man in the world. (Condensed from *Bukhari*)

By Allah's command, Moses (set out on a journey to seek a man wiser than himself). He said to his servant, *"I won't give up until I've reached the junction of the two seas or until I've spent years traveling."* [60]

When they finally did reach the junction, (they made camp for the night), but they forgot all about their fish, (which then leapt out of its container) and made its way into the sea through a tunnel. [473] [61] After

---

[473] The commentators explain this part of the episode thusly: the pair traveled down the coast to the tip of the Sinai Peninsula, and the servant was charged with carrying the container in which the fish was kept. At some point, the two travelers stopped to sleep near the junction of the two seas by a spring named *al-Hayat* (the life giving), which (unbeknownst to them) was reputed to be a miraculous spring that brought any dead animal to life. Accordingly, the fish came to life, flipped out of the container and landed in a crevice, perhaps between the rocks near the shore. It swam through the water-filled

they (arose the next morning and) traveled (some distance farther), Moses said to his assistant, *"Bring us our breakfast, for as it is we've endured so much fatigue on our journey."* [62]

"Did you see (what happened) when we were resting on that boulder (the night before)?" (the servant exclaimed). [474] *"I forgot (to tell you about) the fish, and only Satan could've made me forget to mention it. It (leapt out of the container) and made its way back into the sea in an amazing way!"* [63]

"That was it!" Moses cried. *"That was (the sign) for which we were looking!"* Then they retraced their footsteps [64] and found one of Our servants upon whom We had granted mercy from Our Own presence and whom We had taught from Our Own knowledge. [475] [65]

"Can I follow you," Moses asked, *"so you can teach me something of the good sense that you've been taught?"* [66]

"You won't be able to have patience enough (to learn) from me," (Khidr) replied, [67] *"for how could you have patience in situations where your knowledge is incomplete?"* [476] [68]

"Allah willing, you'll find me patient," (Moses) replied, *"and I won't disobey your commands."* [69]

"If you really want to follow me," (Khidr) said, *"then don't ask me about anything until I've spoken about its meaning first."* [477] [70]

---

tunnel it found out into the sea. The servant saw what happened, but he was too tired to stop it. He then forgot to tell his master. (Perhaps he thought it was a dream.) (*Ibn Kathir, Bukhari*)

[474] Some commentators think his assistant might have been none other than a young Joshua, who would later lead the Israelites into the promised land.

[475] The man Moses found was a wise sage named Khidr. His name means *green* in Arabic, and the Prophet said he had that name, because he once sat on a patch of pale, withered vegetation, and it turned green with new plant growth. (*Bukhari*)

[476] The Prophet said, "A strong believer is better than a weak believer, though there is good in both, so work for things that will be to your benefit, and (avoid) things that you're not able to handle. If you're ever overcome by some situation, then say, 'Allah has planned as Allah willed.' Beware of saying, 'What if,' for, 'What if,' begins the work of Satan." (*Ibn Majah*)

[477] 'Ali ibn Abi Talib said, "Don't speak on a topic about which you know nothing, or else you may be accused (of ignorance when you speak) on topics of which you do know." (*Nahjul Balagha*)

The Mysterious Journey

Then they proceeded on (and took passage on a ship), but then (Khidr) damaged (the boat and caused it to take on water). [478] (Moses) cried out, *"Have you damaged it in order to drown those within it? What an awful thing you've done!"* [71]

"Didn't I tell you," (Khidr) intoned, *"that you would have no patience with me?"* [72]

"Don't hold my forgetfulness against me," (Moses) cried, *"nor be hard on me in my position."* [73]

So then they proceeded on until they met a young man, but then (Khidr) killed him. *"Have you killed an innocent person,"* (Moses) cried out, *"who hasn't murdered anyone! What a horrible thing you've done!"* [74]

"Didn't I tell you," (Khidr) answered, *"that you would have no patience with me?"* [75]

Then (Moses) beseeched him, saying, *"If I ever ask you about anything after this, then you have every right to part ways with me, and you would be fully justified as far as I'm concerned (to make me leave)."* [479] [76]

Then they traveled farther until they came to some people in a town. They asked them for food, but the (townspeople) refused to give them any hospitality. (As they passed through the town,) they came upon a wall that was about to collapse, but then (Khidr)

---

[478] The Prophet's narration adds that the sailors mentioned in this verse had let Khidr and Moses aboard for free and that he damaged a bottom part of the hull by prying up a plank with an ax. After Moses objected, Khidr stood by the railing and watched as a bird came near the side of the boat. It dipped its beak once or twice in the water. Then Khidr turned to Moses and said to him, "My knowledge and your knowledge, in comparison to Allah's knowledge, is like what this bird took out of the sea." (*Bukhari*)

[479] The Prophet said, "May Allah's mercy be upon us and upon Moses! If he had stayed with his companion, he would have seen amazing sights, but he said, 'If I ever ask you about anything after this, then you have every right to part ways with me, and you would be fully justified as far as I'm concerned (to make me leave).'" (*At-Tabari*)

repaired it. *"If you want,"* (Moses) remarked, *"you could ask them for some payment for (your labor)."* [77]

"This is where you and I will go our separate ways," (Khidr) announced, *"but first let me tell you the full meaning of those things for which you had no patience."* [78]

"As for the boat, it belonged to some poor (sailors) who used it on the sea, and I only desired to make it (temporarily) unserviceable, for there was a certain king coming up ahead of them, seizing every boat by force." [480] [79]

"As for the young man, his parents were believers, and we were afraid that he was going to bring sorrow down upon them due to his rebellious and thankless nature. [80] *Therefore, we only desired that their Lord give them (a better son) in exchange, one who would be purer and nearer to a merciful disposition."* [481] [81]

"As for the wall, it belonged to two young orphans of the town. Below it was a buried treasure that was their due right. Their father had been a moral man, so your Lord desired that they should reach maturity and find their treasure, as a mercy and favor from your Lord. [482] *I didn't (do all those things) from my own motivations. This is the meaning of (all of those things) for which you had no patience."* [483] [82]

---

[480] Apparently, the boat was owned by ten brothers, half of whom were handicapped. The able-bodied brothers used the boat and its produce to support their needy relatives. (*Ma'ariful Qur'an*)

[481] The Prophet said, "The boy that Khidr killed was on the path to becoming a rejecter (of Allah) from the day he was born." (*Muslim*) The Qur'an, of course, is not offering murder as a way to deal with children who are on the road to evil behavior, and there are no Qur'anic verses or prophetic traditions that advocate such a doctrine. Remember that the Qur'an is recounting a journey that Moses made and things he saw in the company of a kind of guru. The principle of killing a bad child is, however, enshrined in the Old Testament, in a passage supposedly written by Moses. In Deuteronomy 21:18-21, parents of a bad son are counseled to denounce him publicly and have him stoned to death. (Also see Exodus 21:15, 17.) Islam has no such provision. (See 16:125)

[482] The Prophet said that the treasure was a chest full of gold and silver. (*Tirmidhi*)

[483] When Moses realized that his own people were impatient with him just as he was with Khidr, he became a wiser and better leader. Thus, the management principle is offered in the Qur'an that a true leader never loses touch with the perspective of his or her underlings.

Background on verse 83: The following subject, that of the story of the "Master of the Two Horns," is one of the topics that visiting Jews from Medina told the Meccans to ask Muhammad about. Who was the Master of Two Horns? It was hoped by the Arabs and Jews that Muhammad would stumble on this issue and expose his lack of knowledge. Yet, when the revelation of this story came to him, the Jews realized that Muhammad was a man with which to be reckoned, and the pagans were further dumbfounded. The Master of Two Horns refers to King Cyrus the Great of Persia, who was spoken about in glowing terms in the Jewish scriptures in the book of Daniel (8:20) and also in the book of Isaiah (verse 45:1), where he is called (in Hebrew) the *Messiah*.

Now they're asking you about the Master of the Two Horns. Say (to them), *"I'll narrate for you something of his story."* [484] [83]

---

[484] No record or opinion as to the identity of this figure has survived from the time of the Prophet and his companions. Early commentators were divided among themselves as to which historical figure *Dhul Quarnayn* could be. However, by the end of the classical period, many commentators, after having been exposed to the stories and legends of Alexander the Great (d. 323 BCE), applied the title to him and were elated that such 'a great man' was mentioned in their holy book. Those who still subscribe to this opinion, that Alexander is being spoken of here in verses 83-101, point out that Alexander traveled widely and often wore a pair of ram's horns on his helmet, a decoration commemorating the Egyptian god Ammon-Ra, which even found its way onto coins minted during the ill-fated ruler's reign. However, putting these two inconclusive and incidental details aside, could *Dhul Quarnayn* really be Alexander of Macedon? That question can only be answered by first defining the character of the man mentioned in this chapter and then comparing it with all the available historical accounts that we have of Alexander. *Dhul Quarnayn* is presented as a pious man who ruled with justice. He also traveled generally west, then generally east and then generally north. Alexander the Great traveled east *first*, then north, and finally south before going back west, so the chronology of travel doesn't fit here. This is not the only thing that disqualifies him, however, for Alexander was a polytheist who thought of himself as the son of Zeus! He was also fond of wine, murdered some of his friends and conquered for no other purpose than to be famous forever. (He got what he wanted!) So Alexander doesn't fit very well with the description of *Dhul Quarnayn*. So who was *Dhul Quarnayn*, or the *Master of the Two Horns*? It was the Jews of Medina who had suggested to the Meccans that they ask Muhammad this question. This story was revealed in response. A Persian king named Cyrus the Great (d. 529 BCE) is the definitve candidate, and the proof is very convincing. If we remember the origin of the question that the Meccans put to the Prophet, that it came from the Jews of Medina, and if we also remember that every other similar question the Jews proposed originated from their religion, historical experience and their scripture, then we need do no more than look to the Jewish scriptures for the source of the reference. The Jewish prophet Daniel, who was living in captivity in Babylon, saw a vision of a ram with <u>two horns</u> of different heights (Daniel 8:20). (Thousands of Jews, including Daniel, had been forcibly relocated from Israel to Babylon by the Babylonian tyrant Nebuchadnezzar many years before.) Then Daniel saw a goat (in his vision) with one small horn breaking the two horns of the ram, and then the goat's horn broke into four pieces in turn. According to Daniel, Angel Gabriel came and explained the meaning of the vision. It

We established him in the earth and gave him the means to reach every (place he wanted). [485] [84] He followed one way [85] until he reached the setting of the sun, and it appeared to him to set (behind) a murky body of water. [486] Near it he found a people (who were given to misbehavior, but who had no power to resist him). We said, *"Master of the Two Horns! Either punish them or treat them well."* [487] [86]

---

was that the nations of the Medes and the Persians (symbolized as two horns) would unite to make a great empire spanning a huge territory (under Cyrus's rule) and further that a Greek king, (Alexander the Great,) would then vanquish that empire, and in turn his kingdom would break up into four smaller kingdoms. (See Daniel 8:1-22) In Daniel's lifetime, the Babylonians were in fact defeated by Cyrus the Great, the first king and uniter of the Medes and the Persians (see Daniel 5:30-31), and on a map Cyrus's empire looks roughly like two horns arcing up to the east and west with Persia as the epicenter, while the eastern half of his empire arcs up further north than the western half. (As Biblical scholars admit, the book of Daniel erroneously rearranges the chronology of the two Persian kings, Cyrus and Darius I and mistakenly identifies Darius I, the third reigning Persian king, as the *first* Persian king and conqueror of the Babylonians. Ezra 4:3-5, however, gets the chronology right.) Cyrus the Great has been beloved of Jews ever since that time on account of the fact that he let the Jewish captives return home to Israel. He is also revered by Jews as having been a righteous man, devoted to Allah, (see Daniel 6:26-28) and the renovator of many holy places in Jerusalem. Thus, *Dhul Quarnayn* can be none other than Cyrus the Great of Persia, as the Jews knew him to be the meaning of the vision of the master of the two ram's horns. (*Ma'ariful Qur'an, Tafhimul Qur'an*)

[485] Daniel 8:4 specifically says the king of the two-horned empire could go wherever he wanted, unimpeded by anyone. Cyrus never lost a battle (save for his last with a Central Asian warrior queen in which he died), nor was he deterred by any obstacle. He even bridged impassable rivers with pontoon floats! The Persians, by the way, were great road builders, and one of Cyrus's successors, Darius I (d. 486 BCE), would eventually build the world's first transnational highway called the Royal Road.

[486] Some critics of Islam, who seem to have no imagination for literary devices, have charged that the Qur'an somehow promotes the idea that the sun sets *inside* a murky pool! Besides the fact that the Arabic words don't give that exact impression, if you get to the actual meanings of the words used, for anyone who has ever witnessed a sunset behind a body of water, without ever believing the sun touches the water, doesn't it look like it's setting *in* it? Such critics who advance literalisms seem to contend that Allah has no license for imagination or for a sense of literary flourish. (No Muslim scholar to the best of my knowledge has ever interpreted this verse to say that the sun sinks in a well! Even Ibn Kathir pointed out that this phrase was an idiom that meant Cyrus conquered as much as he wanted until he came to the limits of the land, bounded by the sea. In Medina, the Prophet himself once said that the sun sets between the horns of Satan - another romantic flourish that means that nightfall is a time when people become more prone to risky behavior, - as some modern studies have confirmed.) Unfortunately for such critics, the Qur'an is full of such charming descriptions. The commentators from the very beginning (Ibn Kathir, etc...) have understood this verse as it is, that it means the king reached a dark-hued shallow body of water or inland sea of some sort (but less than an ocean) and saw the sun go down on the other side of it.

[487] With the help of ancient historians (Herodotus, Xenophon, etc.), we can definitively place the travels of Cyrus the Great and match them with those of *Dhul Quarnayn*. (The

"The one who does wrong shall be punished," he announced. *"Then he'll be sent back to his Lord, and He'll punish him with a harsh penalty.* [87] *However, the one who has faith and does what's morally right will be well rewarded, and we'll issue easy commands to him."* [488] [88]

Then he followed another way [89] until he came upon the rising of the sun. He found it rising upon a people who had not been provided

---

fact that Cyrus's expeditions match the order given in the Qur'an is quite astounding!) After uniting the Medes and the Persians (the two horns of Daniel's vision), Cyrus led his army westward into Asia Minor (present-day Turkey) in the year 547 BCE. Even a cursory glance at a map of Cyrus's travels to the west shows that he passed through what is today known as Turkey. In central Turkey there is a 580 square mile salt lake known as Tuz Golu, which is shallow and muddy, due to the high rate of annual evaporation it experiences for much of the year. The empire of Lydia was located in this region, and its eastern border lay right on the western shore of this lake. (Some have suggested that Cyrus went straight to the Aegean Sea, and beheld the sun setting in its murky darkness, and the Arabic word used here is not bahr (ocean) but 'Ain or Sea, though there is scant historical evidence that Cyrus personally went to the shores of the Aegean Sea.) Thus, when Cyrus's forces reached the border of Lydia, Cyrus would have seen the sun setting beyond this dark, shallow lake to the west. Cyrus passed around this lake on his way into Lydia to take its capital city of Sardis. He waged war on the people of Lydia because their despotic ruler Croesus had attacked the city of Pteria and enslaved its people against all right. (Pteria was a part of Cyrus's grandfather's possessions, against whose corrupt rule Cyrus was first encouraged to revolt. Indeed, the reason Cyrus traveled so widely was that he was securing the far flung provinces of his grandfather's realm.) The Lydian army was nearly bested at the battle of Pteria and withdrew into the walls of its fortress at Sardis.

[488] Cyrus laid siege to the Lydian capital of Sardis. The Lydians tried one last effort to oppose Cyrus on the battlefield but were forced to withdraw. After Cyrus' men secretly gained entrance into Sardis, Croesus was forced to surrender After taking possession of the city in 546 BCE, Cyrus ordered that Croesus and his band of corrupt nobles be executed. According to Herodotus, at the last minute, Cyrus changed his mind and spared the life of Croesus and his men. (Croesus, about to be publicly thrown in a fire, repented of his evils, remembering the words of an old Athenian acquaintance named Solon, who had chastised him for his arrogance and greed.) Cyrus even befriended Croesus after that display of remorse! Then Cyrus established just laws among the people of western Anatolia so they would not fall under the spell of corruption again. The grateful Greeks of the Anatolian coast, for example, even labeled Cyrus as the 'Law Giver.' (An original clay cylinder inscribed with the tolerant and humane principles of Cyrus has survived to this day.) After Cyrus departed from Lydia, a local strongman named Pactyas revolted, promising riches to his people, but he was soon captured by a Persian general and sent in chains to Cyrus for punishment. Thus, verses 84-88 are fully identified. In summary, Cyrus traveled west to a land containing a murky body of water, uprooted a despot, had the choice to forgive him or not, forgave him, rewarded righteousness, reformed the laws of the land, and punished someone (the rebel) who did wrong.

by Us with secure shelter. [90] (He left them alone) as they were, for We knew better what he had there before him. [489] [91]

Then he followed another way [92] until he came upon (a land) between two mountain (ranges). He found beneath them a people who could barely understand a word (of his language). [490] [93]

---

[489] Historical records tell us that Cyrus then traveled in an easterly direction out of Asia Minor. He mopped up the last remnants of resistance to his rule along the way, including taking the city of Babylon without a fight. It was then that he earned the eternal favor of the Jews by letting them return home to Palestine (See Ezra 1:1-8). Some commentators believe that the 'people who had no shelter' were the captured Jews of Israel who had been sent there in exile. There is also an alternative view that puts Cyrus even further East. From Babylon Cyrus then continued in an easterly direction and entered into the wilds of the easternmost reaches of the empire that he was trying to solidify. He traveled deep into such uncivilized northeastern lands as Arochosia, Bactriana (southern Afghanistan), Sattagydia and Mardiania. Here we find Cyrus in the shadow of the Hindu Kush mountains in a region collectively known as Greater Khurasan, which is Persian for '**the place of the rising sun**.' Thus, the metaphor of the 'rising of the sun,' for it would have certainly looked like the sun arose from behind the mountains. (Ibn Kathir, among others, explain that verses 86 and 90 mean that *Dhul Quarnayn* traveled from one end of his empire to the other, an idea which fits here splendidly.) This region was, indeed, an area inhabited by uncivilized nomads such as the Paktyan and Rhoplutae tribes of Arachosia, peoples who were not worth trying to subjugate. Cyrus left such peoples alone as he was more interested in subjugating settled towns and cities. Thus, by way of summary again, the Qur'an tells us that *Dhul Quarnayn* traveled east to the farthest point that he could reach, into a land inhabited by uncivilized nomads, and that he did not oppress nor subjugate the uncivilized peoples he encountered there. This is exactly the course of action that Cyrus followed and it may hold more weight as an interpretation rather than holding that the peple mentioned in this verse were the exiled Jews, and Allah knows best.

[490] Again we find that the route of Cyrus and *Dhul Quarnayn* match each other. He had already gone west as far as he could, then he had gone east as far as he could. Now he went *another way*, in this case, northeast through Bactria into Central Asia and the lush Ferghana Valley. The 'two mountains' mentioned in verse 93 are the Himalayas to the north and the tip of the Hindu Kush (known as the Pamirs) to the south. This new land that Cyrus entered, Sogdiana by name, was a settled and fertile valley between the mountains whose people were under constant threat of attack from barbarian nomads who flooded in through a narrow pass from time to time. (Modern-day Samarqand was the capital city of Sogdiana.) The Sogdians, being only distantly related to Cyrus's own people (the Medes and Persians), could *barely understand a word* of his language. Thus, communication would have been very difficult at first, *but not impossible,* until some common way of harmonizing the different dialects could be devised. When they could communicate with each other, the Sogdians told Cyrus of their great nemesis to the north.

They told him, *"Master of the Two Horns! The Yajuj and Majuj (tribes) cause great destruction in the land.* [491] *Could we pay tribute to you so you can build a strong barrier between us and them?"* [94]

"(The wealth and power) that my Lord has granted me is better (than any tribute you could give). Help me instead with your strength (and labor), and I will build a barrier between you and them. [95] *Now bring me pieces of iron!"*

(Then he ordered the people to build) until he had filled the space between the steep mountains (with strong fortifications). [492] *"Blow (with your bellows!"* he then commanded), and when he had made it as hot as fire, he said, *"Now bring me molten copper so I can pour some of it over (the iron to reinforce the defenses)."* [493] [96]

---

[491] The two nomadic tribes whose violent raiding struck fear in the hearts of people from Europe to China were called the Sacae (Scythians) and the Massagetes by the Greeks. (The Persians called them the Apa Saka and the Ma Saka.) Ibn Kathir was also of the opinion that the *Yajuj* and *Majuj* were tribes from somewhere north of the Black Sea. Unfortunately, many modern translators identify the Yajuj and Majuj with the Biblical Gog and Magog, though the two have nothing to do with each other, as the Gog and Magog of the Bible are described quite differently and serve a different purpose in Biblical theology than the Yajuj and Majuj of the Qur'anic story, and Allah knows better.

[492] Cyrus is credited with building a string of fortifications throughout Sogdiana up to and along the Jaxartes (Syr Darya) river to protect the people of the region from the barbarian raiders, who were being led by a warrior queen named Thamaris. The crowning jewel of these fortifications was the fortress of Kurushkatha (Cyropolis to the Greeks, or City of Cyrus). Cyrus built it in 530 BCE to protect the entrance to the heavily populated Ferghana Valley. Indeed, the narrow Khudjand Pass, which Cyrus's main fort was meant to guard, has been the traditional invasion route for the nomads of the steppe for ages. Sadly, Thamaris was able to draw Cyrus out into the wilds of Central Asia, and after he had pursued her tribe for some miles, she surrounded his army and slaughtered them. His fortresses, however, still stood and prevented the worst of the raids. Today, the ruins of this fortress are located in the country of Tajikistan, in an area known as Kurkath. The ruins are just south of a later fortress built by Alexander the Great for a similar purpose.

[493] While it is obvious that the major building material for the fortress in question would have been stone and brick, metals at key points such as gate jambs would have added strength and stability. Sadly, any metals used in the construction of the fortress would have rusted away long ago. Some classical and even modern commentators such as 'Abdullah Yusuf Ali have proposed that Dhul Quarnayn built a gate made of iron to keep the invaders out. As proof they note that an iron gate in the Caucasus mountains was written about by early travelers, both Arab and Chinese, between the seventh and ninth centuries. The problem with this theory, besides the fact that neither Cyrus nor Alexander ever traveled in the Caucasus mountains, is that the Arabic text here in this verse says the king erected a *sudda*, or barrier (fortification, deterrent, fort, line of control, etc...) and not a *baab*, or gate. Thus, it is a strong fortress or string of such deterrents that

226

And so the (enemy) was rendered helpless to climb over (the walls of the forts), nor could they penetrate them from below. [494] [97]

(When he saw that the enemy was powerless to invade the valley,) he remarked, *"This is a mercy from my Lord,* [495] *but when my Lord's promise comes to pass, then He'll reduce (the deterrent) to dust, and my Lord's promise is a true one."* [98]

On that day, We're going to let (the barbarians) surge forward like waves, one after the other. [496] Then the trumpet will be blown, and We'll collect them all together. [99] We'll present the full expanse of

---

must be identified. I personally am of the opinion that the walled fortress of Cyropolis, which is the crowing jewel of a string of forts, is the *sudda* or barrier in question. I base my position on the following points: on the prominent strategic location of Cyropolis and its sister forts, which together guarded the pass into the valley; the fact that it was meant to deter the Scythians and Massagetes (Yajuj and Majuj?) and succeeded in doing so; because of the barrier's location in between two mountain ranges and because the barrier protected a valley; the Jews who asked the question of Muhammad took a direct reference to Cyrus from their scriptures (the book of Daniel); and also because of the fact that this fortress was built in a land whose inhabitants had some (but very little) knowledge of Cyrus's own language. Couple these points with the fact that Cyrus is, as many modern commentators (including Maulana Maududi) have shown, the most like *Dhul Quarnayn* in all respects, though Allah knows better.

[494] The Arabic word used here (*naqba*) is usually translated as dig or tunnel, perhaps in the sense that the invaders could not tunnel under the walls of the fortifications. Since it was a string of hilltop forts at intervals that Cyrus built, then the alternative meaning of the word can be used here, namely, that the invaders could not pass through or penetrate the line of defenses from below.

[495] Cyrus apparently did believe in One God. Daniel 6:26 records this in witness (even as the previous verse in that book incorrectly names the king as Darius. Ezra 4:3-5 gets the right chronology.)

[496] The Prophet once had a nightmare, and he woke up his wife Zaynab and said, "There is no god other than Allah! The Arabs are ruined on account of a misfortune that is approaching: a little gap has been opened today in the barrier of Yajuj and Majuj!" Then he made a circle with his index finger and thumb. Zaynab asked him, "Messenger of Allah, will we be destroyed even though there will be righteous people among us?" The Prophet replied, "Yes, if sinfulness increases." (*Bukhari, Muslim*) Some classical commentators say that this doom upon the Arabs probably refers to the devastating Tartar and Mongol invasions that brought Arab rule in the Middle East to an end in the thirteenth century and wiped out the last vestige of the Abbasid Caliphate in 1258. (Those two groups were the loose descendants of the Central Asian Scythians.) The Mongols, in particular, were so savage that they massacred millions of Muslims all across Persia, Iraq and Syria. Eventually, the descendants of the Tartars and Mongols accepted Islam, but they were never fully Islamized, and this has been a thorn in the side of the Muslim world even to this day. If that is what happens when a small gap is opened in the barrier, how will it be when the barrier is crumbled to dust just before the Day of Judgment, and barbarian hordes are once again released upon the world!

Hellfire for the faithless to see [100] - *those whose eyes had been under a veil against remembering Me* - moreover they were (unwilling) even to listen (to the message)! [101]

A Day of Winners and Losers

Do the faithless think that they can take My (created) servants as protectors besides Me? Well then, We've made Hellfire ready to entertain all those who suppressed (their ability to believe)! [102] Say (to them), *"Should we tell you about those who are going to lose the most in their deeds?* [103] *(It's) those whose life's work has been wasted, even as they thought they were getting something good for their efforts."* [104]

They're the ones who denied the (revealed) verses of their Lord and their meeting with Him. Their works will be rendered void, and on the Day of Assembly We'll give them no weight (in the balance of deeds). [497] [105] That's their reward – *Hellfire* – because they rejected (their Lord) and took My (revealed) verses and messengers as a joke. [106]

Those who had faith, however, and did what was morally right will be entertained in an exclusive garden in Paradise. [498] [107] There they shall remain, never wishing for anything to change! [108]

Allah is without Limit

Background on verse 109: This verse was revealed in response to a Jewish man who boasted to the Prophet that the Old Testament was a lengthy text; thus, his people could claim a greater amount of knowledge and legitimacy on account of its massive size. (*Asbab ul-Nuzul*)

Say (to them), *"If the ocean were made of ink (and it was used to write out) the words of my Lord, the ocean would run dry first before the words*

---

[497] The Prophet said, "A very fat man will come forward on the Day of Judgment, and he will weigh no more than a gnat's wing to Allah. So recite if you will, '*…on the Day of Judgment We will give them no weight.*'" (*Bukhari, Muslim*) In other words, those who had the power on earth to stuff themselves and live a life of leisure will have no power on the Day of Judgment.

[498] *Firdaws* is considered the most exclusive garden in Paradise. The Prophet said, "If you ask Allah for Paradise, then ask Him for *Firdaws*, as it is the highest part of Paradise, in the midst of Paradise, and from it spring the rivers of Paradise." (*Bukhari*)

of my Lord would be exhausted, even if we added another ocean just like it to help!" [109]

Muhammad is no More than a Man

> **Background on verse 110:** Apparently this verse was revealed in the Medinan Period in response to a Muslim man who told the Prophet that he did good deeds for the sake of both Allah and his reputation and that this dual purpose of his was good enough for him to satisfy his own sense of duty. (*Ma'ariful Qur'an*) This verse warns against adding any 'partners' in one's service to Allah, even if that 'partner' is one's own sense of self-satisfaction or pride in one's reputation.

Say (to them), "I'm just a man like yourselves. I've received inspiration (that commands me to inform) you that your God is One God and that whoever expects to meet his Lord, let him do moral deeds and let him not join any partners at all in the service of his Lord." [499] [110]

---

[499] In a narration, the Prophet explained that if a person does a good deed and he has any other goal in mind besides pleasing Allah, even slightly, then Allah will reject the entire good deed. In another, longer narration, he said, in part, that Allah will say on the Day of Judgment, "Whoever used to associate anyone with Allah in the deeds that he did, let him seek his reward from someone else besides Allah, for Allah is the least in needing any partner or associate." (*Ahmad*) Abu Hurayrah was concerned about the implication of this verse. He told the Prophet that when people call on him while he is at home, if he happens to be praying, he gets happy that people found him at prayer. So he wanted to know: was that showing off? The Prophet replied in the negative and explained that it was the source of two rewards: one for praying in secret and the other for setting a good public example. The Prophet also explained that if people praise a good deed that it is merely good news for a believer. (*Ma'ariful Qur'an*)

Mary

19 Maryam

Middle Meccan Period

This chapter was revealed in approximately the year 614. By that time, the Meccan leaders had failed in their initial efforts to break the will of the Prophet and his followers. Their next major policy initiative involved open persecution and economic pressure. After some months passed, and the travails and suffering of the Muslims of Mecca became unbearable, the Prophet told his followers that they could migrate to Abyssinia if they chose, that the government there was overseen by a just king, a Christian king, and that they could stay there until Allah had made a better situation for them in their homeland.

The first migration was of eleven men and four women, who narrowly eluded capture. A few months later, in the year 615, a much larger group of refugees, consisting of over eighty men and eleven women, escaped Mecca, leaving only about forty or fifty Muslims behind in Mecca with the Prophet. The migration of so many people caused a great amount of consternation in Mecca, as every family had at least one member who left, even close relatives of Abu Jahl, Abu Lahab and Abu Sufyan had migrated.

The leaders of the Quraysh decided to send a delegation to Abyssinia to petition the king to return the refugees to Mecca. The two men they chose soon arrived at the court of the king of Abyssinia, bearing expensive gifts. At first they lavished offerings upon the king's officials, and then they met with the king in person and asked for the return of the Meccans who had taken refuge in his kingdom. They explained the refugees were religious rebels who gave up the religion of their people and didn't embrace Christianity, either. The king, being a fair man, decided to let the Muslims plead their case, saying, "I'm not going to give them back without a proper hearing, for these people have put their trust in my country, rather than in any other country. They've come here to seek shelter, and I won't betray them. Thus, I'll send for them first and investigate the charges that these people have made against them. Then I'll make my final decision."

The leaders of the Muslim migrants were brought to the king, and their spokesman was Ja'far ibn Abi Talib, who said, "O King! We were a people lost in ignorance and had become very corrupt. Then Muhammad came to us as a Messenger of Allah. He did his best to reform us, but the Quraysh began to persecute his followers, so we've come to your country in the hope that here we will be free from persecution." Then Ja'far was asked to recite some of the

Qur'an, and he recited verses from this chapter that relate to Mary, Jesus and John the Baptist. The king began to weep, and he said, "Most surely this revelation and the revelation of Jesus have come from the same source. By Allah, I will not give you up into the hands of these people."

The Meccans weren't about to give up so easily, however, and the next day they met with the king once more to press him to turn over the Muslims. They told the king that the Muslims denied the divinity of Christ and thus hoped to inflame hatred in his heart towards the Muslims. When the king summoned Ja'far again and asked him what the Qur'an said about Jesus, Ja'far answered, "He was a servant of Allah and His Messenger. He was a spirit and a word of Allah, which had been sent to the virgin Mary." The King then traced a line on the floor with his staff and said, "By Allah, the difference between us and you is no thicker than this line." Then he returned the gifts of the Quraysh, saying, "I can't be bribed." He then sent them away, while giving permission to the Muslims to remain in his kingdom in peace.

In the Name of Allah,
the Compassionate, the Merciful

Kāf. Hā. Yā. 'Ayn. Sād. [1]

(This is) a reminder of the mercy of your Lord to His servant Zachariah [500] [2] when he called out to his Lord in private supplication, [3] saying, *"My Lord! My bones are weak, and my head is sparkly grey.* [501] *However, I've never been left without blessings when I've called upon You, my Lord."* [4]

"Now I'm worried about what my relatives (will do) after me, and my wife is barren, so grant me an heir from Yourself, [5] *one who will inherit (the mantle of righteousness) from me and from the family of Jacob. Make him, My Lord, someone with whom You'll be pleased."* [6]

---

[500] Zachariah was a family elder and religious leader. He held his fractious relatives together on the path of faith by sheer force of his personality. Like parents everywhere, when he became old he began to look down the path of the future and worry about all those generations who would come after him. Since he had no son of his own whom he could groom to be a leader after him, he called upon Allah to bless him with one. The knowledge he inherited from his forefathers, going all the way back to Jacob, could then be passed on to his satisfaction. The Prophet said that Zachariah was a carpenter by trade and that he used to eat from what his own earnings provided him. (*Muslim*)

[501] According to Zamakhshari, Zachariah was emphasizing that he was so old his head was shooting sparks of grey hair.

231

"Zachariah," (a voice called out to him), *"we've come to give you the good news of a son who shall be called John.* [502] *We've never called anyone else by that name before."* [7]

"My Lord!" (Zachariah) replied. *"How can I have a son, seeing that my wife is barren and I'm weakened by old age?"* [8]

"And so it shall be," (the voice) answered, *"for your Lord says, 'That's easy for Me, for I already created you before when you were nothing.'"* [9]

"My Lord," (Zachariah) implored, *"give me a sign!"* (The voice) replied, *"Your sign shall be that for three nights you won't be able to speak to anyone, even though you're not mute."* [10]

Then Zachariah left his private chamber and came out among his people, inspiring them (through hand motions) that they should glorify Allah in the morning and at night. [503] [11]

The Nature of John the Baptist

"John! Take hold of the scripture firmly!" [504] We made him wise, even from his youth, [12] and (gave him) sympathy from Us towards (every living thing), for he was pure-hearted and mindful (of Allah). [13] He was also kind to his parents and was neither aggressive nor rebellious. [14] So peace be upon him the day he was born, the day that he died and the day that he's raised to life again. [15]

Mary Receives Her News

Mention in the Book (the story of) Mary when she withdrew from her family to a place in the east. [16] She erected a curtain (to

---

[502] The name John (*Johanan*) literally means in Hebrew *a gift of God*. He is John the Baptist, and was a gift from God to his father. In Arabic, his name is *Yahiya*, and it means *to be made alive.*

[503] The Prophet said, "All you people! Spread peace (to all), feed others, care for relatives, and pray at night while others are sleeping, for then you will enter Paradise in peace." (*Tirmidhi*)

[504] According to the Qur'anic commentary of Abu Nasir al Haddadi (d. abt 1009), this verse is saying, in other words, for John to be faithful to the Torah and live by it, as his father Zachariah, taught him. (*Tafsir-Munir*)

screen herself) off from (her family), and then We sent Our angel to her, who appeared like a mortal man in all respects. [505] [17]

"I seek the protection of the Compassionate from you!" she cried out (when she saw the stranger approaching). *"If you're wary (of Allah, then you'll leave me alone)!"* [18]

"Truly, I am a messenger from your Lord," he answered, *"(sent to tell) you about the gift of a pure boy."* [19]

"But how can I have a son," she asked (in surprise), *"when no man has ever touched me, and I'm not a loose woman?"* [506] [20]

"And so it will be," he answered, *"for your Lord says, 'That's easy for Me.' (Your son) will be appointed as a sign for people, as well as a (source of) mercy from Us, and thus it's been decided!"* [21]

Then she conceived him [507] and withdrew with him to a far off place (outside the city). [508] [22] The labor pains soon drove her to the

---

[505] When Mary became a teenager, it became more difficult for her to continue her religious studies publicly, as girls weren't allowed to study rabbinical knowledge in those days. This may have been the reason she moved to the eastern side of either the town or her family's compound and then set up a private area for herself, enclosing it with a curtain. Indeed, there is value in privacy for more sincere religious devotions. Ibn Taymiyyah (d. 1328) once wrote of solitude thusly: "It's important for the worshipper to be isolated from others at the time for (personal) prayers, remembering Allah, reciting the Qur'an and evaluating himself and his actions. Also, isolation allows a person to supplicate, seek forgiveness, avoid evil, and more besides."

[506] The Arabic term *baghi*, literally means a loose woman who fornicates without regard for morality.

[507] According to Ibn 'Abbas, when the angel had put Mary at ease, he approached and blew his breath through her robe and into her womb, causing the start of her pregnancy. (*Zamakhshari*)

[508] Notice how the character of Joseph, whom Christians claim was Mary's husband, plays no role in the Qur'anic story. (The New Testament asserts that Mary went to a village named Bethlehem with a new husband named Joseph, but the Qur'an makes no mention of this and merely intimates that the birth was performed some distance from her hometown.) Some scholars of Christianity have even asserted that Joseph was a fictional character added to the story later on to give legitimacy to the pregnant Mary, who in those days would have been considered scandalous if she were pregnant and unmarried – even in a written story. Interestingly enough, some segments of Christianity have held that Mary was a "perpetual virgin" her whole life, but Matthew 1:25 asserts that Joseph "knew her" after her firstborn son Jesus was born. Having a firstborn also implies *"other borns,"* and it has long been assumed that Jesus had siblings, (with at least one brother).

trunk of a palm tree, and she cried out, "Oh! *If only I had died before this and become something forgotten or lost to sight!*" [509] [23]

"Don't be distressed!" a voice called out from under her. [510] "*Your Lord has provided a spring for you.* [24] *Now shake the palm tree towards you, and it will shower ripe dates upon you.* [25] *So eat, drink and rest your eye, and if you happen to see any man, tell him, 'I've vowed a fast for the Compassionate, and I won't talk to any person at all today.'*" [26]

Jesus Spoke as an Infant

In time, she went back to her people, carrying (the baby, but when they saw her) they cried out, "Mary! *You've come to us with something bizarre!* [511] [27] *O Sister of Aaron!* [512] *Your father wasn't a bad man, and your mother wasn't a loose woman!*" [28]

---

[509] When Mary began to show her pregnancy, she knew she couldn't remain in her hometown, surrounded by people who might accuse her of promiscuity. She packed up some belongings and left the village. When her food ran out and the pain of her pregnancy got to her, she cried out in desperation at the trunk of a tree. Allah answered her prayer.

[510] The commentators usually explain that this was the voice of an angel sent to calm Mary in her frightened moment of pain and distress. Food and water would be provided for her in her last stage of pregnancy, and she was given a convincing statement to use to ward off any strangers who might wonder about the young woman sitting under a tree in the middle of nowhere. Her statement that she was fasting was not a lie, however, for fasting (*sawm*) in Islam doesn't mean to fast from food exclusively. It can be applied to other aspects of self-denial, such as giving up arguing, talking, drinking or any other thing for a set time period.

[511] Mary's relatives thought she had committed fornication, and they berated her, reminding her that she was descended from the House of Aaron and that her parents had been fine, upstanding people. How could she have dishonored her status and parents?

[512] Some critics of Islam assert that verse 28 inaccurately calls Mary the 'sister' of Aaron, a man who lived many centuries before. Such critics must be forgiven for their ignorance of how language is used in human cultures, for a person can be associated with a noble ancestor as a sister or son or daughter, even though they are not immediately related to that distant ancestor. (In a tradition the Prophet explained this verse in this very same way.) Even the Christian New Testament calls Elizabeth, the wife of Zachariah, one of Aaron's daughters, even though Aaron was from the distant past (Luke 1:5). Also see 66:12 and footnote about the use of ancestor references in Semitic parlance.

(Mary was speechless and frightened), and she merely pointed to the baby. (Her family looked surprised) and asked, *"How can we talk to a baby in a cradle?"* 513 [29]

(Then the baby Jesus spoke out), saying, *"I am a servant of Allah. He's given me (knowledge of) the scripture and made me a prophet.* [30] *He's placed blessings upon me wherever I may be and has made me prayerful and charitable for as long as I live.* [31] *(He also) made me gentle towards my mother, being neither aggressive nor rude.* 514 [32] *So peace be upon me the day that I was born, the day that I die* 515 *and the day that I'll be raised to life again."* [33]

This was Jesus, the son of Mary, and that's an exposition of the truth about which they're arguing. [34] It's not right (to say) that Allah has taken a son. All glory be to Him! Whenever He decides something, all He has to do is say, *"Be,"* and it is! 516 [35]

---

513 Jesus spoke one time as an infant by a special miracle from Allah in order to defend his mother from the accusations of infidelity hurled at her by her angry relatives. The Prophet said, "No infant spoke from the cradle except for three: Jesus, the boy during Jurayj's time, and one other." (*Bukhari*) The story of Jurayj (George) is told in the prophetic traditions. Jurayj was a righteous man falsely accused of fornication and fathering a child out of wedlock with a prostitute. When Jurayj was being beaten by the people for fornication, the baby boy spoke in his defense and said that his father was a shepherd with whom the prostitute slept. The third baby who spoke did so, according to an obscure prophetic tradition, after his mother made value judgments about two people who had passed by. The mother praised a haughty nobleman and then disparaged a slave girl who was being falsely accused of a crime. The baby told the mother that the man was a tyrant and the slave girl was innocent. In Christian tradition, St. Anthony of Padua (d. 1231) caused a newborn baby to speak in defense of its mother, who was being accused of adultery by her husband.

514 A child must be gentle and respectful to his mother for life. The Prophet once said, "May his nose be rubbed in dust." He repeated saying this two more times and then added, "the one who finds that one or both of his parents became old, and he failed to enter Paradise because he didn't serve them." (*Ahmad*)

515 Jesus was not crucified or killed, but rather Allah saved him and took him into the next realm to await the End Times when he will be returned to earth to fight the Anti-Christ. (A second century Gnostic Christian text found at *Nag Hammadi*, known as the Second Treatise of the Great Seth, also makes this claim.) After winning the battle, Jesus will marry, have a family and then die of old age. This information is all culled from the traditions of the Prophet Muhammad. This verse [19:33] and the earlier verse about John the Baptist of a similar type [19:15] are interesting because they use a different tense for the verb "to die." In the verse about John, it says, "the day that he died" (*yawma yamutu*) whereas in the verse about Jesus it says, "the day that I die" (*yawma amutu* which is implied future tense).

516 The Prophet said, "Whoever testifies that there is no god besides Allah, alone, Who has no partners, that Muhammad is His servant and Messenger, that Jesus was Allah's

(Jesus, himself, said), *"Allah is my Lord and your Lord, so serve Him, for that's the straight path."* [517] [36] However, the various factions (among the Christians) differed amongst themselves (about the true nature of Jesus). Those who cover up (the truth) will be doomed at the sight of a momentous day. [518] [37] Oh, how they're going to hear and see (the truth) on the day when they appear before Us.

As of today the wrongdoers are clearly mistaken, [38] but warn them still of the stressful day when the issue is going to be decided once and for all. They're careless, and they don't believe (in the truth). [519] [39] (In the end, however,) We're going to inherit the earth, as well as whoever's upon it, and then they're all going to come back to Us. [40]

---

servant and Messenger, and a *word* that He bestowed upon Mary and a spirit from Him, and that Paradise and Hell are both real, then Allah will admit him into Paradise regardless of anything else he did." (*Bukhari, Muslim*)

[517] John 14:12 and 24 quotes Jesus as saying people must obey what he (Jesus) is telling them to do, and if they don't listen to and implement his sayings, then they are not of him. Thus, the words of a true prophet. John 12:49 clearly lays out how Jesus thought of himself: "For I have not spoken of myself; but the Father which sent me, He gave me a commandment, what I should say, and what I should speak." (KJV) Can anyone read this, and numerous others sayings attributed to Jesus, and come away with any other conclusion than that he, himself, felt subordinate to God?

[518] Muslims must believe in Jesus, but they must also hold the line against turning him into another god alongside of God. Christians were divided as to the nature of Jesus in the first four centuries of their religious movement, with different groups holding different opinions about his nature. Unfortunately, the most successful group was the Trinitarian party (three gods in one), whereas the Unitarians (who believed that Jesus was not Allah) and the Gnostics (who were like Christian Sufis) lost the battle. Christians today say that the Trinitarians won because it was planned so by God. This is a shaky position upon which to base the crux of their entire movement, for then anything can be attributed to God, even idol-worship, which the pagans offered as proof of God's will for them! Trinitarianism prevailed because it was adopted by literate Greeks and Romans who had the will and power both to propagate their views widely and to suppress those who differed with them. The Unitarians, who were mostly concentrated in North Africa and the Middle East (Jesus' home turf), were weaker, less organized, less literate and had no imperial power to back up their views. When Islam came many centuries later, the bulk of the Unitarian Christians, tiring of persecution from Trinitarian Europe, gradually (and freely) converted to Islam over the course of two hundred years.

[519] The Prophet said that on Judgment Day, the very institution of death will be given the shape of a black and white ram. Then Allah will call the attention of both the saved and the damned to it, and the ram will be slaughtered. (In other words, death will be dead and no one will ever die again.) Then an angel will say to everyone, "People of Paradise! Forever for you and no more dying. People of Hell! Forever for you and no more dying." Then the Prophet recited this verse [19:39] for emphasis. (*Bukhari*)

Abraham and His Father

Mention in the Book (something about) Abraham, for he was an honest man and a prophet. [41] He said to his father, *"My father! Why are you worshipping things that can neither hear nor see nor bring you any benefit at all?* [42] *My father! Some teachings have come to me that haven't reached you, so follow me, and I'll guide you to an even path.* [43] *My father! Don't be in the service of Satan, for Satan is a rebel against the Compassionate.* [44] *My father! I'm afraid that a punishment might befall you from the Compassionate that might cause you to be included among Satan's allies."* 520 [45]

"Are you talking against my gods?" (his father) demanded. *"Abraham! If you don't back off, then I'll stone you! Now get yourself away from me!"* [46]

"So peace (and good bye) to you then," 521 (Abraham) answered. *"However, I'm still going to pray to my Lord for your forgiveness, because He's always been kind to me."* 522 [47]

"Now I'm going to turn away from you and from those whom you call upon besides Allah. All I can do is call upon my Lord and hope my prayer to my Lord doesn't go unanswered." [48]

And so he turned away from (his people) and from those (false gods) that they worshipped besides Allah. (In time), We granted him Isaac and then Jacob, and We made each one a prophet. 523 [49] We granted Our mercy to them and gave them high honors that are (still spoken of by the) honest tongues (of those in later generations). [50]

---

520 In other words, he was afraid that his father might die while being a sinner and that in the next life he would be grouped with the followers of Satan.

521 This is a polite way of saying, "Good-bye, forever."

522 See 9:113-114 and footnotes where the result of this prayer is discussed.

523 The Prophet was once asked who the best people were, and he replied, "The Prophet of God Joseph, the son of the Prophet of God Jacob, the son of the Prophet of God Isaac, the son of the Friend of God Abraham." (*Bukhari*)

Other Prophets also had their Commission from Allah

Mention in the Book (something about) Moses, for he was selected (by Allah) and was both a messenger and a prophet. [51] We called out to him from the right side of the mountain and brought him close to Us for an intimate conversation. [52]

Out of Our mercy, We granted (him the help of) his brother Aaron, and he was made a prophet (alongside of him). [524] [53] Also mention in the Book (something about) Ishmael, for he was true to his word, and he was a messenger and also a prophet. [525] [54] He used to order his people to pray and to give in charity, and his Lord was pleased with him. [55] Mention further in the Book (something about) Idrís. [526] He was an honest man and a prophet [56] whom We exalted to a high place. [527] [57]

---

[524] Moses was apprehensive about possibly stuttering in front of Pharaoh, so out of His mercy Allah elevated his more eloquent older brother Aaron to prophethood to reassure him and strengthen him. See 28:34.

[525] Generally, a messenger is the next level in status above a prophet. A messenger has all the abilities of a prophet, such as prophecy and leadership capacity, along with the added benefit of getting some type of codified scripture or body of organized teachings. Of course, Abraham still had contact with his son Ishmael even after he set him and his mother in the wilderness of central and northern Arabia (see Genesis 25:9), so what then was the message of Ishmael? Consider the many customs from time immemorial that were practiced by the Arabs of northern and central Arabia. Many of the rituals of the pilgrimage to Mecca predated Muhammad's mission by millennia, and the pagan Arabs still had some ideas about angels, the Supreme God and some legends from the days of Ishmael. Thus, something of his message survived, though it had been horribly mutated by the time of Muhammad's mission.

[526] Some early commentators, have held that Idrís is the same person as the Biblical Enoch mentioned in Genesis 5:21. Early Islamic scholars have also said that he is synonymous with Hermes Trismegistus, a mythological composite of an ancient Greek philosopher and the Egyptian god Thoth whose purported scripture is the 'Emerald Tablet." Some others have suggested that Idrís could have been a prophet completely out of the Biblical sphere of influence, from any known land, from anywhere in the world. So who was he? Speculation can go in any direction, so the most logical position is to assert that he was one of the ancient prophets with whom Allah was pleased, and his exact identity may have been lost to us. His name, itself, is related to the Arabic verb, *darasa*, which simply means *to study or teach*. Thus, Idrís was a purveyor of knowledge or someone who taught. Muhammad said, "Idrís was the first person who made a pen and used it to write." The world's first writing instrument that is in the form of what we would call a pen was a simple reed, the use of which was first invented in the fourth millennium BCE in the vicinity of Egypt. Therefore, this early prophet was from extremely ancient days and most assuredly outside of the Hebrew tradition!

[527] During his night journey to Jerusalem and subsequent ascension to Heaven, Prophet Muhammad saw Idrís in the fourth level of Paradise.

Those were some of the prophets from Adam's offspring who were favored by Allah. (Some of them were descended) from those whom We carried (in the boat) with Noah, and some of them (were descended) from Abraham and from Israel. [528] They were among those whom We guided and selected. Whenever verses (revealed from) the Compassionate were recited to them, they would bow down prostrate in tears. [529] [58]

After them came generations (of people) who missed their prayers [530] and followed their own whims. [531] Soon enough they're going to be lost in disillusion, [59] but that's not the case with those who repent and believe and who do what's morally right.

They're going to enter the Garden, and they won't be wronged in the least. [60] (For them) are gardens of delight - the same ones that the Compassionate promised to His servants in the realm beyond human perception. His promise will surely come to pass! [61]

They'll hear no useless chatter (in Paradise), but rather the greetings of peace. They'll have whatever they need there for their survival every morning and evening. [62] That's what the Garden will be like, and that's the place We're going to give as an inheritance to those servants of Ours who were mindful (of their duty to Allah). [63]

The Statement of the Angels

Background on verses 64-65: When the pagans were asking the Prophet questions about the Companions of the Cave, the Master of the Two Horns and other topics, the Prophet said that he would answer them the next day, but he failed to say, "As Allah wills", (hence the reminder in 18:23-24). A full fifteen

---

[528] *Israel* was a nickname for Jacob, Abraham's grandson.

[529] After reading this verse, it is customary for the one who has faith in Allah to prostrate himself on the floor and praise Allah.

[530] The Prophet said, "May Allah have mercy upon the man who gets up at night to pray and awakens his wife. If she refuses to get up, he sprinkles water on her face. May Allah have mercy upon the woman who gets up at night to pray and awakens her husband. If he refuses to get up, she sprinkles water on his face." (*Abu Dawud, Ibn Majah*)

[531] The Prophet's companions took prayer so seriously that the second caliph, 'Umar ibn al-Khattab, wrote official letters to his governors telling them that if they didn't establish official public prayer on a solid basis in their territories, then they would be defective in everything else they did. (*Ma'ariful Qur'an*)

days passed, during which the pagans began taunting the Prophet for his lack of response from Allah to their questions. When Gabriel finally did go to the Prophet with the new revelations of most of chapter 18, the Prophet expressed his gratitude at finally seeing him. He also asked why he didn't come sooner. This passage here was revealed to him to explain that the angels only go where they are commanded and serve at Allah's pleasure – not at the pleasure of a mere human being. (*Asbab ul-Nuzul*)

(Angel Gabriel told Muhammad), *"We don't descend (down to the earth) without your Lord's command. Whatever is in front of us and behind us and all things in between belong to Him, and your Lord never forgets* [532] [64] *- the Lord of the heavens and the earth and everything in between! So serve Him, and be constant in your service to Him! Do you know of any other who can be named (as an equal) with Him?"* [65]

The Bridge over Hellfire

Background on verses 66-70: This passage was revealed in response to Ubayy ibn Khalaf, a pagan leader who picked up an old bone in his hand and said, "Muhammad is pretending that we're going to be raised up after death!" (*Asbab ul-Nuzul*)

The human being says, *"So then when I'm dead, am I really going to be raised back to life again?"* [66] Doesn't the human being recall that We created him from nothing already once before? [67]

By your Lord, We're certainly going to gather them back together, along with all the devilish (jinns). Then We'll bring them forward on their knees and gather them all around Hellfire. [68] We'll then drag out from every faction all those who were the most rebellious against the Compassionate. [69] *We know best who deserves to be burnt in (the fire)!* [70]

There's not one among you except that you're going to have to pass over (the bridge than spans over Hellfire). This is an outcome that your Lord will bring about, [533] [71] but We're going to save those

---

[532] The majority of commentators explain that this refers to the beginning of time, the end of time and everything in between.

[533] This refers to a razor thin bridge that spans the chasm of Hellfire. All people will be made to approach this bridge after the judging by Allah is completed. The wicked will get snagged on jagged edges straightaway and tumble in (or be pushed in by the angels if they were particularly bad), while those who are destined for Paradise will pass over it

who were mindful (of their Lord), even as We're going to leave the wrongdoers on their knees. [534] [72]

Allah Gives Us All a Chance

> **Background on verses 73-76:** These verses echo the common Meccan objection to the Prophet's preaching. Muhammad was attracting converts mostly from the lower classes in society, and the wealthy Meccan leaders mocked this trend, pointing out that they dressed better and looked more refined due to their affluence.

When Our clear verses are recited to them, the (well-to-do among) the faithless say to the (common) believers, *"Which of these two sides is in a better position? Which group seems more impressive in the public forum?"* [73] Yet, how many generations before them have We destroyed who were better equipped and more impressive in their appearance (than they)? [74]

Say (to them), *"If anyone goes astray, the Compassionate will hold out (the rope of salvation) to them, up until the point they see the promised (penalty of Allah coming to pass), whether it be the punishment (of destruction) or the coming of the Hour. Then they're going to realize who it was that was in the worst position and who it was that had the weakest influence (among men)!"* [535] [75]

Allah increases the guidance of those who seek to be guided. Moral deeds that endure are the best in your Lord's sight for repayment and the best for profitable returns. [76]

(with some being cut along the way as payback for some sins). This bridge is called the *sirat*.

[534] There will be some people who fall off the bridge and tumble into Hellfire, perhaps due to some unfulfilled oath, even though they were believers. (*Bukhari, Muslim*) After they've served their sentence, the angels will enter Hellfire and look for them, only recognizing them by the marks of ablution on their bodies that the Fire is not allowed to burn off. They will be removed from Hellfire, then reformed anew in perfect bodies and will thus enter Paradise fully cleansed of their shortcomings. The Prophet remarked that even if someone has faith in their hearts equal to a mustard seed, they will be eventually taken out of Hellfire. Hell is forever only for certain categories of hopelessly wicked people, such as brazen hypocrites, the most morally depraved wrongdoers, the open enemies of Allah and His prophets and those who never gave up idolatry, even though they heard or felt that there might be something wrong with it.

[535] "Weakest influence": *lit.* the smallest posse or entourage.

Allah Records Everything

Background on verses 77-87: A follower of the Prophet named Khabab ibn al-Aratt, who was a blacksmith, went to a pagan named Al-As ibn Wa'il to collect payment for a sword he had made for him, but Ibn Wa'il refused to pay him what he owed unless Khabab renounced his faith in the Prophet first. Khabab refused, saying he would never do that even until the day Ibn Wa'il died and was raised to life again. Ibn Wa'il then asked Khabab if he really believed that there would be a heaven filled with gold and silver after death. When Khabab nodded in the affirmative, Ibn Wa'il then boasted, "And so after I've been brought back to life and been given wealth and children, then I'll repay you your money!" This passage was revealed in comment on this episode. (*Bukhari, Muslim*)

Have you seen the type (of person) who rejects Our (revealed) verses; yet, they have (the audacity) to say, *"I'm certainly going to be blessed with abundant wealth and children."* [77] Have they peered into what's beyond human perception or made a deal with the Compassionate? [78]

No way! We're going to record what they said, and We're going to increase their allotted share of punishment! [79] Everything that they've said will come back to Us, and they're going to appear before Us bare and alone. [80]

They've taken other gods in place of Allah and expect to get power (from them)? [81] Absolutely not! Those (false gods) are going to reject the service they offer to them, and they're going to be their opponents (on the Day of Judgment)! [82]

Haven't you seen how We've riled up the devils against the faithless to make them furious with anger? [83] So don't be in a hurry against them, for We're merely counting down (the days they have left before We punish them). [84]

One day We're going to gather the righteous before the Compassionate like an honored delegation, [85] even as We're going to drive the wicked into Hellfire like a thirsty herd (of cattle) being driven to a well. [86] No one will have any power to intercede, except for the one who has permission from the Compassionate. [87]

Ascribing Children to Allah

They're claiming that the Compassionate has taken a son! [88] They've uttered an outrageous statement! [89] It's as if the skies are ready to explode, as if the earth is ready to crack apart, as if the mountains are ready to crumble to pieces [90] that they should call for the Compassionate to take a son! [91] It's not conceivable for the Compassionate to take a son! [92]

There isn't a single being in the heavens nor on the earth except that it must come as a (humble) servant to the Compassionate. [93] He's counted them and numbered them all precisely! [94] Everyone of them will come before Him alone on the Day of Assembly, [95] and He'll bestow His love upon those who believed and did what was morally right. [536] [96]

And so, We've made (this Qur'an) easy on your tongue, [537] so you can use it to give good news to those who are mindful (of their duty to Allah), as well as warn those people who are given to senseless opposition. [538] [97]

---

[536] The Prophet said that Allah, Himself, said, "My servant draws closer to Me through the religious duties I placed upon him. My servant then continues to draw closer to Me with voluntary (good actions) until I love him. When I love him, I become his ears that he uses to hear, his eyes that he uses to see, his hand that he uses to strike and his foot that he uses for walking. If he then asks Me for anything, I would surely grant it to him, and when he asks for My protection, I will surely give it to him. I don't hesitate in anything I have to do as much as I hesitate in taking the life of My believing servant. He hates death, and I hate to hurt him." (*Hadith Qudsi*)

[537] The Qur'an has a pleasant, well-ordered rhyme scheme. It's presented in a style reminiscent of dramatic poetry and prose. It's easy to remember, delightful to recite and compelling when heard - qualities that are impossible to carry over into English translation.

[538] Some critics of Islam argue for no other reason than out of a desire to confuse others. For example, there are those critics of Islam who spend a great amount of time trying to "prove" that the God of the Qur'an is not the same God as in the Judeo-Christian tradition. (They assert that "Allah" is an Arabian moon goddess and other such nonsense!) It's a futile point, however, for the Qur'an says that Allah is the same monotheistic and unseen God that spoke to Abraham, Moses and Jesus. It even argues tirelessly against idol-worship, anthropomorphism and such. Still these critics try to tie people up in circles over a moot point to keep them from ever delving into the real heart of Islamic teachings. (*Allah* is merely the Arabic word for *God*, like *Dios* is the Spanish word for *God*, and Arabic speaking Christians say 'Allah,' even as translations of the Bible into Arabic use 'Allah' for God.) Talking in circles does nothing more than confuse the ones doing the talking, thus carrying them farther and farther away from ever

How many generations before them have We destroyed? Can you find a single one of them (still surviving) or hear so much as a whisper from them? [98]

understanding the truth! Let such critics tackle the question of whether the God of Judaism and the God of Christianity are the same! The theologies are completely opposed to each other to an even greater degree than the ideology of Islam! (Even the Hebrew word for God is *Elah*, which is linguistically the same word as *Allah*!)

244

Ta Ha

20 Tā Hā

Middle Meccan Period

This chapter was revealed in approximately the year 615. This was near the time of the migration of over eighty Muslim refugees to Abyssinia. They were desperate people who sought protection from the violent Meccan persecution. The city of Mecca was so torn by upheaval with the introduction of Islam that one pagan named 'Umar ibn al-Khattab decided to end the problem once and for all.

He vowed to his fellows that he would go and kill the Prophet right away. Accordingly, he drew his sword and stormed through the streets of Mecca, looking for Muhammad. As he passed by one street, an acquaintance of his named Nu'aym saw him and asked him what he was going to do. When 'Umar mentioned his grim purpose, Nu'aym told him, "You should look to your own first, for your own sister and brother-in-law have embraced Islam." 'Umar became enraged, and he set off towards his sister's house in a fuss.

When he arrived, he heard some chanting coming from inside the front door. He burst inside and found one of Muhammad's followers, Khabab ibn al-Arat, sitting with 'Umar's sister Fatimah and her husband Sa'eed. Fatimah was holding a leather scroll. She tried to hide it, but 'Umar had already heard them reading from it, and he started shouting at them. Khabab ran into another room to hide (for 'Umar was something of a tough and fearsome man), while 'Umar began beating Sa'eed.

Fatimah rushed to shield her husband, and 'Umar swung his fist at her in his madness and struck her across the face, causing her to bleed. 'Umar froze when he saw his sister on the floor in pain, and he surveyed the scene of destruction he had just caused with his own hands. He cooled down and asked Fatimah for the scroll. She made him promise not to tear it up, and then she asked him to go home and take a quick bath before she would let him touch it.

When he returned, he read the scroll, which contained chapter 20 of the Qur'an. After reading only a few lines, he exclaimed, "This is something amazing." Khabab came out of hiding (for he had hidden again when he heard 'Umar returning), and said, "By Allah, I have high expectations that Allah will get great service from you to propagate the message of His Prophet, for just yesterday I heard the Prophet praying to Allah saying, 'My Lord, make Abul Hikam ibn Hisham (Abu Jahl) or 'Umar ibn al-Khattab a supporter of Islam.' In that case then, 'Umar, you should turn to Allah. Turn to Allah!" 'Umar was persuaded by these words, and he immediately accompanied Khabab to see the Prophet, and there 'Umar embraced the faith.

In the Name of Allah,
the Compassionate, the Merciful

Background on verses 1-4: The pagans used to tease the Muslim converts about their frequent prayers – even into the late night – saying that the Qur'an only brought them hardship and difficulty. This passage was revealed to answer this taunt. (*Ma'ariful Qur'an*)

Ṭā. Hā. [1]

We didn't send this Qur'an down to you in order to give you a hard time, [2] but only as a reminder for those who fear (Allah). [3] It's a revelation from the One Who created the earth and the lofty heavens. [4]

The Compassionate [539] is firmly set upon the throne (of power), [540] [5] and to Him belongs whatever is in the heavens, whatever is on the earth, as well as everything in between and even under the ground! [6]

(It doesn't matter) if you talk out loud (or keep your thoughts to yourself), for He knows every secret - *even what's concealed (in your*

---

[539] *Ar-Rahman* is a frequently used attribute and name of Allah in the Qur'an. The Prophet explained the significance of this name, which when translated means '*The Compassionate*.' He said that Allah, himself, said, "I am the Compassionate (*ar-Rahman*). I created the womb (*raham*) and derived My Own Name out of it. Thus, whoever keeps relations with it, I will keep relations with him, while whoever severs it, I will sever ties with him." (*Tirmidhi*) Therefore, the believers don't sever their ties with their families, especially their mothers.

[540] What does it mean that God is sitting on a 'throne?' Since Islam is very strict about not ascribing to the Divine human qualities, such as sitting down somewhere, this verse was the subject of much debate in the early days of *tafseer* development. Some traditional commentators held that the Lord indeed has some type of Throne, but we do not know what it is, whereas others, particularly those identified as 'Rationalists' or *Mu'tazili*, have suggested that the Arabic term *'arsh* is figurative only and is meant for people to understand that God is in control, using the imagery of a throne, for that is how we understand the position of leadership. In later centuries, a compromise position was reached between the Traditionalists and Rationalists which basically said that "the servant knows that, just as God the Lord says, He alone sits on the throne, how this is we do not know, for more than this He did not say." (*Hadaddi, Tafseer-i Munir*)

hearts!) [7] Allah! There is no god but He! The most beautiful names belong to Him! [8]

The Story of Moses

Has the story of Moses reached you? [9] He saw a fire (in the distance) and said to his family, *"Wait here for I see a fire. Maybe I can bring you back a burning branch or perhaps find some kind of useful news."* [541] [10]

When he went to the fire, a voice called out (to him, saying), *"Moses!* [11] *I am your Lord! Remove your shoes, for you're in the valley twice sanctified.* [542] [12] *I have indeed chosen you, so listen to the inspiration."* [13]

"I am Allah. There is no other god than I, so serve Me (alone) and establish prayer, so you can remember Me." [543] [14]

"The Hour (of Judgment) is coming, though I plan to make its (arrival) obscure, so that every soul can be repaid according to what it has earned. [15] *Don't let those who have no faith in it, who merely follow their own whims, steer you away from it, or you'll be ruined."* [16] *Now, Moses, what's that in your right hand?"* [17]

---

[541] Keeping in mind the life of nomadic people, a lifestyle which Moses was living at the time, when a fire is seen in the distance, it means the possibility of meeting others and either learning some news (*lit.* guidance) or at the very least getting a burning branch to light one's own campfire more easily.

[542] Consecrated and holy places are not places where shoes should be worn. The Prophet once saw a companion named Bashir ibn Khasasia walking through a graveyard with his shoes on. The Prophet told him, "When you pass by a place that needs to be respected, take your shoes off." (*Ma'ariful Qur'an*) Muslims also remove their shoes when they enter the prayer area of a mosque. The only time a Muslim may wear shoes when at prayer is when on the road traveling far distances in areas where it would be difficult to remove his or her shoes at prayer time.

[543] The Prophet said, "Whenever one of you sleeps past the prayer time, or if he forgets to pray, then let him pray when he remembers it, for Allah has said, '...and establish regular prayer so you can remember Me.'" (*Ahmad*)

"It's my staff," (Moses) replied, *"and I use it to lean on and to beat down fodder for my flocks to eat, and it has other uses, as well."* [544] [18]

"Throw it down!" (Allah) commanded. [19]

When (Moses) threw it (on the ground, suddenly) it became a slithering serpent! [20] *"Now pick it up,"* (Allah) commanded, *"and don't be afraid, for We're going to transform it back to what it was before.* [21] *Now place your hand in your shirt. It will come away (glowing) white, though causing no pain. (This is) a further token (of Our power) that We're showing to you,* [22] *so We can show you (two of) Our mighty miracles.* [23] *Now go to Pharaoh, for he's (a tyrant who's) out of control."* [24]

Moses Makes a Request

"Increase me in my intelligence," (Moses) prayed. [25] *"Make my task easy for me,* [545] [26] *and remove the stutter from my speech,* [27] *so they can understand what I'm saying to them.* [28] *Give me an assistant from my family* [29] *– my brother Aaron -* [30] *and strengthen my resolve through him.* [31] *Let him share in my task,* [32] *so we can glorify You often* [33] *and remember You often,* [34] *for You're the One Who watches over us."* [35]

"So that's how it will be, Moses, just as you've requested," (Allah) replied. [36] *"We were already favorable to you, even before this,* [37] *when We directed your mother with inspiration,* [546] *(saying,)* [38] *'Put (your baby) in the box, and drop it in the river. The river will deposit him on the shore, and he'll be found by someone who is an enemy to both him and Me.' I covered you in love from Myself so you could be raised under My watchful eye."* [39]

---

[544] Of course, Allah already knew what Moses was holding, but by asking Moses to testify to the plainness of his staff, it made the coming miracle of turning into a snake that much more astonishing to him. (*Ibn Kathir*)

[545] The Prophet said, "Religion is very easy, and whoever overburdens himself in it will not be able to continue in that way. So you should try not to be extremists but try to be near to perfection and accept these good tidings that you may be rewarded. Gain strength by worshiping in the mornings, afternoons and during the last hours of the night." (*Bukhari*)

[546] Two women are mentioned in the Qur'an as receiving communication from Allah. Although they are not considered prophets, it does advance the point of view that Allah has communicated to both males and females, as exemplified in His communications with Mary, the mother of Jesus, and here with the mother of Moses.

"Then your sister went forward and said (to the people of Pharaoh's house), 'Would you like me to show you someone who can nurse him?' [547] And so, We returned you back to your mother, so that her (anxious) eye might be cooled, and also so she wouldn't be stricken with grief. Then, you later killed a man, [548] but We saved you from distress, and then We tested you in many different ways. You stayed a number of years with the people of Madyan, and finally you arrived here as you were supposed to, Moses." [40]

"And so have I prepared you for My Own (service). [41] So go now, you and your brother, with My miraculous signs. Never falter in your remembrance of Me. [42] Go to Pharaoh, for he's (a tyrant who's) gone out of control. [43] Speak mildly to him, however, for he might heed the reminder or fear (Allah)." [44]

In the Land of the Pharaohs

(Just before they met with the pharaoh, Moses and Aaron prayed), "Our Lord! We're afraid that he might mistreat us or that he might get out of control!" [45]

"Don't be afraid," (Allah) replied to them, "for I'm with you, and I hear and see (everything). [46] Go before him and say, 'We are indeed messengers sent by your Lord, so release the Children of Israel to us, and oppress them no further. We've come here before you with proof from your Lord. Peace be upon the one who follows (His) guidance. [47] Truly, it's been revealed to us that punishment will befall all those who deny (their Lord) and turn away.'" [48]

(When they said these things to Pharaoh), he asked, "Moses! Who is this Lord of yours?" [549] [49]

---

[547] The new found baby wouldn't take milk from any of the palace nursemaids, and Pharaoh's wife was afraid the baby would die. It was then that Moses' sister Miriam sent word to the palace servants (that she might know) of a good nursemaid who was in need of employment.

[548] See 28:15-21 for this incident.

[549] The plural form of 'yours' is used here in the Arabic text to include Aaron in the address of Pharaoh.

"Our Lord," (Moses) replied, *"is the One Who gave everything its basic nature and then guides (all things to their ultimate end)."* [550] [50]

"So what about (our) previous generations (who didn't serve your Lord alone)?" [551] (Pharaoh) asked. [51]

"That knowledge is recorded in my Lord's presence," (Moses) answered, *"and my Lord never makes a mistake, nor does He forget.* [52] *He's the One Who spread the earth out wide for you.   He opened roads for you upon it, and He sends water down from the sky."*

As a General Comment for All

(Know then, all you people), that We use that (very same water) to produce every kind of diverse vegetation (which you find so useful). [53] So eat (of those plants as you like), and pasture your herd

---

[550] Being well aware of Egyptian religious beliefs, Moses took the issue directly to the heart of the matter by asserting that the 'unseen' Allah is the One Who began creation and guided it to fruition, and not the idols decorating the temples of the land. Indeed, in the pantheon of gods of ancient Egypt, there was, in fact, an all-powerful god who was considered to be the hidden force behind all of creation. This deity, known as Âmen, was an ancient god - even in the days of Moses - and Egyptologists believe that knowledge of this deity was handed down from the most ancient of days preceding the formation of Egyptian civilization proper. In hieroglyphic texts, Âmen is described as "hidden," "unseen," "the creator of all things," "of unknown form," "the one who speaks and things come into being" and other such epithets which clearly point the way, as far as the Islamic theory of the corruption of religion over time goes, to the probability that Âmen is the name of God for the Egyptians of the most ancient days. Following this line of reasoning, even as the Arabs after the time of Abraham added idols, a wife, children and other false attributes to God, the Egyptians did so likewise. Given that Islam teaches that prophets were sent to all nations in antiquity, it is not preposterous to assume that Moses called to the original unseen god of the Egyptians to make the point that they were steeped in an idolatry of their own making that has nothing to do with the ultimate and ancient truths of the unseen God of all the worlds.

[551] At the time of Moses, Egyptian civilization was already old, with many previous dynasties having already passed away. Pharaoh, who was being confronted by an upstart Hebrew, must have mused over the longstanding line of pharaohs that preceded him and how this line of continuity seemed more concrete to rely upon than the words of a man who was raised as an orphan child in his own palace. He also was questioning the fate of those previous generations, for Egyptians believed that the dead continued to live in an afterlife that was something of a mirror image of this life. If Moses was claiming that Egyptian gods were false and that there was only One True God, then what happened to all the rulers of the past? Did they have some other fate in the afterlife than they had expected?

animals, also, and there are signs in this for people of reason. [552] [54]
We created you from (the earth), and We will surely return you to it;
then We shall draw you out from it once again (at the resurrection)!
[55]

Pharaoh Reacts

And so it was that We showed each of Our miracles to Pharaoh,
but he denied them all and refused (to believe). [56] *"Moses!"* he said.
"Have you come to drive us away from our land with your magic? [57] *(If so),
then we can produce magic that will match yours! Let's schedule a match
between us, and it will be binding upon us both to attend. We'll even hold
it on neutral ground."* [58]

"The date of your match, then, will be during the great festival," (Moses)
answered, *"so gather the public (there) after the sun has risen."* [553] [59]

Then Pharaoh withdrew (for private consultations with his
advisors). He gathered together the details of his plan, and then he
returned (to address Moses). [60]

"You're doomed!" Moses said to them, *"Don't craft a lie against Allah,
or He might destroy you completely with (His) punishment, for the one who
crafts (a secret plan against Allah) will fail in frustration."* [61] So the
(pharaoh and his nobles) argued over what they had been arranging,
but they kept their discussions a secret. [554] [62]

(Pharaoh's nobles) said, *"These two are just sorcerers. Their goal is to
drive you out of your land with their magic and also to abolish your honored*

---

[552] Humans eat plant foods such as vegetables and grains but cannot eat most of the
grasses that herd animals do. However, humans can eat the meat that was grown from
those inedible plants and that was deposited on the frames of so many types of
domesticated and wild animals. Is there not a miraculous sign in this from the Creator?
[553] The Egyptians, being a very religious people, had numerous festivals and solemn
ceremonies throughout the year, both to honor their gods and celebrate the harvests.
[554] Being a prophet has its advantages. Moses was intuitive enough to realize that
Pharaoh and his officials were concocting a plan. He warned them not to try and put
one over on Allah, for Allah would then punish them.

traditions. 555 [63] *So finalize your plan, and assemble (your people) in rows (to watch). Whoever wins that day will have the advantage."* [64]

The Great Showdown

(When the appointed day arrived, Pharaoh's sorcerers) said, *"Moses! Will you cast (your spell) first, or should we be the first to cast?"* [65]

"No," (Moses) replied. *"You cast first!"* Then, after (they had cast down) their ropes and rods, it seemed to him that, due to their magic, they really had come to life! [66] Moses began to feel afraid inside himself. [67]

"Don't be afraid," We said, *"for you have the advantage!* [68] *Throw down what's in your right hand, and it will quickly swallow up all that they've faked.* 556 *What they've faked is nothing more than a sorcerer's trick, and a sorcerer is never successful anywhere he goes."* [69]

Then the sorcerers fell down prostrate (in wonder), saying, "We believe in the Lord of Aaron and Moses!" [70]

"Are you believing in him without my permission!" (Pharaoh) exclaimed. *"He must have been your leader all along! (He's) the one who taught you your magic! I'll order your hands and feet to be cut off on opposite sides, and then I'll hang you on tree trunks. That way, you'll know for certain who it is that can give a more brutal and conclusive punishment!"* [71]

"We'll never hold you as more important than the evident proofs that have come to us, nor will you ever be more important (to us) than the One Who originated us," they cried. *"Order whatever you want to order, for your orders can only affect what's part of the life of this world.* [72] *As for us,*

---

555 The ancient Egyptians believed that a balance had to be maintained between heaven and earth, and this delicate balance was embodied by the goddess *Mott.* If imbalance came due to a lack of devotion to the ancient rituals of Egyptian religion, then disaster would strike the land. Thus, the officials were appealing to Pharaoh with the greatest thing in their belief system: these two foreign men want to upset the balance of all things by abolishing our way of life!

556 The serpent that Moses produced swallowed up all the wiggling ropes and sticks of the court magicians.

we now believe in our Lord, and we (hope) He forgives us for our mistakes and for the magic that you made us do. Allah is far better (than you) and more lasting." [73]

Indeed, whoever comes before his Lord in a state of wickedness will have Hellfire, within which he'll neither die nor live. [557] [74] The one who comes to Him as a believer, however, and who did what was morally right – they're the ones who will be ranked highly! [75] For them are everlasting gardens beneath which rivers flow, and there they shall remain. That's the reward of those who kept themselves pure! [76]

The Escape from Egypt

And so it was that We sent a revelation to Moses that said, *"Travel by night with My servants, and strike a dry path for them through the sea. Have no fear of being overtaken (by Pharaoh's army), and don't be terrified (of him), either."* [77]

Then Pharaoh pursued them with his forces, but they were completely overwhelmed and smothered under the sea. [558] [78] And so, Pharaoh led his people astray instead of guiding them. [559] [79]

---

[557] The Prophet said, "The people of Hellfire – the ones who deserve it – will not die in it, nor will they be alive. Instead, they'll be people who will be justly punished by the Fire for their sins. It will only gradually kill them and devour them until they become like burnt charcoal. Then intercession will be allowed. They will be brought out (of Hellfire) group by group, and they'll be spread upon the rivers of Paradise. Then it will be said, 'People of Paradise! Pour (water) over them.' Then they'll start to regenerate like a seed growing on the muddy banks of a flowing river." A man listening nearby said of the Prophet and how he described the scene, "It's like the Messenger of Allah had lived in the desert (and been as eloquent a narrator as the desert folk)." (*Ahmad*)

[558] See Exodus 15:1-21 where the Hebrews are shown celebrating just after Pharaoh and his legions were drowned.

[559] Some time after the Prophet arrived in Medina in the year 622 C.E., he came to know that the Jews of the city held a fast on a day called *Ashura*. When he asked them why they held a fast on that day, they replied, "This is a blessed day. Allah saved the Children of Israel on this day from their enemy (in Egypt), so Moses fasted this day to give thanks to Allah." The Prophet replied, "We are closer to Moses than you are, so (we will) fast it." (*Bukhari, Muslim*) The day of Ashura falls on the tenth of the month of Muharram. The Prophet made it an obligatory fast, but the following year, after the Qur'an made fasting in the month of Ramadan obligatory, the fast of Ashura was made optional. Some time later, a group of Muslims asked the Prophet if it was good to fast on the same day of Ashura as the Christians and Jews did. The Prophet answered them by giving permission

Children of Israel! We saved you from your enemy and made an agreement with you on the right side of the mountain. We even sent manna and quails for you (to help you survive your flight from Egypt). [80] So eat of the wholesome things that We've provided for you. Don't go beyond (what you've been allowed), or My condemnation might befall you. Whosoever has My condemnation descend upon them, thus shall they perish! [81] Even still, I forgive anyone who repents, believes, behaves morally and then accepts guidance. [82]

The Plot of the Storyteller

"*What made you hurry back here (to the mountain) ahead of the rest of your people, Moses?*" [560] (Allah asked). [83]

"*They're following in my tracks,*" (Moses) replied. "*I only hurried back to You, My Lord, to please You.*" [84]

"*We have given your people a test in your absence,*" [561] (Allah) said, "*and the Storyteller [562] has led them astray.*" [85]

---

to celebrate the fast of Ashura on any or all of three days in Muharram from the ninth to the eleventh (as long as the tenth day is observed at the very least) The Prophet once remarked that by fasting the day of Ashura, Allah might erase the sins committed by a person in the previous year. (*Muslim*) The scholars agree that this refers to minor sins only, as major sins are in a different category all together from such meritorious acts as voluntary fasting. This is also the anniversary day when the Prophet's grandson Husayn fell in battle while fighting the forces of the second Umayyad caliph Yazid in the year 680 C.E. Shi'a Muslims commemorate the anniversary of this tragic event while Sunni Muslims do not.

[560] Moses left his people encamped near the sacred mountain, which was located somewhere in northwestern Arabia. Then he went up the slopes alone for forty days to commune with Allah.

[561] Exodus chapter 32 mentions this story, though with significant differences from the Qur'anic rendition.

[562] Who was the Storyteller, or *as-Saamiri* mentioned here? To begin, the term *saamiri* is probably not being used here, as some people claim, as a reference to a person from Samaria, (i.e., a *Samaritan*,) which was a later territory near historical Israel. (Though Jewish sources point out that the term for *samaritan* used in the Bible in II Kings 17 is actually a title for a religious group among Jews (*shomronim*) that predates the actual founding of Samaria - and even Moses. See entry for *samaritan* in the Encyclopaedia Judaica.) The Qur'an generally refrains from assigning a title to a person based solely on his country of origin, and it is highly unlikely that obscure place names in Palestine were known to most Meccans, who did most of their travels in Syria and Iraq. When we look

Then Moses angrily returned to his people and said, *"My people! Didn't your Lord make a good enough promise to you? Did you think the promise wouldn't be fulfilled for a long time? Were you looking for your Lord's wrath to come down upon you? Is that why you broke your promise to me?"* [86]

"We didn't break our promise to you of our own accord," they answered. *"We were forced to carry the heavy ornaments of the nation (of Egypt when we left that land.* [563] *It was for this reason that) we threw them in (the bonfire), and that's what the Storyteller suggested we do.* [87] *Then he brought out (of the fire) the image of a calf, and it seemed as if it were making a sound.* [564] *It was then that (some people) said, 'This is your god and the god of Moses, but Moses has just forgotten.'"* [88]

---

into the actual meaning of the Arabic term *saamiri* we must first look at its root which is *samara*. From this root, a variety of meanings are formed, including the terms *brown, pleasant nightly chat, to be nailed down, entertainer* and *teller of fictitious tales*. It can also mean a *watcher* or *lookout*. The actual designation of *saamir*, according to the common Arabic usage, is conversationalist, storyteller or entertainer, and this is what the unnamed man in this verse engaged in. (Verse 23:67 uses the exact same word in a slightly different grammatical form for the same purpose.) The tenth-century scholar, Muhammad ibn Is-haq ibn al-Nadim, using the definition of *saamir* in the same way, noted that the fictitious tales of a storyteller (*al-asmar*) are fit only for nightly entertainment! (From *al-Fihrist*) Do we know the name or true identity of this Storyteller? Many commentators, going back to Ibn 'Abbas (d. 687), have held that he was either an Egyptian (who followed Moses out of Egypt) or he was a Hebrew who had been living completely according to Egyptian culture while the Hebrews were still in bondage. One classical commentator, al-Baydawi, even assigned a name to this man, calling him Musa ibn Zafar, though the source for this name is most probably spurious. When Moses was away receiving Allah's commands, the Storyteller convinced the Hebrews through his stories and persuasive arguments that they needed to make a god they could see – a god of gold!

563 Some scholars are of the opinion that in Moses' absence, the Hebrews debated whether it was right for them to take the property of the Egyptians. Aaron (or the Storyteller) ordered all the gold to be thrown in a pit, and they would await the return of Moses for a decision. The Storyteller then suggested to make the gold into an idol and somehow got the figure to make a sound, causing the people to think it was a real god. (*Ma'ariful Qur'an*) See Exodus 12:35 where the Hebrews "borrowed" the gold of Egypt as they left.

564 Ibn 'Abbas (d. 687) said that the sound came from wind passing through a hollow part of the idol, and the foolish people took it as the actual mooing of a calf. (*Ibn Kathir*) Such devices (idols with special noise-making holes for wind to pass through) were used in antiquity in later Egyptian and even some Greek temples.

Couldn't they see that (the statue) had no power to reply to any word (they spoke to it) and that it had no power to do them any harm or benefit? [89]

Aaron had already said to them before (they started worshipping it), *"My people! You're being tested in this (situation). Your Lord is Compassionate, so follow me and obey my orders!"* [90] However, they replied to him, *"We're not going to give this (idol) up, and we'll keep on (worshipping) it until Moses comes back to us."* [91]

"Aaron!" (Moses) shouted, (when he returned). *"What stopped you from (opposing them) when you saw them going astray?* [92] *Were you disobeying my orders?"* [93]

"Son of my mother!" (Aaron) cried out. *"Don't grab me by my beard nor by my head! I was afraid that you might say to me, 'You caused a split among the Children of Israel and didn't respect my word.'"* [565] [94]

(Moses turned towards the man who crafted the idol) and said, *"So, Storyteller, what (do you have to say) about yourself?"* [95]

"I saw (something) that they couldn't see," he replied. *"So I took a handful of the traces that the messenger left behind and tossed it in.* [566] *That's what I felt that I should do."* [96]

"Get out of here!" (Moses) ordered. *"Your (curse) in this life is that (you'll be an outcast) and will have to say, 'Don't touch me,' (for you'll be stricken with disease).* [567] *Beyond that, you'll have the unbroken promise (of*

---

[565] The book of Exodus charges that it was Aaron himself who made the idol. (See Exodus 32:2-5, 35.)

[566] There are two interpretations of this verse. The first is that the Storyteller tried to defend himself by saying that he mixed some traces of the teachings left behind by Moses with some ideas of his own and influenced people that way. Other commentators have explained this enigmatic verse by saying that the Storyteller took some dirt from a footprint, either left behind by Moses or an angel, and threw it on the golden cow, (dramatically, no doubt,) causing it to make a sound. The Arabic word used here is *athar*. It means many things, including relics, marks, tracks, teachings, reports, sources, influence and also exclusive knowledge, among a dozen other things. Only Allah knows which interpretation is right.

[567] What was the sign of his being an outcast? Some have suggested that the Storyteller was stricken with leprosy. Others have suggested it was a self-imposed exile from social

eternal punishment waiting for you). Now look at your 'god,' the thing to which you've become a devoted worshipper. We're going to melt it in a bonfire and scatter its particles far and wide!" [568] [97]

Our Lives will Seem Like Nothing on that Day

Truly, your only god is Allah, the One before Whom there are no other gods. He is expansive and fully aware of all things. [98] And so We've narrated to you some stories of what happened in days that have passed away. We've sent a message to you from Our Own presence. [99]

Whoever turns away from it will bear a heavy burden on the Day of Assembly. [100] They'll remain in that (condition), and their burden that day will be awful, indeed! [101]

On the day when the trumpet is blown, that day We'll gather the sinful, bleary-eyed (with fright). [102] They'll be whispering to one another, saying *"You stayed (in the world) no more than ten (days at the most)."* [103] We will certainly know better (than they) what they're talking about, and then the best behaved among them will say, *"You stayed (on the earth) for no more than a day!"* [569] [104]

Understand the Magnitude of Judgment Day

Now they're asking you about the mountains - (will they really be crumbled to nothing)? Say (to them), *"My Lord will pull them out from their roots and scatter them like dust,* [105] *leaving a smooth, level plain*

---

contact brought about by shame. Only Allah knows the truth of this matter, though it seems likely to me that since the Old Testament is full of examples of Allah throwing plagues on the people of Moses that this would be the most likely reason for the Storyteller to become an outcast.

[568] Moses ordered the calf to be melted and pulverized. He forced some of the guilty people to drink water mixed with the powder of it. See 2:93 and footnote.

[569] It has often been said that the older one gets, the more it seems as if life is literally the blink of an eye. On Judgment Day it will be so weighty and serious a time that our entire earthly life will seem to have passed in an instant.

behind. [570] [106] *Nothing bumpy will you see, nor anything uneven remaining there."* [571] [107]

On that day, (all people) will follow (the voice of) the caller without deviation. All noise will be hushed in the presence of the Compassionate, and you'll hear no more than the sounds of shuffling feet. [108] On that day, no one's intercession will do any good, save for those who were given permission (to intercede) by the Compassionate, and whose speech is acceptable to Him. [109]

He knows what lies before them, as well as what lies behind them. Yet, they can't comprehend Him at all in their knowledge! [572] [110] Faces will be lowered in humility before (Him) – the Living, the Everlasting! Whoever carries the burden of evil (on his back that day) will be in utter failure, [111] while the one who behaved morally and who believed will have no fear of being wronged nor of having anything (due to him) withheld. [112]

And so We've revealed (this scripture) as an Arabic recital. We've mentioned within it some of what's been forewarned, so that perhaps they can be mindful (of Allah) - or at they least they can be reminded (of the truth)! [113]

Background on verse 114: Whenever the Prophet used to receive revelation, he used to try to memorize it as quickly as possible for fear of forgetting it. This verse is telling him to slow down and ask Allah to help him remember it. Also see 75:16-19.

Allah is high above all others – the Ruler, the Reality! So don't be hasty with the Qur'an before its revelation is completed to you,

---

[570] It's interesting that the Qur'an puts forward the notion that mountains have roots. This was not something that was known in the ancient world and is an accurate description of actual geologic structures found deep under mountain ranges and rooted in the activities of plate tectonics.

[571] The Prophet said, "On the Day of Judgment, all people will be gathered on a white (featureless), flat land that looks just like a piece of wheat bread, for it will have no landmarks anyone can recognize." (*Bukhari, Muslim*)

[572] The Prophet said, "The Exalted (Allah) will say, 'Bring out of the Fire anyone who has a seed's weight of faith in his heart.' So a large number of people will be brought out. Then He will say, 'Bring out of the Fire anyone who has half a seed's weight of faith in his heart. Bring out anyone who has the weight of a speck of dust's worth of faith in his heart. Bring out anyone who has the weight of an atom of faith in his heart.'" (*Bukhari*)

(Muhammad). Rather, you should say, *"My Lord! Help me to know more!"* [573] [114]

The Fall of Adam

And so it was that We had made a covenant with Adam, but he was careless about it, and thus We found no firmness in his resolve. [115] When We said to the angels, *"Bow down to Adam,"* they all bowed down. However, (a jinn named) Iblis didn't bow down, for he refused. [574] [116]

Therefore, We (warned him,) saying, *"Adam! This is an enemy to both you and your wife, so don't let him get you thrown out of the garden, for then you'll be miserable.* [117] *There are enough (comforts) for you here to keep you from starving or feeling naked,* [118] *nor will you suffer from thirst or sunburn."* [119]

Then Satan whispered to him, saying, *"Adam! Should I lead you to a tree of eternity and to a kingdom that will never pass away?"* [120] Then both (Adam and his wife) ate from it together, and the awareness of their nakedness came to their senses. They began to sew leaves

---

[573] This short supplication (*"Rabbee zidni 'ilma."*) is popular among Muslims in their private devotions.

[574] This story (of the angels being made to bow down to Adam and Satan refusing to follow suit) was also known to the Jews and is contained in a section of ancient Jewish writings that are called the Old Testament Pseudepigrapha. The Midrashic literature, which was written by ancient rabbis to supplement Jewish teachings, also makes mention of these events. One piece of literature from these sources is entitled, "The Life of Adam and Eve." The Midrashic account reads as follows. "(How did) Adam the protoplast (do so)? The day when he was endowed with his knowledge, the Holy One, blessed be He, commanded the ministering angels: 'Enter and bow down to him!' The ministering angels entered to perform the will of the Holy One, blessed be He. (However,) Satan, who was the mightiest of all the angels in heaven, said to the Holy One, blessed be He, 'Master of the universe! You created us from the Divine Glory, and now You say to us, 'Bow yourselves down!' before one whom You created from the dirt of the earth??!?' The Holy One, blessed be He, answered him: 'This one who originates (from) the dirt of the earth possesses some wisdom and intelligence which is not in you!'" (Albeck H (ed.): *Midrash Bereshit Rabbati.* Jerusalem, Mekize Nirdamim, 1940.) In this story from the Midrash, Satan (or Iblis) is identified as an angel, while in the Qur'an he is labeled as a jinn.

together from the garden to wear as clothes. Adam had disobeyed his Lord and let himself be deceived! [575] [121]

Later on, his Lord chose him, turned to him (in forgiveness) and guided him. [122] He said, *"Both of you go down and away from here, though (your descendants will be) enemies of one another. However, if there ever comes any guidance from Me, (and it will surely come), whoever follows My guidance will never lose his way nor fall into misery.* [123] *However, the one who turns away from My message will have a constricted life,* [576] *and We'll raise him up blind (to faith) on the Day of Assembly."* [124]

---

[575] There is a fascinating conversation between Adam and Satan, after Satan tricked Adam into sinning, that is preserved in the Midrashic literature selection called, "The Life of Adam and Eve." In this selection, Satan tries to explain why he hates Adam and will always seek to tempt both he and his descendants forever. The conversation is as follows: And the devil sighed and said, "O Adam, all my enmity and envy and sorrow concern you, since because of you I am expelled and deprived of my glory which I had in the heavens in the midst of angels, and because of you I was cast out onto the earth." Adam answered, "What have I done to you, and what is my blame with you? Since you are neither harmed nor hurt by us, why do you pursue us?" The devil replied, "Adam, what are you telling me? It is because of you that I have been thrown out of there. When you were created, I was cast out from the presence of God and was sent out from the fellowship of angels. When God blew into you the breath of life and your countenance and likeness were made in the image of God, Michael brought you and made (us) worship you in the sight of God, and the Lord God said, 'Behold Adam! I have made you in our image and likeness.' And Michael went out and called all the angels, saying, 'Worship the image of the Lord God, as the Lord God has instructed.' And Michael himself worshiped first, and called me and said, 'Worship the image of God, Yahweh.' And I answered, 'I do not worship Adam.' And when Michael kept forcing me to worship, I said to him, 'Why do you compel me? I will not worship one inferior and subsequent to me. I am prior to him in creation; before he was made, I was already made. He ought to worship me.' When they heard this, other angels who were under me refused to worship him. And Michael asserted, 'Worship the image of God. But if now you will not worship, the Lord God will be wrathful with you.' And I said, 'If he be wrathful with me, I will set my throne above the stars of heaven and will be like the Most High.' And the Lord God was angry with me and sent me with my angels out from our glory; and because of you, we were expelled into this world from our dwellings and have been cast onto the earth. And immediately we were made to grieve, since we had been deprived of so great glory. And we were pained to see you in such bliss of delights. So with deceit I assailed your wife and made you to be expelled through her from the joys of your bliss, as I have been expelled from my glory." (Life of Adam and Eve 12:1-16:3) Taken from: Johnson MD: Life of Adam and Eve. In Charlesworth JH (ed.): *The Old Testament Pseudepigrapha: Volume Two*. Peabody, Hendrickson Publishers, 2011, page 262.

[576] Despite whatever worldly success they achieve, their horizons will become narrower and narrower. No matter how rich and successful they become, their focus will literally be squeezed so that even wealth will no longer bring them joy and satisfaction – and they'll be unable to see anything beyond it. Oh, what a cursed way to live!

"My Lord!" he'll cry. *"Why have You raised me up blind (to faith) when I used to be able to recognize (things clearly)?"* [577] [125]

"Wasn't it the case that whenever Our (revelations) came to you, that you ignored them? So today you're going to be ignored!" [126]

That's how We're going to compensate the one who went out of control and who didn't believe in the (revealed) verses of his Lord. *Yet, the punishment of the next life is even more serious and lasting!* [127]

Isn't it guidance enough for them to consider how many generations before them We destroyed and in whose ruins they now move about? There are signs in this for reasonable people. [128] If it wasn't for the fact that their Lord (had already decreed) the verdict (that all nations will have a specific deadline, then their punishment) would've come upon them already. However, there is a set time limit. [129]

Prayer Strengthens Resolve

So be patient with what they're saying. Glorify the praises of your Lord before the rising of the sun, before it sets and during some hours of the night. Glorify (Him) at the two ends of the day, as well, so you can have (even more spiritual) satisfaction. [578] [130]

Don't let your eyes gaze longingly at those (material goods) that We've given to some groups among them to enjoy, (for it's only) the

---

[577] As the commentators explain, it is not their eyesight that will be blinded, but rather their capacity to understand and accept faith. (This is clarified in verse 20:126 where the blindness is essentially that they will be ignored by Allah's light and grace.) They will, in effect, be spiritually blind on Judgment Day, almost as if they've had the light of their souls put out. This makes Hellfire the only option they have left to them. There is a prophetic tradition that confirms this interpretation, as well.

[578] Some commentators say that this verse mentions the five daily prayers that were first enjoined upon the Prophet and that were later made obligatory upon all Muslims. The prayers are 1) *fajr* i.e., before sunrise; 2) *'asr*, i.e., before sunset; 3) *'isha'* i.e., the hours of the night; 4) *zuhr*; and finally 5) *maghrib*. The last two are what are called the prayers at the two sides of the day. *Zuhr* is the first prayer after the sun has come up and is performed in the early afternoon, while *maghrib* is the prayer performed when the ball of the sun disappears. Other commentators regard this verse as more general and assert it mentions suggested times for prayer and contemplation without being specific as to prayers that became required later on.

splendor of this world through which We test them. The provisions that are with your Lord are better and more lasting. [579] [131]

Background on verse 132: Several members of Muhammad's extended family had accepted Islam by the time of this revelation. This verse is asking him to institute prayers as a habit among them. (*Ibn Kathir*)

(Muhammad,) command your family to pray, and (ask them to) commit themselves to it. We're not asking you to procure any resources (for Us), for We're going to provide them to you, and the final destination is for the mindful. [132]

They may ask, "*So why isn't he bringing us some kind of miracle from his Lord?*" [580] But hasn't enough clear evidence already come to them in the ancient scrolls of revelation? [581] [133]

If We *would* have inflicted punishment upon them before this, then they would surely have cried out, "*Our Lord! If only You would've sent us a messenger, then we would've followed Your (revealed) verses long before we would've ever needed to be humbled or disgraced!*" [134]

---

[579] 'Umar ibn al-Khattab once went into a small upper floor apartment in which the Prophet was staying after he had begun a boycott of his wives. He noticed the Prophet had nothing with him other than a rough straw mat, a few implements hanging on the wall and a pile of edible tree pods. 'Umar took in the scene, and then his eyes filled with tears. When the Prophet asked him why he was crying, 'Umar replied, "Messenger of Allah! Khosroes (of Persia) and Caesar (of Byzantium) are living in luxury; yet, you're the One that Allah chose for a friend among all of creation?" The Prophet then said, "Are you in doubt, O son of al-Khattab? Those people have merely had their good fortune hurried on for them in the life of this world." (*Bukhari*)

[580] The pagans of Mecca already knew there were Jews and Christians in the world who spoke of one God, prophets, a life after death and such. Didn't the pagans realize the miraculous nature of those earlier revelations, which were also messages carried by mortal men? People don't always have to be dazzled with supernatural miracles. At some point, they have to use their reason and consider a message based on its own merits.

[581] It is verses like this one that can dispel many of the legends of Muhammad that grew up in classical Muslim civilization. (Some of these legends have even made it into some of the books of *hadith*!) In those tales, the Prophet is credited with literally hundreds of fantastic miracles. When we strip away all the legends, however, we find that the Prophet was sent with only one main miracle and that was the Qur'an. There are a handful of bona fide miracles that are affirmed in the Qur'an and that are reliable in the *hadith* collections, but most of the other stories that have come down to us do not stand up to the test of credibility, nor are they needed to prove the truth of the Prophet's mission.

Say (to them), *"Each of us is waiting, so you just wait, and soon you'll know who were the companions of a straight way and who were truly guided."* [135]

The Prophets

21 Al Anbiyā'
Middle Meccan Period

This chapter presents a series of arguments for Prophet Muhammad to employ against the pagans who questioned that Allah would actually choose prophets from among human beings to deliver His messages. It must be remembered that the idol-worshippers had no concept of divine revelation, let alone of it coming to a human being. Their culture was filled with superstition and idolatry. The only value that any man could have in the eyes of his fellows was in the raw courage and reputation for bravery that he could amass through the rough and tumble world of the desert. The pagans knew that Jews and Christians claimed something similar to what Muhammad was bringing, but those beliefs held little sway in most of Arabia where animism was the religion of prominence. The Qur'an, however, was a challenge coming from within their own society. Thus, their rejection of it was more pointed and even desperate. The many stories of the various prophets mentioned in this chapter were a way for the pagans to open their imagination and thoughts to the prospect that Allah did, indeed, communicate His messages to human beings many times in the past and that He was doing it once again!

In the Name of Allah,
the Compassionate, the Merciful

People get closer and closer to their reckoning; yet, they're careless about it and just turn away. [1] No fresh message ever comes to them from their Lord without them listening to it as if it were a joke [2] – all the while their hearts are occupied (with trivial things).

The wrongdoers hide their secret discussions (in which they say), *"Is this (man) any different from the rest of you? Are you going to fall for (his) magic while you see it (for what it is)?"* [3]

Say (to them), *"My Lord knows (everything) that's spoken within the heavens and on the earth, for He's the Hearing and the Knowing."* [4]

"No way!" they say. *"It's just a bunch of jumbled dreams! No way! He made it up! No way! He's just a poet! So let him bring us a miracle like the ones that were sent down in ancient times!"* [5] The (people of) those previous settlements that We destroyed didn't believe, so will these (people) ever believe? [6]

Before you, We sent messengers who were (ordinary) men whom We inspired (with revelation). [582] If you're not sure about it, then ask those who (already) possess (previously revealed) messages. [583] [7] We didn't give (any prophets before you) bodies that could go without food, nor were they immortal. [8]

In the end, We fulfilled Our promise to them and saved them, along with whomever else We wanted to save, and We destroyed those who went out of control (in their wickedness). [9] And so it is that We've revealed a book to all of you that contains a message directed towards you. Won't you at least reflect (upon it)?" [10]

History is Proof of Allah's Will

How many settlements have We destroyed completely on account of their corruption and then established other people in their place? [584] [11] Whenever they sensed Our punishment (coming for them), they tried to run away from it! [12]

---

[582] Prophets of Allah have special missions and divine support. As far as miracles are concerned, the overwhelming majority of prophets were not granted spectacular miracles, and those who were given such needed them for their daunting task. Prophet Muhammad had Allah's favor, and as his story bears witness, his miracle was the fact that an orphan boy in the desert brought a scripture and religion that triumphed against all odds and created a world civilization that spanned from Spain to China in only about a hundred years.

[583] The pagans objected to Muhammad's claims of prophecy, saying that he was just a man like themselves. This verse is asking them to talk to Jews and Christians and find out from them if previous prophets were men or some kind of supernatural beings.

[584] 'Abdul Rahman ibn Khaldun (d. 1408) wrote extensively on the cyclical nature of history. He penned an exhaustive treatise on the causes of the rise and fall of nations entitled *Kitab al-'Ibar*. In his prologue volume, which is an often separately published book entitled *al-Muqaddimah*, Ibn Khaldun lays out a cyclical pattern that goes something like this: less advanced people, whether driven by religious zeal or the ambitions of powerful personalities, overthrow more advanced nations that had become weak with the passage of time. Then those conquerors settle down and eventually become civilized enough to become soft themselves one day – only to be overthrown by a new rising tide of less developed, though intensely focused invaders. No doubt verses like this one inspired Ibn

Oh, don't run away now! Go back to your luxuries and your dwellings, so you can be questioned (about them)! [13] They would cry out, "We're doomed! We were truly wrong!" [14] and their cry never ceased until We cut them down to dry stubble. [15]

We didn't create the heavens and the earth and everything in between them for a mere diversion. [16] If We had wanted to be entertained, then We could've chosen (Our entertainment) from that which is with Us – that is if We were ever so inclined! [17]

But no! We hurl the truth against falsehood and knock out its brains! And so falsehood passes away! (If you don't stop making false statements about Allah,) then you'll be destroyed on account of how you're (wrongly) defining (Him). [18]

All those (who reside) within the heavens and the earth belong to Him. Even those (angels) who are closest to Him are not too proud or weary (to serve him). [19] They glorify Him throughout the night and the day, and they never pause or falter (in their praise)! [20]

There are No Equals With Allah

Have they taken gods from the earth who can raise (the dead to life)? [585] [21] If there were other gods in (the heavens and on the earth) besides Allah, then there would've been chaos in both! Glory be to Allah, the Lord of the throne, for He's high above what they attribute to Him! [586] [22] He can't be questioned for what He does, but they'll be questioned (for what they do). [23]

Khaldun in the formulation of his theories! A recent book by Gregory Clark entitled, "*A Farewell to Alms*," (Princeton University P., 2007) also complements Ibn Khaldun's many economic theories quite well.

[585] This is possibly a reference to the Christians having taken Jesus, a man, to be their god. He did not raise the dead to life by his own power, but it was a miracle that Allah granted to him, just as the prophet Elisha allegedly did the same (see II Kings 8:1; also see Qur'an 3:49 and 5:112-115).

[586] If people have a theological view of the world that involves an entire pantheon of gods, such as can be found in Greek mythology, with many gods, half-gods and the like, and further still if they make their gods out to be nothing more than humans with super powers, then it is entirely plausible to assume that such gods would never work together and would always be trying to undermine each other, even as the myths of the Greek,

Have they taken other gods for worship besides Him? Say (to them), *"Bring me your evidence. This (Qur'an) is the (proven) message of those with me and the (proven) message of those who came before me."* [587] But no! Most of them don't know the truth, and so they just turn away. [24]

We never sent any messenger before you without giving him this inspired message: *'There is no god besides Me, so serve Me.'* [25] Yet, they say, *"The Compassionate has taken children for Himself."* Glory be to Him! No way! The (beings that you call His children) are only honored servants. [26] They don't speak before He speaks, and they do what He commands. [588] [27]

Roman, Oriental and Hindu gods attest. (Think about the war between the Greek gods and the Titans, for instance.) If there were many gods, then the chaos would be evident and would engulf the natural world, as each god strives to gain power over the regions controlled by other gods.

[587] In other words, the pagans claim their gods are real, but they cannot bring any proof or corroboration from any other religious group, nor can they produce any ancient scripture or obvious signs. The revealed message of the Qur'an, however, is the proof that Allah is One, even as it is a continuation of that tradition of revelation from God that included messages to Abraham, Moses and Jesus.

[588] This verse mainly refers to the pagans who thought Allah had daughters from among the angels, but it also answers the doctrine of the Christians, who said God had a baby boy who was carried in the womb of a human girl named Mary. It is an inescapable fact that even when one reads the four Gospels in the Bible, the distinct impression is given that Jesus is not equal to God and that he is subservient to Him. It is unfortunate that the rest of the New Testament spends much of its time trying not only to overlook this fact, but also to turn the situation on its head and make it seem as if Jesus and the separate 'Father' are co-equals (see Philippians 2:5-11), with a holy *ghost* to round out the three-in-one equation. This is like the Roman Triumvirate of Julius Caesar, Pompey and Marcus Crassus or the later one of Octavian *aka* Caesar Augustus, Marcus Lepidus and Mark Antony, which was a known political structure in the first century CE when early Christian doctrines were being formulated. Perhaps this notion of the trinity of co-equals was a mere extension of this Roman political concept, and it allowed non-Jews to understand and find familiar ground with the new religion when Paul and his followers began to spread their version of Christianity outward from its Jewish roots. (Also note the contemporary triumvirate of the Greek religion in Zeus and his two brothers, Hades and Poseidon.) The idea of God having children was also a known and accepted concept among the Greeks and Romans of that time, making them undoubtedly even more comfortable with the new faith, as it was presented to them. In John 8:42-47, during a lengthy exhortation to the Jews to follow him, Jesus is purported to have said, "If God were really your Father, then you would love me. I came from God, and now I am here. I did not come by my own authority. God sent me. You don't understand these things I say. Why? Because you cannot accept my teaching. Your father is the devil. You belong to him. You want to do what he wants. The devil was a murderer from the beginning. He was always against the truth. There is no truth in him. He is like the lies he tells. Yes,

He knows what's (coming) ahead of them and what's (happened) behind them. They can't intercede at all unless they're acceptable to Him, and they hold Him in fear and reverence. [28] If any of them should ever say, *"I'm a god in place of Him,'* then We would reward him with Hellfire, and that's how We reward the wrongdoers! [29]

Isn't Nature Proof Enough of Allah?

Don't those who suppress (their awareness of the truth) see that the heavens and the earth were once fused together in a single piece, and then We split them apart? (Don't they see) that We made every living thing from water? So won't they believe? [589] [30]

We placed firmly rooted highlands in the earth so it wouldn't shake along with them, [590] and We made broad passes (between them) for them to travel through, so that (through these landmarks) they could be guided (in their travels). [31]

We made the sky as a sheltering canopy, as well. [591] Yet, they turn away from these miraculous signs (in nature that point to an

---

the devil is a liar. He is the father of lies. I speak the truth. That is why you don't believe me. Can any of you prove that I am guilty of sin? If I tell the truth, then why don't you believe me? The person that belongs to God accepts what God says. But you don't accept what God says, because you don't belong to God." After reading a passage like this, can anyone doubt that Jesus and Muhammad have the same status as created beings before God? (Also see Mark 12:29.)

[589] Previous generations of commentators have not fully known how to interpret this line. Many modern commentators hold that it is a clear reference to the Big Bang theory, which asserts that all matter, including the earth, was once fused together in a compact unit that suddenly split apart, eventually resulting in the galaxies, planets, stars and other heavenly bodies over billions of years. This is a plausible interpretation as the plural word *samawat* (heavens) is used here, which is usually used in Qur'anic parlance to refer to all the zones of space outside the earth. (Compare with verse 21:32 where earth's specific 'sky' is mentioned in the singular.)

[590] The plates that make up the surface layer of earth's crust continually move and slowly grind against each other, causing earthquakes and other disasters. The formation of mountains, through gradation and uplift, act as a sort of stabilizer between the plates. If mountains were not formed when the plates collided, but rather the plates would merely crumble each other, then there would be far more earthquakes and volcanic eruptions in the world.

[591] The sky, including the ozone layer, protects the earth from harmful radiation and the like, as well as mitigating the effects of small meteorites, which often burn up in the atmosphere. Were it not for the sky as it is, life could not exist on the planet.

intelligent Creator). [32] Moreover, He's the One Who created the night and the day and the sun and the moon; each of them swims [592] gently along in its rounded (orbit). [593] [33]

> **Background on verse 34:** The pagans wanted to see Muhammad dead so they wouldn't have to hear his message of monotheism and accountability before Allah, and they often told him so. However, even that wouldn't save them from still having to face their Lord one day. That is the reason for the revelation of this verse.

We didn't grant immortality to any mortal being before you, so if you died all of a sudden, (Muhammad), would they get to live forever? [34] Every soul will taste of death, and We're testing you through both disaster and good fortune, and (in the end) you'll all be brought back to Us. [594] [35]

The Foolish Reject Faith

When the faithless see you, (Muhammad,) they treat you with nothing but contempt, saying, *"Is this the one who's talking (against) your gods?"* (Worse still), they reject the Compassionate whenever He's mentioned! [36] Human beings are indeed impulsive from their very creation! Soon will I show you My signs, and then you won't ask Me to hurry them on any more! [37]

"So when will all of this come to pass," they ask, *"if you're really being so honest?"* [38] Oh, if only the faithless knew (for sure about the time) when they'll be powerless to keep the fire off their faces and their backs, and when they'll be quite beyond help! [39]

But no! It'll come upon them all of a sudden, leaving them perplexed! They'll have no power to keep it away, nor will they be

---

[592] The Arabic term used here (*yasbahoun*) literally means that they're gently floating, as if swimming. This is precisely the effect of weightlessness in space, even as astronauts train under water here on earth for their space missions.

[593] The Arabic word *falak* means a rounded path or curved way, i.e., orbit. Thus, the sun and moon have orbits of their own in some type of rounded path.

[594] The Prophet said, "A person will be tested according to his level of religious commitment. The stronger his religion, the harder he'll be tested." (*Ahmad*) The second caliph, 'Umar ibn al-Khattab, once said, "We were tested through hardships, and we bore them with patience; yet, when we were tested with pleasures, we were impatient (in enjoying them and were thus thankless to Allah.)" (*Ma'ariful Qur'an*)

given a break! [40] Many messengers were ridiculed before you, but their critics were eventually surrounded by the very thing at which they scoffed! [41]

Heed the Warning Before It's Too Late

Ask them, *"Who can keep you safe throughout the night and the day from (the command) of the Compassionate?"* Yet, still they turn away from the remembrance of their Lord. [42] Is it because they have gods that can protect them from Us? They don't even have the power to help themselves, nor can anyone protect them from Us! [43]

> **Background on verse 44:** Even though this chapter was revealed in Mecca during a time when the Muslims were suffering from pagan persecution, the pagans were, nevertheless, losing some control and influence around them. Within Mecca, people were converting to Islam, mostly from the poor classes. Thus, they no longer obeyed the tribal chiefs of the city. Outside of Mecca, Muhammad was making converts from tribes both distant and near. This, as this verse suggests, was slowly resetting the strategic map in favor of Islam.

No way! We've given the luxuries of this life to these (people) and to their ancestors, until their time seemed to extend indefinitely. Indeed, don't they see that We're gradually reducing the land (that they hold influence over) from its outlying borders? (Do they still think) they're going to win? [44]

Say (to them), *"I'm only warning you as the revelation (dictates me to do)."* However, the deaf can't hear the call, even when they're issued a warning! [45] If only a slight breath of your Lord's punishment were to touch them, they would surely cry out, *"We're doomed! We were truly in the wrong!"* [46]

On the Day of Assembly, We're going to set up the scales of justice, so that no soul will be treated unfairly in the least. [595] If there's

---

[595] A man who had beaten his servants went to the Prophet and said, "Messenger of Allah. I have servants who lie to me, deceive me and disobey me. Therefore, I shout at them and beat them. How do I stand with respect to them?" The Prophet replied, "On the Day of Resurrection, an account will be taken of the extent of their deceit, disobedience and lying towards you and of the punishment you administered to them. If your punishment was commensurate with their offences, its being exactly equal will count neither for you nor against you. If your punishment was less than their offence deserved, it will be something extra to your credit. However, if your punishment was greater than

something even as light as a mustard seed, We're going to bring it (to the scale). We're sufficient enough to take an account (of all things). [596] [47]

And so it was that We gave the standard (of judgment) to Moses and Aaron, as well as the illuminated (Torah) and a reminder for those who would be mindful (of Allah). [597] [48] They were the ones who feared their Lord sight unseen and who were in awe of the Hour (of Judgment). [49] Now this (Qur'an) is a blessed message that We're sending down (to all of you), so are you just going to dismiss it? [50]

Abraham had a Similar Challenge

And so it was that We gave clarity of thought to Abraham, and We knew everything about him. [51] He had said to his father and his people, *"What are these images to which you're so devoted?"* [598] [52]

"We found our ancestors worshipping them," they replied. [53]

"Well, both you and your ancestors have been clearly mistaken!" (Abraham) declared. [54]

---

their offences deserved, then compensation will be taken from you on their behalf for the excess." Then the man began to weep, so the Prophet asked him if he had ever heard the words of Allah, the Most High. Then the Prophet recited this verse. The result of this was that the man freed his servants in the hopes of salvation from Hell. (*Tirmidhi*) For his part, the Prophet forbade unjustly beating or slapping servants for no reason, requiring that the price of doing that would be that they must be freed. (*Muslim*)

596 The Prophet's wife A'ishah asked him one day if he would remember his family on Judgment Day. He replied to her, saying that there were three times when people would not have the presence of mind to think of anyone else but themselves. These three times will be the day when people will be brought before the scales for their deeds when they don't know how they will fare, when one's record of deeds is passed to them and placed in either their right or left hands, and finally when they have to pass over the bridge spanning the chasm of Hellfire. (*Ma'ariful Qur'an*)

597 The bright light and reminder given to Moses was the Torah.

598 There are other versions of this story in Jewish and Christian lore, but the Qur'anic version is different in many important details and includes dialogue not to be found in any other source. In the many competing Jewish versions, Abraham first destroys the idols in his father's workshop before taking on the temple idols. It is also said that he was thrown in the fire pit with a whole crowd of relatives and other people, though only he survived, and that over 900,000 people came to watch him burn, though he remained unharmed for three days. A Muslim would hold that the Qur'anic narrative is a correction of previous versions of the tale that were corrupted over the long centuries of transmission. See 2:258 and footnote.

"Have you really brought 'the truth' to us," they asked, *"or are you only joking?"* [55]

"Certainly not!" he answered. *"Your Lord is the Lord of the heavens and the earth, and He's the One Who brought them into being! I'm just a witness to this (truth).* [56] *By Allah! I have a plan for your idols after you've turned your backs!"* [57]

And so he broke them to pieces, all except the big one, so (the priests) could return (and find it standing alone, unscathed amidst the rubble). [599] [58]

(When the priests returned and saw what had happened), they said, *"Who did this to our gods? He must have been a criminal!"* [59]

(Some people in the crowd) said, *"We heard a young man named Abraham talking out against them."* [60] The (priests) said, *"Then bring him before the eyes of the people, so they can witness (his confession)."* [61]

(When he was brought), they asked him, *"Are you the one who did this to our gods, Abraham?"* [62]

"No way!" (Abraham) answered. *"Someone must have done it – ah, there's the big one. Just ask (all the broken idols about it), that is if they're able to speak."* [63]

Then (the people) turned towards each other (to discuss the matter amongst) themselves, and they said, *"You were all wrong (in trying to get a confession from him, for the biggest idol must have done it)."* [600] [64]

---

[599] Abraham entered the temple when the priests were away for festivities; then he broke all the smaller idols with a hammer or an axe. He hung the tool he used to break the idols hanging around the neck of the biggest idol, which was left unscathed. (The largest idol was probably Nanna-Sin, the ubiquitous moon god of much of Mesopotamia.)

[600] Some commentators suggest that verse 64 should be understood to mean that the people almost realized that their idolatry was indeed false. (One old Jewish tale quotes the king as admitting, "Idols neither speak nor eat nor move.") At the last moment, however, the idolaters snapped back into defending their beliefs. I prefer the alternative view that Abraham confused the people into admitting their idols were lifeless and dead. That was why they were so angry that they wanted to burn him alive on the spot.

Then their thoughts became muddled, and they reversed course saying (to Abraham), *"You know full well that they can't speak!"* [65]

"So are you worshipping besides Allah," (Abraham) asked, *"things that can neither benefit you nor harm you?* [66] *Shame on you and the things that you're worshipping besides Allah! Don't you have any sense?"* [67]

"Burn him!" they shouted. *"Protect your gods if you must do something!"* [68]

We said, *"Fire, cool down and be a place of safety for Abraham!"* [69] But then (the nobles) made a plan against him, but We caused them to fail. [601] [70] We saved (Abraham) and Lot (and directed them) towards the land that We blessed for (all the nations) of the world. [602] [71]

We granted (Abraham a son named) Isaac and (a grandson named) Jacob as an extra gift, and We made each of them righteous. [72] We also made them into leaders to guide (their people) by Our command. We inspired them to do good, to establish prayer and to give in charity, and they always served Us. [73]

We also gave discernment and knowledge to Lot and saved him from the city that was steeped in filthy behavior. [603] They really were an evil and rebellious people! [74] We admitted him into Our mercy, for he was one of the righteous. [75]

---

[601] After Abraham escaped the fire unhurt, the stunned crowd let him go. He was soon taken in front of the king and interrogated. Why did the king want him killed? During his meeting with the king, Abraham had dumbfounded him with the logic mentioned in verse 2:258, so the king ordered Abraham to be punished, though he escaped, as this verse asserts. The young Abraham had a small window of opportunity to escape. The book of Genesis says that Abraham's father moved his family out of Ur to a northern city named Harran, possibly to protect him. Abraham eventually left his father and moved into Palestine.

[602] This refers to the Holy Land which encompasses the modern nations of Jordan, Israel and greater Palestine. These lands were specially blessed by Allah. Due to their significance and strategic value, they have been fought over for thousands of years.

[603] Although he lived in the wicked city of Sodom, Lot never became corrupted.

When Noah called to (Us) in the past, We listened to him and saved him and his family from the great anguish. [76] We helped him against the people who denied Our signs. They really were an evil people, so We drowned them all together! [77]

> **Background on verse 78:** There was a very interesting court case in Solomon's time which is the subject of this Qur'anic verse. Some sheep wandered into another man's fields by night and ate up all the young shoots, causing the farmer's crops to be ruined. David ruled that the farmer should be allowed to keep the sheep in compensation, but his young son Solomon, who was not yet a teenager, suggested that the farmer should be allowed to keep the sheep and use them only until he recouped his losses (by taking their milk, wool and young lambs). This way the farmer could be compensated, and the shepherd wouldn't be ruined for something he never intended to happen. David accepted his son's suggestion, and it was a very wise ruling, indeed.

When David and Solomon rendered their verdict concerning the case of some people's sheep that had wandered by night into the field (of someone else, causing crop loss), We (were there), witnessing their verdict. [604] [78] We endowed Solomon with a clear understanding of the matter, and to each of them We gave discernment and knowledge. We caused both the mountains and the birds, along with David, to glorify Us, [605] and We made it happen. [606] [79]

---

[604] In another case put before David, two women came fighting over custody of a baby. (A wolf had come and taken one of the women's children; thus, they each claimed ownership over the one surviving baby.) David ruled that the child belonged to the older woman, but Solomon came and asked for a sword and threatened to cut the baby in half so each woman could share it. The younger woman gave up all rights to the child immediately, and this is how Solomon showed to whom the baby really belonged. Thus, the younger woman got her baby back. (*Ahmad*)

[605] This is a reference to what is reported in Psalm 148:1-14 where the order is given to everything living and non-living to praise God. The birds, mountains, etc. are all mentioned there.

[606] The Prophet was passing by a home at night when he heard a man named Abu Musa al-'Ashari reciting the Qur'an in an exceptionally beautiful voice. He remarked about it, "That man has been given one of the flutes of the people of David." Abu Musa heard what the Prophet said and came out, saying, "If I knew you were listening, then I would've done my best for you!" (*Fath al-Bari*)

We also taught (David) how to make coats of armor for your benefit, so you could be protected from each other's violence in combat. Won't you then be thankful? [607] [80]

Solomon had the very winds themselves at his disposal, and he used them (to propel his ships) towards the land that We had blessed, and We knew all about everything (he did). [608] [81] (Solomon also had control) over some of the devilish ones who (were forced) to dive (in the sea to collect pearls) for him, and who did other work, besides. We were guarding them (so they couldn't do mischief or flee). [609] [82]

There were other Prophets Who were Blessed

When Job cried out to his Lord, saying, *"Misery has come upon me, but You're the most merciful of the merciful,"* [83]

We listened to him, took away his misery, restored his family to him and doubled their number – all as a mercy from Our presence and a reminder for those who serve Us. [84]

Ismael, Idrís and Ezekiel – each of them was patient, [610] [85] so We admitted them into Our mercy, for they were among the righteous. [86]

---

[607] David was able to integrate armor technology into his armed forces. He did not necessarily invent the technology, and this verse doesn't say that he did, but he did learn how to craft it and make improvements upon it. David was probably keen on acquiring such an advantage for his armies, given that as a boy he witnessed the well-armored Philistines facing off against the armies of his predecessor, King Saul.

[608] There have been two opinions about this power of Solomon. Some have said it means that Solomon could order the wind to move at his command. Others have said it refers to Solomon's fleet of ships, which plied the region under favorable winds and brought him vast riches through trade (see I Kings 9:26-28). (See 34:12 where the purpose of the wind for Solomon is mentioned.) The land that Allah had blessed, by the way, refers to the land of Palestine, which was known as Israel in Solomon's day.

[609] See 34:12-14 for an explanation of Solomon's control over these *hidden ones*.

[610] Ismael (Ishmael) was patient due to his having to endure possibly being sacrificed by his father. (At-Tabari thought it was Isaac who was to be sacrificed, though Muslim scholars generally believe is was Ishmael and not Isaac who was in that incident, as explained by Ibn Taymiyyah and Ibn Kathir..) Idrís taught for many years and was not always listened to, while Ezekiel, according to Biblical sources, had to tell the people of Jerusalem they were going to be conquered, without being too specific as God warned him the people would ignore him (Ezekiel 3:26-27), and his wife also died of the plague and he was told not to mourn her in the traditional way, but use her example as a sign of what was to come from the Babylonians. (Ezekiel 24:15-24)

And the fish master, (Jonah) [611] - he left in anger and thought We had no power over him, but he cried out in the darkened (belly of the fish), [612] *"There is no god besides You! Glory be to You! I was truly wrong!"* [613] [87] We listened to him and saved him from his distress. That's how We save those who have faith! [88]

When Zachariah called upon his Lord, saying, *"My Lord! Don't leave me childless, though You're the best inheritor (of the future),"* [89]

We listened to him, too, and granted him (a son named) John. And so We cured his wife's (infertility!) These prophets were quick to do good.

They used to call upon Us in hope and trepidation, and they were humble towards Us. [90]

And (Mary), the one who had maintained her virginity - We breathed Our spirit into her and made her and her son a sign for all the worlds. [91]

---

[611] Jonah was originally from a small town in Nazareth named Gath-heper. He was sent to dwell among the Assyrians in their capital at Nineveh in order to preach to them. The Assyrians were a ruthless and cruel warrior race, and the prospect of living among them must have been abhorrent to a man like Jonah. Therefore, he turned back in anger (possibly mixed with fear) and tried to flee Allah's command. He took passage on a boat to Tarshish, but wound up being thrown overboard by frightened sailors seeking to placate the sea during a storm. He was quickly swallowed up by a large fish instead of drowning! Jonah survived and later convinced the people of Nineveh to repent, and he dwelt among them to guide them for a time. (See 10:98 and footnote for more information concerning his story.)

[612] There are documented cases of people who have been swallowed by fish and survived. One large species of fish common throughout the world is the "Sea Dog" or *carcharodon carcharias* which swallowed a fallen sailor in the year 1758. The man was saved when his captain shot the fish, which can grow as long as forty feet, with a cannon ball. Sperm whales have also been known to swallow humans. In 1891 a sailor from a ship named "Star of the East" was swallowed by one after he fell overboard, and he was found alive – two days later – when the whale was harpooned and brought aboard a whaling vessel. The sailor, James Bartley, described his time in the belly of the whale as a place of heat, darkness and stinging fluids.

[613] The Prophet once remarked that any supplication made by a person, coupled with the cry of Jonah, would surely be accepted by Allah Who would then remove his distress and misfortune. (*Ahmad, Tirmidhi*) The Biblical book of Jonah records the lament of our hero of the same name in Jonah 2:2.

Truly, this community of yours is one community, and I am your Lord, so serve me. [92] (It will come to pass that later generations will) divide their affairs amongst themselves (by breaking up into sects), but they're all going to return to Us. [614] [93]   Whoever does a moral deed and has faith, his effort won't be rejected, for We're going to record it. [94]

A Sign of the End Times

It's forbidden for any settlement that We destroyed to ever return (to life) [615] [95] until (the people of) *Yajuj* and *Majuj* are unleashed and they swoop down from every hill. [616] [96]

When the true promise draws near, that's when the eyes of those who covered (the light of faith within their hearts) will be staring – unblinking in horror. *"We're doomed! We never thought about any of this! We were truly wrong!"* [617] [97]

---

[614] Verses 91-92 here are both a statement of principle and a prediction of what eventually came to pass. The Muslim community is meant to be united, and the standard of membership in the fellowship of Islam is very simple. The Prophet once remarked that any person who says that there is no god but Allah and who eats halal meat is a Muslim. Variations after that are acceptable (within some well-defined yet generous limits). Yet, within a generation of the Prophet's passing, new sects arose that claimed exclusive truth, and dissension arose in the Muslim world that has remained to this day. Allah will bring all people back to Him, and He will tell them the truth of all that they did. Also see 6:159, 23:53-54 and 30:32.

[615] This refers to cities specifically destroyed by an act of Allah's will. Normal natural disasters or other calamities can strike a land and its people can rebuild.

[616] The *Yajuj* and *Majuj* are invaders who will invade and conquer much of the Middle East. Translators usually label them as the Biblical Gog and Magog, but this may not be a valid linkage. These two tribes (at least their ancestors) are mentioned in chapter 18, verses 83-101, along with the story of Cyrus the Great, and were originally most likely two bands of fierce nomadic warriors of Central Asia: the Scythians and Massagetes, as the Greeks knew them. Later invaders from the same region were the Mongols and the Tartars who between them devastated much of the world from Europe to China. Interestingly enough, many scholars of the thirteenth and fourteenth centuries considered those two tragic depredations the fulfillment of this Qur'anic prophecy. It may be possible.

[617] Psalms 9:17 echoes a similar theme when it says, "The wicked shall be turned into hell, and all the nations that forgot Allah."

The Fate of False Gods

Background on verses 98-100: The Prophet was sitting with some prominent pagans near the Ka'bah and preaching to them one day, when the eloquent speaker, an-Nadr ibn al-Harith, came to the gathering and started disputing with him. The Prophet won the argument and then recited this newly revealed passage to the gathering. Then he got up and went to sit with some other people. (*Asbab ul-Nuzul*)

To be sure, both you and (the false idols) that you worship besides Allah will be no more than fuel for Hellfire, *and you're going to reach it!* [98]

If those (idols) were really gods, then they would never even have to go near it, but each of them will be made to stay in it! [99] For them there will be nothing more inside than weeping and crushing silence. [100]

Background on verses 101-103: After the Prophet had left the gathering (see background for verses 98-100), one of the pagans remaining in that group, al-Waleed ibn al-Mughirah, said, "By Allah, an-Nadr ibn al-Harith couldn't beat the son of 'Abdel Muttalib in an argument. Muhammad even claims that both we and these gods that we worship are fuel for Hellfire." Another man named 'Abdullah ibn az-Zab'ari, who had some knowledge of Christian and Jewish doctrines, said, "By Allah, if I met with him, I'd beat him in an argument. Ask Muhammad whether everyone who is worshipped instead of God will be in Hellfire along with those who worshipped them, because we worship the angels, the Jews worship Ezra, and the Christians worship the Messiah, Jesus the son of Mary." Al-Waleed and the other men in the group were impressed with his tactics and thought he had made some good points.

Then the pagans approached the Prophet, who was still with the new gathering, and asked him about this. The Prophet replied, "Everyone who desires to worship something other than God will be with the one who is worshipped, for indeed they're worshipping Satan and whoever told them to worship that object." Just before the pagans could object that this would also put Jesus in Hell, the Prophet recited these new verses [101-103], which made the caveat that good people who were worshipped against their will would be exempted from going to Hell along with those who worshipped them. Then verse 21:26 was revealed, which called the idea of assigning children to Allah ludicrous. Az-Zab'ari then accused Muhammad of wanting to be worshipped as a part of God, like the Christians called Jesus a part of God. Thereafter, to the amazement of al-Waleed, who had accompanied az-Zab'ari to watch, the Prophet recited the following additional verses: 43:57-61. (*Ibn Kathir*)

However, those who already had a good (record) with Us will be far removed from that place. [101] They won't hear even the faintest sound of Hellfire, for they're going to be in the place for which their souls had hoped. [102]

The Great Distress won't bother them at all, for instead they'll be met by angels (who will say), *"This is your day that you've been promised!"* [103]

This is a Message for People to Consider

One day We're going to roll up the sky like a written scroll. Even as We began creation in the beginning, so shall We produce a new one. That's a promise binding upon Us, and We can certainly fulfill it! [618] [104]

And so it was that We wrote in the Psalms, which came after the message (of Moses): *"The land shall be inherited by My righteous servants."* [619] [105] There's a lesson in this for people who serve (Allah). [106]

(Muhammad,) We didn't send you except to be a mercy to all the worlds. [107] So say (to them), *"It's been revealed to me that your God is One God. So will you now submit (to Him)?"* [108]

If they turn back, then tell them, *"I've expressed the message to you evenly and fairly, and I don't know if what you've been promised is near or far.* [109] *He knows what's being uttered openly and what's being held in private.* [110] *I don't know if (the delay in punishment) is meant to be a test for you or merely a time for you to live for a while."* [620] [111]

---

[618] Some modern commentators have postulated that this phrase, '*roll up the sky like a written scroll*' is a veiled reference to the antithesis of the Big Bang, a phenomenon known as the Big Crunch. According to this theory, even as all the matter of the universe has been steadily moving away from the epicenter of the Big Bang, one day the acceleration will slow and then reverse itself until all matter comes together and recompacts itself. Besides the fact that this theory is only a hypothesis, the word used in this verse is the singular *as-sama'* or sky, which is usually indicative of the immediate zone around the earth. Thus, this verse speaks only of the destruction of the earth's atmosphere, at the most.

[619] See Psalms 37:29 where Allah is reported to have said, "The righteous shall inherit the land and dwell therein forever." Most commentators have suggested that the 'land' in question here in this verse is really a reference to Paradise. Thus, only the righteous will inherit the eternal home. See 39:74 and 23:10-11. (*Ma'ariful Qur'an*)

[620] The Prophet said, "Indeed, the immensity of the reward is commensurate with the immensity of the test. Truly, if Allah loves a people, He tests them. Whoever then is

279

Then say (to them), *"My Lord! Judge truthfully (between us). Our Compassionate Lord is the One to Whom We should look for help against all (the false things) you attribute (to Him)."* [112]

contented (after hardship), he shall have joy, while whoever gets angry (at his misfortune), anger will come down upon him." (*Tirmidhi*)

The Pilgrimage

22 Al Hajj

Late Meccan to Early Medinan Period

This is a transitional chapter. Verses 1-18 were most likely revealed in the Prophet's last months in Mecca. The remaining verses are definitely Medinan in their tone and structure and were probably revealed within the first year or two after the Migration to Medina in the year 622. The name of this chapter indicates that after the Muslims had migrated to Medina, they had begun to grow nostalgic for their hometown of Mecca, especially when the month of *Hajj* had arrived. Many wondered what the future held and about relations with the Meccan pagans they had left behind. The point is also made in this chapter that the Quraysh had no right to prevent people from visiting the public shrine, known as the Ka'bah, located within their city. It was also during this first two years in Medina that Meccan raids on the Muslims in Medina began in earnest, and many Muslims wondered when they would be given permission to fight back. Verse 39 of this chapter is universally recognized as the first verse to authorize self-defense. Shortly after it was revealed, the Prophet authorized the first Muslim expedition to quell some bedouin raiders near the coast of the Red Sea early in the year 624.

In the Name of Allah,
the Compassionate, the Merciful

O you people! Be mindful of your Lord! The convulsions of the Hour (of Judgment) will be a terrible thing! [1] On the day when you see it, every nursing mother will forget her suckling babe, and every pregnant woman will have a miscarriage.

You'll see people (stumbling about) as if they were drunk; yet, they won't be drunk! Allah's punishment will be that intense! [621] [2]

---

[621] The Prophet was traveling with some companions in the countryside, and they had fallen behind him. Then the Prophet started to recite this passage in a loud voice, and the men quickly caught up to him to hear what he had to say. After the men heard the message of the verses, the Prophet said, "Do you know what day that is? That's the day when Adam will be called. His Lord will call to him and will say, 'Adam, bring forth those of your descendants who are to be put in the Fire.' (Adam) will reply, 'Lord! How

Even still, there are some people who have no knowledge; yet, they continue to argue about Allah, and they follow every rebellious devil. [622] [3] It's (a principle that's) already been recorded that whoever inclines towards (Satan) will be misled by him and guided by him towards the punishment of the raging blaze. [4]

Consider the Origin of Man

O you people! If you have any doubts about the resurrection, then (consider how We brought you into being the first time). We created you from dust, then from a drop of mingled fluids, then from a clinging thing, and then from a chunk of partially formed and partially unformed flesh, so that We could make (the course of your development) obvious to you. We cause whomever We want to reside within the womb for a set time period. [623]

---

many are to be put in the Fire?' (Allah) will answer, 'From every thousand, nine hundred and ninety-nine will be put in the Fire, and one will be in Paradise.'" When his companions heard this, they became despondent and stopped smiling. One companion even sighed despondently, "O Messenger of Allah, who can escape that terrible fate?" When the Prophet saw the concern on all the peoples' faces, he said, "Be of good cheer and strive hard, for by the One Who holds the soul of Muhammad in His hand, you're going to be as numerous as two other creations in numbers, the *Yajuj* and *Majuj* and those who've already died of both Adam and Iblis's descendants." The companions began to smile again, and the Prophet continued, saying, "Strive hard and be of good cheer, for by the One Who holds the soul of Muhammad in His hand, in comparison to the rest of humanity, you're going to be like a mole on the side of a camel or a mark on the foreleg of an animal." (*Ahmad, Tirmidhi, Nisa'i*) In another report of the same incident it's added that the Prophet began calling out that he hoped the Muslims would be the majority of the people of Paradise, and his companions shouted, "Allah is greater!" in unison.

622 The commentators say that this is a reference to wicked human beings who goad their people into endless and futile theological debates about Allah, resulting in widespread confusion and disillusionment among the masses. By extension, the blame goes ultimately back to the real Satan, and the next verse gives his fate.

623 'Abdullah ibn Mas'ud (d. 653) said, "The Messenger of Allah, who is the honest and inspired one, told us, 'Every one of you is collected in the womb of his mother for the first forty days, then he becomes a clinging (leech-like) thing for another forty days and then a lump of flesh for another forty days. Then Allah sends an angel to write four statements. He writes what his provision will be, (the nature) of his deeds, the length of his life, and whether he will be blessed or miserable. Then (the angel) blows a spirit (*ruh*) into him." (*Bukhari, Muslim*) Based on this narration, the traditional view has been that after 120 days the fetus is to be considered a full-fledged human being.

Then We bring you out as infants (and allow you to grow until) you reach your age of full strength. Some of you are made to die (young), [624] while others are propelled into a feeble old age with the result that they lose all knowledge even though they had known so much before. [625]

You also see the earth, how it's barren and lifeless. Yet, when We shower rain down upon it, it stirs (to life) and bursts forth with every kind of beautiful growth in paired (plant organs). [626] [5] That's because Allah is the true Reality. He gives life to the dead, and He has power over all things. [6]

The Arrogant will Perish

The Hour (of Judgment) will come to pass. There is no doubt about it, and neither is there (any doubt) that Allah will resurrect those who are in their graves. [7] Yet, there are some people who argue about Allah without any knowledge or guidance or even an enlightened book! [8]

Such (a person then) cocks his head (arrogantly) to the side and distracts others away from the path of Allah. Well, he's going to have nothing but disgrace in this life, and on the Day of Assembly We're going to make him taste the burning punishment! [9] *"This is (what you deserve) because of what your hands sent ahead of you!"* Allah is never unfair to (His) servants. [10]

---

[624] Babies and small children sometimes tragically die, as do people in the prime of their lives. This is the way of things, even as the same happens all throughout the web of life that makes up our world. For those who bear with patience the loss of those whose time seemed to be inadvertently shortened, they can still hope for rewards from Allah and an eventual reunion with their dearly departed ones. The Prophet once promised Paradise to those women who lose their babies and then bear the loss with patience.

[625] The onset of age can bring on a loss of neurological functioning and memory loss, such as from Alzheimer's Disease, which makes a grown adult as innocent and unable to care for himself as a child. It has been shown that regular brain "exercise" by remembering old events, reading for enjoyment, doing logic puzzles and other things can mitigate these ill-effects.

[626] This reference to beauty and paired growth is to flowers which have paired organs.

When Faith is Fickle

Background on verse 11: Ibn 'Abbas (d. 687) explained the reason for this verse by saying, "People would come to Medina (to declare their conversion to Islam). If their wives bore sons and their mares gave birth to foals, then they would say, 'This is a good religion,' but if their wives or mares didn't give birth, they would say, 'This is a bad religion.'" (*Bukhari*)

There are some people who serve Allah as if they were standing squarely [627] (on the edge of fickle whims). If something good happens to them, they're content with it, but if some misfortune befalls them, they turn their faces away (in disappointment). They're going to lose both this world and the next, and that's a loss for all to see! [11]

They call upon others in place of Allah (for good luck and fortune). Yet, (those idols) can do them no real harm nor bring them any benefit at all! (Believing in idols) is the most obvious loss! [12] In fact, it may be the case that (such a person) is really calling upon something that will harm him even more than it could ever possibly benefit him! That's the worst kind of patron to have and the worst kind of follower, as well! [13]

Allah's Plan will Prevail

Allah will allow those who believed and did what was morally right to enter into gardens beneath which rivers flow, for Allah fulfills what He plans. [14] If anyone thinks that Allah's not going to help (His Prophet) in this world and in the next, then they should stretch a rope up to the sky and (climb up there so they) can cut off (Allah's help) by themselves, (if they think they can stop it). [628]

Then let them see if this scheme of theirs will do away with the source of their tension! [15] This is the way in which We send down

---

[627] The Arabic word used here means they are 'standing' firm in a certain way or in a situation that can be fluid depending on variables.

[628] The pagans were complaining that Muhammad's preaching was causing stress and dissension in the city. This verse dares them to prevent Allah from helping His Prophet, if they can. Some commentators think this verse is saying that if they really want to stop the Prophet, then the faithless should hang a rope from the sky and hang themselves with it, if they think it will bring them peace of mind. (*Asbab ul-Nuzul*) Either interpretation is valid in this ambiguous verse.

verses with precise (challenges so they can be warned), and Allah guides whomever He wants! [16]

Truly, the believing (Muslims), (the followers of) Judaism, (the followers of) the Sabian faith, [629] the Christians, the Magi (who follow Zoroaster) and the idol-worshippers - Allah will judge among them on the Day of Assembly, for Allah is a witness over all things. [630] [17]

---

[629] See 2:62 and 5:69 for an explanation of the Sabian faith. Before accepting Islam or understanding it, 'Umar ibn al-Khattab thought Muhammad was a Sabian.

[630] Islam is the only world religion that makes room for and recognizes the status and rights of those of other religions. No other religion in the world names other competing religions in its scripture in a favorable light and then (scripturally) affords that competing religion the right to exist free from oppression, harassment and forced conversion. (See 2:256 and the book entitled, *Peace Be Unto You*, by Zachary Karabell, Alfred A. Knopf Pub., 2007.) Contrary to the unfortunate and *highly inaccurate myth* that "Islam was spread by the sword," Muslim civilization has been the most tolerant of all *religiously-oriented* or *religiously-motivated* societies (when compared in all respects). The early Muslim state did have military conflicts with the Christian Byzantines first and then the Zoroastrian Persians, but those were contests between governments that the Muslims did not start and later happened to win. (See the book *The Great Arab Conquests* by Hugh Kennedy for more on how Ithe new empire spread so fast.) On the ground, official policy under the first four caliphs of the seventh century was to leave conquered peoples to their own religion. The non-Muslims merely had to pay a tax to the state to exempt their males from the draft and to pay their fair share of their government's operating expenses. This policy continued, with very little aberration, throughout Umayyad and into 'Abbasid times in the thirteenth century. (It has long been noted that under Umayyad rule, conversion to Islam was often *discouraged* by the government, which benefited from the *jizyah* tax. This because unlike the collected *zakah* tax, *jizyah* funds could be spent in any way.) It has been estimated by modern historians that by the end of Umayyad rule in the eighth century, more than 80% of the population in the Islamic Empire was still either Christian, Zoroastrian, Hindu or Jewish. Muslims, by contrast, only formed a majority in urban areas. The same general statistic holds true for Muslim-ruled Spain, even after 700 years of Muslim rule. (That's why it was so easy for Christians to retake the land later on – most of the population was still Christian!) The later Seljuk and then Ottoman Turks continued to practice generally tolerant policies well into modern times. Although there were occasional bouts of persecution against Hindus in India, in the main such aberrations were not sustained, nor were they successful, for when the British wrested control of the Subcontinent from the last of the Mughal emperors, (a Muslim dynasty that ruled India for three centuries), the Muslims made up less than 15% of the population. In addition, no Muslim governments ever conquered southeast Asia, where most of the Muslims of the world now reside. Contrast this with the results of Christian rule in North and South America where the native peoples were forcibly converted under pain of death. (That's also how Northern Europe was converted to Christianity under Charlemagne, by the way, for he decreed that all who resisted conversion would be '*put to the sword*.') There are still religious minorities living in nearly every Muslim nation that *predate* the coming of Islam to those places. Can the same be said of Christian nations? Today there is religious freedom in the *secular* West, but at the price of removing religion from government policies, given that warfare and intolerance among Christian nations

Don't you see that everything within the heavens and the earth bows (in submission to His will) - the sun, the moon, the stars, the hills, the trees, the animals and a large number of people, as well? At the same time, there's another large number (of human beings) who have had due punishment justified against them. Whomever Allah humiliates, there can be no one to honor him, for Allah does whatever He wants. [631] [18]

The Faithless have No Chance of a Final Victory

Background on verses 19-24: This passage refers to the Prophet's uncle Hamza, who along with 'Ali and 'Ubaydah, were arguing with the pagan leader 'Utbah and two of his friends, Shaybah and Al-Walid, just before the two trios engaged in single combat before the Battle of Badr began. 'Ali finished the argument saying, "I'm going to be the first one to kneel down before the Compassionate so that the dispute can be settled on the Day of Judgment." The three Muslim fighters killed the three pagans in the duel, and then the full battle got under way. (*Bukhari*)

(There were) two opposing groups who argued with each other about their Lord (at the Battle of Badr). Those who rejected (faith in Him) will have clothes made of fire tailored just for them and (buckets) of boiling muck poured over their heads! [19] It will melt their guts away, as well as their skins! [20] They'll also have iron hammers (used against them to drive them on), besides! [21] Every time they'll wish to get away from it - *from their torment* – they'll be forced back into it, (and they'll be told), *"Suffer the burning punishment!"* [22]

(However,) Allah will allow those who believed and did what was morally right to enter into gardens beneath which rivers flow. They'll wear bracelets of gold and pearls, and adorn themselves with clothes made of silk! [23] They had been guided towards the purest speech of

---

devastated Europe and held back its progress for countless centuries. For contrast, also see Deuteronomy 7:2-3.

[631] It is customary that when this verse is recited, the reader or listener should bow down humbly and prostrate to Allah for a moment. The Prophet said, "When the son of Adam recites the verses containing (required) prostrations, Satan runs away weeping and says, 'Oh! I'm ruined! The son of Adam was commanded to prostrate, and he prostrated, so he will be given Paradise. When I was commanded to prostrate, I refused, so I'm doomed to Hellfire.'" (*Muslim*)

all, and thus they were guided towards the path of the Praised One. [632] [24]

The Meccans Prevented the Pilgrims

Those who reject (Allah) and who've been holding others back from the way of Allah and from the Sacred Mosque (in Mecca), which We had (intended to be) open for all people [633] – *both the resident and the visitor are equal there* [634] – and those who want to do (any type of) evil or injustice there - *We're going to make them all suffer a painful punishment!* [635] [25]

The Origin of the Pilgrimage

When We showed Abraham where to build the (Sacred) House, [636] (We told him), *"Don't take anything as a partner in My divinity. Purify*

---

[632] What is the 'purest speech?' The Prophet said, "They will be inspired (to say) words of glorification and praise, just as they are inspired to breath." (*Muslim*) Some scholars think this verse also refers to the *kalimah*, or essential statement of 'There is no god but Allah.' (*Ma'ariful Qur'an*)

[633] See verse 9:28 and footnote.

[634] While property can be owned, bought, sold and inherited in Mecca, many commentators are of the opinion that no one is allowed to charge rent to another person living there. 'Umar ibn al-Khattab, during his rule, said, "People of Mecca! Don't put gates on your houses, and let the bedouins stay wherever they want." (*Ibn Kathir*) Also see 9:28 and footnote for a discussion of the open nature of the city of Mecca.

[635] The commentators have offered many interpretations about what kinds of evil or injustice a person might commit in Mecca. Among these are hoarding essential goods, mistreating others, killing any living thing and keeping people out of the city unjustly. The Prophet, himself, made a prediction about a future invading army when he said, "This House will be attacked by an army. Then when they are in a wide open space, the first and last of them will be swallowed up by the earth." (*Bukhari*) Thus far, the only army that ever fought in Mecca was led by the forces of the Umayyad leader Abdul Malik ibn Marwan under the command of Hajjaj ibn Yusuf (d. 714). However, that army was not attacking the Ka'bah as it's target, but rather the forces of 'Abdullah ibn az-Zubayr (d. 692), who led a rival caliphate from Mecca. (The Ka'bah was damaged by a catapult shot, and the Umayyads were victorious after a bloody siege and battle. This brazen assault on Mecca has earned Hajjaj a great amount of disgrace in Muslim historical circles)

[636] The Ka'bah is the oldest continuously used religious shrine in the world. Its history goes back nearly four thousand years to the time of Abraham. Since that time, it has been built and rebuilt as necessary. How did Allah show Abraham where to build the Ka'bah? Here is one possible explanation. A very small meteorite fell from the sky and landed in the valley of Becca, which would later be the site of the city of Mecca. Abraham saw this sign from afar and thus knew that that valley was the place where he had to leave

My House for those who walk around it, stand (near it) or bow down in prostration." [637] [26]

"Declare the pilgrimage ritual to all people. They're going to come to you on foot and on every type of well-worn transportation, traveling from every deep canyon (on earth), [27] *so they can bear witness to things that will benefit them, and so they can remember the name of Allah during the appointed days."* [638]

"Then after they've (slaughtered) the livestock that He's allowed for them, you can eat from them and feed those who are in desperate need. [28] *Thereafter, let them clean themselves up,* [639] *fulfill their vows and then walk around the Ancient House."* [29]

This is (the origin and purpose of the Pilgrimage to Mecca). Whoever honors the sacred rituals of Allah will have the best (reward waiting for him) in the presence of his Lord. You're allowed to eat any type of livestock (during the Pilgrimage), except for (the

---

his second wife Hagar and his son Ishmael. Later, he would build a religious shrine there when he came back for a visit and saw his son had survived. Abraham recovered the meteorite and placed it as a decoration in the side of his shrine. That is the Black Stone, which still sits in one corner of the Ka'bah shrine in Mecca to this day. Muslims do not worship this stone, nor do they ascribe any special significance to it other than as a revered link back to Abraham. During the pilgrimage season, devout people try to touch or kiss the stone in respect to Abraham. Those who cannot reach it point to it when they pass by it.

[637] There is a small enclosed area just behind the Ka'bah that was originally part of the shrine built by Abraham. When the Ka'bah was damaged by a flood in the days before Muhammad was made a prophet, the Quraysh rebuilt the Ka'bah. However, due to lack of funds, they didn't extend the Ka'bah to cover this small semi-circular section – they just left it as is. The Prophet explained that that this more ancient section was a part of Abraham's original design. Thus, he included it as part of the footprint of the sacred site around which the pilgrims would walk while praising Allah. Some commentators suggest that the Arabic word *atique*, (used in verse 29,) which is defined as 'ancient,' may also mean unconquered, in that the Ka'bah has always remained a fixture of the city from time immemorial. Some scholars believe the site of the Ka'bah was taken as a place of worship even earlier in the time of Adam and Eve.

[638] The *appointed days* are the first ten days of the Islamic month of *Dhul-Hijjah*, during which all the rituals of the Pilgrimage are performed. The Prophet said, "There are no days that are more important in the sight of Allah or in which deeds are more loved by Him than these ten days, so increase your (saying of the testimony of faith), your extolling of Allah's greatness and your praising (of Him)." (*Ahmad*)

[639] When the main portion of the *Hajj* is completed and the animals have been sacrificed, then the pilgrims may cut their hair, trim their beards, cut their nails and wear regular clothes, as some of the restrictions of the journey have been lifted.

forbidden things) that have already been mentioned to you. So shun the abomination of idols, and shun false doctrines. [30]

Follow the natural (monotheistic) way of life for Allah's sake, and never make any partners with Him. If anyone makes partners with Allah, it'll be as if they fell from the sky and was snatched up by birds or as if they were carried away by the wind and thrown in a faraway place! [640] [31] That's (exactly what their situation would be like)!

Now whoever truly wishes to honor the symbolic (ritual of sacrifice ordained) by Allah (should know) that it can only (be done properly) by a (person who has a) heart that's mindful (of its duty towards Him). [641] [32]

There are certain benefits for you to enjoy for a while in the (animals that you raise and then dedicate to Allah for the Pilgrimage). Then they're to be brought (near the vicinity) of the Ancient House (for sacrifice). [642] [33]

The Purpose of the Sacrifice during the Pilgrimage

We've appointed religious rituals for every community (on earth), so they could commemorate the name of Allah over the resources He gave them from among (the many types of) livestock

---

[640] The Prophet said, "When the angels of death take the soul of a faithless person at death, they take his soul up to the sky, but the gates of heaven are not open for him. Instead, his soul is thrown down from there." (*Ahmad*)

[641] The Prophet forbade the sacrifice of animals that were lame or deformed and also those that had their ears mutilated according to pagan customs and superstitions. That is to what this phrase here alludes.

[642] The sacrificial animals are brought near to Mecca but are not sacrificed within the city limits, based on the prohibition of killing anything within the city's boundaries. The place of slaughter is at Mina, which is about five miles away. The meat is then used to feed both the pilgrims and the poor. (Thus, there can be no objection to the ritual as the animals are eaten and not wasted.) This exercise is a way to commemorate the story of Abraham and his test, in which he almost sacrificed his (then) only son to demonstrate his obedience to Allah. Thus, the other benefits that come from their slaughter are Allah's rewards for your obedience, as well as food for you to eat. Even prior to this, the animals might have provided labor and milk for years. The Prophet said, "Eat (some of it), and give (some of it) in charity, and make use of the skin, but don't sell it." (*Ahmad*)

(animals). [643] Your God is One God, so submit yourselves to Him and give good news to the meek [34] whose hearts are filled with awe whenever Allah is mentioned, who are patient with what troubles them, who maintain their prayers and who spend in charity out of the resources that We've provided for them. [35]

The sacrificial animals that We've made for you are symbols of (obedience) to Allah. [644] There are benefits in them for you, so pronounce the name of Allah over them as they're lined up and also when they've been laid down on their sides (after slaughter). Then you may eat from them and feed those poor people who are quietly enduring (their misfortune), as well as those poor people who come begging in desperation. This is why We've placed the animals under your control, so you can be thankful. [645] [36]

---

[643] Nearly every community on earth eats some type of animals for food. The principle in religions all over the world, which has still carried over from ancient days, is for people to give some type of thanks to Allah for the animals they kill for food. For example, Native Americans had special prayers they recited before a hunt and after they felled a creature. Judaism has long had its own rituals for slaughter, and even Christians are taught to say a prayer over their meals to thank their Lord. Some religious traditions have dispensed with eating animals all together, such as orthodox Buddhism and Hinduism, which require their most ardent followers to be strict vegetarians. Taking an animal's life is not supposed to be an easy thing for a believer in Allah, for religion teaches us to hold all life as Allah's miraculous gift. People who take the lives of animals must do so only reluctantly and with a humble heart. A man once went to the Prophet and said, "Messenger of Allah, when I slaughter a sheep, I feel sad for it." The Prophet replied, "You're going to be rewarded for that." (*Ahmad*) When we mention Allah at the time of slaughter, we're acknowledging our use of His resources for our survival. Any animal that is killed without paying respect to Allah is impure for a true believer to eat. It shows a lack of respect both for the animal and for its Creator!

[644] It is not allowed that every individual person should sacrifice an animal for themselves. A narration in the collection of Imam Muslim states, "The Messenger of Allah commanded us to share in offering the sacrifice, a camel for seven people and a cow for seven people." It is also reported that the Prophet allowed people to sacrifice one sheep or similar animal on behalf of their whole family. Even those who do not attend the Pilgrimage are required to make some sort of arrangements to slaughter an animal to feed the poor. (*Ibn Kathir*) Today, many people pay organizations to slaughter an animal on their behalf, with the resulting meat being used to feed the poor and the needy in foreign countries.

[645] People have control over animals so they can use them to survive and to feed the poor people among them. Islam teaches that animals do have some rights, such as the right to be treated humanely, not to be overworked, and not to be bothered with in nature for no good reason, etc... The Prophet said, "Allah has ordained efficiency in everything, so if you have to kill, then kill well, and if you have to slaughter (an animal), then slaughter well. Let each of you sharpen his blade, and let him spare suffering to the animal he slaughters." (*Muslim*) If an authentically constituted Islamic government were

It's not their meat nor their blood that reaches Allah, but rather your mindfulness (of your duty to Him) that reaches Him. [646] That's why He placed them under your control, so you could extol Allah's greatness for the guidance He gave to you, and also so you could give good news to those who do good. [37]

Permission is Given to Fight Back Against Oppression

Background on verses 38-40: After enduring persecution for thirteen years in Mecca, the Muslims finally fled from the city for the safer city of Yathrib (Medina) to the north in the year 622. Then they endured two years of Meccan and bedouin raids that kept them in a constant state of fear. During these many years the Muslims were not allowed to fight back or defend themselves. This approach of non-violence, even though by all rights they would have been justified to fight back earlier, helped to test the believers and solidify their resolve. (The theory is that non-violence only works for so long and only against an opponent with a conscience to which you can reasonably appeal.) Finally, in the year 624, this passage was revealed, giving the Muslims permission to fight against their oppressors. The Prophet immediately began organizing patrols to curtail the bedouin raiders. Later in the same year, the Battle of Badr took place, which showed the Muslims that they could achieve victory with Allah's help against superior odds.

Allah will defend those who believe, for Allah has no love for thankless traitors. [38] Those who've been attacked now have permission (to fight back) because they've been wronged, and Allah can provide them with powerful aid. [39]

They're the ones who've been driven from their homes against all right and for no other reason than that they've said, *"Our Lord is Allah."* If Allah didn't use one set of people to check (the ambitions) of another, then there would've been many monasteries, churches, synagogues and mosques, which are used to commemorate the name

---

functioning today, it would have strict humane laws, derived from the letter and spirit of the Qur'an.

[646] The Bible explains that God finds the aroma of a sacrificial animal to be 'pleasing' (see Leviticus 1:9), but the Qur'an says that only the act of obedience is pleasing to God and that nothing else from the act of sacrifice reaches Him. (There are, in fact, 24 separate verses in the Book of Leviticus that emphasize that God *enjoys* the roasting smell of the burnt offerings.)

of Allah abundantly, pulled down and ruined. [647] Allah will definitely support those who support Him, for Allah is strong and powerful! [40]

(He helps) those who would establish prayer and spend in charity and who would encourage what is recognized (as right) and forbid what is unfamiliar (to Allah's way of life) – (these things they would do) if We ever made them dominant in the land. [648] Indeed, all final results are with Allah! [41]

If You are Rejected, Others Were Before You

If they deny you, (Muhammad,) well then it was the same with other peoples before them who also denied (their prophets), such as the peoples of Noah, 'Ad and Thamud, [42] as well as the peoples of Abraham and Lot [649] [43] and the companions of Madyan. *Even Moses was denied (by his people), too!* I gave a break to those who suppressed (the light of faith within their hearts), but then I seized them, *and oh, how terrible was my repudiation (of them)!* [44]

---

[647] In the Islamic world view, it is natural to live in a multi-racial and multi-religious society. This was the reality of Islamic civilization from the very beginning. A Muslim is required to protect the houses of worship of other religions, even as they protect their own, for Allah does not like any place to be despoiled or ruined, since His praise is being done there. (Remember that Allah has many names! See 17:110) Despite the chaos and upheavals current in many parts of the Muslim world today, the traditional view of Islam is one of extreme tolerance. When 'Umar ibn al-Khattab traveled to Jerusalem to accept the surrender of that city, some of his men asked him to pray in a Christian church near the Temple Mount. He refused, citing his fear that future generations might forcibly turn it into a mosque. Prophet Muhammad, himself, joined in several treaties with Jews and Christians in which the sanctity of all houses of worship was guaranteed. In the 16th century, when the Ottoman Sultan Sulayman (d. 1566) was informed that the Jewish Wailing Wall was long buried under debris, he ordered it repaired for Jewish use. Up until the fall of the Ottoman Empire after World War I, the various Islamic leaders through the centuries often paid for some of the expenses and upkeep of the churches and synagogues in their territory. See the book by Abdul-Latif Hussayn entitled, *Tasamuh al-Gharb Ma'l-Muslimeen*.

[648] Some scholars have said that this verse obligates Muslim rulers to emulate the example of the first four caliphs of Islam, Abu Bakr, 'Umar, Uthman and 'Ali, for they were righteous leaders and were specifically praised by the Prophet on many occasions as being the best examples of his followers. Today, Muslims call their period of enlightened rule as the time of Right Guidance in the caliphate. (*Ma'ariful Qur'an*)

[649] The people of Abraham were his community in Mesopotamia, while the people of Lot were the people of Sodom, the city in which he and his family and retainers eventually settled and assimilated.

How many settlements did We destroy (in the past) that were given to practicing oppression (and wrongdoing)? Now they lie in ruins under shattered roofs! How many wells and mighty castles now lie deserted, crumbling and abandoned? [45] Why don't they travel through the world, so that their hearts can gain insight from the (relics of the past) and so that their ears can hear (the tales of days gone by)? [650] Truly, it's not their eyes that are blind, but the hearts within their chests! [46]

Yet, they're asking you to hurry the punishment forward! Even still, Allah won't fail in His promise, for a day in the sight of your Lord can be like a thousand years of your estimation. [651] [47] How many settlements were there that were given to oppression but to which I gave a break? In the end, I seized them all, and the final destination (of all things) is back to Me. [48]

Satan Brings Opposition to the Messengers

Say (to them), *"People! I'm a clear warner for you!* [49] *Those who believe and do what's morally right will get forgiveness and a generous share!* [50] *However, those who campaign against Our (revealed) verses, trying to prevent them (from achieving their purpose), shall be companions of the raging blaze!"* [51]

---

650 The Qur'anic principle is thus enshrined that ruins and relics of the past cannot be destroyed for they are sources of spiritual lessons. In addition, the study and investigation of history, according to this verse, has a useful purpose related to strengthening faith and realizing the power of Allah in human society.

651 The day mentioned here being a thousand years to Allah in comparison to how we understand the passage of time is to emphasize that while the wheels of history seem to move slowly for us, Allah takes the long view and is not under any compulsion to accomplish things by our puny and short-sighted timetable. (See II Peter 3:8 in the New Testament where *an unknown author* writes that a day to God can also be like a thousand years. Even as the Bible uses this general metaphor, so does the Qur'an. Also see Psalm 90:4 for a particularly beautiful expression of the same idea.) The Arabic prefix *ka*, which precedes the word for 1,000 means *can be like* or *as if it is*. (Also see 32:5 and footnote.)

We never sent any messenger or prophet [652] before you that didn't have Satan try to disrupt his plans when he formulated them. [653] However, Allah erases whatever Satan throws in, and Allah will confirm His verses, for Allah is full of knowledge and wisdom. [52]

(He allows) Satan to instill doubts (in people's hearts) so He can make it a test for those who have a sickness in their hearts or who have hardened hearts. The wrongdoers are in extreme opposition (to the truth)! [53] (He allows doubts to exist) so that those who have deep knowledge can come to realize that (the Qur'an) is the truth from your Lord, and also so they can believe in it and have their hearts softened towards it. Indeed, Allah guides those who believe towards a straight way. [654] [54]

The faithless will never stop doubting (the truth of the Qur'an), even until the Hour (of Judgment) comes upon them all of a sudden, or until some punishment overtakes them on a gloomy day. [55] The right to rule on that (final) day will belong to Allah, and He's going to judge between them. Those who believed and did what was

---

[652] There is a well-known, though disputed, report that says the Prophet was asked how many messengers and prophets were sent by Allah to the world. He replied, "There were 124,000 (prophets) and 313 messengers." The difference between the two is that a messenger receives a scripture or organized body of teachings, such as a Moses or Muhammad, while a prophet receives predictions of the future and the commission to warn his people to reform, such as an Ezekiel or Daniel. Both offices can be assigned to one person.

[653] Satan tries his best to dash the inner hopes of prophets and messengers by sowing doubts and fears in their minds. The men that Allah chooses to be His message-bearers are only human, and they're subject to the normal range of human emotions. If people don't listen to them, if they reject them and hurl insults at them, they're going to feel it. Satan or satanically-minded people use these human emotions to disrupt people's hopes that they can ever succeed. The forces of evil also continually tempt the prophets and try to make them go astray. Even Jesus was tested by the devil in a relentless contest of wills! (Matthew 11:1-4 and Luke 4:1-14. See 6:112 also.) In addition, Satan also tries to sow confusion among the followers of the prophets.

[654] The appearance of doubts or unsettled issues forces people to double-check what they had already assumed to be true. If their doubts are satisfied, then their belief is doubly strengthened. Thus, a Muslim is not afraid of objections and doubts that are raised either from outside critics of Islam or from within their own souls. Only a faith that has been backed up by research, inquiry and evidence can be called a solid faith. The key is to embrace your doubts and not try to bury them, for they will make your faith stunted or imbalanced. The cure for doubts is in education, observation, service to humanity and the world and reflection on the meaning and shortness of life. Sometimes such paths do more than heal one's doubts – they strengthen the faith of millions!

morally right will be in gardens of delight! [56] Meanwhile, those who rejected and denied Our (revealed) verses will have a humiliating punishment. [57]

Allah will Reward the Martyrs

Those who migrate (from their homes as refugees) in the cause of Allah, and then who are subsequently killed or die – they're going to have a wonderful share of resources granted to them by Allah, for Allah is the best provider of resources! [655] [58] He'll admit them to a place that will bring them complete satisfaction, for Allah is full of knowledge and is forbearing. [59] That's (going to be their reward)!

The one who doesn't retaliate more than he's been injured, and who is further attacked without warning, then Allah will help him, for Allah erases (sins) and forgives. [656] [60] That's (within His power to do) because Allah merges the night into the day, and He merges the day into the night.

Allah listens and watches (over all things). [61] Moreover, (it's within His power to help you, for He is) Allah, the ultimate Reality. Whatever they call upon besides Him is nothing more than falsehood, and Allah is the Highest and the Greatest. [657] [62]

Don't you (people) see that it's Allah Who sends down water from the sky, and thereafter the earth blossoms forth with green (plants)? Allah understands (the details of) every type of intricate arrangement.

---

[655] A man named Shurahbil ibn as-Samit reported the following incident, which took place many years after the Prophet's passing, during a campaign in Syria. He said, "We had a Roman fortress under siege for a long time when Salman al-Farsi passed by and said, 'I heard the Messenger of Allah say, 'Whoever dies while guarding the borders of Islam, Allah will reward him like (a martyr) and will provide for him and keep him safe from trials (on the Day of Judgment). Recite if you would like (verses 22:58-59).'"" (*Ibn Kathir*)

[656] Thus, the principle of self-defense in Islam is a fully justified one.

[657] See 112:110 where the principle is mentioned that the forces of evil may seem to triumph for a time, even to the point where even a prophet would lose hope, but then Allah's aid will come and evil will be vanquished.

Whatever is within the heavens and on the earth belongs to Him, for Allah is the Self-sufficient and the Praiseworthy. [64]

Don't you (people) see that Allah has tamed whatever is on the earth for your use, even the ships that sail through the sea by His command? He prevents the sky from falling on the earth, except for whatever He allows (to fall from it, such as rain), for Allah is kind and merciful to people. [65]

He's the One Who brought you to life, and then He causes you to die - only to bring you to life once more! Yet, human beings are thankless! [66]

Allah Made many Religions over the World

Background on verses 67-69: The pagans were disputing with Muhammad about whether it was allowed to eat animals that died by themselves, for, as they reasoned, Allah caused their death, and they should be as fine to eat as the animals that had been slaughtered in the ritual way. It was the pagan custom, after all, to kill animals as they pleased (even by beating them to death with clubs) or to eat dead carcasses they found. This passage here is telling them that Allah always established methods of correct slaughtering and that the pagan method was not correct by any standard of Allah. Islam forbids eating animals that died by themselves, nor can animals be cruelly killed. (*Asbab ul-Nuzul*)

We appointed religious rituals for every community (on earth) to follow, 659 so don't let them argue with you on this point. Rather, keep on calling them to your Lord, for you're definitely following the correct guidance. [67] If they keep arguing with you, tell them, "*Allah knows best about whatever you're doing.*" 660 [68] Then Allah will judge

---

658 With our limited natural abilities, we can see rainfall and the resulting plant growth, but Allah knows about the mysteries of life down to the molecular and subatomic levels and beyond. As Isma'il al-Farooqi (d. 1986), a modern Muslim philosopher, said, "Every Muslim is a scientist." In other words, the Qur'an repeatedly calls upon us to look for signs of Allah's handiwork in all aspects of the natural world around us.
659 Previous religious codes include the laws of Moses and the teachings of Jesus. The Qur'an superseded them both, as all earlier codes were compromised by the hands of men who added or subtracted what they desired over many centuries. (*Ma'ariful Qur'an*)
660 In other words, the Qur'an accepts that there are many different religions and religious customs among the people of the earth. Why shouldn't there be when the roots of all true religions come from Allah? Religions and customs were shaped by the local needs of the people to whom they were revealed, and later generations added to or altered the customs over many centuries. The pagans of Mecca kept trying to argue with the Prophet about this, using it as a justification for their own eccentric rituals. The Qur'an here is

between you on the Day of Assembly (and solve) your disagreements. [69]

Don't you know that Allah knows about all things within the sky and the earth? (Every event) is recorded in a ledger, and that's easy for Allah. [661] [70] Even still, they worship (idols) in place of Allah, having no clear mandate to do so nor any accurate knowledge. Those who are corrupt will have no one to help them! [71]

When Our clear verses are read out to them, you can clearly see the defiance on the faces of those who suppress (their awareness of the truth), as if they were about to pounce on those who are reading Our verses to them! [662]

Say (to them), *"Should I tell you about something that you'll dislike far more than these verses? It's the Fire that Allah has promised to the faithless, and that's the worst destination!"* [72]

Idol Worship is Foolish and Illogical

O people! Here is a comparison, so listen to it! Those (idols) that you call upon besides Allah can't create as much as a fly, even if they all got together to do it. [663] Further still, if a fly were ever to take something away from them, they wouldn't have any power to get it back from that fly! How weak is the one who seeks (knowledge from

---

telling the Prophet to agree with them that there are many different customs that exist, and if they continue arguing further, then Allah knows that their real intention is merely to create discord and drama.

[661] The Prophet said, "The first thing that Allah created was the Pen. He said to it, 'Write!' It asked, 'What shall I write?' He said, 'Write about what will happen.' Thus, the Pen wrote down everything that will happen until the Day of Judgment." (*Abu Dawud*)

[662] What a clear picture of the discrimination and persecution the Muslims faced from the hostile Meccans! You can just imagine a believer walking in the street, humming some Qur'anic verses, all the while being mindful of the venomous stares of all those around him or her. See 68:52 for a similar mention.

[663] The Prophet said that Allah, Himself, said, "Who does more wrong than the one who tries to create something like My creation? Let them create an ant or a fly or a seed like My creation!" (*Ahmad*) Based upon this and other narrations, many modern commentators hold that genetic manipulation, cloning and other bioengineering enterprises are forbidden in Islam because it is tampering with Allah's creation when we have no right to alter what He has designed simply for our own convenience.

idols), and how weak are (the idols) from whom they seek (to learn)! 664 [73]

They haven't thought highly enough of Allah, for Allah is strong and powerful! 665 [74] Allah chooses messengers from among both angels and people, and Allah hears and sees (all things). [75] He knows what's in front of them and what's behind them, and all decisions go back to Allah (for their resolution). 666 [76]

O you who believe! Bow down, and prostrate yourselves (in prayer). Serve your Lord. Do what's best so you can be successful. 667 [77]

Strive in His cause with honest effort, for He's chosen you and hasn't made any difficult (regulations) for you to follow. 668 This way of life is no less than the creed of your forefather Abraham.

---

664 Salman al Farsi, who was a Persian convert and close follower of the Prophet, was giving a speech in which he told a very interesting story. He said, "Once upon a time, two men had a unique experience with a fly. When they died, one of them entered Hellfire because of it, while the second one entered Paradise. In days long ago, these two men were traveling in a far off land. On their way, their journey led them to a road where they happened to meet some idol worshippers. The people had placed their idol at the crossroads and were forcing everyone who passed by to make an offering to their idol. When the two men arrived at the junction, the idol worshippers said to them, 'You must make an offering to our god.' The first man said, 'I have nothing to offer.' 'You can sacrifice anything,' they answered, 'even a fly will do!' The man agreed and started running after a fly and caught it. He then sacrificed it to the idol, and the people around him were happy. That man later entered Hellfire because of his action. When the idol worshippers told the second man to do the same thing, he declared, 'I don't give any offerings to anyone or anything besides Allah.' The idol worshippers became angry and argued with him furiously. They finally became so mad that they grabbed him and killed him. When he died, he entered Paradise because of his true belief in only one God."
665 The Prophet said, "Satan comes and whispers to people, 'Who created this and that? Who created this and that?' Until he says, 'So who created Allah?'" The Prophet then advised people to ignore such a question and seek refuge with Allah. (Asbab ul-Nuzul) (Allah is uncreated, and the human mind cannot fully fathom what that truly means).
666 This is a way of saying that Allah knows their future and their past.
667 The great jurist, Imam ash-Shafi'i (d. 820), recommended that after reading this verse, those who have faith in Allah should prostrate themselves on the floor and praise Allah. It is not agreed upon by all jurists, as are the other fourteen places of prostration.
668 The Prophet said, "This religion is easy. Whoever makes it harder will be a loser. Follow it with moderation, stick by it, give good news (to others) and follow it in the morning, during the day and at night." (Bukhari)

(Allah) is the One Who has named you *Submitters*, [669] both before and in this (revelation), so that the Messenger could be a witness for you, and so you could be witnesses (to your faith) before all people.

Establish prayer, give in charity, and hold firmly to Allah. He is your protector, and (He's) the best for defense and the best for giving help! [670] [78]

[669] This is the translation of the word *Muslim*. Thus, the Qur'an has coined this term to describe the followers of Allah. Abraham called people to become submissive or compliant to Allah, and so it is perfectly fine to say he labeled his followers as Muslims, as well. See 2:128 where the meaning of Muslim is explained in Abraham's speech.
[670] Whenever the Prophet would feel stress or worry, he would sometimes call for Bilal, the official caller to prayer in Medina, and say to him, "Bilal, comfort us with (prayer). The peace of my eyes is kept for me in prayer." (*Ibn Kathir*)

The Faithful

23 *Al Mu'minūn*

Late Meccan Period

This chapter was revealed during the days of famine in Mecca that chapter 44 had foretold. It goes over the familiar themes of Allah's signs and the need for people to recognize Allah as their Creator and ultimate judge. It also contains some words of advice to the Prophet to help him cope with the persecution of the Meccans. 'Umar ibn al-Khattab said of this chapter: "This chapter was revealed in my presence, and I, myself, saw the condition of the Prophet during its revelation. When the revelation was finished, the Prophet (turned to us and) said, 'On this occasion, ten verses have been sent down to me that, for the one who measures up to them, will most surely make him enter Paradise.' Then he recited the first verses of this chapter." (*Ahmad, Tirmidhi, Nisa'i, Hakim*) In later years, a man named Yazid ibn Babnūs asked the Prophet's widow A'ishah to describe for him the habits and behavior of the Prophet. She replied to him that he followed the message as it was revealed in the Qur'an. Then she recited the first ten verses of this chapter. Afterwards she said, "These verses describe his behavior." (*Nisa'i*)

In the Name of Allah,
the Compassionate, the Merciful

So it will be that the believers will succeed [1] – those who are humble in their prayers, [671] [2] who avoid useless chatter, [672] [3] who

---

[671] The Prophet said, "Allah keeps watch over His servant while he's praying as long as he is concentrating on Allah, but when he turns his attention elsewhere, Allah turns away from him, likewise." (*Ma'ariful Qur'an*) In another incident, the Prophet was observing a man at prayer, but the man was fiddling with his clothes and playing with his beard. The Prophet remarked that if that man had any humbleness in his heart, it would have been clearly shown in his body. In other words, he would have stood still and respectfully while at prayer.

[672] Mindless gossip and pointless conversations lead people into sin. How many people have been hurt by the idle wagging of a careless tongue! The New Testament similarly advises people to leave off profanity and speaking of useless things in II Timothy 2:16 where we read, "...shun profane and vain babblings, for they will increase unto more ungodliness." The Prophet Muhammad once said, "Allah doesn't like foul language nor the use of it." He also said, "A person who believes in Allah and the next life should speak about good things, or else he should keep silent." (*Bukhari*) Thus, a Muslim is not allowed to speak badly or use profanity. Abu Hamid Muhammad al-Ghazali (d. 1111) once

engage in charity, [4] who guard their modesty [5] - except with their spouses and those (maidservants) under their control (whom they've married), [673] for there's no blame for them in this. [6] Whoever goes beyond (these limits), they're indeed going out of bounds. [7]

(True believers) are those who faithfully discharge their trusts and agreements, [8] and they guard their prayers strictly. [9] They'll be the inheritors [10] who will inherit an exclusive garden in Paradise, and there they shall remain! [674] [11]

The Reality of a Temporary Life for Human Beings

We created (each) human being from minerals extracted from clay, [675] [12] and then We placed him as a mingled drop, securely held in place. [676] [13] Then we transformed that drop into a clinging thing. Then out of that clinging thing, We formed a chewed up lump. Out of that chewed up lump, We fashioned bones and clothed them in flesh. [677]

---

wrote: "People count with self-satisfaction the number of times they've recited the name of Allah on their prayer beads, but they keep no beads for counting the number of useless words they speak."

[673] The servants they marry are also lawful for them, and this is pointed out specifically so there can be no doubt that former bonded-servants have equal status with people who were always free, lest some people look down upon others. The Prophet said, "There are three types of people who will be given their reward twice: a person from among the Followers of Earlier Revelation who believed in his prophet and then believed in me; a servant who performs his duty well towards Allah and for whomever he works; and a man who has a maidservant and then educates her, teaches her refined manners, frees her and then marries her." (*Bukhari*) Also see 24:32 and 70:30 and footnote.

[674] The Prophet explained what this passage was about when said, "There are none of you except that you have two homes, a home in Paradise and a home in Hellfire. If he dies and enters Hell, the people of Paradise will inherit his home. This is what Allah meant by, 'They'll be the inheritors...'" (*Ibn Majah*)

[675] When human biological compounds are broken down and examined, we find that we are little more than a complex arrangement of minerals and organic compounds that can easily be found in rich loam or clay.

[676] Once the sperm and egg join together, it descends as a mingled or mixed drop into the uterus where it attaches to the uterine wall by 'clinging' to it like a leech. (Even the shape looks like a leech!) From there the clinging 'leech,' known as a zygote in medical terms, gets its nourishment from the mother's blood and grows into the various stages described above until it becomes another human being! This one verse, which so accurately describes the process of gestation, is cited as one of the most miraculous verses of the Qur'an in terms of scientific accuracy. Also see 22:5.

[677] 'Umar ibn al-Khattab was in the presence of the Prophet when verses 12-14 were revealed and recited aloud. After the line was read, "...We made another creature,"

So then out of (that initial tiny drop), We made another creature! So blessed be Allah, the best of all creators! [678] [14] Then after (your life span has passed), you're going to die. [15] Then after that, you're going to be raised to life again for the Day of Assembly! [16]

The Fruits of the Earth

Above you We made seven layered tracts, [679] and We're not unmindful of Our creation. [17] We send a measured amount of water down from the sky and lodge it in the earth. We can drain it off, as well. [18]

We use (that water) to grow gardens of date palms and vineyards for you, in which you can find abundant fruit that you can eat. [19] (We also grow a type of olive) tree, (the best of which) sprouts near Mount Tur, from which you get olive oil and relish for your meals. [680] [20]

'Umar interrupted and exclaimed excitedly, "*So blessed be Allah, the best of all Creators!*" The Prophet smiled at him and told him that this was the very next line that Allah had revealed. This is a phenomenon, known to commentators, of Allah putting into the heart of the listener the prediction of what would be revealed next based on the initial flow of the verses. (From the *tafseer* of al-Muqatil and As-Suyuti)

[678] From nearly nothing a new life form grows. Science, which has done an excellent job in describing *how* the various processes of life work, has ultimately failed in answering the question as to *why* they work. Why does life seem to *want* to grow and develop? Why is it that genetic coding exists in the first place? Further still, *why* does the process work as it does? We know how it works, but from where does life get its spark, its impetus, its blueprint? Religion asserts that Allah is the force behind it, but the various religions have taken different attitudes towards their relationship with science. While Christianity views science as suspect, (Martin Luther, for example, called Copernicus crazy for suggesting that the earth spun like a top, for it contradicted the Bible,) the Qur'an, on the other hand, takes science as Exhibit A in proving the existence of Allah, as the hundreds of Qur'anic verses that reference nature demonstrate.

[679] *Taraa-iq* literally means tracts or areas. These are the seven distinct atmospheric layers that surround our planet in an envelop of protection from the vacuum of space and the harmful radiation of the sun. See footnote to 41:12 for the names of these seven layers that encircle the earth. Some commentators think that these tracts refer to the seven types of heavenly bodies such as stars, planets, and such, but this is not really plausible given that they do not exist in layers or sections as this verse is referencing.

[680] The standard olive of the type *olea europaea* has been cultivated in the Middle East for nearly five thousand years, and its earliest known growers were the Phoenicians. It grows well in poor soil and in dry climates, making it the perfect food for many civilizations that grew around the Mediterranean world. The best olives in the seventh century came from

You can even find a lesson in domesticated livestock, [681] for We produce (milk) from within their bodies for you to drink. There are many other benefits in them for you, as well, such as their meat that you can eat, [21] and also in the fact that you can ride upon them like ships (traversing the land). [682] [22]

The Saga of Noah

And so it was that We sent Noah to his people. He said (to them), *"My people! Serve Allah! You have no other god than Him! Won't you be mindful (of Him)?"* [23]

The chiefs of the faithless among his people said, *"He's no more than a mortal man just like the rest of you! He only wants to have an advantage over you! If Allah really wanted to send someone to us, then He could've sent down angels. Really now, we've never heard anything like this coming (down to us from the traditions) of our ancestors!* [24] *He's just a man who's been possessed (by evil spirits), so wait a while (for him to go away)."* [25]

"My Lord!" Noah cried out. *"Help me against their lies!"* [26] And so We revealed to him: *"Build a boat under Our sight and inspiration. When Our command arrives and the heated banks (of the river)* [683] *give way (and cause a flood) upon the land, take on board a pair of every (kind of useful livestock animal), both male and female.* [684] *Also bring your family aboard,*

---

the region around northwestern Arabia, and they were particularly sought after by people at that time.

[681] The Arabic term *an'am* (cattle) refers to all domesticated herd animals such as cows (including oxen), sheep, goats, camels and horses.

[682] The imagery of people riding on horseback or camelback over the landscape paints a pretty picture as serene as the tall ships that sail smoothly over the ocean.

[683] The term *tannur* literally means a hot surface such as an oven or the heated surface of the earth. It also means a high embankment. The imagery used here, then, is of the waters of the earth bursting forth from river banks and flooding the sun-baked land. Mesopotamia is a hot, dry land punctuated by two mighty rivers. The imagery is perfect!

[684] Muslim commentators have always assumed that the animals that Noah was to take were from his local area – animals that he would need to rely upon for rebuilding his community after the flood, such as sheep, goats and other similar things. Muslim theologians have generally never promoted the idea that a pair of every animal *on earth* went in the boat with Noah. It has been the general trend in Muslim scholarship to assume that only the people of Noah's region were destroyed by great flooding. Noah's descendants then went on to repopulate the region.

except for those who will have the sentence proven true against them. [685]
*Don't appeal to Me any further on behalf of the wrongdoers, for they're going
to be drowned."* [27]

*"When you and everyone with you have gone on board the boat, then say,
'Praise be to Allah, the One Who has saved us from these corrupted people.'*
[28] *Then pray, 'My Lord! Let me also leave this boat (at a future date) with
Your blessings, for You're the best One to allow (us) to leave.'"* [686] [29] There
are signs (in this story for people to consider), for We're always
testing (people in their faith). [687] [30]

The Cycle of History Continues Unabated

Then We raised another generation (of people) after them, [31] and
We sent them a messenger (drawn) from among their own, (who
said), *"Serve Allah! You have no other god than Him! Won't you be
mindful (of Allah)?"* [688] [32]

The leaders among his people who rejected and denied their
rendezvous in the next life, and upon whom We had showered the
luxuries of this world, [689] said, *"He's no more than a mortal man just like*

---

[685] Noah's own wife and son did not believe in his prophethood and refused to board the
boat. See 38:84-85 for the proverbial 'sentence' or verdict of Allah.

[686] Abu Dharr al-Ghiffari once saw the Prophet holding the door of the Ka'bah, and he
heard him praying, "My family among you is like Noah's boat: whoever sails upon it will
be safe, and whoever holds back from it will perish." (*Tirmidhi*)

[687] The old sayings of, "Practice makes perfect," and "Use it or lose it," apply to the state
of a person's faith, as well. Allah constantly gives us challenges to renew our commitment
to faith and to rescue us from complacency, for Satan preys upon the relaxed and
unconcerned mind. The Prophet said, "When Allah loves a person, He tests him." Thus,
if there doesn't seem to be any challenges in your life, watch out, for you may have been
abandoned to your life of pleasure and carelessness, only to find yourself suddenly seized
one day. Then you'll cry out, "What! What happened? Oh no, I'm now among those
who are lost!" This is the exact same message that this Qur'an is trying to get across in
so many ways and in so many verses. Isn't it time we took notice and woke up to the
reality of our lives?

[688] This passage [23:32-44] summarizes succinctly the struggle of all those prophets who
lived between the time of Noah and Moses. This snapshot of prophetic history could
roughly correspond to chapters 9-50 in the book of Genesis.

[689] Why does arrogance seem to settle within the circles of power in any society? Recent
research into the behavior of those who are blessed with abundant wealth has identified
some surprising answers. It seems that the wealthier one becomes, the more focused he
is on the rewards and pleasures that are within his reach, even as he becomes less
concerned with the welfare of those around him who are less well-off. By way of contrast,

the rest of you. He eats the same food that you eat and drinks the same liquids that you drink. [33] If you were to obey a mere mortal who's no different than the rest of you, then you'd truly be lost. [34] Is he promising you that after you've died and become rotten bones that you'll be brought (to life) again? [35] That's a far off prospect that you've been promised!" [36]

"There's nothing else (for us) other than our lives here in this world! We (humans) die, and (new generations are then given) life, but we'll never (individually) be raised to life again! [37] (This) is just a man who's made up a lie about Allah, and we're never going to believe him." [38]

(Their prophet) cried out, "My Lord! Help me, for they're accusing me of a lie!" [39]

"They're going to be sorry in just a little while," (Allah) replied. [40] Then the blast rightly overtook them, and thus We reduced them to nothing more than scattered debris. So away with the wrongdoers! [41] Then We raised other generations after them. [42] No community can advance its final time limit, nor can it delay it. [43]

And then We sent Our messengers one after another, and every time a messenger went to his community, they accused him of lying. So We made them follow one after another (in destruction), reducing them to mere historical accounts. [690] So away with the people who won't believe! [44]

---

those with scarce resources tend to behave in a more deliberate and guarded fashion. This has been labeled the approach/inhibition theory, and the Qur'an has long accepted this line of thought as a matter of indisputable fact. Greater resources equals an increased likelihood of self-aggrandizement.

690 During the rule of Harun ar-Rashid of Baghdad (d. 809), a wandering preacher named Ibn Sammak came to meet with him. After some time had passed in conversation, the caliph felt thirsty and asked for water to be brought to him. Ibn Sammak offered to get the water himself, and he returned with a cup a moment later. When ar-Rashid reached for the cup, Ibn Sammak withdrew it from his reach and said, "Commander of the Faithful, if you were thirsty and water was withheld from you, would you trade half your empire for it?" The caliph readily agreed, knowing that without water a man would die. Then Ibn Sammak gave him the cup. After the caliph finished his drink, Ibn Sammak asked him, "If for some reason, perhaps an illness, you were unable to discharge the water you just drank, would you trade half your empire to be relieved of it?" Again, the caliph agreed, recognizing the discomfort that would come from being unable to answer the call of nature. Then Ibn Sammak said, "So what is the value of a kingdom that isn't worth more than a drink of water and some urine?"

Then We sent Moses and his brother Aaron with Our signs and a clear mandate [45] to Pharaoh and his nobles, but they acted arrogantly and were quite a conceited people. [46] (Pharaoh and his nobles) said, *"Should we believe in two mortal men who are just like us, especially since their people are our slaves!"* [47] So they denied them and were thus plunged into destruction. [48] And so it was that We gave Moses the Book, in order for (his people) to be guided. [49]

We also made the son of Mary and his mother a sign, as well, and We sheltered them securely on high ground in comfort and with flowing streams. [691] [50] *"All you messengers! Eat only wholesome (foods), and do morally upright deeds, for I know what you're doing."* [692] [51]

Be United for the Truth

(O you who believe!) Truly, this community of yours is one community, and I am your Lord, so be mindful of Me. [52] (People) have divided their way of life into sects among them, with each faction satisfied with its own doctrines. [693] [53] Leave them alone in their confusion for a while. [54] Do they think that just because We've granted them wealth and children [55] that We're (always) going to rush every type of good (fortune) their way? Certainly not! They just don't understand. [56]

---

[691] Some commentators say that this refers to the place where Mary bore Jesus - that it was on a safe, dry hill near a spring (see 19:22-26), while others think that this refers to Jesus and Mary being in a beautiful place in Paradise. Yet a third interpretation is that Jesus had enemies who wanted to kill him as a child, but Allah gave him and his mother a safe place to live so he could grow into manhood. Any of these interpretations could be subscribed to, though the first makes more sense in the context of what is actually stated in this verse.

[692] The Prophet said, "All you people! Allah is wholesome, and He only accepts what is wholesome. Allah commands the believers just like He commanded the messengers by saying, 'All you messengers! Eat only wholesome (foods)...'" Then the Prophet also recited verse 2:172, which has a similar message. Finally, the Prophet mentioned a man who was dirty, dusty and disheveled from traveling, and he said, "...his food, drink and clothes are impure, and he's fed himself with what's forbidden. If he extends his hands towards the sky and says, 'Lord! Lord!' How can his prayer be answered?" (*Muslim*)

[693] The varied nature of religions all over the world is almost bewildering; yet, even still, they all share some basic moral and conceptual characteristics. This is a sign that religions have evolved over time from earlier and more harmonious doctrines that all came from a single source: Allah.

Truly, those who anxiously fear their Lord, [57] who believe in the signs of their Lord, [58] who don't make partners with their Lord [59] and who give whatever they give (in charity) with nervous hearts, (knowing that) they're going to return to their Lord, [60] they're the ones who rush forward (to do) every type of good deed. [694] They're foremost (in doing what's pleasing to Allah). [695] [61]

You have no More Excuses with Allah

Background on verses 62-74: Ibn 'Abbas was of the opinion that this passage is a reference to the leaders of the Quraysh tribe of Mecca and that this was a veiled threat to them that because they were persecuting Allah's Prophet, they were in for trouble at a later date. Their downfall at Badr, then, would be the fulfillment of this threat. (*Ma'ariful Qur'an*)

We don't place a burden upon any soul that's greater than it can bear. We have a record before Us that shows the truth, and they won't be treated unfairly. [62] But no! Their hearts are overwhelmed in confusion about this. More than that, there's still some (sinful) things that they're doing - and that they'll keep on doing - [63] even until the moment comes when We seize in punishment all those who had the luxuries of this world (and who were thus heedless). *Oh, how they'll cry out (for mercy) then!* [64]

"Don't cry out (for mercy) today!" (they'll be told,) *"for you'll find no help from Us! [65] My (revealed) verses were read out to you, but you used to turn back on your heels [66] arrogantly, saying bad things about them like a storyteller in the night."* [696] [67]

---

[694] The Prophet's wife A'ishah asked the Prophet about this passage [57-61], wanting to know if the people who had fearful hearts were fearful because they were committing sins like drinking alcohol or stealing. The Prophet replied, "No, O daughter of the Truth-confirmer (Abu Bakr), it's not like that. They're the ones who pray and fast and give in charity while being afraid that their deeds won't be accepted by Allah because of their own shortcomings. They rush forward to do good deeds, and they're in the forefront in doing them" Then the Prophet recited verse 61. (*Ahmad, Ibn Kathir*)

[695] For a further description of the reward of this type of sincere believer, see 56:19-26.

[696] Some commentators are of the opinion that this verse implies that storytelling in the late night is undesirable and that after the last prayer of the day ('*isha*) a conscientious believer should go to bed in the hopes that he may have the will to wake up in the dead of night to pray. 'Umar ibn al-Khattab used to promote this very thing during his rule whenever he came upon people listening to storytelling after '*isha* prayer. (*Ma'ariful*

Haven't they thought seriously about the word (of Allah), or has something come to them that's never come to their ancient ancestors? [68] Is it that they don't recognize their messenger? Is that why they're refusing him? [69] Do they say, *"He's possessed"*? Certainly not! (On the contrary), he's bringing them the truth, but most of them hate (to hear) the truth! [70]

If the truth were shaped according to what they would like it to be, then the very heavens and the earth and every (creature) within them would've been warped (out of all recognition)! But no! We're giving them their reminder, but they're turning away from their reminder! [71]

Is it that you're asking them for some kind of reward? Your Lord's reward is far better (than anything they can give), for He's the best One to provide. [697] [72] You're calling them to a straight path, [73] and those who don't believe in the next life are veering away from that path. [74]

If We were merciful to (the idol-worshippers of Mecca) and relieved them of the agonizing (famine) from which they've been suffering, then they would still eagerly persist in their rebelliousness, wandering all around in distraction. [698] [75]

We punished them with this (famine so they could learn a lesson), but they've neither humbled themselves before their Lord, nor have they begged Him (for relief). [76] (Their arrogance will continue) - even until We open a door for them that will lead to a painful punishment. Then they'll be in abject despair within (their place of doom)! [77]

Qur'an) Of course, today's version of storytelling would be watching digital media such as television.

[697] Compare this with 18:94-95 where even a king refuses payment because he appreciates what Allah has given him.

[698] See the introduction to chapter 44 and 44:10-12 and commentary for the details of this foretold famine that eventually struck Mecca. The Prophet had beseeched Allah saying, "Allah! Help me against them by sending on them seven years (of famine) like the seven years of Joseph's (famine in Egypt)." (*Bukhari*) Abu Sufyan, the *de facto* leader of the pagans in Mecca, eventually approached the Prophet when he was settled in Medina and begged him to ask Allah to lift the famine and drought. The Prophet prayed for relief, and the heat wave abated soon thereafter. (*Ma'ariful Qur'an*)

Our Senses Tell Us the Truth

He's the One Who endowed you with hearing, sight, sensitivity and self-awareness. Yet, you're hardly thankful at all! [78] He also multiplied you throughout the earth, and in the end you'll (all) be gathered back to Him. [79] He's the One Who gives life and death. The alternation of the night and the day is His (doing), so won't you understand? [80]

But no! They repeat the same kinds (of denials) that the ancients said! [81] They say, *"When we've died and become rotten bones, are we really going to be raised to life again?* [82] *These things were promised to us and our ancestors before, but they're no more than the tales of the ancients!"* [699] [83]

Ask them, *"To whom belongs the earth and all beings upon it? (Speak) if you know!"* [700] [84] They'll (be sure) to say, *"To Allah!"* Then say (to them), *"So won't you take a reminder?"* [85]

Then ask them, *"Who is the Lord of the seven heavens and the Lord of the great throne (of power)?"* [701] [86] They'll (be sure) to say, *"Allah is!"* Then say (to them), *"So won't you be mindful (of your duty to Him)?"* [87]

---

[699] Hasan al Basri (d. 737) once said, "I'm astonished at those people who are ordered to prepare their provisions, but then when the start of the journey is announced, they remain unmindful in their useless talk and wasted deeds."

[700] It's really amazing that every polytheistic religion, which contains countless mini-gods and independent supernatural actors, still holds that there is some type of an unseen overlord over all the universe. For the Egyptians it was Âmen, for the Greeks it was Chaos (Zeus was not the source of the universe), and a similar "chief god" can be found in other belief systems, as well. The point of these types of questions is that from their own mouths, idol-worshippers must acknowledge that the Supreme God is in charge at the end of the day. As such, won't they reconsider the many idols they've set up for themselves?

[701] In Arabic idiom, the seat or throne of a king was synonymous with and symbolic of his power. Thus, when the Qur'an mentions that Allah has a throne, it doesn't necessarily mean that Allah literally *sits on a chair*, and no Muslim scholar would ascribe such literal imagery to Allah, even though we sometimes talk in these anthropomorphic terms. Rather, Muslim theologians have usually understood that this is a reference to Allah's *power*, and at least some of the pagans of Mecca would have understood this in the same way, as well. Muslims also don't believe that when Allah's 'hand' or 'eye' is mentioned that He has a *hand* or *eye* like us created creatures.

Now ask them, *"In whose hands is the control of everything, and who protects all and doesn't need protecting? (Speak) if you know!"* [88] They'll (be sure) to say, *"Allah!"* Then say (to them), *"So how can you be so deceived (into worshipping idols)?"* [89] By no means! We've sent them the truth (which they affirm with their own tongues); yet, they practice lies (in spite of it)! [90]

Allah never took any son, nor is there any other god with Him. (If there were many gods), then each god would've taken (control) over what it had created, and some of them would've tried to dominate the others! Glory be to Allah (above all) they're making Him out to be! [91] He knows what's beyond human perception and what's plain to see, and He's high above what they're joining with Him! [92]

Be Strong, Prophet of Allah

(Pray to your Lord), saying, *"My Lord! If you're going to show me (the punishment) that they've been promised,* [93] *then, my Lord, don't place me among the people who do wrong!"* [702] [94] Oh, indeed, it's entirely possible for Us to show you (the punishment) about which they've been warned! [95]

So ward off the evil (things they say) with (a state of) goodness, for We know what they're describing (you to be). [703] [96] Say, *"My Lord! I seek Your protection from the incitement of devils,* [97] *and I seek Your protection, My Lord, from them ever coming near me."* [704] [98]

---

[702] The Prophet sometimes made this supplication: "Allah! I seek Your protection from old age. I seek Your protection from being crushed or drowned, and I seek Your protection from being assailed by Satan at the time of death." (*Abu Dawud*)

[703] The Prophet said, "Among the manners of a believer are these: when he speaks, he speaks nicely; when someone speaks to him, he listens attentively; when he meets others, he welcomes them with a smiling face; and when he makes a promise, he fulfills it." (*Ad-Daylami*)

[704] This passage addresses the Prophet and how he should handle all the horrible insults he was receiving. The "devils" mentioned here refer to both the Prophet's human detractors, as well as possibly the doubts and gnawing misgivings that can come from having to bear insults on a daily basis. In that, there is a wide lesson for all people here. Verse 97 specifically is a plea to Allah to help a person overcome his anger when being insulted by someone who wants to get a rise out of him.

There are no Confessions accepted when Life is Over

(The faithless will remain blind to the truth) - even until death comes upon one of them, and they cry out (in their grave), *"My Lord! Send me back (to life)* [99] *so I can act righteously in those things that I neglected!"* [705] (However, it will be said of them), *"No way! It's just something they're saying!"* Then a barrier will be raised before them until the day they're resurrected. [100]

When the trumpet will be blown, all relations between them will cease, nor will anyone (even think to) ask about anyone else that day! [101] Then those whose scales are heavy (with good) will be successful, [706] [102] while those whose scales are scarce (of good) will have lost their own souls and be relegated to Hellfire. [707] [103] The fire will burn their faces, and they'll scowl horribly (in pain). [104]

"Weren't My verses read out to you?" (they'll be asked). *"Didn't you treat them as lies?"* [105]

---

[705] Here we have mention of the Islamic doctrine of *barzakh*, or the barrier. When a person dies, the angels draw his soul out of his throat. The soul hovers near the body until it's buried or otherwise disposed of. Then the soul sinks in the earth and remains in a state of suspended animation until the Day of Judgment when the soul is brought out and used to recreate the human being anew. The Prophet said, "When the coffin is ready and people lift it above their shoulders, if the body is that of a virtuous person, it urges, 'Take me ahead; take me ahead.' If it is the body of a wrong-doer, it says, 'Curses! Where are you taking me?' Its screams are heard by everything except humans, and if they could hear it, they would faint." (*Bukhari*) When first laid to rest, two angels will come to the dead soul and ask it three questions. (Who is your Lord? What was your religion? Who was your prophet?) Our answers will determine what happens next. The barrier is the partition between life and death. No soul may cross it and return to life. Good souls will rest peacefully and not feel the passage of time, while the souls of the wicked will be quite awake. The wicked will be tormented every day by angels who will come and beat them and berate them for their wickedness. The Prophet often prayed to Allah for protection from the punishment of the grave.

[706] Interestingly enough, the Prophet once said that on the scales set up on Judgment Day, the ink used by scholars will weigh more than the blood of martyrs. (*Ma'ariful Qur'an*) This tradition has been one of many prompts that has made the desire to be a learned scholar a common goal of Muslims throughout the ages.

[707] According to numerous prophetic traditions and the concurring consensus of all major scholars, even a person who claims to be a Muslim can go to Hellfire if his sins are more numerous than his acts of goodness. For such a one, Hellfire is a time of purging and purification, and he may eventually be released and admitted to Paradise (unless, of course, he was a die-hard hypocrite, in which case he may never get out). (*Ma'ariful Qur'an*)

"Our Lord!" they'll cry. *"Our own misfortune overtook us, and we were a people who went off course.* [106] *Our Lord, take us out of this. If we ever return (to sinful ways after this), then we would really be wrongdoers (and would deserve this punishment)!"* [107]

"Get back into it even further!" (Allah) will reply, *"Speak no more to Me!* [108] *There was a group of My servants who used to pray, 'Our Lord! We believe, so forgive us and have mercy on us, for You're the best One to show mercy!'* [708] [109] *Yet, you laughed at them, even until your ridicule of them made you forget My message!* [110] *I've rewarded them this day for their patience, and they're the ones who've triumphed."* [111]

Then (Allah) will ask them, *"How many years did you stay on earth?"* [112]

"We stayed for a day or part of a day," they'll reply. *"Just ask those who keep track."* [113]

"You stayed only for a little while," He'll exclaim, *"if only you would've known!* [114] *Did you think that We created you just for fun and that you wouldn't be returned to Us?"* [709] [115]

Glorify Allah in the Highest

(O you who believe!) [710] Extol (the glory of) Allah! The Ruler, the Reality! There is no god besides Him, the Lord of the throne of honor! [116]

If someone calls upon any other god alongside of Allah, they don't have any right to do so! Their record (of deeds) will stand in the sight

---

[708] This is a popular supplication, and most Muslims learn it from a young age.

[709] The classical poet, Hakim Sanai (d. 1150), once wrote, "While mankind remains mere baggage in the world, it will all be swept along, as if in a boat, asleep. What can they see in sleep? What real reward or punishment can there be?" Indeed, as 'Ali ibn Abi Talib said, "People are asleep (in the world), and when they die they wake up."

[710] 'Abdullah ibn Mas'ud recited this verse in the ears of a person who was ill. The man recovered in record time, and when the Prophet heard about it, he asked Ibn Mas'ud about it. When Ibn Mas'ud confirmed what he had done, the Prophet said, "I swear by the One Who has power over my life, if a true believer were to recite these verses on a mountain, the mountain itself might even move from its place." (*Qurtubi*)

of their Lord, and the faithless will never be successful! [117] So pray then, *"My Lord! Forgive and show mercy, for You are the best One to show mercy!"* [118]

The Light

This chapter was revealed in approximately the year 627. It was a tense time for the Muslims who had lost face among the tribes of the desert, due to their being defeated at Uhud. Hostilities arose from every quarter. Indeed, seeing that the Muslims were not invincible after the Battle of Uhud in 626, Abu Sufyan left a challenge for the Muslims to fight the Quraysh once again at the Wells of Badr the following year (no doubt wanting to erase their earlier defeat there).

Accordingly, the Prophet marched a force of some 1500 fighters there at the appointed date, but the Quraysh failed to show up. Instead, Abu Sufyan tried to break the Muslim resolve by sending a man to spread rumors in Medina about how fearsome the Quraysh army would be, hoping to prevent the Muslims from accepting his challenge! The Prophet camped with his men at Badr for eight days and then marched his men back home.

A few weeks later, the Prophet received reports that two bedouin tribes were preparing to launch an attack on Medina, so the Prophet again assembled a force (this time of 400 men) and marched out to prevent their assault. Finding the bedouins had fled rather than risking a fight, the Prophet once again returned to Medina with his men. Then word of a new threat from the powerful Banu Mustaliq tribe reached Medina, and the Prophet assembled yet another force (this time of 700 men) to meet the foe before it could strike. He came upon the tribe's encampment while they were unaware of his march.

The tribe was defeated, and its people taken into custody. (It was a pre-emptive attack, and this is allowed in Islam if it is clearly known that an enemy is already making preparations to attack you first.) The Prophet was assigned Juwayriyyah, the daughter of the Banu Mustaliq chief, as his share of the booty, but he freed her and married her. Then all the other captives were freed by the enthusiastic companions. Due to his gracious treatment, the tribe accepted Islam.

On the return trip from the campaign, the Prophet's wife A'ishah was inadvertently left behind in one of the campsites when she went looking for a lost piece of jewelry. A companion of the Prophet, finding her there, escorted her to Medina, arriving a day behind the main body of the army. Hypocrites immediately seized upon this to spread rumors and slander that A'ishah had been unfaithful with her escort. This grieved the Prophet, A'ishah and many others, as baseless accusations tend to take on a life of their own.

This chapter was eventually revealed to the Prophet from Allah, absolving A'ishah of any guilt. In addition, harsh words are directed against slanderers and those who falsely question a woman's honor without proof or sincerity. Other miscellaneous matters of social interaction are also addressed.

In the Name of Allah,
the Compassionate, the Merciful

This is a chapter containing Our regulations that We're sending down. We've included self-evident verses within it so you can be reminded. [1]

Any woman or man who is guilty of adultery or fornication [711] is to be whipped with a hundred lashes each. Don't let compassion sway you regarding their case, for it's part of Allah's way of life - that is if you're (sincere) believers in Allah and the Last Day. Also arrange for some believing witnesses to observe their punishment. [712] [2]

---

[711] The term used here (*zina*) is a generic term for any unlawful sexual relations outside of marriage and is commonly applied to both adultery and fornication. (*Ma'ariful Qur'an*)
[712] Although no one disputes that a fornicator would get a whipping, after the Prophet's passing there was some confusion among his companions and their students about the punishment for adultery. Based on this verse, some said it was lashes, while others, citing *hadith* reports, said the punishment was elevated to stoning by prophetic injunction (or divine revelation). (*Bukhari, Muslim*) This second position was strongly advanced by 'Umar ibn al-Khattab, among others. The latter position eventually rose to prominence in the succeeding years, (with some dissenters), and it became the common legal position in the classical period of Islamic scholarship that a married adulterer is to be stoned to death, while an unmarried fornicator is to be whipped with a hundred lashes (administered in such a way that it causes no bleeding or permanent scarring) and banishment for a year. (The latter punishment being outlined in the Bukhari collection.) The proponents of stoning base their position on several *hadith* reports in which it appears that the Prophet called for this more drastic punishment. Other commentators assert that the Qur'anic punishment of whipping is to be applied to both the adulterer and the fornicator in preference to the stoning that is contained in the *hadith* reports. Their argument is based on the common position that the Qur'an trumps what the Prophet may (or may not) have said and that no *hadith* report can abrogate a Qur'anic injunction. Why would there exist *hadith* reports that suggest that the Prophet called for the stoning of adulterers rather than a whipping? It must be remembered that the injunction for stoning adulterers is from the Torah, that no such verse appears in the Qur'an, and that the Prophet recommended to the Jews who came to him with at least two adultery cases that they must follow what's in *their* scripture, the Torah. (See Qur'an 5:41 and footnote where one of these cases is recounted.) The Qur'an, which abrogated or superseded both the Torah and the Gospel, has its own outlined punishment of whipping. It cannot be abrogated, opponents of stoning assert, by any human source. Some pro-stoning scholars take the position that the Qur'an does say to flog adulterers, but that it's *really* calling for stoning them. They justify this by saying that there is an 'uncollected' or 'forgotten' verse of the Qur'an that ordered stoning that the Prophet at some point stopped reciting out of dislike

Don't Match the Pure with the Tainted

Background on verse 3: The exact reports differ slightly, but the basic issue surrounding the revelation of this verse is that some poor believer(s) asked about marrying prostitutes. Either they wanted them to keep plying their trade and thus have money coming into their coffers, or the women themselves wanted to keep doing it so they would be financially independent. This verse forbids chaste people from marrying people who did *zina*, or adultery and fornication, and those who led that lifestyle can only marry others like them or pagans (who have no prohibition against committing adultery or fornication, and who might presumably fall into it again).

---

for it. There is also an odd mention in the Ibn Majah and Ahmad collections that the so-called 'stoning verse' was written on a leather parchment and kept in A'ishah's house and that a goat came in and ate the leather piece while the Prophet's funeral was being performed, resulting in the verse being lost forever! Besides that report sounding a bit whimsical, the untenable nature of such a position is in the fact that staunch Muslims readily charge that the Jews of Medina had hidden a verse of their Torah that called for stoning (Deuteronomy 22:22), dishonestly reducing the penalty for adultery from death to flogging, while at the same time, these same Muslims are saying they want to eliminate the ruling of the existing Qur'anic verse that calls for adulterers to be flogged in favor of the harsher penalty of stoning, based on a verse that *doesn't even appear* in their own book. When the Jews of Medina asked the Prophet for a ruling on this issue, he *did* order them to follow their religious law to the letter. Thus, the Prophet technically did call for stoning. Yet, in later years, he actually refused to repeat the order for stoning, even though 'Umar wished to hear it from him. *Could it be that the ruling on stoning was never a Qur'anic verse, but was instead the Prophet's opinion based on his respect for the law of Moses, and that he later received direction from Allah to drop that idea, with that divine commandment being backed up by an actual Qur'anic verse that outlines flogging as the punishment Allah decrees?* (Thus, the issue of the existence of a stoning report supposedly left out of the Qur'an can be reconciled.) Allah only knows and only He knows which legal position is right. I take no firm stance either way other than to say that there is a serious punishment to be suffered for this serious crime. By the way, four witnesses must catch the person in the act of adultery or fornication for the punishment to be due, and if a spouse accuses another of it on his or her sole testimony, the accused can swear to Allah that he or she is innocent and have the guarantee to be found not guilty in a court of law. Thus, the only practical way anyone would get either of these punishments (whipping or stoning) is if they volunteered for it! Now about "uncollected" verses, would any of the companions willfully let any verse go unrecorded in the official text if they knew it existed and was supposed to be preserved? Could a verse be 'lost' because a goat ate it, when there were so many companions who had the entire Qur'an memorized? When Uthman ibn Affan (d. 656) was asked by his nephew, Ibn az-Zubayr, why he included a particular verse in the finalized edition of the Qur'an that he had ordered to be compiled - a verse that some people at the time thought was abrogated by another verse (2:240 was abrogated, some say, by verse 2:234), he replied, "My nephew, I shall not change any part of the Qur'an from its place." Thus, Uthman, one of the Prophet's closest companions and a member of his inner-circle, testified from his own mouth that he collected the Qur'an in its full form as the Prophet envisioned it, regardless of what others would think about the continued validity of individual verses. (*Fath al-Bari, Ibn Kathir*)

Thereafter, don't let any man guilty of adultery or fornication marry anyone except a woman who is also guilty of the same crime, or (he can marry) a pagan. Likewise, let no woman who is guilty of adultery or fornication marry anyone except a man who is guilty of the same crime, or (she may marry) a pagan. (Marrying someone guilty of unlawful sex) is forbidden for the believers. [713] [3]

Don't Slander Respectable Women

Those who make an accusation against a respectable woman, and who don't produce four witnesses (who caught her in the act of adultery or fornication), then whip (the ones who brought the unsubstantiated charge) with eighty lashes, and never accept any testimony from them ever again, for they're disobedient troublemakers. [4] If they repent afterwards and reform themselves, then Allah is forgiving and merciful. [714] [5]

---

[713] There are many dangers involved with people who are so out of control in their intimate lives that they have unlawful sexual relations against Allah's orders. (Both Christianity and Judaism have traditionally forbidden adultery and fornication as strongly as Islam does.) How can a chaste person of good reputation and disposition be paired with someone who did not obey Allah's strict orders in this regard? Worse still, perhaps such a risky lifestyle may bring horrible diseases such as AIDS down upon an innocent and chaste person? How can a person who may have had many partners outside of a marriage bond, in defiance of all religions, be expected to be faithful to the marriage bond in the same way as someone who believes marriage is the only lawful outlet for passion and waits patiently for it? Such people may not be ideal partners for those who have led a life of chastity and who expect to find the same in their life partner. (See 24:26) Thus, people who have committed adultery or fornication are only allowed to marry each other. It must be noted that a person who accepts Islam is forgiven all their past sins and is thus exempted from this ban, as they lived in ignorance before. (This position is proven by the fact that most of the male and female companions had lived in the same kind of ignorance before the coming of Islam and were under no relationship restrictions after converting to Islam. Also see 16:119.) However, if converts fall into sin again after claiming to believe, then they will be subject to this verse's strictures after that and can only seek marriage with a similar type of person or a non-Muslim (whom they can eventually convert). The Prophet once advised men thusly, "Don't divorce women unless they've committed the evil act (of adultery), for Allah doesn't like men and women who merely wish to experience the taste of sex." (*Ma'ariful Qur'an*)

[714] If they publicly repent for slandering a woman and thereafter lead a righteous life in the eyes of their fellows, then such people can, at least in theory, regain Allah's favor and perhaps the right to have testimony accepted again, provided they admit to having lied. (There is no way, however, to avoid the whipping.) The reputation of a woman is her honor. If anyone questions it without foundation or makes false charges, they've done tremendous harm to a potential mother, wife, sister or daughter. By the way, the culturally-based practice of so-called *honor killing*, in which a family member kills a female

Addressing Accusations of Adultery

Background on verses 6-10: Ibn 'Abbas (d. 687) related that some companions had been discussing what should happen if they were by themselves and they caught their spouse in the act of adultery with someone else. Would they themselves get the 80 lashes because they could not produce four witnesses? Who would ever report a case of adultery then? Their concern was soon answered. A man named Hilal ibn Umayyah went to the Prophet and swore that he found his own wife cheating on him with a man named Sharik ibn Sahma. The Prophet disliked hearing such an accusation, since the Qur'an had already laid down the rule that four witnesses must be brought if someone wants to lodge a charge of infidelity against someone, so he asked Hilal if he were prepared to accept 80 lashes because he lacked corroborating witnesses.

Another companion nearby named S'ad ibn 'Ubadah mused to his friends that he thought the Prophet would declare all the future testimony of Hilal to be unreliable and void. Hilal was very upset, and he beseeched the Prophet for some ruling from Allah. The Prophet was about to order the man whipped (based on the previously revealed verses 4-5 of this chapter), but then he suddenly froze and began to look as if he were under great strain, (signaling to those around him that he was receiving a new revelation). When he became relaxed again, the Prophet recited verses 6-10, and he said to Hilal, "A bargain for you, since Allah found a solution for you and absolved you, and I hoped for that from my God."

Later that day, Hilal and his wife went before the Prophet in the mosque, and the Prophet made each of them swear to Allah about their statements and invoke His curse upon them if they were lying, and both sides did so as this passage [24:6-9] outlines, thus canceling each other's accusations. (Hilal's wife did hesitate before taking the fifth oath as to her innocence, but then she said, "I will not dishonor my family today.") With that done, the wife escaped the accusation and the punishment for adultery. Then the Prophet predicted that she was pregnant, and then he annulled their marriage and forbade anyone from ever accusing her of adultery or accusing the child of being illegitimate. Next, he said that if the child was born with reddish hair, then it was Hilal's child, but if it were born with curly hair, dark eyes and was heavy-set (like Sharik looked), then it was not Hilal's child. Later she gave birth to a child that fit the second description, and the Prophet said, "If it wasn't for the oath that she swore, I would have dealt with her." Her son took his mother's family name and was never attributed to any father. He eventually grew up to be a governor of Egypt. (*Ibn Kathir*)

---

relative for fear she has *dishonored* the family, a practice that is prevalent in some backward countries in the Middle East, Asia and Africa, has absolutely no legal basis in Islamic Law (though it is in the Bible in Deuteronomy 22:21). 'Honor' killing is routinely spoken against by Islamic legal scholars, and it falls under the crime of murder. Those who practice this unnatural and extra-legal custom are blameworthy and will have to answer for it on the Day of Judgment, that is if they escape prosecution in this life. Verse 24:2 is the only legally-sanctioned punishment, and it can only be applied if four witnesses catch the people in the act and testify before a judge in a court, and the penalty must be applied equally to both the male and the female.

As for those who make an accusation (of adultery) against their spouses, and who don't have any witness other than themselves, their sole testimony (can be accepted) if they swear to Allah four times that they're telling the truth [6] and then swear a fifth time that the curse of Allah should come upon them if they're lying. [715] [7]

However, (the spouse) can avert the punishment if they swear to Allah four times that (the accuser) is telling a lie [8] and then swears a fifth time that Allah's wrath should come down upon them if (the accuser) was telling the truth. [716] [9] If it wasn't for Allah's favor and His mercy towards you, (then you would've committed injustice in disputes involving infidelity), but Allah accepts repentance and is wise. [10]

The False Charge against A'ishah

Background on verse 11: Whenever the Prophet led a large expedition, one of his wives would usually accompany him to look after him. When the Prophet set out at the head of several hundred men to attack the Banu Mustaliq tribe, which was secretly preparing to attack the Muslims first, A'ishah was the one who came along. On the return journey, the Muslims made camp, and it was there that A'ishah noticed that one of her prized pieces of jewelry was missing.

As the men prepared their mounts to resume the journey home, A'ishah, not realizing the pace of packing, walked back along the trail hoping to spot her gold necklace. When she returned to camp after finding her necklace, she found that the men had all gone and moved on. Her palanquin, or camel mounted chamber, was always covered in a curtain, so no one noticed that she wasn't inside when the party set out once again. A'ishah remained in the abandoned camp, confident that her absence would soon be noticed and that someone would be sent to look for her.

One Muslim man named Safwan ibn al-Mu'attal, who had been given the chore of collecting any lost baggage, came upon A'ishah and found her sitting in the campsite. He placed her on his camel and set off immediately after the main body of the army. They reached Medina about a day behind the army. When people saw the young man leading A'ishah into the city, the tongues of the hypocrites began to wag. 'Abdullah ibn Ubayy, in particular, began avidly spreading the rumor of adultery, and even some sincere believers got caught up in the rumor-mongering. The Prophet immediately defended A'ishah and Safwan as honest and trustworthy in a public speech, and when he asked for help against the gossip campaign from Ibn Ubayy, the Muslims in the mosque broke up into two factions along tribal lines and began quarrelling. The Prophet was stunned, and A'ishah was heartbroken over the accusations.

---

[715] The process works the same way whether the accuser is the husband or the wife.
[716] Accusations of infidelity are grounds for automatic divorce, and the couple can never remarry.

A'ishah soon moved back in with her parents and stayed with them for a month to rest, and the Prophet checked in on her from time to time as he consulted with his companions about the rumor-mongering that was going on. The issue continued to divide the Auws and Khazraj companions who continued to argue over the matter. A'ishah described her heartache as the worst thing she ever felt in her life, saying, "I cried continuously every day and couldn't sleep, so that my parents expected me to die from my extreme sorrow."

Safwan was equally in despair and protested his innocence profusely. Then, after one month passed, the Prophet visited A'ishah and said, "There is no god but Allah. I've been told (rumors) about you, but if you're innocent, then Allah will prove it (today), though if you've committed a sin, then ask forgiveness of Allah and repent to Him, for if a servant of Allah admits his sin, then his repentance will be accepted."

A'ishah began to feel better, and she motioned for her parents to answer for her, but they declined, citing the fact that they didn't know what they were to say. Then A'ishah said, "Even though I'm still young and I haven't read much of the Qur'an, I do know what you've heard and thought about me. Even if I said that I'm innocent, and Allah knows it, you probably wouldn't believe me, and if I admitted to something of which Allah knows I'm innocent, then you'd probably believe me then. So I haven't found for you and me any other saying than what the father of Joseph said." Then she recited Joseph's quote from verse 12:18, and afterwards she turned away and laid down on her bed.

The Prophet went out into another room, and a few moments later this passage was revealed [24:11-26], which proved A'ishah's and Safwan's innocence and exposed the plotting of the hypocrites. The Prophet laughed joyfully and announced first, before reciting the verses, "A'ishah! Good news for you! Allah has proven your innocence!" A'ishah was overjoyed when she heard the news, and she soon moved back into her own apartment fully exonerated.

Those who brought out the slanderous (charge of adultery against the Prophet's wife A'ishah) are nothing more than a gang among you (who tried to stir up trouble). [717] Don't think of it as a bad thing, however, for it was ultimately a good thing for you (that this issue was dealt with openly). [718] Every person among them will have his

---

[717] This 'gang' is a reference to 'Abdullah ibn Ubayy (and his henchmen) who did the most to keep the scandal alive and in constant circulation.

[718] Gossip is one of the most natural things for any group of people to engage in, and it is also one of the most destructive behaviors out of the many in which people indulge. The Prophet was sensitive to people's tongue-wagging, for he understood well how idle chatter can divide people and create scandals and hatreds in society. One night he was walking his wife Safiyah to her home after a late night of worship in the mosque. Two men were passing by in the street. When they saw the Prophet in the dim light walking with a woman, they hurried on, not wanting to bother him. The Prophet, fearing the men might think something bad about him, (that he was with a woman to whom he was not married), called out to them and said, "I am here walking with my wife Safiya." The men said they thought nothing bad, and the Prophet explained that he wanted to make sure no one would be plagued with thoughts from Satan. (*Ibn Kathir*)

sin recorded, and the one who was the most involved among them will have a terrible punishment (from Allah). [11]

When you first heard of the situation, why didn't the men and women of faith think better (of A'ishah) to themselves and say, *"This is obviously a false charge"*? [719] [12] Why didn't they bring four witnesses to prove it? When they failed to bring witnesses, they were (proven) to be liars in the sight of Allah. [13]

If it wasn't for Allah's favor towards all of you and His mercy - *both in this world and in the next* - then a terrible punishment would've certainly befallen you on account of your indulgence in this affair. [720] [14] While you (people) were eagerly passing (this lie along) with your tongues and saying with your mouths things you knew nothing about, you thought it was just a trivial matter, but in Allah's sight it was a serious issue. [721] [15] When you (first) heard about it, why didn't you say, *"It's not right for us to talk about this. Glory to You, (Our Lord), this is an awful rumor!"* [16]

---

[719] When the gossip began to spread around Medina, Umm Ayyoub, the wife of Abu Ayyoub al-Ansari, said to her husband, "Have you heard what the people are saying about A'ishah?" He replied, "Yes, and it's all lies. Would you ever do that, mother of Ayyoub?" She answered, "No, by Allah! I would never do that!" Then Abu Ayyoub said, "A'ishah is even better than you." (*Ibn Kathir*) It is also important to note in this case that Safwan brought A'ishah into Medina openly, in front of everybody, while she was mounted on his camel. If something shameful had occurred, then they would have come into town at night in a sneaky way. So the question remains, "Why didn't people think more highly? Why were some people's minds so intent on thinking the worst?"

[720] A number of men and women repented of their involvement in this affair, including the Prophet's own brother-in-law and sister-in-law, Hassan ibn Jahsh and Hemnah bint Jahsh, and they were forgiven. The Prophet once remarked, "Don't speak ill of my companions for I like to leave each of you with a clear mind." The principle is that no matter how we feel about someone else, we should not try to prejudice others against them. Rather, we should let other people form their own opinions by themselves based on their dealings with others.

[721] The Prophet said, "A man may say a word that makes Allah angry without realizing how far it will go, and because of it he will be thrown into Hellfire a distance greater than what is between the sky and the earth." (*Bukhari, Muslim*)

Allah is warning you seriously not to repeat this (vicious rumor-mongering), that is if you're (sincere) believers. [722] [17] Allah makes His verses clear for you, for Allah is full of knowledge and wisdom. [18]

Those who love to spread scandalous accusations among the believers will have a painful punishment in this life, as well as in the next life. Allah knows (all about their evil intentions), even though you don't know. [19] If it wasn't for Allah's favor towards you and His mercy, (then you believers would've been punished for your participation, too), but Allah is kind and merciful. [20]

Maintain Good Relations

O you who believe! Don't follow in the footsteps of Satan. If anyone follows in Satan's footsteps, then he'll order (them to do) what's shameful [723] and despicable. If it wasn't for Allah's favor

---

[722] The Prophet said, "Don't annoy Allah's servants or abuse them or look for their hidden faults. Whoever seeks out the faults of his Muslim brother, Allah will expose his faults and embarrass him, even if he's hiding in his house!" (*Ahmad*)

[723] *Fahsha-i* implies outrageous sexual or lewd conduct such as prostitution, homosexuality, pornography, obscenity, rape, molestation, etc.... It is sometimes associated with adultery and fornication, but the Qur'an generally uses a different word (*zina*) for those two sins. (See 24:2) On the issue of rape, it is a crime in Islam, and the unfortunate misapplication of Qur'anic principles by extremists and certain men of a rustic mental nature, in which they blame the victim and punish her, has unnecessarily given critics of Islam a reason to complain. That Islam outlaws a believer from raping a woman is undisputed. (See verses such as 5:5, 24:30, 6:120 and 24:33. Compare with Deuteronomy 22:28-29.) The problem arises when a victim of such a crime reports on her assailant. Those of a rustic mental capacity then invoke verse 24:4 and demand that the victim produce four witnesses. When she can't, which is to be expected, they then invoke against her the charge of adultery and lobby for lashes or stoning. This is a preposterous insult and injustice to the victim. For those who like to be absolutely specific in Qur'anic injunctions, it must be noted that the verse requiring the production of witnesses specifically states that it is for those who launch a charge of adultery against a woman, and in general Qur'anic usage, when both males and females are covered under an injunction, the masculine pronouns are used. However, when women are specifically addressed (to the exclusion of men), then feminine pronouns and word forms are employed. Thus, in cases of rape, the strictures of verse 24:4 do not apply at all. Therefore, in Islamic law, the crime of rape is an assault for which a single person's witness is acceptable and for which a court judge must rule. (Contrary to popular mythology, the Qur'an does not have a blanket rule that a woman's testimony is worth half of a man's as a matter of policy. Only in 2:282 is it mentioned that a woman should have a second woman to back up her testimony in business dealings, and the reason is given for that, as explained in the footnote for that verse. Verse 24:9 specifically accepts the single testimony of a woman, for example, if she is accused by her husband of

towards you and His mercy, then none of you would've ever been sanctified. Allah sanctifies whomever He wants, and Allah listens and knows (all things). [21]

Don't Hold a Grudge Against Family

Background on verse 22: Abu Bakr found out that one of the men who kept the false charges against his daughter A'ishah circulating was none other than his poverty-stricken cousin, Mistah ibn Uthathah, to whom he had always given money in the past. Thus, Abu Bakr vowed to cut off any support for him. A'ishah learned of her relative's slandering of her one night from Mistah's own mother, who said, "Mistah should be ruined!" A'ishah incredulously asked, "Are you abusing someone who was present at the Battle of Badr?" Mistah's mother replied, "Oh my, haven't you heard what he's been saying?" Then she told A'ishah about his part in the rumors and gossip, causing her to feel even more terrible. This passage asks Abu Bakr, and by extension anyone else with wayward relatives, to forgive their faults out of a spirit of charity and generosity. When the line was read to him, "Don't you want Allah to forgive you," Abu Bakr replied, "Of course, we would love, Our Lord, for You to forgive us." (*Ibn Kathir*) The Prophet reiterated this Qur'anic concept by saying that the real test of kindness towards relatives is not just by helping them when they are friendly towards you, but by helping them still after they've cut you off. (*Ma'ariful Qur'an*)

Don't let those who've been endowed (with great wealth and status) among you swear that they're no longer going to help their relatives, the needy or those who've migrated in the cause of Allah (simply because those people might have behaved poorly). Forgive them, and overlook (their faults). Don't you want Allah to forgive you, too? Allah is forgiving and merciful! [22]

---

committing adultery.) Did the Prophet ever deal with this issue in the community? A man named Wa'il ibn Hujr reports of an incident when a woman was raped. Later, when some people came by, she identified and accused the man who had raped her. They seized him and brought him to the messenger of Allah. He said to the woman, "Go away, for Allah has forgiven you," but of the man who had raped her, he said, "Stone him to death." (*Tirmidhi, Abu Dawud*) A single woman's testimony was accepted, she was not penalized, and her attacker was punished quite harshly. In classical Islamic civilization, rape was under the criminal category of *hiraba*, or terrorizing. Ibn Hazm defined *hiraba* as: "One who puts people in fear on the road, with or without a weapon, at night or day, in urban areas or in open spaces, in the palace of a caliph or a mosque, with or without accomplices, in the desert or in the village, in a large or small city, with one or more people... making people fear that they'll be killed, or robbed, or raped... whether the attackers are one or many." Thus, in classical Islamic law, rape was not put under the category of *zina* (adultery and fornication) at all, but under the crime of *terrorism*!

The Punishment of Slanderers

Those who make false charges against naive, yet respectable, believing women, are cursed in this life, and in the next life they're going to have a terrible punishment [23] on the day when their tongues, their hands, and their feet will testify against them as to what they've done. [724] [24] On that day, Allah will repay them for the genuine results of their way of life. Then they'll (finally) realize that Allah is the Obvious Truth. [25]

Tainted women are for tainted men, and tainted men are for tainted women. Wholesome women are for wholesome men, and wholesome men are for wholesome women. [725] (Respectable people) are not affected by what (slanderers) say (about them), and they're going to have forgiveness and a generous share (in Paradise). [26]

Asking Permission to Enter a Home

Background on verses 27-28: A woman went to the Prophet and said, "Sometimes when I'm in the privacy of my own home, I don't want to be seen by either my father or my son, but my father still enters while I'm (not fully dressed). So what can I do?" (Pre-Islamic Arab culture had previously no restrictions on entering another person's home at will.) This passage was revealed in answer and lays down the principle that people's privacy must be respected. (*Asbab ul-Nuzul*)

O you who believe! Don't go into anyone's homes other than your own unless you've asked permission first and greeted those who (live) within them. [726] That's the best (practice) for you (to follow) so

---

[724] The Prophet was grinning broadly one day when he asked those around him if they knew why he was smiling so much. When they replied that both Allah and he knew best, he replied, "Because of the way someone will be arguing with his Lord (on Judgment Day). He's going to say, 'O Lord! Didn't You try to protect me from doing wrong?' Allah will reply that He had. Then the person will say, 'Then I'm not going to accept anyone testifying about me other than myself!' Then Allah will say, 'Then you are quite enough to testify against yourself!' Then his mouth will be sealed, and his limbs will be ordered to speak. So they will speak about his deeds, and after the man will be allowed to speak again, he'll cry out to them, 'Get out of here! I was only speaking to defend you!'" (*Muslim, Nisa'i*)

[725] This passage is saying that morally upright people don't cavort with immoral people, and thus a moral person has nothing to fear from slanderous accusations against his or her reputation.

[726] The Prophet once counseled a man that he must ask permission to enter even his mother's home when he visits her lest he come upon her when she is *indisposed*. Even when

you can be reminded (of the importance of respecting the privacy of others). [27]

If you find no one in the house, (or if no one answers you), then still refrain from entering until you've been given permission. [727]

If you're asked to leave, then leave, for that's the purest course of action for you (to follow), and Allah knows what you're doing. [28]

> **Background on verse 29:** Abu Bakr, when he heard verses 24:27-28 being recited, asked the Prophet about the abandoned homes people would sometimes find and sleep in on their trading trips to Syria. This verse was revealed in response. (*Asbab ul-Nuzul*) It also covers going into stores and other places of business. Obviously, if the store or office is closed, the visitor will have to wait for normal business hours before entering.

It's not wrong for you to enter buildings (without permission) if they're not used for habitation, and which serve some other (public) purpose for you. Allah knows what you reveal openly and what you (try to) hide. [29]

Modesty Begins With the Eyes

Tell the believing men that they should lower their gaze [728] (and not stare lustfully at women) and that they should guard their modesty. That's the purest course of action for them to follow. Allah is well-informed of everything they do. [729] [30]

---

a person enters his own home, if there are others living in the house, he must make some noise while entering so people know he has come home. (*Ma'ariful Qur'an*)

[727] A Muslim must say the full greetings of peace before entering someone else's home. (*Ahmad*) The Prophet taught that if, after three salutations (or knocks) at the door, no one answers, then you should leave. (*Bukhari*) He also forbade people from peeking into other people's homes to snoop or spy if the door is open (or if there is no door). Once the Prophet noticed a man peeking into his house through the key hole in the door. The Prophet picked up a stick and poked the man in the eye. If the people in a house don't want to answer the door, then we should not try to barge in or make ourselves a nuisance.

[728] The Prophet once advised his followers not to sit idly by the roadside, but they complained, saying it was the only place they could meet people to talk. Then the Prophet said, "If you insist, then give the street its rights." When they asked him what those were, he replied, "Lower your gaze, return the greetings of peace, encourage the good and forbid the wrong." (*Bukhari*)

[729] No one can underestimate the temptation that outright staring at the opposite sex can bring. It is so serious a moral issue that Prophet Jesus is quoted in the New Testament as saying that a man who stares lustfully at a woman has already committed adultery in his

Likewise, tell the believing women that they should lower their gaze (and not stare lustfully at men), that they should guard their modesty, and that they shouldn't display their attractions - other than what must ordinarily show. [730]

They should also draw forth their headscarves over their bosoms and not let their curves be seen except by their husbands, their fathers, their husbands' fathers, their sons, their husbands' sons, their brothers, their brothers' sons, their sisters' sons, their female (relatives and acquaintances), [731] their bonded maidservants, their menservants who have little sexual interest (such as the very old), and children who are innocent of intimate attraction. [732]

---

heart! (Matthew 5:27-29) Some critics of Islam have questioned Islam's emphasis on moral purity, modesty, chastity and gender conscious restrictions, saying that Islam takes a dim view of people and their ability to control their sexual desires and impulses. (They say this while seemingly completely ignorant of the strict traditions of personal morality found in traditional Judaism and Christianity!) What must be remembered is that Islam is not so much a cure for social ills as it is a preventative measure designed to *preempt* the behavior that leads to such ills to begin with.

[730] The Qur'an established a more modest dress code to protect the dignity of women, a dress code that is nearly identical to the code of female modesty practiced in Judaism called *tznius*. Thus, women are advised not to cheapen themselves so much that they become a kind of show for men, and also so that they need not feel inadequate over their level of attractiveness in public. The Prophet explained the public veiling requirements for the general female population (after puberty) as follows. "When a girl reaches the menstrual age, it is not proper that anything should remain exposed except this and this." Then he pointed to his face and hands. (*Abu Dawud*) The "ordinarily shown" category covers, in the view of most scholars, things such as the feet (for Arabia was a sandal culture) or the basic shape of the body that no amount of covering can conceal. The eminent commentator Zamakhshari wrote the following about the Prophet's permission of a woman to show her face, hands and feet in public: "Why is a woman permitted to display, '*other than what must ordinarily show*'? Because to conceal that would cause her inconvenience. A woman is forced to deal in commodities with her hands. She is compelled by genuine need to expose her face, especially at the time of giving evidence, litigating in court, and marriage. She is compelled to walk the streets and expose her feet, especially poor women." Other commentators such as al-Qurtubi and Razi were of the same view.

[731] The classical scholars have suggested that a Muslim woman should be wary of removing her head covering in front of non-Muslim women because they have no equivalent concept of modesty and may describe them and how they look to their husbands. The Prophet said, "No woman should describe another woman to her husband as if he were looking at her." (*Bukhari, Muslim*)

[732] Many (but not all) pre-Islamic Arab women used to wear head coverings called *khimars* over their hair, but they wore them loosely and showed their forelocks and such. They also wore gowns of varying lengths, but they were often tight and short with low cut necklines. Thus, many women exposed a great deal of themselves in public. Once Asma',

(Also tell them) that they shouldn't stamp their feet in order to draw attention to their hidden (charms and jewelry). O you who believe! Turn together towards Allah so you can be successful! [733] [31]

Get Married when You Can

Single people among you should get married, [734] and the morally upright among your bonded servants and maids (should get married,

---

the daughter of Abu Bakr, saw some women in Medina coming to her house dressed like that, and she commented, "How revolting!" As Zamakhshari explained, "Women in those days used to cover their heads with the headscarf (*khimar*), throwing its ends upon their backs. This left the neck and the upper part of the chest bare, along with the ears, in the manner of the Christians. Then Allah commanded them to cover those parts with the headscarf." The idea is that when a woman is in public and in full view of men who are not supposed to see her hidden charms, she should conceal her feminine attributes by draping the ends of her headscarf over her chest in front. The Muslim woman is to be a dignified woman and shouldn't wantonly parade her beauty in front of strange men. The Prophet said, "The worst among women are those who leave their homes without a headscarf. They are hypocrites, and few of those will enter paradise." (*Bayhaqi*) Traditionally, Judaism also required women to cover their hair, though many modern Jewish sects allow women to wear berets, kerchiefs or wigs (*shaytal*) in place of the veil. (Jewish men also are exhorted to wear a yarmulke on their head.) Christianity also traditionally required women to cover their hair in public (see I Corinthians 11:1-13 where the Greek word for veil or *katakalupto* is ordained for women), though this Biblical commandment has been largely abandoned by most modern Christians since the early part of the nineteenth century (save for some regions of eastern Europe and Africa and also among the Amish, some Greek Orthodox, some Pentecostals and nuns of the Catholic church). The traditional wedding veil used in Christian marriages is a vestige of both the required veil and also of arranged marriages, which used to be the norm among Christians until the early nineteenth century.

[733] Muslim men also have a kind of obvious identity badge not unlike the female *khimar* or headscarf, as explained by the Prophet, and that is to grow a beard (if physically possible) and to wear a turban, headscarf or cap. (*Bukhari, Muslim*) The Prophet sometimes wore a cap and at other times he wore a head-cloth draped over his hair, and this was also called a *khimar*. (See the book entitled, *Niqab: A Seal on the Debate*, by Kamillah Khan. Dar al Wahi, 2008.)

[734] Does Islam forbid people from marrying outside their culture, class or race? Again, this is another myth, based upon popular fiction, that has given rise to the false belief that marriages between people of the same race, class or culture are superior to interracial or interclass marriages. The Qur'an says in 49:13: "People! We created you from a single pair of a male and a female and made you into nations and ethnic groups so you can come to know one another. The noblest among you in the sight of Allah is the one with the most awareness (of the truth of Allah)." In addition, the example of the Prophet is telling: he married a Jewish woman (Safiyah), and later he brought a Greek Christian convert (Maria) into his household; he arranged the marriage of his African-Arabian companion Bilal to a local pure-blooded Arab woman; and he even broke class lines by arranging several marriages between wealthy people and poor people. Religion and

as well). If any of them are too poor (to support a family), then Allah will enrich them from His bounty, for Allah pervades all things and has knowledge. [735] [32] Those who don't yet have the financial means to marry [736] should keep themselves chaste until Allah enriches them from His bounty. [737]

Don't Prevent Bonded Servants from Working for Their Freedom

Background on the middle part of verse 33: Suba'ih, the servant of a man named Huwaytib, asked for an emancipation contract, but Huwaytib refused. This verse was revealed in response. (*Asbab ul-Nuzul*)

Also, if any of your bonded servants ask you for a written contract (to buy their freedom), then give them one. [738] If you've found

---

sincerity are the best qualities to look for in a mate or in-law, as evidenced by the well-known saying of the Prophet in which he enumerated the reasons that people look for to marry someone (religious adherence, wealth, status, good looks), and he concluded that sincere religious practice was the best criteria to consider! (*Bukhari, Muslim*)

[735] Merely being of humble means is no reason to postpone marriage. A person who has only a little can improve himself and gain greater wealth over time. In Islam, a person's bank account does not define his worth, as a person's wealth comes and goes. Only a person's character, manners and his faithfulness to his Lord and to his obligations matter. When 'Ali ibn Abi Talib went to the Prophet to ask for his daughter's hand in marriage, he had no worldly wealth. The Prophet asked him what he could offer as a dowry. When he said he had nothing, the Prophet suggested he could sell his shield and thus gain some funds. 'Ali went to sell his shield, and Uthman bought it for 400 silver coins. Then he gave the shield back to 'Ali as a wedding gift for his marriage to Fatimah.

[736] When a man asks a woman to marry him, he must pay her a marriage gift or dowry, and the bride sets the amount. This verse refers to those men who cannot afford to give what the woman asks and she is unwilling to accept a down payment.

[737] Born and raised Muslim males and females must remain virgins until marriage. They are advised not to postpone marriage for too many years after they've reached the marriageable age, especially if they're financially able, in order that they may channel their youthful vigor in lawful ways. The Prophet once advised those who had a hard time controlling their sexual energies outside of marriage to practice fasting because it dampened sexual feelings. (*Bukhari, Muslim*) The Prophet always urged young adults to marry, and it has never been a Muslim cultural custom (until recently) to postpone marriage merely on account of waiting for long-term educational or financial goals to be completed. There is also no stigma in Islam in marrying people who are divorced. The Prophet, himself, married mostly divorced and widowed women.

[738] Bonded-servants who want to be free can demand a fair written contract outlining a price for their release based on market value for their labor or worth. Since no one can overwork his or her bonded servant or make him work the entire day, there is free time in which a servant can seek other employment and save his money to purchase his own freedom from servitude. (The commentators agree that installment payments are legitimate.) The retainer is even counseled to help his bonded servant gain his or her freedom, if he's found him or her to be of good character. While in Medina in the

them to be good (in character), then give them some money yourselves out of what Allah's provided you (to aid them in buying out their contracts).

Don't Send Women into Prostitution

> **Background on the last part of verse 33:** 'Abdullah ibn 'Ubayy had several slave girls, including two women named Mu'adhah and Musaykhah. In pre-Islamic days, he had forced them to become prostitutes to make money off of them. After Islam came to Medina, the women converted to Islam and were sincere in their conversions. They wanted to know if what they were being made to do was allowed in Islam, so Musaykhah, accompanied by her mother, went to the Prophet and asked about it. This verse was revealed forbidding the evil practice, and thus they were able to stop being a part of that unwholesome lifestyle. (*Asbab ul-Nuzul*)

Don't turn your maid-servants into prostitutes just so you can make some money off the goods of this world, especially since they desire to be chaste, though if any (unscrupulous man unlawfully) forces them (to be prostitutes), then even after (they've been) forced, Allah (will forgive those maid-servants), for Allah is forgiving and merciful. [739] [33]

Prophet's time, 'Umar ibn al-Khattab had a slave named Abu Umayyah, for whom he wrote an emancipation contract. When Abu Umayyah made his first installment payment, 'Umar gave it back to him and said, "Take it as a help for your emancipation contract." (*Zamakhshari*) During his rule as caliph, a bonded servant named Sirin went to 'Umar to complain that his retainer, Anas bin Malik, would not write up an emancipation contract for him. When Anas was summoned, he refused 'Umar's order to do so. Therefore 'Umar hit him with his stick and recited this verse. Then Anas wrote the contract. (*Bukhari*) This entitlement for bonded servants to emancipation contracts, along with other Islamic reforms, revolutionized the age-old institution of slavery by first affirming the human equality of those in bondage, then elevating them to servants rather than slaves, then restricting the means by which servants can be obtained (only on the battlefield) and finally allowing marriage between retainers and their servants or maids. With all these reforms, as has been pointed out by many Muslim thinkers, unIslamic chattel slavery and even Islamic bonded servitude were institutions whose existence would ultimately fade away.

[739] Thus, with this ruling we find that prostituting one's maid-servants (or any women) is forbidden in Islam. This verse is also a message of hope to those two women and to all women everywhere who are forced into prostitution that Allah will not hold them accountable for what they've been forced to do, even as the evil-doers who force them will be punished either in this life, the next or both. Forced prostitution is so prevalent in today's world that all governments would do well to enact the total Islamic ban on prostitution.

And so We've sent down to you evident verses and examples from (the lives of) those who came before you, as a way of forewarning those who are mindful (of Allah). [34]

Allah is the Light...

Allah is the Light of the heavens and the earth.

The example of His Light is like a nook.

Within that nook is a lamp,

and the lamp is encased in crystal.

The crystal resembles a star, glittering (like a pearl)

whose (flame is) lit from a blessed tree –

an olive (tree) - neither from the East nor the West, [740]

whose oil is glistening and glowing, even before it's been lit!

Light upon Light!

Allah guides whomever He wants towards His Light, and (this is how) Allah gives examples to people, for Allah knows about all things. [741] [35]

Background on verses 36-37: It is said that this passage is a reference to a blacksmith and a sword maker, both of whom literally used to drop everything and rush to the mosque when the call to prayer was announced. (*Qurtubi*)

---

[740] The symbolic 'olive' that is mentioned here, from which the oil for the holy lamp is lit, is of the Syrian variety of olive, which was highly prized, being better than olives produced to the east or west of Arabia. (*Ibn Juzayy*)

[741] The Prophet said, "Allah, the Exalted One, created His creation in darkness, and then later that day He sent His Light upon them. Whoever was touched by His Light on that day will be guided, and whoever was missed will go astray. Therefore I declare, 'The pens have dried in accordance with the knowledge of Allah, may He be glorified!'" (*Ahmad*)

(His Light shines forth) in houses (of worship) that He's allowed to be built and sanctified, [742] and in which His name is remembered and His glorification is done, both in the mornings and the evenings, [36] by men who let neither business nor trade divert them from the remembrance of Allah, [743] nor from establishing prayer nor from giving in charity.

They fear the day when hearts and eyes will be all aflutter (at the horrors of Judgment Day). [744] [37] And so, Allah will reward them according to the best of their deeds, *and He's going to add even more for them besides out of His bounty,* for Allah gives resources to whomever He wills without limitation. [38]

---

[742] The Prophet said, "Whoever builds a mosque for Allah's sake, Allah will build the same for him in Paradise." (*Bukhari, Muslim*) A Muslim house of worship should be simple, however, and not overly decorated, for it defeats the purpose of the place, which is to focus the worshippers' minds on the true destination of us all. The Prophet said, "The Hour will not come until people start showing off in building mosques." (*Ahmad*) The Prophet also said, "Whoever Allah loves should love me. Whoever loves me should love my companions. Whoever loves my companions should love the Qur'an. Whoever loves the Qur'an should love the mosques, for they are the courtyards of Allah, which were built with the permission of Allah. They should be raised up, and He has blessed what is in them. Its people are blessed, and its people are protected while they are in their prayers. Allah is seeing to their needs while they are in their mosques and Allah is before them."

[743] Within the mosque all business transactions are discouraged. The Prophet said, "If you see someone buying or selling in the mosque, say to him, 'May Allah never make your business profitable,' and if you see someone calling out about lost property, say, 'May Allah never return it to you.'" (*Tirmidhi*)

[744] There is a group of Muslims who consciously try to distance themselves from the material world and focus on spirituality, repeating religious phrases (*dhikr*) and doing good deeds above all else. These devotees are often called Sufis, after the wool clothes they used to wear in medieval times. Among the catalysts that fuel their inspiration is the following saying of the Prophet: "The utterly devoted ones (*mufarridun*) are racing ahead (of other believers)." He was asked, "Who are the utterly devoted ones?" He replied, "Those men and women who frequently celebrate the remembrance of Allah (*dhikr*)." (Muslim) The Prophet also said, "Anyone who loves the idea of living in the Garden of Paradise should remember Allah often." (*Ibn Abu Shaybah*) While not all Sufi groups maintain orthodox beliefs, there is something to be said for spiritual exercise. While odd practices done by some groups such as whirling, saint veneration and prayers to old masters are disallowed in Islam, most Sufi groups adhere to Islamic teachings and provide colorful and intense spiritual succor for the mosques and other places they visit. The famous conservative scholar Ibn Taymiyyah (d. 1328), approved of *authentic* sufi practices such as those by spiritual masters such as Abdul Qadir al Jilani (d. 1166), Ibrahim ibn Adham (d. 782) and Sahl ibn 'Abdullah al-Tustari (d.896).

The Futile Works of this World

The deeds of those who suppress (their faith) are like a mirage in the desert, which a thirsty man mistakes for water, until he comes up to it and finds it to be nothing at all! [745] He will, however, find Allah there with Him, and He's going to pay him back what is due to him, for Allah is quick to settle accounts. [39]

(Their example is also) like (that of a man, trapped under) the darkness of a deep ocean, overwhelmed under a great wave, topped by another great wave, topped by a dark cloudiness - darkness in layers one above another! If he stretches out his hand (before his face), he can hardly see it! [746] For the one who has not been granted any light from Allah, there can be no light! [40]

All Things Praise Allah's Glory in their Own Way

Don't you see that all creatures within the heavens and the earth glorify Allah, even the birds as they fly with their wings spread out wide? Every (creature) knows how to make its own kind of prayer and glorification, and Allah knows what they're all doing. [747] [41] The control of the heavens and the earth belongs to Allah, and back to Allah is the final destination (of all things). [42]

Don't you see that it's Allah Who moves the clouds gently, then joins them together and then piles them up in a heap? Then you see

---

[745] There is a story collected by the classical writer, Sa'di Shirazi (d. 1291), in which the following lines are found: "A man once lost his way in the desert and wandered aimlessly for several days. He ran out of food and thought he would surely die. Then he saw a bag lying on the sand. He opened it and saw what he thought were barley grains. He was ecstatic and laughed for joy. When he tried to eat them, however, he discovered they were pearls and fell into deep despair." (*Ghulistan.*)

[746] There is a well-known modern anecdote connected to this verse about a man who was a sailor by trade. He read this verse and asked a Muslim he knew if Muhammad had ever sailed on the ocean before. The Muslim said that he hadn't. Then the sailor asked if Muhammad had ever seen the ocean before, and again the Muslim replied that he hadn't. Then the sailor remarked that only someone who had been deep under the sea, such as in a deep sea diving suit or submarine, would have known that that's how the environment appears there if one were deep under water and looking up – waves under waves of current, with darkness in layers, one above the other with a cloudiness beyond. Then the sailor accepted Islam. Also see 6:25.

[747] Psalms chapter 148 echoes a similar theme of universal praise.

332

raindrops issuing from within them. (Don't you see that) He sends *mountains of clouds* down from the sky? [748]

Hailstones come from within them, and He uses them to pelt whomever He wants, and He turns them away from whomever He wants. (Indeed,) the blinding flash of (one of) His lightning bolts can blind (your very) sight! [43] Allah alternates the night and the day, and in these (signs) are lessons for those who are perceptive. [44]

Allah created every creature from water. Among them are some that crawl on their bellies, some that walk on two legs and others that walk on four. Allah creates whatever He wants, for Allah has power over all things. [45] And so it is that We've sent down evident signs, and Allah guides whomever He wants towards a straight path. [46]

The Problem of False Obedience

Background on verses 47-52: A hypocrite named Bishr was disputing with a Jewish man over ownership of some land. The Jew wanted to go to Muhammad for a settlement, but the hypocrite wanted to go to another man for judgment, saying that Muhammad would not judge fairly. (Bishr knew he was in the wrong, and he wanted to go to K'ab ibn Ashraf, a Jewish chief, for a ruling.) This passage was revealed concerning this issue. (*Asbab ul-Nuzul*)

(The hypocrites) say, "*We believe in Allah and in the Messenger, and we obey,*" but even after (saying all of that), some of them turn away, for they're not (really) believers. [47] When they're called (to appear before) Allah and His Messenger, so He can judge between them, some of them refuse (to come)! [48] However, if the truth is on their side, then they'll come to (the Prophet), acting all cooperative and compliant. [49]

---

[748] During the rule of the second caliph, 'Umar ibn al-Khattab, the caliph came upon some young men who had taken up residence in one of the mosques. The mosques were traditionally open for the poor to sleep in, but 'Umar noticed that there was nothing physically wrong with the young men that would prevent them from finding a job. He became angry at their laziness and began roughly pushing them out of the mosque. He shouted at them, "Go out and earn a living, for the sky doesn't send down rain made of gold or silver."

Is it because there's a sickness in their hearts, or are they just uncertain, or are they afraid that Allah and His Messenger will treat them unfairly? No way! They're the ones in the wrong! [50]

The reply of the believers, when they're called (to appear) before Allah and His Messenger so He can judge between them, is nothing else besides, *"We hear, and we obey."* They're the ones who will be successful! [51] Whoever obeys Allah and His Messenger and fears Allah, while being mindful of Him, will be among the winners. [749] [52]

(The hypocrites) swear to Allah adamantly, claiming that if you but gave the command, they would leave (their homes and march with the militia in times of war). Tell them, *"Don't just swear on it, for actual obedience is a more fitting (way to prove your sincerity), and Allah is well-informed about what you're doing."* [53]

Say (to them), *"Obey Allah, and obey the Messenger, but if you turn away, then (the Prophet) is only responsible for his own duty, even as you're (only responsible) for what's been placed upon you. If you obey him, then you will be guided rightly, for the Messenger's only duty is to convey (the message) clearly."* [54]

Allah's Promise of Relief will come to Pass

Background on verse 55: In the early years of Islam, the Muslims were beleaguered and under fire from all sides. Some companions asked the Prophet, "Will there ever come a time when we can live in peace and put down our weapons?" The Prophet replied, "Yes, and that time is coming very soon." Then this verse was revealed. (*Qurtubi*) The Prophet also told his companions, "You won't stay like this for long, and then each of you will sit in dignified meetings where there will be no (need for) weapons (at hand's reach) anywhere." (*Ibn Kathir*)

Allah has promised to those among you who believe and who do what's morally right that they'll inherit the land, even as He had

---

[749] During the rule of 'Umar ibn al-Khattab, a Byzantine Roman citizen journeyed to Medina and declared to 'Umar that he had accepted Islam. 'Umar, who was startled from sleep by this unexpected visitor, asked him why. The Roman explained that he had studied the Torah, the Psalms, the Gospels and several other books, but when he heard a Muslim prisoner of war recite this passage [24:51-52] he realized that the Qur'an encapsulated the essential message of all other previous religious books, and thus he accepted Islam and entered Muslim lands. (*Qurtubi*)

granted it to those who came before them. (He's also promised) that He'll firmly establish the way of life that He's chosen for them and that He'll transform the fear that they've been living under into a sense of security. [750]

(In order for this to happen), they must serve only Me and not make any partners at all with Me. If anyone thanklessly suppresses (their awareness of faith) after this, then they're rebellious and disobedient. [55]

Be constant in prayer, and give in charity, as well. Obey the Messenger so you can receive (Allah's) mercy. [56] Never assume that the faithless are going to hold back (Allah's plan) in the land, for their resting place is in the Fire. *Oh, how awful a place in which to reside!* [57]

Teaching People to Respect Your Privacy

> **Background on verse 58:** A woman named Asma' bint Marthid went to the Prophet and complained about how sometimes young children or servants were coming in upon her at home when she wasn't decently dressed. 'Umar ibn al-Khattab also came to him with a similar complaint, and he asked if Allah could make a ruling about this situation, so people could have their privacy at home respected. This verse came in answer to this problem. (*Asbab ul-Nuzul*)

O you who believe! Make your bonded servants and the young (children) among you ask your permission (before coming in a private room to see you) at these three times: before the pre-dawn prayer, when you've disrobed for an afternoon rest, [751] and after the time of

---

[750] These three predictions of the Qur'an came to pass in the Prophet's lifetime. 1) The Muslims eventually had complete control in Arabia, even though they were only a small, weak community. 2) Islam became so spectacularly successful that the Islamic world expanded faster than any empire in history; thus, Islam became firmly rooted. Finally, 3) the Muslims, who had been living under a constant state of fear from the Meccans, the bedouins and others, eventually tasted the fruits of peace in their land. When this verse was revealed, all of these three predictions seemed unattainable. Indeed, ever since they had fled from Mecca, the Immigrants used to keep their weapons close by their beds at night, fearing a sudden attack from the pagans in the dark.

[751] The cultural pattern in Arabia at the Prophet's time included taking an afternoon rest or siesta, even as many cultures today still retain such a custom. Taking a nap at mid-day has recently been shown by preliminary medical studies to be effective in reducing stress and also in reducing the rate of heart problems. Thus, many in our modern world are looking into reestablishing this refreshing habit (which the Qur'an assumes people will be prone to indulge in as a matter of course.)

the late-night prayer has ended. These are the three times when (people are likely) to be undressed.

Outside of these times, it isn't wrong for you or for them to move around and interact with each other (in the home). This is how Allah clearly (explains) the verses to you, for Allah is full of knowledge and wisdom. [752] [58] After those young children among you reach puberty, they still must ask for permission, even as those older than they must, and (again) this is how Allah clearly (explains) His verses to you, for Allah is (indeed) full of knowledge and wisdom. [59]

Elderly Women Have Fewer Dress Restrictions

It isn't wrong for elderly women who are past the prime age of marriage [753] to abandon wearing their outer cloak, as long as they don't display their beauty in an obvious manner. However, it's still best for them to be modest, for Allah listens and knows (about all things). [60]

---

[752] Few people appreciate how radically different the manners were that the Prophet was teaching his followers to adopt, as opposed to what was considered good etiquette in Arabia. Before Islam hygiene was almost non-existent among the Arabs, but the Prophet taught his followers to brush their teeth several times a day, to bathe daily (as was his custom), to knock on doors before entering and even something as simple as not walking around wearing only one shoe, which Arabs would sometimes do. He taught them to wash their hands before and after eating, to eat only from the plates that were closest to them, to not waste food and even to share food with a neighbor whenever possible. He taught them how to greet each other, how to make proper small talk, how to shake hands and also to comb their hair daily. These verses in this section of chapter 24 are another example of how literally Islam completely changed the standards of etiquette in Arabia. (There are so many points of good etiquette taught by the Prophet that entire books are written collecting the information together.)

[753] The comprehensive terminology used here, *la yarjun nikahan*, means a woman who can no longer bear children and who is not really in the marriage-market any more such as a younger woman might be. They can leave off their *thowb*, or overcoat, when they go out in public, though they should still avoid any tight fitting clothes and only use loose fitting pants, shirts or dresses. A *thowb* is basically one's outer covering, like a suit jacket or an over-coat, or even a long shirt worn over an inner shirt. If you hearken back to standards of proper dress in the West until the mid twentieth century, then you get the idea of what proper dress is for Muslims when they go out in public. Today, the term *thowb* is applied to a type of long gown worn by men in the Middle East.

It isn't wrong for the blind, the handicapped, the ill, [754] or yourselves if you eat (your meals) in your own homes, or in those of your fathers, your mothers, your brothers, your sisters, your father's or mother's brothers and sisters, or in homes to which you have the keys [755] or in the homes of your close friends. [756]

> **Background on the last part of verse 61:** Some people of Medina wondered if it was allowed to eat alone, as was their habit before Islam. They felt guilty about it, thinking that since Islam emphasized community so much that it might also require communal family dinners. This part of the verse addresses that concern. (*Asbab ul-Nuzul*)

It isn't wrong if you eat together or separately, but if you enter a home, then greet each other (with the words) of peace, blessings and goodness, (which are a greeting) from Allah. [757] This is how Allah

---

[754] It had been the custom in pre-Islamic times for people to forbid the blind, the handicapped and the ill from coming to their dinner parties, on the belief that the misfortune of those people would befall the hosts, too. Also, handicapped people in those days would often feel embarrassed at their condition and usually refrained from going out to peoples' houses for dinner parties, even if their relatives wanted to take them along with them. This verse forbids such disdain for the handicapped and encourages people to invite those with disabilities to their tables, even as it tells handicapped people not to be ashamed of their state. In addition, dinner parties that are segregated by social status or wealth are also forbidden. A prominent companion, 'Abdullah ibn Mas'ud (d. 653), once said, "If only the rich are invited and the poor are left out, we have been ordered (by the Prophet) not to respond to such an invitation."

[755] This refers to house-sitters who might be afraid of eating the food in the house they've been asked to look after, even after they've been expressly told that they can. When the companions used to go out on military campaigns, they would give the keys to their homes to the ill and lame and would tell them they could eat what they liked in return for looking after their property. The handicapped people used to hesitate eating any food out of shyness. (*Ma'ariful Qur'an*)

[756] Dinner parties in the homes of friends are an integral part of life. Once the Prophet was invited to the wedding feast of one of his companions, Abu Usayd as-Sa'idi. Abu Usayd's own new wife was serving a drink to the Prophet made of water that had been sweetened with dates. (*Bukhari*) Although traditional Muslim cultures today often observe strict separation of the genders at social gatherings, such was not the case in the Prophet's time or in the immediate centuries thereafter.

[757] Thus, Muslims often add extra greetings to their basic greeting formula, wishing not only peace, but Allah's blessings and goodness. The full greeting that is even more blessed than the standard, "Peace be upon you," is *"Assalamu 'alaykum wa rahmatullahi wa barakatuhu."* "Peace be upon you, and Allah's mercy and His blessings." The reply is to say the same thing, merely reversing the order of the first two words and adding the conjunction *"wa"* or "and" in the very beginning.

(explains) the verses for you, so you can understand (what proper manners are). [61]

How to Behave in the Presence of the Prophet

Background on verse 62: This verse was revealed while the Muslims were digging a trench in front of the city of Medina just before the Battle of the Trench in the year 626. Everyone was assigned a quota of digging — even the Prophet fulfilled his share — but some hypocrites would dig a little and then slink away. This verse was revealed about them. (*Bayhaqi, Ibn Is-haq*)

True believers are those who believe in Allah and His Messenger. When they're with (the Prophet in the midst of important) communal affairs, they don't leave until they've asked him if they could be excused.

Those who ask you to be excused are those who (have shown that) they believe in Allah and His Messenger, so when they ask you to be excused for some business of theirs, then excuse whomever you want, and ask Allah to forgive them, for Allah is forgiving and merciful. [758] [62]

Don't consider the call (to attend a meeting) with the Messenger like any ordinary call from each other. Allah knows those among you who slip away (from his meetings without asking permission), holding to some (lame) excuse.

Let those who oppose the Messenger's command beware, for some chaotic situation might befall them, or a terrible punishment might afflict them. [63]

There's no doubt that whatever is in the heavens and on the earth belongs to Allah. He knows what you're up to, and one day you're going to be brought back to Him. Then He's going to tell you the meaning of all that you did, for Allah knows about all things. [759] [64]

---

[758] The Prophet said, "When any of you joins a gathering, let him say peace, and when he wants to leave, let him say peace. The first time is not more important than the last time." (*Abu Dawud*)

[759] The eighth-century scholar, Hasan al-Basri (d. 737), once wrote, "The Muslim takes an account of himself more vigorously than a businessman does of his partner."

The Standard

25 Al Furqān
Middle Meccan Period

This chapter was revealed in response to the many challenges the Prophet was receiving from the Meccan pagans who were adamant in their belief that there were many gods, not just one. They pointed to their idols made of wood, sticks and stone and challenged the Prophet to bring them proof more convincing than that physical evidence there before them. They also called into question the fact that the Prophet was not endowed with supernatural powers and lived as any other human being did. The Prophet was well into the public phase of his ministry and oftentimes found himself overwhelmed with questions, accusations and taunts. Through this chapter he was able both to steady his resolve and to answer many of the issues raised by his critics. Although the bulk of this chapter dates from the middle Meccan period, many scholars feel that verses 68-70 were revealed in Medina.

In the Name of Allah,
the Compassionate, the Merciful

Blessed be the One Who sent down the *Standard* [760] to His servant, so it could be a warning to all the worlds. [761] [1] He's the One Who controls the heavens and the earth. He hasn't taken any son, nor does He have any partners in His dominion. He created everything and measured their proportion exactly. [2] Yet, still they've taken in His place other gods that can't create anything at all and that were themselves created! They have no control over the harm or good that befalls them, nor do they have any power over death, life or resurrection! [3]

---

[760] The Qur'an here is called *al-Furqān*, or the *Standard*, for it set the standard for identifying what was truth and what was falsehood.
[761] In general, the phrase 'all the worlds' signifies 'all living things on earth' in Arabic.

The Accusations of the Critics

Background on verses 4-6: This passage was revealed in response to the taunting of the popular Meccan poet, an-Nadr ibn al-Harith. He told his fellow Meccans one day, "By Allah, Muhammad cannot tell a better story than I, and his speech is only of old fables that he has copied, as have I." He also said the quotes that are reproduced in verses 4-5. (*Asbab ul-Nuzul*)

The faithless say, *"This is all just a pack of lies that he's made up, and some people helped him do it!"* They're the ones who've brought an unfair charge and an unsubstantiated accusation. [762] [4] Then they say, *"It's all just tales from long ago that he's ordered to be written down.* [763] *They're being dictated to him in the morning and at night."* [5]

Say (to them), *"This (message) was sent down by the One Who knows the mysteries of the heavens and the earth, and He's forgiving and merciful."* [6]

Now they're saying, *"What kind of a 'messenger' is this? He eats food (just like we do) and walks around in the markets! Why hasn't an angel been sent down to him to warn us alongside of him?* [764] [7] *Why hasn't he been given a treasure or a nice garden in which to have his meals?"* [765]

Then these same corrupt (critics) say (to the believers), *"You're following some kind of lunatic."* [8]

---

[762] In Arabia at the Prophet's time, poetry was taken seriously, and the reputation and even life of an individual could be put in jeopardy due to the slanderous activities of poets who influenced people with their words in a way that powerful politicians might today. An-Nadr ibn al-Harith, the man whose quotes are reproduced here, was one of those who continually urged his pagan fellows to attack Muslims on sight. When the Muslims and pagans met in the Battle of Badr a few years after this chapter was revealed, an-Nadr was one of the Meccan pagans captured. He was also one of the two or three prisoners not ransomed back to Mecca. (Another virulent poet named 'Uqbah was also not returned.) They were executed for the crime of incitement, for their words of hate had contributed to the deaths of many innocent people over the years.

[763] The pagans were acknowledging that Muhammad could not write anything himself, for he did not know how to write. Thus, he had a number of companions acting as scribes.

[764] A similar charge is echoed in 6:8-9.

[765] The pagans mentioned a garden here to mock the idea of a garden paradise in the next life.

Do you see, (Muhammad,) how they're making you out to be? However, they're the mistaken ones, and they'll never be able to find a path (to salvation). [9]

Blessed be the One Who could grant you far better things than those if He so desired: *gardens beneath which rivers flow and lofty palaces!* [10] But no! They're just denying the Hour (of Judgment). We've prepared a raging blaze for all those who deny the Hour! [11]

When (Hellfire) sees them in the distance, they'll hear its fury and overwhelming roar, [12] and when they're tied up together and cast into a tight crevice within, they'll beg to be obliterated at once! [13] *"Don't beg for just one obliteration today! Beg for endless obliteration!"* [14]

Ask them, *"Is that (fate) better or the Eternal Garden that's been promised to the mindful?"* That'll be their reward and also their final destination. [15] They'll have everything within for which they ever wished, and they can dwell within it forever. Now that's a promise from your Lord for which to pray! [16]

On the day when He's going to gather them all together - *they and the things they used to worship besides Allah* - He's going to ask (those objects of worship), *"Are you the ones who led My servants astray, or did they veer off the path by themselves?"* [17]

"Glory be to You!" they'll cry. *"It wasn't our right to take any protectors besides You. You provided them with abundance, and their ancestors, too, until they finally forgot the message. And so, they were (proven to be) a worthless bunch of people!"* [18]

(Then Allah will say to the sinners), *"Now (your idols have testified) that what you've been saying is a lie! Now you can no longer avoid (the punishment you deserve), nor will you (find anyone) to help you. Anyone among you who did wrong will now suffer a massive punishment."* [19]

The messengers that We sent before you, (Muhammad), were no more than (ordinary men) who ate food and walked through the markets, and that's how We've made some of you (people) to be a test

for others. [766] Won't you be patient then, for your Lord is watching?
[20]

They do Nothing but Deny

Those who think that they're never going to meet Us say, "*So why aren't any angels being sent down to us? Why aren't we seeing our Lord (face to face)?*" They think so highly of themselves, and their audacity is enormous! [767] [21]

When the day comes that they finally do see the angels, the sinners won't have any good news at all that day! They'll cry out (in fear), "*(Where can we hide) to be safe?*" [768] [22] Then We'll turn towards whatever (good) deeds they (accumulated in this life) and transform them into mere scattered dust! [23] On that same day, however, the

---

[766] The idea behind our free will to choose or deny our Creator is that Allah won't prejudice or tip the scale in His favor by dazzling us with fantastic miracles or angels blazing with light all the time. How could we then make an honest choice based on our own conviction, the evidence in nature and our own free will in such a case? Of course, everyone would believe if the supernatural were a part of ordinary life. Out of all creation Allah gave us the power to choose Him after having an equal opportunity of also denying Him. When he appoints a human being as His messenger and gives him messages to share with others, that's where people are tested in their beliefs. Can they believe a man like themselves is in communication with Allah? Do they really believe in Allah, after all? If they reject that Allah would send revelation to one of their fellows, what does it say about their conception of Allah? If a seemingly poor man comes to you and asks to be taken care of, promising that he's really a rich man who lost his way, what do you think? Do you care for him out of the goodness of your heart, regardless of any future supposed reward? That would be the highest level of faith. Do you care for him longing for the promised payback? That is also good, in that you at least chose the right thing, though without as noble a motivation. Do you call the poor man a liar and turn him away, perhaps only to find out later that he was telling the truth and that he was bestowing his rewards upon another? Even if he was truly poor all along, if you denied him, what does that say about you? Remember that all our choices made today have their consequences in the future, and given that religion is as old as humanity, might there not be something there worth paying attention to? For those who advance the argument that relgions have been abused and have been the source for terribly oppression, it might be useful to not that atheism, the official ideology of communism, has caused more deaths than all world religions combined. Religious teachings are not to be judged by ignorant men who twisted them for their own purposes. Rather, they should be judged on what they plainly say and the best examples that they can produce.

[767] The Prophet said that Allah, Himself, said, "Glory is My robe, and pride is My garment; whoever rivals Me in either of them, I will make him dwell in the Fire." (*Abu Dawud*)

[768] There is an alternative interpretation to the ending quotation in this verse, and that is that instead of the sinners crying out for a safe place to hide, the angels will be telling them that Paradise is a refuge they cannot ever hope to enter. (*Ma'ariful Qur'an*)

companions of the Garden will have the best place of rest and the finest sanctuary! [24]

The Remorse of an Apostate

Background on verses 25-31: This passage was revealed with regards to 'Uqbah ibn Mu'ayt. 'Uqbah used to be friendly with Muhammad and often invited him over to dinner. When Muhammad became a prophet, he told 'Uqbah that he would no longer be able to dine with him unless he stated that there was only one God and that Muhammad was His messenger. 'Uqbah repeated the words forthwith. The next day, Ubayy ibn Khalaf, a severe critic of the Prophet, found out about 'Uqbah's apparent conversion, and he was very angry with him. Ubayy confronted 'Uqbah about it, and even though 'Uqbah protested that he only said what he said to please Muhammad, Ubayy wasn't convinced. After a lot of arguing, Ubayy got 'Uqbah to renounce Islam. To confirm his rejection of Islam, Ubayy told him to disrespect Muhammad publicly. Thus, 'Uqbah went out and either spit in the Prophet's face or threw animal guts on him in the street. The predicted lamentations of men such as 'Uqbah on Judgment Day are contained in verses 27-29. (*Qurtubi, Asbab ul-Nuzul*)

The day when the sky will be shredded by a (descending) cloud, [769] angels will descend (from within it) in ranks! [25] That will be the day when ultimate control will rightfully belong to the Compassionate. It's going to be a sore day for those who suppressed (their ability to believe). [26]

That's the day when the one who did wrong will bite his hands and say, *"If only I would've joined with the Messenger on a path (to truth)!* [27] *I'm doomed! If only I would've never taken (Satan) for a friend!* [770] [28]

---

[769] This verse is interpreted to mean that after the first blast of the horn, signaling the end, and after the second blast of the horn, signaling the start of Judgment Day, on the plain of judgment, the clouds will part due to the descent of some cloud-like object in which Allah's power will be made manifest. It will be borne by the angels. (*Ma'ariful Qur'an*)

[770] One night a man went to Imam Abu Hanifa (d. 767) and told him that he had buried a bag of money somewhere but that he had now forgotten where he hid it. He asked for the Imam's help in finding it, but Abu Hanifa protested that it wasn't in his expertise to find someone's lost money. The man persisted in seeking the Imam's help, so finally Abu Hanifa told him to go home and pray all night until dawn, and then he would remember where he hid it. So the man did as he was told, and during his prayers, he suddenly remembered where he buried his money. He promptly went and retrieved it. The next morning he returned to the Imam and thanked him. Then he asked the Imam how he knew he would remember his money while he was praying. Abu Hanifa replied, "I knew that Satan wasn't going to leave you alone during your prayers. He kept you busy with thoughts of your money, rather than you concentrating on your prayer."

He led me away from the message after it had come to me! Satan is a traitor to all humanity!" [29]

Then the Messenger [771] will say, "My Lord! My people took this Qur'an as a joke." [30] And so it is that We've set up an adversary for every prophet from among the wicked (among his people, whom he must confront), [772] but your Lord is (powerful) enough to guide and to help. [31]

Then the faithless ask, "So why isn't the Qur'an revealed to him all at once?" (It's being revealed at this gradual pace) so We can strengthen your heart with it, for We're releasing it in slow, well-ordered stages. [32] They don't bring any issue before you without Us revealing to you the most straightforward and appropriate counterpoint. [773] [33] Those who will be cast down prone on their faces as they're being gathered together for Hellfire will be in the worst position and the furthest off the way! [34]

---

[771] The Messenger is Prophet Muhammad.

[772] This is an answer to the Prophet as to why he had to face such bitter and wicked foes: it strengthens the resolve of the Prophet, gets every issue out in the open for the masses to consider and enables the patient to acquire good deeds on account of their perseverance. The most prominent enemy for Muhammad during his days in Mecca was his indirect paternal relative, Abu Jahl. In Medina it would be the hypocrite, 'Abdullah ibn Ubayy.

[773] Thus, this is one reason why some passages of the Qur'an were revealed for specific situations or to answer specific issues raised by the people around the Prophet, both his followers and enemies. Thus, the Qur'an is, in some respects, an interactive revelation from Allah that not only communicated Allah's will, but also guided people in many situations, much like the Gospel of Jesus did. The term *tafseer*, which comes from the root-word *fassara*, means explanation, interpretation, commentary or to give an answer to an issue (counterpoint). This term, which is present here in this verse, has become the term that Muslims have adopted to use for commentary on the meaning and background of the verses of the Qur'an. *Tafseer* is used by judges, scholars, government officials and even ordinary people in their efforts to understand how to apply the Qur'an to the various issues of daily life. The two main modes of *Tafseer* research are known as *Tafseer bil ra-iy* (interpretation by opinion and logic) and *Tafseer bil ma'thur* (interpretation based on prophetic sayings, opinions of the Prophet's companions and the understandings of the generation that came after that). The heyday of classical *Tafseer* was from the ninth to the fourteenth centuries. The works of at-Tabari, as-Suyuti, Ibn Kathir, Zamakhshari, Ibn Rushd, Wahidi, al-Alusi, Abu al-Layth al-Samarqandi, Baydawi, Razi and others represent the most well-known of the classical works.

And so it was that We sent the Book to Moses and set up his brother Aaron to be his assistant. [774] [35] We told them, *"Go, both of you, to the people who've denied Our signs."* Then We destroyed (those people) completely! [775] [36] Likewise Noah's people – when they denied the messengers, [776] We drowned them all and made (their story a lasting) legacy for people (to remember). We've prepared a painful punishment for the wrongdoers! [37]

And (what of) the 'Ad, Thamud, and the Companions of the Shallow Pool, [777] and the many generations that passed between them! [38] We sent examples to each of them (to convince them to believe), but then We ruined them completely (on account of their sins). [39]

Already (these pagans of Mecca) must have passed by the (remnants of) the nation (of Sodom and Gomorrah), which (was destroyed) under an awful shower (of brimstone and fire). [778] Haven't they seen (that broken land)! But no! They never expect that they'll be raised to life again! [40]

When they see you, they treat you with scorn, saying, *"Is 'this' the one whom Allah sent as a messenger?* [41] *He almost got us to abandon our gods, except we were so stable (in our devotion to them)."* Soon enough,

---

[774] The term *wazeer* means a top aide or right hand man and has become the term of choice in Islamic civilization to describe the chief minister of state under the caliph or sultan.

[775] Both Pharaoh and the greater part of his army were overwhelmed and destroyed, leaving Egypt weaker than ever before. Eventually, Egypt fell to outside powers, including the Assyrians, the Babylonians, the Persians, the forces of Alexander the Great, the Romans, the Arabs, the French and finally the British!

[776] This implies that they had more than one messenger sent to them in their history, or it could include non-divinely commissioned religious missionaries who called them to faith along with the officially sanctioned Noah.

[777] Who were the Companions of the Shallow Pool? The commentators differ in their views, but a majority think it refers to a tribe that lived along a trading route in Yemen and that had abundant wells and oasis pools. They are thought to have been a remnant of the previously destroyed tribe of Thamud from the far north of Arabia. Thus, their land is called *Hadramawt*, or "After the Death."

[778] The city in which Lot lived was utterly destroyed by a cataclysm consisting of a terrible blasting sound, an earthquake that turned the city upside down, and showers of stones and hardened clay. That was quite an enormous punishment!

when they see the punishment before them, they'll know who was the furthest off the path! [42]

Have you seen the one who takes his own whims for a god? Could you ever manage his affairs? [779] [43] Do you think that most of them are listening to you or understanding you? They're nothing more than cattle! Even more than that, they're the furthest astray! [44]

Take Note of the Signs of Allah's Power

Have you ever noticed how your Lord lengthens the shadow, (as the afternoon progresses)? If He had wanted, He could've made it stand still, but We've made the sun to be its guide, [45] and then We draw it in towards Us in slow, easy stages. [780] [46] He's the One Who made the night as a cloak for you and sleep as your manner of rejuvenation, even as He made the daylight for going abroad once more. [781] [47]

He's the One Who sends the winds as heralds of good news going forth from the hands of His mercy. [782] We send cleansing water pouring down from the sky [48] and use it to give life to the barren land, and also to quench the thirst of the herd animals and the many peoples that We've created. [49] And so We distribute it among them so they can remember (the gifts We give to them), but most people are thankless. [783] [50]

---

[779] There was a poor man among the pagans of Mecca who could not afford to purchase an idol of his own. He was forlorn on account of this, as it was the custom that every family would have their own "house idol" to worship. So he took a date that he had, carved a face on it, and then proceeded to worship it as his god. Later in the day, however, he became hungry. After some thought, he popped his "god" in his mouth and ate it. How can you reach a person so fickle as that! These were the kinds of people that the Prophet was trying to reach.

[780] As the sun rises and then falls, the length of shadows likewise transforms. If Allah had wanted, He could have changed the rotational orbit of the earth or placed binary stars in our solar system, so that we would suffer from unending sunshine, causing our shadows never to transform throughout the day.

[781] One of the possible meanings of the Arabic word *nushura* is arising or resurrection, but it also means to propagate, to go abroad, and many, many other similar meanings.

[782] Wind heralds the arrival of rain clouds and is thus a portent of good news for people.

[783] This also means that people deny that Allah caused the rain and, instead, attribute it to astrology, random wind patterns, etc…

If We had wanted, We could've sent a warner to every town (in the world). 784 [51] So don't pay attention to those who suppress (their faith), but rather strive against them using (the logic) of this (Qur'an) with your utmost capacity. 785 [52] He's the One Who let loose the two types of flowing waters: one is fresh and sweet, while the other is salty and bitter. Yet, He made a firm barrier between them. 786 [53] He's the One Who created mortals from water, (and then He) established ties of lineage 787 and marriage, for your Lord has also measured (the form of human society). [54]

Yet, still they're worshipping things besides Allah that can bring them neither benefit nor harm! 788 The rejecter (of truth) is ever a collaborator against his Lord! [55] We didn't send you for any other purpose than to give good news and warnings, [56] so say (to them), *"I'm not asking you for any reward (for this choice I lay before you) that each of you should choose whether or not they would like to take a path towards their Lord."* [57]

Put your trust in the One Who's always alive and never dies. Glorify His praise, for He's capable enough to know the shortcomings

---

784 The Qur'an already says that Allah sent a warner to every people; thus, the record of countless religious leaders throughout human history has come down to us. Here Allah is saying He could have sent a warner to every *individual town* if He wanted. This is meant to reassure the Prophet that Allah does send warners as He wills.

785 This verse was revealed in Mecca, long before any order to fight back was given. Therefore, it refers to the mental, logical, theological and verbal struggle that the Muslims were locked into with the pagans.

786 When a fresh water river flows into the sea, it continues to flow as a fresh water current deep out into the ocean. Salt water and fresh water don't mix easily, due to their different densities and salinities. Eventually they do mix together, but not for some time. It is assumed that this verse is referring to the Tigris and Euphrates rivers, which pour so much fresh water into the Persian Gulf that returning tides are often mostly of fresh water. It can also be assumed that this phenomenon was not unknown to the Arabs, for it was a phenomenon that was commented on as far back as the first century by Pliny the Elder.

787 A Muslim is allowed to keep track of his lineage and family tree. In fact, there are traditions that specifically mention the merits of this pastime, such as when the Prophet said, "Preserve your family trees through which you can preserve your family ties, and you will thus be able to fulfill your obligations." (*Tirmidhi*) This is how relationships among people are known and established over many generations. A Muslim is forbidden, however, to use his lineage as a source of boasting, like the pagans and faithless people do, for no one becomes special on account of who his or her distant ancestor was.

788 In other words, the idols can't really bring them good luck or fortune, nor can the idols punish them or strike them down if they are disobeyed. They're just objects of wood and stone!

of His servants. [58] He's the One Who created the heavens and the earth and everything in between them in six stages, and then He mounted the throne (of power). (He's) the Compassionate! Just ask anyone who has information (about Him)! [789] [59]

When they're told, *"Bow down and prostrate yourselves to the Compassionate,"* they say, *"Who's the Compassionate?* [790] *Are we really supposed to bow down prostrate to what you're ordering us?"* And so, their aversion (to Allah) grows! [791] [60]

Blessed be the One Who placed constellations in the sky and Who placed therein a lamp and a lighted moon. [792] [61] He's the One Who made the night and the day to follow each other (as a sign) for any who wish to be reminded or who wish to be thankful. [62]

Walking the Path of Salvation

The (true) servants of the Compassionate are those who walk humbly through the earth. Whenever the ignorant try to engage them (in futile argument), they say (to them), *"Peace."* [793] [63]

(Allah's true servants) are those who pass the night in worship, prostrating and standing (obediently). [794] [64] They're the ones who

---

[789] A person who is unsure about the nature of Allah can look around and find the world full of religions that talk about Him in one way or another. Although theologies may differ, even greatly, all religions portray the Supreme Deity in a very common way: He is for justice and against sin, He calls to righteousness and punishes evil, He is wise and will pardon many, etc…

[790] The Arabs had never known *Allah*, or the Supreme God, by the name of *Compassionate*. Therefore, when the Qur'an started calling Allah by that designation, the Meccans were resistant to adopt that new title for Allah.

[791] After reading this verse, it is customary for the one who has faith in Allah to prostrate himself on the floor and praise Allah.

[792] Throughout the night and the day, these heavenly bodies are the most prominent features in the sky. To the Arabs, both the sun and the moon were gods, and some of the stars were gods, too. This verse is making the case that those objects in the sky were merely created things from a supreme being besides Whom there are no other gods.

[793] Imam ash-Shafi'i (d. 820) once said, "When a dull person comes to visit me, I start to feel as if the earth beneath him is sinking from the heaviness of his presence." The Qur'anic principle, when faced with people who are hopelessly ignorant or unreasonably critical is to say, "peace," to them, which, as everyone knows, is the Muslim way of saying good-bye and farewell. See 19:47 where this principle is demonstrated practically.

[794] This verse calls for the practice known as *qiyam ul-layl*, or night vigil. It is basically an all night marathon session of worship, prayer, supplication, repentance and personal and

pray, *"Our Lord! Steer the punishment of Hellfire away from us, for its punishment is horrible.* [65] *Oh, what an awful place in which to reside, and (what an awful place in which) to rest."* [795] [66]

When they spend (in charity), they're neither extravagant nor stingy but maintain a position in between. [796] [67] They never call upon anyone else besides Allah, nor do they ever take any life that Allah made sacred, except for a just cause, nor do they commit adultery or fornication.

Anyone who does those things will have to pay the price, [68] and the punishment (they'll face) on the Day of Assembly will be doubled for them. They'll remain there in disgrace [69] unless they repent, believe and do what's morally right (before they leave this life), for then Allah will transform their evil (nature) into goodness, for Allah is forgiving and merciful. [70] [797] Whoever repents and does what's morally right has genuinely repented to Allah. [71]

---

group discussions on topics related to piety and self-renewal. Today such events are usually organized either monthly or at least several times a year in mosques or in peoples' homes.

[795] It is said that a very old man with sunken eyes approached the Prophet one day and said, "Messenger of Allah, a man betrayed others and did sinful deeds, and there wasn't a single type of sin except that he did it. If (his numerous sins) were parceled out among all the people of the world, they would all be doomed. Is there any repentance for him?" The Prophet asked, "Have you become a Muslim?" The man answered, "As for me, I testify that there is no god but Allah, the One, Who has no partner, and that Muhammad is His servant and Messenger." The Prophet then said, "Allah will forgive you whatever you have done like that, and he will replace your evil deeds with good ones." The man exclaimed, "Messenger of Allah! Even my betrayals and sins?" The Prophet answered, "Even your betrayals and sins." The man then went away, saying repeatedly, "There is no god besides Allah," and "Allah is great." (*Ibn Kathir*)

[796] The Prophet said, "The thoughtful man adopts a middle course in his spending habits." In a related saying he explained that a person who is moderate in his spending would never become destitute. (*Ma'ariful Qur'an*)

[797] When verses 25:68-69 and 4:93 were revealed, they stated that idolaters and any who killed a Muslim intentionally and unlawfully would go to Hellfire. Some Meccan leaders who were still pagans then wondered if they had any hope of salvation if they were considering converting to Islam as by that time some of them had been complicit in the murder of Muslims. One of them publicly asked, "We have taken lives that Allah has declared sacred. We have worshipped other gods alongside Allah, and we are guilty of fornicating." Then verse 25:70 was revealed that offered the exception. Repentance with true remorse forgives all sins of the past. As the early scholar Mujahid said, "The one who regrets their crime is excepted." (Bukhari)

(Allah's true servants) are those who (keep themselves away from situations) where they would witness fraud or corruption. [798] If they pass by foolishness, they pass by it with dignity. [799] [72] Whenever (Allah's true servants) are admonished with their Lord's (revealed) verses, they don't act as if they're deaf or blind to them. [73] They're the ones who pray, *"Our Lord! Grant us spouses and children who will be a comfort to our eyes, and make us leaders in righteousness."* [74]

These are the ones who will be rewarded with a lofty place (in Paradise) on account of their perseverance, and they're the ones who will be met with welcome and peace. [75] They'll remain there, *and oh, what a beautiful place in which to reside, and (what a beautiful place in which) to rest!* [800] [76]

(So now say to the faithless), *"My Lord won't have any regard for you unless you call upon Him, but you're denying (Him), so soon your (lack of faith) will keep you tied (to an awful doom)."* [77]

---

[798] *Zura* has several meanings, such as crookedness, forgery, fraud, falsity and such. The basic idea is that a believer does not put him or herself into situations where he or she will have to witness corruption, crime and deceit. The Muslim does not keep company with dishonest people, nor does the Muslim get involved in shady schemes.

[799] Living in our world, it is impossible to isolate oneself completely from the foolishness and corruption that goes on all around us. As believers, we must try to keep as much of it away as possible, for Islam has no conception of accommodation or assimilation into godless cultures, despite what some modernists would like to believe. (See 18:28). A believer must spend the lion's share of his or her waking hours among other believers, and he or she must spend the bulk of his or her time in a wholesome, Allah-oriented environment. When the believer does witness foolishness or immorality, such as people dancing shamelessly in public, lewd advertisements, shameless public displays of intimacy or drunkenness and such, he or she is to hold his or her head up high and pass by without giving such displays any credence or undue attention. Basically, a Muslim has to ignore it with dignity and get away from it as quickly as possible.

[800] Critics of Islam sometimes point out the sensual and very material nature of the Islamic conception of Paradise, suggesting that Islam promises its followers a very pleasurable rather than spiritual afterlife. Besides the fact that no other promise would capture the imagination of large numbers of people and make them willing to forgo pleasure in this world for the sake of the next, the Qur'an emphasizes that spiritual concerns will reign supreme there. People will be praising Allah and interacting with each other in righteousness. Doesn't the New Testament of the Bible contain tantalizing hints of a sensual and material afterlife, with references to pearly gates, streets paved with gold, and banquets prepared for the faithful?

The Poets

26 Ash Shu'arā'
Middle Meccan Period

The idol-worshippers of Mecca persistently denied the message of the Prophet. They made up one excuse after another for rejecting it. These ranged from denying that their idols were false inventions to complaints that Muhammad wasn't showing them spectacular miracles. This chapter opens with words of encouragement to the Prophet that he shouldn't let grief and sorrow over the disbelief of his people weigh down too heavily upon him. Thereafter, it discusses, in various ways and through various stories of the past, that Allah's signs are evident both in nature and in the course of human history.

It must be remembered that Muhammad *was* given powerful miracles, as well, such as the Qur'an, itself (a nearly illiterate man from Arabia suddenly spouting literature and poetry of the highest order, whose message was more than mere poetry), to more concrete things such as making true predictions, making the moon appear to split, and preaching a message that brought out the very best in its followers. However, the pagans made excuses for those things, as well. (Not finding any human explanation for the Qur'an, they took to saying Muhammad was possessed by a jinn who gave him the words. For the moon, they said Muhammad had cast a spell over them and bewitched their eyes. For the good conduct of his followers, they said his followers were just low common people who didn't know any better.)

In the Name of Allah,
the Compassionate, the Merciful

Tā. Seen. Meem. [1]

These are the verses of the clear Book. [2] Maybe you'll worry yourself to death because they won't believe. [3] If We had wanted, We could've sent a miracle from the sky down upon them that would've definitely made them bow their necks in humility! [4]

However, a fresh reminder from the Compassionate never comes to them without their turning away from it. [5] And so it is that they've denied (this message). Yet, (the effects) of the prophecy at which they're laughing will soon come down upon them! [6]

Haven't they looked at the earth and how many wonderful pairs of things We've grown upon it? [801] [7] These are indeed miracles, but most of them put no faith (in them). [8] Yet, even still, your Lord is the Powerful and the Merciful! [9]

Moses and Aaron are Sent to Pharaoh

When your Lord called out to Moses, He said, *"Go to the people of corruption!* [10] *Go to the people of Pharaoh. Won't they be mindful (of Allah)?"* [802] [11]

(Moses) said, *"My Lord! I'm afraid they're going to call me a liar!* [12] *(I'm afraid) that I might be stricken with fright and that I might stammer in my words! So send (my brother) Aaron (along with me to help).* [13] *What's more, I've been charged with a crime (in that land), and I'm afraid they're going to kill me."* [803] [14]

"By no means!" (Allah) replied. *"Both of you go forth with Our signs, for We're going to be with you, and We're going to listen (to your prayers).* [15] *Go then to Pharaoh and say to him, 'We've been sent by the Lord of All the Worlds,* [16] *so send the Children of Israel with us!'"* [17]

---

[801] This is a reference to the pairs of males and females among nearly most creatures. Even most plants have pairs of organs of different genders that are fertilized by the actions of insects and other creatures.

[802] Is there any evidence that a man named Moses existed and lived during Egyptian times? Yes, there is, and it comes from a monument crafted during the thirteenth dynasty. (It is on display in the British Museum.) Ancient Egyptian hieroglyphics, that have only recently been translated, say that during the rule of Pharaoh Khenephres, an expedition was sent to subdue the aggressive people of Nubia and Ethiopia. The Egyptian forces were under the command of a man named Mousos (Moses?), and the foray was wildly successful under his direction. The ancient historian Josephus (assuming it was the Moses of the Bible being talked of) writes of this account in these words: "The Egyptians, under this sad oppression, betook themselves to their oracles and prophecies, and when Allah had given them this counsel, to make use of Moses the Hebrew and take his assistance, the king commanded his daughter to produce him, that he might be the general of their army... So Moses... cheerfully undertook the business and defeated the African invaders by marching through a snake-infested region and taking them by surprise. When he had therefore proceeded thus on his journey, he came upon the Ethiopians before they expected him, and, joining battle with them, he beat them and deprived them of the hopes they had of success against the Egyptians. He then went on overthrowing their cities and made a great slaughter of those Ethiopians."

[803] Moses got involved in a fight between a Hebrew slave and an Egyptian. Moses punched the Egyptian and accidentally killed him. That's why he fled Egypt in fear of his life so many years previously. See 28:15-21.

The Showdown

(When Moses arrived in Egypt and delivered his message to Pharaoh), the (Pharaoh) said (to Moses), *"Didn't we take care of you as a child, and didn't you live among us for many years of your life?* [18] *Then you (killed a man) like you did, and you were thankless (for all our kindness towards you)!"* [19]

"I did do it," (Moses) answered, *"but it was a mistake,* [20] *and I ran away from you because I feared you. Since then my Lord has granted me sound judgment and has chosen me to be one of the messengers.* [804] [21] *What's more, for what 'favor' are you scolding me? You're keeping the Children of Israel in bondage!"* [805] [22]

"And just who is this 'Lord of All the Worlds' (of whom you speak)?" (Pharaoh) asked. [23]

"The Lord of the heavens and the earth," (Moses) answered, *"and everything in between, if you really want to be sure."* [24]

"Do you hear that?" (Pharaoh) said to those around him. [806] [25]

"(He's) your Lord and the Lord of your ancestors from the very beginning," (Moses) continued. [26]

"This 'messenger' who's been sent to you (Hebrews) is crazy!" (Pharaoh) exclaimed. [27]

---

[804] Allah forgives sins for the people who honestly repent to Him, even the crime of unintentional murder can be forgiven. A humble heart and a desire for righteous living are the beginnings of new life, and hope in Allah is the mortar that makes that new structure strong. There is only one sin that Allah will not forgive, if a person dies while still doing it, and that is the sin of holding others equal with Him.

[805] Yes, Moses did accidentally kill a man when he was young and impulsive, but Pharaoh's attempts to shame Moses on account of his life of privilege falls flat on its face – Moses only got into the house of Pharaoh after the previous Pharaoh ordered a whole generation of baby boys to be murdered! The new Pharaoh still kept Moses' people in abject bondage! So much for spurning the Pharaoh's generosity.

[806] One can imagine Pharaoh turning to his courtiers and laughing, "Did you hear what this man has said? What nonsense!"

"(He's) the Lord of the East and the West and all points in between," (Moses) intoned, "*if you only understood!*" [28]

(Then Pharaoh addressed his court), saying, "*If any of you choose a god other than me, then I'll put you in prison!*" [29]

"*Even if I was able to bring you something that clearly (proves the truth of what I'm saying)?*" (Moses) asked. [30]

"*Then bring it on, if you're really so honest!*" (Pharaoh) replied. [31]

So (Moses) threw his staff down, and suddenly it became a serpent, clear (as day)! [32] Then he drew out his hand, and it radiated white (light) for all to see! [33]

Moses Duels With the Sorcerers

(Pharaoh whispered) to his nobles around him, "*Now that's one skilled sorcerer,* [34] *but his aim is to drive you (and me) out of the country with his magic, so what do you suggest (we do)?*" [807] [35]

"*Keep him and his brother preoccupied,*" (his nobles replied), "*and then send couriers to every settlement to collect* [36] *back to you all of our most skilled sorcerers.*" [37]

Then the sorcerers were gathered in due course for the reserved day (of the showdown). [38] The spectators were asked, "*Are you all gathered here (and ready to watch),* [39] *so we can all (reaffirm our faith) in the ways (of our master Pharaoh) if the sorcerers win?*" [808] [40]

When the sorcerers arrived, they (first) addressed Pharaoh, saying, "*Of course, (we assume) we're going to be well rewarded if we win?*" [41]

---

[807] Being a materialistic man, Pharaoh automatically assumed that Moses and Aaron were merely trying to supplant him in his rule and take over the country. Given that Moses, according to the historian Josephus, had military experience in his younger years, this was a very real possibility.

[808] What better way to show up Moses and assert his power. Pharaoh arranged for a public refutation of Moses, so both the Egyptians and the Hebrews would see that Pharaoh's power was supreme. If the sorcerers won the showdown, then the people would have no choice but to continue to worship Pharaoh as a god.

"Of course," (Pharaoh answered), "and when you (do win), you're going to be (promoted) to my inner (council)." [42]

Moses said to them, "Cast whatever you're going to cast!" [43]

So they threw down their ropes and their rods and chanted, "By the power of Pharaoh, we shall be victorious." [44]

Then Moses threw down his staff, and (suddenly it became a huge serpent). It swallowed up all the tricks they had devised! [45] Then (the stunned) sorcerers fell down and lay prostrate (on their faces.) [46] "We believe in the Lord of All the Worlds," (they cried), [47] "the Lord of Moses and Aaron!" [48]

(Pharaoh was shocked, and) said, "Have you believed in him before you have my permission? He must have been your leader all along - the one who taught you magic! Well, soon you'll know (who has the real power), for I'm going to cut your hands and feet off from opposite sides, and then I'll hang you all from wooden stakes (to die)!" [49]

"It doesn't matter (what you do to us)," they replied, "for we're going back to our Lord (after we die). [50] We only hope that our Lord will forgive us for our mistakes, given that we were (among) the first (of our people) to believe." [809] [51]

---

[809] The medieval poet, Abul A'la of Ma'arri (d. 1057), summed up this very Islamic attitude succinctly when he wrote, "There's a tower of silence; ah! the bell has swung high - another man is meant to be! For some years the song of the bell and the man's life will move in harmony. But alas, when your song ends, so shall your life end, as well! There is no sword necessary for Death to arrive, for he's already here and waiting to strike. Neither helm nor shield will save you from his sudden, fateful swing, for we're all no more than letters, the crooked alphabet of Allah, and He will read us well, before He wipes us all away."

The Great Escape

We inspired Moses, saying, *"Travel with My servants by night, for you're certainly going to be pursued."* [810] [52] Then Pharaoh sent heralds to every city (to gather his forces.) [53]

(When the army was assembled, he said to them), *"Those (Hebrews) are only a small group,* [54] *and they've brazenly defied us.* [55] *Now we're gathered in our multitudes, and we were warned well enough in advance (of their plans)."* [56]

And so We lured them (from their land) and from (its) gardens and springs [57] and opulent wealth. (And in this way they were deprived of) their noble position! [811] [58]

Well there it is, but We made the Children of Israel inherit those (very same things when We established them in the fertile land of Palestine). [59] Meanwhile, (the hordes of Pharaoh) pursued (the Hebrews) at dawn, [60] and when the two groups saw each other, Moses' people cried out, *"Surely we're going to be overtaken!"* [61]

"By no means!" (Moses) cried out, *"for My Lord is with me, and He will guide me (in what to do next)!"* [62] Then We inspired Moses: *"Now strike the sea with your staff!"* Then it divided in two, and each of the sides became as solid as cliffs! [63]

---

[810] After some time had passed, perhaps a few years, Pharaoh lost control over the Hebrews who were now united in their determination to follow Moses. Although the Jewish account of this story contains a dramatic announcement of permission from Pharaoh to leave Egypt (Exodus 12:31-32), the Qur'an seems to suggest it was more of a well-coordinated escape by night. Only after the Hebrews had left from northeastern Egypt, heading towards the Sinai Desert, did Pharaoh decide to pursue them and annihilate them.

[811] Look at Pharaoh's address to his troops! He's doesn't want to lose face, so he asserts that *he* ordered the Children of Israel to leave as part of his strategy against them and that *he* deprived them of their comfortable life in Egypt where they were lucky to serve their masters. He tells his people that the thanklessness and plotting of the Hebrews has enraged him and all of Egypt. Thus, he called for their complete destruction. This passage [26:57-58] is sometimes translated as Pharaoh's statement of comment, rather than Allah's. However, given the context of verse 59, I've opted for the more common understanding.

We made (the pursuers) come close (to the center of the path as they pursued the Hebrews in their blind rage). [812] [64] And then We saved Moses and everyone else who was with him, [65] while We drowned all the rest! [66] There is indeed a sign in this (story), but most of them don't believe (enough to see it). [67] Your Lord is the Powerful and the Merciful. [68]

Abraham and His Father Speak

Narrate for them (something of) Abraham's (story). [69] He said to his father and people, *"What are you worshipping?"* [70]

"We're worshipping idols," they replied, *"and we're utterly devoted to them."* [71]

"But do they hear you when you call (on them)?" (Abraham) asked. [72] *"Do they bring you any good (when you worship them) or cause you any harm (if you neglect them)?"* [813] [73]

"Not at all!" they replied. *"However, we found our ancestors doing like this, also."* [814] [74]

"Have you taken a good look at what you've been worshipping," (Abraham) asked, [75] *"both you and your ancestors before you? [76] (All those things) are my enemies except for the Lord of All the Worlds. [77]*

---

[812] Different routes out of Egypt have been proposed by historians. Some suggest that the Hebrews crossed into northern Sinai through an area of shallow lakes and that Pharaoh's army was overtaken there. Others suggest that the Hebrews crossed from Egypt into a shallow area of the Red Sea that was miraculously (or plausibly) open for them and that this path led from Egypt into the southernmost tip of the Sinai Peninsula or even northwest Arabia. We may never know for sure the exact route, but the story of this great escape has captivated the imagination of countless generations.

[813] The Prophet was walking near the Ka'bah one day when he saw a group of pagans worshipping their idols. They set them up and adorned them with ostrich eggs and earrings. Then they started bowing to them. Muhammad exclaimed, "People of Quraysh! You're going against the creed of your fathers, Abraham and Ishmael, who both submitted (to Allah)." The pagans replied, "Muhammad, we're only worshipping them so they bring us closer to Allah." (*Asbab ul-Nuzul*)

[814] The Prophet said, "On the Day of Judgment, Abraham will see his father covered with dust and darkness." (*Bukhari*) See 9:113-114 for more discussion about the meaning and result of Abraham's request for forgiveness for his father.

" (He's) the One Who created me, Who's guiding me [78] and Who provides my food and drink. [79] When I'm sick, He cures me. [80] (He's the) One Who will cause me to die and bring me back to life, [81] and He's the One Who, I hope, will forgive my faults on the Day of Judgment." [82]

(Abraham then prayed), "My Lord! Endow me with wisdom, and make me one of the righteous. [83] Let (my reputation be carried) on the tongues of honest (people) in coming (generations). [84] Make me one of those who inherit the Garden of Delight." [85]

"Forgive my father, for he's among the mistaken. [86] Don't let me suffer any disgrace on the Day of Resurrection, [87] the day when no amount of wealth or children will do any good, [88] (and when everyone will lose) except for the one who presents a submissive heart to Allah." [815] [89]

There will be Regrets for Sinfulness

The Garden will be brought near to those who were mindful (of Allah), [90] while the Fire will come in full view of those who were hopelessly lost. [91]

Then they'll be asked, "Where are those things you used to worship [92] besides Allah? Can they help you now? Can they even help themselves?" [93]

Then they'll be thrown inside of it, both the (idols) and those who were hopelessly lost, [94] along with the hordes of Iblis all together! [95]

---

[815] In the second generation of Islam, there was a woman named Rab'iah bint Ismai'l who reported that she once went to the home of Hukaymah bint Umaymah of Damascus for advice. When she entered her chambers, she saw Hukaymah reading the Qur'an. Hukaymah looked up at her and said, "Rab'iah, I've heard that your husband (Ahmad ibn Abi al-Hawari) is taking a second wife." When Rabi'ah replied in the affirmative, adding, "How could he?" Hukaymah replied, "Given all that I've been told about his good judgment, how could his heart be distracted away from Allah by two women? Haven't you (both) learned the meaning of the verse: "*except for the one who presents a submissive heart to Allah*"? "No," Rabi'ah replied. Hukaymah then said, "It means that when someone encounters Allah, there should be nothing in their heart other than Him." Rabia'h said later of this incident, "When I heard her words, I went out staggering into the streets. I was afraid that people might see me lest they assumed I was drunk." When her husband heard her tale, he exclaimed, "By my father! This is the only form of delirium (a Muslim should feel)!"

After they're inside (of Hell), they're going to argue (with their lifeless idols), saying, [96] *"By Allah we were clearly mistaken* [97] *when we thought you were equal with the Lord of All the Worlds.* [98] *What were they, those (people) who seduced us (into idol-worship), except for wicked (liars)!* [99]

"Now we have no one to speak out for us [100] *nor a single friend to feel (sympathy for us).* [101] *If only we had the chance to go back (to our former lives), then we would surely be among the believers!"* [102]

There is a sign in this (realization of theirs); yet, most of them don't believe. [103] Yet, even still, your Lord is the Powerful and Merciful One. [104]

The People of Noah Denied

Noah's people denied the messengers. [105] Noah, their brother, said to them, *"Won't you be mindful (of Allah)?* [106] *I'm a trustworthy messenger for you,* [107] *so be mindful of Allah and obey me.* [108] *I'm not asking you for any reward for this (preaching), because my reward is due from none other than the Lord of All the Worlds,* [109] *so be mindful of Allah and obey me!"* [110]

"Should we believe in you," they asked, *"seeing that only low class people are following you?"* [816] [111]

"Just what do I know about what they're doing?" [817] he replied. [112] *"Their account is with none other than my Lord, if you only understood.* [113]

---

[816] There was a poor bedouin named Zahir ibn Haram who used to bring small presents to the Prophet whenever he came to Medina to trade. The Prophet used to praise him and called him, "…our bedouin and our villager." Zahir was a very unattractive, ugly-looking man, however, and he had always been teased when he was younger. Thus, he had very low self-esteem. One day, the Prophet saw him in the marketplace, and he approached Zahir from the back and gave him a hug. Zahir didn't recognize who was hugging him, so he said angrily, "Let me go. Who is this?" When he turned around and saw the Prophet, he felt ashamed at his gruff reply, and he turned back around in sorrow, leaning on the Prophet's chest. Zahir then cried out somberly, "Who will buy me as a slave? O Messenger of Allah, you can see that I'm worthless, by Allah!" The Prophet answered him, saying, "But in Allah's sight you are not worthless." (*Sharh as-Sunnah*)

[817] Noah is emphasizing that he doesn't know or care about anybody's social status. He must give the message to all, and he won't be bothered with the reputation of anyone in the eyes of others. Only Allah knows about their inner value.

I'm not going to drive away those who believe, [114] for I'm no more than a clear warner!" [115]

"If you don't stop (what you're doing)," they threatened, "then we're going to stone you!" [116]

"My Lord!" (Noah) cried. "My people have denied me, [117] so make an open decision between us, and save me and those believers who are with me!" [118]

And so We saved him and those who were with him in a crowded boat, [119] and then We drowned all those who remained behind. [120] There is a sign in this; yet, most of them don't believe. [121] Yet, even still, your Lord is the Powerful and Merciful One. [122]

The People of 'Ad Denied

The (people of) 'Ad denied the messengers. [123] Hūd, their brother, said to them, "Won't you be mindful (of Allah)? [124] I'm a trustworthy messenger for you, [125] so be mindful of Allah and obey me. [126] I'm not asking you for any reward for this (preaching), because my reward is due from none other than the Lord of All the Worlds." [127]

"Are you erecting monuments [818] on every high place just to amuse yourselves? [128] Are you constructing buildings for yourselves that will last forever? [129] When you exercise your power, will you do it with more force than necessary? [130]

"Be mindful of Allah, and obey me! [131] Be mindful of the One Who taught you everything you know [132] and Who gave you livestock and children [133] and gardens and springs. [134] I fear for you the punishment of an awful day." [135]

"It's all the same to us," they said, "whether you inform us or don't inform us, [136] for (your teachings) are no more than the invention of the

---

[818] The word ayah is used here, which usually signifies a sign, miracle or revealed verse. However, in preIslamic tradition, the Arabs would build alters on hilltops to their idols as 'signs' of veneration for their gods.

ancients. [137] *We're certainly never going to get any kind of punishment!"* [138]

Then they denied him, so We destroyed them. There is a sign in this; yet, most of them don't believe. [139] Yet, even still, your Lord is the Powerful and Merciful One. [140]

The People of Thamud Denied

The (people of) Thamud denied the messengers. [819] [141] Salih, their brother, said to them, *"Won't you be mindful (of Allah)?* [142] *I'm a trustworthy messenger for you,* [143] *so be mindful of Allah and obey me.* [144] *I'm not asking you for any reward for this (preaching), because my reward is due from none other than the Lord of All the Worlds."* [145]

"(Do you think) you're just going to be left alone in safety with all that you have here, [146] *with (your) gardens and springs* [147] *and crops and fruitful date palms?* [148] *You confidently carve your homes out of mountain sides,* [149] *(but that won't keep you safe from Allah's wrath), so be mindful of Allah and obey me.* [150] *Don't obey (the ways) of the high and mighty* [151] *who cause chaos and disorder in the land and improve nothing."* [152]

"You've been bewitched!" they cried. [153] *"You're no more than a mortal man like the rest of us. So bring us a miracle if you're telling the truth!"* [154]

"Here's a camel," he replied. *"She has her turn to drink (water from the well), and you'll have your turn to water (your animals) on your reserved day.* [155] *Don't let any harm come to her, or punishment will take hold of you on an awful day."* [156]

Then they crippled her, and although they came to regret it, [157] the punishment seized them nonetheless. There is a sign in this; yet, most of them don't believe. [158] Yet, even still, your Lord is the Powerful and Merciful One. [159]

---

[819] The Thamud are a people who lived centuries before the time of the Prophet in an area that encompasses part of northern Arabia and southern Jordan. Their homes, which were carved in the sides of cliffs and small mountains, can still be seen today.

The People of Lot Denied

The people of Lot denied the messengers. [160] Lot, their brother,
[820] said to them, *"Won't you be mindful (of Allah)?* [161] *I'm a trustworthy
messenger for you,* [162] *so be mindful of Allah and obey me."* [163]

*"I'm not asking you for any reward for this (preaching), because my
reward is due from none other than the Lord of All the Worlds.* [164] *Out of
(everyone available to you) in the whole world, are you approaching (other)
men (for your lusts)* [165] *and leaving behind the ones whom your Lord created
for you to be your mates? No way! You're a people who are completely out
of control!"* [166]

"If you don't stop (what you're saying)," they threatened, *"then we're
going to drive you away!* [167]

"I detest what you're doing!" he replied. [168] *"My Lord! Save me and
my family from what they're doing!"* [169] So we saved him and his family
all together, [170] save for an old woman who remained behind. [821] [171]

Then We destroyed (the others) to the last (man)! [172] We rained a
shower (of brimstone) down upon them, and it was a terrible
downpour upon those who had been warned! [173]

There is a sign in this; yet, most of them don't believe. [174] Yet, even
still, your Lord is the Powerful and Merciful One. [175]

---

[820] Lot settled in Sodom (Sadum), which (is generally believed) to have been located
somewhere near the present-day Dead Sea. His extended family, friends and servants
assimilated into the culture of the locals, and he dwelt among them for many years. This
is why he is also called 'their brother,' which is a term in Arabic (and English) that can be
used in the sense of a companion, a citizen of a place, an ideological convert or
compatriot, or someone who becomes part of the people they live among by virtue of
time. The Qur'an affirms that Lot was the blood relation of Abraham and that they both
left their homeland to flee idol-worship and then parted ways at some point, with Lot
going to the city and Abraham living as a bedouin. The use of 'brother' in the Qur'an
doesn't always mean a direct blood relation, and the other prophets mentioned in this
chapter, such as Salih, Hud and Shu'ayb, who are also called 'brothers' to their people,
are not technically being called the blood relative of everyone in their tribe. The Meccan
Muslims and Medinan Muslims were called 'brothers' in the Qur'an, as well, even though
they were often unrelated, simply on account of the fact that they dwelt in each other's
company and developed a strong bond of solidarity. Further still, all Muslims are called
the brothers (and sisters) of every other Muslim by virtue of group identity.
[821] Lot's wife didn't want to leave, as she was enamored of the culture of the people. She
was a traitor to her husband and used to tell the men of the street whenever Lot had
visitors. (See 66:10.)

The People of Madyan Denied

The Companions of the Thicket denied the messengers. [176]

Shu'ayb [822] said to them, *"Won't you be mindful (of Allah)?* [177] *I'm a trustworthy messenger for you,* [178] *so be mindful of Allah and obey me.* [179] *I'm not asking you for any reward for this (preaching), because my reward is due from none other than the Lord of All the Worlds."* [180]

"Measure (what you sell) fairly, and don't shortchange, [181] *and weigh with accurate scales.* [182] *Don't withhold what people are owed, and don't cause chaos and disorder in the land.* [183] *Be mindful of the One Who created you and the people of old."* [184]

"You've been bewitched!" they cried. [185] *"You're no more than a mortal man like the rest us, and we think you're a liar.* [186] *So make a piece of the sky fall down upon us if you're really telling the truth!"* [187]

"My Lord knows best about what you're doing." he replied. [188] And so they denied him and thus were seized with punishment on a dark and gloomy day - *and that was a tremendous day of punishment!* [189]

There is a sign in this; yet, most of them don't believe. [190] Yet, even still, your Lord is the Powerful and Merciful One. [191]

So Now Listen to Your Lord

Truly, this revelation is from the Lord of All the Worlds. [192] It was revealed by the Trusted Spirit [823] [193] to your heart, so you could become a warner [194] in the plain Arabic language. [195]

---

[822] This time, the pattern of this chapter is broken in that Shu'ayb is not called 'their brother.' According to Ibn Kathir, it is because this group of people, who were the people of Madyan, are given the title here of the idol they worshipped, which was a unique tangle of twisted trees in a single formation. Their 'goddess' resided within the thicket, or *aykah.* Neither Prophet Shu'ayb nor any other prophet should be called the 'brother' of a people if their idol's name is given in their specified title. (In 7:85 he is called 'their brother', but the nation is referred to as the 'People of Madyan.' This is a very fascinating and often overlooked aspect of the precise nature of many Qur'anic details.)

[823] This refers to the archangel Gabriel, who carries the divine revelation from Allah to Allah's chosen prophets. He is also sometimes called the Holy Spirit in the Qur'an (see 2:87).

Indeed, it was (foretold) in (the scriptures) of old, [824] [196] so isn't it proof enough for them that the scholars among the Children of Israel knew about it? [825] [197]

If We would've revealed it to a non-Arabic speaker, [198] and if he would've (tried to) recite it (with an accent) to them, then they would never have believed in it. [199]

That's how We've caused the wicked to (reject it) in their hearts (of their own accord, after hearing its message recited clearly). [826] [200]

---

[824] Even though the basic Muslim position is that the Bible is not fully accurate, Muslims do recognize that the words of the ancient prophets can still be found scattered within its various histories, biographies and tribal writings. Muslims have sometimes identified possible prophecies in the Bible that could point to Muhammad, and some of them have been startlingly precise. Among these are the following verses. In Jude 14-15 we read about ten thousand saints who will accompany the victory of the Lord against those who have worshipped idols and spoken out against God. This mirrors the Prophet Muhammad's march into pagan Mecca at the head of ten thousand followers to show the Meccans that idols were wrong and to redress their vicious opposition to Allah. Deuteronomy 18:15-22 foretells of a prophet who will be from the 'brethren' of the Jews. Ishmael and Isaac were brothers, and thus the Arabs are the metaphorical 'brethren' of the Jews. Furthermore, this predicted man would be raised up in their midst. Muhammad was born in Arabia, a land that included many Jewish tribes, and when Muhammad lived in Medina he lived near many Jews. Christians have long supposed that this prophecy is a reference to Jesus; yet, when you read the verses, a man "like Moses" is clearly being described. (Muhammad and Moses have far more in common than Moses and Jesus, and the man in question is certainly not assumed to be a god on earth.) Isaiah 42:1-13 contains verses that are also very specific to Muhammad, rather than to Jesus. The foretold prophet here is referred to as God's servant, and if Jesus were a part of God, then how could he be God's servant? Muhammad's official title, after the ubiquitous *Messenger of God*, is *God's servant*. Verse 11 specifically mentions this man will come from the villages of Kedar (one of Ishmael's sons), which was synonymous with the Arabs whose range extended from Syria to Arabia. It also says that the message will go forth among the gentiles, or non-Jews. Jesus generally did not preach to or heal non-Jews as a matter of policy, equating it with giving crumbs to dogs, though he supposedly once (grudgingly) helped a *gentile* after he was defeated by her logic. (See Matthew 15:21-28.) There are many more such possible Biblical prophecies that could point to Muhammad, and you will find them mentioned in this book where relevant.

[825] This is an apparent reference to some Jewish scholars who had come to Mecca to investigate the man who was claiming revelation from God, namely, Muhammad. From the context it is clear that they publicly endorsed that it was at least similar to what they had. The details of this encounter have not survived, however. Perhaps verses 198-199 are an answer to the issue of why the Qur'an was being revealed in Arabic, when the book of Moses was revealed in Hebrew, and Allah knows best.

[826] The pagans of Mecca are asked if it's really so far-fetched an idea that Allah would chose a native Arab to be their messenger. If he would have chosen a Greek, a Persian or someone else to bring a message to the Arabs, the custodians of the Ka'bah, Allah's original shrine, then the Arabs would have laughed at the poor foreigner who would have

They're not going to believe in it until they see the painful punishment. [201] Even still, it's going to come upon them suddenly when they're not expecting it, [202] and then they're going to cry, *"Won't we get any break?"* [203]

So are they asking for Our punishment to be hurried on? [204] What do you think? (Should We) let them enjoy themselves for a few years longer [205] and then bring down upon them what they've been promised? [206]

Oh, but nothing they enjoyed will do them any good then! [207] We never destroyed any town without (sending) warners [208] to remind (them about Allah) first, and We were never unfair (to any of them). [209]

Evil Cannot Produce Good

This (Qur'an) is not being revealed by any devils, [210] for it's not in agreement with (their values), nor could they ever (make something like this). [827] [211] On the contrary, they're far removed from ever even hearing (anything like this from their own kind)! [212]

Don't call upon any other deity besides Allah, for if you do, then you'll be punished. [213] Warn your nearest relatives, [828] [214] and lower your wing (in kindness) to the believers who follow you. [215] If they ever disobey you, then say, *"I'm not responsible for what you've done."* [216]

---

had a hard time speaking in the local tongue. By choosing an Arab, all Arabs had no choice but to understand the message, at least on the surface, and the truly wicked people would have no way to complain or feign ignorance on the Day of Judgment!

[827] An echo of what Jesus said when he was accused of being in league with Satan. "A house divided against itself cannot stand." (See the incident in Matthew 12:24-28.) After the pagans failed to identify any human source or explanation for Muhammad's revelations, they began to accuse him of being insane. When that charge didn't hold water, they started saying that evil demons were bringing him the Qur'an. As this verse points out, demons don't command good and righteous behavior. They don't call people to give up falsehood and to look to God alone for guidance. Only a holy source would call to holiness, and thus this is another aspect of the Qur'an that people must consider.

[828] The Prophet was commanded to warn his clan, the Banu Hashim, and other related clans. Once he approached the people of a clan near to his own and said to them, "O Banu Abd' Munaf! I'm a warner. My example is that of a man who sees the enemy, so he rushes to save his family, fearing that the enemy will reach them before he does." (*Muslim, Nisa'i*)

Trust in the Powerful and Merciful, [217] Who sees you standing upright (when you pray), [218] even as He sees your movements when you're among (people) who are prostrating (to Allah in unison). [219] He is the Hearing and the Knowing. [220]

Poetry can be Used in a Positive or Negative Way

Should I inform you about those upon whom the devils really descend? [221] They descend upon every lying, sinful (fortune-teller), [222] who listens to (the evil things) that they're told, and most of them are liars. [829] [223]

As (for the slanderous words) of (hostile) poets, only the hopelessly lost follow them. [224] Haven't you seen how they wander aimlessly in every valley [225] and how they speak about things they don't even do? [830] [226]

Exempted (from this blanket condemnation) are those (poets) who believe and do what's morally right, and who remember Allah often and defend themselves (in verse) only after they've been unfairly

---

[829] Devils or evil jinns descend upon fortune-tellers and whisper secrets into their minds. Once some people asked the Prophet about fortune-tellers, and the Prophet answered, "They're nothing." Then the people pointed out that sometimes they made true predictions, whereupon the Prophet said, "That's just a true report that the jinn snatched (by spying on the angels), then he babbles it like the clucking of a chicken into the ear of his friend, but he mixes it with more than a hundred lies." (Bukhari) In another narration the Prophet said that people hear one true prediction from a fortune-teller, and based on that they decide to believe everything he says, just because he got something right once. (Bukhari)

[830] The poets of Arabia were essentially the wandering comedians, propagandists and entertainers of their age. Many pagan poets turned their verbal talents against the Muslims and viciously ridiculed them at every turn with great venom. The Muslims had their own poets, as well, and they were sometimes employed in answering the enemy poets in the ongoing propaganda wars. See 49:5 for one such episode when there were dueling poets. One famous poet named 'Abdullah ibn az-Zab'ari told the Prophet upon his conversion, "Messenger of Allah! My tongue will surely try to make up for the things it said when I was bad - when I used to go along with Satan during my years astray." (Ibn Kathir) The Prophet himself explained that verses 221-226 apply only to poets who use their talents for evil, while verse 227 applies to poets who use their talents for good. (Ma'ariful Qur'an)

attacked. [831] Soon enough those who are wrong will know by what kind of damage they're going to be vanquished! [832] [227]

[831] Despite the assertions of some puritanical extremists, Islam does not forbid the use of poetry. The Prophet is on record quoting the lines of at least two poets approvingly (Labid and Abu al-Ala). The Prophet also said, "Poetry is a form of writing. If its subject is good and useful, then it's good, but if its subject is sinful, then it's bad. (*Fath ul-Bari*) On another occasion he said, "Some poetry is wisdom, while some speeches are like magic." (Quoted from *In Pursuit of Virtue*, by M. Abu Laylah.)

[832] In the ninth century, Egypt was ruled by a tyrant governor named Ahmad ibn Touloun. The people beseeched a local female religious scholar named Fatimah at-Tahirah for help in persuading him to reform. (She was also a descendant of the Prophet through his grandson Hassan.) Fatimah asked about the governor's schedule, and she learned at what hour he toured the city the next day. She wrote a short letter in which she scolded him for treating people badly and oppressing them. Among the things she wrote were the following words, "You were chosen by people, but you became a wrongdoer...Don't you know that the arrows of the dawn prayers are accepted by Allah? You may continue to oppress the people, but with Allah we are counted as the unjustly oppressed." Then she concluded her letter by quoting this verse from the Qur'an [26:227]. The next day, as the governor was passing by, she handed him the letter. He read it and understood it. Thereafter, he reformed his method of governance and treated the population with justice.

The Ant

27 An-Naml

Middle Meccan Period

This chapter presents a series of dramatic episodes in the lives of several previous prophets. There are various lessons that can be gleaned from this chapter. Thus, it is something of a "teachable moment" for those who listen to it and ponder over its meanings. The chapter also introduces the concept that non-human creatures also communicate with each other and that human beings can also learn to communicate with some of them.

In the Name of Allah,
the Compassionate, the Merciful

Tā. Seen.

These are the verses of the Qur'an and the clear Book. [1] (It's) a guide and a source of good news for the believers. [2] They're the ones who establish prayers, [833] give in charity, and have full confidence of the next life. [3]

We're going to make the deeds of those who don't believe in the next life appear dazzling to them so they can wander around confused. [4] They're the ones who will have a painful punishment, and in the next life they're going to be losers. [5] As for you, (Muhammad,) you're receiving the Qur'an from the very presence of a wise and knowing Being. [6]

---

[833] Ibn Sina (aka *Avicenna*, d. 1037) wrote: "Prayer is the thing that allows the soul to realize its connection with the Divine. Through prayers, human beings worship the truth and look forward to an everlasting reward. Prayer is the cornerstone of the religion, and the religion is the means by which a soul is cleansed of all that defiles it. Prayer is the worship of the Originator of all things, the Supreme Ruler of the World, the Source of All Strength. Prayer is the adoration of the One Whose existence is needed." (*Kitabul Najat*)

The Day Moses was Chosen

Moses said to his family, "*I noticed a fire (on the mountain). I'll (go there) and bring you some news (if it's from a traveler's campfire), or (if not,) then I'll at least bring you a burning branch to light our campfire so you can be warm.*" [7]

When he approached the fire, a voice called out, "*Blessed be whoever is within this fire, and whoever is around it, and all glory be to Allah, the Lord of All the Worlds.* [8] *Moses! I am Allah, the Powerful and the Wise.* [9] *Now throw your staff down (on the ground)!*"

(So Moses did as he was told), but when he saw it start to move and wiggle like a snake, he turned to run away.

"*Moses! Don't be afraid, for in My presence those who are messengers need not fear,* [10] *but if any commit injustice and then afterwards trade their evil ways for good; yet, still, I'm forgiving and merciful.* [11] *Now put your hand in your cloak, and it will come away blazing white (even though you won't be burned). (These are but two) of the nine (miraculous) signs for Pharaoh and his people, for they're a rebellious people.*" [12]

When Our signs reached (the court of Pharaoh), so they might open their eyes, they said instead, "*This is obviously magic!*" [13] And so, they arrogantly scoffed at them, even though they were convinced of them deep down in their souls. Then just see how we defeat the disobedient! [14]

Solomon and the Hoopoe

And so it was that We gave knowledge to David and Solomon, and they both declared, "*Praise be to Allah, Who favored us above so many of His believing servants!*" [15]

369

Solomon was David's heir, and he announced, *"O people! We've been taught the language of the birds, and we've been given (knowledge) of so many things.* [834] *This is clearly a favor (from Allah)."* [16]

The crowds of jinns and men were lined up at attention before Solomon, along with the birds, [835] and they were all kept in ranks. [17] (He marched with them) until they came to a valley full of ants. One of the ants (was alarmed), and she said, *"All you ants! Get in your homes, or Solomon and his huge (army) might crush you without even knowing it!"* [836] [18]

(Solomon) smiled, amused at what she said, and he exclaimed, *"My Lord! Grant me the capacity to be grateful for all Your favors, which You've bestowed upon me and my parents, so I can do what's right and pleasing to You. Admit me, through Your mercy, into the company of Your righteous servants."* [19]

---

[834] Solomon is using the 'royal we' in his speech. Referring to himself in the plural to emphasize his royal being and his authority. The vehicle of talking birds was the inspiration for the famous Muslim fable, *The Conference of Birds*, by Fariduddin 'Attar (d. c. 1220). It is sort of like a Muslim *Canterbury Tales*. The hoopoe bird is the main character and guide for all the other birds who were searching for their king (which was a metaphor for people seeking Allah).

[835] How was the bird able to *speak* to Solomon? Solomon kept a number of birds in his service for sending messages, such as carrier pigeons, which were also used in many other cultures. He may have also had a number of hunting birds such as falcons and eagles. The hoopoe is a bird common to the Middle East. Returning to the original question, could a man ever 'speak' to an animal, or could an animal ever 'speak' to a man? Allah gave Solomon this ability to converse with animals. It is not an unheard of concept, for the Bible records a man having a conversation with a donkey, by Allah's command. See Numbers 22:28-32. In addition, modern researchers have taught certain apes how to communicate with sign language, and some of them have developed quite impressive communication skills.

[836] It's interesting that the word for ant in Arabic, *an-naml*, is a male-pattern noun, while the Qur'an specifically labels the alarmed ant as a female with the verb, *qalat*, or *she said*. In the Prophet's time there was no scientific understanding anywhere in the world that insects such as ants had genders, even more, no one knew at that time that worker ants were all females. (Male drone ants are only produced occasionally when new queens are, and they die off quickly, never doing any field work.) Even the idea that ants could communicate with each other and convey messages was something unheard of. Ants use their antennae and other sensory organs to communicate and work together in their vast network of fellow sisters. The Qur'an uses the verb *to say* without implying that the ants uttered any sounds, for there was no Arabic word at the time to describe communication by chemicals. (Be that as it may, some species of ants also make rudimentary sounds and noises.) The very word chemical wasn't even invented until centuries after the Qur'an was revealed and was first known in Arabic as the science of *alchemy*.

(One day) he was taking a roll call of the birds and said, *"Why don't I see the hoopoe? Is he absent without leave?* [20] *I'll definitely punish him severely or even slaughter him, unless he brings me a good excuse."* [837] [21]

The hoopoe wasn't long in coming, though, and he gave his report, saying, *"I'm coming to you with a report about something of which you're unaware. I've just come back from (the land of) Sheba, and I have an accurate report.* [22] *I found a woman there who was ruling over them with every necessary resource of authority, and she also had a magnificent throne."* [838] [23]

"I found her and her people worshipping the sun in place of Allah. Satan has truly made their actions seem dazzling to their eyes. He's kept them away from the path, so they're without the guidance [24] *that would prompt them to worship Allah alone, the One Who brings to light what's hidden within the heavens and the earth and Who knows what you hide and show.* [839] [25] *Allah! There is no god but He, the Lord of the throne of glory!"* [840] [26]

(Solomon) said, *"We'll soon see whether you told the truth or not.* [27] *Go and carry this letter of mine, and deliver it to them. Then stand back, and wait (for the reply) that they'll send back with you."* [28]

The Queen of Sheba

(The Queen of Sheba, addressed her court), saying, *"All you nobles! A regal letter has been delivered to me.* [29] *It's from Solomon, and it reads as follows:*

---

[837] While it is forbidden in Islamic law to punish wild animals if they do not obey you, domesticated animals can be lightly punished for disobedience or even slaughtered for food if they can no longer serve the function for which they are being kept. (*Qurtubi, Ma'ariful Qur'an*)

[838] This female ruler is traditionally called Bilquis and she was the Queen of Sheba, which was located in modern-day Yemen. The Old Testament and even the Jewish apocrypha (II Targum of Esther) record a similar tale as found here, though with some significant differences. See I Kings 10:1-13 or II Chronicles 9:1-12.

[839] One can imagine that the bird wanted to give a very enthusiastic report, given that his master was already angry at him for his unapproved absence.

[840] After reading this verse, it is customary for the one who has faith in Allah to prostrate himself on the floor and praise Allah.

'In the Name of Allah, the Compassionate, the Merciful. [30]

Don't be too proud to (heed my request),
so come to me submissively.' [31]

"All you nobles," she then asked, *"counsel* [841] *me what I should do about this situation, for I've never decided any issue without your counsel."* [32]

"We're a powerful nation," they said, *"and we can wage fierce warfare, but it's your decision, so think deeply on what you will command."* [33]

"When kings enter a land," she mused, *"they ruin it and turn the best of its people into the worst, and that's just what they do."* [842] [34]

(Then she said), *"I will send him a gift, and then I'll see with what (response) my ambassadors will return."* [35]

When (the ambassadors bearing gifts) came to Solomon, he said to them, *"Are you going to bring me mere treasure, when what Allah has already given me is far better than what He's given to you!* [843] *No way! You're the ones who are pleased with your gifts!* [36] *Return (home) to (your*

---

[841] Here is a use of the word from which the Islamic legal term *fatwa*, or religious opinion is derived.

[842] Despite the fact that there have been – and continue to be – many monarchies in Muslim lands, the institution of hereditary monarchy is forbidden in Islam. The Prophet never instituted it, nor did he speak in favor of it, nor did his next four successors to public office practice it. (The Prophet even forbade one person to bow to another!) Instead, the first four caliphs practiced a kind of hybrid between democracy and parliamentarianism. These caliphs were, more or less, very strong prime ministers for life who were elected by a counsel of elders whom they consulted in all important affairs. They could also resign or theoretically be removed from office, based on some sayings of the Prophet to that effect. Sadly, dynastic rule was forcibly instituted and came to be the norm in the Muslim world scarcely forty years after the Prophet's passing. Most Muslim reform movements in the past several centuries have emphasized a return to the more egalitarian governance structure of the first four caliphs (which was characterized by limited government intrusion in most areas of people's lives). Muslims have not, however, developed a unified theory of how such a system would work in the modern context. The closest effort in recent times has been promulgated by Muhammad Asad in his book, *The Principles of State and Government in Islam.*

[843] The Prophet joined some of his companions after he had bathed and dressed himself. 'Umar ibn al-Khattab remarked, "You're looking happy today, Messenger of Allah." The Prophet replied, "Yes, I am." Then people in the gathering started talking about affluence, and the Prophet said, "Affluence is not a bad thing for someone who has the fear of Allah in his heart, but remember, for a righteous person ,good health is even better than affluence, and being cheerful is a bounty bestowed by Allah." (*Ahmad*)

kingdom), and mark my word that I'll be coming to (your people) with such forces that they'll never be able to withstand, and (unless your queen comes here to meet me), we'll drive them away from there in disgrace, and they'll be humiliated!" [844] [37]

Solomon and the Queen

(Solomon) said, *"All you nobles! Which of you can bring her throne to me before she arrives here to submit?"* [38]

A powerful, yet cunning, jinn [845] said, *"I'll have it brought to you before you even stand up from your meeting, for I'm strong enough to do that, and you can surely trust me (with this task)!"* [39]

(However, another jinn) who was well-versed in knowledge of the scripture said, *"I'll bring it to you in the twinkling of an eye."*

Then when Solomon saw it appear right there in front of him, he said, *"This is by the favor of my Lord as a test to see whether I'm thankful or not. Whoever is thankful (for the blessings that Allah gave him), then his gratitude is for (the good of) his own soul. Whoever is thankless, well, My Lord is self-sufficient and noble."* [40]

Then he commanded, *"Disguise her throne so she won't even recognize it. Let's see whether she (is capable) of being guided (to the truth) or if she's one of those who can't be guided."* [846] [41]

---

[844] Solomon's purpose in writing to the Queen of Sheba (known popularly as Bilquis) was to help her spiritually by revealing the knowledge of the One True God to her. When he saw the ambassadors and their gold and jewels, he became disappointed in her response, for he never wanted tribute or treasure from her or her people. Thus, he made his threat to invade Sheba and remove its rulers from power. The Queen of Sheba decided to take the path of peace and wrote back to Solomon offering to go to Jerusalem in person.

[845] An *ifrit* is a powerful and cunning type of jinn that is ever bent on creating mischief. Solomon chose the second jinn to bring Bilquis's throne because he didn't boast when he offered his services. Perhaps the first one was planning to embarrass Solomon or do some act of mischief. Perhaps this is the jinn of whom fables speak, who was imprisoned in the lamp later found by Aladdin! Thus, Qur'anic stories even informed the fiction and fantasy literature of Muslim civilization.

[846] Her people saw the sun as the most powerful thing in their world and thus worshipped it. The Aztecs, Mayans, Babylonians and Egyptians are among the many civilizations that have done likewise.

So when she arrived, she was asked, *"Is this your throne?"* She exclaimed, *"It looked just like this! We knew about this before, and we hereby submit (to Allah)."* [847] [42] She had only been diverted from (true faith before) by what she used to serve in place of Allah, for she was (raised among) a people who had no faith. [848] [43]

She was asked to enter within (the main hall) of the palace, but when she saw the floor (and how it sparkled translucently), she thought it was a pool (of water). She lifted up the ends of her dress, exposing her legs, (and was about to walk into the room like that), when (Solomon) said, *"This floor is reflective, for it's been polished to a clear shine!"*

(The queen) exclaimed, *"My Lord! I truly did wrong against my own soul. I submit, along with Solomon, to the Lord of All the Worlds."* [849] [44]

---

[847] Some commentators have suggested that the phrase, "We were given knowledge about this beforehand, and we hereby submit (to Allah)," was a comment made by Solomon after the queen recognized her disguised throne. Others say it was an affirmation by the queen that she had thought about the reason why Solomon rejected her treasures, that she came to realize that he was offering her a true religion, and that's why she was ready to submit as soon as she met him. I feel the latter view is most correct given that the phrase in question is grammatically a continuation of the queen's words. In addition, there is a story about this incident contained in Ibn Kathir that reaffirms that Bilquis made up her mind to convert to whatever Solomon would ask of her, given that she understood instinctively that he was no mere king in the usual sense.

[848] In other words, she was one of those insightful people who, even though she was raised among ignorant traditions, knew them to be suspect. Thus, when knowledge of the truth finally came to her, she was already predisposed to accept it. Some commentators understand this verse [43] to mean that Solomon diverted her from the worship of the sun.

[849] The lesson of not taking things according to their surface appearance was driven home with the polished floor that she thought was covered in water. Even as her people thought the sun was a god, so, too, do people take many things in the wrong light. Thus, she exclaimed her full acceptance of Allah and His prophet Solomon. The floor of Solomon's palace, according to I Kings 7:7, was made of cedar. (The nearby temple's floor was made of polished gold.) When cedar is polished profusely with expensive oils, the floor can give off the appearance of translucence, like a thin layer of water was upon it, especially under an arc of sunlight shining in the dim light of a palace throne room. This verse is often mistranslated to mean that the floor of Solomon's temple was made of *glass*. None of the three main Arabic words used here, however, signify glass. (The word for glass in Arabic is *zijaaj*.) The phrase, *"As-sarh mumaraddun min qawareer"* literally means, "The clear (floor) is of a reflective foundation (or bottom)."

The Trials of the Thamud

And so it was that We sent Salih, their brother, to the (people of) Thamud, and he said, *"Serve Allah!"* Thereafter, (his people) divided into two competing factions. [45]

(Salih) said, *"My people! Why are you asking for something dreadful to be hurried on instead of something good? If you would just ask Allah to forgive you, you might receive mercy."* [46]

"We see a bad omen in you," [850] they answered, *"and in those with you."*

(Salih) responded to them, saying, *"Your bad omen is with Allah. No way! You're a people who are being tested."* [47]

The Plot of the Nine Assassins

Background on verses 48-49: The story is told that the nine men mentioned in this passage were noblemen of the tribe. Two pagan women, one who divorced a follower of Salih and an old woman with several beautiful daughters, held a bitter grudge against Salih. The two women publicly offered a reward to anyone who would kill the camel. Finally the two women each recruited a man to do the job. The divorcee promised her assassin money, while the old woman promised her most beautiful daughter to the killer she hired. Seven other men of the clan were also recruited. The nine men ambushed the camel and shot its leg with an arrow. To encourage them, the beautiful daughter of the old woman accompanied the men and showed her face to them. The men set upon the camel and savagely killed it with their swords. When Salih was informed of what had happened, he told the people of his tribe, *"Enjoy yourselves in your homes for three days."* (See 11:65) (*Ibn Kathir*)

Now in the city there lived nine men from one clan who often caused trouble in the land, and furthermore they made no effort to reform themselves. [48] They said to each other, *"Let's swear together in Allah's name that we'll ambush him and his followers by night, then we can*

---

[850] Bad omens or signs are a kind of superstition. For the Arabs (and the Romans before them), they were sometimes represented in the erratic habits of birds. The Prophet said, "(Believing in) omens is like making partners (with Allah). People may see a glimpse of their (portents), but Allah dispels (omens when people) put their reliance (on Him)." (*Ahmad, Abu Dawud*)

(lie) to his patrons later on, saying, 'We never saw any attack on his people, and we're telling the truth!'" [49]

And so, they plotted and planned, but We were planning, too, even though they didn't realize it. [851] [50] So see how their plot was foiled! Then We destroyed them and their people all together! [51] Their houses were left in ruins because of their corruption, and in this is a sign for people who know. [52] We saved those who believed, however, and who were mindful (of Allah). [53]

The Example of Prophet Lot

Lot said to his people, *"Will you do something so perverted,* [852] *even watching it (in public)!* [54] *Are you really using men instead of women for your passions? That's not right! You're an ignorant people!"* [55]

His people gave him no other answer than to say, *"Drive them out! Drive out the followers of Lot from the city - these people who want to be so clean and pure!"* [56] We saved him and his family, except for his wife, for We determined that she would remain behind. [57] Then We rained down upon them a shower (of brimstone), and it was a terrible downpour upon the warned. [58]

Which is Better?

Say (to them), *"Praise be to Allah, and peace be upon His servants whom He has chosen!"* So who's better - Allah or the 'partners' they make with Him? [59] (Which of them) created the heavens and the earth and sends down water from the sky? In fact, We use it to produce the lovely orchards (in which you find so much delight).

---

[851] The nine men plotted to kill Salih before the threatened three-day limit was up. They knew where he used to pray in solitude in the countryside, and they waited to ambush him in a grotto. However, a rock slide covered the plotters in their hiding place, and they were never heard from again. (*Ibn Kathir*)

[852] *Faahishah*, or unlawful, shameful behavior. Thus, the designation that *faahishah* is synonymous with sexual deviancy such as homosexuality.

It's not in *your* power to make the trees within them grow (without Allah's help. So can there be another) god with Allah? No way! (Those who think otherwise) are people with no sense of justice! [60]

Who made the earth a stable place on which to live with rivers flowing in its midst, and (who) placed firm highlands upon it? (Who) settled a boundary between the two bodies of water, (salty and fresh,) so they don't mingle? (Can there be another) god with Allah? No way! Yet, most of them don't know. [61]

Who answers the call of a distressed person when they call upon Him? [853] Who relieves their suffering and makes you inherit the earth? (Can there be another) god with Allah? *Oh, how few reminders you accept!* [62] Who guides you through the darkness of both land and sea, and who sends the winds as bearers of good news ahead of His mercy? (Can there be another) god with Allah? Allah is high above what they associate with Him! [63]

Who initiated the creation (of all things) and then renews it, and who gives you resources from both the sky and the earth? (Can there be another) god with Allah? So say (to them), *"Bring out your evidence if you're really so honest!"* [64]

Then tell them, *"None in the heavens nor on the earth, besides Allah, knows the unseen, nor can they be aware of when they're going to be resurrected."* [65] No way! They can neither understand nor comprehend the (magnitude) of the next life. No way! They're confused about it, and they can never be anything but blind to it! [66]

---

[853] The Prophet said, "Anyone who is overcome by sadness or grief and supplicates in the following words, surely Allah will remove his grief and sadness and exchange them for delight: 'O Allah! I am your servant and the child of your female servant. My forelock is in your hand. Your decision regarding me will surely come to pass. Your judgment is fair towards me. I invoke You by every name You have and by which You call Yourself, as they're sent down in Your Book, taught to any of Your creatures, or kept with You in the knowledge of the unseen that's there with You. Make the Glorious Qur'an the springtime of my heart, the light of my chest, the remover of my grief and the dissolver of my concerns.'" (*Ahmad*)

The Faithless Deny

The faithless ask, *"After we've crumbled to dust, are we really going to be raised (from the dead) – both ourselves and our ancestors?* [67] *Well, both ourselves and our ancestors were already promised this in the past, but it's all no more than ancient fables."* [68]

Say (to them), *"Go abroad in the world, and see how the wicked (civilizations of the past) came to an end."* [69] Then feel no sadness for them, (Muhammad,) nor worry yourself over their plots. [70]

They ask, *"So when will this promise (come to pass), if you're really so honest?"* [71] Tell them, *"It just might be that some of what you want to hurry on could be close behind you!"* [72] Your Lord is favorable towards people, but most of them are thankless. [73] Your Lord knows what's hidden in (people's) hearts, even as He knows what they reveal. [74] There's nothing hidden in the heavens or on earth without it being recorded in a clear record. [75]

The Solution to Jewish Doctrinal Disputes

This Qur'an addresses most of that over which the Children of Israel disagree, [76] and it's a guide and a mercy for those who believe. [77] Your Lord will decide between them according to His judgment, for He's the Powerful and the Knowing. [78] So trust (your affairs) to Allah, for you're on (the path) of clear truth. [79]

You can't make the dead listen, nor can you force the deaf to hear your call - *especially since they're running away in retreat.* [80] You can't guide the blind, either, nor can you prevent them from swerving aside. You can only make those listen who believe in Our signs, and who then submit (voluntarily). [854] [81]

---

[854] A man named Amr went to the Prophet and said, "Give me your right hand so that I may give you my pledge of loyalty." The Prophet stretched out his right hand, but then Amr withdrew his hand abruptly. The Prophet said, "What has happened to you, O Amr?" He replied, "I need to lay down one condition." The Prophet asked, "What condition do you intend to put forward?" Amr said, "That Allah forgives my sins." The Prophet said, "Didn't you know that converting to Islam erases all previous sins?" (*Muslim, Ahmad*)

The Judgment cannot be Denied

When the sentence (of Allah's judgment) is fulfilled against (the faithless), We're going to produce a thing creeping from the earth, [855] and it will speak to them, for humanity has never been convinced of Our miraculous signs. [82]

And one day We're going to collect from every community a group of those who denied Our signs, and they'll (be made to stand) at attention [83] until they come (before Allah for judgment). He'll ask them, *"Did you deny My signs, even though you weren't sure (if you should have done that or not), or were you doing something else?"* [84] And so the sentence will be fulfilled against them on account of their corruption, and they won't be able to offer a defense. [85]

The Final Word

Don't they see that We made the night for them to rest in and the day for them to see? There are signs in this for people who believe! [86] On the day when the trumpet will blow, all beings within the heavens and the earth will be struck with terror, save for those whom Allah wills, and everyone will come forth in utter humility. [87]

You see the mountains now and assume them to be solid, but they'll drift away (on the Last Day), even as the clouds drift by. That

---

[855] The thing *that will creep from the earth and speak* has always been an enigmatic subject for the commentators. The Arabic word *dâbatan* is usually translated as a *beast*, and the Prophet predicted that in the End Times a *dâbatan* will rise from the earth and speak. What does this mean? Is a monster of some sort going to wake up underground and emerge and speak to people? There are a variety of interpretations on this issue. What we can add is that it must be remembered that Arabic words oftentimes have multiple and widely varied meanings. The root word of this term, which is *daba*, means anything from a crawling reptile or a horse or mule to a rushing outpouring of something. Other meanings include vitality, to gain ascendancy and even a sand hill. This verse is saying that in the End Times, when Allah's judgment is about to overshadow the earth and the wicked upon it, that something will come out of the earth and will communicate some type of message to humanity, as something of a final sign to humanity that they never believed in Allah's other signs. What will the *dabatan* actually be? Only Allah knows.

will be Allah's handiwork, for He's the One Who perfects everything, and He's well-informed of all that you do. [856] [88]

If anyone does good, then good will come to him from it, and he'll be safe from terror on that day. [89] If anyone does evil, he'll be thrown on his face in the Fire. Can you ever be rewarded with other than what you did? [90]

(Say to them, Muhammad,) *"As for me, I've been commanded to serve the Lord of this city (of Mecca), the One Who made it holy and Who owns all things. I've been commanded to be among those who submit (to Allah)* [91] *and to recite the Qur'an."* [857]

Whoever is guided is guided for the good of his own soul, while if anyone goes astray, just tell him, *"I'm no more than a warner."* [92] Then say, *"Praise be to Allah, the One Who will soon show you His signs so you can recognize them, and your Lord is not unaware of what you're doing."* [93]

---

856 Even the mighty mountains will be uprooted by Allah when the Last Day is established.

857 The Prophet said, "The one who reads the Qur'an aloud is like someone who gives news of charity, while the one who conceals the Qur'an (by not reciting it aloud) is like someone who conceals acts of charity." (*Abu Dawud*) This means that if someone recites the Qur'an to themselves, even though no one knows what they're doing besides Allah, they will be counted as having given charity in secret. If they recite it aloud for all to hear, they are still rewarded, but at a different scale. See 2:271.

The Tales

28 Al Qasas

Late Meccan Period

This is one of the very last Meccan revelations. While some of it was revealed to Muhammad while he was still residing within the city of Mecca, the first 50 and last 4 verses were revealed later, while the Prophet was on the run in the desert during his migration to Yathrib (Medina) in the year 622. Indeed, the pursuing pagans were difficult to elude, and the Prophet, along with Abu Bakr and a trusty guide, were feeling worn down from the journey. Once, while they were encamped, Angel Gabriel came and asked Muhammad if he was feeling homesick. The Prophet replied that he was, and so the story of Moses contained in this chapter was revealed to him to comfort him and strengthen his resolve (verses 1-50). (*Ma'ariful Qur'an*) In the main, this chapter concentrates on the story of Prophet Moses. It is a metaphor for Prophet Muhammad's own experience and offers the promise of eventual triumph (see verse 5, for example). In fact, many parallels can be drawn between the two prophets, most notably in the way each is presented with a seemingly insurmountable task, which results in their eventually having to depart from their iniquitous people.

In the Name of Allah,
the Compassionate, the Merciful

$T\bar{a}$. *Seen. Meem.* [1]

These are the verses of the clear Book. [2] Now We're going to recite to you some of the story of Moses and Pharaoh in all its truthfulness, for people who believe. [858] [3]

Truly, Pharaoh exalted himself in the land. He divided his people into different social classes, causing the downfall of some of them [859]

---

[858] In other words, this story will be accurate and will not contain the many legends and additions that later generations have added.

[859] He reduced the Hebrews to slavery, even though their ancestors came into Egypt during the time of Prophet Joseph as free people. This oppression was caused by both his xenophobia and the general hatred of the Egyptian ruling class for Semitic peoples, especially since Egypt had been conquered and ruled for a time by other Semites known as the Hyksos. Perhaps after native rule was restored, the Hebrews became prime targets for racial discrimination. See note for verse 12:49.

– even killing their sons but not their daughters, [860] for he was truly evil. [4]

We wanted to empower those who were being oppressed in the land, to make them leaders, to give them an inheritance (in the earth), [5] to establish their nation firmly in the world, and to use them to show Pharaoh, Haman and their hordes that they couldn't (hold back) the very things they were trying to prevent. [861] [6]

Allah Inspired the Mother of Moses

We directed the mother of Moses by telling her, *"Suckle him as usual, but when you're afraid for his safety, set him adrift in the river (Nile). Don't be afraid or feel sad, for We're going to restore him to you and then make him one of Our messengers."* [862] [7]

(When Pharaoh's men were close, she did as she was commanded and set the baby adrift in the river.) Later on, Pharaoh's own family fished him out, (not realizing that) Moses would one day become their enemy and also a source of regret for Pharaoh, Haman and all their hordes. They were grossly mistaken! [8]

---

[860] This Pharaoh sought to control the population growth of the Hebrews by infanticide: ordering the death of baby boys from time to time. By not ordering the death of baby girls, he ensured generations of population imbalance, which would further serve the interests of the Egyptian government.

[861] Their evil policies of abject slavery, discrimination and even murder were designed to ensure Egyptian dominance. The Qur'an is saying here that Allah wanted to use these weakened and oppressed people to show the tyrants of Egypt that nothing they could do could prevent the retribution of Allah upon them for their evil. In other words, He wanted their humiliation to come from where they least expected it.

[862] The Egyptians had a policy of killing Hebrew baby boys in alternate years. This was to ensure that there were at least some male slaves to do the work that the Egyptians, themselves, didn't want to do. Aaron was born before Moses in one of those alternate years and was allowed to live. Moses was born in a year of death, however, but his mother Jochebed concealed her pregnancy from the local midwives whose task it was to monitor births. Moses' mother would suckle her baby and keep him hidden in the house. Whenever someone she feared would come near her home, she would put the baby in a box-like basket and put the basket in a thicket of reeds by the side of the river Nile, tied to a rope. One day she was so spooked by coming visitors that she forgot to tie the rope, and the basket floated away with the baby inside. She sent her daughter to see where the basket went to, and it drifted right towards one of the riverside palaces of the Pharaoh. (*Ibn Kathir*)

The Pharaoh's wife [863] exclaimed delightedly, *"A joy to the eye for you and me! Don't kill him, (my husband), for he might be useful to us, or we might adopt him as a son."* They had no idea (what they were doing). [9]

(When the news reached her that her baby was taken into Pharaoh's house,) Moses' mother felt a great emptiness in her heart. [864] She would've revealed the secret, but We strengthened her heart so she could remain faithful. [10] She had told (the baby's older) sister, *"Follow him (as he floats down the river)."* She had watched him discreetly, and the (Egyptians) didn't catch on. [11]

We forbade (the baby) to suckle (from any of the wet nurses of the palace,) until (Moses' sister approached them) and said, *"Do you want me to show you a family home where (the baby) can be fed and looked after for you by those who will care diligently?"* [865] [12] This is how We restored him to his mother so her eyes could be comforted, so her worry could be abated, and so she could know that Allah's promise is true, but most (people) don't understand. [13]

---

863 The noblewoman mentioned here would be the wife of the pharaoh who ruled when Moses was very young. If this story took place during the rule of Pharaoh Kenephres, then his wife is identified in historical records as Merris. The new, second pharaoh, who ruled Egypt many years later (when Moses was much older and had become a prophet) would have been Kenephres's son, Dudimose. Muslim tradition states that his wife was named 'Asiyah. It has long been discussed as to whether 'Asiyah was present both when Moses was found and later when he was a prophet many decades later. There is no reason to assume that she was or wasn't, for as a member of a royal family, or at least well-connected enough to have later married a pharaoh, she most probably would have known of Moses as he grew into manhood. Also see 66:11.

864 The mother of Moses had sent her daughter to follow the basket. When the daughter saw it pass before one of Pharaoh's palaces and get retrieved, she told her mother, who would have petitioned for the return of her baby, but Allah strengthened her heart, and she held her tongue.

865 After refusing all offers of milk, Pharaoh's wife, who had become attached to the baby, was in a state of alarm. She sent her servants carrying the baby out in the city and searched for a wet nurse for hire. It was at this moment that the sister of Moses recognized the baby one of them was carrying and approached her, suggesting that she knew of a wet nurse where the baby could be raised and fed. Thus Moses would spend a part of each day in the company of his real mother and another part of the day with his adoptive mother, but no one could reveal the secret that Moses was being raised by his biological mother. (*Ibn Kathir*)

The Young Prince

When (Moses) grew into manhood and his character was settled, We bestowed wisdom and knowledge upon him, [866] for that's how We reward the good. [14] (Then one night) he ventured out into the city, unnoticed by others, (and explored its streets) until he came upon two men having a fight. One of them was (a Hebrew), and the other (was an Egyptian) and thus his enemy. [867]

The (Hebrew) man called out to him for help against his opponent, so Moses punched (the Egyptian) with his clenched fist and (accidentally) killed him. (Moses) cried out, *"This is Satan's doing, for he's an enemy who clearly leads (his victims) towards mistakes.* [15] *My Lord,"* he then prayed, *"I've been wrong, so forgive me."* So, Allah forgave him, for He's the Forgiving and Merciful. [16]

"My Lord," he prayed once more, *"Since You've favored me, I swear I'll never help any immoral person (again)."* [868] [17] So he spent (the night hiding) fearfully in the city until the morning broke. Then he saw the same (Hebrew) man who had asked for his help the day before calling for his help yet again! Moses told him, *"You're clearly some kind of troublemaker!"* [18]

However, when (Moses) resolved to restrain the man who was an enemy to both him and the (other Hebrew, the Egyptian attacker) shouted, *"Hey, Moses! Do you want to kill me like you killed a man yesterday? You just want to be a tough guy in the land and not a reformer."* [869] [19]

---

[866] The *knowledge* was that he was really a Hebrew, and the wisdom he received was his beginning to question his identity and what it meant.

[867] Moses learned who he really was while being raised in the house of his own mother, but he had to feign dual loyalties to the royal household. Thus, he knew that the Egyptians were not really his friends or allies.

[868] Moses didn't mean to kill the Egyptian, but by letting the heat of the moment get to him, he joined in the fight when it would have been more prudent to have first found out what the problem was. Here he promises not to help anyone ever again who may be engaged in wrongdoing, for he realized that automatically siding with someone just because they were of the same ethnic group was not a wise thing to do. See 4:135.

[869] Moses' part in the killing the day before was known! This new Egyptian man taunted him, saying that he (Moses) wasn't trying to stop an innocent slave from being beaten, but rather he just wanted to garner a reputation for being tough.

Suddenly, (a friend) came running from the other side of the city and warned Moses, saying, *"Moses! The nobles are meeting to decide your fate. They plan to kill you, so run away. That's the best advice!"* [870] [20]

So he fled the scene in guarded fear and prayed, *"O my Lord! Save me from the tyrants."* [871] [21]

The Fugitive Finds a Home

And so he (fled Egypt) and set out towards (the land of) Madyan, saying, *"My Lord will guide me towards the right path."* [22] Then he arrived at a watering hole in Madyan and found a large group of people gathered there, (watering their flocks).

Meanwhile, two ladies, who sat nearby, were kept waiting (with their sheep). He asked them, *"What's the problem here?"*

They answered, *"We can't get a turn at the watering hole until the shepherds leave, and our father is too old (to stand up for us)."* [23]

So he, himself, watered their flocks, (and when he had finished) he went back to rest in the shade. *"My Lord,"* he prayed, *"I could use whatever good You send me."* [24]

A little while later, one of the ladies came back to him, walking bashfully, and said, *"My father has invited you (to a banquet) to reward you for watering (our flock) for us."* [872]

---

[870] This probably would have been one of Moses' friends from the royal court.

[871] Moses was guilty of unintentional homicide, but he knew he would not get a fair hearing or trial, for it was well known that Hebrews guilty of killing Egyptians were automatically put to death, no matter what the mitigating circumstances were. In addition, Moses apparently had some military skill (as reported by the ancient historian Josephus, who chronicled a military expedition against Nubia led by Moses before this), and perhaps he was seen as a threat in the royal court. Moses had no choice but to leave Egypt.

[872] Without any textual justification whatsoever, some classical commentators have identified the old father of these ladies as Prophet Shu'ayb. As most modern commentators have shown, this is not a correct linkage.

(When Moses arrived at their father's camp), he told him his whole story. (The old man reassured him), saying, *"Don't worry about it. You've escaped from an oppressive people."* [25]

(One of the ladies) said, *"My father, why don't you give him a job, for the best worker is a strong and trustworthy one."* [26]

(Her father) then said (to Moses), *"In fact, I want to marry one of these two daughters of mine to you, but on one condition: that you work for me for eight years. However, if you finish ten years in total, it would be a favor from you, but I don't want to put a burden on you. You'll find that I am, Allah-willing, a morally upright man."* [27]

(Moses) answered, *"Then that's how it will be between you and me. Whichever of the two time periods I (choose to) fulfill, don't let it be held against me. Let Allah's guarantee be on what I say."* [873] [28]

The Burning Bush

After Moses had completed his term of service, (he struck out on his own) and journeyed with his family (in search of opportunity.) [874] (One day, while they were camped in the desert), he saw a fire burning on the slopes of Mount Tur.

"Wait here," he said to them. *"I see a fire. I want to bring you some news from it, or at least a burning branch that you (can use to start your campfire) to warm yourselves."* [29]

(When he finally) reached (the fire, he heard) a voice coming from the right side of the valley, emanating from a tree on blessed ground. *"Moses! I am Allah. The Lord of All the Worlds. Now throw your staff to the ground!"* [30] After he did it, he saw it wiggling like a snake, so he turned to escape and was hesitant to venture back.

---

873 Ibn 'Abbas (d. 687) said that Moses fulfilled the longer term out of his generosity. (*Ibn Kathir*)

874 Some commentators are of the opinion that Moses missed his home and family and wanted to visit Egypt in secret. Enough years had passed, and his appearance as a bedouin might just have enabled him to envision successfully pulling off such a bold visit.

"Moses!" (the voice commanded.) *"Come closer, and don't be afraid, for no harm will come to you.* [31] *Now slip your hand in your shirt, and it will come away blazing in perfect whiteness. Then fold your limb to your side again without fear (of being burned). These are two miracles (that you've been given) from your Lord (to impress) Pharaoh and his nobles, for they've become a rebellious people."* [32]

(Moses) cried out, *"My Lord! I killed one of their men, and I'm afraid they're going to kill me.* [33] *My brother Aaron is a better speaker than I, so send him as my partner to back me up, though I'm still afraid that they'll call me a liar."* [34]

"We'll strengthen your arm with your brother and grant power to you both that will keep them from harming you. (If you employ) Our signs, that will ensure that both of you, as well as any who follow you, will succeed." [35]

Pharaoh

Moses (returned to Egypt) and went to (its leaders) with clear proofs, but they said, *"This is no more than invented sorcery, and We've never heard anything like this (message) from our ancient ancestors!"* [36]

"My Lord knows best," (Moses answered), *"who is coming with guidance from Him and who will have the (best) result in the realm of the next life. Tyrants will certainly never succeed!"* [37]

"O Nobles!" Pharaoh said. *"I don't know of any other god for you than myself. Haman! Fire up the (furnaces to make) bricks of clay, and build me a towering palace so I can climb up to the God of Moses. As for me, I think he's a liar!"* [875] [38]

---

[875] Some issues that need to be addressed here center on Egyptian religious beliefs and architecture. At Muhammad's time, and especially in central Arabia where knowledge of the surrounding world and the cultures of antiquity was extremely scarce, there is no good explanation for why the Qur'an correctly states that the Egyptian pharaohs considered themselves as gods on earth. The reading of hieroglyphics had been lost by that time. Thus, people of the Prophet's day would not have known what the ancient Egyptian rulers really thought of themselves. The second issue is in the massive building projects of the Egyptians. Muhammad never journeyed to Egypt, and in those days most of the grand buildings of the ancient pharaohs were lost to the sands of the desert, nor

Against all right he was arrogant throughout the land, both he and his hordes. They never thought they would come back to Us! [876] [39] So we seized him, along with his hordes, and threw them into the sea! So just look at how wrongdoers are finished off! [40]

We made (their conduct) the pinnacle of all invitations to the Fire, and they'll find no one to help them on the Day of Assembly. [877] [41] A curse will follow them in this world, [878] and on the Day of Assembly they're going to be hideous (to behold, on account of how they're going to be disfigured). [42]

Moses and Muhammad

And so it was that We revealed the Book to Moses, following a time in which We destroyed (many) earlier generations, so that people could be given insight, guidance and mercy and also so they could be reminded. [879] [43]

---

could he have known that Egypt was so scarce of trees, thus requiring the use of baked mud/clay bricks to build practically everything.

[876] Ibn Hazm (d. 1064), the Spanish Muslim writer, once wrote, "If your pride leads you to boast, you will be doubly guilty, for your intelligence will have been shown to be too weak to control your pride."

[877] In other words, Pharaoh and his nobles were so wicked that they set the standard for what will send a person to Hellfire without the possibility of forgiveness. They were idol-worshippers, murderers of children, wasters of resources, unjust enslavers, and to top it all off they were arrogant and refused to listen to their prophet no matter what signs he brought.

[878] To this day, mention of the pharaohs, their beliefs and their tombs evokes images of curses and evil happenings, i.e., the Mummy's Curse, the Mystery of Tutankhamen, the Egyptian Book of the Dead, etc. Whether the curses are real or not is immaterial. The reputation of ancient Egypt and her mysteries in this world is one of dark fascination, intrigue and sometimes raw unnatural power.

[879] Muslims are taught to accept the Torah, Psalms and Gospel as true expressions of divine revelation. As such, a Muslim is not allowed to disrespect a Bible or copy of the Torah. Even though Muslims believe that the original revelations of the former prophets have been edited, added to and otherwise tampered with, they do believe that some portion of those original revelations is still contained within the modern versions of those books of the same name. Muslims are even allowed to research the scriptures of Jews and Christians and quote them for examples of Allah's earlier injunctions, as companions of Muhammad such as 'Abdullah ibn Salam and K'ab al-Ahbar (converts from Judaism) did, and they were never censured by any of their contemporaries. The Qur'an gives permission for this in practice also in verse 3:93.

You weren't there, (Muhammad,) when We gave the commission to Moses on the western side (of the mountain), nor did you witness (his exploits). [44] We raised up other generations that lasted for many ages, and you weren't living among the people of Madyan either, nor were you reciting Our (revealed) verses to them. Yet, We always kept sending (reminders to humanity). [45]

You also weren't there on the side of (Mount) Tūr when We called out (to Moses), but (now here you are:) a mercy from your Lord to warn a people who've never had a warner before you. *So now let them have their reminder!* [46]

If (you) were never (sent to them), and a disaster befell them on account of what they did with their own hands, then they might be (within their rights) to say, *"Our Lord! Why didn't you send us any messenger, for then We would've followed Your (revealed) verses and believed?"* [47]

So now, when We're sending Our own truth to them, they (have the audacity to) say, *"Why hasn't he brought any (miracles) like Moses brought?"* But haven't they already rejected (the miracles) that Moses was given? They said, *"Those are just two kinds of sorcery backing each other up!"* Then they said, *"We reject them both!"* [880] [48]

So say (to them), *"Then bring a book from Allah that's a better guide than both (the Torah and the Qur'an), so I can follow it, if you're really so honest!"* [49] If they don't listen to you, it's because they're following nothing but their own whims. Who can be more wrong than the one who follows his own whims, lacking any guidance from Allah? Allah certainly won't guide people who do wrong. [50]

---

[880] The Qur'an asserted that it was a new revelation from Allah that affirmed the previous revelations of former prophets. The pagan Meccans, upon hearing of the miracles that were given to Moses, such as a staff turning into a snake or a blazing hand, asked where Muhammad's miracles were. Even though he performed some miracles, he always asserted that the main miracle he brought was the Qur'an, itself. However, the pagans merely said that that they didn't believe in either Moses' or Muhammad's miracles at all!

Accepting the Book

Background on verses 51-54: Some commentators believe that this passage was revealed in Medina in the year 628. At that time, forty emissaries from the Christian king of Abyssinia arrived in Medina to extend their king's greetings to Muhammad. The Prophet was in the midst of setting off for the fortress town of Khaybar to subdue it, and these men joined in the campaign. Some were wounded, but none were killed. Before they set off for their return journey to Africa, the ambassadors offered to send some funds to help the economically strapped Muslims, and they affirmed their belief that Islam and Christianity were compatible and complementary. (*Tabarani, Ma'ariful Qur'an*)

And so it is that We've reinforced (Our cascading revelations) by sending the spoken words (of scripture) to them so they can be reminded. [881] [51] Those to whom We sent scripture in the past believe in this one, too. [52]

When it's recited to them, they exclaim, *"We believe in it, for it's the truth from our Lord, and we were already submissive (to Allah's will before.)"* [53] They're going to be rewarded twice, for they persevered, used good to ward off evil and spent (in charity) out of what We gave to them. [882] [54]

When they hear useless talk, they turn away from it and say, *"Our actions count for us, and yours count for you. Peace be upon you; we're not looking (to associate with) ignorant people."* [883] [55]

---

[881] So the pagans of Mecca reject divine revelation? This verse is making the case that all three major texts, the Torah, Gospel and Qur'an, back each other up to such a degree that there is really no practical way for them to deny Allah any longer.

[882] This passage describes the way in which a righteous Jew and Christian will behave both before and after they have accepted Islam. They were the best example of their religion before and will be the best example of a Muslim later. Their reward is twice what others will get, for they believed in two messages from Allah. The Prophet said, "There are three types of people who will be given their reward twice: a person from among the Followers of Earlier Revelation who believed in his prophet and then believed in me; a servant who performs his duty well towards Allah and for whomever he works; and a man who has a maidservant and then educates her, teaches her refined manners, frees her and then marries her." (*Bukhari*)

[883] The commentators say that the best policy when dealing with an ignorant person is to do what this verse suggests. Since the saying *of peace be upon you* is a greeting, as well as a farewell in Islamic culture, the veiled idea is that when a person is confronted by an utterly ignorant fool, he or she should say *good-bye* to them and leave them alone, as nothing is to be gained from talking to a fool but stress and headache. (Also see 25:63.)

When Loved Ones don't Believe

Background on verse 56: This particular verse was revealed to console the Prophet concerning his beloved uncle, Abu Talib, who had just passed away while still unwilling to forsake his idols. (*Muslim*) The Prophet had approached him on his deathbed just before his demise and asked him to recite the testimony of faith. The Prophet's indirect paternal relative, Abu Jahl, was there also, and he kept trying hard to convince Abu Talib to die an idolater. Eventually Abu Talib agreed with Abu Jahl and said he would not forsake the religion of his father, who was an idolater. The Prophet told Abu Talib he would pray for his forgiveness anyway, but then another verse was revealed forbidding a Muslim from praying for forgiveness for an idolater. Some scholars have debated whether prayers for Christian and Jewish relatives are permissible, as they are not in the category of idolaters. (See 9:113) (*Bukhari, Muslim*)

You'll never be able to guide all those whom you love, though Allah guides whomever He wants, and He knows better who it is that accepts guidance. [884] [56]

Belief in Allah is not a Hindrance

Background on verses 57-60: The pagan tribe of Quraysh were the masters of Mecca, a major trading city and religious site of pilgrimage for people all over the peninsula. They were afraid that if they rejected idolatry, the hundreds of tribal groups that housed their idols in the city would revolt and drive the Quraysh from their favored position. Al-Harith ibn Uthman ibn 'Abd Munaf said the statement recounted in the verse below, and it refers to this situation. This passage was revealed to point out to him, and to the Quraysh in general, that their tribe was in power only by Allah's permission and that it was He Who could protect or destroy any nation. (*Nisa'i, Asbab ul-Nuzul*)

They say, *"If we followed this 'guidance' along with you, then we would surely be swept away from this land!"* However, didn't We already establish them in a secure sanctuary where all kinds of fruits are brought (in trade) as a bounty from Us? Yet, most of them don't understand. [57]

---

[884] This verse is a consolation to those who earnestly want their close friends and relatives to believe in Allah and follow the Godly path. In the Prophet's time, there were many heart-rending examples of converts who tried desperately to convince their loved ones to give up idolatry and worship Allah alone. Some were successful; others were not. In the end, we must remember that guidance is not in our power. It is between each individual and Allah.

How many towns have We destroyed that took pleasure in their (wealthy) lifestyles? Their ruins are deserted, and their remnants are few, and thus We were the inheritors (of their wealth and power). [58] And your Lord never destroyed any town unless He first sent a messenger among its main public places who would recite Our (revealed) verses to them. And We never destroyed any town unless its people were wrongdoers. [59]

What you've been given (in this life) is only useful for this life. It's (no more than) dazzling trinkets, [885] but (the rewards) that are with Allah are far better and longer lasting, so won't you think about that? [886] [60]

The Plight of the Doomed

> **Background on verse 61:** Most commentators say this verse refers to Hamza (the Prophet's uncle) and/or 'Ali ibn Abi Talib (the Prophet's cousin), both of whom were on the good side, and Abu Jahl (an indirect paternal relative of the Prophet and an ardent foe), who was on the side of evil. (*Ibn Kathir*)

Are they the same: the one to whom We've made a good promise and who will receive it; and the one to whom We've given the good things of this life, but who will then be dragged back for (harsh judgment on) the Day of Assembly? [61]

On that day, (Allah) will call out to (the sinners), asking, *"Where are My 'partners' that you've been imagining?"* [62] Those whose sentence of guilt will be proven true against them [887] will say, *"Our Lord! These are all the people whom we led astray, but we only led them astray because*

---

[885] The Prophet said, "Whoever has as his ultimate goal the (reward) of the next life, then Allah will endow his heart with richness; he'll be granted a secure and close family environment, and he'll get as much out of life as he wants, despite the uncooperativeness (of the world). However, the one who is obsessed with this life will be made by Allah to see financial ruin always before his eyes; his family ties will be broken, and he'll gain nothing from (the world) except for what he's been allowed to get." (*Tirmidhi*)

[886] The Prophet said, "By Allah, this life compared to the next life is like one of you dipping his fingertip into the sea; let him consider what he brings out." (*Ahmad*)

[887] The people who believed in false gods and idols, and who gained followers on account of it, will be asked to produce their 'partners' with Allah.

we, ourselves, were astray. We renounce them right here in front of You, for they weren't really worshipping us." [888] [63]

Then it will be said to (their sinful followers), *"So call on your 'partners' now!"* But even though they'll try to call upon them, their (heroes and false gods) won't listen. Then they're going to see the punishment that awaits them. *If only they would've listened to the guidance!* [64]

(Allah) will call to them that day, saying, *"How did you respond to your messengers?"* [65] However, all their arguments and excuses will get jumbled (in their minds), leaving them unable even to ask each other anything. [66] However, those who repented, believed and did what was morally right can hold out the hope that they'll be among the successful. [67]

All will Return to Allah Regardless

Background on verses 68-70: A man named Walid ibn Mughirah told the Prophet that Allah didn't have any say in the matter of who was a prophet or not. Thus, he would disbelieve in Muhammad's mission. This passage was revealed in response. (*Asbab ul-Nuzul*)

Your Lord creates whatever He wants and selects the best for (all creatures). [889] Glory be to Allah! He's high above what they join with Him. [68] Your Lord knows everything that their hearts hide and what they show. [69] He is Allah. There is no other god besides Him. All praise belongs to Him in the beginning and the end. The power to command belongs only to Him, and you're all going to go back to Him. [70]

---

[888] Many people throughout human history have claimed to be gods on earth or to have special communion with the supernatural. They will insist that they are not responsible for misleading others, for they themselves were without guidance. It is a lame excuse that passes the blame.

[889] This is a general phrase that points out that Allah made the environment in the best way for living creatures both because He willed it, and also because it was good for the creatures that have to live in it. The last phrase of this verse then, in effect, is telling us to give thanks to Allah for making something so beneficial, and also to realize that a god of wood or stone could not have accomplished such an amazing feat.

Day and Night are Blessings from Allah

Ask them, *"Don't you see it? If Allah made the night last forever, all the way to the Day of Assembly, then what other god besides Allah could bring you any form of light? Won't you listen?"* [71]

Then ask them, *"Don't you see it? If Allah made the daytime last forever, all the way to the Day of Assembly, then what other god besides Allah could bring the darkness of night upon you so you could rest? Won't you see it?"* [72]

It's from His mercy that He's established the (alternating pattern) of night and day, so you can have a rest cycle, and so you can go out in search of His bounty. This is (a reason) for you to be thankful. [73]

He'll call upon them one day, asking, *"Where are My 'partners' that you've been imagining?"* [74] Then We'll bring out a witness from every community and say, *"Now show your proof (that Allah has partners)."* That's when they'll know the truth of Allah, and whatever they invented will leave them to languish. [75]

Korah, the Arrogant

Background on verses 77-84: Korah had been favored under the rule of Pharaoh, even though he was a Hebrew, and he had enriched himself so mightily at their expense that the keys to his strongboxes were metaphorically so numerous it took strong men to carry them all.

Korah [890] was from among Moses' people, but he behaved contemptuously towards his fellows. We bestowed upon him so much wealth that the very keys to (his treasure chests) weighed down a group of strong men.

One day his people told him, *"Stop gloating, for Allah has no love for people who gloat.* [76] *Instead, use (the wealth) that Allah has given you to secure a home in the next life, without having to neglect your own needs in*

---

[890] Many commentators are of the view that Korah (Qarun) was a cousin of Moses, though there is no proof for this position. The story of Korah is also contained in the Bible in Numbers 16:1-35.

this world. Be good (to others), even as Allah has been good to you. Don't cause disorder in the earth, for Allah has no love for troublemakers." [77]

However, he answered them, saying, *"All this is mine from my own efforts and knowledge."* Didn't he know that Allah had already destroyed before him many generations that were far stronger and wealthier than whatever he amassed? However, the wicked are not always made to answer for their sins (in this life). [891] [78]

So (Korah) strutted around among his people in all his finery, and those who only desire what this physical life contains (saw him and) said, *"If only we had (the wealth) that Korah has! He's the master of tremendous good fortune!"* [79]

However, the truly learned people said, *"(We feel) sorry for you. Allah's reward is the best for those who believe and do what's morally right, though no one receives it except the patient."* [80]

We made the earth open wide, and it swallowed both him and his entourage. He didn't have any supporters who could help him against Allah – *he couldn't even help himself!* [892] [81]

Those who had envied his position just the day before were saying the very next morning, *"Allah increases or restricts the resources of any of His servants as He wills. If Allah's favor weren't upon us, He could've made the earth swallow us up, too! Those who reject Him are never successful."* [82]

We're going to grant the realm of the next life to those who have no desire to gloat nor cause trouble throughout the earth. [893] The

---

[891] There have been many sinners who have died before they seemed to receive their proper punishment in this world. We are not to worry, however, for no one can escape the court of Allah.

[892] The Prophet once made mention of Korah, saying, "When a man from among the people who came before your time went out wearing two green garments, walking proudly and arrogantly, Allah commanded the earth to swallow him up, and he will remain sunk in the earth until the Day of Resurrection." (*Ahmad*)

[893] 'Ali ibn Abi Talib is quoted as saying, "If a person wants the straps of his sandals to be better than the straps of his companion's sandals, then he is one of those spoken about in this verse." (*At-Tabari*) To understand the difference between feeling satisfaction and gloating, we can turn to the words of the Prophet who said, "It has been revealed to me

ultimate conclusion (is the best one) for those who are aware (of their duty to Allah). [83]

Whoever does good will be rewarded better than the value of what they did, but whoever does wrong will be punished only according to the value of their deeds. [84]

Continue to Strive despite the Odds

Background on verses 85-88: Ibn 'Abbas said that this passage was revealed to the Prophet when he emerged from the cave he was hiding in while on the run from the Meccans during his migration to Medina in the year 622. The Prophet had looked back in the direction of Mecca and felt sadness, and the angel put these words in his heart to console him. (*Ibn Kathir*)

The One Who bestowed the Qur'an upon you will surely bring you back to the destination. [894] So say (to them), "*My Lord knows better who is coming with guidance and who is clearly wrong.*" [85] You never expected that a Book would be sent down to you, but it was a mercy from your Lord, so do nothing that will help the faithless (against you). [86]

Let nothing turn you away from the (revealed) verses of Allah after they've been revealed to you. Invite all to your Lord, and don't mingle with idol-worshippers. [895] [87]

---

that you should be humble to the extent that none of you boasts to others or mistreats others." (*Muslim*) Are Muslims discouraged from wanting to look nice in public? No, for the Prophet was once asked the following question: "Messenger of Allah, I like to have good looking clothes and shoes – is this a kind of arrogance?" The Prophet answered, "No, for Allah is beautiful and loves beauty." (*Muslim*)

[894] A minority of classical scholars hold that this verse is a prediction to Muhammad that one day Allah will bring him back to Mecca in victory. Most scholars believe it refers to the next life.

[895] Even though a believer is not supposed to mingle freely with idolaters, nevertheless, they are not supposed to shun them insolently or rudely. The basic attitude of a Muslim is that all people are potential believers, and thus we must keep the door of invitation open. Many a convert came into Islam after experiencing the warmth and generosity of a sincere believer. Jalaluddin Rumi once commented on this in one of his teaching stories, saying, "The Jewish man told of his dream (in which he saw Moses) – oh, there are many Jews who have had a praiseworthy end. Don't spurn any unbeliever, for isn't there the hope that he may die as a Muslim? What do you know of his dying day, that you should forever turn your face from him?" *Mathnawi* VI, 2450.

Don't call upon any god other than Allah, for there is no other god besides Him. Everything will pass away except His face. The power to command is His, and you'll all be brought back to Him. [88]

The Spider

29 Al 'Ankabūt
Middle Meccan Period

This chapter was revealed just prior to the immigration of vulnerable Muslims to Abyssinia in the year 615. The grave tone in the first three verses is a clear indication that some of the Prophet's followers began to second guess their decision to join Islam in the face of the relentless persecution they faced at the hands of the Meccan pagans. Using the examples of past nations who were also put to the test, this chapter closes with a direct appeal from Allah to the beleaguered faithful to stand firm for Allah's sake.

In the Name of Allah,
the Compassionate, the Merciful

Background on verses 1-3: Even after the Prophet had left Mecca for the safer environment of Medina, people back in Mecca were still accepting Islam. The Prophet sent messages to them telling them they wouldn't be accepted as true Muslims until they immigrated to Medina. They replied that others who had attempted to leave suffered from the depredations of the idol-worshippers, and they were afraid of being harmed. This passage was revealed to strengthen their resolve, and the slow trickle of emigration resumed. (*Asbab ul-Nuzul*)

*A*lif. Lām. Meem. [1]

Do people think they're going to be left alone by just saying, "We believe," and that they won't be tested? [896] [2] We tested those who came before them, and Allah will make known who is true (in their belief), and He will make known who the liars are. [3]

---

[896] The Prophet said, "The people who are tested the most are the prophets, then the righteous, then the next best and the next best. A person will be tested in accordance with the degree of his religious commitment – the stronger the religious commitment, the stronger his test." (*Tirmidhi*)

Do those who do evil assume they can beat Us? [897] Well, their assumption is plain wicked! [4] Whoever places their hope in their meeting with Allah (should hold firm), for the deadline set by Allah is fast approaching, and He's the Hearing and the Knowing. [5]

Whoever strives (in the cause of Allah) is striving for (the good of) his own soul. Allah doesn't need anything from any part of the universe. [898] [6] Those who believe and do what's morally right will have all their past sins erased, so We can reward them according to what they did best. [7]

When *not* to Obey Parents

Background on verses 8-9: This passage was revealed about a companion named Sa'ad ibn Abi Waqqas, who converted to Islam against the wishes of his mother, yet remained with her, trying to care for her, despite her self-imposed hunger strike to protest his actions. In his own words, Sa'ad recounts: "When my mother heard the news of my conversion to Islam, she flew into a rage. She approached me and said, 'O Sa'ad! What is this religion that you've embraced that has taken you away from the religion of your mother and father? By Allah, either you forsake your new religion, or I will not eat or drink until I die. Your heart will be broken with grief for me and remorse will consume you on account of the deed you've done - people will blame you forever.' 'Don't do (such a thing), my mother,' I said, 'for I won't give up my religion for anything.' However, she went on with her threat... For days she neither ate nor drank. She became emaciated and weak. Hour after hour, I went to her, asking whether I should bring her some food or drink, but she stubbornly refused, insisting that she would neither eat nor drink until she died or until I abandoned my religion. So I said to her, 'O my Mother! In spite of my strong love for you, my love for Allah and His Messenger is indeed stronger. By Allah, if you had a thousand souls and each one

---

[897] During the height of Meccan persecution, one Muslim tradesman, a blacksmith named Khabab ibn Aratt, related the following story: "I used to be a blacksmith in Mecca, and once I did some work for Al-As ibn Wa'il. When I went to collect my payment, he told me, 'I won't pay you unless you renounce Muhammad.'" Later, according to Khabab, while he was sitting with the Prophet near the Ka'bah, he said to him, "Messenger of Allah, now the persecution is out of control, so why don't you pray to Allah (for help)?" The Prophet became distraught and said, "The believers before your time were persecuted much more than you. Their bones were scraped with iron combs, and their heads were cut with saws. Still they didn't give up their faith. I assure you that Allah will fulfill this mission. There will come a time of such peace that someone could travel from Sana to Hadaramawt, and he'll have no fear from anyone, save Allah. However, you people have already become impatient." (*Bukhari*)

[898] Lit. 'from any world.' It must be remembered in all of our practice of religious devotion that Allah does not need it from us, and He is not harmed if people do not worship and serve Him. Rather, we need Allah, and by applying spiritual and religious knowledge and practice within our lives, we are really doing what is ultimately good for us, both in this life and in the next.

departed one after another, I would not abandon this religion for anything.' When she saw that I was determined, she relented unwillingly and then ate and drank." (*Muslim, Tirmidhi, Ahmad*)

We have made it a duty upon every human being that they should show kindness to their parents. However, if (your parents) ever strive to make you set up partners with Me after everything you've learned, then don't obey them. [899] All of you will return to Me, and I will tell you the meaning of all that you did. [8] Those who believed and did what was morally right will be admitted among the righteous. [900] [9]

The Weak in Spirit

Among people there are some who say, "*We believe in Allah.*" However, if they undergo any hardship in Allah's (cause), they act as if the people who were oppressing them were somehow the very punishment of Allah laid upon them! Then, if your Lord provides you with some kind of help, they're quick to say, "*We've always been on your side!*" Doesn't Allah know better what's in the hearts of (all beings) in the universe? [10] Allah knows who the true believers are, and He knows who the hypocrites are. [11]

All are Responsible for Themselves

Background on verses 12-13: Muhammad publicly asserted on many occasions that people will have to answer to Allah for the evil that they do. Some of the idol-worshippers actually taunted the small cadre of Muslims, saying that if they would only rededicate themselves to the idols, then their pagan neighbors would take their sins upon themselves. Since the idol-worshippers didn't believe in sins anyway, they were really being sarcastic. This verse was revealed in response to that situation. (*Asbab ul-Nuzul*)

The faithless say to the believers, "*Follow our way, and we'll pay for your sins ourselves,*" but they'll never be able to pay for anyone else's sins in the least - and they're all liars! [12]

---

[899] Also see 31:14-15.

[900] The scholars are generally of the opinion that verses 8-9 were revealed in the Medinan Period.

They'll have to bear their own load, with much more added besides. Then, on the Day of Assembly, they'll have to answer for all their false assertions. [901] [13]

The Call of the Prophets is often Ignored

And so it was that We sent Noah to his people. He dwelt among them fifty years shy of a thousand. [902] Yet, (even after all his preaching), the flood overwhelmed those who persisted in wrongdoing. [14] We saved him and his followers in the boat, and We made it a sign for all (people) everywhere. [903] [15]

---

[901] The Prophet said, "Beware of doing injustice, for on the Day of Resurrection, Allah will swear an oath, saying, 'By My glory and majesty, no injustice will be overlooked today.' Then a voice will call out, 'Where is so-and-so, the son of so-and-so?' He will be brought forward, followed by his good deeds which will seem like mountains, so much so that the gathered throngs will gaze at them in wonderment, until that person is standing before the Compassionate (Allah). Then the voice will be commanded to say, 'Whoever is owed something by so-and-so or was wronged by him, let him come forward now.' So they will come forward and gather before the Compassionate. Then the Compassionate will say, 'Settle the accounts for My servant.' The (angels) will ask, 'How can we settle the account?' He will say, 'Take from his good deeds and give it to them.' They will keep taking from his good deeds until there is nothing left, and there will still be people with scores to settle. Allah will say, 'Settle the accounts for My servant.' The (angels) will say, 'He doesn't even have one good deed left.' Allah will say, 'Take from their evil deeds and give them to him.'" Then the Prophet recited this verse. (*Ibn Kathir*, with a similar report in *Muslim*)

[902] The Qur'an states that Noah lived 950 years. According to Genesis 5:3-32, many people in ancient times lived for centuries. (Adam lived for 930 years!) Genesis 9:29 states that Noah was 950 years old when he died. (He was 600 years old when the flood began, according to Genesis 7:6.) In modern times, a select few have lived for 120 years or more. If Noah lived as long as he did, then it can be assumed he married and was a widower many times over. In the ancient Sumerian accounts of the survivor of the flood, the name for Noah is Ziasudra. (His father is the author of one of the oldest texts in the world called the Instructions of Shurupak, in which moral precepts are listed.) In later Akkadian and Babylonian versions the name is Utnapishtim. These names mean, "He of long life," and "He found life" respectively. (Genesis 6:4 and Numbers 13:33 in the Bible mention that there were also 'giants' in those days. Although the Qur'an does not say this, there is an obscure prophetic tradition that says that Adam was something of a giant.)

[903] The commentators differ over what this means. Some hold that it means that Noah's boat will remain on the side of the mountain for future generations to discover and take a lesson from it. Others say that Noah, who might have lived as long at six thousand years ago, was the first to develop the concept of a large cargo vessel and that the memory and knowledge of ship building would remain after him. Still a third group believes it is merely the story of Noah and the flood that has remained and enlivened the imaginations of peoples everywhere. Indeed, ancient Sumerian and Babylonian records also make mention of a time of floods, even as the Hebrews carried this story with them for ages.

Abraham (was also sent to his people), and he told them, *"Serve Allah, and be mindful of Him! That's the best thing for you if you only knew!* [16] *You're worshipping idols besides Allah, and you're making up nothing but myths. Those things you worship besides Allah have no power to provide you with resources (for your survival). So look for your necessities of life from Allah. Serve Him, and give Him thanks, for you're all going to go back to Him.* [17] *If you deny this, well, generations before you denied it, as well. The duty of a messenger is only to convey the teachings clearly."* [904] [18]

Haven't they seen how Allah initiated the creation and then repeats it? That's easy for Allah to do. [19]

So say (to them), *"Travel all over the world, and see how Allah initiated the creation. In the same way will He recreate (it all) once more, for Allah has power over all things.* [20] *He punishes whom He pleases and is merciful to whom He wills, and back to Him will you all return.* [21] *Whether you flee through the earth or fly through the sky, you won't be able to elude Him, for you have no one else to protect you or help you besides Allah."* [22]

Those who reject the signs of Allah and their coming appointment with Him, they're the ones who have no hope of My mercy. They're the ones who will suffer a painful punishment. [23]

The Blessings of Abraham

The only answer Abraham's people gave to him was to say, *"Kill him! Burn him alive!"* However, Allah saved him from the flames, and there are signs in this for people who believe. [24]

(Abraham) said to them, *"You've taken idols for yourselves in place of Allah, just because it makes you feel a close bond in this life.* [905] *On the Day of Assembly you're all going to disown each other and curse at each other.*

---

904 The messenger conveys the message, but it is up to the people to choose to listen or not. The messenger will not be blamed if he is ignored.

905 The practice of idolatry in Mesopotamia was elaborate, and the tight rituals lent a certain kind of community spirit to the society. Idolatry became the glue that held the community together. Thus, it was the foundation for their communal love and loyalty.

Your final destination will be in the Fire, and there will be no one to help you!" [25]

The Story of Lot

Lot believed (in what) his (uncle Abraham taught), and he said, *"I'll forsake my home for my Lord, for He's the Powerful and the Wise."* [26] We (further blessed Abraham) with a line of descendants through Isaac and Jacob and instituted prophethood and scripture among them. We rewarded him in this life, and in the next life he's going to be with the righteous. [27]

Lot said to his people, *"You're more perverted than any other people that existed in all the universe!* [28] *Are you approaching other men (for intimacy) and even accosting them on the roads (for your lusts)? You do such abomination in your clubs, as well!"*

His people gave him no other answer but to say, *"So bring Allah's punishment down upon us, if you're really so honest!"* [29]

"My Lord!" he cried. *"Help me against these depraved people!"* [30]

Then Our (angelic) messengers went to Abraham with the awaited news and told him, *"We're going to destroy the people of this place, for they're wrongdoers."* [31] *"But Lot is there!"* (Abraham) interjected.

"We know who's there," they answered, *"and we're going to save him and his followers, but not his wife, for she will remain behind."* [32]

When our messengers went to Lot, he became worried (for their safety). He felt powerless (to protect) them (from his wicked people). (The angels) told him, *"Don't be afraid or worried, for we're here to save you and your followers, though your wife will remain behind.* [33] *We're going to bring (Allah's) punishment down from the sky upon the people of this settlement, for they're in a state of evil rebellion."* [34]

And so it was that We left (the destruction of their land) as an evident sign for people who think. [35]

Madyan and Pharaoh Perish

To (the land of) Madyan went their brother Shu'ayb, and he said, *"My people! Serve Allah, and be mindful of the Last Day. Don't spread the evil of corruption in the land."* [36] Yet, they denied him and were seized by a blast that left them cowering in their homes by the morning. [37]

And (the people of) 'Ad and of Thamud - the ruins of their settlements are laid out clearly for your inspection. [906] Satan made their (evil) deeds seem right to them, and he steered them all away from the path (of Allah), even though they were very far-sighted peoples. [38] And Korah, Pharaoh and Haman - Moses went to them in the past with clear evidence (of the truth). Yet, they acted outrageously in the land, *but they couldn't get away from Us!* [39]

We seized each of (those wrongdoers) for their sins. Among them were some who suffered from deadly sandstorms; some were shattered with deadly blasts; some were swallowed up by the earth, while others were drowned (in the sea). Allah wasn't the author of their harm, however, for they brought harm to their own souls. [40]

The Example of the Spider

The example of those who take protectors other than Allah is that of a spider that builds its dwelling (out of delicate webs), for the flimsiest of homes is the home of the spider, if they only knew. [907] [41]

---

906 The ruins of ancient cities dot northern Arabia on into Jordan. Some of these are associated with the Thamud people. Where are the ruins of the city that the 'Ad used to inhabit? Muslim commentators in the past were unsure of the identity of their capital city of Iram, which was known to the Greeks as Ubar, but the first definitive proof of a city named Iram came in 1975 when archeologists unearthed the ancient city of Ebla in northwestern Syria. There amid the ruins, which were over 4,500 years old, was a huge cache of ancient tablets, which recorded the dealings of Ebla and other cities. One of the cities mentioned was Iram. In the year 1992, archeologists discovered the ancient city of the 'Ad in present day Oman, and its physical description matched that found in the Qur'an. It is also probable that the name of this city survived in legends throughout some parts of Arabia, given that when it thrived it was an important trade center and land of expensive incense cultivation. See 50:13 and footnote.

907 Besides the obvious meaning that a spider's web is easy to break and thus is a good example of the weakness of believing in idols, some commentators have also suggested another dimension to this verse, as the females of many species of spiders often devour their male suitors after mating. This makes the spider's home life even that much more

Allah knows what they're calling upon besides Him, for He's the Powerful and the Wise. [42] These are the kinds of metaphors that We lay out for people; yet, no one understands them save for those who have knowledge. [908] [43] Allah created the heavens and the earth for a truthful purpose, and there are signs in this for the believers. [44]

Stay the Course with Allah's Support

Recite what is being inspired to you of the Book, and establish prayer, for prayer discourages shameful behavior and bad deeds. The remembrance of Allah is even greater, and Allah knows what you're doing. [909] [45]

Don't argue with the Followers of Earlier Revelation except in a better way, unless it's with those who are corrupt among them. [910] Say (to them), *"We believe in the revelation that's come down to us and also in*

---

fragile! Some scholars have suggested that due to this verse, it is undesirable to kill spiders. (*Ma'ariful Qur'an*)

[908] The Prophet once recited this verse to a group of people, and then he said, "That person is knowledgeable, the one who ponders over the message of Allah, acts obediently to Him, and keeps away from those actions that He does not like." (*Baghawi*)

[909] Regular prayer reminds a person to be moral. The ritual prayers in Islam are performed at five strategic points throughout the day. Thus, there is never any period of more than a few hours where prayer isn't performed or has been performed. What of a person who prays and still does bad things? Chapter 107 records the case of such a person who prays 'only for show.' A companion named Abu Hurayrah went to the Prophet and said, "So-and-so prays at night, but when morning comes he steals." At first the Prophet asked, "What are you saying – that (merely praying) will stop him from doing that?" (*Ahmad*) Then the Prophet said, "Soon the prayer will persuade him to stop." The man eventually did reform himself. (*Ibn Kathir*) The prayer is a type of daily spiritual exercise. Those who gain benefit from it excel at moral growth and become more conscious of avoiding sinful behavior. Those who are careless in their prayers still have some good influence from them and perhaps keep from falling further into error. Those who pray, but it has no effect on them, are the most unfortunate of all. It's like a man who eats spoonfuls of food and then spits them back out. No benefit comes from the mere act of chewing unless you're willing to swallow the food, which in this case is the lesson. Once the Prophet saw a man praying in the mosque, and the man kept fidgeting with his beard and clothes all throughout. The Prophet said of him, "If there was any humbleness in his heart, you would have seen it in his body." In other words, he would have been concentrating and meditating upon Allah's praise, not worrying about his appearance.

[910] This verse is commonly interpreted to mean that a Muslim debater should not descend to a vulgar or emotional level in a public dialogue. Rather, he or she should speak in a dignified way, even if the opposing side becomes testy, irrational or rude.

what's come down to you. Our God and your God are the same, and we surrender to His will." [46]

And so We've sent the Book to you, (Muhammad). (Some of) those to whom We've already given scripture in the past have faith in it, as do some of these (former pagans of Arabia). [911] No one repudiates Our (revealed) verses save for those who suppress (their faith). [912] [47]

You were never able to recite a book (of scripture) before this, nor could you have ever written one with your right hand. If you would've (been known to recite verse in public or write) before, then the babblers would have had a valid reason to doubt. [913] [48] But no! The (fact that you never did these things before) is a sign for the insightful. No one repudiates Our (revealed) verses but the corrupt. [49]

Then they say, *"So why are no miracles being sent down to him from His Lord?"* Tell them, *"Miracles are indeed with Allah, but I'm only a plain warner."* [50] Isn't it enough for them that We've sent down a book to you that's recited in front of them? There are merciful (teachings) within it and reminders for the believers. [51]

Say (to them), *"Allah is witness enough between you and me. He knows what's in the heavens and the earth. Those who believe in falsehood and reject Allah – they're going to be the losers."* [52]

---

911 While in Mecca, Muhammad would sometimes preach to visiting Jews and Christians who came for trade and business. Some of them converted to Islam, just as some of the pagan Arabs did, as this verse references.

912 The Prophet said that Allah, Himself, said, "I am testing you and testing others through you, (Muhammad,) revealing to you a book which cannot be washed away by water, which you recite while you're asleep and while you're awake." (*Muslim*)

913 Although Mecca held regular poetry contests, and there were even renowned public podiums for people to display their talent daily, Muhammad was never a participant in these forums. He was not known among his peers as a man of rhymed language, nor did he know how to write. (After prophethood, he employed dozens of scribes to do this for him.) The Qur'an is pointing that fact out here, primarily as a way to remind the Meccans of what has occurred: a man who never recited or wrote before is suddenly blazing with elegant verse and expounding upon organized essays and sermons that are being recorded and distributed. As the next verse offers, there is a sign in this inexplicable phenomenon. If Muhammad were a known poet or writer before the beginning of his ministry at forty years of age, then the people could have fairly accused him of being overly creative or delusional in his own talent.

They're asking you to bring on the punishment (about which you've warned them). If it wasn't for the fact that there's a fixed time limit (for their civilization to exist), then the punishment would've surely come upon them (already) - *and it will come upon them, when they won't even (see it) coming!* [53] So are they really asking you to bring on the punishment?

Truly, Hellfire will surround those who covered up (their ability to believe)! [54] On the day when punishment will overshadow them from above and below, they'll be told, *"Suffer the results of your actions!"* [55]

A Direct Appeal from Allah

Background on verse 57: This verse was revealed before the migration to Medina. As you can see, the Prophet and his followers were being primed for their coming abandonment of their hometown. As hard as it is to move, remaining in an evil city is worse. Medina was going to be much better for Islam to grow and be safe. The Prophet once said, "All cities belong to Allah, and all people are His servants. Therefore, wherever you find goodness, you live there." (*Ahmad*)

My believing servants! My earth is wide, so serve Me, (even if it means migrating to a safer place). [56] Every soul will taste of death, and in the end you'll be brought back to Us. [57] Those who believed and did what was morally right will be given a home in the Garden. They shall dwell within mansions beneath which rivers flow, and there they shall remain (forever)! How excellent a reward for doing (good)! [58] They were patient, and they put their trust in their Lord. [59]

The Contributions of Allah cannot be Discounted

Background on verse 60: The Prophet and Ibn 'Umar, the son of his dear friend, were visiting the home of one of the Helpers, or Medinan converts, and the Prophet began to eat some dates. He saw that Ibn 'Umar wasn't eating. He offered him some, but Ibn 'Umar refused to eat, saying he had no appetite for them. The Prophet then said, "I've got an appetite for them since I've just passed four days without really eating anything, knowing that if I asked my God, He would provide for me like Caesar or the Emperor of Persia. So what do you think about people who earn their own living?" Then this verse was revealed, and the Prophet recited it. (*Asbab ul-Nuzul*)

How many creatures are out there that aren't equipped with the resources they need to survive? [914] Allah provides for both them and you, and He's the Hearing and the Knowing. [60]

If you asked them who created the heavens and the earth and who subjected the sun and the moon (to natural laws), they would surely answer, "*Allah.*" So why are they so confused? [61]

Allah increases the resources of whichever of His servants that He wills, and He likewise restricts them (for whichever of them He wills), for Allah knows about all things. [62] If you asked them who it was who sends down water from the sky and uses it to bring life to the barren earth, they would surely answer, "*Allah.*" Then say (to them), "*So praise be to Allah!*" However, most of them don't reason well. [63]

What is there in this world except distractions and games? The realm of the next life is where the real living is, if they only knew. [64]

Now if they were to set sail on a boat, they would call upon Allah (for safe passage) with sincere conviction, for (in that case they would recognize) that He owns all religion. Then, after He deposited them safely back on the shore, they would go and make partners with Him, [65] thanklessly snubbing what He gave them and plunging themselves into endless diversions! Soon they're going to know (the truth)! [915] [66]

---

[914] In general, living creatures have to go out in search of sustenance – they're not born with some sort of self-replicating food supply built into their bodies. All creatures know how to go out and find their food, and Allah provides the resources they need.

[915] After the Muslims successfully occupied Mecca in a peaceful surrender, a handful of pagans fled, thinking that the Prophet would take vengeance upon them for their criminal deeds during the long years of persecution and conflict that the Muslims endured at their hands. 'Ikrimah, the son of Abu Jahl (who was a bitter foe of the Prophet), journeyed to the Red Sea and booked passage on a ship bound for Abyssinia. During the voyage, a sudden squall overtook the boat, and it began to rock violently in the waves. The crew of the boat began to ask the passengers to pray to Allah for deliverance, for no one could save them except Him. (The sailors were probably Christians.) As 'Ikrimah reports, he said to himself, "By Allah, if there is no one who can save us on the sea except Him, then there is no one who can save us on land except Him, either." Then 'Ikrimah made a vow: "O Allah, I vow to you that if I come out of this, I will go and put my hand in the hand of Muhammad, and I will find him kind and merciful." The boat made it to shore, and 'Ikrimah reversed his journey and returned to Mecca, where he repented to Allah and declared himself a Muslim at the Prophet's hand. In later years, he became a scholar of religious knowledge. (*At-Tabarani*)

Don't (the Meccans) see that although We've granted them a secure sanctuary (in their midst), yet even still people are being swept up (into Islam) all around them? [916] Even so, they're still believing in false things and rejecting Allah's favors! [917] [67]

Who does more wrong than the one who invents a lie against Allah or denies the truth when it comes to him? Isn't there a home in Hellfire reserved for those who (willfully) suppress (their awareness of the truth)? [68]

As for those who strive in Our (cause), We're going to guide them to the paths [918] (that will lead them back to) Us, for Allah is with those who are good. [69]

---

[916] Even though the Quraysh tribe of Mecca lived in a city with a shrine that, by their own admission was built by Abraham and dedicated to the One God, and even though, despite their best efforts to persecute Muhammad and the Muslims, the peoples of surrounding territories were converting to the faith with ever greater frequency, these same 'custodians' of Mecca continued bowing to idols made of wood, stone and even animal bones. They just didn't get it!

[917] This verse continues to have relevance even into modern times. Even though the enemies of Allah seem to have every advantage over the believers, still the numbers of Muslims swell all throughout the world, due to both conversion and natural increase. Even after all the challenges Muslims have faced, Islam has never stopped growing.

[918] There are many different roads that people may take before they reach the path of Allah. Some people must travel through a variety of roads in life, both good and bad, before their hearts ultimately open to the one path of Allah. It is for this reason that Allah gives people (and nations) some time in their lives to make choices, learn and then reassess what they've been doing. Our time limits are all different, and none of us knows how long we have. Therefore, the sooner we stop being deluded by this temporary life of pleasure and get on with the task of learning about the truth, purpose, usefulness and meaning of our lives, the better!

The Romans

30 Ar-Rūm

Middle Meccan Period

Starting in the year 612, the Persian Empire launched a series of devastating attacks against the Byzantine Romans in Syria, Egypt and even into Anatolia itself. With barbarian invaders to the west, governors revolting in the north, east and south and the mighty Persians rampaging through their eastern lands, the Byzantines looked as if they might be wiped out - even their capital city of Constantinople was put briefly under siege.

These events were set in motion within the first two or three years of the Prophet's ministry in Mecca, and as the years passed with greater Persian success, these events had propaganda value for the pagans. The Byzantines were Christians who believed more or less in one God, while the Persians presided over an empire filled with idolatry and who themselves subscribed to the dualistic religion of Zoroastrianism.

The Meccans taunted the Muslims, telling them that this was a sign that their One God was defeated and fleeing. The Muslims were despondent and unable to respond until this chapter was revealed in about the year 620. The opening verses boldly predicted that the Romans would recover and move on to defeat their enemy within three to nine years.

When the significance of this revelation became clear, Abu Bakr cheerfully went through the streets of Mecca telling everyone about it. One of the leaders of the Quraysh, Ubayy ibn Khalaf, offered to make a bet with Abu Bakr about this.

Abu Bakr agreed, but Ibn Khalaf made him agree to the middle figure of six years, which is in between the three to nine years that the word *bid'* implies in Arabic. (This was before betting was made illegal in Islam.) If the Byzantines were not victorious within six years, then Abu Bakr would have to pay.

Six years passed with no clear Roman victory, and Abu Bakr had to pay up. Early the following year, however, the Byzantines inflicted a crushing defeat upon the Persians at Nineveh (in 627) and forced them to flee back to their home territory, and many Muslims told Abu Bakr he was wrong for settling on a single year when *bid'* meant from three to nine years. Because this unlikely prediction made by the Qur'an came true, many new converts entered the fold of Islam. [919] (*Tirmidhi*)

---

[919] Some versions of the story have the Prophet asking Abu Bakr to hold to the full nine years as his bet, and thus he won a hundred camels from the heirs of the recently deceased

In the Name of Allah,
the Compassionate, the Merciful

A*lif. Lām. Meem.* [1]

The Romans have been defeated [2] in the lowest place on earth, [920] but they'll be victorious (over their Persian enemies), in spite of this defeat, [3] in three to nine years time. [921]

> **Background on verses 4-6:** One of the Meccan idol-worshippers had boasted to the Muslims, "You have a scripture, and the Christians also have a scripture, but we are without any scripture. Our Persian brothers have overcome your Roman brothers, and so shall we overcome you if you ever try to fight us." This passage was revealed in response. (*Asbab ul-Nuzul*)

Command over the past and the future belongs to Allah, and when that day (of victory arrives), the believers will be the ones celebrating [4] with Allah's help. [922] He helps whomever He wants, for He's the

---

Ibn Khalaf. The Prophet told Abu Bakr to donate them to charity, as he did not approve of gains made by gambling, even though the Qur'an had not officially prohibited it yet. (*Ma'ariful Qur'an.*)

[920] The Persians defeated the Byzantine Romans on a battlefield by the Dead Sea in about 613, which is a region that has the lowest elevation on earth (approx. 395 meters below sea level). Although many translators usually translate the Arabic term *adna* as *nearest*, the root word *dani* literally means the *lowest*. Besides, northern Palestine is nowhere 'near' to Mecca, being several weeks worth of journeying away by caravan, so the true meaning of *adna* - which is *lowest* - has to be presented as it is. Where is the internal evidence to support the use of the word this way? The Qur'an uses a related form of the word frequently in the phrase *hayat ad-dunya*, which means the life of the *lower* (world), i.e., the life of this physical world as opposed to the Next Life *up* in Heaven. This is a fascinating detail about the geographic lay of the land that would have been completely unknown to anyone alive at that time. News of this decisive battle reached into Arabia, and the pagans of Mecca taunted the Muslims, saying that a monotheistic power (the Byzantine Romans) was defeated by a pagan one (the Persians).

[921] In Arabic parlance, the amount of time mentioned in this verse (*bid'i sineen*) is any number between three to nine years. The Persians began their assaults on the Byzantine lands in the year 612. This chapter was revealed in approximately 620, when the Persians were on the verge of total victory. The Byzantines, however, snatched victory back after almost certain defeat a few years later in 627 and turned the tide against the Persians who steadily had to give ground thereafter. Thus, the prediction of the Qur'an was fulfilled in approximately seven years. The Persians were forced to sign a humiliating peace treaty in December of the year 628.

[922] When the Byzantines did achieve victory, the Muslims were elated, and the idol-worshippers were now despondent, as the forces of monotheism triumphed over the forces of theistic dualism. This swayed some people in Mecca to convert to Islam.

411

Powerful and the Merciful. [5] (This is) Allah's promise, and Allah never backs away from His promise, but most people don't understand. [6]

They only understand the outward aspects of the life of this world, while they're unconcerned with the next life. [923] [7] Haven't they pondered (this question) within themselves, that perhaps Allah didn't create the heavens and the earth and everything in between them except for a valid reason and a limited time? Even so, there are still many people who deny the meeting they have with their Lord. [8]

Haven't they traveled throughout the earth and seen what happened to all those (civilizations) that came before them? They were stronger than (these people here today) and worked the land and populated it in far greater numbers than they ever could've done.

Messengers went to them with clear evidence (of Allah's truth; yet, they rejected them). It wasn't Allah Who did them any wrong; rather, they wronged their own souls. [9] In the end, the final result for evil is greater evil in return, for they denied the signs of Allah and treated them as a joke! [10]

The Verdict is for Allah Alone

Allah is the One Who initiates the creation and then repeats it, [924] and then all of you will go back to Him. [11] On the day when the Hour (of Judgment) is established, the guilty will stagger along in despair. [12] They'll have no one to intercede for them among their 'partners,' and what's more they're going to reject their 'partners' (as false friends). [13]

---

[923] They see the material world and understand it only in terms of how to use it. They see nothing deeper in it, no meaning, no truth and no destiny. Ibn 'Abbas (d. 687) said that this verse means, "The faithless know how to prosper in the world, but they're ignorant in matters of religion." (At-Tabari) Hasan al-Basri (d. 737) said, "The world has reached such a state that any one of them could put a coin on his finger and tell how much it weighed, but he doesn't know how to pray properly." (Ibn Kathir)

[924] This refers to the original creation of the material universe and then to the second recreation when the dead are raised to life for judgment.

On the day when the Hour is established, that will be the day when they'll be divided into categories. [14] Those who had faith and did what was morally right will rejoice in ecstasy, [15] while those who rejected faith and denied Our signs and their meeting in the next life will be taken in for punishment. [16]

So glorify Allah in the evening and when you rise up in the morning [17] - *all praise within the heavens and the earth belongs to Him* - (glorify Him) in the late afternoon and at midday, as well. [925] [18] He brings life from death and death from life, and He gives life to the earth after it was dead. [926] *And that's how you're going to be brought out (of your graves at the resurrection)!* [927] [19]

Evidence of Allah's Hand in Human Society

Among His signs is the fact that He created you from dust. Then from that (simple substance), you became widely scattered mortals! [928] [20] And among His signs is the fact that He created spouses for you from among your own kind so you can dwell with them in harmony.

---

[925] Four of the daily ritual prayers are mentioned here: *Fajr, Zuhr, 'Asr* and *Maghrib*. In English they are the prayers before dawn, just after noon, late afternoon and sunset. The Prophet also was accustomed to praying a fifth time, called *'Isha*, at night, long after sunset. The five daily prayers were not made a duty upon all Muslims until the Prophet and his followers immigrated to Medina in 622. Verses 11:114 and 24:58 specifically mention this fifth prayer (*'Isha*) as a duty. Also see 20:130 where all five prayer times are mentioned in one verse.

[926] The Prophet once said, "Remember death, the destroyer of pleasures, for not a day passes upon the grave except it says 'I am the house of remoteness; I am the house of loneliness; I am the house of dirt; I am the house of worms.'" (*Tirmidhi*)

[927] The Prophet said that whoever recites these verses [17-19] in the morning, then all the deficiencies in his deeds during the day will be repaired, and if one recites them at night, then all the deeds of the night will be repaired of deficiencies, as well. (*Tabarani, Abu Dawud*)

[928] Unlike any other species, humans can be found in nearly every corner of the world, even though our beginnings were as nomadic tribesmen in East Africa, the place where our ancestors were first established. The Prophet said, "Allah created Adam from a handful taken from throughout the earth. Thus, the sons of Adam vary (in color) as the earth varies, so they are white, red, black and in between, and they're both evil and good, easy-going and difficult." (*Abu Dawud, Ahmad, Tirmidhi*) Thus, depending on where people are on the earth, their physical characteristics are shaped by their local environment. This adaptability has allowed humans to flourish all over the globe in many widely diverse regions. Out of many colors, we still all have the same basic form and nature.

929 Indeed, He put love and mercy between you, 930 and there are signs in this for people who think. 931 [21]

Among His signs are the creation of the heavens and the earth and the differences in your languages and skin colors. There are indeed signs in this for people who know. [22] Among His signs are the occasions during the night and day when you sleep, and also your daily search for the resources that His bounty provides. There are signs in this for those who listen. [23]

Among His signs that He exhibits to you is the lightning that causes you to hope (for rain), as well as to fear (for your lives). [932] He

---

929 Marriage is a civil partnership in the Islamic worldview. It is not a dictatorship of the husband, despite what some rustics seek to promote. The wife is not even responsible for doing the housework, as Islamic scholars often point out. If she does it and other domestic chores, it is a favor for the husband for which Allah will reward her. Otherwise he has to hire a housekeeper! (In Islamic law, the wife can have her own job, property and income independent of the man and can use it as she wills without his permission, in addition to getting the benefit of being supported by him in her daily needs for food and shelter.) There is no verse in the Qur'an that tells women that they must 'obey' their husbands blindly, such as one finds in the New Testament in Ephesians 5:22-24, Colossians 3:18, I Peter 3:1-6 and I Corinthians 11:3.

930 The Prophet said, "Allah has divided mercy into one hundred parts, out of which he retained ninety-nine parts with Him and has sent the one remaining to earth. From this one part emanates all the compassion that the whole of creation shows towards each other. So much so that an animal will lift her hoof above her young lest it should get hurt." (*Bukhari*) Also see footnote to 2:24.

931 The Prophet once remarked that when a husband and wife look upon each other with love, then Allah looks upon them in mercy. Muhammad demonstrated how affection and love are expressed in daily life with his own wives. He used to hold hands openly with whichever wife he was walking in public, and sometimes he would walk arm-in-arm with her. He was very patient in his demeanor and would compliment his wives. He also lent a hand in the household chores, washing and mending his own clothes, for example. He once advised people that the best man is the one who is the kindest to his wife.

932 Most people in our modern world are far removed from the raw forces of nature – existing in a world of steel, stone and artificial light. Think back to a simpler time when a person standing on an open plain would see the darkness of an approaching storm, smell the damp air and see the fingers of lightning coming ever closer. In that sense, he or she could literally feel and taste the coming of the storm. We are removed from those realities by our illusion of control over our environment, but sometimes that illusion is shattered when nature overwhelms our puny structures and defenses. The man and woman who would be awakened back to the awe of Allah should step out of doors once in a while and let themselves experience the power of the forces that rage all around us – whether it be a sunny walk in a forest, sitting in the stillness of a cold night, climbing a lonely mountain trail, watching the sun rise from a meadow or a park, wading into the rushing surf or watching an approaching storm in awe of its destructive presence. These

sends down water from the sky and uses it to revive the earth after it was barren. There are indeed signs in this for the thoughtful. [24] Among His signs is the fact that the sky and the earth stand firmly by His command. However, when He calls to you with a single shout, you'll emerge from (your graves) in the earth! [25]

All (creatures) that reside within the heavens and the earth belong to Him, and they're all devoted to Him. 933 [26] He's the One Who initiates the creation and then repeats it. That's easy for Him to do. All throughout the heavens and the earth, the most stunning examples 934 are His, for He's the Powerful and the Wise. [27]

Use Your Common Sense

Now He's going to set out for you an example taken from your own selves. Do you take partners from among your servants to share *equally* in the wealth We've given you? Do you feel the same kind of fear towards them as you would feel fear towards each other? 935 This is how we explain the verses precisely for people who use their reason. [28]

But no! The wrongdoers follow their own whims instead of knowledge. So who can guide those whom Allah leaves astray? They'll have no one to help them (escape from the punishment they deserve). [29]

---

things reconnect us to the world that Allah made for us and teach us to be thankful for the safety we enjoy for a while.

933 While some modern thinkers have taken this verse, and other verses like it, as a hint that there may be extraterrestrial life, the reference to the beings in the heavens could refer either to jinns, angels or the many trillions of tiny microbes that can be found floating in earth's upper atmosphere – some of which have been collected by scientists in the mesosphere, a region as high as forty miles above the earth's surface on the borders of outer space!

934 Whatever examples we can think of to describe Allah's power fall short of reality. Allah's example is more stunning than our minds can conceive. Whatever metaphors and similes we can use to help us understand this point, in our own limited language conceptions, must suffice.

935 This is an obvious address to the pagans, who thought slaves were nothing more than property. Would they take a slave as their equal? Would they ever fear displeasing one, as they would fear displeasing one whom they considered an equal? Then why would Allah make idols of wood or stone His equal?

So set your face firmly upon the natural religion (of monotheism).
⁹³⁶ Allah instilled this instinctive nature upon all of humanity, and
Allah never changes what He creates. ⁹³⁷ This is the straight religion;
yet, most people don't understand. ⁹³⁸ [30] Turn back to Him (in

---

⁹³⁶ In modern times, certain fundamentalist Christian groups have advanced the odd idea
that the God of the Qur'an is not the same as the Judeo-Christian God. They have done
this in an effort to sow suspicion among their flocks towards Islam. While undoubtedly
the conception of God in the Qur'an is more monotheistic than the Christian trinity, the
Qur'an repeats over and over that it is a message from the same God that spoke to
Abraham, Moses and Jesus (see 29:46). Ironically, Islam and Judaism have more in
common in terms of conceptualizing God than either has with Trinitarian Christianity.
One modern Jewish activist, Eliezer Abrahamson, gave this response on the status of
Islam in Jewish law: "According to Jewish law, Islam is a true form of worship of Allah
(*Shu"t HaRamba'm*, 160). It recognizes the One indivisible God as the Creator and Ruler
of the Universe. For this reason, a non-Jew who follows Islam is not considered an idolater
according to Jewish law." Thus, Judaism accepts that the God of Islam is the same God
as its own. Those Christians who try to drive a wedge between the three Abrahamic
faiths don't realize that the wedge would put Islam and Judaism on one side and their
own faith on the other!

⁹³⁷ The commentators explain that this verse refers to Allah's revealed religion and our
natural affinity towards it. If we avoid our own shortcomings of disbelief, temptation,
materialism or arrogance, then we gravitate towards Allah and feel at peace. Even if
environmental influences or personal flaws lead us astray, the seed of faith remains within
each of us, albeit in a dormant state that ever awaits the rain of insight to cause it to grow.
Thus, what Allah created does not change, but we change, at least on the surface.
Regarding religion, the basis of most of the world's religions shows some degree of
uniformity in spiritual practice, regardless of the particular worship methods, and this is
a further sign of the original origin of all religions - from a Being that knows how to touch
our hearts. Is there any religion with no form of prayer or meditation directed towards
personal growth and the eternal truth? Thus, even the principles of divine religion do
not change, even if we alter the forms and invent new doctrines on our own. The Prophet
explained that Allah created everyone as a natural monotheist but that Satan messes them
up in their religion as they grow and mature. (*Muslim*)

⁹³⁸ The Qur'an advances the concept that all human beings are endowed with a spirit
(*ruh*) from Allah while still in their mothers' wombs. If we have something from Allah
within each of us, then it stands to reason that that part of us will always recognize, in a
vague sort of way, where it belongs. Thus, the concept of *fitrah*, as it is mentioned here
in this verse. Our *fitrah*, or inborn inclination towards Allah, is that feeling within all of
us that prompts us to be religious. Science today has even identified such a "Allah gene"
within us that prompts us to believe in the supernatural. It is this inner nature that
logically causes us to doubt the validity of idols, even as it causes us to question the reason
for our existence in this world. Those who don't listen to their *fitrah* and who reject Allah's
proofs warp their souls and become prone to immorality. Allah lets them sink further
into error as a punishment for their willful lack of common sense, though He makes His
signs continually available for them to consider anew. He even lets greater tests befall
them so they have the chance to break out of their negative thinking pattern and embrace
their Creator. On the flip side, those who listen to their *fitrah* seek out Allah's truth and
may travel the world in search of knowledge, perhaps changing religions along the way,
until they are fully satisfied they have found Allah's truth. The innate predisposition to

repentance), and be mindful of Him. Establish prayer, and don't be among those who make partners (with Allah). [31] Those who split their religion up into competing factions – *each side happily assumes it has (the truth).* [939] [32]

Our Lack of Appreciation for Allah's Favor

When misfortune comes upon people, they cry out to their Lord, turning back to Him (in sincere repentance). Yet, when He gives them a taste of mercy from His Own Self, some of them make partners with their Lord [33] - (as if to show) how really thankless they can be for what We've given them. So enjoy yourselves now – *oh, but soon you'll know!* [34] Have We sent down to them some kind of authority that tells them all about the 'partners' they have? [35]

When We give people a taste of mercy, they rejoice in it. However, when hardship comes upon them, because (of mistakes) they made with their own hands, they're plunged into despair! [36] Don't they see that Allah increases or restricts the resources of whomever He wants? There are signs in this for those who believe. [37]

(So don't be afraid to) give what is due to your relatives, the poor and stranded travelers. [940] This is the best course of action for those who seek Allah's face, and they're the ones who will be successful. [38]

---

seek spiritual meaning is often thought of in scientific circles today as some sort of 'Allah gene.'

[939] This is a prescient warning to the followers of Islam not to break up into sects, for each will assume it has the truth, when it may very well be only partially right. The criticism here, however, is a direct reference to the habit among Christians and Jews to break up into competing sects. Although Muslims, too, eventually split up into sects, the Prophet said that the correct one could be identified by seeing which one followed his example and that of his companions. The Prophet also said that his community would never unite on an error. Therefore, we should look for the largest sect that adheres closely to what the Prophet and his companions practiced, without historical or theological oddities or practices that developed centuries later and that can be proven to be invented practices.

[940] The Prophet once said, "Whoever seeks Allah's protection, give that person protection. Whoever asks in the name of Allah, give him a place of safety. Whoever does something nice for you, reward him, and if you don't have anything, at least call upon Allah's blessings on his behalf until you know he has been rewarded (by Allah)." (*Fiqh-us-Sunnah*)

Remember Where the Best Returns Lie

The (false) gifts that you give out to other people, (in the hopes) of making a profit (in return) off their property, doesn't get you any increase (in value) with Allah. [941] However, what you give in charity, seeking only Allah's face, (will increase your value with Him). They're the ones who will get multiplied returns. [39]

Allah is the One Who created you and gave you your resources. Then He'll cause you to die and then bring you back to life again. Can any of your 'partners' do anything like that? Glory be to Him! He's high above the partners they make with Him. [40]

The World is Your Example

Corruption has appeared on land and at sea because of what the hands of people have done. [942] (Allah allows it to go forward) so they can suffer the (bad consequences) of their actions and thus have a chance to return (to Him). [943] [41]

Say (to them), *"Travel all over the world, and see the end result of all those (civilizations) that came before you, and most of them made partners (with Allah).* [42] *So set your face towards the straight religion before a day comes from Allah that can't be put off, a day when people will be divided (into different categories)."* [43]

---

[941] This verse describes a practice in which a person gives a gift in the hopes that he will receive a reciprocal gift of equal or greater value than what he gave. This is giving without good intentions, for the giver wants to hedge his bets and hope for a greater return later. As such, the term that is used in this verse is *riba*, or increase, which later became equated with interest money. I have translated the word as investment money, reflecting the goal of the false-gift transaction, and also because of the fact that at this time in the Meccan Period, charging interest on loans was not forbidden yet. (*Ma'ariful Qur'an*)

[942] Some commentators held that this line also encompasses pollution and humanity's ruining of the environment. The Prophet said, "When an evildoer dies, it is a relief for people, the land, the trees and the animals." (*Tirmidhi*)

[943] This is a clear answer for those who ask why Allah allows corruption and injustice to exist in the earth. The resulting consequences of our actions might cause us to rethink our opposition to Allah and morality. On the Day of Judgment, those who were wronged on earth will be repaid their due, while those who did evil will be punished for what they did. Also see 32:21. (See Jeremiah 18:8 in the Old Testament where the same principle as the above verse is enumerated.)

Whoever rejected faith will suffer from that rejection, while the one who did what was morally right will have prepared a fine resting place for himself. [44] (That's so) He can reward those who believed and did what was morally right from His bounty. Truly, He has no love for those who suppress (their awareness of the truth). [45]

Signs in Nature are to be Pondered

Among His signs are the winds that He sends as welcome news (for sailors), and also so you can have a taste of His mercy. (Those same winds) propel ships (through the sea) by His command, allowing you to search for His bounty, and also so you can be thankful. [46]

And so it was that We sent messengers before you, (Muhammad,) to their respective nations, and they brought clear evidence. We took retribution upon those who were wicked, and it was Our task to help those who believed. [944] [47]

Allah is the One Who sends the winds that form the clouds. Then He spreads them in the sky as He wills and breaks them into fragments until you see water coming out from within them.

Then after He's caused (the rain) to fall upon whichever of His servants that He wills, you see them celebrating, [48] even though they were in abject desperation just a moment before. [945] [49]

---

[944] The Prophet said, "No Muslim defends the honor of his brother except that there would be a right upon Allah to defend him from Hellfire on the Day of Resurrection." Then the Prophet recited this verse. (*Ibn Abi Hatim*)

[945] The great legal scholar, Imam Abu Hanifa (d. 765), demonstrated how a believer can be content with both good and bad fortune. Once, while he was giving a sermon, a man came rushing into the mosque and approached him, whispering something in his ear. Abu Hanifa said, "Praise be to Allah," in an even tone and then continued on with his sermon. A few moments later, the same man came rushing back into the mosque and again whispered something into the Imam's ear, causing him to say once again, "Praise be to Allah." The people were curious, and afterwards they asked him about the man who had come in twice and whispered to him and why he had praised Allah both times. Abu Hanifa replied, "The first time the man came, he told me that a ship that was coming into port full of my trade goods had sunk. When I realized that the loss had no effect upon my faith, I said, 'Praise be to Allah.' The second time he came in, he told me that it wasn't my ship that had sunk, but another. When I realized that having my goods

So examine the results of Allah's mercy: how He gives life to the earth after it was barren. This is how life will come to the dead, for He has power over all things. [50] However, if We happened to send a whirlwind that damaged their crops, leaving them withered and yellow, they would become thankless once more! [946] [51]

What will it Take for Them to Listen?

You can't make the dead listen, nor can you force the deaf to hear the call, especially once they've turned their backs on it, [52] and neither can you lead the blind back from their wandering. [947] You can only convince the faithful to listen, for they've believed in Our (revealed) verses, and they've surrendered (their wills) to Us. [53]

Allah is the One Who created you weak (at birth), and Who gave you your strength after that weakness. Then after that strength, (He will) give you weakness once more and grey hair, as well. [948] He creates whatever He wants, for He's the Knowing and the Determiner. [54]

On the day when the Hour (of Judgment) is established, the wrongdoers will swear that they hadn't lived but an hour - *that's how used to being deceived they were!* [55]

Then the learned people who believed will say (to them), "*You were just passing time within Allah's recorded (plan), all the way up to the Day*

---

restored to me had no effect on my faith, I again said, 'Praise be to Allah.'" When the famous female mystic, Rabi'ah al-Adawiyya (d. 801), was once asked about the point at which a servant of Allah would know if he was truly content with his Lord, she replied, "When his joy in hardship equals his joy in blessings."

[946] The hidden subtext is that people should not tie their faith in Allah to the fact of being in good or bad times. Whether the wind blows one way or the other, our faith should be independent of our life's circumstances. The famous Umayyad caliph, 'Umar ibn 'Abdul-Aziz, once wrote, "Whenever Allah gives a blessing to a servant, then takes it back from him, and the servant endures the loss patiently, then He may reward him with a blessing that's better than the one He took away."

[947] Jesus is quoted as saying something similar in Matthew 13:13, when his disciples asked why he always told parables or stories.

[948] Abu al-Hassan al-Husri, who lived in Cordoba in the twelfth century, once wrote, "If white is the color of mourning in Andalusia, it's a proper custom. Look at me, I dress myself in the white of white hair, in mourning for my youth!"

of Resurrection. Now this is the Day of Resurrection, but you weren't paying attention!" [949] [56] So no excuses the wrongdoers offer that day will do them any good, nor will they be allowed to make amends. [57]

And so We've laid out in this Qur'an every kind of example for people (to learn from), but even if you brought them a miracle (that they couldn't deny), the faithless would say of it, *"You're only talking nonsense."* [58] That's how Allah seals the hearts of those who won't understand. [59] Have patience with them, for Allah's promise is real, and don't let the faithless shake your resolve. [950] [60]

---

949 A famous poet, Mir Mu'izzi (d. 1125), once wrote on the importance of trusting your inner sense of faith with these poignant, yet terse, words: "Written upon the pages of earth and sky, the line: 'Therefore take heed, O you who have eyes.'" Nature itself is sufficient proof of a Designer.

950 The Prophet said, "The believer is like a green plant; the wind blows its leaves to the left and to the right. When the wind is still, it is still. This is the example of the believer. He always has to face difficult and trying situations." (*Bukhari*) The example of an unbeliever is a pine tree, which never is shaken enough to move until Allah cuts it down when He wills. In other words, no matter what detractors and critics might say to shake your faith, a believer will always bend back straight, but the tests will never end. Just accept it and get on with your life. The force of Resilience is built through prayer and supplication, contemplation of the wonders of life, reading spiritual and philosophical knowledge, service to humanity, practicing mercy, being hard on your own shortcomings, asking forgiveness, remembering death will come and also from frequent introspection.

Luqmān

31 Luqmān
Late Meccan Period

This chapter takes its name after a legendary wise man Luqmān whose ultimate identity is unknown. The example of the sage, who was virtually unknown to Arabian lore, is meant to create further connections between the past and the contemporary preaching of the Prophet, in order to show that Allah is ultimately the source for all wise and noble teachings. The remainder of the chapter is dedicated to highlighting more proofs of Allah's power, as well as the reality of the next life.

In the Name of Allah,
the Compassionate, the Merciful

*A*lif. *Lām. Meem.* [1]

These are the verses of the Book of wisdom. [2] (It's a source of) guidance and a mercy to the righteous. [3] They're the ones who establish prayer, give in charity and have the full confidence in their hearts of the next life. [4] They're being guided by their Lord, and they'll be successful. [951] [5]

Background on verses 6-7: There are two references as to the reason for this verse. They both revolve around a man named an-Nadr ibn al-Harith, who had traveled frequently to Persia. He offered the Quraysh his tales of Persian heroes as an alternative to listening to the Qur'an. He also tried to use music to take people's attention away from the Qur'an. He used to bring out a foreign slave girl he owned to sing when Muhammad was preaching. He used to say, "Muhammad makes you listen to the Qur'an; then he asks you to pray and fast, and he makes life hard for you. Come and listen to this music instead, and have some fun." (*Ma'ariful Qur'an*)

---

951 The Prophet said, "The height of wisdom is the fear of Allah. The best thing that can dwell in the heart is certainty (of the truth of Allah). Doubt comes from disbelief. Youth is one branch of insanity. The happiest person is the one who learns a lesson from someone else. The saddest person is one who was sad from his mother's womb. The end is near." (*Bayhaqi*)

There are some among people who buy useless tales that are devoid of knowledge, in order to mislead others from the path of Allah by making a mockery of (knowledge). They'll have a humiliating punishment. [952] [6] When Our (revealed) verses are read out to someone like that, they turn away arrogantly, acting like they didn't hear anything – almost like they were deaf in both ears! Give them the news of a terrible punishment! [7]

Those who believe and do what's morally right will have gardens of delight, [8] and there they shall remain! Allah's promise is true, for He's the Powerful and the Wise. [9]

He created the skies without any supports that you can see. [953] He rooted firm highlands in the earth so it wouldn't shake with you, [954]

---

[952] Some conservative scholars have used this verse to rule that all music and singing is forbidden. This extreme position, however, is not supported by the wider *hadith* literature, which contains several references to incidents of singing that were approved of by the Prophet. In addition, this verse and the background describes to what the *useless tales* refer, in that they are for the purpose of making a mockery of knowledge by using music to *compete* with intelligent conversation when it is being offered. The Prophet specifically allowed women and girls to sing and play drums during times of celebration, such as at weddings and other events. See reports in Tirmidhi, Tabarani and Bukhari. He also sang with his companions when they were digging the trench around Medina. When the Muslims used to travel long distances, drums would be played to lessen the monotony of the road, and songs would be sung, as well. (Drums or small tambourines seem to be the only instruments specifically allowed in the traditions.) The Prophet also composed a suggested wedding song of celebration for girls to sing as they clapped their hands and played tambourines. That song is recorded in Tabarani and goes as follows: "To you we have come! To you we have come! So welcome us, as we welcome you!" (Also recorded in *Ibn Majah*.) Some commentators have attempted to extrapolate even further and have forbidden hobbies and pastimes, in general, on the spurious notion that they distract one from religion. This is an untenable position, for as the *hadith* literature shows, the Prophet engaged in or approved of many different types of sports and pastimes from wrestling and archery to foot races, swimming, horseback riding, target practice, poetry and storytelling. (There are obscure traditions that forbid the playing of backgammon and chess, but these are obviously spurious reports, as those two games were not invented yet in the Prophet's time.) The Prophet said, "Let your heart rest sometimes," and many scholars take this as the permission to engage in recreational activity. (*Ma'ariful Qur'an*)

[953] Even though the sky above the earth seems to be immaterial, the entire structure is held up by an invisible combination of gases, pressure, the earth's gravity and a host of other factors, which keep our atmosphere from collapsing. All the other known rocky planets have non-existent atmospheres with no air as we know it.

[954] Mountains and other highland formations are formed from the action of the tectonic plates that form the topmost layer of the geologic structure of earth. Without mountains being formed with deep roots in the mantle, the plates would move faster and cause

and He raised up all kinds of animals throughout (the earth). [955] We send down water from the sky and produce every type of beneficial species (of plant) in pairs. [10]

That's the creation of Allah! Now show Me something that anyone else besides Him has created - it's just not possible! [956] Therefore, the wrongdoers are clearly mistaken. [11]

The Wisdom of Luqmān

Background on verse 12: Luqmān was not a prophet, but he was a very wise man. It is said that he was offered the choice to become either a prophet or a very wise man. He chose the latter on the reasoning that the office of prophethood carries too much responsibility. He is often thought of as something of an Aesop of the Middle East, if you will. Though it is uncertain when and where he lived, some have suggested he was a citizen of the ancient city of Iram (Ubar), which was a major trading center in present-day Oman nearly a thousand years before the lifetime of the Prophet. Others have placed him outside of Arabia altogether and have suggested that he was an African wise man, a carpenter by trade, who lived in the era of Prophet David. Most commentators seem to favor the latter view. Ibn Kathir records that Luqmān's son's name was Thārān.

---

earthquakes much more frequently than they do now. The mountains act as something like an anchor or peg on the earth.

[955] Animals are a sign of Allah's creative genius. In Islamic law, animals have rights, and the only time a person is allowed to kill an animal is either for food or to protect themselves from attack. Sport hunting is forbidden in Islam, as is treating animals in a cruel or inhumane manner. The Prophet also forbade tying up animals to use for target practice. Ibn 'Umar once came upon a boy who had tied up a hen and was using it for target practice. Ibn 'Umar untied the hen and brought it and the boy to the boy's father and said, "Don't allow your boys to tie up birds in order to kill them, for I heard the Messenger of Allah forbidding the tying up of animals or other creatures in order to kill them." (*Bukhari, Muslim*). The words of the Prophet are contained in the following report: "Do not use anything in which there is a soul as a target." (*Muslim*) The Prophet also forbade people from overworking, beating or overloading their domesticated animals. If a person keeps a pet, he must care for it properly, or the mistreated pet will take revenge upon them on the Day of Judgment. There is a well-known tradition in which the Prophet described a woman who will be punished on Judgment Day because she starved her pet to death. It reads as follows: "A woman will be punished for a cat that she imprisoned until it died, and she will enter Hellfire because of that. She did not feed it or give it water when she locked it up, nor did she let it free to eat the crawling things of the earth." (*Bukhari, Muslim*) Also see the book entitled, *Animals in Islam*, by Anayat Durrani.

[956] Ibn Ata'ullah, an eleventh-century philosopher, wrote, "If you don't love Him on account of His beautiful qualities, then at least love Him for how (well) He provides for you." (*Hikam*)

And so it was that We bestowed wisdom upon Luqmān, (telling him), *"Be thankful to Allah. Whoever is thankful, then it's to the good of his own soul, but whoever is ungrateful, (know that) Allah doesn't need anything and is (already being) praised."* [957] [12]

"My son," Luqmān said to his child during a lesson, *"don't make any partners with Allah, for making partners is the worst offense (against Allah)."* [958] [13]

(On account of the sacrifices that parents make for their children), We made it a duty upon every human being (to be respectful) to his parents. After enduring wave upon wave of pain, his mother finally gives birth to him, and then he's (totally dependent on her) for two years of weaning. So be thankful to Me and to your parents, for the final destination (of you all) is back (to Me). [959] [14]

However, if (your parents) try to force you to set up partners with Me, offering (deities) about which you know nothing, then don't obey them. Yet, still keep company with them in this world in a fair manner. [960]

---

[957] Allah doesn't need our thanks, but if we are thankful, then it is to our own benefit, for it keeps us humble and focused on the brevity of life. If someone is still ungrateful, even after understanding the fragility of life and all it has to offer, then they should know that Allah doesn't need their gratitude anyway and that He is already being amply praised by the believers and also by the angels, who praise Him continuously.

[958] When verse 6:82 was revealed, many of the companions became distressed, for it said that believers are those who don't confuse their faith with oppression and wrong. Some people asked the Prophet the meaning of the Arabic word *zulm*, which means any type of wrong, injustice or offense, and they exclaimed that everyone has done it, so how can there be hope for them? The Prophet said, "That's not what *zulm* means (in this verse). Haven't you heard what Luqman said?" The prophet then recited this verse. (*Muslim*) Thus, the *zulm* mentioned in 6:82 is talking about the practice of offending Allah by making partners with Him.

[959] The famous Muslim missionary and mystic, Bayazid Bustami (d. 874), read this verse as a boy. He soon came to feel that it was too difficult for him to serve both Allah and his widowed mother with equal sincerity, so he left his home as a teenager and set out on the road of service to Allah. After many decades of bringing the wisdom of faith to the masses in Persia and India, he eventually was called to return to his now aged mother, who, he discovered, had become blind. He then resolved to stay by her side for the rest of his life.

[960] A follower of Islam still must maintain kind relations with his or her parents, even if they are of a different religion. This is the importance that the Qur'an places on respecting the ones who carried you and raised you while you were helpless. The commentators say this verse is making reference to an actual situation where a pagan

Keep yourself on the path of those who turn towards Me, for all of you will return to Me, and I'm going to tell you the meaning of everything you did. [961] [15]

"My son," (Luqmān said,) "even if there were a tiny speck of mustard seed lodged within a rock or anywhere else in the heavens or the earth, Allah can bring it out, for Allah is aware of all subtleties. [962] [16] My son, establish prayer, encourage what's known (to be right in Allah's sight) and forbid what's strange (or unfamiliar to Allah's good way). Have patience with whatever happens to you, for that shows determination in dealing with matters. [963] [17]

"Don't puff up your cheek (arrogantly) at other people nor strut around through the earth, for Allah has no love for conceited snobs. [18] Walk moderately, and speak softly, for the most annoying noise of all is the shrill of a donkey." [964] [19]

Asking People to Believe

Don't you see that Allah has tamed everything in the heavens and on earth for you and that He's showered His favors down upon you - favors that you can recognize and others that you can't even fathom?

---

mother tried to force her son to renounce Islam, and he refused. Eventually she gave up her efforts.

[961] It is said that this last line of this verse was revealed for the sake of the Prophet's best friend, Abu Bakr. After he had accepted Islam, being one of the first persons to do so, five of his close friends asked him if his conversion was sincere. When Abu Bakr affirmed his choice to follow Muhammad, each of his friends, who included Uthman ibn Affan and Az-Zubayr, also declared that they believed in Muhammad, as well.

[962] The Prophet said, "Luqman the Wise used to say, 'When something is given into the care of Allah, He looks after it.'" (Ahmad)

[963] A seventh-century convert to Islam, who was known for his prodigious wisdom, named Al-Ahnaf ibn Qays told his son, "My son, when you're selecting someone to be your friend, make him angry first. If he still treats you with fairness while he's angry, then make him your friend. Otherwise, have nothing to do with him."

[964] Among the several nuggets of wisdom that have survived the ages among the Arabs, there is a report that Luqman was once asked how he gained his wisdom. He replied, "By watching ignorant people. Any time I saw faults in such a one, I avoided doing the same."

Still there are some people who argue about (the existence) of Allah without knowledge, without guidance and without a scripture to enlighten them! [965] [20]

When they're asked to follow what Allah has sent down, they say, *"No way! We're going to follow what we found our ancestors doing."* What! Even if it's Satan calling them to the punishment of the raging flame? [21]

Whoever submits his face to Allah and is good, then he's taken hold of the most secure handhold, for the final outcome rests with Allah. [22]

Whoever rejects faith, however - don't let their rejection bother you, for they're going to come back to Us, and then We're going to tell them the meaning of all that they did. Allah knows all the secrets of the heart! [23] We give them time to enjoy themselves for a while, but in the end We're going to drive them ever deeper into relentless punishment. [24]

If you asked them who created the heavens and the earth, they would be sure to say, *"Allah."* So say (to them), *"Praise be to Allah."* Yet, even still most of them don't understand! [25] To Allah belongs whatever is in the heavens and the earth. Allah is the Self-Sufficient and Praiseworthy. [26]

If all the trees of the earth were pens, and the ocean (were made of ink) - even backed up by seven more oceans - still the words of Allah would not be exhausted, for Allah is strong and wise. [966] [27]

The creation and resurrection of you all isn't (any more difficult for Allah than doing both) to a single soul by itself, for Allah hears

---

[965] Malik ibn Dinar, who lived in the seventh century, once said, "If you find your heart hardened, your body weak and your earnings are poor, then you should know that you talked without knowledge about things that did not concern you."

[966] The "words" of Allah are often interpreted as being His commands for the creation and functioning of things. There is an entire universe to oversee, and Allah is capable of running it all, and more besides.

and sees (everything all at once). [967] [28] Don't you see that Allah merges the night into the day and merges the day into the night and that He's the One Who tamed the sun and the moon, each following its own set trajectory?

Allah is well-informed about all that you do, [29] and that's because Allah is the True Reality. Whatever they're calling upon besides Him is falsehood, for Allah is the Highest and the Greatest. [968] [30]

Our Last Hope is with Allah

Don't you see the ships sailing through the sea by Allah's favor, in order for Him to show you some of His signs? In this (example), there are signs for every patient and thankful person. [31] If an overshadowing wave climbs up over (the bow of the ship), the (sailors) cry out to Allah, offering to devote themselves to Him (if He saves them). [969]

Yet, when He brings them safely back to the shore, some of them stop halfway (in between faith and rejection). Yet, no one rejects Our signs except for deceitful betrayers. [32]

O people! Be mindful of your Lord, and fear the day when no parent will be able to do anything for his own child, nor any child for his parent. Allah's promise is indeed the truth, so don't let the life of this world fool you, nor let the Great Deceiver trick you into (rejecting) Allah. [33]

Allah has Knowledge of the Unseen

Background on verse 34: A bedouin came in from the desert with a horse and a colt to sell in the market. He saw Muhammad and asked, "Who are you?" He replied, "I'm the Prophet of Allah." The bedouin asked, "*Who* is the prophet of

---

[967] Allah's powers are so vast, and His abilities so limitless, that He can keep track of all life *forms - as if He were watching only one!*

[968] The Prophet said, "The truest word of any poet was the saying of Labid: 'Truly, everything besides Allah is false.'" (*Bukhari*)

[969] This refers to the phenomenon known today as "rogue waves" in which an unusually high wave (up to eight stories tall) comes from an unknown source and suddenly towers over a ship, threatening to swamp it. If Allah saves people from such unnatural things, they are usually thankless in the end.

Allah?" When Muhammad reaffirmed to him that he was, the man then asked him, "So when will the Hour come to pass?" "It's part of the unseen, and no one can know it save Allah," answered the Prophet. Then the man asked, "So when is it going to rain?" "It's not known except by Allah." "So with what is my horse pregnant?" he asked. "It's not known except by Allah," the Prophet intoned. Then this verse was revealed in response. (*Asbab ul Nuzul*)

The knowledge of the Hour (of Judgment) is with Allah. He's the One Who sends down the rain, and He knows what's in the wombs (of pregnant women). No one knows what he'll earn tomorrow, nor does anyone know in what land he'll die, [970] though Allah is full of knowledge and is well-informed (about all these things). [971] [34]

---

[970] The Prophet said, "If Allah wants to take a person's soul in a particular land, He gives him a reason to go there." (*Al-Hakim*)

[971] On one occasion, the Prophet said, "There are five hidden things that can't be known except by Allah Almighty: the coming of the hour, what is in the womb, the future, the land in which one will die, and when it will rain." (*Bukhari*) Even though ultrasound has given us a way to determine the gender of a child, it still does not reveal the totality of the child who will be born (eye color, physical traits, some hidden defects, personality, growth potential, unknown disabilities, etc). In any case, the grammar construction of this Qur'anic verse does not state that *only* Allah knows what's in the womb (only the hour of the Last Day, and later on our earnings and place of death are specified as the exclusive knowledge of Allah).

The Prostration

32 As-Sajdah
Middle Meccan Period

The tone of this chapter reflects the fact that when it was revealed, the Meccan persecution had not yet reached its height. It answers a number of objections posed by the pagans, as well as emphasizing the utter 'rightness' of submitting to Allah. The Meccans are also asked to consider the fate of previous civilizations who rejected the call of Allah.

In the Name of Allah,
the Compassionate, the Merciful

A*lif. Lām. Meem.* [1]

The revelation of this Book is from the Lord of All the Worlds; there's nothing doubtful within it! [2] So are they saying, "*He must have made it all up*"? No way! It's the truth from your Lord, so you can warn a nation that never had any warner before you, and also so they can be guided. [3]

Allah is the One Who created the heavens and the earth and everything in between them in six stages; then He established Himself upon the throne (of power). [972] There's no one who can protect you nor vouch for you other than He, so won't you be reminded? [4]

He regulates all commands within the sky and the earth, and then after (the end has come, all affairs and matters) will ascend back to Him (for resolution) in a day that is like a thousand years of your

---

[972] The commentators explain this *taking control of the throne* to mean that after Allah created the universe in six stages, or *days*, He affirmed it to be under His law, thus the symbol of the *throne*, which is the traditional symbol of power for a ruler.

estimation. [973] [5] That's what He's like – the knower of the hidden and the clear – the Powerful and the Merciful! [6]

He's the One Who created everything superbly! He initially created the human being from (nothing more) than clay. [7] Then He made his descendants from the extract of lowly mixed fluids. [8]

Then He constructs (each of them in his mother's womb) and then breathes into him something of His spirit.

Then He endows you with (the faculties of awareness): hearing, sight and feeling. [974] (Yet, for all of these gifts), you're hardly thankful at all! [9]

Accepting the Concept of an Afterlife

They say, "What! When we're deep underground (and rotted away), are we really going to be made again like new?"

---

[973] Some critics have suggested that there is a contradiction between the following three verses: 22:47, 32:5 and 70:4. The first two verses [22:47 and 32:5] are often interpreted to mean that a day to Allah is like a thousand years of our time, while the last verse [70:4] is often said to mean that a day to Allah is like fifty thousand years. This misunderstanding is easily dispelled upon a close examination of what each of these verses is *specifically* referencing, for the verses in question apply to completely different things. Verse 22:47 states (in general terms) that a day to Allah *can be like* a thousand years of our own time. So verse 22:47 is a general statement that is unrelated to the subject matter of the remaining two verses. Verse 32:5 states that Allah rules the universe, and then *after that* (i.e., after He shuts down humanity's term) it will take a day that is like a thousand years (refer to 22:47) for all the *affairs* (records) to be assembled in the place on high. Now what is verse 70:4 referencing? Verse 70:4 is saying that *the angels* and *spirit* (Gabriel) will ascend to Allah (for the Day of Judgment, as verses 70:1-3 imply) which itself is a 'day' (or time period) that will last for *fifty thousand years*. This figure is confirmed in a tradition of the Prophet when he said that the Day of Judgment (where punishment will be meted out) will, in fact, last for fifty thousand years. In addition, verse 32:5 ends with the phrase, *of your estimation*, while verse 70:4 does not reference human timekeeping, so the number in 70:4 is a specially fixed duration from Allah (confirmed by prophetic tradition). Thus, the Prophet confirmed that this one 'day' (of Judgment) will last a lot longer than any other time period. Thus, there is no contradiction among these three verses on account of what each is referencing.

[974] It is interesting to note that the development of the senses in the womb listed here are in the exact order that a fetus develops them: the internal ear appears before the eyes start to develop, and the brain's capacity to feel sensations communicated by the nerves surfaces last.

But no! (They're) rejecting their appointment with their Lord. [10]

Tell them, *"The Angel of Death* [975] *will be put in charge of you, and he's going to collect your souls and take you back to your Lord."* [11]

If only you could see how the guilty will be hanging their heads dejectedly before their Lord. *"Our Lord!"* (they'll cry out in despair). *"Now we see it, and now we've heard (our records read out to us). Please, send us back (to earth), and then we'll reform ourselves, for now we really do believe!"* [976] [12]

If We had wanted, We could've guided every soul, but the truth of My sentence will come to pass: *"I will fill Hellfire with jinns and people all together!* [13] *So suffer it! You forgot this appointed day of yours, so now We're going to forget you! Suffer the eternal punishment for your deeds!"* [14]

The true believers are those who, when they hear Our verses being read out to them, fall down in adoration and praise of their Lord. They're never too proud (to bow down before their Lord). [977] [15]

Their bodies propel them to rise restlessly from their beds (at night) so they can call upon their Lord earnestly in hope and fear, [978]

---

[975] According to a saying of the Prophet, when Angel Azra'il was chosen to be the Angel of Death, he complained to Allah, saying, "O My Lord! You've given me such a task that the entire race of the children of Adam - *throughout the entire world* - will think badly of me on account of this, so much so, that every time I am mentioned, I'll be considered an evil thing." Allah replied to him, saying, "We've taken care of that by implementing such clearly recognizable diseases and other causes of death in the world that everyone will attribute death to those causes and diseases, and thus you will be shielded from their remarks." (*Qurtubi*)

[976] Uthman ibn Affan (d. 656) once said, "Allah gave you life in this world so you could ask for the next life from here. He didn't give you life so you could stay here. Life here will perish while life in the hereafter will last forever. Don't be fooled by this temporary life, and don't be so busy that you (forget) the eternal one."

[977] It is customary that those who believe in Allah will stop reading after this verse and prostrate themselves in awe of Allah.

[978] This verse refers to those who give up sleep in favor of prayer, whether by getting up early for the predawn prayer, not napping before the night prayer, or getting up in the darkness of the night to perform the late night, optional prayer known as *tahajjud*. A famous companion named Mu'adh ibn Jabal once asked the Prophet, "Prophet of Allah, tell me of a deed that will grant me admittance into Paradise and save me from Hellfire." The Prophet said, "You've asked about something of great importance, and it's easy for the one who has it made easy for him by Allah. Serve Allah, don't make 'partners' with

and they spend (in charity) out of the resources that We've given them. [979] [16]

No soul knows what delights of the eye are kept hidden from it as a reward for the (good) they have (all) done (during their time in the world). [980] [17]

The Twisted are not Equal to the Righteous

Background on verses 18-22: This passage was revealed concerning the case of 'Ali ibn Abi Talib and Walid ibn 'Uqbah ibn Abi Mu'it. Walid boasted to 'Ali, "I'm stronger than you, more eloquent and a more powerful fighter than you." 'Ali said, "Shut up, you twisted deviant." (*Asbab ul-Nuzul*)

And so is the one who believes no better than the one who is a twisted deviant? No, they're not equal at all! [981] [18]

Him, establish prayer, pay the required charity, fast in the month of Ramadan and perform a pilgrimage to the House." Then he said, "Shouldn't I tell you about the gates of goodness? Fasting is a shield; charity wipes out sin, and the prayer of a person in the middle of the night (brings forgiveness)." Then he recited this passage. Afterwards he said, "Shouldn't I tell you of the greatest of all things and its pillars and highest peak?" Mu'adh answered, "Of course, Messenger of Allah." Then the Prophet said, "The greatest of all things is Islam; its pillars are the prayers, and its highest peak is *jihad* for the sake of Allah." Then he said, "Shouldn't I tell you upon what all of these things depend?" Mu'adh again answered, "Of course, Messenger of Allah." Then the Prophet took hold of his tongue and said, "Control this." Then Mu'adh asked, "Messenger of Allah, are we going to be held accountable for what we say?" The Prophet answered, "May your mother lose you, Mu'adh! Will people ever be thrown into Hellfire for any other reason than because of what their tongues say?" (*Ahmad*)

979 The Prophet once remarked that faith lies in between hope and fear. We fear disobeying Allah's limits and laws, more so than we would fear disobeying our own parents for the utter shame with which it would fill us. Then we hope in Allah's immense forgiveness and mercy, thus giving us the courage to continue in this life of testing, for Allah has promised in this Book that salvation is for the *sincere*, not necessarily the *perfect*.

980 The Prophet said, "Whoever enters Paradise, he will enjoy a life of luxury and never feel deprivation. His clothes will never wear out, and his youth will never fade. In Paradise there are things that no eye has ever seen, no ear has ever heard and no person has ever conceived of." (*Muslim*)

981 It has to be remembered that what seems obvious for us today was a new concept to the idol-worshippers of Mecca, who didn't believe in an afterlife, let alone accountability for one's faith and actions.

Those who believe and do what's morally right will be given gardens for their welcoming place as a reward for what they used to do (in the world). [982] [19]

Twisted deviants will have for their place of welcome (nothing else save) the Fire, and every time they want to get out of it, they'll be pushed back into it.

They'll be told, *"Suffer the punishment of the Fire – (the punishment) that you used to call a lie!"* [20]

However, before We condemn them to that (dreaded) punishment, We let them experience some (lesser) forms of punishment here (in the) lower (life of this world), so they can at least have (a chance to repent of their evil) and return (to the path of Allah). [983] [21]

So who's more wrong than the one who is reminded of the signs of his Lord but then turns away from them? We're indeed going to get retribution from the wicked! [22]

---

[982] One night, a burglar looking to steal something crept into the house of Malik bin Dinar, who was in the first generation of Muslims. The burglar was disappointed to find nothing worth stealing. He then noticed that the owner of the house was busily praying in the night. When Malik noticed the thief, he calmly told him, "Brother, may Allah forgive you. You entered my home and didn't find anything worth taking, but I will not let you leave without gaining any benefit." Malik brought him a jug of water and told him, "If you were to perform ablution and pray two units of prayer, you would leave with something better than that which you came to find." Needless to say, this shocked the burglar. He was quite humbled by this request, and he agreed. After performing his ablution and praying, the thief said, "Malik, would I be imposing on you if I were to pray two more units of prayers?" Malik told him he could pray as much as he wanted, and the thief kept on praying till morning. After finishing his night prayers, he asked Malik, "Malik, would I be imposing on you if I were to spend the day with you, for I intend to fast." Malik told him he could stay as long as he wanted, so he stayed a few days with him, fasting in the day time and praying in the night. When he left Malik's house, he met a thief whom he knew, and the thief saw happiness in the repented one's face. He told him, "I think you must have found your treasure," to which he replied, "I found Malik bin Dinar. I went to steal from him, but he ended up stealing something from me, my heart!" (Adapted from *Encyclopedia of Islam*, Brill)

[983] The Prophet once recited this verse; then he said, "By the One Who holds my life in His hands, the pain suffered by a person from a minor scratch done by a wood chip, a misstep or an itch in the skin are all the after-effects of some sin (the person did), and Allah, the Exalted, forgives many sins." (*Baydawi*) Also see 42:30.

Take the Lesson for What it Is

And so it was that We gave a scripture to Moses; therefore, (Muhammad,) have no doubt (that a scripture is coming to you, too).

We made (the Torah) to be a guide for the Children of Israel, [23] and We set up leaders from among them who guided them by Our command. 984

(We favored them) for as long as they patiently persevered and believed in Our signs, 985 [24] but your Lord will judge between them and their points of difference on the Day of Standing (for judgment). [25]

Haven't they learned any lessons from all those generations that We've destroyed before them, and among whose ruins they now explore?

There are signs in this, so aren't they listening? [26] Don't they see how We drive the water to barren land and use it to grow plants for their cattle to eat, and for them, as well? 986   Don't they see (any of those things)? [27]

They just ask, "*So when will this all come out in the open, if you're really so honest?*" [28]

Say (to them), "*When the Day of Victory (arrives), believing then won't do any (good) for the faithless, and they won't be given any break, either.*" 987 [29] So turn away from them and wait, for they'll be waiting, as well. [30]

---

984 In other words, even as Allah revealed a scripture to Moses, so, too, should the Meccans accept that Allah is revealing a new scripture as a source of guidance to a man from among their own people.

985 As elegantly expressed in II Chronicles 15:1-15.

986 Since this verse mentions water specifically and not rain, the commentators explain that this refers to rivers that flow through deserts as well as underground water sources that can flow and bubble up through the earth even in dry regions. (*Ma'ariful Qur'an*)

987 Some commentators hold that this verse refers to the Judgment Day; others feel it is a prophecy about the Battle of Badr, when Islam was finally settled on a solid footing, and many pagans were vanquished on that day of victory.

The Allied Forces

33 Al Ahzāb

Middle Medinan Period

Early in the year 627 CE, the largest Arab army that had ever been assembled marched on Medina to destroy Islam and the Muslim community forever. In preparation for this impending assault, the vastly outnumbered Muslims hastily dug a large trench along the exposed outskirts of the city. (This was the suggestion of the Persian convert, Salman al-Farsi.) The rear of the city, which contained many walled houses, was fortified together, and the disjointed walls were sealed with heavy brickwork.

The twelve-thousand strong allied army, cobbled together by the leaders of the banished Banu Nadir Jews, was a formidable coalition made up of well-armed Meccans and men from five large bedouin tribes. When the jubilant horde approached the city and found a wide trench laid out before them, they scoffed and hesitated, for traditional battles among the Arabs had always involved simple frontal assaults of armed men against each other.

The trench made their cavalry useless, and the attackers were thus forced to order a series of infantry charges. Their men were unable to cross the deep ravine in sufficient numbers, however, to overwhelm the defenders on the other side, who assailed them with arrows. Thus, the Allies settled in upon a strategy of blockading the city. It would be only a matter of time before Medina would be starved into submission, they reasoned.

After some relatively uneventful weeks, one of the organizers of the coalition, Huyyay ibn Akhtab, persuaded the one remaining Jewish tribe in Medina, the Banu Qurayzah, to repudiate their treaty with the Muslims and join in a coordinated assault to overwhelm the Muslims from all sides. The situation for the Muslims was truly bleak. To make matters worse, a large number of hypocrites within the city were counseling their fellows either to break with the Prophet and join the enemy or, at the very least, to escape and flee into the desert.

The Muslims had never faced such a dire situation. However, through the skillful use of a double agent and an understanding of the fragile nature of the coalition facing him, the Prophet was able to split the resolve of the Allies and cause them to doubt each other's intentions. A sudden desert storm that arose one night convinced the demoralized attackers to lift the siege and flee - almost one month to the day after the attack began.

In the Name of Allah,
the Compassionate, the Merciful

Background on verses 1-3: There are several different, yet complementary, reports as to the references for the revelation of this passage. The most common of them is as follows. Some months after the Battle of Uhud, a delegation of Meccan pagans was allowed to enter Medina to parlay with the Prophet under a guarantee of safety. They included Abu Sufyan, 'Ikrimah, the son of the slain Abu Jahl (at Badr), and Abdul A'war as-Sulaymi. The delegation met first with 'Abdullah ibn Ubayy and some of his hypocrites. Then the Meccans, accompanied by two hypocrites named 'Abdullah ibn Sa'd and Ta'ma ibn Ubayrak (who is mentioned in the background to verses 4:105-112), went to hold a meeting with Muhammad.

Abu Sufyan began his address, exclaiming, "Don't say anything about our gods Lat, 'Uzza and Manat, except that they have the power to advocate and that they bring benefits for their worshippers, and then we'll leave you alone with your Lord." The Prophet didn't agree, and 'Umar ibn al Khattab (d. 644), who was also present, asked for permission to kill them. "But I have guaranteed their safety," the Prophet objected. So 'Umar told the delegation, "Go with Allah's curse and anger upon you." The Prophet then asked the delegation to depart the city. These three verses were then revealed. (*Ma'ariful Qur'an*)

O Prophet! Be mindful (of Allah). Pay no mind to those who suppress (their awareness of the truth) nor to the hypocrites, for Allah is full of knowledge and wisdom. [1] Instead, follow the inspiration that's coming to you from your Lord, for Allah knows exactly what you're doing. [2] Put your trust in Allah, for Allah is enough to look after (your) affairs. [3]

Adopted Children must Retain their Own Family Names

Background on verses 4-6: One day when the Prophet was praying in congregation he trembled momentarily. Some hypocrites then said (oddly enough) that the Prophet was wavering between his adopted home of Medina and his love of his hometown, and thus they said, 'He has two hearts.' The first part of verse four was revealed to affirm that the Prophet has a single heart and a single purpose. (*Ibn Kathir*) The remainder of this passage was revealed to settle the status of actual blood relationships versus adoptive ones.

Allah hasn't placed two hearts in any man's chest, nor has He made the wives whom (some of) you (have wrongfully) divorced by (saying they're like your mothers), *equivalent* to your mothers, [988] nor has He made your adopted children your actual (biological) children. [989]

All these pronouncements are merely phrases from your mouths. Allah explains (how it's really meant to be) in all truth, and thus He guides you on the path. [4]

Call (your adopted children) by the surnames of their fathers, for that's the right thing to do in the sight of Allah. [990] However, if you don't know (the surnames) of their fathers, then call them your brothers in faith and your protected ones. There is no blame if you make a mistake in this, for it's your heart's intentions (that matter). Truly, Allah is forgiving and merciful. [991] [5]

The Prophet is closer to the believers than they are to themselves, and his wives are like their mothers. [992] Blood-relatives have closer ties to each other (in inheritance rights) than (the wider fellowship)

---

[988] See 58:1-2 and introduction to the chapter for an explanation of the odd pre-Islamic custom of *zihar*, whereby a man could say that he had the same feelings towards his wife that he has for his mother and thus he won't sleep with his wife any further, while not fully divorcing her so she can marry someone else.

[989] There is a misconception that Islam does not allow adoption. This is untrue. What Islam doesn't allow is taking a child and giving it one's own family name, so that the child grows up not knowing who he or she really is. An extreme danger is that such a person may wind up unknowingly marrying his own sibling who was adopted by someone else, or at the very least, when an adoptee finds out they were adopted, they begin to long for their real parents and seek them out. Islam is very insistent that taking orphans into one's home and raising them with love is praiseworthy and of the highest good. It merely stipulates that their identity should not be hidden from them.

[990] This passage was revealed a short time before the Prophet's adopted son, Zayd ibn Harith, had divorced his wife Zaynab, and the continuation of this issue is taken up in verses 36-40 of this same chapter. In the past, people had always called Muhammad's adopted son Zayd ibn Muhammad, but after verse 5 was revealed, people began calling him by his real surname, Zayd ibn Harith. (Zayd later married Muhammad's childhood caretaker, an African lady named Barakah!)

[991] The Prophet said, "If a judge uses independent reasoning (*ijtehad*) and reaches the right decision, he will have two rewards. If he uses independent reasoning and reaches the wrong decision, he will have one reward." (*Bukhari*) The meaning is that a judge is still rewarded by Allah, even if he makes an honest mistake, because he at least tried to think a problem through with logic when the Qur'an and sayings of the Prophet didn't exactly cover an issue or dilemma.

[992] The wives of the Prophet were given the honored title of "Mothers of the Believers" or "*Ummahat al Mu'mineen*," and their status required them to set the best example. They served as teachers, resource people for questions and also as community leaders.

of believers and immigrants (who fled oppression), according to the decree of Allah. [993] However, continue to do the right thing for your close associates, as that's decreed in the Book (of Allah). [994] [6]

All Prophets were the Same in Purpose

Recall that We took an agreement from (all the prophets), even as We (took such an agreement) from you, (Muhammad,) and from Noah, Abraham, Moses and Jesus, the son of Mary.

We took from them a formal agreement [7] (that stipulated that Allah) would question the honest (messengers) about their sincerity (in conveying the messages to their peoples). He's prepared a painful punishment for those who (ungratefully) suppress (their natural disposition to believe in Him). [8]

---

[993] After the Treaty of Hudaybiyyah was signed in the year 628, in which the Meccans agreed to a ten-year truce with the Muslims, the Muslims were allowed to perform a pilgrimage the following year. When the Muslims arrived the next year and performed their pilgrimage, they were making ready to leave when suddenly the very young daughter of the Prophet's uncle Hamza (who was killed in the Battle of Uhud in 625) followed after the Prophet, saying, "Uncle! Uncle!" (She wanted to leave Mecca and go to Medina where all her father's friends and close relatives had settled.) 'Ali took her by the hand and led her to Fatimah and said to her, "Take care of your uncle's daughter." So Fatimah picked her up, but then two other men came (Zayd and Ja'far) and disputed as to who should have custody of her. 'Ali said, "I have more right because she's the daughter of my paternal uncle." Zayd said, "But she's the daughter of my brother (in faith)." Ja'far said, "She's the daughter of my paternal uncle, and I'm married to her maternal aunt, Asma' bint 'Umays." The Prophet came and settled the dispute, saying the girl should be in the custody of her maternal aunt. Then he said, "The maternal aunt has the same status as the mother's." (*Bukhari*)

[994] When the immigrants from Mecca settled in Medina, they began to share inheritance rights with the Medinan Muslims, or *Helpers* (as they were forbidden to leave their property to their non-Muslim relatives back in Mecca). After Mecca and Medina were united, this verse stopped this practice, as inheritance, in normal circumstances, is based only on blood-relations. The Prophet said, "There is no believer except that I'm the closest of all people to him in this world and in the hereafter. Recite, if you like, 'The Prophet is closer to the believers than themselves.' If any believer leaves behind any wealth, let his own relatives inherit it. If he leaves any debt or orphans, bring them to me and I will take care of them." (*Bukhari*) Some scholars have suggested that the last portion of this saying obligates a Muslim government to support orphans and debt relief for the destitute who left their families with debt.

The Great Siege of Medina

Background on verse 9: The Great Siege of Medina was the most harrowing time for the Muslims. The pagans expected a speedy victory. Instead, due to the many defenses erected by the Muslims, especially a five-yard deep trench across the exposed front of the city, the Allies had to settle in for a blockade. After a month the alliance collapsed, and a fierce sandstorm drove the hoard away.

O you who believe! Remember the favor of Allah upon you when an overwhelming horde (of enemies) came down upon you (to attack you right at Medina). We let loose against them a fierce desert sandstorm and other forces you couldn't even see, for Allah is watching everything you do! [9]

Background on verses 10-12: When the pagan forces, over twelve thousand strong, arrived, some of the pagans made camp on low ground in the plain, while others made their camps in the hills overlooking Medina. The sight of their many campfires must have been frightening indeed to those mere 3,000 Muslim fighters within the city walls! One man named Mu'attib even publicly shouted, "Muhammad promised us the treasures of Khosroes and Caesar, but look. We can't even (go out of the city gates) to go to the bathroom!" A more faithful man named Abu Sa'eed asked the Prophet, "O Messenger of Allah, is there anything we can say, for our hearts are in our throats?" The Prophet replied, "Yes, say, 'O Allah, cover our weaknesses and calm our fears.'" This passage was revealed in comment. (*Ibn Kathir*)

The (enemy) came upon you from above you and below you - eyes lost hope, and hearts leapt up to their throats, (as some of you) imagined all sorts of (treasonous) thoughts against Allah. [995] [10] That was traumatic for the faithful, and they were shaken with intense trembling. [11]

The hypocrites and the sick at heart (panicked and) cried out, *"Allah and His Messenger have promised us nothing more than a fantasy."* [12]

Background on verse 13: It was a man named Auws ibn Qayzi of the tribe of Banu Harithah who said the following statement on behalf of his clan, but his people were really more interested in fleeing a potentially catastrophic battle. (*Ibn Kathir*)

---

[995] The pagan Ghatafan tribe attacked the trench from the eastern high ground while the Quraysh and their allies concentrated their efforts on the western side of the trench which was at a lower elevation.. (*Zamakhshari*) Seeing these assaults, some Muslims, especially the hypocrites, were greatly alarmed and fearful, and their penchant for panic caused them to spread discord in public at every turn.

Some of them said, *"People of Yathrib! You can't withstand (this assault)! Pull back now, (and protect your own homes)!"* A group of them even went to the Prophet and asked to be excused from the defense (of the city), saying, *"Our homes are exposed and undefended."* Their homes were not exposed, nor were they without defense. They only wanted to run away (from the front lines). [13]

If there had, in fact, been a way (for the enemy to slip through) from the sides (of the city), and if (those infiltrators) called to (the hypocrites) to betray (the believers) and join them, then (know that) they wouldn't have hesitated for an instant to do it! [14]

(Indeed, they would've turned on you), even though they had already made an agreement with Allah not to turn their backs on you, and an agreement with Allah must be answered for! [15]

Say (to them), *"Running away won't do you any good if you're just trying to escape death or (a fierce) battle, for even if you did (get away), you wouldn't enjoy more than a moment's rest."* [16]

Then ask them, *"Who could shield you from Allah if it were His desire to punish you or to show you mercy?"* They'll find neither any best friend nor any helper apart from Allah! [17]

Indeed, Allah knows about those among you who tried to discourage (people from joining in the defense of Medina) and also about those who said to their brothers, *"Come over here with us,"* but who then participated in the fighting for only a short while. [18]

They held back from (committing fully) to you. When they're terrified, you'll see (people like that) looking to you (for help), with their eyes swiveling around like someone about to die!

When the fear is past, however, they'll stab at you with their sharp tongues and stretch themselves out to grab whatever goods they can. These kinds of people have no faith, so Allah has cancelled the value of their deeds, and that's easy for Allah to do. [19]

They think that the Allied Forces are still lurking (in the countryside somewhere). Well, if the Allied Forces did happen to appear (before the walls of Medina once more), then (the hypocrites) would (once again) wish they were wandering around in the deserts with the bedouins, asking for the latest news (from a safe place). However, if they did stay in your company, they would hardly aid in the battle. [20]

Courage and Faith

The Messenger of Allah provides you with a beautiful example (to follow), for anyone who longs for Allah and the Last Day and who remembers Allah often. [996] [21]

Indeed, when the believers (in the city of Medina) saw the Allied Forces (approaching in the distance to attack), they said, *"This is what Allah and His Messenger promised us (would happen), and Allah and His Messenger told us the truth."* [997] (The specter of desperate battle) did no more than increase their faith and submission (to Allah). [998] [22]

---

[996] This is one of the verses used to justify following the prophetic traditions, or *hadiths*, as this verse says to follow the Prophet's example. Since we learn about his example from the voluminous *hadith* reports that have come down to us, we must, therefore, follow the example of his conduct as outlined in those traditions (as long as they're well-proved as authentic, of course). Imam ash-Shafi'i once asked a group of people to ask him any question, and he would answer from the Qur'an. Then a man asked about the case of a person who killed a wasp while under pilgrimage restrictions. The Imam recited verse 59:7, which states that we must take whatever the Prophet gives us, and then the Imam narrated a *hadith* in which the Prophet talked about the permissibility of killing certain creatures, such as stinging insects if they attack you, even though during the pilgrimage no killing of living creatures is otherwise allowed. (*Qurtubi*) Thus, the common phrase is said among Muslims that a believer must follow the Qur'an and the *Sunnah*, or Prophet's example. The Prophet said, "I am leaving two things with you. You will never go astray as long as you hold to them tightly: the Book of Allah, and the example (*Sunnah*) of His Messenger." (*Muwatta*) He also said, "…whatever the Messenger of Allah has declared to be forbidden, it is the same as being forbidden by Allah." (*Abu Dawud, Ibn Majah*)
[997] This is precisely the meaning of 2:214 where the Qur'an explains that believers will be tested with tremendous trials to purify their hearts and bring them closer to Allah and to purity.
[998] When the two opposing sides drew up for the first day of battle, the Muslim fighters, who numbered less than three thousand, took up positions in front of Medina, while the pagans formed ranks in the plain outside the city. Only the wide trench separated the two sides. The trench made cavalry charges useless, and infantry charges were repelled by squads of Muslim archers in foxholes. The women and children were holed up in fortified sections of the city, and the fortress of the Jewish tribe of Banu Qurayzah

Those Who were True to their Oath

Background on verses 23-24: A man named Anas ibn al-Nadir was unable to participate in the Battle of Badr, and he made an oath, saying, "I swear that if I have another chance, I'll make people notice what I'll do." When the Battle of Uhud was at hand, he prayed for forgiveness from Allah and declared he was free of what pagans believe. He entered the battle and told one of the companions, "I swore by the One Who owns my soul that I'll be the first one to enter Paradise." Then he fought without hesitation until he was killed. The companions later reported that when they found his body it had over 80 wounds on it, and they didn't know if it was him for certain until his sister was able to identify the shape of his fingertips. This passage was revealed concerning his case and the case of others who were likewise martyred. (*Bukhari*)

There are some men from among the faithful who've been true to their promise with Allah. Some have completed their oath (by sacrificing their lives in Allah's cause), while others are still waiting (to prove themselves), and they've never swerved (in their determination) at all. [999] [23]

(They know that) Allah will reward the truthful for their truthfulness and punish the hypocrites, if He so desires, though He may be merciful to them, for Allah is forgiving and merciful. [24]

Allah turned back the faithless in all their fury, and they gained no advantage at all! Allah is enough (of an ally) for the believers in their battles, for Allah is strong and powerful. [1000] [25]

---

protected the rear approaches of the city with its 800 fighting men. (After being swayed by secret promises of victory, the Banu Qurayzah switched sides and the Muslims were faced with a two-front war!) When the Prophet initially saw the horde of Arabs approaching the city, he invoked Allah, saying, "O Allah, Who revealed the Book and is quick in calling to account, defeat the Allies. O Allah, defeat them and shake them up!" The only serious incident of hand-to-hand fighting happened midway through the siege when a fearsome pagan warrior named 'Amr led a small cavalry charge that actually made it over the trench by forcing the horses to leap further than they should have been able to under normal circumstances. The Prophet called for volunteers to mount horses and repel the threat, and no one answered the call due to their fear. Then 'Ali ibn Abi Talib came forward and challenged 'Amr to a duel, which was a common Arab custom. 'Ali wound up winning, rallying his men and causing the remaining cavalrymen to flee.

[999] When the Prophet commented on the case of a man named Talha, who he learned later had lost both arms in the battle and died, he recited this passage, saying he was of those who had completed their oath (to serve in Allah's cause even unto death).

[1000] After the siege of Medina was lifted and the stunned Muslims began to count their blessings, the Prophet took to saying a kind of victory song that is still recited around the

He brought the Followers of Previous Revelation who had joined the (enemy's) side down from their strongholds and caused their hearts to panic. You killed a portion of the (Banu Qurayzah) [1001] and took another portion (as bonded-servants). [1002] [26] He made you

---

world today as part of a longer chant by Muslims as they await their holiday or *'eid* prayers. The words are translated as: "There is no god other than the One God. He was true to His promise, and He helped His servant. He strengthened His soldiers and defeated the Allies by Himself, and there is nothing else after Him."

[1001] The betrayal of the Banu Qurayzah could not be overlooked. No sooner had the Allies left than the Muslims laid siege to the fortress of the Banu Qurayzah. The siege lasted about twenty-five days. At the end, the Banu Qurayzah agreed to surrender only if they could choose the one who would judge them. The Prophet agreed, and the Banu Qurayzah chose their old friend, the chief of the Auws tribe to decide their fate. The Auws chief, Sa'd ibn Mu'adh, had been wounded during the siege from the Allies and was recovering in a tent when he was brought on a specially outfitted donkey to give his verdict. The Prophet said to him, "(These people)," and he pointed to the gathered leaders of the Banu Qurayzah, "have agreed to accept your judgment, so pass judgment on them as you wish." Sa'd asked, "My judgment will be carried out?" The Prophet said, "Yes." Then Sa'd asked the leaders of the Banu Qurayzah what the punishment for treachery was in the Torah. The Banu Qurayzah hung their heads in shame, for they knew that it was death. Then Sa'd decreed that the leaders were to be executed and the non-combatants, women and children were to be taken as bonded servants. (Is this an unreasonable verdict against those who betrayed and almost caused the downfall of their former allies? Remember that after World War II was over, the victorious powers of the United States, Britain, France and the Soviet Union held public trials of the leaders and war criminals of Germany and Japan, and thereafter they executed many of them.) The Prophet did intervene in the parceling out of the civilians as bonded servants, ordering that no mothers should be separated from their children. He also offered to spare the life of any of the condemned men who agreed to convert to Islam, returning their property in the bargain. Only two of the leading men of the Banu Qurayzah took up the offer.

[1002] It has long been assumed that the fighting men of the Banu Qurayzah were executed as traitors after the tribe surrendered to the Muslims, (upon the ruling of Sa'd ibn Mu'adh,) and that the elderly, the women and their children were given over to bonded servitude. New research into the sources for these reports has shown that there was no wholesale execution of the men of the tribe, and the Qur'an, itself, bears witness to it in the choice of grammar used. The verse here uses the masculine gender when referring to those who were taken into servanthood (*tasiroun fariqan*, literally: 'a portion (of them) you took into custody (to be servants).' In Arabic, the masculine gender would not have been used if only (or mostly) women and children were taken into servanthood. Furthermore, there are no mass graves anywhere in or around Medina (especially not in the main market where the unsubstantiated report incredulously asserts that up to 700 men were beheaded and then buried – the Prophet would have never buried anyone in so public a square). Thus, we are forced to look at the sources of the report that claims *all* the men were killed for treason. As it turns out, that report is traced to descendants of the Banu Qurayzah, and it was incorporated by one of the earliest historians of Islam, Ibn Is-haq (d. 783), without question or verification, into his monumental work of biography. He even named each of the Jewish men to whom he spoke, as well as their sources, going back to two men of the Banu Qurayzah tribe (giving further evidence that the men were not killed wholesale). It must be remembered that some of the compilers

inherit their lands, houses and goods. (Then, later on), you also (gained control) over (the distant city of Khaybar), a place where you had never been before, for Allah has power over all things. [1003] [27]

An Option for the Wives of the Prophet

Background on verses 28-29: The Prophet's wives were upset and annoyed that they had to live an austere life of poverty. The Prophet, himself, owned practically nothing, for he constantly gave whatever came into his possession

---

of the Prophet's biography, such as Ibn Is-haq, were not always as strict as the scholars of *hadith* in verifying the truth of all the reports they received. (In his introduction, Ibn Is-haq said of the information he collected, "Only Allah knows which of these narrations are true or not.") This is a small blemish on the otherwise exemplary efforts of such men. Scholars in Ibn Is-haq's own time and afterwards, such as Imam Malik and Ibn Hajar, denounced Ibn Is-haq for including such spurious tales as this one that were not investigated properly. (Unfortunately, other writers, who did their work centuries later, such as Ibn Kathir and at-Tabari, merely parroted this particular story without trying to ascertain if the facts were right.) It was never the precedent in the Prophet's policies to kill wholesale the men of his enemies, and both Jewish tribes he fought earlier were merely exiled – and they took their wealth with them. Even after the final episode with the Banu Qurayzah, Muhammad thereafter continued his strict policy of merely exiling or subduing any other Jewish tribes who made war against him. When the northern Jewish settlement of Khaybar was taken the following year, (from which the plot to invade Medina was hatched,) the Muslims found a remnant of the previously exiled Jewish clan of the Banu Nadir residing there among the Khaybari Jews. Even though they were guilty of inciting great enmity against the Muslims, the Prophet merely told them, "Sons of Abu al-Huqayq! I have known the extent of your hostility to Allah and to His Messenger; yet, that does not prevent me from treating you as I treated your brethren." In other words their punishment was *exile*, and that expedition was *after* the surrender of the Banu Qurayzah. (The original Khaybari Jews, incidentally, were allowed to remain on their land with the payment of tribute.) Therefore, most probably only a handful of men of the Banu Qurayzah, known to have been the leaders of the betrayal, were executed. (Ibn Kathir even records how during the rule of 'Umar ibn al-Khattab, the caliph had a religious conversation with a former rabbi *of the Banu Qurayzah*, who had recently converted to Islam! This account is taken from his commentary of chapter 37 of the Qur'an.) In addition, the report in Bukhari of S'ad ibn Mu'adh's verdict specifically says only the 'warriors' or 'fighting men' were to be executed for treason. (*Bukhari*, 5, 58, 148) So we can conclude that after the traitors were taken into custody, their leaders and warriors were killed, with the rest of the non-combatant men, elderly and women and children taken into bonded servitude, and thereafter their descendants carried the grudge and told the tale in an exaggerated way to make it look like their forebears were punished more harshly than they were, and Allah knows best.

[1003] About ten or twenty days after the conclusion of the Treaty of Hudaybiyyah with the Meccans, the Prophet marched his followers northward to subdue the hostile Jewish settlement of Khaybar. This was where the previously exiled Banu Nadir had settled and from where the entire grand alliance of Jews and pagans against Medina was forged. The settlement capitulated after some days of fighting, and the local Jews were allowed to remain on their land upon the payment of a yearly tribute to Medina. The Banu Nadir were exiled yet again and moved to Syria.

away to charity. It often happened that his wives had barely enough food for a proper diet. Thus, they began to grumble and ask for a material lifestyle that would seem more appropriate to their higher status as wives of the Prophet of Allah. Even as another family crisis was solved through a Qur'anic dispensation (see 66:1-5) that offered his wives the choice to divorce him and have a nice and enriching settlement, here also the same offer is given.

O Prophet! Say to your wives, "*If you want the life of this world and all its glitter, then come on! I'll set you up in style and then set you free in a fine manner.* [28] *However, if you're longing for Allah and His Messenger and the home of the next life, (know that) Allah has prepared a tremendous reward for the good among you."* [1004] [29]

Women of the Prophet! If any of you were ever proven guilty of outrageous acts, then the punishment would be doubled for her, and that's easy for Allah. [30]

If any of you are devoted to the service of Allah and His Messenger and do what's morally right, then We'll double her reward and provide her with a generous amount of benefits. [31]

Special Regulations for the Prophet's Household

Background on verses 32-34: The Prophet was having a meal at the home of one of his wives named Umm Salamah, when she brought out a particularly tasty dish. He asked her to go and invite his daughter Fatimah, her husband 'Ali and

---

[1004] The Prophet was completely dedicated to a life of prayer and charity. As some commentators have noted, after his only wife Khadijah died, he might not have ever married again, but for the practical purposes of alliance building and supporting widows. This verse tries to make an important point clear to his nine wives of the time: if they want more material wealth and comfort, then they don't belong with the Prophet. If they can bear with patience their straightened circumstances in this life, Allah will give them a great reward in the Afterlife. When these verses were revealed to confirm that choice, the Prophet went to A'ishah first and said, "I'm going to tell you something, and you don't have to be quick in your answer until you talk with your parents." Then he recited this passage. A'ishah answered, "What do I need to talk to them about? I choose Allah and His Messenger and the home of the next life." (*Bukhari*) A'ishah then asked the Prophet not to tell his other wives about her decision to stay with him, but he said, "Allah didn't send me to be harsh; rather, He sent me to teach in a gentle and easy manner. If any of them asks me what your decision was, I will tell her." (*Ahmad*) Later, Abu Bakr and 'Umar ibn al-Khattab went to visit the Prophet when he was sitting with all his wives. They began berating the women saying, "You're asking the Prophet for what he doesn't have!" The Prophet stopped the two men, and then his wives said, "By Allah, after this we will not ask the Messenger of Allah for anything that he doesn't have." (*Ahmad*)

their two small sons, Hassan and Husayn, to share in the meal. After they arrived and began to eat, Husayn began to play with a cloak in the back of the room.

Suddenly, this passage came to the Prophet, and he recited the verses. Then he asked the four guests to gather close to him. He wrapped the cloak around them and lifted his hands heavenward saying, "My Lord! These are my family, and they're special to me, so remove all shortcomings from them and make them pure and spotless." Umm Salamah came closer and said, "And me among them, too!" The Prophet said to her, "Truly, the best for you. Truly, the best for you." (*Asbab ul-Nuzul*)

W omen of the Prophet! You're not like other women. If you have the awareness (of Allah in your hearts), then don't be too soft spoken when you speak (with men in public), otherwise a person with a warped heart might become (infatuated) with you. [1005] So speak firmly and forthrightly. [1006] [32]

[1005] The Prophet's wives lived in private apartments attached to the mosque in Medina. Several of them conducted women's study circles, while the remainder devoted their lives to acts of piety and charity. Both men and women often approached them with questions regarding Islam. To forestall any possibility of causing infidelity in some men's minds, these women were asked to live humbly and modestly and not to speak to men in soft feminine voices, but rather in an even tone.

[1006] There is an inaccurate belief among some of the more conservative Muslim sects that suggests it is forbidden for a woman to speak with a man to whom she is not married or related. They consider a woman's voice to be part of the *'aurah*, or concealed things, and that merely hearing a woman's voice will cause uncontrollable desire to well up within a man. This well-intentioned belief is faulty and not based upon Prophetic principles. Women and men in the Prophet's time, and for centuries thereafter, interacted with each other in the market and other public places, and there was no taboo in communication. (Women even spoke up in the mosque without hesitation, well into the rule of the first four caliphs!) There is an etiquette, however, that is to be followed in inter-gender interactions among unmarried or unrelated individuals. Chief among them is that women should speak with *an even voice* and avoid speaking softly, coyly or in any way that seems *inviting*, as that may lead to interest on the part of one or both. (Men must also follow the same protocol.) This verse advises the Prophet's wives of this, for they often had male inquirers asking questions about Islamic practices. For women in general, there is also a tradition from the Prophet that advises women, likewise, to speak with even firmness. Unmarried and unrelated women can speak with men when there is a legitimate need, such as in business dealings, at school, etc, but they must, however, speak firmly and never be alone together unchaperoned, especially if they're courting each other! They also should avoid too much eye contact (by lowering their gaze) and must not touch each other, such as with handshakes and the like. All of these requirements, which are proven in reports from the Prophet, help to protect society from adultery, fornication and many of the kinds of chaotic social problems currently undermining the very foundation of modern societies everywhere. Can Islam be faulted if it nips in the bud most of the 'provocations' that lead to sexual anarchy and unfaithfulness? Islam is not so much a cure as it is a preventative measure!

Stay quietly in your homes, [1007] and don't make a dazzling spectacle (of yourselves) like (women used to do) in the backward days before (Islam). [1008] Establish prayer, give in charity, and obey Allah and His Messenger.

[1007] Some very conservative commentators have extrapolated from this verse that *all* women are forbidden to leave their homes as a general rule and, furthermore, that the very voice of a woman is not to be heard in public places. Thus, the adoption of the practice of *purdah*, or female seclusion, that became widespread throughout the Middle East and parts of Asia during the last five centuries. But is this what the Qur'an is calling for? To begin with, the term *purdah* is of Persian origin and appears nowhere in the Qur'an or *hadith* literature. (*Purdah* describes a pre-Islamic Persian custom in which well-to-do women were kept at home at all times to emphasize the fact that they were wealthy enough not to have to work in the fields and thus to be browned by the sun.) This position, that women are forbidden to leave their homes save for the direst of needs, is a fallacious leap of doctrine. First of all, this verse is addressed specifically to the wives of the Prophet, and even still it does not categorically forbid them from ever leaving their homes, for the Prophet's wives <u>did</u> continue to go out and move about in society (with the Prophet's approval), only more discreetly and infrequently than before. Ordinary women in the Prophet's time and for many centuries beyond did not remain in their homes as a matter of policy, for many needed to work (and they were frequently in the public sphere – even in the mosques), and there is voluminous evidence from the traditions, biographical literature and history books to demonstrate this. (Compare this verse with the biblical verses of I Timothy 2:11-12 or I Corinthians 14:33-35!) Save for the harsh rulings of some modern extremists and the assumptions of certain rustics, who mistake long-standing cultural practices for religion, the general opinion of most mainstream scholars is that women can hold jobs, go to the mosque and go to school, even as they can go out for other needs. (*Ma'ariful Qur'an*) The Prophet said, "You (women) have been allowed to go out for your needs." (*Muslim*) Furthermore, what gives men the right to determine what the specific needs of individual women are?

[1008] Is there a principle that all women can glean from this verse? The commentators say that in pre-Islamic times some women used to flirt with men shamelessly, and that's what this verse is seeking to bring to peoples' attention. The famous commentator Mujahid said, "Some women used to go out purposefully walking in front of men (to attract their attention), and this was from the days of ignorance." Another commentator named Qatadah wrote, "When they went out of their homes, (some women in pre-Islamic times) used to walk in a shameless and flirtatious manner, and Allah, the Exalted, forbade that." (*At-Tabari*) The Prophet allowed women to leave their homes for their legitimate needs and tasks. Despite the illogical position of some extreme conservatives, women cannot be excluded from the social and religious life of the community. The Prophet said, "Do not prevent the female servants of Allah from (attending) the mosques of Allah, just let them go there wearing no perfume." (*Abu Dawud*) By the way, there were no partitions of any kind separating men from women in the mosques in the Prophet's time or in the time of the caliphs, even into Umayyad and early 'Abbasid times. Both sexes prayed and listened to speeches in the same space, with men sitting in the front and women sitting in the back. (The practical effect of this seating arrangement is so that men, who are universally recognized as more susceptible to *distraction*, can keep focused on the proceedings there before them.) According to a *fatwa*, or legal ruling by Islamic scholars, contained in the book *Majalat al-Buhuth al-Islamiyah*, erecting a partition in the mosque to separate men from women is an innovation in religion and is thus forbidden. (pub. 1979, *fatwa* #2611.)

Allah wants nothing more than to cleanse you of any blemishes (in your character), O you people of the (Prophet's) household, [1009] and to make you pure and spotless. [33] Meditate on what is recited to you in your homes of the verses of Allah's (Book) and His wisdom, for Allah is well-informed of the deepest mysteries (of the soul). [34]

Men and Women have Equal Status before Allah

Background on verse 35: The Muslims who had fled to Abyssinia during the worst days of Meccan persecution gradually began to migrate to Medina to join the Muslims who had already settled there. Among these latecomers was a woman named Asma', who was wife of Ja'far ibn Abi Talib. She went to some of the Prophet's wives and asked, "Is there anything revealed in the Qur'an with regards to us (women)?"

When they told her that there was not, she then went to the Prophet and lamented, "Why are women always hopeless and shortchanged?" When the Prophet asked her what she meant, she explained, "Because (women) haven't been mentioned in righteousness the same as men." Umm Salamah, the Prophet's wife, also asked something similar. The Prophet waited for guidance from Allah, and soon this verse was revealed to assuage and assure women of Allah's equal estimation of both. (*Asbab ul-Nuzul*)

For men and women

who have surrendered (their wills to Allah),

for men and women who believe,

for men and women who are devout,

for men and women who are honest, [1010]

for men and women who are patient,

for men and women who are humble,

[1009] The Prophet's family was given the nickname of "Kindred Ones of the House," or "People of the House," which is *Ahl al-Bayt* in Arabic.

[1010] The unfortunate misconception among many is that Islam does not hold women in equal status with men. Besides the fact that this and other verses prove otherwise, there is a proven track record of the Prophet fighting for the rights of women, as his sayings and even the divinely revealed Qur'an attests. Backward cultural practices found in the modern Muslim world are proof of nothing more than the ignorance of the people about their religion and progressive roots.

for men and women who donate to charity,

for men and women who fast,

for men and women who guard their modesty,

and for men and women who remember Allah often –

for them Allah has prepared forgiveness and a great reward. [35]

The Case of Zayd ibn Harith

Background on verses 36-40: Long before he had become a prophet, Muhammad had adopted a son named Zayd ibn Harith while he was living in Mecca. Originally, the boy was a Syrian slave that his wife Khadijah had given to him, but Muhammad had freed him and taken him as his own. Thus, he was known as Zayd ibn Muhammad. Zayd's Syrian father later came in search of his son and found him living safely in Mecca.

Zayd, who had grown up from boyhood in Mecca in Muhammad's household, politely told his father he wanted to remain where he was. Years later, after the commencement of the prophethood of Muhammad and after the Muslims were settled in Medina, the Prophet brokered a marriage between his distant cousin, Zaynab bint Jahsh (d. 642), and Zayd. The marriage didn't work out, however, for the upper class Zaynab was not content to be married to a common man who was a former slave, and she treated him with veiled contempt (in her belief that he was beneath her nobility).

As time passed, however, Zayd did not like how he was being treated by the haughty Zaynab, and he asked the Prophet about divorcing her. The Prophet counseled him to remain married, but the love was gone in that marriage. Thus, despite Muhammad's efforts to preserve the marriage, Zayd wound up divorcing Zaynab.

A short time later, the Prophet proposed to her, and she readily accepted the offer. This situation, however, created a minor scandal - with the Jews and hypocrites of Medina accusing Muhammad of marrying his own son's former wife. This passage was revealed after verses 4-6 of this chapter, clarifying that there is no harm in marrying someone who was married to an adopted person, as the adopted person is not a biological relative, and thus the usual restrictions do not apply.

It's not right for a believer, whether male or female, to second guess a decision about a matter that's been decided by Allah and His Messenger. Whoever disobeys Allah and His Messenger is clearly mistaken in error. [1011] [36]

[1011] Only the Arabs had a taboo against marrying the divorced spouses of adoptees. Judaism, Christianity and even modern legal traditions have no such restriction. This

(Muhammad, when Zayd wanted to divorce his wife Zaynab,) you had said to (your adopted son Zayd, a man) who had received Allah's grace and your favor, *"Stay (married) to your wife and be mindful of Allah."*

However, you were hiding something in your heart that Allah was about to disclose. [1012] You were afraid of (what) people (would think if you were to marry the woman that Zayd divorced, but it's more appropriate) for you to fear Allah.

Then, after Zayd dissolved (his marriage) to her, following all the proper procedures, We joined her in marriage to you, so that there wouldn't be any more (confusion) among the faithful about (the permissibility) of marrying the ex-spouses of their adopted children, after all the proper procedures (of divorce) have been followed, for Allah's command must be fulfilled. [1013] [37]

There shouldn't be any obstacles for the Prophet in discharging the duty that Allah has laid upon him. This principle of Allah was practiced by those who passed before, and the command of Allah is an irresistible decree. [38] (The principle outlined above is accepted by) those who convey the messages of Allah and who fear Him. So fear no one besides Allah, for Allah is enough to make an accounting (of what people do). [39]

Muhammad is not the father of any of your men, [1014] but he is the Messenger of Allah and the Seal of the Prophets. [1015] Indeed, Allah knows about all things. [40]

---

action of the Prophet abolished this pagan taboo among the Arabs. The Qur'an affirms this right, for the adopted and the adopter have no immediate blood ties whatsoever.

[1012] Before Zayd divorced Zaynab, the Prophet knew that their marriage was about to end. He felt that Allah would use this situation to make a point; yet, he had to suppress his feeling that he might be married to Zaynab later on, and he continued to counsel to Zayd to stay married to Zaynab. (*Zamakhshari*)

[1013] See 33:4-6 and footnote for details on why this symbolic marriage was important to show that ties of adoption do not equal ties of blood.

[1014] Although the Prophet had several sons, all of them died in early childhood. Thus, he was the father 'of no men' in the community.

[1015] Muhammad is the "Seal of the Prophets." In other word he is the cap on the bottle of divine revelation. He once said, "My example in relation to the prophets who came

Allah's Message of Hope in Tough Times

O you who believe! Remember Allah with great remembrance. [1016] [41] Glorify Him in the morning and at night. [42] He's the One Who sends down blessings upon you, and the angels do so as well, in order that He can bring you out of darkness into the light, and He's merciful to the believers. [43]

On the day when they're going to meet Him, they'll greet each other by saying, "*Peace.*" He has indeed prepared a generous reward for them. [44]

Instructions for the Prophet

O Prophet! We've sent you to be a witness, a bringer of good news, a warner [45] and also a caller to Allah's (path), by His leave, like a lamp shining light in dark places. [46] So give good news to the faithful that they'll have great favor from Allah (waiting for them). [47]

Don't obey those who suppress (their faith) nor the hypocrites, and pay no mind to their pestering ways. Rather, put your trust in Allah, for Allah is enough to take care of all matters. [48]

---

before me is that of a man who built a house beautifully and well, except that one brick in its corner was missing. The people went around it and wondered at its beauty, but said, 'If only that final brick were put in its place!' I *am* that brick, and I am the last of the Prophets." (*Bukhari*, also see Matthew 21:42-44 for an interesting statement from Prophet Jesus.) Thus, Muhammad is the conclusion of all of Allah's direct communication with man. Therefore, any person who claims to be a prophet after Muhammad is not accepted as authentic by the mainstream majority of Muslims. (*Ma'ariful Qur'an, Ibn Kathir*)

[1016] The Prophet said, "Any people who sit together without mentioning Allah will see it as regretful on the Day of Resurrection." (*Ahmad*) The classical philosopher, Muhyiddin ibn 'Arabi (d. 1240), once wrote: "There are places that offer but scant consolation, while others offer a person great delight. However, make the Lord the mainstay and refuge of your soul, wherever and however you may be." Thus, there should be mention of Allah in all meetings, for that reminder brings one's heart back into focus on the sweetness of faith, as opposed to the pedestrian nature of worldly affairs.

Divorce before Consummation

O you who believe! When any of you marries a believing woman, but then divorces her without ever having had intimate relations with her, then there's no need for you to keep track of her waiting period. Give her a gift, and then set her free graciously. [1017] [49]

The Prophet's Defined Marriage Rules

O Prophet! We've made lawful for you your wives to whom you've given their dowries, as well as those (maidservants) under your control who've been acquired through spoils and were assigned to you by Allah. [1018]

(Also lawful for you in marriage are) the daughters of your paternal and maternal aunts and uncles, (as long as they've demonstrated their loyalty to Islam) by migrating (from Mecca to Medina) with you, [1019] and any believing woman who offers herself (in marriage) to the Prophet, if the Prophet wishes to marry her.

[1017] This teaching is explained more fully in 2:236-237.

[1018] A'ishah said, "I often felt jealous of those women who offered themselves (in marriage) to the Prophet." (Bukhari) A woman named Khawlah bint Hakim walked into the mosque one day and proposed to the Prophet, offering herself in marriage. The Prophet remained silent for a few moments, and then a man stood up and said, "Messenger of Allah, marry her to me." The Prophet asked the man about the potential dowry he could offer her, and it turned out he had no possessions, so the woman accepted for her dowry that the man teach her what he knew of the Qur'an. On another occasion, a woman named Umm Sharik entered the mosque and also offered herself in marriage to the Prophet. The Prophet again declined the offer. A'ishah, who was present, remarked (out of jealousy) that she thought any woman who so brashly offered herself in marriage to a man was something of a lowlife. This verse was revealed to the Prophet to lay out specifically what sort of women he was allowed to take as wives. It is said that Maymunah bint al-Harith, whom the Prophet did accept after she offered herself, is especially referenced here.

[1019] While Muhammad was still living in Mecca, he had asked for the hand of his cousin, Umm Hani bint Abi Talib, in marriage, but she politely declined, and he accepted her excuse. This verse was later revealed in the Medinan Period, and Umm Hani explained that she was now forever forbidden in marriage to the Prophet, as she had not migrated to Medina and was still a pagan at the time that Mecca was liberated. (Zamakhshari)

These (specific marriage regulations) are only for you, (Muhammad), and not for any other believers. [1020] We know what regulations We've already stipulated for them with regards to their wives and (the maidservants) under their control. [1021]

(We've spelled out your allowances specifically here) so that you won't have any difficulty (in knowing what you're allowed to do), for Allah is forgiving and merciful. [50]

A Dispensation for the Prophet

Background on verse 51: The Prophet had been dividing up his scant free time equally among his wives, and this was a hardship for him for two reasons: he was generally busy with worship and community work and found it hard to keep a regular family schedule, and he also had more fondness for some of his wives and preferred to spend more of his free time with them in their apartments. A'ishah reports that he said in exasperation one day, "O Allah, I've done as much as I can with regard to what's under my control, so don't blame me for what's under Your control and not mine." (*Ahmad*) In other words, he had no control over his feelings and heart. The Prophet, therefore, desired to be granted flexibility with regard to his scheduling, for he had to ask permission from the wife whose turn it was to see him if he wanted to spend time with another, and this new verse was revealed to give that flexibility to him.

You can postpone any of (your wives' turns to be with you), as you like, or you can see whichever one of them as you like. You won't be blamed in either case if you call upon one of them whose turn you had postponed. [1022]

[1020] The Prophet received specific instructions and allowances for his own personal life. He was allowed to have more than the maximum legal limit of four wives, due to his status, which made it possible to broker alliances through marriage, support widows and also marry those who were unwilling to marry others, such as Zaynab, who had very high standards regarding who her husband would be. The Prophet married a total of eleven women (after his first wife died) while in Mecca and Medina, (though he was monogamous with his first wife Khadijah for over twenty-three years in Mecca until she died, bringing the total number of women he married in his lifetime to twelve). He never had more than nine living wives at one time, for he had married several older widows, and some of them passed away before he did. All of his marriages after Khadijah passed away were to support widows, demonstrate legal rulings, or cement alliances.

[1021] The marriage regulations for all other people are contained in 4:23-25.

[1022] A'ishah said of this verse, 'Why would any woman offer herself (in marriage to the Prophet) when Allah revealed this verse?" A'ishah also said to the Prophet when she heard this verse, "I see that your Lord hastens to fulfill your desires." (*Bukhari*) A'ishah also told him, "If I could forbid you from seeing any of your other wives, I wouldn't allow your favor to be bestowed upon anyone but me." (*Bukhari*)

(Your exemption from having to follow a rigid, fixed schedule among your wives) is so that their eyes may be cooled, that their anxious feelings (may be answered), and that they can be satisfied with whatever you can offer them. Allah knows what's in your hearts, and Allah is full of knowledge and forbearance. [51]

(Now that some time has passed, Muhammad,) you're forbidden to marry any more women after this (new verse revealed here now), nor can you substitute any of them for (other) wives, even though you might be attracted by their beauty, except for any (handmaiden you wish to marry) who may be under your authority. [1023] Allah watches over all things. [52]

Etiquette in the Prophet's Household

O you who believe! When you're coming for a meal, don't enter the Prophet's house without permission, and don't arrive so early that you're waiting around for (the food to) finish (cooking). [1024] When you're invited inside, come in. Then, when the meal is over, leave in a timely fashion without trying to engage in small talk.

This annoys the Prophet, but he's too shy to ask you to leave - though Allah isn't too shy to tell you the truth. [1025] When you ask (his

---

[1023] This verse, which was revealed about seven years after the migration to Medina, forbade the Prophet from marrying any other free women, except for maidservants whom he could marry. He married Maria the Copt, who was a gift from the ruler of Egypt, and she bore him a son named Ibrahim (who tragically died in infancy).

[1024] The Prophet was a human being and had his own particular habits. He was generous and friendly with everyone, but all of us have our limits. He used to see and talk to so many people throughout each day that at times he longed for some peace and quiet. When he gave a dinner party to celebrate his marriage to Zaynab bint Jahsh in the year 626, his many guests ate their fill and then departed, but three men remained sitting and didn't leave for a long time. Zaynab, herself, felt embarrassed at these men who couldn't take the hint to leave, so she turned her back to them and faced the wall. Eventually, they left. The Prophet was too shy to tell those people that they had tarried in his home for too long after the meal, so after they left, Allah, Himself, Who promised to look after the Prophet's peace of mind, revealed this passage to ask the faithful to give the Prophet some personal space. (*Bukhari*)

[1025] The faithful were so eager to observe everything that they could about the Prophet that they would peek into his keyhole, climb up on his roof to see into his courtyard and wait outside his door to get a glimpse of him or to get some advice. This is how much they loved him. Sometimes they forgot that he had only the endurance of a single man.

wives) for something, ask them through a *hijab*. [1026] This is more wholesome for the sake of both your hearts and theirs.

(Know that) it's not right for any of you to annoy the Messenger of Allah, nor should you marry any of his widows after he has passed away. That would be going too far in the sight of Allah. [53] Whether you show something or hide it, (remember that) Allah knows about all things. [1027] [54]

[1026] There are various stories to explain why this verse was revealed, and all of them revolve around 'Umar, who was apparently concerned that the Prophet's wives were free to go out in society without a head covering and looked upon by all. In one instance, he accidentally touched A'ishah's finger while a food bowl was passed to him, and this caused him great consternation. Ever concerned that the Prophet's family be protected from strange men and false accusations, it seems he was lobbying for a ruling from Allah to govern public interactions between the Prophet's wives and the general male public. When this verse was revealed, the Prophet's wives were asked to conduct their public business dealings with unrelated men through a *hijab* (a screen divider in a room or a face veil. (*Ibn Ati Hatim, al-Tabarani*, et al) Certain rustic cultures have assumed that the regulations laid out here (and in verse 55) that ask the Prophet's wives to speak to unrelated men from behind a face veil or curtain apply, by extrapolation, to all women. This is an extreme view, as the general lot of women in the community of Medina did not implement this for themselves. They still went out with faces uncovered (though with hair covered), and spoke to men in public places as the need dictated, such as in the bazaar, the mosque and other, similar public places, without being segregated into all female zones in every place. (Even into the times of the caliphs, how could there have been all those heroic Muslim female warriors at such battles as Qadasiyya and Hattin if they were hiding behind screens or in a full face veil?) In a narration of A'ishah, she said that the ordinary women of Medina, when they heard this verse, made head scarves for themselves by cutting up curtains, and that was all they did. (Not all women covered their hair fully in public before the revelation of this verse.) (*Abu Dawud*)

[1027] This is a subtle way of saying that no man should even harbor the desire in his heart for one of the Prophet's wives. This may seem an odd thing, that the Muslims of Medina were asked not to let themselves be attracted to a member of the Prophet's household, but in reality it was absolutely necessary for the Prophet's peace of mind. (One tribal chief in Medina named Uyayna, following pre-Islamic customs, actually proposed trading wives with the Prophet: his own wife for A'ishah! The Prophet flatly refused, saying, "Allah forbids such things.") The Prophet's wives were major sources of information about Islam, and both men and women would make appointments to see them to ask them questions about Islam. Because of their elevated position, even a good man might start to feel an attraction. How could the Prophet, or any man in a similar position, give his undivided attention to his all important mission if he is worried about the fidelity of his spouse or the amorous glances of strange men upon her? Islamic teachings accept the fact that some men, no matter how righteous they appear, can be plagued by inner desires that they seemingly have little control over. The Prophet once said, "Satan runs through a person's veins like their blood." He added that we should then control that *Satan* (i.e., our urges) through hunger and fasting. So the community could still have access to his wives, but they should be behind a screen when they answer questions. Although this commandment never applied to women in general and was not practiced among the

456

There is no blame on the (wives of the Prophet if they see and converse with the following categories of men, without a partition between them): their fathers, their sons, their brothers, their brothers' sons, their sisters' sons, their female (friends and relatives) and the servants under their authority. Be mindful of Allah, for Allah is a witness to all things. [55]

Allah and His angels send blessings down upon the Prophet. O you who believe! Call for blessings to be sent down upon him, and wish him peace with due respect. [1028] [56]

Those who (deliberately) annoy Allah and His Messenger are cursed by Allah in this world, while in the next life, He has prepared a humiliating punishment (especially) for them. [57]

Further still, those who (deliberately) annoy the believing men and believing women, without a valid reason, take upon themselves the crime of slander and also an obvious sin. [58]

---

masses in those days as such, later generations of Muslims, thinking they were being extra pious, began literally screening women out of the public space to the extent that today one can find walls and screens separating female and male worshippers in Mosques, as well as at public functions and in other instances. There is no official sanction in the Qur'an or *hadith* literature promoting this for the general public. It is accepted by all, even those who practice it, that the Prophet did not have a barrier separating men and women in his mosque. In fact, he merely made the men wait to leave while the women existed from the building first.

[1028] This verse is often quoted in Friday sermons near the close of the main speech. When people heard this Qur'anic verse being recited, they asked the Prophet how they could send prayers down upon him. He then taught the people a prayer formula that is commonly called the *durud sharif*. It is a supplication which asks Allah to bless Muhammad like He blessed Abraham. The Prophet once said, "The person nearest to me is the one who asks for blessings upon me the most." On another occasion, the Prophet said that if someone hears his name and doesn't wish him blessings, then that person is like a miser. Why the eagerness to be blessed, even after departing from this world? In Islamic belief, the supplications of the living can still be of benefit for the dead. (Once the Prophet described it like rain falling in the grave to nourish the souls of the departed.) The common formula Muslims use when they hear the Prophet's name being mentioned is, "*Salallahu 'alayhi wa sallem*," which means, "The prayers of Allah be upon him and peace." Muslim writers have taken this injunction to heart and have produced many extended benedictions to the Prophet, such as the *Dalai'l al-Khayrat* of 'Abdullah Al Juzuli (d. 1465) and the *Burda* of Sharafuddin Al Busayri (d. 1296). The Prophet once said that anyone who wishes blessings on him, then that person will get ten good deeds. (*Ahmad*)

Dress Code for Women in Public

Background on verse 59: Although the Prophet and his followers had migrated to Yathrib, soon to be known as Medina, and established themselves there from the year 622, the Muslims did not rule over the whole city as if it were their own city-state. It wasn't until the year 628 that Muslim sway over the city was fully cemented. Prior to this, Muhammad and his followers had to maintain a delicate balance between many competing interests, such as the Jewish tribes, the hypocrites, and the large number of pagans that remained among the local bedouin population. Thus, not every vice could be eliminated or policed right away. One of these vices was prostitution.

Although it was forbidden to Muslims, the many non-Muslim residents and visitors in the city still sought out prostitutes for their services. If a woman walked outside in the streets at night and her hair was unveiled and her clothes were loosely draped, it was taken as a sign that she was "available-for-hire." Thus, to help Muslim women avoid being accosted by such lecherous men, this verse was revealed, advising them how to dress so the non-Muslims seeking prostitutes wouldn't molest them.

O Prophet! Tell your wives and daughters and the believing women that they should draw their outer garments [1029] closely over their bodies (when they go out in public).

That's the easiest way for them to be known (as respectable), so that they won't be accosted (by strange men). Allah is forgiving and merciful. [1030] [59]

Warning the Hypocrites of Medina

In all seriousness, if the hypocrites, the sick at heart and the rabble-rousers who try to stir up sedition in the city don't stop (their treasonous activities), then We'll certainly stir you up against them! Then they won't be able to remain (in the city) as your neighbors for very long! [60]

[1029] The outer garments or *jilbab* mentioned here is often considered to be an outer cloak, coat, robe, long shawl or an over shirt. It is not synonymous with an all-enveloping tent-like structure called a *burka*, which is a later cultural invention of Persia and India. (Also see 24:30-31)

[1030] It is not commonly known in the West that Muslim men also have a dress code and that it is nearly identical to the requirements for women in that the body must be covered. (Proper public dress is a fully covered body, though men who need to work or dive in the sea and such can wear shorts, as long as the area between the navel and below the knees is fully covered.) Men's clothes must be loose, and a turban or cap is preferable to wear.

They'll be cursed, and wherever they'll be found they'll be captured and slain completely. [61] This is the same practice of Allah (that's always been) enforced by those who lived in the past, and you won't find any change in the practice of Allah. [62]

The Coming of the Hour

People ask you (when) the Hour (of Judgment will come to pass). Tell them, *"Only Allah knows the answer (to that question)."*

How can you be made to understand? *The Hour could be very near!* [1031] [63]

Allah has truly cursed the faithless and prepared for them a blazing fire, [64] and there they shall remain forever – and they'll neither find any best friend nor any helper (to aid them)! [65]

The day when (the haughty expressions on) their faces will be turned upside down (by the humiliation of the) fire (is the day) when they'll cry out, *"We're doomed! If only we had obeyed Allah and obeyed His Messenger!"* [66]

They'll also say, *"Our Lord! We obeyed our leaders and our heroes, and they misled us on the path. [67] Our Lord! Give them twice the punishment, and curse them terribly!"* [68]

Follow Allah's Command

O you who believe! Don't be like those who troubled Moses – *even Allah had to clear him of all the things they said of him* - for he was honorable in Allah's sight. [1032] [69]

[1031] The Prophet said, "From among the signs of the (final) Hour are the following: religious knowledge will be taken away, ignorance will increase, fornication will be widespread, the consumption of alcohol will be common, the population of men will decrease and the population of women will increase, so much so that fifty women will be looked after by one man." (*Bukhari*)

[1032] The Israelites were disobedient to Moses because they had lived in Egypt for generations and picked up many bad habits, along with a skeptical and disobedient attitude. The pure faith of their ancestors, Jacob and Isaac, was all but gone. After Moses

O you who believe! Be mindful (of Allah), and always speak in a straightforward manner, [70] so He can reform your behavior and forgive you your sins.

Whoever obeys Allah and His Messenger has already achieved the greatest success! [1033] [71]

We offered the commitment (of self-awareness) to the heavens, the earth and the mountains, but they all refused to accept it out of fear (of the consequences). [1034]

---

led them to freedom, he had to endure their ignorance, even as he had to try and teach them to be faithful and obedient to Allah again. The following story, related by the Prophet Muhammad, illustrates the extent of Moses' predicament: The Israelites used to bathe naked together in communal places. Moses used to take his baths alone (for he was very shy and meek, as Numbers 12:3 asserts). Some of the Israelites started spreading the following rumor: "The only thing that's keeping Moses from bathing with the rest of us is that he has a defect on his body." Once, when Moses went out to take a bath, he put his clothes over a stone. (When he had finished bathing and went to retrieve his clothes), the stone miraculously bounced away with his clothes still on top of it! Moses ran after that stone yelling, "My clothes! Hey, stone! My clothes! Hey, stone!" He ran past the Israelite camp, and when they saw him they exclaimed, "By Allah, Moses doesn't have any defect on his body." The stone abruptly stopped, and Moses quickly grabbed his clothes. Then he took up a big stick and began to beat the stone so hard that it made deep marks in it. (*Bukhari*)

[1033] The Prophet said, "Allah will bring a servant close (to Him) on the Day of Judgment and make him confess all of his sins. This will go on until the servant thinks that he's about to be destroyed. Then Allah will say, 'I've hidden these sins for you in the worldly life, and I'm forgiving them for you today.' Then he will be given his book of good deeds in his right hand. For the rejecter and the hypocrite, the witnesses will say, 'These are the ones who lied against their Lord, and the curse of Allah is upon the corrupt.'" (References verses 7:44-45, with reports from *Bukhari, Muslim, Ahmad*)

[1034] *Al Amanah* means commitment or trust. Atiyah Al `Awfi (d. 729) reported that Ibn `Abbas said, "*Al Amanah* means obedience. This was offered to them before it was offered to Adam, and they could not bear it. Then Allah said to Adam: `I have offered the *Amanah* to the heavens and the earth and the mountains, and they could not bear it. Will you take it on' He said, `O Lord, what does it involve' He said, `If you do good, you will be rewarded, and if you do evil, you will be punished.' So, Adam took the *Amanah* and bore it, and this is what is referred to in the Ayah." This is why we human beings are to be held accountable for our deeds and either rewarded or punished in an afterlie. It is literally imprinted on our DNA, and that helps explain why humans understand the concepts of right and wrong, justice and injustice, oppression and salvation, and sometimes willfully engage in wrong, but then can be redeemed back into the light.

Humanity agreed to undertake it, *though it overstepped and was foolish,* [72] so much so that Allah now has to punish hypocrites, both male and female, and also the faithless, both male and female.

Allah turns in mercy, however, to the believers, both male and female, for Allah is forgiving and merciful. [73]

This Concludes Volume 2

Made in the USA
Monee, IL
29 April 2022

1811aec7-a0c1-4e50-b90b-153bacd7b7d2R01